Philosophical Consciousness and Scientific Knowledge: Conceptual Linkages and Civilizational Background

Publications in PHISPC-CONSSVAY Series

HISTORY OF SCIENCE, PHILOSOPHY AND CULTURE IN INDIAN CIVILIZATION

General Editor & Project Director: D.P. Chattopadhyaya

Conceptual Volumes

*	Part 1	Science, Philosophy and Culture: Multi-disciplinary Explorations	D.P. Chattopadhyaya & Ravinder Kumar	(eds.)
*	Part 2	Science, Philosophy and Culture: Multi-disciplinary Explorations	D.P. Chattopadhyaya & Ravinder Kumar	(eds.)

Volume I The Dawn and Development of Indian Civilization

*	Part 1	The Dawn of Indian Civilization (up to *c*.600 BC)	G.C. Pande	(ed.)
*	Part 2	Life, Thought and Culture in India (from *c*.600 BC to *c*. AD 300)	G.C. Pande	(ed.)
*	Part 3	India's Interaction with Southeast Asia	G.C. Pande	(ed.)
*	Part 4	A Golden Chain of Civilizations: Indic, Iranic, Semitic and Hellenic (up to *c*.600 BC)	G.C. Pande	(ed.)
>	Part 5	A Golden Chain of Civilizations: Indic, Iranic, Semitic and Hellenic (from *c*. 600 BC to *c*. AD 600)	G.C. Pande	(ed.)
>	Part 6	Purāṇas, History and Itihāsa	Vidya Nivas Misra	(ed.)

Volume II Life, Thought and Culture in India (AD 300-1100)

*	Part 1	Life, Thought and Culture in India (AD 300-1000)	K. Satchidananda Murty	(ed.)
*	Part 2	Advaita Vedānta	R. Balasubramanian	(ed.)
*	Part 3	Theistic Vedānta	R. Balasubramanian	(ed.)
*	Part 4	Origin and Development of the Vaiśeṣka System	Anantalal Thakur	
*	Part 5	A Social History of Early India	B.D. Chattopadhyaya	(ed.)
*	Part 6	Pūrvamīmāṁsā from an Interdisciplinary Point of View	K.T. Pandurangi	(ed.)

Volume III Development of Philosophy, Science and Technology in India & Neighbouring Countries

*	Part 1	History of Indian Science, Technology and Culture (AD 1000-1800)	A. Rahman	(ed.)
*	Part 2	India's Interaction with China, Central and West Asia	A. Rahman	(ed.)
*	Part 3	Development of Nyaya Philosophy and its Social Context	Sibajiban Bhattacharyya	(ed.)
*	Part 4	Philosophical Concepts Relevant to Sciences in Indian Tradition	Pranab Kumar Sen	(ed.)
*	Part 5	Philosophical Concepts Relevant to Sciences in Indian Tradition	Pranab Kumar Sen	(ed.)
*	Part 6	India and China: Twenty Centuries of Civilizational Interaction and Vibrations	Tan Chung & Geng Yinzeng	(ed.)
>	Part 7	The Trading World of the Indian Ocean, AD 1500-1800	Om Prakash	(ed.)

Volume IV Fundamental Indian Ideas of Physics, Chemistry, Life Sciences and Medicine

*	Part 1	Chemistry and Chemical Techniques in India	B.V. Subbarayappa	(ed.)
*	Part 2	Medicine and Life Sciences in India	B.V. Subbarayappa	(ed.)
*	Part 3	Indian Perspectives on the Physical World	B.V. Subbarayappa	
*	Part 4	The Tradition of Astronomy in India: Jyotiḥśāstra	B.V. Subbarayappa	

Volume V Agriculture in India

*	Part 1	A History of Agriculture in India (up to c.1200 AD)	Lallanji Gopal and V.C. Srivastava	(eds.)
>	Part 2	A History of Agriculture in India (c. 1200 AD onwards)	Lallanji Gopal and V.C. Srivastava	(eds.)

Volume VI Culture, Language, Literature and Arts

*	Part 1	Aesthetic Theories and Forms in Indian Tradition	Kapila Vatsyayan and D.P. Chattopadhyaya	(eds.)
>	Part 2	Architecture in India	M.A. Dhaky	(ed.)
*	Part 3	Indian Art: Forms, Concerns and Development in Historical Perspective	B.N. Goswamy	(ed.)
>	Part 4	Language, Grammar and Linguistics in Indian Tradition	V.N. Jha	(ed.)
*	Part 5	The Life-World of the Tamils: Past and Present - I	R. Balasubramanian	(ed.)
>	Part 6	The Life-World of the Tamils: Past and Present - II	R. Balasubramanian	(ed.)
<	Part 7-11	PHISPC in Regional Languages and Literature	(Under Plan)	

Volume VII The Rise of New Polity and Life in Villages and Towns

*	Part 1	The State and Society in Medieval India	J.S. Grewal	(ed.)
*	Part 2	Religious Movements and Institutions in Medieval India	J.S. Grewal	(ed.)
>	Parts 3, 4, 5	Religious Systems of India	S.R. Saha, N.S.S. Raman, M. Rafique and Others	(eds.)

Volume VIII Economic History of India

>	Part 1	Economic History of India from Thirteenth to Seventeenth Century	Irfan Habib	(ed.)
*	Part 2	Peasant History of Late Pre-Colonial and Colonial India	B B Chaudhuri	
*	Part 3	Economic History of India from Eighteenth to Twentieth Century	B B Chaudhuri	(ed.)

Volume IX Colonial Period

*	Part 1	Medicine in India: Modern Period	O.P. Jaggi	
*	Part 2	Women in India: Ancient and Medieval Period	Bhuvan Chandel (ed.)	(ed.)
*	Part 3	Women of India: Colonial and Post-Colonial Periods	Bharati Ray (ed.)	(ed.)

Volume X Towards Independence

*	Part 1	Development of Indian Philosophy from Eighteenth Century Onwards	Daya Krishna	
>	Part 2	Colonial Development, Education and Social Awareness up to 2000	S. Gopal, Ravinder Kumar & S.Bhattacharya	(eds.)
*	Part 3	Historical Perspectives of Warfare in India: Some *Morale* and *Material* Determinants	S.N. Prasad	(ed.)
*	Part 4	Cultural Foundations of Mathematics: The Nature of Mathematical Proof and the Transmission of the Calculus from India to Europe in the 16th c. CE	C.K. Raju	

* Already Published
> In the Process of Publication
< Under Plan

History of Science, Philosophy and Culture in Indian Civilization

General Editor D.P. Chattopadhyaya

Volume XI Part 1

Philosophical Consciousness and Scientific Knowledge: Conceptual Linkages and Civilizational Background

edited by

D.P. CHATTOPADHYAYA
in association with
A.K. Sen Gupta

Project of History of Indian Science, Philosophy and Culture [PHISPC]
Sub Project: Consciousness, Science, Society, Value and Yoga [CONSSAVY]

CENTRE FOR STUDIES IN CIVILIZATIONS

Publication of this Volume and much of the research it represents has been made possible by continuing grants with full financial assistance from the Department of Higher Education, Ministry of Human Resource Development, Government of India, which has supported multidisciplinary exploration of the Project of History of Indian Science, Philosophy and Culture.

First published in 2004
Re-printed in 2009
by Professor Bhuvan Chandel, Member Secretary, CSC,
DD-24, (Near Nehru Enclave), Kalkaji, New Delhi-110019

Distributed by
Motilal Banarsidass
Bungalow Road
Jawahar Nagar, Delhi-110 007

ISBN: 81-87586-15-X

Typeset in Pratap, 11/14.5 pts.

Typeset by Digigraphics and
Printed at Durga Print-O-Graph, Delhi-110091

Centre for Studies in Civilizations

Governing Board

Contents

II. Science in its Larger Perspective

III. Interplay of Science on Consciousness

IV. Traditional Linkage of Philosophy and Science

Preface

Encouraged by the reception of 29 Volumes, published till date, of the PROJECT OF THE HISTORY OF SCIENCE, PHILOSOPHY AND CULTURE IN INDIAN CIVILIZATIONS [PHISPC] THE CENTRE FOR STUDIES IN CIVILIZATIONS [CSC]and Government of India, have jointly decided to bring out 28 additional Volumes. Besides the original Project named PHISPC under which a total of 68 Volumes and Monographs have been planned, till date, these additional Volumes, 28 are being brought out by March 2010. In the extended part of the PHISPC, called CONSSAVY, the major themes which have been planned to cover are closely related to the subjects of PHISPC itself. It has been designated as CONSSAVY, acronym for CONSCIOUSNESS, SCIENCE, SOCIETY, VALUE AND YOGA. Formally CONSSAVY has been launched, after long deliberation, in 2002.

When in the past the PHISPC itself was launched, two Launching Volumes, SCIENCE, PHILOSOPHY AND CULTURE: MULTIDISCIPLINARY EXPLORATIONS, **PART ONE** and **PART TWO** were brought out under the editorship of the late Ravinder Kumar and myself during the years 1996 and 1997. Advised by many distinguished philosophers and scientists we tried to spell out in those works the basic themes to be covered by the Project in its original form. Initially it was thought that we will be able to complete the Project by publishing 30 Volumes. Organic growth of the Project due to its internal impulsion led CSC to the conclusion that the work would require at least 50 Volumes, 30 Main Volumes and 20 Monographs, to make justice to the interdisciplinary study already undertaken.

The projected work and publication has been progressing in full swing, thanks to sincere cooperation of our editorial colleagues and contributors. At this stage I thought it would be academically advisable to undertake a similar exercise of bringing out two Launching Volumes on the eve of going out into the specifics of Main Volumes and Monographs under the CONSSAVY SUB-PROJECT. Accordingly my colleagues and I have organized several well-designed Seminars from 2002 to 2004, discussed the themes of the work undertaken to prepare a few Launching Volumes, introducing the basic areas and issues of CONSSAVY. The titles of the Volumes are (i) PHILOSOPHICAL CONSCIOUSNESS AND SCIENTIFIC KNOWLEDGE: CONCEPTUAL LINKAGES AND CIVILIZATIONAL BACKGROUND, (ii) SELF, SOCIETY AND SCIENCE : THEORETICAL AND HISTORICAL PERSPECTIVE, (iii) CONSCIOUSNESS YOGA AND INDIAN PSYCHOLOGY, and (iv) THE ENWORLDED SUBJECTIVITY: ITS THREE WORLDS AND BEYOND.

Some very basic points regarding this search and publication must be stated here. First, the Volumes under CONSSAVY will be devoted to both Indian and European ideas on the basic concepts of Consciousness, Science, Society and Value. Secondly, Yoga will be treated from various points of view, and from its spiritual, psychological, parapsychological and therapeutic aspects. Thirdly, the basic concepts of physics, biology and sociology, in that order, together with their epistemological and methodological presuppositions and implications, will also be dealt with. Volumes consisting of research papers on different types of natural sciences and social sciences, with particular emphasis on their interfaces, will be published under this extended SUB-PROJECT of **PHISPC**. Fourthly, like the **PHISPC** volumes, these volumes will be addressed to the educated general readers, not specialists. But each volume will have its occasional glimpses of specialization under thematic compulsion. Fifthly, most of these volumes will be edited, not authored, volumes. Several very distinguished natural scientists, life scientists, social scientists and historians have already joined this Sub-Project and started their editorial work, identifying specialist contributions and organizing Seminars with them. Finally, it may be added here that preparation of some these volumes is at an advance stage and may hopefully be published during the years 2005 or 2006.

The majority of the volumes planned under this SUB-PROJECT basically would be more modern and less historical in their scope and composition. The underlying logic of this partly changed orientation is somewhat like this. Approximately speaking, from the sixteenth century onward, one finds that because of the availability of developed navigational technology in Europe, the western presence started assuming a global character. This presence turned out to be both intellectual and political. The direct effects of this global presence of Europe in other countries were gradually reflected in the history of science, technology and economics of the concerned peoples. Different imperial powers of Europe cast their hegemonic shadows on different countries. By the eighteenth century the world of ideas, in general, and those of science and technology, in particular, started taking a universalistic but euro-centric character. The European scholars' understanding of distant Asian and African civilizations, to start with, had been understandably ill informed, highly coloured and prejudiced in most, but not all, cases. This cultural fallout of European hegemony will be reflected in some of the studies to be brought out under this Project. But conscious attempts will be made to represent this historical trend of euro-centricity as objectively and truthfully as possible. But the negative effects of imperialism and exploitation can hardly be blotted out *in toto*.

The homogenizing impact of science and technology of the European origin on other countries could not naturally be very uniform. The extent, degree and duration of the imperial powers on the colonial peoples certainly made a difference. Japan, for example, could largely escape the negative effects of colonial rule. The fact that a substantial part of China did not experience colonial subjugation has enabled it to retain, at least to a certain measure, its cultural identity. In this respect the story of countries like India and Indonesia has been significantly different.

Naturally, the civilizational self-perception of India during the colonial period, from the late eighteenth century to the early nineteenth century has its own distinct features. Most of the people of this country were more or less overwhelmed by the mighty cultural presence of the foreign rulers. Their language and literature, socio-political theories and rapidly growing scientific tradition deeply impressed the intelligentsia of India. The institutions which came up during the period bore the distinct imprints of the colonizers' national tradition. From schools and colleges to general and judicial administrative systems, all were being steadily shaped by the British model.

In the process two major trends came into effect. At the level of education and administration the Islamic influence of the previous centuries suffered a setback. The classical Indian tradition, which partly assimilated the influence of the Islamic rule and culture, had substantially succeeded in retaining its own identity before the beginning of the colonial rule. But under the colonial rule both the classical heritage and the Islamic tradition of India were being consciously suppressed. The hidden assumption is clear. Unless the ruler's ideas were imposed as the ruling ideas, the colonial rule could not be successful.

Paradoxically enough, in their limited self-interest, to make their rule effective or workably acceptable to the resenting or withdrawn Indians, the British rulers had to make some tactical concessions to the then existing state of affairs and people's aspirations. For example, three notable institutions—Sanskrit College in Benaras, Calcutta Madrassa, and The Asiatic Society, were all established in 1780s. Fort William College was functioning mainly as a sort of Academic Staff College for educating and qualifying the young administrators of the time. Incidentally, of course, some traditional trends of education and research received limited attention and patronage. But, broadly speaking, all the indigenous systems of education and forms of production, both material and intellectual, were objectively suppressed.

Towards the end of the nineteenth century and more clearly in the first quarter of the twentieth century, one perceives a distinct shift in the self-perception of India. The simmering resentment of the people found its first widespread expression in the Sepoy Mutiny of 1857. The establishment of three Universities at Calcutta, Bombay and Madras and the transfer of ruling power from the East India Company to the British Crown symbolized the beginning of a new era of a mixed character. The establishment of Indian National Congress in 1884 turned out to be an event of legitimizing the dissident Indian view articulated in obedient idioms. The partition of Bengal (1905), the establishment of the Muslim League (1906), the Surat Session of the Congress (1907), Non-Cooperation (1921), Civil Disobedience (1931) and Quit India (1942) movements under the leadership of Gandhi are among the major milestones on India's road to freedom. Right from the first decade of the twentieth century to the uprising of the Naval Ratings in Bombay and Karachi in 1945, a fallout of the Subhash Bose-led INA movement, one can clearly discern two parallel forms of the struggle for national independence, one non-violent and another pro-violent.

For understanding the changing scenario of India under the colonial rule one must take note not only of the overt political development but also, perhaps more so, of the social and cultural change in the temper, conduct and self-expression of the seemingly silent masses and the literati.

The introduction of steam ship in 1830s and the running of the trains in 1850s to the establishment of jute mills around Calcutta and textile mills around Ahmedabad marked the beginning of a new techno-economic era in the history of India. Around the same time, some Engineering Schools and Colleges were established in different parts of the India, viz., Madras (1840), Bombay (Elphinston Institution, 1844), Roorkee (Thomason Engineering College, 1847) and Calcutta (Bengal Engineering College, 1856). Later on, some of these institutions changed names and sites. The spread of scientific and technological education was followed up by some research interests and activities in those areas. No modern history of India can be complete unless the development in the fields of science and technology are duly studied and traced.

In the new series of PHISPC-CONSSAVY publications attempt will be made to highlight not only scientific and technological developments but also the developments of social and political ideas from the colonial period to the post-colonial period. While the material conditions of life and living shape the ideational and finer aspects of the society, the latter have their own impact on the former. The character and development of intellectual ideas and practical activities are inseparably related to the concerned social milieu. All things, abstract and concrete, are human in their roots. Without reference to human needs, production and consumption of ideas and ideals and their historical development can hardly be meaningfully related and narrated. That explains, in part, why the extended **PHISPC-CONSSAVY** Project is paying so much attention to the material and ideational aspects of India to make its history of the colonial and post-colonial periods really comprehensive. The contributions to the concerned Volume, it will be noticed, are not only descriptive but also critical and evaluative in all necessary contexts.

It is clear that the editors and contributors of the volume under this Project have paid studied attention in tracing the long ancient and medieval heritage of India. But this has been a part of their aim to bring those findings to bear upon the history of our own time. Every history is unfolded sociology or social accounts of human ideas and actions. Conversely speaking, it may be justifiably affirmed that every stretch of sociology is enfolded history, showing how the received ideas of the past have moulded the contemporary views, values and actions. What is more is this. Historical consciousness, reinforced and modified by contemporary events and ideas, propel human existence together with its social heritage towards the future. Rightly understood, there is no sharp line of demarcation between the past, present and future. It is a continuum. For pressing practical reasons we slice up time arbitrarily. Time's intrinsic metric, if any, is neither known nor respected by us. Somewhat similarly it may be pointed out that cultural space has no perceptible boundary of its own. It is a plenum. Admittedly it is uneven due to different and changing forms of human thought and actions, the basic and dynamic constituents of culture.

In the very titles of the **PROJECT** [**PHISPC**] and its **SUB-PROJECT** [**CONSSAVY**] one can find the basic themes and sub-themes which are being covered in these two related series of publications. Ancillary to the main themes and sub-themes several other related issues have also been taken up in these volumes. The number and variety of the themes and sub-themes found in these volumes are mainly due to the comprehensive scope of the civilizational study and the interdisciplinary character of that study. The interpenetration of the said themes and sub-themes are partly natural and partly interpretative, substantially due to the concerned writers' perception of the subject. Earlier it has been said that within a cultural subjects there exists no unsurpassable natural bounds. Somewhat similarly one may point out that in an interdisciplinary study of a civilizational subject different areas of organized knowledge like philosophy and science, science and society, psychology and sociology cannot be clearly distinguished. One subject gets merged into another. For example, it is well known that Theoretical Physics in its higher reaches is highly philosophical. In the ancient Indian and Hellenic history, for example, philosophy and cosmology, mainly speculative in character, are not distinguishable. In the relatively recent past in the European tradition science is to be referred to as Natural Philosophy or Experimental Philosophy. Even in the late nineteenth century this practice was there.

Admittedly things have changed since. In the twentieth century in Europe, India and elsewhere the relation between philosophy and science is being redrawn and are redefined. Broadly speaking, science is defined mainly in terms of its method. The basic components of scientific methods are quantitative, experimental and, in some cases, axiomatic. Both in terms of its method and subject matter philosophy is more or less, but not entirely, different from science. In philosophy while some philosophers follow analytic method, many others, particularly of Europe, follow the method of phenomenological description and reduction or existential analysis. After the rise of analytical school and post-modernism in which *difference* figures as the basic category, the general run of philosophers in Europe and America, unlike their predecessors of the nineteenth century, do not claim to be system-builder. In place of systematic philosophy we find the dominant influence of logical analysis or ordinary language analysis.

But this Euro-American picture is not exactly what we find in the countries of Asia and Africa. This is not to deny that the influence of western philosophy on the philosophies of all these countries is more or less clear. Partly because of the colonial system of education and partly because of the intensive exposure of African and Asian philosophers to the ideas of their Euro-American counterparts, a new kind of philosophy has been emerging in the ancient countries like China and India. Classical systems of ideas in all their variety are being reinterpreted in the light of new scientific development of Europe and America. In the process classical faithfulness to the ancient texts is being partly replaced by creative synthesis and interpretation. Understandably, in the light of contemporary ideas the ancient categories of thought are being reinterpreted and often proliferated.

Another development which merits special attention is this. Most of the philosophers of our time in their works are found to deal with some or other finds of *social science* or *natural science* or even both. In some cases, philosophy turns out to be a bridge between relatively abstract theoretical principles and empirical findings. In brief, philosophy is philosophy of this or that social science or natural science. To think of philosophizing in a vacuum is idle. Both natural scientists and social scientists try to be conscious of their theoretical pre-suppositions and, on request, are prepared to explain the same. Without theories facts cannot be related meaningfully and intelligibly. Mere description of facts without theoretical cover or linkage leads to a kind of *fact-fetishism.* The other extreme is excessive reliance on abstract theories without trying to relate or apply the same to concrete facts. The opposite of fact-fetishism is *theory-intoxication.* The judicious blend of theories and facts is found in the discourses of science, sociology, empirical psychology and transcendental epistemology, in that order. There we frequently hear of such composite disciplines like *sociology of science* and *psychology of science.*

In the CONSSAVY Volumes the reader will find many composite subjects in their best possible integrity. The inter-disciplinary method which is the heart of the extended **PROJECT, PHISPC-CONSSAVY,** demands that theories and facts should be studied in their mutual relationship. Truly understood, theories are clustered or systematic, not isolated. Similarly, facts or objects exist and change in and through their relational interaction, and not in isolation. Conscious attempts have been made to capture these basic truths about knowledge in different volumes which are being published under the extended PROJECT.

Centre for Studies in Civilizations
Kolkata and New Delhi
February 13, 2004

D.P. Chattopadhyaya

Acknowledgement

It is always a pleasure to acknowledge the debt which one incurs in preparing these kinds of scholarly works. The persons and institutions to which we remain deeply grateful are too many to be mentioned individually. Certainly some deserve special mention and thanks. The Indian Council of Philosophical Research (ICPR), the Indian Institute of Advanced Study (IIAS), Shimla, the Indian Council of Historical Research (ICHR), National Institute of Advanced Studies (NIAS), Bangalore, the Indian Council of Social Science Research (ICSSR), Auroville Foundation, Ministry of Human Resource Development (Department of Secondary and Higher Education), Ministry of Culture and Tourism, India International Centre (IIC), Nehru Memorial Museum Library, Indian National Science Academy (INSA) and Ministry of Science and Technology have been helping us in very many ways. The advice and guidance of the Members of the Governing Body of the Centre for Studies in Civilizations (CSC) has been of much value to us in executing the PHISPC-CONSSAVY Project.

Our foremost debt is of course towards the learned Editorial Fellows of different Volumes and their Parts and the scholarly contributors to those works. Whatever the Project has been able to achieve is substantially due to these academic personalities and kind cooperation.

In the production process of the Volumes being published under the PHISPC-CONSSAVY PROJECT we have been consistently assisted by numerous experts, administrative and academic. In this connection I must put on record our deep sense of gratitude to Professor Kireet Joshi, Professor Bhuvan Chandel, Shri A.K. Sen Gupta, Professor (Ms.) A.K. Anand, Dr. Arun Mishra, Dr. Vikram Singh Sirola, Dr. (Ms.) Mira Roy, Ms. Moitreyee Chatterjee, Mr. Swaraaj Chauhan, Mr. S. Banerjee and Mr. Satkari Mukhopadhyaya. I must take this opportunity to thank heartily Mr. Sreekumaran, S., Mr. Sehdev Ram, Mr. Paramesh Ganguly, Mr. M. Lakshmanan, Mrs. Mukta Gosain, Mrs. Sadhana Nagar, Mrs. Neerja Chogtu, Mr. Ajay Kumar, Mr. Indranil Das, Mr. Partap Singh Sharma, Mr. S. Ghosh, Mr. C.L. Jose and Mr. K.S. Bisht for their painstaking and devoted administrative and secretarial support.

I would like to thank the policy-makers and in-house staff members of our Publishers and Distributors like Oxford University Press, Munshiram Manoharlal and Motilal Banarsidass.

Centre for Studies in Civilizations
New Delhi, March, 2004

D.P. Chattopadhyaya

Contributors

A.V.Afonso is the Head of Department of Philosophy and Dean of Faculty of Languages and Faculty of Social Sciences at Goa University. He taught for several years in colleges affiliated to University of Pune and Bombay and Post-graduate Centre of University of Bombay. He is the author of the book *Essays on Methodological Individualism* and several articles on philosophy of natural and social sciences.

T.R. Anantharaman, who runs a spiritual research centre at Gurgaon, had earlier held the posts of Professor of Metallurgy at Banaras Hindu University; Director, Thapar Institute of Engineering and Technology at Patiala and Senior Scientist (INSA) at National Physical Laboratory, New Delhi. His publications include *Bhagavad Gita* in German, *Rapidly Solidified Metals: A Technological Overview, The Rustless Wonder: A Study of the Iron Pillar at Delhi* and a large number of research papers encompassing a broad spectrum of topics in physical metallurgy.

Prajit K. Basu worked in the Departments of Humanities and Social Sciences of I.I.T Delhi and I.I.T Bombay. Presently he is employed in the Department of Philosophy of the University of Hyderabad. His teaching and research interests include history and philosophy of science and science, technology and society interface areas.

Sibajiban Bhattacharyya, a National Fellow in Indian Institute of Advanced Studies (IIAS), Shimla, was, till recently an Editorial Fellow of the Project of History of Indian Science, Philosophy and Culture (PHISPC). He was formerly B.N. Seal Professor of Mental and Moral Philosophy, Calcutta University and was also a National Fellow of ICPR. He taught philosophy in various Indian and foreign universities for more than 40 years and has written over a hundred articles in Indian and foreign journals and encyclopaedias.

Amita Chatterjee, Professor, Department of Philosophy, Jadavpur University, Kolkata. Her main areas of interest and contribution are logic, cognitive science and Indian Philosophy.

D.P. CHATTOPADHYAYA., M.A., LL.B., Ph.D. (Calcutta and London School of Economics), D. Litt., (Honoris Causa), studied, researched on Law, philosophy and history and taught at various Universities in India, Asia, Europe and USA from 1954 to 1994. Founder-Chairman of the ICPR (1981-1990) and President-cum-Chairman of the IIAS, Shimla (1984-1991), Chattopadhyaya is currently the Project Director of the multidisciplinary 96 volume PHISPC and Chairman of CSC. Among his 36 publications, authored 18 and edited or co-edited 18, are Individuals and Societies (1967); *Individuals and Worlds (1976); Sri Aurobindo and Karl Marx (1988); Anthropology and Historiography of Science (1990); Induction, Probability and Skepticism (1991); Sociology, Ideology and Utopia (1997); Societies, Cultures and Ideologies (2000); Interdisciplinary Studies in Science, Society, Value and Civilizational Dialogue (2002); Philosophy of Science, Phenomenology and other essays (2003). Self, Society and Science : Theoretical and Historical Perspectives (2004); Religion, Philosophy and Science (2006)* and *Aesthetic Theories and Forms in Indian Tradition (2008).* He has also held high Public offices, namely, of Union cabinet minister and state governor. He is a Life Member of the Russian Academy of Sciences and a Member of the International Institute of Philosophy, Paris. He was awarded Padma Bhushan in 1998 and Padmavibhushan in 2009 by the Government of India.

Mahashweta Chaudhuri, a University Grants Commission Emeritus Fellow, was earlier awarded Fellowship by Indian Council of Philosophical Research (ICPR), IIAS Shimla, Indo French Fellowship and Summer Research Fellowship of Maison de sciences de I'homme, Paris. Her collaboration with French philosophers of CREA, Paris, took place in three International colloquium. Besides numerous articles, her major publications include *Epistemology with or without Knowing Subject, Facets of Rationality* and *Bounds of Freedom.*

AMITABHA DASGUPTA, Professor, Department of Philosophy, Central University of Hyderabad, was earlier awarded a Fullbright Fellowship to carry out his post-doctoral research at MIT, Cambridge, Mass. He has held research and teaching positions at the Centre for Philosophy of Science, Boston University, Tilburg University (The Netherlands) and Maison Des Sciences De L'Homme, Paris. He has authored several papers and books including *The Second Linguistic Turn: Chomsky and the Philosophy of Language.*

PARTHA GHOSE, is an Honorary Professor & Member, Board of Trustees, Centre for Philosophy and Foundations of Science, New Delhi; a former Professor and Academic Programme Coordinator, S.N. Bose National Centre for Basic Sciences, Kolkata; Fellow, The National Academy of Sciences, India & West Bengal Academy of Science and Technology; winner of the Indira Gandhi Prize for Popularisation of Science awarded by the Indian National Science Academy. He has published a large number of papers in theoretical physics in international journals and edited a number of conference proceedings. One of his books, *Testing Quantum Mechanics on New Ground,* published by Cambridge University Press, UK, has won critical acclaims.

RAVI GOMATAM (a.k.a. Rasaraja Dasa Brahmacari), Director of Bhaktivedanta Institute in Mumbai as well as in Berkeley, USA, is an Adjunct Professor, Birla Institute of Technology & Science, Pilani, Rajasthan. He holds a masters degree in Electronics Engineering and a Ph.D. in philosophy and science.

DIPANKAR HOME, Professor of Physics in Bose Institute, Kolkata, has done Post-Doctoral work at University of Manchester, University of Southampton, University of Cambridge and Queen's University of Belfast. He has written 81 research publications apart from 4 review articles. His book, *Conceptual Foundation of Quantum Physics* has a Foreword by Novel Laureate Anthony Leggett. He has won sever awards, including the Jawaharlal Nehru Fellowship, Homi Bhabha Fellowship, B.M.Birla Science Prize and Indian National Science Academy Young Scientist's Medal.

SWAMI JITATMANANDA, a monk of the Ramakrishna Mission since 1964, has written eight books, including *Swami Vivekananda: Prophet and Pathfinder, Modern Physics and Vedanta, Holistic Science and Vedanta* and *Indian Ethos for Modern Management.* Since 1986, the Swami has been representing India in various international conferences held in India and abroad.

KIREET JOSHI, Chairman of ICPR, Chairman of Auroville Foundation and Vice Chairman of Maharshi Sandipani Rashtriya Veda Vidya Pratisthan, is also an Editorial Fellow of PHISPC. Earlier he held the posts of Education Adviser to Government of India, Special Secretary in the Union Ministry of Human Resource Development and Registrar of Sri Aurobindo International Centre of Education, Pondicherry. His books include *Sri Aurobindo and Integral Yoga, A Philosophy of Evolution for the Contemporary Man, Glimpses of Vedic Literature, The Veda and Indian Culture, Portals of Vedic Knowledge, Education for Tomorrow, A National Agenda for Education, Philosophy of Value-Oriented Education: Theory and Practice* and *The Good Teacher and the Good Pupil.*

SUBHASH KAK, a Delaune Distinguished Professor of Electrical Engineering and Professor in the Asian Studies Programme at Louisiana State University, Baton Rouge, USA, is the author of numerous papers on history of science, information theory, quantum mechanics, and Indian science, art and philosophy and neural networks. Fifteen books authored by him include *The Astronomical Code of the Rigveda, The Wishing Tree, The Gods Within* and *The Asvamedha.* He has written a monograph, *The Architecture of Knowledge* for PHISPC.

RAJESH KOCHHAR, a distinguished astro-physicist. He is currently Director of National Institute of Science, Technology and Development, New Delhi.

R.A. MASHELKAR, Director General of Council of Scientific and Industrial Research, (CSIR), Government of India, has done pioneering research in polymer science and engineering. He is only the third Indian engineer to have been elected as Fellow of Royal Society (FRS), London in the twentieth century. Fifteen universities have honoured him with honorary doctorates. He was awarded Padmashri (1991) and Padmabhushan (2000) in recognition of his contributions to nation building.

KAMALAKAR MISHRA, former Head of the Department of Philosophy and Religion, Banaras Hindu University, has specialized in Tantric Philosophy, particularly in Kashmir Saivism. In addition to the two books authored by him, *Significance of the Tantric Tradition* and *Kashmi Saivism: The Central Philosophy of Tantrism,* he has written and published several articles on the topic of Tantra, Yoga, Value-education, Applied Indian Philosophy, Mental Health, Rational Religion, etc. A monograph entitled *Maitri-bhavana: the Miracle Yoga of Mental Health and Happiness* is under preparation.

A.K. MUKHOPADHYAY, a Member in the Faculty of All India Institute of Medical Sciences, New Delhi, is an acknowledged authority on Supracortical Consciousness, the bridging concept to reconcile brain-bound consciousness and brain-independent consciousness. He has authored several papers and four books entitled *Frontiers of Research for human Biologists, The Dynamic web of Supracortical Consciousness, Conquering the Brain* and *The Millennium Bridge.*

MOHINI MULLICK, is specialized in logic and taught for a long time at the Department of Technology, Social and Science, IIT, Kanpur.

RODDAM NARASIMHA, a Fellow of the Royal Society and a Foreign Associate of both the U.S. National Academy of Sciences and the U.S. National Academy of Engineering, has held various positions like Director of the National Institute of Advanced Studies and Chairman of the Engineering Mechanics Unit at the Jawaharlal Nehru Centre for Advanced Scientific Research, Bangalore, Director of the National Aerospace Laboratories at Bangalore and President of the Indian Academy of Sciences. He has also held various positions at the Indian Institute of Science.

S. PANNEERSELVAM, Professor of Philosophy, University of Madras, has published one book, *The Problem of Meaning with reference to Wittgenstein and Sankara*, co-edited two volumes, *Post-modernism and Critical Theory* and *Conspectus of Philosophy, History and Religion* and also published number of research papers in the leading philosophical Journals. He was Indo-

Shastri Canadian Institute's Fellow in the year 2003. He is the associate editor of *Indian Philosophical Annual*, University of Madras, Chennai and also the Advisory Committee member of the *Sathya Nilayam: Chennai Journal of Intercultural Philosophy*.

R.C. Pradhan, Professor of Philosophy at the University of Hyderabad, had held the post of Member-Secretary of I.C.P.R. He was also Commonwealth Academic Staff Fellow at Oxford University, UK. He has authored several books including *Language Experience: An Interpretation of the Later Philosophy of Wittgenstin; Truth, Meaning & Understanding; Philosophy of Meaning & Representation; Recent Developments in Analytic Philosophy and The Great Mirror.* He has also contributed many papers to philosophical journals.

Rajendra Prasad, former Professor of Philosophy and Chairman, Department of Humanities, I.I.T, Kanpur, is also an Editorial Fellow of PHISPC. The areas which are of special interest to him include Analytical Philosophy, Ethics and Logic, His publications include six books authored, one edited, and more than hundred research papers.

N.S.S. Raman, an Editorial Fellow of PHISPC, was Head of the Department of Philosophy and Religion and Dean, Faculty of Arts, Banaras Hindu University. He was also a Visiting Professor of Philosophy at the University of Mainz in Germany and also at the IIAS, Shimla. He is editing a Volume on Hinduism for PHISPC.

C. Ramanathan, former Professor and Principal of APS College, Bangalore, has served PHISPC as a Research Assistant for over 7 years. He is presently engaged in the translation of a Sanskrit commentary on the Ramayana into English under a Project undertaken by Sanskrit Vidyapeeth, Tirupathi.

Raja Ramanna, Founder Chairman of the National Institute of Advanced Study, Bangalore, is an eminent scientist and formerly Chairman of the Atomic Energy Commission of India. He contributed not only to science but also to philosophy and music.

Minakshi Roy Chowdhury, Professor of Philosophy, Rabindra Bharati University, Kolkata, has done works in the fields of metaphysics and theory of scientific knowledge. She has published many papers in journals and anthologies e.g. *Myth, Metaphysics and Science* and *Re-enactment or Reconstruction? – On Collingwood's Historical Understanding.*

A.K. Sen Gupta, a Consultant with PHISPC and ICPR, has been a journalist and a civil servant for over three decades. He has held the position of Director General of media units of the Union Ministry of Information and Broadcasting and has edited many Government books and journals. He was Special Correspondent for Prasar Bharati in Africa in the nineties and a Commercial Representative of India in Europe in the eighties.

Ramakant Sinari, Professor Emeritus and former Professor and Chairman of the Department of Humanities and Social Sciences at IIT, Mumbai, was earlier a Fulbright-Smithmundt scholar in U.S.A., a British Council grantee, an invitee Fellow at the East-West Philosophers' Conference at the University of Hawaii, a visiting Professor of Philosophy in the U.S.A., a National Lecturer of the U.G.C., Professor and Head, Department of Philosophy, Goa University, and a National Fellow of the I.C.P.R. He has published several papers and is the author of *Reason in Existentialism, The Structure of Indian Though* and *The Concept of Man in Philosophy* (Ed.).

YOGENDRA SINGH, Professor (Emeritus) in Jawaharlal Nehru University, New Delhi, taught Sociology for many decades and was the Founder Chairperson of the Centre for the Study of Social Systems. The books authored by him include *For a Sociology of India, Towards a Sociology of Culture in India, Towards a Sociology of Non-violence & Peace, Modernization of Indian Traditions, Traditions of Non-Violence in the East and West, Social Stratification and Social Change, Social Aspects of Scientific and Technological Revolution, Essays on Modernization, Image of Man: Ideology and Theory in Indian Sociology, Indian Sociology: Social Conditions and Emerging Concerns, Sociology of Culture, Social Change in India: Crisis and Resilience* and *Culture Change in India: Identity and Globalization.*

RAGHAWENDRA PRATAP SINGH, an Associate Professor and Chairperson, Group of Philosophy, School of Language, Literature & Culture Studies, Jawaharlal Nehru University, New Delhi, was awarded MAN OF THE YEAR 2001 by American Biographical Institute of International Research for his outstanding contributions in the field of education. He has to his credit nine books: *A Critical Examination of Immanuel Kant's Philosophy Kant and Hegel: Methodology, Ontology Epistemology, Dialectic and Ought, Dialectic of Reason: A Comparative Study of Kant and Hegel; Philosophy: Modern and Postmodern; Freedom and Causation: With Special References to Hegel's Overcoming of Kant; The Buddhist World-view; Reason, Dialectic and Postmodern Philosophy; Applied Philosophy;* and *Philosophy: Modern and Postmodern.*

B.V.SREEKANTAN, a visiting Professor at the National Institute of Advanced Studies, Bangalore, was earlier Director of the Tata Institute of Fundamental Research (TIFR) Mumbai. He carried out experimental research in Cosmic Rays, High Energy Physics, and High Energy Astronomies and published over 200 papers. He received many awards including Padma Bhushan Award from the President of India, the Rajyotsava Award from the Karnataka Government, the Jawaharlal Nehru National Award from the Madhya Pradesh Government and the Yodh Prize of the Cosmic Ray Commission of IUPAP and the University of California, Irwine for his lifetime contributions to Cosmic Ray Research.

B.V. SUBBARAYAPPA, an Editorial Fellow of PHISPC, is a Honorary Director of the Centre for History and Philosophy of Science at the Indian Institute of World Culture, Bangalore. He was formerly Executive secretary of the Indian National Science Academy, New Delhi; Project Coordinator and Member Secretary of the National Commission for the History of Science in India; Director, Discovery of India Project, Nehru Centre, Mumbai, President of the International Union of History and Philosophy of Science (related to UNESCO) and full Member of the International Academy of History of Science (Paris). Author and editor of 10 books on History of Science in India, over 80 of the papers were published in national and international journals.

P.N. TANDON, Meghnad Saha Distinguished Fellow and President, National Brain Research Centre, New Delhi, was a Professor at the All India Institute of Medical Science, New Delhi for a long time. He has done considerable research in the frontier areas of Neurology and has written a number of papers on consciousness and neurology.

C.S.UNNIKRISHNAN, Senior Reader at TIFR, Mumbai, Adjunct Professor at Indian Institute of Astrophysics, Bangalore, Faculty Associate at CPFS, Delhi, and Visiting Professor at Ecole Normale Superieure, Paris, has researched on topics including experimental gravitation, conceptual issues and foundational aspects of gravity and quantum mechanics.

General Introduction

I

It is understandable that man, shaped by Nature, would like to know Nature. The human ways of knowing Nature are evidently diverse, theoretical and practical, scientific and technological, artistic and spiritual. This diversity has, on scrutiny, been found to be neither exhaustive nor exclusive. The complexity of physical nature, life-world and, particularly, human mind is so enormous that it is futile to follow a single method for comprehending all the aspects of the world in which we are situated.

One need not feel bewildered by the variety and complexity of the worldly phenomena. After all, both from traditional wisdom and our daily experience, we know that our own nature is not quite alien to the structure of the world. Positively speaking, the elements and forces that are out there in the world are also present in our body-mind complex, enabling us to adjust ourselves to our environment. Not only the natural conditions but also the social conditions of life have instructive similarities between them. This is not to underrate in any way the difference between the human ways of life all over the world. It is partly due to the variation in climatic conditions and partly due to the distinctness of production-related tradition, history and culture.

Three broad approaches are discernible in the works on historiography of civilization, comprising science and technology, art and architecture, social sciences and institutions. Firstly, some writers are primarily interested in discovering the general laws which govern all civilizations spread over different continents. They tend to underplay what they call the noisy local events of the external world and peculiarities of different languages, literatures and histories. Their accent is on the unity of Nature, the unity of science and the unity of mankind. The second group of writers, unlike the generalist or transcendentalist ones, attach primary importance to the distinctiveness of every culture. To these writers human freedom and creativity are extremely important and basic in character. Social institutions and the cultural articulations of human consciousness, they argue, are bound to be expressive of the concerned people's consciousness. By implication they tend to reject concepts like archetypal consciousness, universal mind and providential history. There is a third group of writers who offer a composite picture of civilizations, drawing elements both from their local as well as common characteristics. Every culture has its local roots and peculiarities. At the same time, it is pointed out that due to demographic migration and immigration over the centuries an element of compositeness emerges almost in every culture. When, due to a natural calamity or political exigencies people move from one part of the world to another, they carry with them, among other things, their language, cultural inheritance and their ways of living.

In the light of the above facts, it is not at all surprising that comparative anthropologists and philologists are intrigued by the striking similarity between different language families and the rites, rituals and myths of different peoples. Speculative philosophers of history, heavily relying on the findings of epigraphy, ethnography, archaeology and theology, try to show in very general terms that the particulars and universals of culture are 'essentially' or 'secretly' interrelated. The spiritual aspects of culture like dance and music, beliefs pertaining to life, death and duties, on analysis, are found to be mediated by the material forms of life like weather forecasting, food production, urbanization and invention of script. The transition from the oral culture to the written one was made possible because of the mastery of symbols and rules of measurement. Speech precedes grammar, poetry prosody. All these show how the 'matters' and 'forms' of life are so subtly interwoven.

II

The PHISPC publications on History of Science, Philosophy and Culture in Indian Civilization, in spite of their unitary look, do recognize the differences between the areas of material civilization and those of ideational culture. It is not a work of a single author. Nor is it being executed by a group of thinkers and writers who are methodologically uniform or ideologically identical in their commitments. In conceiving the Project we have interacted with, and been influenced by, the writings and views of many Indian and non-Indian thinkers.

The attempted unity of this Project lies in its aim and inspiration. We have in India many scholarly works written by Indians on different aspects of our civilization and culture. Right from the pre-Christian era to our own time, India has drawn the attention of various countries of Asia, Europe and Africa. Some of these writings are objective and informative and many others are based on insufficient information and hearsay, and therefore not quite reliable, but they have their own value. Quality and view-points keep on changing not only because of the adequacy and inadequacy of evidence but also, and perhaps more so, because of the bias and prejudice, religious and political conviction, of the writers.

Besides, it is to be remembered that history, like Nature, is not an open book to be read alike by all. The past is mainly enclosed and only partially disclosed. History is, therefore, partly objective or 'real' and largely a matter of construction. This is one of the reasons why some historians themselves think that it is a form of literature or art. However, it does not mean that historical construction is 'anarchic' and arbitrary. Certainly, imagination plays an important role in it.

But its character is basically dependent upon the *questions* which the historian raises and wants to understand or answer in terms of the ideas and actions of human beings in the past ages. In a way, history, somewhat like the natural sciences, is engaged in answering questions and in exploring relationships of cause and effect between events and developments across time. While in the natural sciences, the scientist poses questions about nature in the form of hypotheses, expecting to elicit authoritative answers to such questions, the historian studies the past, partly for the sake of understanding it for its own sake and partly also for the light which the past throws upon the present, and the possibilities which it opens up for moulding the future. But the difference between the two approaches must not be lost sight of. The scientist is primarily interested in discovering laws and framing theories, in terms of which, different events and processes can be connected and anticipated. His interest in the conditions or circumstances attending the concerned events is secondary. Therefore, scientific laws turn out to be basically abstract and easily expressible in terms of mathematical language. In contrast, the historian's main interest centres round the *specific* events, human ideas and actions, not *general* laws. So, the historian, unlike the scientist, is obliged to pay primary attention to the circumstances of the events he wants to study. Consequently, history, like most other humanistic disciplines, is concrete and particularist. This is not to deny the obvious truth that historical events and processes consisting of human ideas and actions show some trend or other and weave some pattern or other. If these trends and patterns were not there at all in history, the study of history as a branch of knowledge would not have been profitable or instructive. But one must recognize that historical trends and patterns, unlike scientific laws and theories, are not general or purported to be universal in their scope.

III

The aim of this Project is to discover the main aspects of Indian culture and present them in an interrelated way. Since our culture has influenced, and has been influenced by, the neighbouring cultures of West Asia, Central Asia, East Asia and South-East Asia, attempts have been made here to trace and study these influences in their mutuality. It is well known that during the last three centuries, European presence in India, both political and cultural, has been very widespread. In many volumes of the Project considerable attention has been paid to Europe and through Europe to other parts of the world. For the purpose of a comprehensive cultural study of India, the existing political boundaries of the South Asia of today are more of a hindrance than help. Cultures, like languages, often transcend the bounds of changing political territories.

If the inconstant political geography is not a reliable help to the understanding of the layered structure and spread of culture, a somewhat comparable problem is encountered in the area of historical periodization. Periodization or segmenting time is a very tricky affair. When exactly one period ends and another begins is not precisely ascertainable. The periods of history designated as ancient, medieval and modern are purely conventional and merely heuristic in character. The varying scopes of history, local, national and continental or universal, somewhat like the periods of history, are unavoidably fuzzy and shifting. Amidst all these difficulties, the volume-wise details have been planned and worked out by the editors in consultation with the Project Director and the General Editor. I believe that the editors of different volumes have also profited from the reactions and suggestions of the contributors of individual chapters in planning the volumes.

Another aspect of Indian history which the volume-editors and contributors of the Project have carefully dealt with is the distinction and relation between civilization and culture. The material conditions which substantially shaped Indian civilization have been discussed in detail. From agriculture and industry to metallurgy and technology, from physics and chemical practices to the life sciences and different systems of medicines—all the branches of knowledge and skill which directly affect human life—form the heart of this Project. Since the periods covered by the PHISPC are extensive—prehistory, proto-history, early history, medieval history and modern history of India—we do not claim to have gone into all the relevant material conditions of human life. We had to be selective. Therefore, one should not be surprised if one finds that only some material aspects of Indian civilization have received our pointed attention, while the rest have been dealt with in principle or only alluded to.

One of the main aims of the Project has been to spell out the first principles of the philosophy of different schools, both pro-Vedic and anti-Vedic. The basic ideas of Buddhism, Jainism and Islam have been given their due importance. The special position accorded to philosophy is to be understood partly in terms of its proclaimed unifying character and partly to be explained in terms of the fact that different philosophical systems represent alternative world-views, cultural perspectives, their conflict and mutual assimilation.

Most of the volume-editors and at their instance the concerned contributors have followed a middle path between the extremes of narrativism and theoreticism. The underlying idea has been this: if in the process of working out a comprehensive Project like this every contributor attempts to narrate all those interesting things that he has in the back of his mind, the enterprise is likely to prove unmanageable. If, on the other hand, particular details are consciously forced into a fixed mould or pre-supposed theoretical structure, the details lose their particularity and interesting character. Therefore, depending on the nature of the problem of discourse, most of the writers have tried to reconcile in their presentation, the specificity of narrativism and the generality of theoretical orientation. This is a conscious editorial decision. Because, in the absence of a theory, however inarticulate it may be, the factual details tend to fall apart. Spiritual network or theoretical orientation makes historical details not only meaningful but also interesting and enjoyable.

Another editorial decision which deserves spelling out is the necessity or avoidability of duplication of the same theme in different volumes or even in the same volume. Certainly, this Project is not an assortment of several volumes. Nor is any volume intended to be a miscellany. This Project has been designed with a definite end in view and has a structure of its own. The character of the structure has admittedly been influenced by the variety of the themes accommodated within it. Again it must be understood that the complexity of structure is rooted in the aimed integrality of the Project itself.

IV

Long and in-depth editorial discussion has led us to several unanimous conclusions. Firstly, our Project is going to be *unique*, unrivalled and discursive in its attempt to integrate different forms of science, technology, philosophy and culture. Its comprehensive scope, continuous character and accent on culture distinguish it from the works of such Indian authors as P.C. Ray, B.N. Seal, Binoy Kumar Sarkar and S.N. Sen and also from such Euro-American writers as Lynn Thorndike, George Sarton and Joseph Needham. Indeed, it would be no exaggeration to suggest that it is for the first time that an endeavour of so comprehensive a character, in its exploration of the social, philosophical and cultural characteristics of a distinctive world civilization—that of India—has been attempted in the domain of scholarship.

Secondly, we try to show the linkages between different branches of learning as different modes of experience in an *organic* manner and without resorting to a kind of reductionism, materialistic or spiritualistic. The internal dialectics of organicism without reductionism allows fuzziness, discontinuity and discreteness within limits.

Thirdly, positively speaking, different modes of human experience—scientific, artistic, etc., have their own individuality, not necessarily autonomy. Since all these modes are modification and articulation of *human* experience, these are bound to have between them some finely graded commonness. At the same time, it has been recognized that reflection on different areas of experience and investigation brings to light new insights and findings. Growth of knowledge requires humans, in general, and scholars, in particular, to identify the distinctness of different branches of learning.

Fourthly, to follow simultaneously the twin principles of: (a) individuality of human experience as a whole, and (b) individuality of diverse disciplines, are not at all an easy task. Overlap of themes and duplication of the terms of discourse become unavoidable at times. For example, in the context of *Dharmaśāstra*, the writer is bound to discuss the concept of value. The same concept also figures in economic discourse and also occurs in a discussion on fine arts. The conscious editorial decision has been that, while duplication should be kept to its minimum, for the sake of intended clarity of the themes under discussion, their reiteration must not be avoided at high intellectual cost.

Fifthly, the scholars working on the Project are drawn from widely different disciplines. They have brought to our notice an important fact that has clear relevance to our work. Many of our contemporary disciplines like economics and sociology did not exist, at least not in their present form, just two centuries ago or so. For example, before the middle of nineteenth century, sociology as a distinct branch of knowledge was unknown. The term is said to have been coined first by the French philosopher Auguste Comte in 1838. Obviously, this does not mean that the issues discussed in sociology were not there. Similarly, Adam Smith's (1723–90) famous work *The Wealth of Nations* is often referred to as the first authoritative statement of the principles of (what we now call) economics. Interestingly enough, the author was equally interested in ethics and jurisprudence. It is clear from history that the nature and scope of different disciplines undergo change, at times very radically, over time. For example, in India '*Arthaśāstra*' does not mean the science of economics as understood today. Besides the principles of economics, the *Arthaśāstra* of ancient India discusses at length those of governance, diplomacy and military science.

Sixthly, this brings us to the next editorial policy followed in the Project. We have tried to remain very conscious of what may be called indeterminacy or inexactness of translation. When a word or expression of one language is translated into another, some loss of meaning or exactitude seems to be unavoidable. This is true not only in the bilingual relations like Sanskrit-English and Sanskrit-Arabic, but also in those of Hindi-Tamil and Hindi-Bengali. In recognition of the importance of language-bound and context-relative character of meaning we have solicited from many learned scholars, contributions, written in vernacular languages. In order to minimize the miseffect of semantic inexactitude we have solicited translational help of that type of bilingual scholars who know both English and the concerned vernacular language, Hindi, Tamil, Telugu, Bengali or Marathi.

Seventhly and finally, perhaps the place of technology as a branch of knowledge in the composite universe of science and art merits some elucidation. Technology has been conceived in very many ways, e.g., as autonomous, as 'standing reserve', as liberating or enlargemental, and alienative or estrangemental force. The studies undertaken by the Project show that, in spite of its much emphasized mechanical and alienative characteristics, technology embodies a very useful mode of knowledge that is peculiar to man. The Greek root words of technology are *techne* (art) and *logos* (science). This is the basic justification of recognizing technology as closely related to both epistemology, the discipline of valid knowledge, and axiology, the discipline of freedom and values. It is in this context that we are reminded of the definition of man as *homo technikos*. In Sanskrit, the word closest to *techne* is *kalā* which means any practical art, any mechanical or fine art. In the Indian tradition, in *Śaivatantra*, for example, among the arts (*kalā*) are counted dance, drama, music, architecture, metallurgy, knowledge of dictionary, encyclopaedia and prosody. The closeness of the relation between arts and sciences, technology and other forms of knowledge are evident from these examples and was known to the ancient people. The human quest for knowledge involves the use of both head and hand. Without mind, the body is a corpse and the disembodied mind is a bare abstraction. Even for our appreciation of what is beautiful and the creation of what is valuable, we are required to exercise both our intellectual competence and physical capacity. In a manner of speaking, one might rightly affirm that our psychosomatic structure is a functional connector between what we are and what we could be, between the physical and the beyond. To suppose that there is a clear-cut distinction between the physical world and the psychosomatic one amounts to denial of the possible emergence of higher logico-mathematical, musical and other capacities. The very availability of aesthetic experience and creation proves that the supposed distinction is somehow overcome by what may be called the bodily self or embodied mind.

V

The ways of classification of arts and sciences are neither universal nor permanent. In the Indian tradition, in the *Ṛgveda*, for example, *vidyā* (or sciences) are said to be four in number: (i) *Trayī*, the triple Veda; (ii) *Ānvīkṣikī*, logic and metaphysics; (iii) *Daṇḍanīti*, science of governance; (iv) *Vārtta*, practical arts such as agriculture, commerce, medicine, etc. Manu speaks of a fifth *vidyā* viz., *Ātma-vidyā*, knowledge of self or of spiritual truth. According to many others, *vidyā* has fourteen divisions, viz., the four Vedas, the six *Vedāngas*, the *Purāṇas*, the *Mīmāṁsā*, *Nyaya*, and *Dharma* or law. At times, the four *Upavedas* are also recognized by some as *vidyā*. *Kalās* are said to be 33 or even 64.

In the classical tradition of India, the word *śāstra* has at times been used as a synonym of *vidyā. Vidyā* denotes instrument of teaching, manual or compendium of rules, religious or scientific treatise. The word *śāstra* is usually found after the word referring to the subject of the book, e.g., *Dharma-śāstra, Artha-śāstra, Alaṁkara-śāstra* and *Mokṣa-śāstra.* Two other words which have been frequently used to denote different branches of knowledge are *jñāna* and *vijñāna.* While *jñāna* means knowing, knowledge, especially the higher form of it, *vijñāna* stands for the act of distinguishing or discerning, understanding, comprehending and recognizing. It means worldly or profane knowledge as distinguished from *jñāna,* knowledge of the divine.

It must be said here that the division of knowledge is partly conventional and partly administrative or practical. It keeps on changing from culture to culture, from age to age. It is difficult to claim that the distinction between *jñāna* and *vijñāna* or that between science and art is universal. It is true that even before the advent of modern age, both in the East and the West, two basic aspects of science started gaining recognition. One is the *specialized character* of what we call scientific knowledge. The other is the concept of *trained skill* which was brought close to scientific knowledge. In the medieval Europe, the expression 'the seven liberal sciences' has very often been used simultaneously with 'the seven liberal arts', meaning thereby, the group of studies by the *Trivium* (Grammar, Logic and Rhetoric) and *Quadrivium* (Arithmetic, Music, Geometry and Astronomy).

It may be observed here, as has already been alluded to earlier, that the division between different branches of knowledge, between theory and practice, was not pushed to an extreme extent in the early ages. *Praxis,* for example, was recognized as the prime *techne.* The Greek word, *technologia* stood for systematic treatment, for example, of Grammar. *Praxis* is not the mere application of *theoria,* unified vision or integral outlook, but it also stands for the active impetus and base of knowledge. In India, one often uses the terms *Prayukti-vidyā* and *Prayodyogika-vidyā* to emphasize the practical or applicative character of knowledge. *Prayoga* or application is both the test and base of knowledge. Doing is the best way of knowing and learning.

That one and the same word may mean different 'things' or concepts in different cultures and thus create confusion has already been stated before. Two such words which in the context of this Project under discussion deserve special mention are *dharma* and *itihāsa.* Ordinarily, *dharma* in Sanskrit-rooted languages is taken to be conceptual equivalent of the English word *religion.* But, while the meaning of religion is primarily theological, that of *dharma* seems to be manifold. Literally, *dharma* stands for that which is established or that which holds people steadfastly together. Its other meanings are law, rule, usage, practice, custom, ordinance and statute. Spiritual or moral merit, virtue, righteousness and good works are also denoted by it. Further, *dharma* stands for natural qualities like burning (of fire), liquidity (of water) and fragility (of glass). Thus one finds that meanings of *dharma* are of many types—legal, social, moral, religious or spiritual, and even ontological or physical. All these meanings of *dharma* have received due attention of the writers in the relevant contexts of different volumes.

This Project, being primarily historical as it is, has naturally paid serious attention to the different concepts of history—epic-mythic, artistic-narrative, scientific-causal, theoretical and ideological. Perhaps the point that must be mentioned first about history is that it is not a correct translation of the Sanskrit word *itihāsa*. Etymologically, it means what really happened (*iti-ha-āsa*). But, as we know, in the Indian tradition *purāṇa* (legend, myth, tale, etc.), *gāthā* (ballad), *itivṛtta* (description of past occurrence, event, etc.), *ākhyāyikā* (short narrative) and *vaṃśa-carita* (genealogy) have been consciously accorded a very important place. Things started changing with the passage of time and particularly after the effective presence of Islamic culture in India. Islamic historians, because of their own cultural moorings and the influence of the Semitic and Graeco-Roman cultures on them, were more particular about their facts, figures and dates than their Indian predecessors. Their aim to bring history close to statecraft, social conditions and the lives and teachings of the religious leaders imparted a mundane character to this branch of learning. The Europeans whose political appearance on the Indian scene became quite perceptible only towards the end of the eighteenth century brought in with them their own view of historiography in their cultural baggage. The impact of the Newtonian Revolution in the field of history was very faithfully worked out, among others, by David Hume (1711–76) in *History of Great Britain from the Invasion of Julius Caesar to the Revolution of 1688* (6 Vols., 1754–62) and Edward Gibbon (1737–94) in *The History of the Decline and Fall of the Roman Empire* (6 Vols., 1776–88). Their emphasis on the principles of causality, datability and continuity/linearity of historical events introduced the spirit of scientific revolution in European historiography. The introduction of English education in India and the exposure of the elites of the country to it largely account for the decline of the traditional concept of *itihāsa* and the rise of the post-Newtonian scientific historiography. Gradually, Indian writers of our own history and cultural heritage started using more and more European concepts and categories. This is not to suggest that the impact of the European historiography on Indian historians was entirely negative. On the contrary, it imparted an analytical and critical temper which motivated many Indian historians of the nineteenth century to try to discover and represent our heritage in a new way.

VI

The principles which have been followed for organizing the subjects of different volumes under this Project may be stated in this way. We have kept in view the main structures which are discernible in the decomposible composition of the world. The first structure may be described as physical and chemical. The second structure consists, broadly speaking, of biology, psychology and epistemology. The highest and the most abstract structure nests many substructures within it, for example, logic, mathematics and musical notes. It is well known that the substructures within each structure are interactive, i.e., not isolable. The more important point to be noted in this connection is that the basic three structures of the world, viz., (a) physico-chemical, (b) bio-psychological, and (c) logico-mathematical are all simultaneously open to upward and downward causation. In other words, while the physico-chemical structure can causally influence the bio-psychological one and the latter can causally influence the most abstract logico-mathematical, the reverse process of causation is also operative in the world. In spite of its relative abstractness and durability, the logico-mathematical world has its downward causal impact on our bio-psychological and epistemological processes and products. And the latter can also bring about change in the structures of the physical world and its chemical composition. Applied physics and bio-technology make the last point abundantly clear.

Many philosophers, life-scientists, and social scientists highlight the point that nature loves hierarchies. Herbert Simon, the economist and the management scientist, speaks of four steps of partial ordering of our world, namely, (i) chemical substances, (ii) living organisms, tissues and organs, (iii) genes, chromosomes and DNA, and (iv) human beings, the social organizations, programmes and information process. All these views are in accord with the anti-reductionist character of our Project. Many biologists defend this approach by pointing out that certain characteristics of biological phenomena and process like unpredictability, randomness, uniqueness, magnitude of stochastic perturbations, complexity and emergence cannot be reduced without recourse to physical laws.

The main subjects dealt with in different volumes of the Project are connected not only conceptually and synchronically but also historically or diachronically. For pressing practical reasons, however, we did not aim at presenting the prehistorical, proto-historical and historical past of India in a continuous or chronological manner. Besides, it has been shown in the presentation of the PHISPC that the process of history is non-linear. And this process is to be understood in terms of human praxis and an absence of general laws in history. Another point which deserves special mention is that the editorial advisors have taken a conscious decision not to make this historical Project primarily political. We felt that this area of history has always been receiving extensive attention. Therefore, the customary discussion of dynastic rule and succession will not be found in a prominent way in this series. Instead, as said before, most of the available space has been given to social, scientific, philosophical and other cultural aspects of Indian civilization.

Having stated this, it must be admitted that our departure from conventional style of writing Indian history is not total. We have followed an inarticulate framework of time in organizing and presenting the results of our studies. The first volume, together with its parts, deals with the prehistorical period to A.D. 300. The next two volumes, together with their parts, deal with, among other things, the development of social and political institutions and philosophical and scientific ideas from A.D. 300 to the beginning of the eleventh century AD. The next period with which this Project is concerned spans from the twelfth century to the early part of the eighteenth century. The last three centuries constitute the fourth period covered by this Project. But, as said before, the definition of all these periods by their very nature are inexact and merely indicative.

Two other points must be mentioned before I conclude this General Introduction to the series. The history of some of the subjects like religion, language and literature, philosophy, science and technology cannot for obvious reason be squeezed within the cramped space of the periodic moulds. Attempts to do so result in thematic distortion. Therefore, the reader will often see the overflow of some ideas from one period to another. I have already drawn attention to this tricky and fuzzy and also the misleading aspects of the periodization of history, if pressed beyond a point.

Secondly, strictly speaking, history knows no end. Every age rewrites its history. Every generation, beset with new issues, problems and questions, looks back to its history and reinterprets and renews its past. This shows why history is not only contemporaneous but also futural. Human life actually knows no separative wall between its past, present and future. Its cognitive enterprises, moral endeavours and practical activities are informed of the past, oriented by the present and addressed to the future. This process persists, consciously or unconsciously, wittingly or unwittingly. In the narrative of this Project, we have tried to represent this complex and fascinating story of Indian civilization.

Centre for Studies in Civilizations
New Delhi

D.P. Chattopadhyaya
General Editor

I
Science and Philosophy

CHAPTER 1

Some Considerations on Philosophical Consciousness and Scientific Knowledge: Conceptual Linkages and Civilizational Background

Sibajiban Bhattacharyya

It is usual to suppose that scientific knowledge is the best form of knowledge. This assumption, however, is wrong for various reasons. One reason is that scientific knowledge is abstract in two senses. In one sense, all sciences deal with different parts of nature. Sometimes the same object is studied from two different points of view. For example, both physics and inorganic chemistry deal with inanimate matter. But the scientists make a distinction between physical properties of matter and chemical properties of matter. All these distinctions are abstract in the sense that they are not so in reality. In reality nature is one undivided whole along with human beings. There are no parts of nature. In the second sense, all sciences are abstract for the scientific laws are general, either causally or statistically. The differences between the objects are ignored. So all sciences involve abstract universals.

Philosophical consciousness is all-comprehensive and concrete. Moreover, it is entirely rational. We may remind ourselves of the Hegelian dictum that whatever is rational is real, and what is real is rational. According to Hegel, philosophy is rational. According to him, sciences are products of the understanding which is a lower faculty than reason. This is true both of idealistic philosophy and materialistic philosophy. For example, dialectical materialism is not merely a natural law but is also a law of human history.

There is also an attempt to unify sciences. Even if this be possible, this unity of sciences cannot be philosophy, for the unity of science presupposes philosophy (of science), so it cannot be philosophy. Another reason is that all sciences ignore the subject or the knower. Sciences claim that they are completely objective. But this is unjustified because there can be no science without a scientist who explains the scientific laws. In comtemporary quantum mechanics where measurement changes what is measured shows the importance of the subject. It has been pointed out by existentialist philosophers that to study any object, a thinker is necessarily presupposed.

Moreover, it has been claimed that the progress of science depends upon the use of mathematics. This theory is wrong because "Mathematical models rarely agree *exactly* with physical reality. . .. All the 'laws' of physics that we arrogantly impose on the universe seem condemned to remain partial models, approximate mental representations that we ceaselessly improve."[1]

There is another reason to criticise scientific knowledge. All scientific theories are philosophy-laden. This is how progress in science is made possible. For example, when the atomic theory of matter was first proposed, it was confidently believed that atoms are the smallest particles of matter. But later on it was found out that atoms can be split. Newton also discussed space and time as separate. But Einstein has a theory that space and time are not different; time is only the fourth dimension of space. There are more examples which we shall discuss later on.

I

PHILOSOPHY OF MATHEMATICS

The question here is what is the nature of mathematical objects? Three types of theories have been proposed—Platonism, Formalism and Intuitionism. Thomas Hardy and the French mathematician Charles Hermite as well as many other mathematicians believe in the reality of mathematical objects. But Platonism leaves in the dark how a mathematician in the flesh could ever explore the abstract realm of mathematical objects.

David Hilbert, head of the Formalist Movement, holds that "The existence of the mathematical objects is meaningless. Mathematics is only a game in which one manipulates symbols according to precise formal rules. Mathematical objects such as numbers have no relation to reality: they are defined merely as a set of symbols that satisfy certain axioms."[2] According to Wittgenstein's famous statement "All mathematical propositions mean the same thing, namely nothing."[3] This is not true that the whole of mathematics can "be reduced to an exploration of the consequences of purely arbitrary choices... most mathematicians do not just manipulate symbols according to purely arbitrary rules."[4]

"A third category of mathematicians is that of the 'intuitionists' or 'constructivists', who believe that mathematical objects are nothing but constructions of the human mind. In their view, mathematics does not exist in the outside world, but only in the brain of the mathematician who invents it. Neither arithmetic, nor geometry nor logic predate the emergence of the human species. It would even be conceivable for another species to develop radically different mathematics." "The founders of intuitionism have stressed the primitive and irreductible nature of numerical intuition." "As demonstrated by the mathematics historian Morris Kline, the roots of intuitionism go back to Descartes, Pascal, and of course, to Kant." "Kant stated that 'the ultimate truth of mathematics lies in the possibility that its concepts can be constructed by the human mind.'"[5]

A theory of number is based upon the distinction between numbers and numerals. "Judged by today's standards, the Babylonian system had one final drawback: for fifteen centuries, it lacked a zero. ... Not until the third century before Christ did the Babylonians finally introduce a symbol to fill this gap and explicitly denote absent units. Even then, this symbol served only as a placeholder. It never acquired the meaning of a 'null quantity' or of 'the integer immediately below I' which we attribute to it today."[6]

Now we shall discuss a diversity of number languages. The first question to be decided is the base of the number language. Base 20 ruled "Aztec, Mayan, and Gaelic languages and is still in use in Eskimo and Yoruba. Traces of it can still be found in French, in which 80 is '*quatre-vingt*' (four twenties) and in Elizabethan English, which often counted in scores (twenty)."[7] "Memory Span in China soars to about nine digits, while it averages only seven in English. Why this discrepancy? Are speakers of Chinese more intelligent? Probably not, but their number words happen to be shorter." "Chinese number words are remarkably brief. Most of them can be uttered in less than one-quarter of a second (for instance, 4 is 'si' and 7 'qi'). Their English equivalents—'four', 'seven'—are longer: pronouncing them takes about one-third of a second. The memory gap between English and Chinese apparently is entirely due to this difference in length. In languages as diverse as Welsh, Arabic, Chinese, English, and Hebrew, there is a reproducible correlation between the time required to pronounce numbers in a given language and the memory span of its speakers. In this domain, the prize for efficacy goes to the Cantonese dialect of Chinese, the brevity of which grants residents of Hong Kong a rocketing memory span of about 10 digits."[8]

II

MATHEMATICS AND AXIOMATICS

As has been shown by Śrinavasa Rāmānujan lyengar, although it is usual to formulate mathematics axiomatically, this is not necessary. "Rāmānujan claimed that his theorems were 'written on his tongue' during the night by the goddess Namagiri. On getting out of bed, he would often feverishly write down some unexpected result that would later stun his colleagues."[9]

There is a difference between the Indian way of doing mathematics and western mathematics. So British mathematicians were at pains to provide rigorous proofs or refutations for the hundreds of formulas. We quote here a statement which shows the genius of Rāmānujan. "The following dialogue took place between Hardy and Rāmānujan while the Indian mathematician was slowly dying of tuberculosis in a sanitarium. 'The taxi that I hired to come here bore the number 1729', said Hardy. 'It seemed a rather dull number.' 'Oh no, Hardy', retorted Rāmānujan. 'It is a captivating one. It is the smallest number that can be expressed in two different ways as a sum of two cubes—$1729 = 1^3 + 12^3 = 10^3 + 9^3$!'"[10]

III

THE NATURE OF MATHEMATICS

"Mathematics is often called the only science that is cumulative—its results, once acquired, are never questioned or revised." Mathematics is often called 'a temple of rigour'. But there are many counter-examples to this view. "Monumental volumes have become obsolete with the advent of general methods for solving polynomial equations of the second, third, and fourth degree. A demonstration, which is once found valid, may be judged inadequate or downright false by the next generation of mathematicians."

Take, for example, the infinite sum 1 – 1 + 1 – 1 + 1...infinitely alternating the addition and subtraction of 1. "Today, any university student can prove that this sum has no meaningful value (it oscillates between 0 and 1). Yet in 1713 a mathematician as talented as Leibniz *proved*—incorrectly, of course—that this infinite sum was equal to ½!"

This is because mathematics is a result of evolution. "Mathematics is a human construction and hence a necessarily imperfect and revisable endeavour." This evolution is not merely biological but also cultural. This may be seen from the different languages of number developed in different cultures. It is to be noted that mathematics, though considered an intellectual enterprise, depends upon various subjective factors. For example, children of equal initial abilities may become excellent and hopeless at mathematics depending on their love or hatred of the subject. "Passion breeds talent"[11]. This explains the possibility of genius mathematicians. All geniuses are extremely fond of mathematics.

"To affirm that arithmetic is the product of the human mind does not imply that it is arbitrary and that, on some other planet, we might have been born with the idea that 1 + 1 = 3. Throughout phylogenetic evolution, as well as during cerebral development in childhood, selection has acted to ensure that the brain constructs internal representations that are adapted to the external world. Arithmetic is such an adaptation."

There is also another point about mathematics which should be noted. "Mathematicians generate an enormous amount of pure mathematics. Only a small part of it will ever be useful in physics. There is thus an overproduction of mathematical solutions from which physicist select those that seem best adapted to their discipline."[12]

There is also the problem of the relation between pure science and technology. Previously there was a fundamental difference between pure science and technology. Science gives us knowing that, technology gives us knowing how. In modern times, this distinction between knowing that and knowing how is gradually vanishing. So even researches in pure science involve use of high technology. Thus researches in atomic or quantum science involve cyclotrons, which are the products of technology, so also in other areas of pure science. Moreover, researches in pure science and even in humanities are not possible without the use of sophisticated computers. For example, in order to solve problems of, AI, digital computers are often used.

Professor Jayanta Viṣṇu Nārlikar once said that Government determines various fields in which researches in pure science can be carried out. This is because researches in pure science require so much money that can be supplied only by a government. Moreover, there is a matter of policy involved. For example, there are many countries like Japan and West Germany, which could easily develop atom bombs but the governments of these countries do not allow the scientists to do research in this area. Cloning of human beings may be scientifically possible. But many governments do not allow research in the area. Thus governments determine the areas where research is possible.

IV

PHILOSOPHY AND SCIENCE

Kant, in his *Critique of Pure Reason*, has asked three fundamental questions:

1. How is pure mathematics as a science possible?
2. How is pure physics as a science possible?
3. How is metaphysics as a science possible?

According to him the first two are possible because they involve synthetic *a priori* judgements. The third is not possible for there is no intuition corresponding to the Ideas of Pure Reason. There can be only antinomies when one comes to settle metaphysical questions.

However, Kant's questions are not justified. For example, there is no certainty in pure physics. Thus, Einstein's General Relativity Theory is based on the assumption that the velocity of light is ultimate. There cannot be anything which can exceed the speed of light. Now many physicists have challenged this assumption. They hold that there is a particle called 'tachyon' which can move faster than light. As time is connected in relativity theory with light, a particle which moves faster than light, will pass from the future to the past through the present. But the existence of tachyon is not accepted by all physicists.

This proves that physics is not absolutely certain. There is a fundamental difference between different physicists. There are schools of physics as there are schools of philosophy. This shows that there is no difference in kind between science and philosophy.

There is, however, an aspect of pure mathematics which shows that mathematics and philosophy are very different. It is probably Einstein himself who, in a letter published by Hadamard in his famous *Essay on the Psychology of Invention in the Mathematical Field*, articulated most clearly the role of language and intuition in mathematics. "Words and language, whether written or spoken, do not seem to play any part in my thought processes. The psychological entities that serve as building blocks for my thought are certain signs or images, more or less clear, that I can reproduce and recombine at will."[13] Great mathematicians' intuitions about numbers and other mathematical objects do not seem to rely so much on clever symbol manipulations as on a direct perception of significant relations.

If it be true that even the greatest mathematicians do not use language to do mathematics it seems that philosophy in the western tradition has to use language. But philosophy itself is culture-bound and there are many systems of Indian philosophy which transcend language altogether. So there will be no difference in kind between science like pure mathematics and Indian philosophy.

V

PHILOSOPHY AND CULTURE

There is a radical distinction between western philosophy and Indian philosophy. Western philosophers are intellectuals, perhaps intellectual giants, whereas all schools of Indian philosophy are rooted in intuitions of the sages. All Indians philosophical systems are based on aphorisms (*sūtra*) which record intuitions of the sages who are the authors of the

Indian philosophical systems. Thus even in science, we may find difference in attitude of the western interpreters of science and Indian theories.

Here we mention only one science, namely, ecology. I shall discuss here two different interpretations of ecology by western philosophers. According to one interpretation, nature has to be protected, including prevention of global warming, for the sake of man. Because man lives in nature and nature has to be protected, sound and air pollution cured, only to make man healthy. Man is the highest form of creation and therefore nature, and flora and fauna, are to be treated as an instrument for man's happiness. A second interpretation of ecology is to regard nature as having supreme value. Nature is to be protected only for the sake of nature, it has nothing to do with human existence.

Indian culture seems to combine the two interpretations. According to Indian culture, man and nature constitute an organic unity. One has to protect nature for the sake of nature as also for the sake of man. So also one has to protect man for the sake of man, and also for the sake of nature. You cannot harm one without harming the other. Just as man without nature is an abstraction, so also is nature without man. Neither man nor nature in isolation has any separate reality. In the *Ṛg Veda*, the seers have repeated a number of times that nature and man are united in an all-embracing consciousness. Nature is as much important as man.

Indian culture is a composite of various strands. There were technological developments, like metallurgy, medicine and commerce, and there was also a very developed theory of language. Moreover, there is an emphasis on the ethical and the spiritual side of man. It has been pointed out that war is never prohibited. For example, it is pointed out that in the *Gītā* the Lord himself urges Arjuna to fight. This war-cry has been given a wholly spiritual colour. For example, it has been stated in the *Gītā* that human agency is illusory and that the Lord himself is the doer. Moreover, the whole world is in God who is really the doer. A man is said to be only an instrument of action for God (*nimittamātraṁ bhava savyasācin*). Then there is a classification of men and worshippers of God. So the *Gītā*, though it enjoins war, is read only by wise men of culture, not by soldiers who know only to fight. Thus the *Gītā* is recommended for spiritual realization.

It has been pointed out that man cannot claim as a matter of right to be an instrument of divine action. The Lord will have to will someone to be His instrument. That is why the Lord specifically asserts that Arjuna be His instrument.

In India, society is traditionally divided into four castes, but now this caste system is almost gone from some parts of India. In the USA the Africans have many disadvantages compared to white Americans. It may be argued that in every society, people have to be differentiated on the basis of their intellectual and social power. Thus workers are untied to fight for their rights. In offices, there is a union of office-workers. There are also students unions and so on. They fight for their social, economic and political rights against their respective authorities. Then there are soldiers. In many countries, soldiers control political power. In India, soldiers are only used to fight, political power is vested in the government elected by the people.

It is not merely the *Gītā* but all schools in Indian philosophy have a theory which is peculiar to Indian culture. This is the theory of rebirth of the individual. In no other culture we have a theory of rebirth. Usually in all religions like Christianity and Islam, the individual self is regarded as eternal, waiting for the day of the last judgement by God. Then those who are found wanting are condemned to an eternal stay in hell; and those who are virtuous are rewarded by eternal stay in heaven. This, according to Indian philosophers, is contrary to both the causal principle and ethics. Even if a person is a born sinner, he can perform only a limited number of sinful actions in his whole life. For performing a limited number of sinful actions a person certainly does not deserve eternal hell. So also the virtuous do not deserve eternal heaven. According to Indian philosophers, a sinner or a virtuous person is given a number of chances to improve his character and destiny.

There is also no difference in kind between man and woman. The only difference is in the physical body. A person who is born a man in this life may be reborn in the next life as a woman, and vice versa.

The law of *karma* which is connected with rebirth is present in all schools of Indian philosophy but in no system of western philosophy.

VI

NYĀYA-NAVYA-NYĀYA THEORY OF COGNITION

The Sanskrit term '*jñāna*' is usually translated into English as 'cognition' or 'awareness'. I shall use the word 'cognition' as English translation of the Sanskrit word. The denotation of the word 'cognition' is at once wider and narrower than that of the English word 'knowledge'. Cognition is wider in denotation because it includes false belief non-verdical perception, supposition memory as also the usual verdical perception, valid inference testimony, introspection and other forms of knowledge.

It is narrower than the denotation of 'knowledge' because the word 'knowledge' is often used both in the episodic and dispositional senses, while 'cognition' is used only in the episodic sense.

There is a fundamental difference between the senses of '*jñāna*' and 'knowledge'. The word 'knowledge' is usually defined in contemporary western philosophy as justified true belief. But in Indian philosophy in general as also in Nyāya, there is no concept of justification. So instead of justified true belief we have merely true belief. It is true that according to Nyāya the object of perception is a cause of the perceptual cognition. It maybe regarded as a sort of causal justification. But this sort of causal connection between the object and cognition of the object cannot be present in inference for the object inferred may be a past or a future object which cannot cause the present inference; so also with testimony. So the causal explanation cannot be valid for all true belief.

It has also been argued that true belief *pramāṇa* is invariably caused by an instrument of true belief (*pramāṇa*). But this causal theory of 'true belief' is defined as belief corresponding to the object (*yathārthānubhava*). The instrument of true belief is defined in terms of true belief. So it is not proper to say that an instrument of true belief causes true belief, for it will be analytically true.

Cognition in general is classified differently on different principles. The first classification of cognition is into informative and recollective cognition. Only informative cognition can be true but no recollective cognition, i.e. memory can be true. Another classification of cognition is into true cognition and false cognition. A true cognition is a true belief; false cognitions maybe false beliefs, i.e. illusory perception, or maybe doubt, supposition etc. which are not beliefs about anything.

According to Nyāya there are four sources of true belief, i.e. true cognition. There are instrumental causes of true belief (*pramāṇa*). As true belief is of four kinds, the instrumental causes are also four. The true beliefs are: perception, inference, analogy or identification, and testimony. These four kinds of beliefs are mutually exclusive, as is evidenced by introspection. In introspection these four different kinds of awareness are quite distinct. We shall now explain these four different kinds of true beliefs. In one kind of definition the instrumental cause of the belief is stated.

Navya-Nyāya defines perception in three ways. The first definition is in terms of the instrumental cause of perception. Perception is defined as a cognition produced by the instrumentality of sense-organs. Six sense-organs are admitted in this system, five external senses, and *manas*, the internal sense-organ. The sense-organs are the instrumental cause of perceptual knowledge, because they produce perception through an operation which is the characteristic relation of the sense-organs with their objects.

This definition is rejected as too narrow because it does not apply to God's perception. Navya-Nyāya philosophers postulate one omniscient God who perceives everything, past, present and future. This divine perception is one eternal perception which cannot be produced by anything. Moreover, according to Navya-Nyāya philosopehrs, God does not have any body, any *manas*, or any sense-organs. So God's perception cannot be defined as produced through the instrumentality of sense-organs. So a second definition is proposed. Perception is that cognition which does not have any cognition as its instrumental cause. It is to be noted here that Navya-Nyāya philosophers do not deny that many cognitions play causal roles in the production of perception. For example, *viśeṣaṇa*. So also in many other cases of perception. But these causal factors are not instrumental causes. There is a third definition of perception which applies to the perception of yogins. Perception is defined as that which is known in introspection as having the universal of perception. An undisputed instance of perception is chosen in introspection. This is cognized as an instance of the universal of perception. Then perception is defined as that which is an instance of this universal.

VII

CLASSIFICATION OF PERCEPTION

Perceptions are classified into indeterminate (*nirvikalpaka*) and determinate (*savikalpaka*). *Nirvikalpaka* perception is negatively characterized as not involving any relation between *viśesya* and *viśeṣaṇa*. About what exactly is the object of *nirvikalpaka* perception, there are three views among Nyāya philosophers. (i) According to some we perceive only an undifferentiated mass (*piṇḍā mātra*) in *nirvikalpaka* perception, and express it just as something. (ii) According to others, we perceive only universals and other class characters which function in later *savikalpaka* perception as *viśeṣaṇa* in the perception of a jar.

(iii) According to Viśvanātha and others, we perceive both the *viśeṣya* and the *viśeṣaṇa*, although not as *viśeṣya* and *viśeṣaṇa*, but as unrelated items. For example, we perceive both the substance jar and the jarness as unrelated items. Both (i) and (iii) involve difficulties and (ii) propounded by Gaṅgeśa seems to be the most satisfactory theory.

Nyāya philosophers have an elaborate theory of doxastic relation (*sannikarṣa*) in explaining the theory of perception of different kinds of objects. Thus when someone perceives a jar by his eyes his eyes come into relation with the jar. This relation is contact. When a person perceives by his eyes the colour inhering in a jar, his eyes have to be related to the colour of the jar. But this relation is not a single relation. For his eyes come into contact with the jar in which the colour of the jar inheres. So in this visual perception of the colour of the jar the relation of the eyes with the colour of the jar is contact-cum-inherence (*saṁyukta samavāya*). When someone perceives by his eyes the colour universal present in the colour of the jar, his eyes have to be related to the colour universal. This relation is, again, an indirect relation. It is contact-cum-inherence-cum-inherence (*saṁyukta samaveta samavāya*). The eyes of the person come into contact with the jar in which the colour inheres and in which the colour universal inheres.

It maybe argued that it is not possible to see the colour of a jar without seeing the jar itself. For it maybe pointed out that to relate eyes to the colour of the jar, it is necessary to connect the eyes with the jar by contact. But this theory is not correct. For example, the air cannot be perceived at all but its qualities like coolness, hotness, can be perceived by touch. So without perceiving the substance (air) one can perceive its qualities.

When someone hears a sound the sound is a quality of *ākāśa* which restricted within the ear-hole is the sense-organ of hearing. Now the relation between the sense-organ and sound is inherence. When someone hears a sound, he also hears the universal of sound which inheres in that particular sound. The relation of the sense-organ of hearing to the universal of sound is an indirect relation, inherence-cum-inherence (*samaveta samavāya*).

When someone perceives there is no jar on the ground, i.e., there is absence of the jar on the ground, the ground here is the qualificand and the absence is the qualifier. The eyes of the person perceiving the absence of the jar as qualifying the ground are related to the absence by qualificand-qualifier relation (*viśeṣyaviśeṣaṇabhāva*). These are all forms of the ordinary type of perception (*laukika pratyakṣa*). Thus in *laukika* perception we know substances, attributes, motions, universals, inherence, and also negations, all categories of reals except *viśeṣa*. For perception adequate magnitude (*mahatva*) of the substance is necessary, for perception of attributes, they must be manifest (*udbhūta*).

Savikalpaka perception, again, is classified into (a) *laukika* and (b) *alaukika*. There are three forms of the special type of perception (*alaukika pratyakṣa*). Of these three forms first two are common to all individuals and the third one is special to the yogins. Among systems of Indian philosophy only Navya-Nyāya philosophers have assumed this type of perception.

(i) The first kind of these types of perception is perception of all instances of universals. When we perceive an elephant, we also perceive ordinarily the universal elephantness inhering in the elephant These are all cases of ordinary perception. But Navya-Nyāya philosophers argue that by perceiving one elephant as possessing elephantness, we perceive in a special way, all instances of elephantness, i.e., all elephants, past, present and future, near and far. When we perceive one elephant, we have perceived all elephants merely as elephants. This is why when we see a second elephant we *recognize* it as an elephant. But recognition is not possible if we had not already known the elephant. It is for the first time that we are seeing the second elephant. How can we then recognize it as an elephant? According to Navya-Nyāya philosophers this experience or recognition is possible only if we hold that by perceiving one elephant in the ordinary way, we perceive all elephants in the special way.

This Navya-Nyāya theory of perceiving in a special way all instances of a universal by perceiving the universal in the ordinary way in one instance of the universal avoids a difficulty of the conceptual theory of universals. According to this western theory we perceive a number of elephants, compare and contrast them and abstract their common properties and generalize. This theory is unsound because after seeing an elephant we may see another elephant after a long time and we might have forgotten by that time that first elephant that we have seen. Moreover, when we see a second elephant we cannot know it as an elephant, for, we have not yet got the concept of elephant. If we cannot know the first and second perceived elephants as elephants, we shall not be able to connect them. We shall not be able to form a generic image of an elephant unless we see many elephants of different shapes and sizes at the same time. This coincidence of perceiving many instances of the same universal at the same time is very rare. But without this coincidence of perceiving many instances at the same time, forming a generic image will not be possible. Navya-Nyāya philosophers cannot accept this generic image because they do not admit any image at all.

Every perception requires a doxastic relation (*sannikarṣa*) between the sense-organ and the object perceived. In this kind of special perception of all instances of a universal it is the universal as ordinarily and actually cognized which functions as the doxastic relation. The universal is actually perceived in the instances present here and now. This kind of special perception used in Navya-Nyāya to explain the perception of the invariable uncomitance of smoke with fire. No one can see ordinarily, all cases of smoke. Then how can one know, as one actually does, that all cases of smoke are related in the appropriate manner with fire? The reply is that by seeing one case of smoke possessing smokeness, one sees all cases of smoke. This explains the possibility of perceiving the pervasion of smoke by fire.

(ii) The second kind of special perception is the perception of objects by a sense-organ although these objects are not the proper objects of perception by the sense-organ. As an example, we may take a visual perception of a piece of sandalwood as fragrant.

Fragrance is not an object of visual perception. Yet when we see a piece of sandalwood we see it as fragrant. This is possible only if we have smelt the piece of sandalwood when we saw it before. It is the memory of the fragrance which functions as a very special kind of doxastic relation between the sense-organ of vision and the fragrance. It will not do to say that we see the piece of sandalwood and remember that it is fragrant. Our experience is of visual perception of the piece of sandalwood as fragrant. To explain this experience it is necessary to postulate this kind of special perception. There are six more different cases in which this kind of special perception is used in Navya-Nyāya to explain various types of experience.

(a) The first case is of recognition. We saw Devadatta before; when we see him now we recognize him to be that person. The recognition is perception and it takes the form, "this is that Devadatta". Now in this recognition the memory of Devadatta whom we saw before functions as the doxastic relation between the eyes and the past Devadatta to produce this perception.

(b) According to Nyāya we can know one cognition of an object in a higher order introspective cognition. The object of this higher order introspective cognition of a cognition has this form. "I know the jar." When I perceive the jar I am aware only of the jar, but not of my perceiving it. If I have to know my perception I have to perform a higher order introspective act. This introspective act has as its object the first order act. Yet the first order act cannot be cognized in a second order act unless and until the object of the first order act is also cognized.

The second order act cognizes the first order act as the second order act is introspection or inner perception. It perceives the external object of the first order act only so far as it is cognized in the first order act. Here, the doxastic relation between the second order inner perception and the external object of the first order act is the first order act of the cognition itself. So in this case also a cognition becomes the doxastic relation between *manas* which is the sense-organ of inner perception and the object of the first order perception.

(c) The third case of this type of perception explains the illusory perception of a piece of rope as a snake which is not present here and now. When we mistake a piece of rope for a snake we do not mistake the piece of rope for an idea or a memory of a real snake; we perceive the snake which is not here and now. But how can the sense-organ of vision be related to a snake not here and now? According to Nyāya, this is due to the doxastic relation between the sense-organ of vision and the absent snake.

(d) This is the case of introspection due to an illusory perception. For example, when we mistake a column of dust as smoke, the column of dust becomes the qualificand and smokeness the qualifier of this illusory perception. When we in introspection cognize the perception of the column of dust the eyes are related to the column of dust only through the illusory perception of the column of dust as smoke.

(e) In the case of a perception of a negative object the sense-organ has to be doxastically related to the object. For example, when we perceive that there is no jar on the floor, we have to know the jar before. We cannot simply perceive absence, the absence has got to be the absence of something. Even though the absence is before our eyes, the jar which is absent is not. Yet unless and until we can see the jar we cannot see the absence of the jar. In this case also the memory of the jar functions as the doxastic relation between the visual sense-organ and the absent jar.

(f) Navya-Nyāya philosophers hold that the meaning of word maybe known in different ways. One way is to identify an object as the meaning of a word based on perception of similarity. For example, a forester tells a citydweller that a *gavaya* is similar to a cow. When that man goes to a forest and perceives an animal similar to a cow he knows that the meaning of the word *gavaya* is any animal of this kind. Now the problem is that a person has to *see* the similarity of *gavaya* which is present and a cow which is absent. How can one perceive the similarity between a present and an absent thing? According to Nyāya philosophers the perception of the similarity requires the perception of the two objects which are similar. How can an absent cow be perceived? It is not ordinary perception, and it is the memory of the cow seen before which functions as the doxastic relation between the visual sense-organ and the absent cow.

(iii) The special perception of this kind is not common to all individuals, but is the prerogative of yogins. Yogins can see small things like atoms, distant and past and future things which cannot be perceived normally. In the case of a yogic perception the doxastic relation of *manas* to objects is a special cognition in the mind resulting from yogic exercises.

Moreover, science has developed into newer forms. Classical Physics, for example, has developed into quantum science, which has developed very new principles of quantum matter. For example, there is indeterminacy in quantum science. This means that measurement changes or modifies the matter measured. So when the rate of movement i.e. velocity, of sub-atomic matter is measured its position cannot be measured. On the other hand, if the position of sub-atomic matter is measured, then its velocity cannot be measured. Many scientists hold that even the law of causal determination does not hold in the sub-atomic matter. There was also development of relativity theory of Einstein. According to it, time is only a dimension (the fourth dimension) of space, so that space and time are not different. The basic idea is the idea of movement, which involves both space and time.

Science is different from science culture. A scientist is engaged in his own science. Science culture is the theory that science is the best form of knowledge and also involves common sense philosophy about scientific knowledge. For example, unobservables in nuclear science, like energy, electron, etc. are given two different interpretations. One is anti-realism, according to which the unobservables are mere theoretic terms used in science to explain nuclear theory. The other is the realistic interpretation, according to which the unobservables are real. Science culture accepts the second interpretation. Although many spectacular discoveries of Science and Technology have been made in recent times, there has not been much change in the medical sciences and also in the moral attitude of man.

VIII

INDIAN CONCEPTIONS OF SCIENCE

There are different theories about science in different schools of Indian philosophy. For example, in Nyāya and Vaiśeṣika systems, there is pluralistic realism. The nature of the object is not at all changed or modified by knowing it. This is a fundamental principle of all science and science culture. But as we have already noted, according to quantum mechanics measurement affects the sub-atomic matter. However, in all other cases whether in classical science or quantum science, knowledge does not affect the nature of the object.

It may be argued that according to Nyāya philosophers not in all cases is the object independent of knowledge. For example, knowledge of a particular kind (*apekṣābuddhi*) produces the numbers from 2 onwards in the objects. But the reply to this objection is that this kind of knowledge is only a cause of numbers 2 onwards in the objects. After producing the number in the objects, it is known without being modified in any way.

Now it maybe aruged that as knowledge produces the number in the objects, so the number is knowledge-dependent. But this objection is not justified. Knowledge of this sort can produce an objective property because according to Nyāya, the self or the knower has many properties common with material objects, like number, magnitude, separateness, conjunction and disjunction. Just as we can enumerate physical objects so we can enumerate the individual selves; just as material objects possess magnitude (space, time, *ākāśa* are material objects which have the greatest magnitude) so also the individual selves have greatest magnitude and so on. Thus there is no difficulty on the Nyāya-Vaiśeṣika theory of knowledge which belongs to the knower, in explaining how a property of the self can produce a property in the object. The causal relation between knowledge and number cannot make number dependent on knowledge. For example, fire causes smoke. But to know smoke it is not necessary to know its causal relation to fire. Every thing finite is caused by many factors. But to know any object it is not necessary to know all its causes.

There are two more points to be noted about the Nyāya-Vaiśeṣika theory. One point is that every substance has magnitude (*parimāṇa*). Magnitudes are of three types—(i) smallest magnitude, (ii) intermediate magnitude, and (iii) the greatest magnitude (*paramamahat parimāṇa*) which belongs to only ubiquitous substances (*vibhu dravya*). This magnitude belongs to material objects like space, time etc. as also to individual selves, and to God. According to Nyāya-Vaiśeṣika theory, the individual selves and God have the greatest magnitude in the same sense.

The second point concerns the smallest magnitude. All objects of intermediate magnitude can be analyzed into indivisible parts which cannot be further sub-divided. These are called *paramāṇus*. This term is often translated as 'atom'. But this translation is not quite correct. For example, the *paramāṇus* of earth have the special attribute of earth, namely, smell. According to western science, an atom does not have attributes of gross matter. For example, water is analyzed into H_2O, i.e., 2 hydrogen atoms and one oxygen atom, arranged in a special way. But none of these atoms has the attribute of water, liquidity etc. As a matter of fact, only *molecules* have the same attribute as gross matter. So perhaps the Nyāya-Vaiśeṣika concept of *paramāṇu* may be compared with molecules of western science rather than with atoms. But there is a difficulty in thus identifying *paramāṇus* with molecules; for molecules are not indivisible while *paramāṇus* are. As atoms happened to be sub-divided into electrons, protons etc., *paramāṇus* are indivisible. But they are not of the form of energy. The Nyāya Vaiśeṣika theory of *paramāṇus* has got two characteristics—(a) they are indivisible parts of gross matter like earth, water, air, fire; (b) they have the attributes of gross matter. Neither *paramāṇus* nor their attributes can be perceived ordinarily. They can be perceived only by yogins. The two characteristics of Nyāya *paramāṇus* are contradictory, according to the western conception of physics.

There is another point about substances having the greatest magnitude. Though the substances are infinitely extended they cannot be analyzed into parts. To have the greatest magnitude, i.e., to be a *vibhu dravya* the substance has to be in contact with substances having the smallest magnitude and intermediate magnitude. To be in contact with all substances of restricted magnitude is to have the greatest magnitude. Moreover, substances having the greatest magnitude can never be the loci of contact. (*Vibhutvaṁ sarva-mūrta-saṁyogitvam; mūrtatvaṁ paricchinna-parimāṇavattam*) Substances having the greatest magnitude cannot be located in any object.

Now we discuss the possibility of having psychology as a science. There are two different conceptions of psychology in the West—psychology as a study of one's own consciousness, and psychology as the study of the other. In many Indian philosophies both the western conceptions of psychology present difficulties. Thus according to Nyāya-Vaiśeṣika systems, a person cannot look into his own mind. For example, according to Nyāya-Vaisesika theory, consciousness is identified with cognition (*jñāna*). No cognition can cognize itself. A first-order cognition of an external object can be cognized in a second-order, after-cognition (*anuvyavasāya*). As this after-cognition is internal perception, the first-order cognition endures when the second-order after-cognition originates. So the second-order after-cognition can directly perceive internally the first-order cognition. Thus there is a moment's difference between the origin of the first-order cognition and the after-cognition.

But there are other states of the self only some of which can be directly perceived. For example, pleasure, pain, desire, aversion can be perceived internally by a cognition which arises one moment after these internal states arise. According to Nyāya-Vaiśeṣika, neither pleasure nor pain, neither desire nor aversion is a state of consciousness. At the moment of their origination these internal states are not conscious states, they are cognized always only one moment after their origination by a mental perception, although one moment after their origination, after-cognition of a primary cognition is not necessary, it can occur only when the person having the primary cognition desires to cognize this cognition in after-cognition. If the after-cognition were automatic, then there will be a third-order cognition of the second-order cognition and then a fourth-order cognition and so on *ad infinitum.*

Then there is a theory of origin of life. According to Nyāya, life may originate from non-living matter. This means that Nyāya accepts the theory of abiogenesis. About the nature of life Nyāya holds that there are basically two different forms of life—life which does not and which does come out of a woman's womb. Examples of the first type are plants, worms and animals which come out of eggs, and the bodies of those who are in hell. Examples of the second type are other animals and men living on earth. There are other internal states of the self which cannot be directly perceived either in after-cognition or in mental perception. They are traces (*saṁskāra*) and virtue or merit (*dharma*), and demerit (*adharma*).

Two types of traces common to material objects and selves are cognitive and of another kind. As an example of a material object the usual example given is stretching a rubber band which at once returns to its former shape as soon as this stretching is ended. According to Nyāya this return of the external thing, rubber band, to its former state is due to traces left in the rubber band.

Actions are of two types, voluntary and involuntary; voluntary actions are, again, of two types: good or bad actions. Good actions produce pleasure, bad actions produce pain.

Involuntary actions involve life-saving actions (*jivanayoni*) like breathing, digestion which go on even when the person is fast asleep. Such actions are caused by the stock of merit and demerit, which is unseen (*adṛṣṭa*). The traces of action can be inferred from the feeling of pleasure or pain which is due to traces of good or bad actions. The cognitive traces are left behind in the self by a past experience. Such traces can be inferred only from their effect, namely, memory cognition.

It maybe noted here that Bernard Williams, the western philosopher, has said that a relation between propositions maybe logical, but belief in propositions causes another belief in another proposition. Thus he explains memory only causally; memory is caused by previous experience.

According to Nyāya, a previous experience cannot be bodily present to cause memory. Only traces of the previous experience remain in the self, and, when activated, cause memory. So from the fact of memory which is a present cognition we can infer the presence of the traces.

Thus in a psychology of action we have to depend only on inference. In psychology of cognition, sometimes we depend on observation, and sometimes on inference. When, for example, we want to find out causes of memory we have to depend on inference. So also according to Nyāya, it is not clear how experiments can be performed to study mental states. According to Nyāya, it is possible to study consciousness which is identified with cognition. But neither according to Advaita Vedānta nor according to Sāṁkhya, is it possible to study consciousness which can never be made an object of study. It is to be noted here that experiments are not possible in all sciences. For example, astrophyiscs cannot have any experiments. The scientists only observe astral phenomena in different conditions. So also in the introspective method of psychology, no experiments can be made.

Then in western philosophy, different subjects are separated like epistemology, metaphysics, theory of mind, ethics, logic, aesthetic and so on. In Indian philosophy no such separation of subjects is made. For example, in Nyāya Vaiśeṣika, all subjects are studied together in one book of philosophy. In this system even science, and the theory of natural numbers are also studied. For example, there is physics in Nyāya (*paramāṇuvāda* and theories of space and of time), chemistry (theory of *pāka*), biology (theories of origin of life and of the nature of life), psychology (theory of cognizing internal states), astronomy bt%earth (*vūh*), starry heavens (*bhūvaḥ*) and other worlds, like *varuṇaloka* tb%.

Some contemporary western philosophers have argued that the separation of subjects prevents a deeper study. For example, a thoery of mind naturally presupposes many metaphysical points which cannot be discussed in the theory of mind. So the discussion on theory of minds is incomplete. So also ethics involve a philosophy of action without which ethical study remains superficial. Moreover, thought and action are naturally related, and a study of thought involves, naturally, a reference to the thinker which can be studied only in a philosophy of mind. So all subjects are naturally connected with one another.

There are different forms of science in Navya-Nyāya. Thus, (a) in physics there is a discussion of the nature of space and time. (b) In Chemistry there is the theory of *pāka*. (c) In biology there is a theory of origin of life and a classification of different forms of living beings. Life may originate from non-living matter. Navya-Nyāya philosophers distinguish between three forms of life—(i) life which does not require the womb of a woman, for example, plants, insects and all forms of life which come out of an egg; (ii) then there is the usual forms of life which come out of a woman's womb; (iii) there are bodies in hell or in heaven. They are not created in any ordinary way. There are also different worlds like the world of water (*varuṇaloka*) where the bodies are made up of water. (d) Then there is psychology which discusses the nature of consciousness, of mental actions, memory and its causes and so on. (e) There is also a theory of man. There is the theory of highest good (*niḥśreyasa*) which is identified with ultimate release (*apavarga*). This is the highest ideal of man. It presupposes an eternal self of the individual. Ultimate release is to be achieved only by knowledge of the real nature of the self (*jñānamārga*). Thus, according to Nyāya what is called science is a part of philosophy.

IX

INFERENCE

The term 'inference' is used in Navya-Nyāya in two senses. For example, inference is cognition of the conclusion of an inference (*anumiti*). In the other sense, it is used in the sense of instrumental cause which produces inference in the first sense. In the stock example we have four cognitions:

(1) Smoke-possessing (is the) hiss—(perception)
(2) Wherever there is smoke, there is fire—(pervasion—memory)
(3) (The) hill possessing smoke pervaded by fire—(consideration)
(4) ∴ (The) fire-possessing (is the) hill—(conclusion)

This is what is called inference for one's own sake (*svārthānumāna*). Then there is inference for the sake of others (*parārthānumāna*). This involves communication and therefore language. There is one long sentence which has five parts or members (*avayava*). They are, (i) proposition (*pratijña*), (ii) statement of the probans (*hetu*), (iii) example with pervasion (*udāharaṇa* with *vyāpti*), (iv) application (*upanaya*), and (v) conclusion (*nigamana*). The first and the fifth member must be the same. But the difference is fundamental. In (i) the proposition is merely proposed, in (v) it is proved.

There are three points to be noted about the Navya-Nyāya theory of inference. The first point is that the distinction between inference for one's own sake (*svārthānumāna*) and inference for the sake of others (*parārthānumāna*) is not known in western logic. In inductive logic there is a distinction between discovery and proof. Discovery is to be made by the person himself; so it maybe compared to inference for one's own sake. But this is not correct, for proof maybe used for what is discovered by the person himself or by others. The hunch had to be proved by the person himself. So proof is not inference for the sake of others.

The second point is very fundamental. As is evident all inferences in Indian philosophy in general and Navya-Nyāya in particular are causal. The cognition of the conclusion is indirect cognition causally produced by other cognitions. Thus in Indian philosophy there is no concept of reason. In western philosophy, reason is intuitive knowing forms or universals as in Plato. The usual concept of reason is that of a faculty of a power of the mind to know rational truths and to draw inferences. There are different conceptions of reason in western philosophy. There is a theory of universal reason; man is defined as rational animal. There is also a theory of different reasons in different cultures as in Rorty. This is also the theory of post-modern philosophers, who deny that there is a universal reason. "Post modernism hails freedom, doubt, uncertainty and unpredictability."[14] There are others who have argued that reason in economics is different in kind from reason in physics. There are as many reasons as there are different subjects.

Indian philosophy in general is very different from western philosophy. There is neither any concept of universal reason, or any concept of different reasons. The third point about Indian philosophy in general, and Navya-Nyāya in particular is that there is no distinction between deductive and inductive logic. In every inference there are both induction and deduction. Moreover, there is no concept of formal truth which is necessary for testing the validity of deductive inferences. According to Indian philosophy, there is truth which is both formal and material.

X

WESTERN LOGIC AND NAVYA-NYĀYA THEORY OF INFERENCE

Western logic has some characteristics some of which we explain below.

(i) Western logic is formal; it is based on a distinction between formal truth and material truth. Only Inductive logic, mostly created by J.S. Mill, is based on material truth.

(ii) Western logic is normative. This characteristic distinguishes logic from psychology. In psychology we study thinking as it is, whereas in logic we study thinking as it should be.

(iii) Western logic, both traditional and modern, studies propositions or sentences which are objects of knowledge, but not in relation to knowledge or belief.

(iv) Modern western logic or symbolic logic makes a distinction between a singular proposition or sentence and a general proposition or sentence. We shall explain this difference in Navya-Nyāya in detail later.

There is no concept of normative science or normative philosophy in Navya-Nyāya theory. This is because Indian philosophy in general, and Navya-Nyāya in particular, deals with beliefs and not propositions. Bernard Williams[15] has stated that propositions may be related logically to one another but belief in a proposition is causally connected with belief in other propositions (exceptions are some Buddhistic theories which we do not discuss here).

There is no concept of proposition in Indian logic. Usually sentences mean propositions while terms mean objects. But according to Indian philosophy in general and Navya-Nyāya in particular, sentences mean qualified objects. Thus, according to Navya-Nyāya there is no distinction in meaning between the two expressions (the) 'brown table' and 'the table (is) brown'. There is no distinction between the attributive use and the predicative use, for both the expressions mean the same qualified object—'the brown table'.

In traditional western logic deduction is of two types, mediate and immediate. Mediate deductive inference is syllogism, which as we have explained, is not present in Navya-Nyāya theory. Immediate deductive inferences like obversion, conversion etc. are also not possible in Navya-Nyāya. Obversion, for example, is not possible for obversion requires two types of negation.

(a) Obvertend: All men are mortal.

(b) Obverse: No men are non-mortal.

Thus in Obversion we have two types of negation, 'no' and 'non'. In Navya-Nyāya there is one type of negation which attaches what is usually called in traditional western logic a predicate. So the Obverse (b) 'No men are non-mortal', becomes (c) 'men are not non-mortal' which is really a case of double negation, not of obversion.

Conversion, too, is not possible because it requires a theory of distribution of terms. Thus it is said that an A proposition distributes its subject but not its predicate; an E proposition, on the other hand, distributes both its subject and its predicate. This theory of distribution is possible only when the predicate also is taken in its denotation. But according to Navya-Nyāya, the so-called predicate stands for an attribute or a property. In traditional western logic particular or singular propositions and universal propositions are interpreted in the same way.

(d) The sentence or the proposition 'Socrates is mortal' is interpreted to contain a subject and a predicate. So also the proposition (e) 'All men are mortal' is interpreted to contain one subject and one predicate. Now in modern symbolic logic a fundamental distinction is made between a singular or particular proposition and a universal proposition.

Navya-Nyāya cannot admit inductive inference. J.S. Mill has once argued that all syllogisms involve *petitio principii.* Navya-Nyāya philosophers argue in all inductive inferences, there is a partial petitio. This maybe explained as follows:

From, some men (i.e., all men whom we observed) are (uniformly) mortal.

Therefore, all men are mortal.

Now Navya-Nyāya philosophers argue that the men whom we have observed to be mortal are included in 'all men' of the conclusion. This is fallacy of partial petitio (*bhāgāsiddhi*). To avoid this fallacy it will be necessary to argue

Some men are mortal.

∴ All other men are mortal.

Now this inference avoids the fallacy of partial petitio, but is yet invalid, because the premise is not relevant to the conclusion. As the premise and the conclusion are not logically related, the inference is invalid.

Navya-Nyāya holds that by observing at least one man to be mortal, we perceive, in a special way, that all men are mortal. Thus generalization, according to Navya-Nyāya philosophers, is a matter of a special type of perception (*sāmānya lakṣaṇa pratyakṣa*). We have already explained this type of perception.

XI

THE NAVYA-NYĀYA THEORY OF RELATIONS

When a dyadic relation holds between two objects, one object becomes the first term of the relation and the other object the second term of the relation. According to Navya-Nyāya philosophers, the second term qualifies the first term by the relation. The first term of the relation is called the qualificand and the second term of the relation the qualifier, and the relation is the qualification. Awareness of a relation, according to Navya-Nyāya philosophers is a qualificative awareness. It is the awareness of the second term of the relation qualifying the first term by the relation. Thus every qualificative awareness is the awareness of a qualifier qualifying a qualificand. There is also a difference in the expression of a relation. Thus the relation of *a* in *b* (in English one says that a relation is of *a* to *b*), is expressed as *bRa*, where *b* is the first term of the relation, and in the awareness of the relation it is the locus, and *a* is the second term, and in the awareness, it is the qualifier. In western logic the order of the terms is reversed thus—*aRb*. In Navya-Nyāya the term following the preposition 'of' is the second term and the term following the preposition 'in' is the first term.

In every qualificative awareness, there are three objects—the qualificand, the qualifier, and the qualification. In a non-qualificative, primitive awareness there is only one object which is known in and through itself. Usually only universals are known in a non-qualificative awareness. A qualificative awareness in which something is known in and through something else, maybe expressed symbolically in language—*a*-possessing-*b* (*bRa*), where *b* is the qualificand and *a* is the qualifier; possessing denotes the relation of *b* to *a* (in Navya-Nyāya terminology, it will be the relation of *a* in *b*).

This relation of qualifier and qualificand may be contrasted with the relation of subject and predicate. According to Navya-Nyāya philosophers, every qualificative awareness has a three-fold object, a qualificand, a qualifier, and the qualification. But every qualificative awareness does not involve a relation of subject and predicate. For example, when we see a brown table there is no distinction between subject and predicate. This subject of an awareness is that about which something is known and the predicate is that which is known about the subject. In qualificative perception there is no awareness of something about which something is known. So there is no distinction between subject and predicate in qualificative perception. But in inference and verbal testimony there is always an awareness of subject and predicate. There is much confusion among western philosophers about the notions of subject and predicate. For example, the simple subject-predicate sentence

(S1) Socrates is wise

has been analyzed in various ways. From the different answers given, without trying to be exhaustive, we list the following:

Grammatical Analysis

Subject-expression	Predicate-expression
(1) 'Socrates'	'wise' (traditional logicians)
(2) 'Socrates'	'is wise' (Strawson)

Quine contrasts predicates (in his sense of the term) not with subjects but with singular terms. His analysis of (S1) will be into (i) a singular term, and (ii) a predicate, thus:

Singular term		Predicate expression
(3) 'Socrates'		'(1) is wise' (Quine)
	Categorial Analysis	
Subject		Predicate
(4) Socrates		Wisdom (Strawson, Copi)
(5) Socrates		that he is wise (suggested and discussed by Cook Wilson)
(6) Socrates		Wisdom or Wisdom Socrates (Rannsey)

There are many who are undecided between (1) and (2). Wilfrid Sellars, for example, holds that the predicate in 'S is white' is 'is white'. Now this diversity of analysis is not due to any peculiarity os (S1), for it is a typical subject-predicate sentence. Any subject-predicate sentence will be analyzed into its subject and predicate in all these and possibly other ways.

We thus find that the word 'predicate' is highly ambiguous. When we want to refer to a particular sense, we shall use 'predicate (1)', 'predicate (2)', etc. instead of simply 'predicate'. It may appear from the list that although there is a wide divergence of views regarding the predicate in a sentence, there is near unanimity about the subject. But this is not correct, for 'subject' and 'predicate' are correlatives. (Geach, however, has suggested senses of these terms in which they no longer remain correlatives, but as he himself points out, these senses are 'inconvenient'). And, so, if the concept of the predicate changes there is a corresponding change in the concept of the subject. So when we want to be specific we shall use 'subject (1)', 'subject (2)', etc., in place of the ambiguous 'subject'.

According to Navya-Nyāya philosophers awareness of subject and predicate is the awareness of a qualified object; for the predicate qualifies the subject. Although the awareness of the subject and the predicate is the awareness of the qualified object which contains a qualificand and a qualifier, still the distinction between the subject and the predicate is not always the same as the distinction between the qualificand and the qualifier. As an example in the awareness of the conclusion of the classical instance of Navya-Nyāya inference we may have—

(a) (the) hill (is) fire-possessing

The Navya-Nyāya rule of determining the predicate is to drop the suffix 'possessing' to get the predicate term. The predicate is what is denoted by the term. Thus dropping the suffix 'possessing' we get the predicate term 'fire'. But the predicate is the object fire, not the word 'fire'.

In every inference, according to Navya-Nyāya philosophers, there are three objects—probandum, probans and locus of inference. The Navya-Nyāya rule is that the predicate of the conclusion is the probandum (very roughly corresponding to the major term of traditional syllogism). In the present case, the predicate is fire which is the probandum in the inference. This is also the qualifier of the awareness of the conclusion. But the conclusion may take another form:

(b) fire (is) on (the) hill

In this awareness fire is the qualificand and the hill is the qualifier and *being on* is the relation. Yet fire remains the predicate and is the probandum. Thus is this case the predicate is the qualificand, whereas in (a) it is the qualifier. Thus the qualificand and the qualifier change with the form of the awareness, but the subject and the predicate remain the same. This is because whatever be the form of the awarenss of the conclusion, something which is said about something, i.e., the predicate and the subject remain invariant. So in both (a) and (b) fire is the probandum, and (the) hill is the locus of the inference.

An example, which is usually given in Navya-Nyāya books is the following-

(1) Smoke is prevaded by fire (wherever there is smoke there is fire).

(2) The hill possesses smoke.

(3) The hill possesses smoke prevaded by fire.

(4) ∴ The hill possess fire.

This looks like a western syllogism except the step (3). This is peculiar for Navya-Nyaỵa philosophers to insist that (3) is necessary for the inference. According to western philosophers, the conclusion of a syllogism follows necessarily from the two premises taken together. According to traditional western syllogism, the premises are taken together in the sense of conjunction. According to Navya-Nyāya philosophers, this conjunction of two premises cannot be accomplished in all cases. For example, in the following case of inference—

(5) Something (smoke or light) is prevaded by fire.

(6) The hill possesses (has) something.

(g) ∴ The hill possesses fire.

Now it is impossible to simply conjoin (5) and (6); for the something in (5) may not be the same as something in (6). So we shall have to have a more difficult way of combining (5) and (6). This may be explained symbolically as:

(7) $(Ex)\ (xPf.\ hHx)$

$xPy = x$ is pervaded by y.

$xHy = x$ has y.

where the 'x' being within the scope of the same quantifier, must be substantiated in the same way, both in (5) and (6). (7) is called 'consideration' (*parāmarśa*) which is a doubly qualificative awareness. For, as (3) makes it clear, the predicate smoke is already qualified by pervasion by fire. This smoke which is already qualified, further qualifies the hill, so this awareness is doubly qualificative. As (5) and (6) make clear this doubly qualificative awareness (7) is necessary to explain how the conclusion follows necessarily from the two premises taken together.

All inferences are explained in causal terms as being produced by a belief in pervasion. This belief maybe true or false, but must not be even doubted as false. Thus even a false belief in pervasion, when firmly held, will lead to belief in the conclusion.

Moreover, there is a similarity between modern symbolic logic and Navya-Nyāya theory of inference. This concerns the analysis of universal propositions. According to modern symbolic logic, the interpretation of 'All *a* is *b*' is that whatever has the property of being *a*, has the property of being *b*. Here there are two properties. Thus in the proposition 'All men are mortal', there are two properties, humanity and mortality. The entire proposition means 'whatever has humanity has mortality', (*x*) (*Hx* en% *Mx*), where there are two predicates, namely, '*H*' and '*M*'. According to Navya-Nyāya theory, there is pervasion between two properties. But this is not so in the case of a singular preposition. To say that the hill is fiery is to say that the locus of the property of being a hill is co-present with the property, fire.

Here we should note the Navya-Nyāya use of the term 'property'. 'Property' does not always mean an abstract property. In English the term is also used in a legal sense, as in the expression 'a man of property', the term 'property' means land, house, wealth, none of which is an abstract object. According to Navya-Nyāya theory, the term 'property' may sometimes mean an abstract object. When, for example, we talk about the classifying character of a cow, which is cowness that inheres in all and only cows. But when a particular book is on the table, the particular book becomes the property of the table; the table is differentiated from all other objects, specially tables, by having that particular book on it.

This leads Navya-Nyāya philosophers to uphold double or multiple abstracts. For example, cowness inheres in all and only cows; so cowness has the property of inhering in all and only cows. This property of cowness is cowness-ness. So also there are concrete terms that are made from any term whatever by adding the suffix 'possessing'. A book is bookness possessing, a table is book-possessing, i.e., bookness-possessing-possessing. This is a doubly concrete term. This form of abstraction and its reverse, concretisation, cannot go on for long; for Navya-Nyāya philosophers object to unnaturally long abstracts or concrete terms ('*atidūra-paramparāyā-mānābhāvāt*').

XII

NAVYA-NYĀYA THEORY OF LANGUAGE

Language is articulate speech. Sign-languages like showing two fingers to mean two and other gestures to mean that one is hungry, thirsty, etc., are languages only in a derivative sense just as written language. The Navya-Nyāya theory is that spoken language is language in the primary sense, whereas gestures and written language are languages only in a derived sense, for the gestures and the written signs remind one of the spoken words which would have been used to convey the same sense. It is only by 'suggesting' spoken words that these become a 'language'. The commentators of Viśvanātha make a distinction between the so-called gesture-language and written language by describing the former as language of a different kind (*vijātīya*) and the latter as of the same kind as the spoken language, by contrast, *sajātīya*. But even though gesture-language and written language are thus different from each other in kind, still both of them differ from spoken language. They are called 'language' in the wider sense because gestures and written characters 'suggest' ('*bodhaka*', '*saṅketita*') spoken words which alone constitute language proper.

This Navya-Nyāya theory is based on the presupposition that written language is parasitic on spoken language, even though writing makes possible long and complicated constructions which would have been impossible without writing. Even admitting the fact that the art of writing not merely gives permanence to speech so that it can be repeatedly observed, and also makes possible the development of language in newer directions, the fact remains that written language would have been impossible without spoken language. Thus spoken language is logically prior to written language. In their theory of meaning, Navya-Nyāya philosophers, therefore, regard spoken language alone as primarily significant and written language is taken as derivatively significant in so far as it suggests the spoken words. It is only through spoken words suggested by the written words that they become instruments of communication.

About gesture-language too, Navya-Nyāya philosophers hold the same theory of the primacy of spoken language. Here this primacy is not apparent; for, apparently, gesture-language precedes articulate speech in the process of evolution. Animals use body signs to communicate with each other without sounds. Yet it is a fact that articulate speech is different in kind from gestures which can be used to communicate only the barest information. Emergence of articulate speech marks a total break in the process of evolution. Many western philosophers have even identified rationality of man with articulate speech which, then, is the differentia of man from other coordinate species. (Of course, Navya-Nyāya does not contain any ideas of biological evolution). Moreover, it is not clear if two deaf and mute persons can communicate by means of gesture language, for none can be reminded of the spoken words 'suggested' by the other's gestures, as none of the two can possibly know any spoken words.

XIII

SANSKRIT AS THE OBJECT-LANGUAGE

All systems of Indian philosophy offer a theory of only Sanskrit language and a theory of meaning of words and sentences of Sanskrit. It is necessary to note some special features of this language. One feature of Sanskrit as a language is that it is a frozen language; only as a frozen language it serves as the object-language in the Navya-Nyāya theory as also in Indian theories of meaning generally. Sanskrit, therefore, has a very rigorous grammar starting with alphabets classified into vowels and consonants, rules of formation of words from basic elements, rules of formation of sentences, and so on. Pāṇini's grammar with its rigorous definitions explicitly stated as rules of abbreviation, and rules with an enumeration which uniquely determines their order, with various devices for determining the scope of the rules and the order of their precedence, stands out as one of the best examples of the science of grammar. Still Sanskrit differs from a rigorously constructed artificial language as we have now, in so far as it allows ambiguous words, figures of speech and some freedom to analyze a given expression in different ways. A complex expression, therefore, is, in general, not uniquely analyzable even in the most technical language of Navya-Nyāya.

Dealing only with Sanskrit as the language of study gives rise to the problem of explaining the possibility of regional languages and languages other than Sanskrit. An extreme theory, supported by Gadādhara, is to treat all expressions of regional languages as really devoid of meaning but used in practice as significant only by mistake. Expressions of regional languages create only an illusion of sense.

This extreme theory has not been accepted by many Navya-Nyāya philosophers. Annaṁ Bhaṭṭa, for example, in his commentary *Uddyotana* on Kaiyata's *Pradīpa* gives an argument of some Navya-Nyāya philosophers against the theory supported by Gadādhara. We now explain this argument.

Like words in Saṅskrit, words of regional languages, too, have meanings. For, there is no way of determining whether Sanskrit words have primary meaning and regional languages have only derivative meaning or conversely. The determinant here cannot be equiformity of words in all countries, for the meaning of 'equiformity' is vague and unclear. It may mean one of three different things—

(i) 'equiformity' may mean that Sanskrit words are used in all countries;

(ii) 'equiformity' may mean that words which are used in a particular region have a recognizable identical pattern;

(iii) 'equiformity' may mean absence of usage of regional languages.

Now, sense (i) cannot be accepted because in some foreign lands (*kvacin mlecchadeśe*) there is no trace of Sanskrit (*Saṁskṛta-gandhâbhāvāt*). Sense (ii) cannot be accepted because equiformity in this sense is common to all languages. Sense (iii) also cannot be accepted because it violates what has been stated in the *Bhāsya* which in many places emphasizes use of different nonstandard words among people. Even the way the elite speak cannot be the determinant, for this is common to all languages. According to these philosophers who oppose the theory which Gadādhara supports, God created the world of objects and also their names at the same time. It cannot be said that God created only Sanskrit language and no others. When God created the Ionians, He created their language at the same time. It cannot be said that those languages where originally Sanskrit, from which they evolved.

The attempt of the modern comparative philologists to postulate and construct a proto-Aryan language from which all indo-European languages have evolved according to rules of phonology, philology and grammar tends to support the theory that originally God created only one language, be it Sanskrit or some other language from which all other languages have evolved. The consequence of this theory of the origin of languages for the theory of meanings according to Gadādhara, is that the exclusive concern of the theory of meaning should be with the original language as the object-language. Now this is a further theory which need not be accepted even if one accepts the theory of evolution of different languages from one mother language. Thus the arguments given above of those who propound the theory which Gadādhara rejects are invalid, because like Gadādhara they assume the debatable theory of the logical connection between the mother language and the theory of meaning. Even if it be admitted that the regional languages in North India have evolved from Sanskrit, it does not follow that words and sentences in them do not need to be explained and that no theory of meaning over and above the theory of meaning of Sanskrit is needed. This is the point which Jagadīśa and other Navya-Nyāya philosophers have made. According to these philosophers, there is a possibility of developing different theories of meaning for different regional languages; only they are not interested in developing such theories. They are concerned only with Sanskrit as the object-language.

XIV

ONTOLOGY OF SPOKEN SENTENCES

I shall discuss here first the problem whether a spoken sentence can be regarded as a picture of what it means. One initial difficulty is that the structures of synonymous sentences in different languages are very different. So it is not clear which sentences of which language can be a picture of what it means. This difficulty is present in the case of written sentences also. Wittgenstein, for example, says, "In Russian one says 'stone red' instead of 'the stone is red.'"[16] This difficulty maybe sought to be solved by formulating a symbolic canonical form of all synonymouns sentences with different structures in different languages. But formulas of symbolic language, of symbolic logic, for example, are always written expressions. We have already discussed why written sentences cannot be regarded as pictures even by using conventions of projection.

There is, however, a more serious ontological difficulty about spoken words or sentences. One cannot speak a whole sentence or even a word of more than one syllable, one can only utter sounds in succession; when the first syllable or phoneme is uttered the second is not yet uttered. When the second is uttered the first sound has vanished. So it is impossible to speak a whole sentence as one entity. As uttered sounds are necessarily successive, they cannot be regarded as pictures which are wholes of coexisting parts.

The Navya-Nyāya philosophers explain the experience of the common man who perceives a whole sentence. These philosophers make use of a special form of perception due to *jñāna-lakṣaṇa sannikarṣa* to explain how past sounds can also be said to be perceived. When one hears the sounds as successively uttered, one remembers them in their order. This memory of the earlier sounds functions as a *sannikarṣa* which together with the hearing of the last syllable or phoneme, produces the perception of the whole sentence. If such a special form of *sannikarṣa* is not admitted, can there be any explanation how a whole sentence can be perceived, through hearing successive momentary sounds? There are different philosophical theories which I explain very briefly.

There are philosophers who distinguish between the act of speaking and a spoken word or sentence. They point out various difficulties in the Navya-Nyāya theory of perception of a whole word or sentence. If the last syllable presented together with impressions of the earlier syllables can cause perception (hearing) of the whole word or sentence, then even if the syllables are uttered with long temporal gaps in between, the perception of the last syllable together with the impressions of the earlier ones ought to cause perception of the whole word or sentence. But no one accepts this as a cause of the perception of the whole expression. The case is not different even if the syllables are uttered in quick succession. Secondly, "If the sounds are remembered in the same order in which they are uttered, how could they be simultaneously grasped?"

Hence grammarians like Bhartṛhari do not accept the theory that speaking is ontologically identical with what is being spoken. A spoken word or a sentence, according to this theory, is a type of reality different from speaking.

The theory that words are ontologically different from noises which can be uttered by a speaker involves difficulties of all sorts. One difficulty is how to explain whether a speaker speaking words and sentences performs two acts—producing sounds and speaking words. Then there is also the difficulty from the hearer's point of view. Does a hearer hear two things—sounds and words? The following three different answers apart from their own difficulties are inadequate chiefly because they fail to explain what the speaker does in speaking. (a) One answer is that sounds are heard as identical with words. There are no two objects which are heard when one hears words or sentences. But this answer does not explain how noises and words can be ontologically different and yet the hearer can hear them (correctly?) as identical. (b) The second answer is that sounds are imperceptible and only words can be heard. What is necessary and sufficient to explain the perception of words and sentences is that there be sounds, not that the sounds be perceived. A difficulty of this theory is that a deaf person who cannot hear sounds should be able to perceive spoken words, if objectively there are appropriate sounds. (c) Words are manifestors of objects, and so different from mere sounds. But when one does not clearly hear the words because they are, say, spoken at a distance, one hears only the sounds. Quine cites many examples of 'listening to a lecturer with an odd accent or unusual diction'. 'Accents may bewilder, and they can cause misapprehension without bewilderment.' A difficulty of this theory is that it has to postulate two different causal relations—one for perception of words as fused with sounds, and another when they are not so fused. When we hear sounds we cannot hear the words, for perception of sounds prevents perception of words. Yet when we perceive words we also perceive sounds as identical with the words. But then the question is: if noises and words are ontologically different, words can at best be confused with, not fused with sounds. So the problem of reality of words confused with the ephemeral sounds producing correct perception of words remains.

XV

THE METHODOLOGY OF NAVYA-NYĀYA

Navya-Nyāya is not just one system of philosophy. It has developed a technical language, which is rigorous. It eliminates the ambiguities of ordinary Sanskrit. For example, the expression in ordinary Sanskrit 'negation of a jar' does not show whether the negation is of one jar or the negation of all jars. The Navya-Nyāya technical language uses the concepts of limitor, limiting relation, and determiner. The distinction between two types of negation of a jar is explained by using the concept of limiting property. Thus when the limiting property of counterpositiveness is jarness, we have the negation of all jars. When the limiting property of the counterpositiveness is this jar then we have the negation of a particular jar, this jar, and so on.

The point is the Navya-Nyāya cannot use adjectives of quantity like *all, some* etc. for when words are used they become the content or the object of knowledge. But quantity is a formal character of sentences. In order to show the form it is necessary not to use any word. For by using a word, a form is promoted to the content of the sentence.

Although this language was developed by Navya-Nyāya philosophers who are realists and pluralists, still this language was seen to be metaphysically natural. This is because this technical language expresses rigorously what is said in ordinary Sanskrit. Thus this language could be used not merely in different systems of ontology, like *Advaitasiddhi* by Madhusūdana Sarasvatī and Pūrṇimā commentary by Pañcānana Tarkaratna on *Sāṁkhyakārika* and so on, this language was extensively used in rhetoric and grammar. As a matter of fact, this technical language developed by Navya-Nyāya philosophers was used by them in discussing perception, inference, analogy and testimony. This language gradually became the language of all serious discourse.

XVI

CLASSICAL SYSTEMS OF INDIAN PHILOSOPHY

Now we shall discuss the different theories of Indian philosophy, instead of only one school like the school of Nyāya-Vaiśeṣika. As we shall see, different Indian philosophical systems, although rooted in Indian culture, still have many points of fundamental differences. In this section we shall discuss the different systems of Indian philosophy topic-wise. First of all, in the introduction we shall explain the scope of Indian philosophy.

Introduction

It will be necessary to eliminate the Vedas, the Upaniṣads, the epics, and Purāṇas from the scope of classical philosophy. Classical systems of Indian philosophy are usually classified into two classes—orthodox (*āstika*) and heterodox (*nāstika*). Usually six systems of Indian philosophy are regarded as orthodox systems—Pūrva Mīmāṁsā, Uttara Mīmāṁsā or Advaita Vedānta, Sāṁkhya, Yoga, Nyāya and Vaiśeṣika. It is usual to enumerate three systems as heterodox—Bauddha, Jaina and Cārvāka. It is usual to define an orthodox system as that system which accepts the validity of Vedas, and a heterodox system is usually defined as that which does not accept the validity of Veda. Thus all systems of Indian philosophy, whether orthodox or heterodox are based on the Vedas, positively or negatively. In what follows we shall explain only some concepts as formulated in the different systems.

I. The Concept of Cause

There are three different theories about the causal relation obtaining between the cause and its effect. According to Sāṁkhya and Yoga systems, an effect is pre-existent in the material cause in a latent form. For example, from the seed of a mango tree only a mango tree can develop, whereas from a mustard seed only a mustard plant can come out. This is possible according to the Sāṁkhya and Yoga philosophers if only the mango tree is present in a latent form in the mango seed; and the mustard plant is present in latent form in mustard seed. So also in all other cases. The difference between a cause and an effect is the difference between a latent form and a manifest form.

The Nyāya and Vaiśeṣika philosophers criticize the Sāṁkhya and Yoga theory by pointing out that the manifest form which is the effect is not present in the latent form. So the manifest form is without a cause at all. According to the Nyāya and Vaiśeṣika philosophers, the effect is produced for the first time and is not present in the material cause. The effect is something totally new and comes into existence for the first time. The effect is produced by the cause. An effect is usually defined as that which was not present before its production. This prior absence of the effect (*prāgabhāva*) is one of the causes for the production of the effect.

Nāgārjuna, however, denies the relation of causality all together. According to him neither one of the four alternatives is acceptable : (a) the cause and effect are identical; (b) they are different; (c) they are neither identical nor different; (d) they are both identical and different. Obviously (d) is impossible being self-contradictory. The first two alternatives are the theory of Sāṁkhya and Yoga and the theory of Nyāya and Vaiśeṣika philosophers. Nāgārjuna finds fault with both of these alternatives. As only these four alternatives are possible and none of them is acceptable, the causal relation cannot be real.

II. Ontology

There are four different theories on ontology: pluralism, dualism, monism and nihilism.

(a) According to Nyāya and Vaiśeṣika philosophers there is a plurality of reals. Almost an infinite number of atoms, earth-atoms, water-atoms, fire-atoms and air-atoms, space and time, *manas*, individual selves and the supreme self or God, universals and many other eternal entities are postulated. God creates the world out of the atoms according to the merit and demerit of individual selves. The Nyāya philosophers hold that the relation of inherence also is an eternal relation. Thus Nyāya and Vaiśeṣika philosophers are pluralists in ontology.

(b) According to Sāṁkhya philosophers, there is one primodial source of the material universe, namely, *prakṛti* and a plurality of individual selves which are of the nature of consciousness. It is usual to regard Sāṁkhya philosophers as dualists because they postulate two types of reality—one *prakṛti* and a plurality of individual selves which, of course, belong to one type of reality. Thus Sāṁkhya philosophers admit two realities *prakṛti* and *puruṣa* and they are usually regarded as dualists.

(c) The third type of ontological theory is abstract monism, or non-dualism of Advaita Vedānta. Advaita Vedānta philosophers have given many arguments to prove the concept of duality, hence of plurality, is inconsistent. We shall state here briefly two types of arguments of Advaita Vedānta philosophers to prove that the concept of duality is inconsistent.

The first argument which Advaita philosophers have given to establish the theory of non-dualism is to show that the concept of duality (*a fortiori*, that of plurality) is inconsistent. Their argument may be explained by means of examples of contemporary concepts.

Example 1. One km and another km make two kms.

Example 2. One kg and another kg make two kgs.

The third example is really a question.

Example 3. One km and one kg make two what?

It maybe said that km is a measure so also kg is a measure. So they make two measures. But this procedure will not be valid if we point out that km is a measure of distance and kg is a measure of weight.

As the third example makes clear that two objects in order to count as two, must not be entirely different. In order to count as two the objects must be different and not different. Thus the very concept of two or duality is inconsistent.

Against the Advaita Vedānta theory of the inconsistency of dualism, opponents point out that although to make two, objects must be different and not different; still there is no inconsistency here. This may be explained by an example. One red patch and another red patch make two red patches. One green patch and another green patch make two green patches. But one red patch and one green patch make two patches of colour. But this identity between the two specific colours is generic identity. Because the identity is in the genus and the difference is in the species, there is no inconsistency here.

Against this argument of the opponents Advaita philosophers point out a fundamental inadequacy. How are we to distinguish between the genus and species? There is no generic identity between genus and species. So they cannot count as two. If one finds out some generic identity between genus and species then how does one distinguish it from the generic identity between genus and species? This will lead to infinite regress. So the argument of the opponents is not valid.

It may be argued here that originally Advaita Vedānta philosophers tried to prove that the concept of duality involves inconsistency. But now they point out that there will be infinite regress if duality is admitted. But as inconsistency and infinite regress are very different logical defects Advaita Vedānta philosophers have changed their original position fundamentally.

Against this reply of the opponents Advaita Vedānta philosophers point out that there is no change in their position. They only point out that there will be infinite regress in the opponents' position under certain conditions. Advaita philosophers have not changed their original position that the concept of duality is inconsistent.

A second argument of the Advaita philosophers centres round the concept of relation. If there are two or more realities then they have to be related to each other or both (all of them are realities). Now if the very concept of relation is unintelligible, then there cannot be more than one reality. The argument basically is of infinite regress. If a and b are related by relation R then R has to be related to a and b by other relations *ad infinitum.* Thus the very concept of relation involves an infinite regress.

Against this argument of Advaita Vedānta philosophers it maybe questioned why R has to be related to a and b in order that a and b are to be related by R? If R has not to be related to both a and b, there will not be any infinite regress.

Advaita Vedānta philosophers refute this argument of the opponent. If R can be related a to b by not being related to them, the R will relate any two terms, say, c and d for R is also not related to them. In order to avoid this undesirable consequence that any relation R would hold between any two objects of the world, it is necessary to hold that if R obtains between a and b then R has got to be related to both a and b by other relations. This leads to infinite regress.[17]

In this way Advaita Vedānta philosophers establish their theory of non-dualism.

(d) Usually Nāgārajuna's *śūnyavāda* is regarded as nihilism. Nihilism has many difficulties, but here we shall discuss only one difficulty, namely, the difficulty of explaining the possibility of attaining *nirvāṇa*. In this connection we shall discuss many other theories and try to support the Advaita Vedānta theory.

If bondage is unreal then there cannot be any real release from bondage. For example, according to Nāgārjuna, bondage is unreal so *nirvāna* also is unreal.[18] Candrakirti in his commentary *Prasannapadā* has raised a question: if *nirvāṇa* is unreal then what happens to Buddha's teachings to others for attaining liberation? Candrakīrti himself has replied to this objection. His answer is that if there is any real *dharma*, if Buddha himself be real, then there would be real *nirvāṇa*. Nāgārjuna has proved that there is no real *dharma*, no real hearers of Buddha's teachings and there is no real Buddha, so Buddha could not have taught others about attaining *nirvāṇa*.[19] Hence Candrakīrti concludes that there is no *nirvāṇa*.[20]

The point is that if bondage is not real, how can there be any real release from bondage? Here we shall explain the Advaita Vedānta theory. According to Advaita Vedānta philosophers, the world is an appearance. So also the individual who is bound in this world is also an appearance. Now according to Advaita Vedānta, appearance is neither real nor unreal. It is not real because it is contradicted by knowledge of reality. It is not unreal like a golden mountain for the world is perceived, whereas a golden mountain is never perceived correctly. The ultimate reality, according to Advaita Vedānta philosophers is universal, impersonal consciousness. This consciousness alone is reality. The plurality that we experience in the world is illusory. So the individual self is really identical with the universal self. We do not have any direct experience of our identity with *Brahman* because of *māyā* or *avidyā*, (nescience) which blinds us to this reality. *Māyā* as the material cause of the world which includes ourselves, is neither real nor unreal. *Māyā* can be dispelled only when the individual realizes his identity with *Brahman*. Thus liberation becomes possible, although everyone is always liberated. So Advaita Vedānta philosophers have used the metaphor of getting back a necklace which one already has one's neck in, but has forgotten that one has it (*prāpataprāpti*). Thus according to Advaita Vedānta there is no real attainment of liberation. Liberation is eternally achieved.

Against the Nyāya theory the Advaita Vedānta philosophers point out that if bondage were real, then liberation becomes impossible. For, what is real cannot be undone, cannot be made unreal, by any means.

Without the concept of *māyā* or *avidyā* (nescience) it is not possible to explain attainment of liberation. For example, in the Sāṁkhya system of Iśvarakṛṣṇa, the problem of liberation becomes unsolvable. Thus in the verse 62 of *Sāṁkhyakārikā*, Īśvarakṛṣṇa says that the spirit is neither bound nor liberated. He asserts that it is *prakṛti* which is bound and liberated.[21]

But the question is: how can *prakṛti* which is material and unconscious ever be bound or liberated? Thus the problem of liberation remains unsolved in Sāṁkhya.

XVII

INDIAN THEORIES OF THE SELF

There are different theories of the self in different systems of Indian philosophy. We may classify Indian theories of the self into four different types. (1) According to I-philosophies, the self is what is primarily meant by 'I'. (2) According to We-philosophies, the self is really what is meant by 'we'. (3) According to You-philosophies, the self is really what is meant by 'you'. (4) According to impersonal philosophies, the self is really impersonal consciousness, neither I nor we nor you. We shall explain these four types of theories of the self briefly.

(1) The Self as I

The self may, apparently, be defined simply as the referent of 'I'. Everyone thinks himself as I. Now this apparently simple definition of the self is really ambiguous, for there is no definite referent of 'I'. (i) In waking consciousness I identify myself with my body. In expressions like 'I am sitting, 'I am running', the 'I' refers to my body. (ii) In dream I forget my body and identify myself with a forester, or an old man or a child or whatever. (iii) In many cases the referent of I is the self apart from the body, as in Descartes 'I think, therefore, I am.'

An argument for (i) maybe stated thus. Suppose that I dream that I am a forester and suddenly a tiger chases me. I run for my life in the dream and pant. But when in extreme fright I wake up I find that it is the body with which I identify myself in the waking state which is panting. This shows that my identification with the forester in the dream is not independent of the body. Even in the dream when I identify myself with a forester, by 'I' is meant the body in the waking state.

Problems of self-identity maybe viewed in two ways—horizontally, as problems of referring thoughts, feelings, emotion attitudes, etc., to the same person over time, and vertically, as problems of identifying the self with a not-self. This difference in points of view is not the same as that between 'the third-person version' and 'the first-person version', in the sense in which Shoemaker uses these terms, for even the first-person version of the problems is that of ascribing past and present experiences to me, and is thus the problem of self-identity across time. This is the usual point of view of western philosophers, while Indian philosophers are concerned with the problem of explaining how the self can identify itself whatever it is identified with. To explain this Indian point of view, I begin with a quotation from William James:

"The following vivid account of a fit of hasheesh—delirium has been given to me by a friend:

...I next enjoyed a sort of metempsychosis. An animal or thing that I thought of could be made the being which held my mind. I thought of a fox, and instantly, I was transformed into that animal. I could distinctly feel myself a fox, could see my long ears and bushy tail, and by a sort of introversion felt that my complete anatomy was that of a fox...I was next transformed into a bomb shell, felt my size, weight, and thickness, and experience the sensation of being shot up out of a giant mortar, looking down upon the earth, bursting and falling back in a shower of iron fragments."

This shows that identification in dream is not necessary in terms of the body in waking consciousness.

As a matter of fact, identification admits of degrees. *In Prince and Pauper*, this degree of identification is made clear.

"By and by Tom's reading and dreaming about princely life wrought such a strong effect upon him that he began to act the prince, unconsciously...but at last his thoughts drifted away to far, romantic lands, and he fell asleep in the company of jewelled and gilded princelings who lived in vast palaces, and had servants salaaming before them, of flying to execute their orders. And then, as usual, he dreamed that he was a princeling himself."

The difference between the usual problem of self-identify and self-identification becomes clear if we realize that in self-identification, the self that identifies itself with anything whatever, maybe ontologically just the living body (materialism), a momentary idea or perception (a self-less person); whatever be the ontological status of the self, it is the I-sense that is transferred from it to that with which the self identifies itself. The ontological self does not enter into this transference of I-sense.

According to Advaita Vedānta, I identify myself only occasionally with my son, friends or desired objects, for attachment to them is not as intense as it can be; most of the time they are experienced as mine. I usually identify myself with my body in the waking state, for my attachment to my body is more intense and intimate. In dream I may forget this identification. My attachment to my ego is closest, because even in dream I continue to have the I-sense although I may be a child or whatever. It is only in deep dreamless sleep that I transcend this identification, for then I lose my I-sense totally; I have no sense of being the person that I am in the waking state or in dream. If one can go beyond this state of dreamless sleep, then one can realize the true nature of the self. Only at that stage is the self known with clarity and certainty; at all other stages, the self remains as an unclear, elusive, ever-being background which, however vaguely felt, remains the hidden foundation of my being in all my activity. As I become conscious of myself when engaging in activities of life, this self-consciousness cannot be regarded as involving a reflexive relation. I am conscious of myself only when involved in cognitive acts or practical activities. In introspection myself as the owner of my mental states or as that to whom the states are ascribed, eludes my grasp. The owner or the subject himself cannot be brought to the focus of attention.

There is another type of self-identification, i.e., self-realization. I have already stated that self-awareness during waking state is of the vaguest kind and is confused with awareness of objects. But there is a deepening of awareness of the self and at the deepest level there is immediate, indubitable, clear awareness of one's own self which if self-realization. According to Advaita Vedānta, this realization is of impersonal consciousness which is the foundation not only of the psycho-physical complex of the individual which is me, but of the whole world. So by identifying oneself with that impersonal consciousness one identifies oneself with the world. This type of self-realization requires total surrender of one's individual self, its dissolution in the universal consciousness.

Self-surrender, like self-awareness, has many levels, self-surrender at the superficial level is just relaxation, but when it is total, it is effacement, annulment of my being. The metaphor used here is of a dollop of salt that goes to fathom the sea; it melts without residue and loses its being totally. In this type of self-surrender, one can surrender oneself only to a superior person, not to any inferior being or inanimate object. If self-surrender is total, there is no I-consciousness. One experientially identifies oneself with the impersonal universal consciousness. As this self-identification is self-realization, it can be objectively verified by others. Christian saints meditating on Jesus have been reported to develop stigmata. Sri Rāmakriṣhna is reported to have felt unbearable pain when people walked on the grass. People saw marks on his body when one boatman slapped another in a boat. One may identify oneself in this sense not merely with a supreme person, but also with the entire universe.

There are different kinds of self-surrender. Self-surrender may admit of degrees, may be temporary or permanent, may be a result of effort or may be spontaneous or automatic. Thus one may have even a knack of temporarily putting oneself to sleep or blotting oneself out, as when a medium vacates his mind and hands it over to an invited or sometimes uninvited spirit. The medium does not identify himself or herself with the alien spirit; self-surrender is not self-identification. In this type of self-surrender, when one comes to, one does not have any memory of what happened through oneself. But in other types of cases of temporary relinquishing of charge, one still remains in the background, has memory of what happens to oneself during the interval, as for example, when a poem gets composed in a dream and one remembers it on waking.

Against (i) there is a point which we should note. Even though we accept the theory that there is graded identification we may point out that even at the most intense form of identification, it is not the whole body with which one is identified. It maybe that the 'I' refers to the body, but it is not the body as a whole. There are parts of the body with which one does not identify oneself. For example, hair, nails which maybe cut without the person feeling any pain. Apart from these external elements, there are white and red blood corpuscles which fight with foreign and harmful germs and keep the body fit. Yet these blood corpuscles have their own life. They come into being, do their work and then die. Yet a person is hardly aware of these blood corpuscles within the body. As a matter of fact, a person, even though intensely identifying himself with the body, does not identify himself with the whole body.

Moreover, there is outward-going attitude of every person. He is hardly aware of himself, i.e., his body; most of the time he thinks of his problems, of his friends and of his family. He is hardly aware of his body except when he slips or otherwise has some trouble with his body. We forget ourselves most of the time.

There are various sorts of problems connected with the notion of the body, i.e., the living body of a man. In the western philosophies of the body, three basic questions are usually discussed. (1) Can the concept of the body be defined without a prior presupposition of the concept of a person? It is generally agreed that this is not possible. (2) Is the relation between body and mind an extraneous or a necessary, logical, relation? This question relates to the problem of explaining the reason for the union of a particular body with a particular mind. This problem is important for deciding issues of transmigration of souls, or doctrines of 'metamorphosis' or 'metempsychosis'. Thus the problem of the body is basically the problem of the relation between body and mind. (3) Another major problem of the relation between the human body and the human soul is found in Wittgenstein's *Philosophical Investigations*—"The human body is the best picture of the human soul."

In Indian philosophy, the body of any living being is regarded as belonging to a *jīva*, which maybe very roughly and inadequately regarded as corresponding to the western concept of 'person'. Thus there is no question of regarding the body as extraneous to the *jīva*. The reason for a particular *jīva* assuming a particular physical body is both causal and moral. The problems of mind-body relation become, at their deepest level, problems of incarnation (i.e. associating consciousness with a body) and liberation (i.e. dissociating consciousness from the body). Problems of incarnation, again, may be of two types—(i) general problems of how consciousness can have a body at all; and (ii) special problems of how a particular self or center of consciousness can have the particular body which is his body. Problems of liberation are problems of explaining how the reverse process of dissociation from a body can be made significant and shown to be possible. In both the types of incarnation, and in liberation, the crucial problems is to understand the meaning of 'consciousness having a body'.

At another level the problem of a person assuming a body and discarding it is the problem of birth and death—i.e., the problem of *jīva* assuming a physical body and giving it up. I shall discuss the problem of birth and death after explaining the problem of incarnation.

I have stated that according to Indian philosophy one can identify oneself with anything, living or non-living, through intense attachment, love or empathy. There is, however, a sense in which one is naturally identified with what one calls one's body. I shall now explain this sense.

A new-born child does not distinguish its body from the environment. As sensations gradually crystallize into a sense of its body, its conception of itself, too, crystallizes to that extent. The first point to be noted here is that all individual selves are not at the sense level of perfection—spiritual, moral, intellectual or emotional; therefore, all selves do not have their bodies in the same sense. This is because their bodies do not have the same value, the same importance, the same function for them. For ordinary men, i.e., men living a life of self-interest, having a body is to be identified with it. This is the case with children, for they are openly, unabashedly, selfish. So we may say that every man is born with this attitude, that this is the original, natural, attitude of men. Many men never grow out of it in their lives. A man at this level of life is just conscious, self-conscious, living body, which is felt as one with his ego, with himself.

Our immediate awareness of ourselves is as bodies. The empirical subject 'knows' itself as identical with the body. This 'knowledge', however, is really a false belief. I 'know' what is actually my body as myself even though I say, 'my body'. The expression 'my body' implies a distinction between myself as the owner and the body as the owned, yet I am not clearly aware of this distinction. My body is felt as myself, at the empirical level the body is the self; yet no one can say 'I am the body', unless one has at least the concept of a body different from the self, a concept which one can acquire only from the *śāstras*. The expression 'my consciousness' is also impossible, because at all stages of subjectivity, I am myself, 'myself' is not my self if it implies a distinction between me and myself; 'my self', therefore is the same as 'myself' i.e., 'I'; that the whole of the individual's existence is bodily existence is shown not merely in his attributing the so-called M-predicates to his body like 'reclining' 'six feet tall', but also in attributing the so-called P-predicates not applied to a non-bodily entity, for at this stage, the individual is incapable of thinking, imagining, feeling himself except in terms of what we (at a superior level of conception or of existence) call his body. (He himself does not call it his body, for it is he himself). At this level of existence, I act in this world with 'my body', I know things by means of 'my body' (sense-organs, brain, etc.); I satisfy my desires by means of 'my body'. It is only by being in the body, i.e., by being identical with it, that the self, i.e., myself, is in effective communciation with the world, is in the world. 'To contemplate this truth is to realize that the body is not a prison house but a living link of the individual with the universe.'

"The feeling that the body is integral to the universe, creates a sense of wholeness that can help the body to attain perfect health." "So we can understand how I can exclusively own the body, and yet go far beyond it. As the body is limited to superficial view, so am I. But as the body is really one with the universe, so am I, too. The second view would be the view of those who care to look deeper and wider into fact." The ego identifies itself with the body only through the nervous system—central, sympathetic, and parasympathetic, consciousness spreads itself all over the body through the afferent and efferent nerves. The blood cells have their own cell structure, their own bodies, their own lives. They are not felt as 'I' or as a part of 'I', simply because the nervous system, though sustained by blood circulation and various functions of the blood cells does neither pervade them, nor control their lives.

Secondly, although consciousness is felt as spread all over the body, i.e., it is the body as a whole which is felt as 'I', yet the ego, at this stage of human existence, is located or rooted in the lowest part of the spinal cord. The ego is felt as being there, and views the entire world from there. The point of view of the ego is that of the lowest form of self-consciousness. That there is such a thing as the location of the ego in some portion of the nervous system which becomes its stand-point is experienced in suitable circumstances. Thus when one trips and has a sense of suddenly being supportless, one has a feeling of emptiness in the pit of one's stomach. This sickening feeling of emptiness, of being supportless, also comes when one unexpectedly confronts a very grave personal danger for which one is not all prepared, when one's very existence is threatened. Only in such times of crisis do we have immediate and overwhelming experience of ourselves as being located in a part of the body.

(1) The Self As I

Everyone is a unique individual, but this ontological uniqueness, unlike the uniqueness of, say, a grain of sand, is identical with the I-sense, an awareness of being a unique individual. I am myself, not you, he or she. Thus 'I' in this sense is opposed to 'you', 'he' or 'she'. Often this 'I' is explained in terms of private ownership. The 'I' is the unique owner of thoughts, feelings emotions, desires and actions; they are thus mine—no one else can own them.

This explanation of the I-sense in terms of ownership is an inadequate explanation, for I do not own thoughts in the same way as I own emotions or as I own actions. In deep, concentrated thinking, it is the object that determines the process of thinking and not the subject. In rigorous logical thinking, in the syntax of propositional logic, for example, the subject has to follow the rules almost mechanically, cannot read any meaning into the defined terms other that what has been stated in the definitions. In logical thinking the subject has no role at all. In emotion man sees the object as deeply suffused by subjective colours. The emotions are not merely determined by the subjects, but affect the subject also a consequences—my emotions move me in a way in which my thoughts do not. My actions reveal what I am now and determine what I shall be in future in a way which neither my thoughts nor my emotions can do.

It may be argued here that from the fact that my emotions effect me, move me, while my thoughts do not, it does not follow that I own my emotions in a different way than I own my thoughts. My emotions move me, while my thoughts do not, not because they are *my* emotions, but because they are my *emotions*, and not thoughts. It is the very nature of emotions to affect me more strongly than thoughts, but this does not mean that they are my emotions in a special sense.

This argument misses entirely the fact that I get more deeply involved in emotions than in thoughts; that is why emotional disturbance may lead to problems of identity. So also action, i.e. voluntary, purposive behaviour, flows from my very being. Success in action tends to promote self-confidence, while failure tends to undermine it. This is why in Indian philosophy we have a law of *karmā* (interpreted to mean both action and intention to act) as determining what I shall be and become. My thoughts are important only in so far as they may lead to attachment to the objects I think about and, eventually, to action, or failing that, to desire to act in order to obtain them.[22]

(2) We-Philosophies

We-philosophies emphasize the basic nature of We-consciousness, I-consciousness being an abstraction from it. 'We' the plural of 'I' cannot mean just a plurality of I's, i.e., a plurality of individuals each of whom knows himself as an I. For the concept of a plurality of I's contains a contradiction. Any individual knowing himself as I emphasizes his individuality, isolates himself conceptually and experientally from all other individuals; hence a plurality of individuals all knowing themselves as so many I's will be so many different individuals—all isolated from each other. The plurality which is We must not be severally many, but a collection, a group, and isolated I's resist being herded together into even a loose unity. The concept of I the result of conceptual or existential individuation which must be undermined in the concept of We. I consider other individuals as 'you', 'he', 'they' and so on. But I and you and he or they can not be collected together into we.[23] This shows that We-consciousness cannot result from broadening, widening, of I-consciousness to encompass others, you, he or they, and also that the We-concept cannot be a logical construction from a plurality of I-concepts; it is not a construction or a summation.

This impossibility of attaining We-consciousness starting from I-consciousness, either by logical construction or by broadening of I-consciousness, should make clear the basic character of We-consciousness which encompasses many individuals who, however, are seen or felt to be on one side. United we stand, divided we fall; and the essential unity is a basic experience. 'We', being grammatically the plural form of the first person pronoun, cannot cncompass all individuals, but is essentially opposed to you and them. The felt unity of we is built into the very concept, so much so that 'we' simpliciter is only elliptical. This semantical incompleteness of 'We' is different from the systematic ambiguity of 'I'. The ambiguity of 'I' is resolved by knowing who the speaker is, perhaps in an extra-linguistic context. But the semantic incompleteness of 'we' cannot be solved by knowing who the speaker is. The complete form of expression has to have the principle of unity built into it—'we, men of this earth' (as opposed to beings from some other planets).

This shows that We-consciousness is a group-consciousness which also opposes the group to other groups. This incompleteness of 'we' contrasts with the lack of incompleteness of 'I' or 'your'. To say, 'I, the son of Abraham—' or 'I, Mr. so and so...' is to give additional information just as in 'you, Mr. A'. Here we may distinguish between two types of expectancy. Expectancy arising from incomplete expression is of one type, and expectancy which can be raised about something said is of another type. Thus we do not understand the meaning of 'We' unless it is further explained; but we may ask for further information about the person spoken to, when the third person pronoun 'he' or 'they' almost robs the individual(s) spoken of, of their individuality, turns persons into nameless, amorphous, substances.[24] Hence using this pronoun indicates contempt on the part of the user of the expression who deliberately wants to humiliate the person pronoun 'you' indicates due recognition of the personality almost on par with the personality of the speaker. Hence 'you and I' can be combined into 'we', while 'he and I' or even 'you and he and I' can never be so combined. There is a corresponding semantic incompleteness of the plural 'you'.

This singular 'you' is semantically ambiguous and this ambiguity can be resolved by knowing the person addressed, perhaps in an extra-linguistic context. But the plural 'you' is like 'we' in that it is semantically incomplete and its meaning remains incomplete unless the principle of unity is built into the expression : 'you men', 'you Bengalis', 'you artists' and so on. The third person singular 'he' or plural 'they' can be used only when some person or persons have alreadybeen referred to by the use of nouns or other descriptive expressions.

We can now see that starting from the We-concept we arrive at the I-concept by a sort of limiting process. We may progressively reach the I-concept thus 'we three...', 'we two ...', and the 'I'. But this I concept is still fundamentlaly different from the I-concept of I-philosophies, for this I-concept is essentially a we-cannot although vacuously so in the absence of others, but I-concept of I-philosophies is one of self containment and self-sufficiency.

Self-realization is also different in We-philosophies. One cannot attain individual liberation. Liberation will be either for all or for none. According to Sri Aurobindo, no one has so far been liberated because all are not liberated. Gopinath Kaviraj distinguishes between Yoga and *Akhaṇḍa-Mahāyoga*. Yoga liberates individuals, but *Akhaṇḍa-Mahāyoga* will liberate all.

(3) You-philosophies

Philosophies of the self of this type emphasize that consciousness is always directed to something other than itself. Even in the case of the so-called self-consciousness there is a distinction between the self as the subject and the self as the object. Consciousness is not complete in itself but requires something else for its existence. (i) We may realize this dependence of the notion of I on that of you if we note how children learn to use 'I'. Many children say 'you are hungry' when they mean 'I am hungry' because they themselves are addressed by others as 'you'.[25] Some children use proper nouns, i.e., names by which others address them, when they should use 'I'. Instead of saying, for example, 'I am hungry', a child sometimes says, 'John is hungry'. The awareness of myself as 'I', as an individual is a later development from awareness of myself as 'you'. (ii) The concept of soliloquy or monologue is parasitic on the concept of dialogue. (iii) So also the subjective act of judgement is merely an internalization of the act of speaking. Thought may even be identified with sub-vocal speech. Speech or using language is the essence of consciousness, at least of human consciousness. But speaking necessarily involves the existence and presence of a hearer, i.e., another person. Use of demonstratives like 'this', 'that', etc., will be impossible if there were no other persons to address—as Frege pointed out. (iv) So also, as the existentialists argue the subjective feeling of shame is not possible in the absence of other persons. (v) The moral values like truth, non-stealing etc., will be impossible without the presence of others. (vi) In religion, too, God is regarded as the indwelling spirit controlling everything thought, felt and willed by the individual. The sense of I is really due to ignorance. Self-surrender to God is the only way to attain liberation. 'Thy will be done', is the attitude of the devotee. The individual merely reflects the glory of God, the individual self is nothing without its relation to God who is addressed as 'Thou'.

Vaiṣṇava philosophers distinguish between five different types of devotion to God. (i) Master-Servant relation: This relation between a devotee and God is possible only when God is realized as infinite in glory and grandeur. The devotee serves God with no ulterior motive of personal gain or even of pleasing God. It is absurd to imagine that a finite individual can ever please God even by his whole-hearted service. The devotee serves God only because he cannot help it; in service he finds his own fulfilment, the satisfaction of his innermost urge. (ii) Friendship: Thin relation is possible only when the devotee forgets God's grandeur, and treats Him more or less as his equal. Yet this friendship is much more than between two kindred spirits; this is the relation of the devotee with his own innermost being; God is realized as the inalienable partner.[26] (iii) Tenderest feeling to God as that of a mother to her child. (iv) Love of a wife for her husband: The devotee loves God as a lover loves her beloved. (v) Total merging: This is merging of one's personality with God. This comes as the culmination of self-effacement in the presence of God. This is the state of perfect calmness.

In all these attitudes the devotee finds his true being only in God who is addressed as 'Thou'. There are two conceptions of liberation—self realization and God-realization. In Sāṁkhya philosophy, for example, the liberated self is the individual self. Self-realization means realization of the individual self as separate from the body, mind, etc. Liberation as

God-realization is the realization that God alone is real, the individual is essentially dependent on Him. There are systems like Yoga which have conceptions of both self-realization and a type of God-realization, but God-realization is regarded as a means to self-realization which is the *summum bonum.* But devotees, specially Vaiṣṇavas, regard desire for self-realization as an impediment to God realization.

The two conceptions of liberation have different practical consequences. To attain liberation in the sense of self-realization, one has to purge the mind of impurities to make it calm. One who has attained liberation in this sense is at peace with himself and with the world. It is inconceivable that such a person would indulge in violence or start a war. But there are many instances of men who have surrendered themselves to God, of God-intoxicated men, who have started wars on a large scale. Even God has been conceived as incarnating himself in order to destroy sinners. Anyone who has surrendered himself to God, has surrendered his reasoning, his sense of morality and his will to God. He will do whatever God asks Him to do, and as God's ways are inscrutable, we cannot be sure that a God-man will not start war at the command of God. Thus while it is unthinkable of a Buddha or a Mahāvīra starting a war and destroying people and even animals, Rāma and Kṛṣṇa are revered for destroying sinners wholesale.

(4) Impersonal Philosophies

Impersonal Philosophies, unlike You-philosophies and We-philosophies, do not deny but rather affirm that out initial experience of ourselves is of personal selves. Yet this initial experience, however basic and direct, is not, for that reason, incorrigible. According to impersonal philosophies like Advaita Vedānta there are deeper levels of consciousness of which one is not directly aware at the surface level. Ordinary experience of the self as personal is an experience of the surface level of consciousness. According to Advaita Vedānta the core of impersonal, pure, universal consciousness is covered with five exterior sheaths which are material. The outermost sheath is the gross body, the second sheath is the vital, the third sheath is the mental, the fourth is of thoughts, and the fifth is of enjoyment. Within this fifth sheath the pure impersonal consciousness which is universal remains hidden; to reach this inner reality one has to make an inward journey and experientially dissociate onself from one's body, life, mind, thoughts and enjoyment. This process of psychological distancing may be gradual or may be achieved at one stroke.

The reason why this universal pure consciousness lies hidden from view at the surface level is that *māyā* which ontologically is the stuff of the world epistemically blinds us. Really it is more than mere blindness, for *māyā* has two functions—that of concealment of the real and that of the projection of the unreal. This dual function of *māyā* is often explained by an analysis of ordinary illusion. When we mistake a piece of rope for a snake, our ignorance of the piece of rope conceals it from our vision and projects the snake out there. When we see the real piece of rope we realize not merely that there was never any, not even when we perceived it; we also realize not merely that there is no perception of snake now, but also we could never have perceived it. Thus knowledge cancels illusion in the sense that the object of an illusory perception as well as the illusory perception is cancelled with retrospective effect. So also a person who has realized his innermost impersonal consciousness realizes that he was never a finite, restricted being, not even when he had a direct experience of it. In Indian philosophies, liberation is either identified with, or leads to, the cessation of all pain and suffering for all time to come. In Nyāya-Vaiśeṣika philosophy it is argued that pain that we have already experienced cannot be undone, so what liberation achieves is the avoidance of all future pain. But according to Advaita Vedānta the pain that we experience now, or that we experienced in the past, being an illusory appearance will be cancelled by realization with retrospective effect. We shall realize not merely that we shall have no pain in the future but also that we never had any in the past. The liberated person while living in this body experiences the world in time, although he 'does not consider it as real': '*Karmāṇi bhujyamānāni bādlhitatvāt paramārthato na paśyati*' Vedāntasāra, 219.

Liberation, according to Advaita Vedānta, is the realization of total identity with impersonal consciousness. This universal impersonal consciousness is eternally there, without any content in it, transcending all relations; to identify oneself with it is to see that one could never have existed at all as a separate individual.

A person who attains liberation while living in this body does not experience himself as an embodied being. He lives mechanically very much as the potter's wheel continues to move with its own momentum even when the potter is no longer moving it. The world is not experienced as real, for, as we have already explained, the body and the world are seen as transparent covering, not concealing, the inner reality of the universe which is the same as the inner reality of the self. The liberated person sees the world as unsubstantial.

The world which the liberated soul sees consists of particular objects although experienced as non-existing. 'A man', says Vedāntsāra, 219, 'who is conscious that a magical performance is being given does not consider it real even though he sees it.'

XVIII

THEORIES OF CONSCIOUSNESS

In Indian philosophy there are four types of theories of consciousness. These theories, however, do not concern themselves with the same level of consciousness. Consciousness has been conceived (i) as purely intentional, (ii) as witness; (iii) as the foundation of my embodied existence or of the whole world; (iv) as reflection.

It is to be noted here that every theory of the self has to explain the nature of consciousness. Even when the body is the only reality (as in *Cārvāka*), consciousness has to be explained if only as an epiphenomenon of the brain. In Nyāya, consciousness is identified with cognition. There is no theory of depth of consciousness in Nyāya. Sāṁkhya and Advaita Vedānta distinguish between empirical and pure consciousness. Kāśmir Śaivism has an altogether different theory, of pure consciousness. We shall, now, explain very briefly these different forms of consciousness.

It is now necessary to explain the different senses in which consciousness is intentional and is the foundation of the universe. According to Nyāya, consciousness is intentional, and there are no levels of consciousness. According to Sāṁkhya and Advaita Vedānta, consciousness is intentional only as empirical consciousness, i.e., consciousness somehow identified with the *antaḥkaraṇa.* But behind empirical consciousness, there is foundational consciousness which is not intentional at all. There is a fundamental difference between what Advaita Vedānta takes to the foundational consciousness and what Kāśmir Śaivism takes it to be. According to Advaita Vedānta, pure consciousness is the foundation of the world of which I am a part in the sense in which the rope is foundation of the illusory snake; that is, consciousness as reality is the foundation of the world-appearance. But, according to Kāśmir Śaivism, pure consciousness is the foundation of the world as the ocean is the foundation of the waves. The world originates in consciousness, endures in it and gets withdrawn into it. The world never gets out of the ambit of consciousness even when it appears as 'out there'. As the metaphor of the ocean and waves on it emphasizes, the world is the content of pure consciousness. This is a peculiarity which distinguishes Kāśmir Śaivism from Advaita Vedānta and Sāṁkhya according to which only empirical consciousness has contents which are really modes of the material *antaḥkaraṇa.* The theory that pure consciousness has contents is a necessary consequence of the concept of reflective consciousness in Kāśmir Śaivism; for reflection or 'looking within' will be otiose if there is nothing in consciousness to see. Reflecting on a pure contentless consciousness cannot achieve anything. Pure consciousness is self-shining but not reflective, according to Advaita Vedānta philosophers. The world is not related in any way to consciousness, let alone being contained in it. So in realizing Brahman one has necessarily to cross a void, for there is no continuous passage from illusion to reality, from the finite to the infinite. The two realms are ontologically and experientially separated by an unbridgeable gulf.

XIX

THE CONCEPTION OF HISTORY AND INDIAN PHILOSOPHY

The conception of history is a western concept. In India, there is only one instance of history. Kalhana's *Rājataraṅgini* gives a history of kings of Kashmir. It is not clear whether Kalhana was influenced by Arab writers. It is not clear how different cultures have interacted. For example, the late Professor Suniti Kumar Chatterjee repeated a number of items where Vālmiki's *Rāmāyaṇa* is influenced by Homer. Now even if many scholars dispute the existence of a historical Homer, still Professor Chatterjee's contention may be correct for even if there is no Homer still the works attribtued to Homer like *Iliad* and *Odyssey* might have influenced Vālmiki's *Rāmāyāṇa.*

Apart from Kalhana's book, there is no other work of history in India. For gathering information of the people one has to read Purāṇas and the epics. Of course, Purāṇas have been traditionally regarded as having five characteristics (*pañca lakṣaṇa*). One characteristics is that in every Purāṇa there is a theory of the origin of the universe. This theory differs from Purāṇa to Purāṇa. In the Vedas it is asserted that the creation of the universe is cyclic. It is also asserted that the new unvierse is like the old universe (*yathāpūrvam akalpayat*).

It has been often asserted that history in the western sense is not known in India. But there is a study of olden times in *Itihāsa.* But this is a popular theory. According to it, in practically all schools of Indian philosophy, time is eternal; there is no succession of past present and future. These are all illusory.

Now we explain Bhartṛhari's theory. "Time is the most important of the powers of the Śabdatattva-Brahman. It is its creative power (*kartṛśakti*). The *Vṛtti* calls it *svātantrya.* It is called *Vibhu,* explained by Helārāja as *svātantra.* The same commentator says that according to Bhartṛhari, times is the *svātantryaśakti,* power of complete Freedom of Brahman."[27] Time cannot change for it is identified with Brahman.

It is interesting to note that Bhartṛhari has said that all the different things, past, present and future are imposed on one, eternal time, "Through its eternal activity consisting of prevention and permission, it is differentiated and it assumes the form of sequence." "When the powers of the accessories of an action are suspended, there is prevention. The opposite of that is permission. The activity of Time in regard to objects is characterized by these two states. As objects are constantly changing something is always being produced and something else is always perishing. This sequence which really belongs to the objects is attributed to Time. Sequence is primarily a property of actions but it is attributed to something else."[28]

"Conditioned by action, Time attains the states of past, future and present." (Verse 37)

"Time, conditioned by an action which, after having been initiated, is over, is called the past. When conditioned by actions whose accessories are present and which are expected to be initiated soon, it is called the future. When conditioned by actions, which have been initiated but not finished, it is called the present. These three, when subdivided, become eleven in number."[29]

"The past is of five kinds, the future of four kinds and the present of two kinds. Thus there are eleven varieties."[30]

"Past in general, *adyatana* = immediate (lit. 'of today'), *anadyatana* = not immediate, including *parokṣa* = distant, *adyatanānadyatanasamudāya* = combination of the two previous ones and secondary (*gauṇa*) past, that is, future treated as past—these make up the five kinds of past. Future in general, *adyatana* = immediate future, *anadyatana* = not immediate future and *adyatanānadyatanasamudāya* = combination of the two previous kinds, these make up the four kinds of future. Primary present, and secondary present (that is, past and future treated as present) are the two kinds of present. *These divisions of time have been mentioned only to explain the tense distinctions mentioned in the Science of Grammar.*"[31] As Bhartṛhari, who is a grammarian, notices what is grammatically important, namely, past, present and future tense, so he makes the distinction of 11 varieties of time. When it is said 'future treated as past', by 'future' is meant 'specious future' which contains elements which are past.

Objects that are past, may be are reserved in memory. The very fact that things are remembered is a proof of the existence of Time (past). The fact that we can conceive of objects yet to come is also a proof of Time (future).

"The appearance of the universe which is really without sequence as something with sequence is the work of Time."[32]

Thus there can be no history in India.

Now we come to the theory of the philosophical system of Nyāya-Vaiśeṣika. According to this system of Indian philosophy time is infinite and eternal. It does not have any origin at all. This theory is different from Hawkin's theory that time originated in the big bang. According to him it does not make sense to ask what is the time of big bang? Now according to Nyāya Vaiśeṣika this question is significant and, not only that, it admits of a definite answer. The point is that the entire universe is destroyed (*mahāpralaya*) and after that, a new creation takes place. But time remains same.

But the question arises if time is one, infinite and eternal, how can there be a distinction between past and present or a distinction between present and future. According to Nyāya, past, present and future in time are imposed on time illusorily. So all these distinctions between past, present and future are unreal distinctions imposed on time.

Now time which is one, infinite and eternal is called *mahākāla* which is distinguished from *khaṇḍakāla*. This part time is sometimes identified with the object which is produced in time, endures in time and is destroyed in time. Thus this time is often identified with the nature, say, of a jar (*ghaṭātmaka kāla*). The Nyāya theory is that everything which is created is created in time. This means that time is a general cause of everything that is created. Even the universe is created and is in time.

Even if we accept the Nyāya theory, historical development in time will be illusory. It is one of the reasons why there has not been any history in the Nyāya-Vaiśeṣika tradition.

There is another fundamental difference between Nyāya theory and western theory of existence of an external object. According to western theory an external object exists if it is in both space and time. According to Raghunātha, and Nyāya philosophers generally, an external object may be viewed in two ways. It may be said that the object is in time, it exists *now*; and then space is a limitor of the object. If, on the other hand, the object is conceived to exist in space, (it is *here*) then time becomes the limitor. The point is that nothing can be both in space and time which are different substances. There is nothing which can belong to different substances, excepting the universals like existence.

Another point to be noted here is that there is no other relation to an object belonging to time, or belonging to space. If an object is conceived to be in time, the relation between the object and the time is time itself (*kālika saṁbandha*). So also an object in space is related to space by space itself (*daiśika saṁbandha*). As there are no past, no present, no future, they are all unreal impositions on time, according to all schools of Indian philosophy. Because of this reason, there could not be any history in India. Because there is no history, there cannot be any historical perspective. To study the development of scientific theories from a historical perspective is to study them from a western point of view. I have given a historical study of scientific theories in the beginning of the paper. All that I would like to say now is that the historical perspective is a totally western method. The point is that all systems of Indian philosophy and scientific theories are rooted in Indian culture; so importing a western idea or method to study them is bound to fail.

XX

CONCEPTUAL LINKAGE

It has been argued that the theory of relativity of Einstein is based upon an assumption, e.g., the velocity of light is constant and cannot be exceeded. But this assumption is not accepted by many physical scientists now. According to them, there is a particle called tachyon which has greater velocity than light. As in Einstein's theory time is relative to velocity, a particle which moves faster than light, can pass from the past to the future, thus reversing the arrow of time.

But this contention is not accepted by all physical scientists. Thus there are different systems of physics, so that physics and philosophy come very close. The point is that, every science is based upon some assumptions which maybe challenged. This is usually done in western culture.

We have already seen that science according to Nyāya is a part of philosophy. This Indian theory of the relation between science and philosophy is often accepted in modern western culture.

Then there is the question of the link among different cultures. There are two theories here—*a priori* and empirical. According to the *a priori* theory, no person brought up in one culture can ever understand another culture. This is why all western scholars have failed to understand the fundamentals of Indian philosophy. A person born in and brought up in one culture can at best study another culture only from his own point of view.

The second approach is empirical. It has been found that a new language, Urdu, was brought into being when Arabian and Hindi were combined. This shows that the cultures of the two nations are united in one form.

It has been suggested by scholars like the late Dr. Suniti Kumar Chatterjee that the *Rāmāyana* was influenced by Homer. This shows that cultural contacts led to newer forms of literature and language. I have been told on excellent authority that the term '*pujā*' was Dravidian in origin, but was accepted in Sanskrit. Moreover, Nagārjuna, Śaṁkarācārya and *Rāmānaya*, for example, were Dravidians, but their work has become a part of Indian culture. As a matter of fact present-day Indian culture is a conglomeration of many different cultures. This is because of the Aryan invasion of India.

It is difficult to decide whether the *a priori* approach or the empirical approach is the correct one. There are many terms, specially astronomy, where Greek words like '*hora*' were adopted in Sanskrit. So also the concept of drop scene was taken from the Greeks and introduced into the performing arts in Sanskrit.

Medical experts like Dr. Ashok Bagchi are of the opinion that many medical terms in Greek, Latin and modern Italian are borrowed from Sanskrit. For example, Dr. Bagchi was surprised to see in an Italian hospital a department called '*nāso-kāno-galā*' which meant the department of ear-nose-throat. Dr. Bagchi has written a book to explain his views—a book for which he got a D. Litt. Degree from Burdwan University. It is not clear how different people came in contact with each other and influenced their cultures. After the invasion by the British people of India, many English words have been taken into Bengali, like 'table', 'chair', 'glass', etc. Moreover, many fruits which were imported from European countries retain their foreign names. Thus 'anānās' is either Spanish or Portuguese. It has become in Bengali '*ānārasa*'. The word 'tomato' has become a Bengali word. As potatoes were imported, they are never used in Hindu ceremonies. The word 'apple' has been accepted in Bengali. It is not merely Bengal, but the whole of India, is influenced by western dress and food. This is an empirical study of cultures.

So far as philosophy is concerned ancient Indian philosophy was developed only when there was philosophy in Greece in Europe. Many scholars have found out the influence of Indian philosophy on Greek philosophy and vice-versa. It seems that there was close contact between the Greeks and Indians, which led to their mutual influence.

NOTES

1. Dehaene, Stanislas. 1997. *The Number Sense.* Oxford University Press. p. 251.
2. Ibid. p. 243.
3. Ibid.
4. Ibid.
5. Ibid. pp. 243-244.
6. Ibid. p. 99
7. Ibid. p. 101
8. Ibid. pp. 102-103
9. Ibid. p. 146
10. Ibid. pp. 147-148
11. Ibid. p. 8
12. Ibid. p. 251
13. Ibid. p. 251
14. Hingran, p. 41
15. Williams, Banard. *Problems of the Self.* p. 141.
16. Wittgenstein. *Philosophical Investigation.* p. 10e.
17. Śāṁkarācārya in chapter 2 of his commentary on the *Brahma sūtras* has pointed out that infinite regress is involved in the Vaiśeṣika relation of inherence (*samavāya*). But the argument can be generlized against the very concept of relation. This is what we have done above.
18. "*Na saṁsārasya nirvāṇat kiñcit asti viśeṣaṇam.*" *Madhyamaka Śāstra* with the commentary, *Prasannapadā* of Candrakīrti, 1987. Darbhanga: Mithila Institute. p. 263.
19. "*Atrāha—yadi evam bhavatā nirvānam api pratisiddham, nanu ca bhagavatā...dharmo desito lokasya nirvānāndhigamṝtham, sa evam sati vyartha eva jāyate.*" Ibid. p. 265.
20. "*Tasmān nirvānam api nāsti iti siddham.*" Ibid. p. 265.
21. "*Tasmān na badhyate nāpi mucyate...kascit...*" verse—62. Manikar, T.C. 1964. *The Sānkhyakārikā of Īśvarakṛṣṇa* : Poona: Oriental Book Agency. p. 155.
22. 'Thinking of objects leads to attachment to them...' *Gītā,* 2, 62.
23. 'Since there cannot be plural *ego et ego, nor tu et tu* without change of person addressed, it follows that ego and tu have no proper plurals. *Ego et tu* is an inclusive form and is naturally a dual (we), while *ego et atu* is exclusive of tu requires a separate plural word (nos).'
    Wistle, William J. 1953. *Aspects of Language,* p. 207. Quoted in "Language of Social Hierarchy". Dr. K. Kunjuai Raja in *Rajasudha.* 1982. Madras, p. 244.
24. This is when further information about the person spoken of is not given earlier on later. The situation is completely different if after describing a person, one uses 'he' in sentences which follow simply as a matter of grammatical property.
25. For a detailed discussion of the role of addressing in communication, see Gandhi, Ram Chandra. 1974. *Presupposition of Human Communication.* Delhi: Oxford University Press.
26. "'The Friend a Persian expression for God' says Dr. Aziz". Forester, E.M. 1985. *Passage to India.* Penguin Books p. 273.

27. Subramania Iyer, K.A. *Bhartṛhari.* p. 111.
28. Subramania Iyer, K.A. *The Vākyapadiya of Bhaktṛhari,* Part III p. 9, 30.
29. Ibid. p. 46.
30. Ibid. verse 38.
31. Ibid. p. 47.
32. Ibid. p. 46.

BIBLIOGRAPHY

1. *Bhartṛhari.* 1969. K.A. Subramania Iyer (trans.), Poona: Deccan College.
2. Clemens, S.L. 1968. *The Prince and the Pauper.* New York: Master Piece Library.
3. Dehaene, S. 1968. *The Number Sense.* Oxford University Press.
4. Hadamard, J. *Essay on the Psychology of Invention in the Mathematical Field.*
5. James, W. 1918. *Principles of Psychology* (2 vols.) Dover, New York: Dover Publishing Inc.
6. Jhingran, S. 2001. *Ethical Relativism and Universalism.* Delhi: Motilal Banarsidass.
7. Lyotard, J. 1992. *Postmodern Conditions.* Bennigton & Massumi (trans.), Manchester: Manchester University Press.
8. Rorty, R. 1979. *Philosophy and the Mirror of Nature.* Princeton: Princeton University Press.
9. *The Vākyapadiya of Bhartṛhari,* Chapter III, pt ii, 1974. K.A. Subramania Iyer (trans.). Delhi: Motilal Banarsidass.
10. Williams, B. *Problems of the Self.* Cambridge University Press.

CHAPTER 2

Philosophical Consciousness and Scientific Knowledge: Conceptual Linkages and Civilizational Background

D.P. Chattopadhyaya

I

MAINLY PHILOSOPHICAL

What is philosophy? What is *philosophical consciousness*? Philosophy is a *cognitive vision.* It is not analytic in an exclusive sense. It is analytic only in a restrictive and precise sense. Within a vision, philosophical vision, *darsan* as *vidyā, theoria,* whole of *noema,* many elements, *noeses,* or aspects are reviewed which may be and, in the philosophical context, should be analyzed, vigorously and as exactly as possible. But, every analysandum (that which is to be analysed) has its limits and bearing which in mind we search for and state our analysans (which are used to make analysandum clear).

Relation between analysis and synthesis. The primitivity claim of synthesis, *theoria,* as exemplified in Absolutism (Advaita Vedānta), Wholism or Holism, Integralism and Organicism. Illustratively speaking, the authors whose views and arguments may be profitably recalled, among others, are: Vedic/Vedāntic (One in Many); Spinoza, (God is Nature), Hegel (Whatever is is *of* the as well as *in* the Absolute), and Bradley (Absolute is pure Sentience and available in every bit of experience); Sri Aurobindo (Integralism), Whitehead (Organicism).

Place of Analysis in the writings of Nyāya-Vaiśeṣika, Buddhist Logicians, Jaina Logicians, Russel, Wittgenstein, Existentialists like Sartre, Phenomenoligists like Husserl, and Post-modernists like Derrida: Analysis involves, if not pre-supposes, synthesis. Synthesis as found in the works of Speculative Metaphysicians (Śaṁkara and Śri Aurobindo) and Scientific Metaphysicians (Spinoza and Whitehead). How analysis involves synthesis?

Reference to different foundationalist approaches in the areas of Mathematics, Geometry, Newtonian Physics (Systematicity sustained by the Three Laws of Motion), Relativistic Field Theorists like Einstein and his followers, and the Quantum Field Theorists of the second half of the twentieth century.

No philosophy without philosophical experience. No synthesis without synthetic or integral or organic (or system-theoretic) experience. The proclaimed breakdown between the analytic and the synthetic and its critical review. No theorization, neither scientific nor philosophical, is available or possible without experience, intuition or vision.

II

MAINLY SCIENTIFIC

What is Science? Science as the modern "paradigm" of knowledge. The requirements of *rigor, precision* and *exactitude* in science. Characteristics of Scientific Objectivity. Objectivity, Externality, Mind-independence and Inter-subjectivity, their interrelations. Does Objectivity mean Neutrality of the subject from the object known? Reference to the knowing-known Interdependence, Complementarity and Cybernaticity in the fields of modern science and technology. [cf. Niels Bohr and Norbert Wiener].

Can Science be really neutral? Is not Science Ideology-linked? Is Science itself an Ideology? Reference to the views of thinkers like Marx, Popper, Adorno and Herbert Marcuse.

Does Scientific Neutrality as Objectivity mean (a) disinterested enquiry, or (b) as Freedom from Prejudices/Biases, or (c) as Non-subservience to this or that interest, or (d) as Freedom from Determinations/Conditionings/ Influences, or (e) Indifference to any end?

Neutrality, Objectivity and Responsibility of the Scientists as rational truth-seeking. Reference to the views of Scientists like Einstein, Robert Oppenheimer and Heisenberg in the context of production and explosion of Atom Bomb. Debate over Disarmament, Peace and Security considerations.

III

PHILOSOPHY→SCIENCES→SCIENTIFIC PHILOSOPHY RELATIONSHIP

Had there been any time in the human past when Philosophy and Science could be completely delinked? Is it not a historically evident fact that the ancient philosophers both in India and in the Hellenic world had been *both* scientists in the modern sense and philosopher in the perennial sense.

Is experiment an essential ingredient of scientific knowledge and scientific truth-seeking? Recalling the works of theoretical Physicists, Cosmologists and Astrophysicists—the disciplines in which the role of testing emerges only after that of speculation or hypothesis-framing. Recalling Vedic and Hellenic cosmological ideas—claiming Water, Air, Fire, etc., the elements of Nature, to be the prime Reality. Limits of experience, limits of experiment and necessity of Speculation, Conjecturing and Hypothesis-framing. Status of scientific hypotheses between their time of formulation, context of discovery, and their time of actual experimentation, context of validation.

Relation between Experience and Experiment

Is not Experiment a type of *controlled* Experience? Can Experimental Conditions be created for testing all types of scientific hypotheses? Controllability of experimental conditions remains always a matter of degree, i.e., a matter of imperfection and approximation, and can never be complete and perfect. This is due, among other things, to irremovable *human* and *instrumenta* factors. The principle of Quantum Mechanics to be recalled in this connection is: interdependence of or mutuality between the observer, the observed and the instrument(s) or experimental conditions.

Why any hypothesis in its singularity or even a cluster of hypotheses (in their togetherness) cannot be *decisively* refuted? Reference to the Duhem-Quine hypothesis, i.e., *continuity* of the past science with the present science. The debate over the continuity and discontinuity between past ("paradigms" of) science and the present ("paradigms" of) science. Ambiguity attending the word "paradigm". Critics have pointed out as many as 18 senses in which Kuhn himself has used the word. Examination and assessment of the arguments for and against (A) "paradigm shift" and (B) relation between "Normal Science" and "Revolutionary Science." Reference to the views and arguments of (I) Thomas Kuhn, Stephen Toulmin, Paul Feyerabend and N. R. Hanson, on the one hand, and (II) their critics such as Popper, Quine, Putnam and Watkins, on the other.

Why these type of debates, (i) the debate of *commensurability versus incommensurability*, (ii) the debate of *continuity versus discontinuity* of (a) philosophical and (b) scientific paradigms/theories, does not figure in the history of the development of Science, Philosophy and Scientific Philosophy in India? Is it due to the prevalence of the *cyclical view* of history or evolution in India? Or is it due to the alleged non-emergence of the quantitative, formal and experimental theories of basic sciences like Physics and Chemistry? Why such sciences as Physics and Chemistry, found in the medieval and modern Europe, did not emerge in India, China or even in the West Asia? Is it a pseudo-question or pertinent question? If it is a pertinent, what can be a plausible answer?

IV

SCIENCE AND PHILOSOPHY ON THEIR CRITICO-COMPARATIVE PERSPECTIVE

Is there any fundamental difference between the *History of European* Philosophy and the European Science, on the one hand, and the *history of Indian* Philosophy and the *History of Indian* Philosophy and *Indian* Science, on the other? Is it misleading to speak of "Indian Science", "European Science"? Must we maintain that Science is country-neutral and that it is necessarily "universal", i.e., has nothing to do with this or that Culture or Civilization?

If philosophy is really believed to be concerned with the *first principles* or *basic categories* of knowledge of different objects of the world, including Matter, Life, Mind, how, if at all, there can be fundamental difference between the Indian and European or, for that reason, between any two or many reconstructed historical accounts of Science and Philosophy in different civilizations?

If it is true, as some comparative historians of Philosophy, Science and Civilizations claim, that there are significant parallels between Philosophy, Scientific and Technological developments in such varied civilizations as Sinic (Chinese), Indic, Semitic and Hellenic-European, how to explain the *distinctness* of philosophy and *uneven* development of science in different civilizations?

Reference to the works of Will Durant, Joseph Needham, the UNESCO History of Humanity and various other works.

Why is it that philosophy of every civilization, in spite of its claim to be concerned with the First Principle or the Basic Categories, exhibits a more or less distinct character of its own? Why the so-called First Principles or the Basic Categories or the Categorial Frameworks are not uniform? Are we, then, to understand that even the so-called *fundamental* Truths and/or the *highest* forms of Knowledge are not uniformly realized or available to all peoples belonging to different civilizations?

Bearing the above questions and their different/alternative answers on the Scientific Mode of Knowledge, in general, and the Modern Science, in particular, when it is said that Scientific Truths, experimentally or observationally established and repeatedly testable, are same all over the world, how are we to understand it? Apparently, the availability of difference and alternativity in Science down the centuries is historically undeniable. To take concrete examples, why the pre-Copernican Astronomical systems—Ptolemic, Āryabhaṭṭa's, Varāhamihir's, etc., both in India and Europe, not only differed from the Copernican system but also between themselves? Does the same set of astronomical or other scientific data lends itself to (a) *alternative* and even (b) *conflicting* interpretations?

Does *alternativity* of alternative interpretations imply weakness or inadequacy of the concerned interpretations? Or, does it mean that Reality, studied by Science and Philosophy and articulated in scientific and philosophical statements, *appear* to be alternative and, at times, even *different* because of cognitive limitations of the concerned human beings—be they Philosophers or Scientists? What about the respectable and time-honoured view that there had been, and still there are, great Seers of reality whose realization and expression of Truths are unquestionable (infallible or *apauraṣeya)* for ever? What about the *difference* between the infallibilists themselves and the *conflict* between their scientific-philosophic claims as found in their recorded views?

V

INFALLIBILITY AND HISTORITY OF PHILOSOPHICAL AND SCIENTIFIC MODES OF KNOWLEDGE

How to understand the question regarding the claim that there are specially gifted, spiritually or intellectually or both, persons who can know Truths about Reality under the aspect of eternity. Are we to understand that these Truths about Reality do *not* lend themselves to time-bound or historical explanation? Can Philosophy, as expression of the highest form of Knowledge, be subject to civilizational variation and historical modification?

In the context of Science one is used to hearing such expression as "development", "growth" and "proliferation". Is one entitled to use in a defensible manner these very expressions and their surrogates in the context of Philosophy as well? Does a *comparative* study and *critical* enquiry into *Histority of Science* and *Histority of Philosophy* show that the term *Histority* in the two contexts is being used in the same sense, or in different senses? Is Philosophy a mere interpretation of Science? Or it has its own *autonomy*?

Does Science need Philosophy for its interpretation? Are not Scientists themselves equipped enough to interpret their views? Investigation into the arguments for and against the claim of *Autonomous Science.*

Revisiting such paired concepts as *jñāna/vijñāna, parāvidyā/aparāvidyā,* and Philosophy/Science. Attempts to understand the opposite claims of subordination and superordination in the context of relation between Science and Philosophy. How one should understand such statements as "Philosophy is Science, nothing more and nothing less", "Philosophy is speculative and inexact approximations of the objects studied rigorously in Science" and "Science is the empirical region of philosophy concerned with the *possible* highest Truths about Reality expressed in quantitative and operational terms?"

BIBLIOGRAPHY

1. Carnap, Rudolf. 1966. *Philosophical Foundations of Physics.* Martin Gardner (ed.). New York/London: Basic Books. (Clear and analytic).
2. Chattopadhyaya, D.P. 1996. *Interdisciplinary Studies in Science, Technology, Philosophy and Culture.* Project of History of Indian Science, Philosophy and Culture. New Delhi: Munshiram Manoharlal (distributors). Delhi, 1996.
3. ———. 2001. *Ways of Understanding the Human Past : Mythic, Epic, Scientific, Historical (and Dialogical).* Project of History of Science, Philosophy and Culture & Motilal Banarsidass: Delhi.
4. Chattopadhyaya, D.P. and Kumar, Ravinder (ed.). 1996-97. *Science, Philosophy and Culture: Multidisciplinary Explorations,* 2 vols. Project of History of Indian Science, Philosophy and Culture. New Delhi: Munshiram Manoharlal (distributors).
5. Collins, Ranald. 2000. *The Sociology of Philosophies : A Global Theory of Intellectual Change.* Camb. Mass.: Harvard University (Belknap) Press. (The work is historically informed, represents scholarship of a high order, interdisciplinary and very comprehensive).
6. Dampier, W.C. 1979. *A History of Science and Its Relations with Philosophy and Religion.* Cambridge and London: Cambridge University Press. (Though a little outdated, the work is very scholarly).
7. Einstein, Albert and Infeld, Leopold. 1971. *The Evolution of Physics.* Cambridge: Cambridge University Press. (Simple, readable and authoritative).
8. Fraassen, B. van. 1991. *Quantum Mechanics : An Empiricist View.* Oxford: Clarendon Press.
9. Fine, A. 1986. *The Shaky Game : Einstein, Realism and the Quantum Theory.* Chicago: University of Chicago Press.
10. Gillispie, Charles Coulston. (ed.) 1981. *Dictionary of Scientific Biography,* vols. 15, Supplement I, *Topical Essays.* New York: Charles Scribner's Sons. See, in particular, David Pingree's "History of Mathematical Astronomy in India". (pp. 533-633; with excellent biography and Astronomical & Scientific thoughts of some such ancient civilizations as Mesopotamia, Egypt, Japan and Maya).
11. Gutting, Gary (ed.). 1980. *Paradigms and Revolutions : Appraisals and Applications of Thomas Kuhn's Philosophy of Science.* Notre Dame and London: University of Notre Dame Press.
12. Mehra, Jagdish and Reichenberg, Helmut. 1982 & 2001. *The Historical Development of Quantum Theory, 1925.* Vol. 9. New York: Springer Verlag. (Very comprehensive, partly technical, but philosophical aspects have been taken care of.)
13. Needham, Joseph. *Science and Civilization in China,* vols. 1, 3 and 4 : 1. Cambridge: Cambridge University Press. (Vol. 1 for the relation of China's scientific ideas with those of Indians, Arabian and European. 1954 & 1975; vol. 3 for Chinese Mathematics and Sciences of the Heavens and the Earth. 1959 & 1975; and Vol. 4 : 1 for Physics and Physical Technology, 1962 & 1972).
14. Popper, Karl R. 1969. *Conjectures and Refutations : The Growth of Scientific Knowledge.* London: Routledge and Kegan Paul. (Authoritative exposition of the Popperian, i.e. critico-positivist point of view).
15. Putnam, Hilary. 1990. *Realism with a Human Face.* James Conant (ed. and intr.). Cambridge, Mass: Harvard University Press.

16. Ray, P.C. 1956. *History of Hindu Chemistry,* 2 vols., as revised by P. Ray. *History of Chemistry in Ancient and Medieval India.* Calcutta: Indian Chemical Society. (Pioneer Interdisciplinary Work).
17. Saraswati, Swami Satya Prakash. 1990. *Founders of Sciences in Ancient India,* 2 Parts. Delhi: Govindaram Hasanand. (Various disciplines are discussed).
18. Sarton, George. 1952. *A History of Science,* vol.1, *Ancient Science Through the Golden Age of Greece.* New York: W. W. Norton. (Though primarily concerned with the Hellenic world but references to other civilizations and historical methodology is very instructive).
19. Seal, B.N. 1985. *The Positive Sciences of the Ancient Hindus.* Delhi: Motilal Banarsidass. (Both substantive and methodological).
20. Subbarayappa, B.V. and Sharma, K.V. (ed.). 1985. *Indian Astronomy: A Source Book.* Bombay: Nehru Centre.

CHAPTER 3

Philosophical Consciousness and Scientific Knowledge: Proper Place of Reason

Mohini Mullick

In Section IV, the working paper asks us to consider the question: "Is there any fundamental difference between the History of European Philosophy and Science on the one hand and the History of Indian Philosophy and Indian Science on the other?"

In posing the issue in terms of 'fundamental difference', the question intentionally or otherwise, immediately problematizes the following:

a) that the terms 'science' and 'philosophy' are applicable to both European and Indian thought (at least in a generic sense) in precisely the same manner;

b) that there exists a history of Indian philosophy and of science in again precisely the same sense as it patently does in the European context.

Indeed given the intimate enmeshing of the modern historiography of science with the overall understanding and even definition of science, the two clauses a) and b) can be shown to telescope into each other; a negative response to either one or both could make it difficult to even pose the question afresh and render any attempt to make comparison of the two 'histories' infructuous. Thus it is to these assumptions that I wish to invite attention in what follows. In doing so I like to think that the implicit purpose of the question is thereby being served...

The concept of science has, in the last century, come under the intense gaze of philosophers, many of whom have themselves been practising scientists, including the most eminent. Einstein is possibly the greatest of them. Though there is no one overriding definition to which all philosophers and scientists alike owe allegiance, there is broad agreement on the view that science is definable in terms of its method. Whereas the empirical methods are of course the most characteristic feature of scientific practice, they are not its monopoly. Some practices that fall under the rubric of 'pseudo-science' do also employ empirical methods. And 'verification in experience' as a touchstone of scientificity was shown by the mid-twentieth century to be a standard both too narrow and too wide. The 'falsifiability' of theories that replaced it as a criterion of science, was also demonstrated to be full of loopholes. Thus it was proposed that the concept of science must be understood diachronically in the sense of the development, evolution and possibly, progress of its theoretical grasp over time of the ever enlarging canvas of the natural universe, in the shape of research programmes involving a community of scientists, in other words, method that comes to characterize a tradition—a scientific tradition. That such a tradition was born and has developed in the western world is not open to doubt, though it could perhaps be argued that such an understanding, i.e. in terms of western history pre-empts the meaningful application of the term in other contexts. For the moment, however, we have little choice but to consider the best case—and that surely is that of western science—from which to extrapolate even a most general understanding of the concept. Thus we are constrained to ask: what has been the motor of its development? The answer on the face of it is: the use of critical reason; it is the openness to the critical evaluation of its theories, even its most valued assumptions, in light of fresh evidence, that has led to constant change (progress?), the very hallmark of modern science. Reason in the form of deductive and inductive logic is its prime instrument. This is not the occasion to relive the course of western history that made such a tradition possible. I will permit myself just one quotation that I feel rather neatly sums up the course of events in the West's own perception of its history. I quote Wilhelm Halbfass as he presents the Hegelian view of European history, which I believe remains essentially unchallenged even today:

"The development of Occidental history, from the Greek and early Christian world to the age of the French Revolution, is the development and self-organization of the substance as *subject,* descent and unfolding of the absolute and divine into the finite and human world, self-discovery and self-affirmation of the autonomous person. The 'phenomenology' or self-manifestation of the absolute merges into man's work in history, into human self-fulfilment. Man becomes 'present God' (*praesenter Gott*) and continues the divine process in his own worldly presence, in taking charge of his world and discovering the dignity of the absolute *in* it. Philosophy has to deal with the present, with *this* world... Philosophy cannot escape from the historical process; it is its mirror as well as its motor."[1] This broad understanding of the genesis of the western mind which eventually gave birth to both modern western science and philosophy, immediately makes questionable the notion of Indian science and philosophy in this given sense. Here in this country Man did not become 'present God'; there was no autonomous person...

Though this position may very well be challenged and I am sure will be challenged right here today, it is not my purpose on this occasion to defend it. My purpose is rather to relate this view of western science and its origins to the view regarding philosophy that is also expressed in it. This is the thesis that only the West has philosophy. To quote one of the most pithy comments made in this context, I turn to Heidegger who says: "the phrase 'Western-European philosophy' is a tautology." Before him, Hegel had already proclaimed: "The real philosophy begins only in the Occident. Here the spirit goes down into itself, immerses into itself, posits itself as free, is free for itself. Philosophy can exist only here; and hence we have free constitutions only in the Occident."[2] And Edmund Husserl argues, "one must not allow the merely morphologically general features to hide the intentional depths so that one becomes blind to the most essential differences of principle". Small wonder then that Husserl then goes on to proclaim that philosophy as first science marks "the *telos* which was inborn in European humanity at the birth of Greek philosophy."[3] Husserl is here comparing Indian and Chinese philosophy on the one hand with Greek philosophy on the other. The issue, of course, is not one that questions the use of a word: it is the entire spirit of western thought that is being characterized here.

This brings me to my present concern: are not the fates of philosophy and science intimately enmeshed? If so, then are not these claims or counter claims if one prefers, cognate? Is there an underlying set of criteria, an ethos, explicitly defined or not, that is the ground of both western philosophy (an originally Greek term) and western science (also defined very late in history, but in the West) as it emerged from the womb of this philosophy, first as natural philosophy and even mechanical philosophy, and finally (having severed the umbilical cord) as Science itself?

The answer: clearly there is. One may in fact extend the metaphor of the parent-child relationship: for just as the child fully grown, begins at first to guide and then to dominate the parent, so also has science laid out the field of philosophy's operations in the modern world. The vicissitudes in the fortunes of science are almost poignantly reflected in the self-images of philosophy[4]. And when the inevitable happens—when first Truth and then Rationality are discovered by philosophers of science to be in fact Gods with feet of clay—then in philosophy too, the idea of rule displaces that of truth, objectivity abdicates in favour of solidarity, and the (anti-)method of narrative supplants that of rational explanation. For if it is the West that so fervently espoused the cause of Reason, then it is the West alone in modern times that has questioned it. Heir to the Romantic tradition, Continental philosophy is quick to deny the hegemony of Reason. Not surprisingly then, it is Heidegger who said of this entire project, "thinking shall only begin once we have learned that this thing, Reason, which has been so magnified for centuries, is the most relentless enemy of thought."[5] Note that Heidegger here refers to all western thought, making no distinction between philosophy and science.

How shall we understand this thing, Reason that Heidegger here denounces? I shall use the term Autonomous Reason for that constellation of attributes that philosophy and science in the West have come to share in the modern period of Europe's history—Reason as it reveals itself in the intellectual life of Hegel's autonomous person. Note that the foundations for this form of reason were in fact laid by the Greeks who sutured philosophy to the 'matheme', the *mathesis universalis*. It is this reason alone, freed from the shackles of authoritarian and traditional underpinnings that can pursue the project of the pure theoretical understanding. And here we are again reminded of Husserl's claim, viz., "... only in the Greeks do we have a universal ('cosmological') life-interest in the essentially new form of a purely theoretical attitude ... and the corresponding, essentially new [community] of philosophers, of scientists (mathematicians, astronomers etc.)...These are the men who... strive for and bring about *theoria* and nothing but *theoria*." Autonomous Reason is conceived as both universal and theoretical, i.e. as unrelated to the differing *practical* concerns of *different* cultures.

When we turn our attention to the broad canvas of Indian thought, we see the reasons for this 'fundamental difference'. Here the umbilical cord was never severed: an holistic search for knowledge, today again much vaunted by scholars and practitioners of the ancient science of Indian medicine, and greatly sought after by the votaries of alternative remedies in the West, was nevertheless perhaps the single most important factor that precluded the possibility of a high degree of specialization which is the very hallmark of modern science. Its attendants, the fragmentation of knowledge and the mutual insulation of the numerous sciences that have emerged in the last century, are of course the price that western science has paid for the rapid strides it has made. Now the facts may belie B.N.Seal's observation that "the various *Pramāṇas*, Proofs, i.e. sources of valid knowledge in Hindu Logic, viz. Perception, Inference, Testimony, Mathematical Reasoning(*sambhav*, including Probability in one view)are only operations subsidiary to the ascertainment of Truth (*tattvanirṇaya*). And the Scientific Methods are merely ancillary to these *pramāṇas* themselves."[6] And Chattopadhyaya has taken him to task for totally ignoring the practices of the scientists themselves.[7] However, that the canonical and received version of the valid sources of knowledge plays at least a regulative role in all cognitive practices can hardly be gainsaid.[8] That canonical version included perception (a notion, be it noted, much wider than that of sensory perception) and inference but in a longer list of sources of knowledge in which (for almost all schools), was also included *śabda pramāṇa*. Quite apart from the purely epistemological enunciations of the high texts is also the crucial role played by the social arrangements which were without doubt entrenched in the more ancient Dharmaśāstras and which without doubt were inimical to the practice of science as a community activity. All this is very convincingly documented in D.P. Chattopadhyaya's work on Indian medicine and does not require recounting here.[9]

The above is meant to serve as a recapitulation of what has already been argued, for and against the legitimacy of the search for modern elements in the practice and theory of ancient 'science' in India. But there is still the important factor of history to which perhaps less attention has been paid. In the *Structure of Scientific Revolutions*, Kuhn observes: "History, if viewed as a repository for more than anecdote or chronology, could produce a decisive transformation in the image of science by which we are now possessed." Kuhn, as is well known, then went on to present his understanding of science in terms of the alternation of what he called the normal and revolutionary periods in its development Despite the strenuous efforts of his numerous detractors, Kuhn has left an indelible impression on the historiography of science and the western world's understanding of the process of its history. That western science has had a dynamic and almost self-propelling history, cannot be denied. Its motor has not always been its greater freedom, but rather a fierce self-belief, called hubris, which alone could drive a Copernicus and a Galileo to defy the powers of the Roman Catholic Church—and pay the price.

The propensity to question, even radically reject, the current state of knowledge which alone might have given rise to a series of philosophical and scientific revolutions, was not given to the Indian thinker, scientist and philosopher alike.[10] Without going into the vexed question of the ahistoricality of Indian thought, the near total absence of the idea of the progress in socio-economic terms of man's destiny, it is still pertinent to remind ourselves of the fact that for these thinkers perfection lay in the past rather than in a human future, that the present was a constant struggle to adhere to what in the past had been laid down as canonical truth. In fact one can truly say that the past never quite became 'past'; dialogues in philosophical texts provide ample evidence of its eternal presence. Sheldon Pollock expresses this very thought in words that I quote: "In India... this mode of discourse... implied that all intellectual generations, disembodied from any spatio-temporal framework, were thought of as coexistent: the past was a very present conversation partner. It was also viewed as a superior partner, the master who made the primary statements in a discussion upon which later participants could only comment.... The universe was systematically entropic, and intellectual effort could be nothing but a quest to recover what had once been known more perfectly, but now was lost."[11] Pollock draws attention to another phenomenon that is worthy of our consideration here. The distinction between the *Mārga* and *Deśi* intellectuals, at no point began to favour the latter. In Europe on the other hand, at around the same time, Descartes began to write in French, and soon after that Galileo published his *Discorsi* in Italian.

I must, at this point, stress the fact that no value-judgements are embedded or implied in the above account. I do not for a moment wish to suggest that the modern notion of progress is superior to alternative notions, or even that it is in itself, a coherent one. I wish only to stress its unique motivating power.

The working paper raises the further question: "Why is it that Philosophy of every civilization, in spite of its claim to be concerned with First Principles or the Basic Categories, exhibits a more or less distinct character of its own?" It asks why fundamental truths are not uniformally realized by all peoples... This question is predicated on the unexamined assumption that there exists a set of uniform fundamental truths and I must leave it alone. In any case, as we all are aware, 'why?' questions are notoriously difficult to answer. For this reason, unsatisfactory as it is, I have sought to paint an impressionistic picture of the distinct character of Indian as opposed to the European consciousness and historical experience. It is no doubt a very sketchy picture to which in the detail there were notable exceptions. The development of a tradition of science, however, requires more than the Indian mind could bring to bear—a completely Autonomous Reason. If so, then we must enquire: just what is the reality behind the construct of an 'Indian science'?

Given India's colonial history, the overwhelming need to reconstruct its 'scientific' past, is not difficult to understand. In *Another Reason*, Gyan Prakash recounts these events of the nineteenth century, thus; "To advance universal claims for a people stigmatised as metaphysical and out of touch with modernity was an act of enormous imagination and ambition. Precisely such a far-reaching project came into view in late-nineteenth-century British India as the Hindu intelligentsia began to identify a body of scientific knowledge in particular Indian texts and traditions. Denying that science was alien to India, they argued with remarkable ingenuity and deep cultural learning that the ancient Hindus had originated scientific knowledge..."[12] Prakash is here concerned to demonstrate the role that the project of the recovery of an Indian science played in the justification of "the modern existence of Indians as a people". This, by no means, is the whole story; I mention it here because we as philosophers, even as philosophers of science, tend to ignore historical contexts, socio-political compulsions and the complicities of power and language, in our search for the 'pure' concept. Nineteenth century efforts towards the recovery of ancient Indian 'science' are fortunately very well documented and historians of the modern period are well aware of them. Yet it has to be said that they seldom come to the fore in reconstructions of classical Indian philosophy and science even today. At least in the realm of philosophy, with which I am more familiar, the question of the rationality of Indian thought is treated in a manner that is completely decontextualized.[13] For philosophers of this persuasion, the argument must go directly into what is seen as the 'objective' structure of ancient Indian thought in order to plead for recognition of the attainment of its autonomy in the course of Indian history. In recent times, J.N. Mohanty and Bimal Matilal have been the most ardent defenders of this view. Aware that at least in its origins, Indian thinking was deeply concerned with the question of self-knowledge, Mohanty says: "In the long run, coming from the western intellectual tradition as also from the tradition of Indological studies, the crucial question remains: can the chapters spread out over the Sanskrit texts of the *darśanas* on perception (*pratyakṣa*), inference *(anumāna),* sentential understanding (*śabdabodha),* truth (*pramāṇya),* — can these chapters, topics, disputations, be separated from the supposedly fundamentally soteriological, theological, and ritualistic thinking of that tradition, and be *elevated to* the status of an intellectual discipline to rank with those of a Plato, Kant, or Husserl? I wish to emphasize that not only can they be so separated, but that the tradition itself achieved the necessary idealization."[14] A little later Mohanty feels compelled to articulate the forbidden question: "Does the Indian *darśana,* by virtue of its subject-matter, its concerns, its methodology come under the purview of the concept 'philosophy'?"[15] A sad question, and one full of anxiety, it is tantamount to asking: is critical reason at the heart of the *darśanas*?

Matilal also burns a candle bright to illuminate the issue of the rationality of Indian philosophy, which he too sees as a state in which soteriological issues are essentially left behind. Thus Matilal says: "These concerns (intellectual concerns sparked by religious and soteriological teachings) are very general, but they obviously lead to issues which are specific, complicated, involved, and intellectually demanding. For these are what we call today philosophical issues and puzzles. And when presented with puzzles and knots it is the nature of the human intellect to keep trying to unwind them. This then becomes part of the philosophical enterprise. After some time, slowly but surely the theological or salvational concerns are replaced almost unconsciously by philosophical ones. This is what has happened in the intellectual history of the medieval (classical) period in India."[16]

Implicit in these very similar accounts is the acceptance that the rationality of a system of thought must follow the pattern of western philosophy, must, in fact, adhere to the dictates of Autonomous Reason. For example, Matilal is clearly affirming that salvational concerns cannot be philosophical ones. The overarching panoply of soteriological issues that looms large over all disputations, accounts for the palpable anxiety displayed by an influential set of Indian philosophers who coincidentally or not, have lived most of their professional lives in the West. But why this anxiety? The reasons are not far to seek, but they must be given full recognition. For a hundred years or more, western rationality has been contrasted with Indian mysticism, spirituality and even obscurantism. We again do not need to relive here today, this period of our political and intellectual history. But do we need to perpetuate our defensiveness? I wish to argue forcefully against this. However, in saying this, must one not first grapple with the fact that the absence of rationality is but the presence of the irrational, the mystical and the obscure? Is that how we must think of the Indian *śruti* texts and the *darśanas* that followed them?

Elsewhere I have examined the arguments and evidences put forward by Mohanty, Matilal to establish what, in their view, guarantees the rationality of Indian philosophy.[17]

They argue for the arrival in the course of time, in Indian intellectual history of what I have labelled Autonomous Reason. They have sought to show that logic not intuition was used and prized by Indian philosophers in much the same way as in the West. Given the intimate historical connection between logic and mathematics from the end of the nineteenth century at least, effort has also not been wanting in the direction of demonstrating their awareness of the importance of mathematics. Thus Ganeri concludes his account of the foundations of Vaiśeṣika philosophy with the words: "The idea that nature exemplifies mathematical structure is not remote from the Indian understanding of natural philosophy, contrary to what is generally believed, but is in fact a fundamental aspect of it."[18] One cannot after all forget that as far back as the fifth century B.C., the entrance to Plato's Academy was marked with the words: "Let no man enter here who is not a geometer." On this point at least there is disagreement in the camp. Mohanty is clearly concerned because he says: "It is noteworthy that in spite of the Hindu love of mathematics, this mathematical conception of nature never took hold of the Hindu mind (in spite of astronomy and its mathematical basis."[19] (Why one may ask, is it noteworthy?) It is perhaps at this point also pertinent to recall the astute observation of B.N.Seal who first noted that "philosophy in its rise and development is necessarily governed by the body of positive knowledge preceding or accompanying it" and goes on to observe: "Hindu Philosophy on its empirical side was dominated by concepts derived from physiology and philology, just as Greek Philosophy was similarly dominated by geometrical concepts and methods."[20] If there is a moral to this confusing story, and I believe there is, it can perhaps be read off the words of Srinivasa Murti, man of medicine, who working at the same time as Seal, crisply declared: "We should not torture Ayurvedic texts to read into them Modern Allopathic teachings through forced comparisons and fanciful interpretations."

Having said this much, let us get back to the burning question: did the ancient Indians valorise logic more than intuition? This is perceived as crucial by Mohanty *et al* in order to establish their major thesis concerning Indian rationality. But even before we dare to address a question couched in these terms, it is imperative that we attend to a prior problem. For we must be quite clear from which vantage point the question of rationality is being admitted as one of genuine concern. In spite of protestations that all concerns must be voiced from an internalist standpoint, these philosophers do not even acknowledge that from an internalist point of view the rationality problem was never posed, and arguably could not be posed in the Indian *darśana* tradition. In the Saṁskṛta language, as Arindam Chakrabarti notes, there is no exact word for 'rationality'. But he too argues that this fact alone does not foreclose the issue of whether the ancient Indians possessed the concept. So let us admit that we speak from the horizon of modernity, the vantage point of a contemporary consciousness in a globally accepted language which may find no reverberations in the texts themselves, and ask: just what is the relation between logic and rationality? Surely the demand that the laws of logic be observed in reasoning speaks to a highly impoverished concept of rationality. John Macintyre, recognizing this fact, notes: "... observance of the laws of logic is only a necessary and not a sufficient condition for rationality whether theoretical or practical. It is in what has to be added to observance of the laws of logic to justify ascriptions of rationality... that disagreement arises concerning the fundamental nature of rationality and extends into disagreement over how it is rationally appropriate to proceed in the face of these disagreements."[21]

This reads like a no-win situation since each step of the way towards the solution is blocked by the problem itself. Indeed the resulting impasse becomes the *reductio ad absurdum* of Macintyre's assumption that something must be added—we know not what—to the observance of the laws of logic that will yield ascriptions of rationality to whatever. For how can we *rationally* decide what this something is? Sylvan displays a greater sensitivity to the problem which he frames thus: "But what a reason is, has been, and remains a matter of much debate mainly because of the evaluative loading of the key terms and the different connected value systems embedded in different underlying world views."[22] Note that Sylvan is still seeking rationality in terms of reasons—good reasons no doubt. And we are well aware how the literature has spilt into the notions of reasonableness, Popper's Situational Logic and all that.

It is clear that as long as the rationality debate is enmeshed in the discourse of reasoning, valid or not, it will remain infructuous and the problem intractable. The real issues remain unaddressed if not actually obfuscated. What does it mean to ask of an entire tradition of thought whether it is rational or not? Which society, be it the most 'primitive', consists of members who are simply unable to reason? The anthropological literature of the early part of the twentieth century is replete with debates surrounding the question of the rational, the pre-rational, the proto-rational or the downright magical nature of these societies. A century later, if we have learnt anything from these tortuous debates, the philosophical literature at least does not reflect it.

In the concluding section of this paper I attempt to make some sense of the rationality question which throws some light on the original problem of the fundamentally different 'histories' of philosophy and science in India and the West. To do this we return to the etymological root of the word: *ratio.* Ratio is a common enough word; it gives us the notion of balance, proportion, a characteristic ordering or configuration. The O.E.D, does give us 'the corresponding relationship between things not precisely measurable; the relation between two similar magnitudes.'(No doubt it gives us 'reason, rationale' as well.) The only sensible search for the rationality of any system of thought then must be a search for the characteristic balance of its elements, the unique configuration that becomes the signature of a civilization. Interestingly, in an essay on Leibniz, Heidegger translates the Latin *ratio* as *grunde* in German, the ground or could we even say, grounding. Thus "there is a ground in nature"—*ratio est in natura*—"why something exists rather than nothing." And so on. Ratio here signifies that which underlies, that which is the principle of configuration and that which limits the range of possible conceptual structures. It is not itself a grey, amorphous substance that either is present or not in a given culture. It is a mode of ordering the elements of a culture: it *is* culture. When we reinterpret the question of the rationality of western science and philosophy in this light, it is not difficult to conclude that since the advent of the Enlightenment, it is Autonomous Reason that has grounded both. This is a contingent fact of history, if we are not given to the notion of historical necessity. It is not, contra Hegel, the unfolding of Universal Reason which it was the privilege of the West to inaugurate and the fate of the rest of the world to emulate.

Note that reasoning, the use of logic is not itself privileged in this understanding. Human reason may have a regulative role to play— and then it may not—in the constitution of this ground, as the rationale of surface structures such as beliefs and practices. It could have a highly delimited role: in the theatre of human action and destiny it could even be just a stagehand.

I will illustrate my thesis with reference to an article entitled "Images of Reason in Chinese Culture". The title is significant in that Reason is invoked, indeed but clearly as figured in a different imagination. (The western mind cannot after all relinquish its own...) A major contrast is drawn here between the logical order and the aesthetic order symbolized by the ubiquitous metaphor of the *yin* and the *yang* (literally the sunny and the shady sides of a hill). This pair of opposites orders or grounds experience, thought and understanding for the Chinese. The author says: "Chinese rationality has more to do with mapping and unravelling than with grasping some formal principle or essence. The Chinese word '*li*' if translated as reason, while foregrounding our philosophical importances pays the unacceptable penalty of concealing those meanings which are most essential to an appreciation of its differences." Again, "the investigation of *li*... is to seek out patterns which relate things and to discover resonances between things that make correlations and categorizations possible." Indeed for *li* "the structure of human rationality is importantly contingent—an ongoing process specific to social cultural and of course natural conditions." In fact, the images of *li* are precisely not the images of reason. Reason, human reason here is not privileged; it is not the ratio, the ground of Chinese thought. To say this, is not to deny rationality to Chinese thought its own distinctive rationality.

To conclude: Indian thought—if one can use this term to refer to a complex set of beliefs that certainly were never cast in the mould of a monolith—possessed a rationality all its own. There appears to be no good reason to think of the Vedāngas and the śāstras as science or to translate *darśana* as philosophy without first entering important caveats that will serve to preserve what is distinctive in Indian rationality in the sense that I have argued for. Perhaps it is time now to adopt original terminologies and talk of the various *vidyās*. This should motivate an unbiased search for their foundations. Similarities with western science and philosophy will then be a matter of serendipity, not an agenda for Indian scholarship.

If this is beginning to sound like a truism, then the purpose of this essay has been achieved.

NOTES

1. Halbfass,W. *India and Europe*. Delhi: Motilal Banarsidas. p. 93.
2. Quoted in, Halbfass, p. 93.
3. Quoted in, Mohanty, J.N. 1992. *Reason and Tradition in Indian Thought*. Oxford: Clarendon Press. p. 7.
4. Nothing bears more eloquent testimony to this fact than the extreme position taken by the Logical Positivists on the question of meaningfulness in the 1930s.
5. Interview given to Der Spiegel, quoted in Badiou, A. 1992. *Manifesto for Philosophy*. New York: SUNY Press. pp. 44-5.
6. Seal, B. N. 1985. *The Positive Sciences of the Ancient Hindus*. Delhi: Motilal Banarasidass. p. 290.

7. Chattopadhyaya, D. P. 1986 *The History of Science and Technology in Ancient India: The Beginnings.* Calcutta: Firma KLM Pvt. Ltd. pp. 29-33.
8. The same holds true of western science. Witness the tremendous preoccupation in philosophy of science during the first half of the twentieth century with deductive logic as the model of almost all scientific reasoning.
9. Chattopadhyaya, D.P. *Science and Society in Ancient India.*
10. What possibilities existed, for instance, for a Buddhist science given that the Buddha did defy the established order, particularly the authority of the Vedas, can only be a matter of conjecture today. I speak, of course, only in the Indian context.
11. Pollock, S. "New Intellectuals in Seventeenth Century India", *The Indian Economic and Social History Review,* 38(1).
12. Gyan Prakash. *Another Reason: Science and the Imagination of Modern India.* Oxford University Press. p. 86.
13. This approach however has its defenders. Jonardan Ganeri seeks to make a subtle distinction between the perspective of a philosopher and that of a historian. He says: "If the historian's worst crime is anachronism, (imposing modern notions of semantics and philosophy on modes of thought which evolved in other historical circumstances) then the philosopher's worst crime is parochialism, failure to decontextualize ideas." See, Ganeri, Jonardan. 2001. *Philosophy in Classical India.* London: Routledge. p. 16. Which makes life rather difficult for the historian of philosophy.
14. Mohanty. p. 297.
15. Ibid.
16. Matilal, B.K. 1986. *Perception: An Essay on Classical Indian Theories of Knowledge.* Oxford University Press. p. 17.
17. Mullick, M. "Rationality and the Limits of Reason" in Raina et al. *Science and Tradition.* Indian Institute of Advanced Study. p. 94.
18. Ganeri. p. 94.
19. Mohanty. p. 221.
20. Seal. Fritz Staal too has argued that it is ritual and grammar that are at the origins of science in India. See, Staal, Fritz. "Ritual and Grammar and the Origins of Science in India". *Journal of Indian Philosophy.* 10.
21. Macintyre, J. 1988. *Which Justice? Whose Rationality?* London: Duckworth. p. 4.
22. Sylvan, R. 1989. "Modern Myths Concerning Rationality". *Rationality in Question.* Biderman and Scharfstein (ed.). E.J. Brill Leiden. p. 36.

CHAPTER 4

On Identifying a Substantive Give and Take between Philosophy and Science

Rajendra Prasad

There has occurred a good amount of give and take between philosophy and science in the past and it is becoming day by day more extensive and intensive. To understand what it actually consists in, or rather, should consist in, is not a serious problem for him who is a participant in this process. But it is a serious problem to an outsider who wants to characterize or describe it in a manner faithful to the real nature or spirit of what happens in this intellectual commerce. It is a serious problem because he has to first have a criterion for identifying a substantive or genuine give and take in order that he may distinguish it from some other activities which, though related to, are different from, it.

It seems to me that, in order to understand properly the nature of (a) substantive (or genuine) give and take between philosophy and science, it is necessary to distinguish it from (b) characterization (or description), including evaluation, of substantive give and take already available in the history of philosophy or of science, and from (c) preparatory work for facilitating a substantive give and take.

I

SUBSTANTIVE GIVE AND TAKE

Without claiming any finality for it, but only to let the discussion go on, I shall start with what may seem to be a stipulative criterion. But even if it is, it has the backing of our intellectual common sense insofar as it captures our ordinary intuitions about the identity of a substantive give and take: a give and take between philosophy and science would be substantive only if it promotes, or is likely to promote, intellectual progress, i.e. only if it enables both philosophy and science, or at least one of them, to make an advance which, in all likelihood, would not have been possible, or would have been extremely difficult, had the two not participated in this commerce. Such a commerce between the two can effectively operate only when a philosophical interest (or problem) motivates a philosopher to undertake a scientific study, or a scientific interest (or problem) motivates a scientist to undertake a philosophical study. This may happen, for example, when a scientist, confronted with a scientific problem, for which he does not find a solution in the available scientific literature, or is not satisfied with its available solution, turns to philosophy. The same thing can be said, *mutatis mutandis*, of a philosopher's turning to science. Such a venture would doubtlessly require a good amount of creativity in the scientist as well as in the philosopher, who undertakes the intellectual task of solving, or even comprehending better, a problem belonging to his area by using some insights available in the other.

A substantive give and take can be exhibited in so many ways and in a more or less extensive manner. For example, a philosophical insight may be used to *strengthen* a scientific view, and a scientific insight a philosophical one. G.E. Moore pointed out to the logical fact that if time is unreal, as St. Angustin and Mctaggart maintained, then all temporal propositions would become false. For example 'A ate breakfast today at 8:00 a.m.' would be false though it is true that A ate breakfast today at 8:00 a.m. This logic did gave to the scientist a good logical, or commonsensical, support to his emphasis on the reality of time. Hume's knowledgeable understanding of the then scientific mode of drawing inferences in empirical sciences, particularly in the then psychology and physics, was used by him to support his philosophical theory of causation. This theory maintains, in contradictinction from what the then rationalist theory did, that true causal propositions are contingently and not necessarily true. The rationalist theory, on the other hand, had maintained that they were necessarily true. Mathematicians' proving that though we cannot exhaust or completely enumerate the members of an infinite series, we can perform certain arithmetical operations on them inspired philosophers like Bradley to argue for the view that, though thought cannot reach the absolute reality the content of which is infinite, we can perform conceptual operations to make it intelligible and discussible in philosophical, or religious transactions. The way the recent psychology of sex has influenced philosophical theories in ethics of sex is well known. But sometimes even a creative mind maybe misled in using a scientific insight to yield an unmaintainable philosophical theory. This happened with Spinoza when he, impressed by the elegance and stringency of valid geometrical deductions in which premises *entail* their conclusions, applied this model even to empirical inferences of causes from effects or of effects from causes on the ground that the relation between a cause and its effect too was one of entailment. A similar thing happened with Hegel when he unsuccessfully tried tc deduce nature, the totality of things which exist in space and time, the subject-matter of empirical science, from logic, which, in his philosophy, is a system of abstract categories, non-spatial and non-temporal. And, when one Herr Krug asked him to demonstrate how the pen he was writing with followed from his logic, Hegel angrily replied that philosophy was not concerned with such petty things as Herr Krug's pen.

What happened with Hegel in making him angry with Herr Krug's question happened because he did not realize that there could be a concept fit for a good number of logical operations even though it does not denote any reality. Had he taken due note of the mathematician's use of a concept in valid mathematical operations, like the concept of a completely frictionless pulley, which cannot have a denotatum, since it is not possible for a pulley to be completely frictionless, he might not have tried to deduce a thing from its concept, or the world of empirical reality from logic, a system of non-empirical categories. This would have changed the entire structure, or character, of his philosophy. His use of the scientific insight might have helped him avoid undertaking a philosophical or metaphysical venture in which he was bound to fail, and thereby saved him from receiving from Bradley, the greatest modern Hegelian, the mild rebuke that all that he gave to philosophy was a ballet of bloodless categories.

II

CHARACTERIZATION OF SUBSTANTIVE GIVE AND TAKE

Characterizing, narrating, or even giving a good account of, the creative commerce between philosophy and science, or between any two disciplines or sets of disciplines, is not creative in the sense in which (I) is. But it is not, on that account, an easy job. Only he, who has a good grasp, an in-depth understanding, of the historical development of at least one of the participating disciplines, or set of disciplines, and a good working understanding of the basics of the other, or the other set, can do it well. In brief, he has to be a knowledgeable scholar of what is called the history of ideas. The characterizer is, indeed, not one whom we should require or expect to actually participate in a substantive give and take. But what he must do is to present an accurate account, as far accurate as the technical nature of the participation allows, of what the participation has produced and with how much of success. By doing his job well, he would contribute to the evaluations, appreciation or criticism, of the process of commerce by enabling others to know what it has really produced. He works very much like a competent business manager. The latter is not a shopfloor worker who himself produces or manufactures any good, but still renders yeomen's service to the proper evaluation of the goods, produced or marketed by his company, by making available to prospective retailers or consumers verifiable information about the goods. This is difficult as well as a highly responsible work. A characterizer, who is confused, prejudiced, or too enthusiastic, etc., may (wrongly) see that there exists a support for, or an affirmation of, a philosophical thesis in a scientific theory, or a consummation of a scientific theory in a philosophical one, even though it is not really the case. He would then mislead the reader of the concerned literature and bring bad name to those who have worked hard to formulate the theory or theories he has talked about.

A characterizer must have equal respect for both philosophy and science, or to say the same thing in another way, he must be intellectually objective or neutral. If he is too reverential towards, or too strongly prejudiced in favour of, any one of them, he would do havoc to the noble venture of trying to ascertain what each one has given to or taken from, or *can* give to or take from, the other. This is particularly to be remembered when one is concerned with the interface between classical Indian philosophy (or science) and modern science. A characterizer, too reverential towards modern science, may see only some junk scientific-looking ideas in classical philosophical-scientific literature. On the other hand, one who is too reverential or patriotic towards classical Indian philosophy-science, may see in the classical literature even some ultra-modern scientific theories, or their seeds, claiming, because of his, what I have been calling, *ṛṣibias*, that all that is worth knowing was unfaultably known by the classical *ṛṣis*.

III

PREPARATORY WORK FOR FACILITATING GIVE AND TAKE

This would consist in making available at one place, in a single volume, or in a series of volumes, materials on a certain theme or set of themes, say, consciousness, from different disciplines, say, philosophy, psychology, physiology, neurology, linguistics including psycholinguistics and sociolinguistics, etc. Such a work too is very important and lack of it generally leads to a truncated approach to a theme the proper understanding of which requires looking at it from more than one point of view. Some of the wrong theories of consciousness itself are results of such one-eyed approaches. Undertaking such a work involves selecting materials from different sources, and selection involves not only sound knowledge of the things out of which some are to be selected, but also sound judgement of the appropriateness of the things, so that only the most pertinent and innovative ones get selected. There is a great lack of such works, particularly concerning some themes dealt within classical Indian literature. This is most glaring in the case of normative, or, axiological, ideas, though the concern with norms, or values, is basic to almost every sector of classical Indian thought.

Preparing a work of this type, in some areas, may require analysis or separation of materials of one type from those of another. In any classical corpus thinking on more than one theme, or of more than one category, may be present in one work. For example, scientific and metaphysical, logical, epistemological and metaphysical, ethical, religious and psychological, etc. materials, can be found put together in many classical Indian works. If analytical-descriptive anthologies are presented on important themes, or a cohesive cluster of themes, then study of these works can immensely help any one see how some classical philosophical inquires are related to some of the then or even, modern, inquiries in some field or fields of science. As an example of a work of such a composite character can be mentioned the *Mahābharata*, Bhārata's *Nāṭya Śāstra*, Vātsyāyana's *Kāmaśastra*, even some Upaniṣads, etc. and definitely the Vedas.

IV

SOME ILLUSTRATIONS OF (I)

Let me illustrate what I have said above about (I) with brief references to some of the works of some western philosophers turning to a science with the motivation to satisfy a philosophical need and of some scientists turning to some philosophical area to satisfy a scientific need. I shall limit myself only to illustrating (I).

(i) Gottlob Frege (1848-1925)[1], basically a mathematician, turns to logic, a philosophical discipline, in his endeavour to axiomatize arithmetic, when he does not find any satisfactory way to do that with the resources which contemporary mathematical researches made available to him. His researches in the systematization of arithmetic and formal logic not only opened up new directions in the two areas but also in many others like philosophy of mathematics and of language. This happened in spite of the fact that he acknowledged Russell's pointing out to him a paradox in his system.

The distinctness of Frege's approach, because of its initiating a given and taken relation between arithmetic and logic, becomes clearer when we compare it with F.H. Bradley's (1846-1924) attempt to recast the then logic. He wants to build a metaphysical theory for which he considers the available logical theory inadequate. He does not feel the need to turn to any science to collect evidence for his projected metaphysics. Instead, he turns to recaste the existing logic and presents one he considers more powerful and relevant for providing the needed logical support to the metaphysics he propounds and considers sounder than the existing specimens. His motivation to construct a metaphysics is, unlike Frege's, philosophical, and to satisfy it he remains inside the boundary of philosophy since he turns to recast logic which is well within that boundary. He does not consider it necessary to turn to any science. In contrast to his procedure Henry Bergson turns to biology, and uses the concept of life as understood and used in the then biology to formulate his philosophical theory of evolution, which is his metaphysical theory, and is known as the theory of creative evolution.

Bertrand Russell (1872-1970), too proceeds on lines similar to Frege's, but his problem, to begin with, is philosophical and not scientific. He is impressed with what he calls the majesty of a mathematical proposition in the sense that if it is true, it is true for ever, and if false, false for ever, and its truth-values are conclusively provable, never needing to be empirically checked. The existing theories of truth, or existing epistemologies and logics, do not seem to offer him an explanation of this fact. He therefore undertakes an in-depth investigation into the foundations of mathematics, and in collaboration with A.N. Whitehead, a mathematician-physicist, arrives at the theory that a true mathematical proposition is a tautology and a false one is a contradiction, and therefore, the former is never false, and the latter never true. This result he achieves by first reducing the whole of arithmetic to logic. It is very similar to that of Frege's and therefore it is generally known as the Frege-Russell reduction of mathematics to logic. It is an achievement which is as much philosophical as mathematical or scientific, an excellent product of the commerce between philosophy and science.

John Dewey (1859-1952), a pragmatic philosopher, is primarily interested in philosophical problems arising out of man's social engagements or concerns, i.e. out of social practice in a broad sense in which it includes ethical and political practice. He, therefore, very often enters into this or that social science as it suits his interest. This he does even in his work on logic which he calls the theory of inquiry and by 'inquiry' he primarily means social-scientific inquiry. Instead of constructing a formal logistic system of logic, as Russell does, he explains how logical techniques, norms, and rules evolve and mature in the course of an inquiry. In a more analytical way, Abraham Kaplan shows what logic has given to as well as received from social sciences, and Arthur Burks uses in a highly rigorous way, logic, computer science, and semantics in his works on philosophy of science.

Dewey's use of social science is more distinctly visible in his works on value-theory. The lead which he gives in the area of value-theory has led to a large number of works in which philosophy and some social science have collaborated. In a similar, but a little more technical way, because of his copious use of logic, C.I. Lewis has presented a comprehensive value-theory, quite sensitive to man's social concerns, in a volume the first part of which is logic-epistemology and the second an inquiry into various problems connected with the characterization and realization of values. Equally, or rather more, comprehensively, R.B. Perry, earlier than Lewis, first presents his studies in a value-theory as a general theory of value and uses extensively in his second book results arrived at in the first work, in conjunction with ideas from more than one social science, in presenting his account of various types of values. The definition of value which he gives in his first work and which guides his other works—value as any object of any interest-shows the close link between a philosophy of value and social sciences. By the way, Perry's definition of value, as any object of any interest, is not very far removed from the classical Indian conception of value, a *puruṣārtha,* since '*puruṣārtha*' too means an object of a human desire (*arthanā*) to have or to not-have something. It is important to remember that the Indian theory of *puruṣārthas* has been developed in the way it has been largely because of the classical Indian socio-cultural contexts being what it then was. Another good example of the cooperation between philosophy and social science is found in the work of Abraham Edel and May Edel, the former a philosopher and the latter an anthropologist, the two joining together to show how anthropological researches can be brought to bear on ethical theory. The philosopher Richard Brandt has gone a little further in this experiment. In order to present a systematization of the ethical codes and norms of Hopis, he lived with them for a year, learnt their language, practiced their rituals, participated in their social-religious-ethical performances, and then wrote a book on their ethics. So has John Ladd done for a tribe of Red Indians.

Social scientists too have come forward to use philosophical advances in formulating their theories. It is well known that Naom Chomsky uses Descartes' conception of the non-mechanical, creative, nature of human mind and its possession of some innate ideas in his hypothesis of the innateness of at least some rules of language and in his theory of human creativity in understanding and constructing so far unknown, entirely new, meaningful sentences or strings of worlds. In addition, a large part of his work can be treated as a reaction against Wittgenstein's and Ryle's making the meaning of an expression consist in its use and an user's mastery of a rule of language in his competence in applying it correctly and in detecting its wrong applications or violations, rather than in a self-conscious comprehension of its nature. Many other linguists, socio-linguists, and psyco-linguists have also made copious use of philosophical theories of language. The psychologist B.F. Skinner's use of Charles Peirce's and Dewey's pragmatism in his theory of verbal behaviour is as obvious as the philosopher W.V.O. Quine's use of ideas from all of the three, Peirce, Dewey and Skinner, in his philosophy of language. Morris Ginsberg, a sociologist of repute, in his writings on socio-ethical topics has made use of some philosophical discussions of those topics to such an extent and in such an incisive manner that in the case of some of his writings it becomes difficult to assign to them the designation 'sociological' or 'philosophical' in an exclusivist sense. This is the case also with some of the works of Edward Westermarck, primarily an anthropologist-sociologist.

Perhaps the most prominent example of a highly productive and creative give and take between philosophy and science is the work of Ludwig Wittgenstein. While studying as a student of aeronautical engineering at Manchester Institute of Technology, when asked to design a propeller which involved the use of a good amount of mathematics, he turned to mathematics and therefrom to philosophy of mathematics, and to logic and metaphysics and philosophy of language, etc. Nothing of any worth in philosophy remained uninfluenced by him, and his writings have made an impact on several natural and social sciences as well.

It should be obvious by now that we cannot say that a give and take between philosophy and science has taken place simply by pointing to an instance in which a philosopher has produced a piece in a science, for example, has written a book on some scientific topic, or to one in which a scientist has produced a philosophical work. We cannot say so, for example, if the philosopher's scientific work has nothing to do with his philosophy, or the scientist's philosophical one with his science. It is important to mention here a possibility in the context of Indian philosophical-scientific scene against which a characterizer of the philosophy-science give and take must be on his guard. This possibility arises from the close link between some classical Indian philosophies and some bodies of religious doctrines.

Suppose a scientist, as a religions person, gets convinced of the overall soundness of the religious doctrines which ensue from a particular school of classical Indian philosophy. His conviction may be the result of his own study of the religious doctrines and the philosophical school which has yielded them, or of his having been born in a family every member of which is, or is required to be, a follower of those religious doctrines. Inspired exclusively by his fervour for the religious doctrines, he writes a book on the metaphysics which is claimed to give them the needed theoretical support. This metaphysics would naturally be the metaphysics of the school of philosophy from which the religious doctrines emerge. Therefore, his book can very well be said to be a book on the metaphysics of that school of philosophy. In this venture of the scientist his science has remained aloof. It has played no role in his writing the book, or in his entry into that school of philosophy, or in philosophy, for that matter. Therefore, what he has done would not constitute an instance of an interaction between science and philosophy. Nor would do the mere fact that a scientist, with no religious concern, has done some good work in an area of philosophy as well as in some area of science, pure or applied, with no link between the two. A work in philosophy by a scientist would be a genuine instance of a give and take between science and philosophy only if, as has been already said, his science has prompted him to do this work; that is, only if it has in some way participated in the execution of his philosophical project. The same thing is true, *mutati mutonelis,* of a philosopher's having done some work in an area of science.

It is possible that one and the same individual does several things without there being any intimate link between them. A mathematician may be a musician. But that would not imply that his mathematics is musical or his music mathematical. Bertrand Russell's mathematics and philosophy participated in his work on the foundations of mathematics, but neither of them had anything to do with his *Satan in the Suburbs,* a work in fiction. The mathematician-logician Charles Lutwidge Dodgson's mathematics and logic played some role in his famous works in fiction, *Alice in Wonderland, Alice Through the Looking Glass,* and

The Hunting of the Snark, which he wrote under the pusuedonym 'Lewis Carroll' by which he is known more than by his former name given to him by his parents. His logic-mathematics is visible in these works in the talks of the characters among themselves using some logical ideas and paradoxes, referred to in a manner generally oblique and satirical.

Good, creative, give and take can take place between philosophy and science, whichever definition of philosophy or of science, among the prevalent definitions, or even a new one, is taken into account, if and only if none of the two, philosophy and science, is taken to denote an inquiry intrinsically inferior or superior to the other. This claim is testified by the history of both philosophy and science.

A distinction between two types of inquiries has been made in some works of classical Indian philosophy, and the two types have been called *parāvidyā* and *aparāvidyā*. The Sanskrit word *'parā'* means *'parama'*, *'sarvoccha'*, the highest, the supreme, and *'vidyā'* means wisdom, knowledge, or inquiry. *'Parā'* is the feminine from of *'para'*, and since *'vidyā'* is also feminine, *'parā'* is used to qualify *vidyā* and, therefore, we have the term *'parāvidyā'*. So is the case with *'aparā'* and *'aparāvidyā'*, *'aparā'* or *'apara'* meaning the opposite or contrary of *'parā'* and *'para'* respectively. Therefore, *'parāvidyā'* means the highest, the supreme kind of inquiry, and *'aparāvidyā'*, the inquiry which is not the highest, or the supreme. Therefore, to call an inquiry *parāvidyā* and another *aparāvidyā* is to consider the latter lower in status than the former.

This distinction has been given an interpretation by many writers which gives to philosophy the status of *'parāvidyā'*, and to science that of *'aparāvidyā'*. The way it has been made and emphasized seems to mean or imply that philosophy as such is superior to science. Therefore, it does not seem to be congenial to promoting or facilitating a respectable collaboration between the two. It may even be obstructive or dissuasive. Moreover, this interpretation of the distinction does not seem to me to be fair to the intention of the classical presentation of the distinction. This interpretation appears to have been made a current coin in our classificatory currency in the early part of the twentieth century by some Indian writers on classical Indian philosophy, and it is even today in good circulation in many circles.

Most of those who initiated this interpretation, meant by science—western science and by philosophy—classical Indian philosophy, or philosophy as understood by classical Indian thinkers, and thereby thought that by emphasizing this interpretation they were emphasizing, or claiming, the superiority of classical Indian philosophy, or of philosophy in the classical Indian sense, over western science—the superiority of something Indian over something western. But they forgot that they were *eo-ipso* also maintaining the superiority of Indian philosophy over Indian science and thereby undervaluing Indian science and weakening the motivation for any collaborative enterprise among Indian philosophers and scientists. They also forgot that philosophy and science were not in classical India rigidly, or absolutely, separate, unconnected, inquiries or *vidyās*. Many of the philosophical schools contained ideas or theories which were more scientific than philosophical, for example, the Cārvāka, Vaiśeṣika, Sāṁkhya etc.

B.N. Seal's *The Positive Sciences of the Ancient Hindus* copiously uses classical Indian philosophies as the source materials for presenting classical Indian achievements in the field of sciences, particularly, natural sciences, because by positive sciences he largely means natural sciences. Even the *Vedas*, which are acknowledged by many as the earliest records of the achievements of the classical Indian's propensity to inquire into the nature of what is, what maybe, and what ought to be, are a rich field containing seeds or sprouts of both philosophy and science. The word *'Veda'* itself means neither philosophy, nor science, if each one of them is taken to denote a specific discipline, or a specific set of disciplines, as is done in current academic usage of the two terms.

Derived from the Sanskrit root '*Vid*', *'Veda'* means *Vidyā*, *Jñāna*, wisdom, knowledge, or inquiry, and therefore can be called the mother of both philosophy and science. This would be more appropriate than following the fashion of calling philosophy the mother of sciences. Doing the latter may suggest to an intellectually unsophisticated or naïve reader that philosophy as understood today, i.e. as a specific discipline or a specific set of disciplines, is the mother of all sciences. That certainly is not the case. In fact, originally even in the western characterization of philosophy as the mother of sciences, the term 'philosophy' was not used to mean a specific discipline, or a specific set of disciplines, but to mean what it etymologically means, i.e., love of wisdom, or simply wisdom, knowledge, or inquiry, as the classical Indian use of *'Veda'* means.

When talking about a work in which both philosophical and scientific ideas occur, care should be taken that from the mere fact of their occurrence one does not jump to the conclusion that philosophy and science have collaborated therein with each other. Collaboration would still need to be proven by providing some logical linkage between at least some philosophical idea and some scientific idea occurring in the work. There is another care which also needs to be taken particularly in talking about a classical work. Suppose a modern scientist makes a discovery. A scholar of classics locates in a classical work a passage, or a set of passages, which now, after having known the modern discovery, he interprets as containing the discovery. Therefore, he claims that the discovery had already been made by the writer of the classical work ages before the modern discovery, even though he admits that nobody read the discovery into those passages before the modern discovery was made known. Passages in classical works are interpretable in more than one way. Therefore, if an interpreter is not very cautious, or is too reverential about them, there is a danger of his being chauvinistic in locating modern ideas into them even when they are not there.

When the classical Indian corpus does not rigidly separate one from the other, as is the case with any classical corpus, it is highly implausible that classical Indian philosophers or thinkers have given a sweeping judgement to the effect that science is inferior to philosophy. Moreover, if the received interpretation of the distinction is stuck to, we cannot plead for a substantive, meaningful, give and take between philosophy and science. A substantive give and take, a fruitful collaboration on equal terms, which a genuine give and take ought to be, cannot take place, as already said, between two unequals. Only two equals can interact with each other on equal terms, that is, without infringing self-dignity and self-respect. And, the possibility of equal-level interaction between philosophy and science, or between any two disciplines, for that matter, is a necessary condition for a creative utilization of an advance in the one by the other.

It seems to me that the *parā-aparāvidyā* distinction, as made in classical Indian philosophy, does not mean or imply that any sort of philosophy is superior to any sort of science. Rather, it is intended to highlight that an inquiry, which enables man to *correctly know* what he should aim at as his ultimate, final, all-consummating, value, the supreme goal of his life, and to *successfully attain* that goal, occupies the highest place among the various kinds of inquiries he conducts or is capable of conducting. *Vidyā* in '*parāvidyā*' is a term having a very broad or wide sense, and the safest word as its English equivalent seems to be 'inquiry', and not 'science' or 'philosophy', because both of these two terms have acquired in current usage a specific denotation and connotation. That is why most of scholars would say philosophy and science denote and connote different kinds of inquiries or enterprises. This does not imply, however, that they cannot interact or collaborate with each other. The *parā-aparā vidyā* distinction, therefore, is made primarily to emphasize the distinction between an axiological inquiry into the nature of the highest value a man can and should aspire after and of the means to attain it *and* any other inquiry which is not concerned with the highest value but with something else, whatever may its methodology, scope, and subject-matter be. It does not have to be totally value-neutral, or unconcerned with any sort of value whatsoever. It would be *aparā vidyā* only because it is not primarily concerned with the highest value. All this does not mean that it has no utility, nor that it is obstructive, or of no relevance at all, to the pursuit of the highest value.

The *parāvidyā-aparāvidyā* distinction figures prominently in the *Mundaka Upaniṣad* when Śaunaka requests Aṅgirā to tell him what is that after definitely knowing which all that there is, is known.[2] In response to his request Angira says that knowers of *Brahman,* the Ultimate Reality, have been definitely saying that there are only two kinds of inquiries worth conducting *parā* and *aparā,* one which is of the highest kind and another which is not of the highest kind. Of the two the lower, *aparāvidyā,* comprises the four Vedas, the method of pronunciation, grammar, performance of rituals, etymology, study of metre, and astrology. The higher, on the other hand, consists of knowing *akṣara,* the unchanging reality.[3]

Parāvidyā, thus, is the kind of inquiry by which the ultimate reality is known or realized (*adhigamyate*). To know it is to realize it. Realizing it, or realizing anything, is not a bare, neutral, intellectual cognition, but an attainment, a kind of becoming, the nature of which being determined by the nature of man and that of the thing attained. The *akṣara,* the unchangeable, unsublatable, reality, according to the *Mundaka,* or even other Upaniṣads, is the *Brahman,* the supreme self. Since *parāvidyā* is knowledge of *Brahman,* it is also called *Brahmavidyā,* knowledge of ultimate reality. *Brahmavidyā* is the basis, ground or justifying reason, of all knowledge (*sarvavidyā-pratiṣṭhā*) obviously because it is the knowledge of the ultimate, highest, reality.[4] The implication is that since *Brahman* is the ultimate reality, one who knows it knows everything that is real. Anything would be real only if it is grounded on it, and to know the ground is to know all that is or maybe grounded on it.

This *Brahman,* which is the subject-matter of *parāvidyā,* is also the highest goal, objective, or value (*mahatpadam*)[5] for every individual. He who knows *Brahman* becomes *Brahman,* nobody is born in his family who does not know *Brahman,* and he himself gets rid of all sufferings and sins. Freeing himself from all kinds of blemishes of his heart, he becomes immortal.[6]

The import of this characterization of *parāvidyā* and its objective is that any other kind of inquiry is *aparā,* or lower in status, than it because it does not lead to the attainment of the goal which *parāvidyā* leads to. Therefore, it is not surprising if such things as inquiry into the right method of pronouncing vedic sentences (*śikṣa*), performance of rituals (*kalpa*), grammar (*vyākaraṇa*), etymology (*nirukta*), and astrology (*jyotiṣa*) are considered to be *aparā*. Even the Vedas, all the four, *Ṛg, Yajur, Sāma,* and *Atharva,* are called *aparā.* This may appear surprising. But it need not because by the Vedas, Aṇgirā seems to mean only those of their parts which consist of injunctions about the performances of sacrifices (*yajña*) and other rituals. *Parāvidyā* is thus that kind of inquiry which enables man not only to know what is the highest value he should aim at but also to attain it. Therefore, any other kind of inquiry, howsoever useful it maybe in some other respects, would be *aparā,* lower in rank, though not of no importance at all.

The heart of the matter lies in the assumption that there is a reality which is the ultimate reality as well as the ultimate value and it is such that it can be reached and attained only by a special kind of inquiry different from any purely empirical and rational inquiry which a natural, biological, social, or formal, science is. And, this special kind of inquiry is also different from a conceptual inquiry like epistemology, logic, even some types of ontology, moral philosophy, pure or applied, philosophy of language, philosophy of science, etc., etc. All of these inquiries would be *aparāvidyā.* Therefore, not only sciences but also the majority of the disciplines which constitute philosophy, would be *aparā.* Another assumption is that the highest reality, *Brahman,* is identical with the self in every individual. On account of this identity an individual's knowing *Brahman* is knowing what he himself really is but has been so far ignorant of this truth. Therefore, knowing *Brahman* is a realization of what oneself really is, and only in that sense a kind of becoming, re-awakening, or recognition. All this is said to be effected not by means of sense-experience or intellection, not by the use of the scientific method consisting of observation, experimentation and hypothetico-deductive reasoning, but by the inculcation of a moral-religions discipline resulting in a non-sensuous, non-rational, direct, experience, of the identity of the self with *Brahman,* an experience which maybe called mystical or intuitional.

In establishing the plausibility or validity of this claim about *parāvidyā,* Upaniṣadic and Vedāntic thinkers use a good amount of logic in addition to their appeal to the views and experiential reports of their respected predecessors. In examining their logic and recorded experiential reports both philosophy and science can cooperate with each other. Philosophers can assess their logic and scientists their experiential claims. For example, as a limited empirical analogue of the mystical experience of the unified, undifferentiated, experience of the identity of *Brahman* and the self deep, or, dreamless, sleep (*susupti*) is referred to. It is said that in dreamless sleep one gets a temporary glimpse of what the mystical experience is. A philosopher can examine the validity of the reasoning given to show that a dreamless sleep is an evidence or illustration of the nature of the reality revealed in the mystical experience of the nature of *Brahman,* or the Self, or the identity of the two. The scientist can cooperate with him by showing whether or not sleep is possible without dreams. This is not a petty empirical matter. Suppose neuro-scientists show that no sleep is dreamless. Then the only empirical example, which the Upaniṣadic, Vedāntic, thinker has to tell an ordinary individual what the mystical experience is like, will become unavailable to him. I am referring to this possibility because a neuro-surgeon of great repute, Professor Rama Murty, once said in a lecture that no sleep was dreamless, and very recently a very bright young neuro-surgeon, Dr. A.K. Agrawal, after consulting a lot of literature on the neurology of sleep and dreams confirms that there is so far no evidence of sleep being any time dreamless. On the other hand, even if sleep is dreamless sometimes, if the philosopher shows that no valid inference can be drawn from an instance of it about the nature of any kind of reality mystical experience is claimed to reveal, this too would very adversely affect the validity of the Upaniṣadic claim about the nature of the highest reality and of the viability of calling an inquiry dealing with it *parāvidyā*[7].

I shall conclude the essay with an apology. My apology is for having given only western examples of substantive give and take between philosophy and science. This I have done because of a personal limitation. I have not come across a distinctively Indian example of a philosopher turning to science to seek the solution of a philosophical problem he is grappling with and not finding it in the relevant philosophical literature available to him. I have not talked of any Indian scientist's having used philosophy in the service of his scientific theory, i.e., turning to philosophy to assist him in solving a scientific problem, because I do not possess the competence to talk about any science in a responsible manner. I have noticed scientists turning to philosophy with a religious motivation and philosophers using lay science, or scientific ideas from secondary, popular, literature, with no first hand acquaintance with scientific practice, to support some philosophical theories like the freedom of the will, rebirth, immortality, etc. But making such uses of philosophy or science is very different from what constitutes a creative or substantive give and take between the two disciplines.

NOTES

1. For relevant works, please see the bibliography.
2. *Kasminnu vijñate sarvāmidam vijñatam bhavati: Mundakopaniṣad,* Mundaka I, Part I: 3, p. 263 in *Kalyāna: Upaniṣad Aṅka.* 1949. Gorakhpur Gita Press: The English translation is the author's wherever given.
3. *Para yāyā tadakṣaramādhigamyate.* Ibid: 5
4. Ibid: 1
5. Ibid. Mundaka II, part II p. 276 : 1
6. Ibid. Mundaka III, part II, p. 287.9
7. For a detailed critical discussion of the concept of dreamless sleep see, Prasad, Rajendra. 1999. *Varnadharma, Niṣkāma Karma and Practical Morality: A Critical Essay on Applied Ethics,* Chapter 4 (New Delhi: D.K. Printworld Ltd.)

BIBLIOGRAPHY

1. Bradley, F.H. 1883. *Principles of Logic.* Oxford.
2. ———. 1893. *Appearance and Reality.* Oxford.
3. Brand, R. 1954. *Hopi Ethics.* Chicago: Chicago Univesrity.
4. Burks, A. W. 1969.*Chance, Cause and Reason.* Chicago: Chicago University.
5. Chomsky, N. 1966. *Cartesian Linguistics.* Harper & Row.
6. Dewey, J. 1938. *Logic: The Theory of Inquiry.* Henry Holt.
7. ———. 1939 *Theory of Valuation.* Chicago: Chicago Univ., Transaction Publishers. USA.
8. Edel, May & Abraham. 1959. *Anthropology and Ethics.* USA: Transaction Publishers.
9. Frege, G. 1966. *Translations from the Philosophical Writings of Gottlob Frege.* Peter Geach and Max Black. (ed.). Oxford.

10. ———. (ed. & trans.). 1964. *The Basic Laws of Arithmetic.* Oxford.
11. Ginsberg, M. 1956. *On the Diversity of Morals.* London: Mercury Books.
12. Kaplan, A. 1964. *The Conduct of Inquiry.* USA: Chandler.
13. Ladd, J. 1957. *The Structure of a Moral Code.* Cambridge, Mass: Harvard University.
14. Lewis, C.I. 1946. *An Analysis of Knowledge and Valuation.* Open Court.
15. *Mundakopanisad in Kalyana: Upanisad Anka.* 1949. pp. 262-288. Gorakhpur: Gita Press.
16 Peirce C. 1955. *Philosophical Writings of Peirce,* Selected and edited by Justus Buckler. Dover.
17. Perry, R. B. 1926. *General Theory of Value.* Cambridge, Mass: Harvard University.
18. ———. 1954. *Realms of Value.* Cambridge, Mass: Harvard University.
19. Quine, W.V.O. 1960. *Word and Object.* Cambridge, Mass: Harvard University.
20. Russell, B. (With A.N. Whitehead). 1910. *Principia Mathematica.* Cambridge University.
21. ———. 1919. *Introduction to Mathematical Philosophy.* Allen & Unwin.
22. Ryle, G. 1949. *The Concept of Mind.* Hutchinson's Univ. Library.
23. Skinner, B. F. 1957. *Verbal Behaviour.* Appliton-Century-Crofts.
24. Westermarck, E. 1906. *The Origin and Development of the Moral Ideas.* Macmillan.
25. ———. 1932. *Ethical Relativity.* Harcourt.
26. Wittgenstein, L. 1953. *Philosophical Investigations.* Blackwell.

CHAPTER 5

Parāvidyā-Aparāvidyā—A Reconstruction: Towards an Objective Phenomenology of Consciousness

Amita Chatterjee

Indian theoretical tradition, uphold many renowned scholars, is characterised by a holistic attitude, which is tolerant of pluralism. It is marked by a remarkable absence of sharp boundaries, including the one that is usually thought to demarcate science from philosophy. Historians and philosophers of science have confirmed that there is as much science in the Indian philosophical systems as there is philosophy in sciences. My main purpose in re-examining the age-old distinction between *Parāvidyā* and *Aparāvidyā* is to see whether it reflects the distinction between philosophical consciousness and scientific knowledge.

The most elaborate account of this distinction is available in the *Muṇḍaka Upaniṣad* commented upon by Śaṁkarācārya from the Advaita point of view. In I.1.4, it has been stated, "There are two kinds of knowledge (*vidyā*) to be attained, the higher (*parā*) and the lower (*aparā*)." These two types of knowledge differ from each other in their objects, their consequences as well as in methods of acquisition. The higher knowledge is knowledge of the *Brahman* which leads to liberation (*niḥśreyasa*) and the lower knowledge is knowledge of empirical objects, means and ends, virtues and vices, which can at best lead to prosperity (*abhyudaya)* and heaven (*svarga*)[1]. It is surprising to note that Śaṁkarācārya includes all the four Vedas, viz., *Ṛg, Sāma, Yajuḥ, Atharvan,* and six ancillary disciplines, viz., *Śikṣa* (phonetics), *Kalpa* (ritual), *Vyākaraṇa* (grammar), *Nirukta* (etymology), *Chanda* (metre) and *Jyotiṣa* (Astronomy) within the lower knowledge (*aparāvidyā)*, while maintaining at the same time that the Upaniṣads, the last part of the Vedas, impart knowledge of the *Brahman.* Anandagiri in his *Tīkā* explains that Śaṁkarācārya's comment is not to be understood literally but by its implied meaning. While explaining the Vedas as lower, Śaṁkara must have meant those empirical (*viṣaya-vidyā*) and ritualistic parts (*karma-kāṇḍa*) of the Vedas, which are responsible for bondage. Rāmānuja and his followers point out that the ritualistic parts of the Vedas are called *aparā* because these have only instrumental value. Vedic rituals, if performed in a detached manner, clean all impurities of the mind and prepare the ground for attaining liberation. The Mādhvas also maintain that the entire Vedas are not to be placed in the lower category of knowledge, but only those parts that are not directly related to knowledge of the *Brahman.*

With respect to methods of acquisition too, there is opposition between two types of knowledge. The higher knowledge is said to be direct and intuitive, i.e., characterised by immediacy, while the lower knowledge has different accredited means like perception, inference, etc. Hence, it is not possible to attain higher knowledge by progressively mastering knowledge of empirical objects; the higher knowledge is not an amalgamation of all pieces of lower knowledge. It is not the case that the higher knowledge is true and the lower knowledge is erroneous or false; truth or falsehood in the logico-epistemic sense can be predicated of the lower knowledge alone. So, the distinction between the higher and the lower knowledge can be better captured by pointing out that the former is complete and the latter is incomplete. However, if the lower knowledge were merely incomplete, the divide between the lower and the higher would not have been so great. What is of the most significance is that the lower knowledge is not even completeable because it will always fall short of the Reality. Why this is so, we shall explain very soon.

From the point of view of an enlightened person, knowledge of the phenomenal world is not merely lower (*aparā*), but also tinged with *avidyā* or root ignorance. The *Muṇḍaka Upaniṣad* says that *aparāvidyā* is *avidyā*, concerned with perishable things, while *parāvidyā* is concerned with the imperishable (*akṣara*) and the impartite. Once *parāvidyā* is attained, every other mode of 'knowing' loses its status of knowledge. However, for common men like us, the lower knowledge is knowledge enough, which guides us through our everyday life, helps us to aspire for and attain our mundane ends like prosperity in this world and in the other world. It is evident from the Upaniṣadic characterisation of two types of knowledge that there is incompatibility between the higher and the lower. In many Upaniṣads, it has been succinctly stated that the higher knowledge is not attainable through thought and ratiocination, nor even through dedicated self-study of the scriptural texts. The more we try to decipher the object of the higher knowledge through phenomenal experience, ratiocination and textual study, the more we are distanced from the *Brahman* or the Self. The 41/12 *śloka* of the *Kathā Upaniṣad* says that conceptual and linguistic approach cover the real nature of the Self, instead of uncovering it.[2] The Self is One and Full; it is of the nature of Consciousness. Ontologically it is the Principle of Non-duality. It is devoid of any distinction — homogeneous, heterogeneous or internal. Both human conceptualisation and language are grounded in a phenomenal experience of multiplicity. The minimal requirement of any predication, conceptual or linguistic, is the admission of duality. A real predication, according to all systems of Indian philosophy, must convey some information. That is why, Indian philosophers do not think that non-informative tautological assertions of the form 'A is A' is either well formed or meaningful. Any information is about something. So even at the level of elementary information, there is a dichotomy between information and object. When this information is coded linguistically, there arises the duality between language and reality, and when represented conceptually there is bound to be some distinction between thought and reality. The truth or falsity of a representation depends on its satisfying or non-satisfying the objects-in-relation, of which it is a representation. Even in a formal language, the moment we go beyond the syntactic level, we need to introduce an Interpretation Function, which makes a representation true or false in a selected model—a surrogate reality. Hence, that which is essentially non-dual must lie beyond language, beyond concept.

Many are of the opinion that there is no real opposition between *parāvidyā* and *aparāvidyā*. These two terms are expressive of only two types of experience. These two experiences are compatible, because the higher being a totality includes all. Empirical knowledge of different objects, on the other hand, should be taken as attempts at conceptualising the highest consciousness. I concede that there is some truth in this view. For, *parāvidyā* and *aparāvidyā* appear incoherent if we take a bottom-up approach. From a top-down approach, however, these two are, in a way, compatible.

Now, we should address the question whether this higher knowledge or non-dual consciousness is philosophical and whether it is possible to have a science of this non-dual consciousness. The question is rhetorical and we know by now that there cannot be any science of this non-dual consciousness. In the Upaniṣadic tradition, *parāvidyā* or *jñāna* has been distinguished from *vijñāna*. *Jñāna*, in the seventh chapter of the *Gītā*, has been described as wisdom or direct intuitive illumination of the Ultimate Reality whereas *vijñāna* has been said to contain ratiocinative principles that govern the knowledge of the phenomenal world. In the thirteenth chapter, *Kṣetra-kṣetrajña-vibhāga-yoga*, the *Gītā* discusses the nature of the embodied self, which is again under the monistic interpretation identical with the Self as the Ultimate Reality. Different commentaries of the *Gītā* mention that there can be various different sciences of the physical body or *kṣetra*, but all of these are lower than the knowledge of the Self (*kṣetrajña*) that lies beyond the grasp of reason. Philosophy, in the western tradition, is also a rational enterprise. Therefore, that which lies beyond the grasp of reason, thought and language cannot be the object of philosophical enquiry. If grasping this ineffable non-dual consciousness is a philosophical enterprise, then the westerners will readily identify this brand of philosophy with spiritualism and mysticism.

I must make it clear at this point that I have nothing against spiritualism or mysticism. Nor am I being driven by the ghost of the colonial reading of Indian philosophy, when I place *aparāvidyā* beyond the realm of philosophy. I do seriously believe that philosophy is a cognitive enterprise per excellence, but *aparāvidyā* is not cognitive in this sense. In cognition, the object/content of consciousness is posited to be independent of consciousness and we focus on the objective[3]; conative and affective sides of consciousness may not be totally ignored but these play second fiddle to the objective. *Aparāvidyā*, says Śaṁkara in his commentary on *Kathopaniṣad* [4], is another name of *adhyātma-yoga*, where consciousness must be withdrawn from the object and directed towards the Self. But the Self, which can be attained through *aparāvidyā*, it will be clear, from the subsequent discussion is not the referent of 'I'. The Upaniṣads prescribe three steps, *śravaṇa* (hearing the scriptural Identity Statements from an enlightened teacher), *manana* (internalising the Identity statements through discursive thinking) and *nididhyāsana* (contemplating on the truth of the internalised statements) to this pure non-dual consciousness. Even in the last step, there is duality between the contemplative and the contemplated consciousness, to start with. With practice the contemplative consciousness merge with the all-encompassing flow of consciousness without any residue. This liberated consciousness, being one, cannot be cognitive. Śaṁkara, we know, called this path '*jñānamārga*'. Here *jñāna* cannot be translated as 'knowledge' that presupposes the distinction between the knower, the known and the act of knowing.

At this stage, I don't want to enter the controversy whether *darśana*, which aims at attaining the non-dual consciousness falls within the ambit of philosophy or religion.[5] I am more interested to understand the nature of pure consciousness in the light of the on-going debate regarding the nature of consciousness, being pursued by the mainstream philosophers all over the world. With this aim in view, I shall focus on the nature of pure consciousness, which is to be attained through the higher knowledge, as explained by Śaṁkarācārya in his different commentaries. David Chalmers, in the introduction of his famous book, *The Conscious Mind*[6], has rightly said that the first constraint that anybody pursuing consciousness study should impose on oneself is to take consciousness seriously. I think that no one in the world took consciousness more seriously than Śaṁkara. In all his commentaries, Śaṁkara has grappled with the problem of expressing the ineffable *Brahman*-experience. Most of the predicates that he has used to describe *Brahman* are not real qualities of *Brahman*, but are terms of *prima facie* apprehension of *Brahman* by man.

Before I take up the task just mentioned, I would like to introduce a few terms widely used in the contemporary studies of consciousness. Consciousness is said to have different aspects, viz., intentional, phenomenal and psychological. Those who do not think that consciousness is a unitary phenomenon, talk about different types of consciousness—intentional, phenomenal, psychological etc. Intentional aspect of consciousness was emphasised by Brentano in the modern period and was later developed by Husserl. In the analytical tradition, generally propositional attitudes have been identified with intentional conscious states. But we shall be using the term in a wider sense to mean any conscious state, which is directed to some object, not necessarily to propositions. But what is considered central to consciousness at present is the subjective feel of conscious experience. The subjective quality of experience varies over a wide range—from the specificity of the smell of jasmine to the generality of one's experience of selfhood. This is the phenomenal aspect of consciousness. It is very difficult to state what this phenomenal aspect of consciousness is and it can be defined only on pain of circularity. Still efforts have been made to identify this aspect with the help of ostension. In current philosophical literature, 'phenomena' has been used mostly to mean sensory qualia or raw feels. As Nelkin wrote, "An ice-cube just feels different from a warm compress, a blue cube just looks different from an image of a red square, and a toothache just feels different from the sensation of relief that occurs when the tooth stops hurting."[7] Many think that this subjective side of consciousness is non-representational and is not amenable to functional explanation. It may be possible to specify the neurological correlate basis of this phenomenal aspect, yet there remains the explanatory gap. Hence, Chalmers has branded it 'the hard problem of consciousness'. Consciousness is said to possess a psychological aspect too. For the psychological aspect it is not important whether a mental state has a subjective feel or not, 'what matters is the role it plays' in our conscious life. The philosophers and psychologists are not sure how these aspects are inter-related, or whether the phenomenal aspect really constitutes the core of consciousness. Let us see whether we can throw some light on the so-called hard problem of consciousness by taking a leaf out of the book of Śaṁkarācārya.

Here we need to take a short detour through the Advaita metaphysics. Besides the pure non-dual consciousness, which according to the Advaitins, is the Ultimate Reality, they admit the witness consciousness (*sākṣin*) or the reference of 'I', consciousness limited by an object (*viṣaya-caitanya*) and consciousness limited by the inner sense (*antaḥkaraṇa*) or the empirical knower (*pramātṛ-caitanya*). The witness consciousness is said to be the subjectivity per excellence whose nature is to manifest everything including itself and ignorance. It can never be the object of cognition because an object needs to be revealed by a revealer. If the witness consciousness were not self-revealing, then there would be an infinite regress. To explain empirical knowledge the Advaitins rely upon the modification of the inner sense. But the inner sense being material cannot reveal anything unless consciousness is reflected in the modified inner sense. This consciousness limited by the inner sense is the empirical knower.

We have seen that the non-dual principle of consciousness cannot be an object of thought, nor can one establish it with the help of reason. Śaṁkara, however, has used a *Cogito* type argument in different places to establish the existence of the individual witness consciousness whose relation with the pure consciousness is that of identity-in-difference. The crux of the argument is: refutation of the Self is impossible, for who will doubt, deny or refute it excepting the Self? This self is undoubtedly the individual Self. Transition from the qualified individual Self to the unqualified non-dual Self is through contemplative abstraction.

The Self, according to Śaṁkara, is neither unconscious nor is consciousness an adventitious quality of the Self. If consciousness were adventitious, then the Self would have lacked it at some stage. But the Self in all its stages is endowed with consciousness. To establish that, Śaṁkara has offered us an elaborate phenomenology of the Self in consonance with the theory of the five-fold sheaths or *pañcakoṣa*-s mentioned in the *Taittiriya Upaniṣad.* The first stage of consciousness is the waking consciousness of an individual self. Waking consciousness is intentional par excellence. For, it is necessarily directed to some object. These objects are the gross objects of the empirical world or internal states like pleasure, pain, etc. Since consciousness has no form of its own, it derives its form from its object. But this state of consciousness is self-aware and never lacks the qualitative feeling or the subjective side. At this stage, an individual identifies himself with his physical body, which is a part of the physical nature. The *Taittirīya Upaniṣad* (II.2) metaphorically describes this stage of self-consciousness as the *annamayakoṣa* or the physical sheath of the self.

The second stage of individual consciousness is dream consciousness. Śaṁkara says (*Brahmasūtrabhāṣya* III.2.4) that in sleep activities of sense organs cease. But the individual creates a subtle body of desires and his dreams are shaped in accordance with the past impressions retained by his intellect. Dream consciousness is also accompanied by a feeling of I-ness or subjectivity. Here also the dreamer stands outside but in relation to the dream objects. Hence, the Dream State is also object-directed; objects are the subtle elements (*tanmātra*-s). The main difference between the objects of the Waking State and those of the Dream State is that the former are constrained by the laws of space and time, but the latter are not. In the Waking State, the experiencer has more control over objects, but the experiencer cannot consciously choose the mode or time of presentation of dream objects. The Dream State is associated with a dream body, a subtle body (*sūkṣma śarīra*) covered by three sheaths one after another. The outermost sheath is that of vitality (*prāṇamayakoṣa*), the next one is that of mentality or sensuality (*manomayakoṣa*) and the innermost one is that of intellect (*vijñānamayakoṣa*). While *prāṇamayakoṣa* comprises five-fold breath, *manomayakoṣa* consists of *manas* and five sense organs, and *vijñānamayakoṣa* is made up of *buddhi* or intellect. The theory of *koṣa*-s actually hints at the physiological basis of consciousness, though physiology remained at a very rudimentary level. The Dream State has all three aspects of consciousness. It is intentional, as it is object-directed. It is phenomenal because each dream has a felt subjective side. It is also psychological because it is causally related with the Waking State.

Sometimes we are in a state of dreamless sleep, what is called the state of non-REM sleep in the scientific parlance. There are philosophers and psychologists, both in India and in the West, who maintain that an individual is devoid of consciousness during dreamless sleep. Śaṁkara, however, points out that the state of dreamless sleep cannot be unconscious since when we wake up from dreamless sleep we can say that we slept soundly and happily. Hence, this state must be a conscious state. In dreamless sleep, the subject/object distinction is kept at abeyance. It is associated with a blissful feeling. The individual self enjoys this state in a causal body (*kāraṇa-śarīra*), the *koṣa* counterpart of which is known as the *ānandamayakoṣa*. Deep sleep consciousness is unified and integrated. Though it is a state of non-duality, the self is still a knowing subject; there is however nothing as such to be known. Knowledge is a pure potentiality in this stage. That is why, Śaṁkara says that an individual in deep sleep perceives pure *avidyā* or the root ignorance. Thus in deep sleep, consciousness is not intentional. We have seen that it has its special qualitative / phenomenal aspect. Its psychological aspect is also evident through its association with a causal body. The body in the deep sleep is called causal because it is the ground of future actions.

These three states exhaust the entire span of our phenomenological life. These states are rich in experiential variety. Yet, they have a common feature and that is consciousness. The order in which the states are mentioned has a special significance. In successive stages, objects of consciousness become subtler and the sheaths become increasingly rarefied. Ultimately, the individual reaches the state of pure consciousness, an exalted state known as the *Turīya* State meaning the transcendent state. This state of pure consciousness is free of all sheaths and is associated with the *Ātman*. I am going to describe the essential features of this fourth state following the *Māndūkya Upaniṣad* (Chapter 6). "It is neither conscious of the internal world, nor conscious of the external world, nor conscious of both worlds, nor a mass of consciousness nor simple consciousness, nor unconsciousness; which is unseen, beyond empirical determinants, beyond the grasp of the mind, undemonstrable, unthinkable, indescribable; of the nature of consciousness alone wherein all phenomena cease, unchanging, blissful and non-dual." It is pure indeterminate intuition of non-duality, realisation of which leads to liberation.

It is obvious from the above description that the state of pure consciousness is neither intentional nor psychological. It is not conscious of anything. Since the *Ātman* in this stage has transcended the subject/object duality, it is not directed to any object, neither towards this or that particular object, nor towards an object-in-general. It has also transcended the principle of causality, which governs the world of space and time. It is neither an agent nor an effect of anything. Can it then be construed as a pure phenomenal state? Let us first consider the arguments in favour of this conjecture.

A. Pure consciousness has been described as blissful, a glimpse of which we can have in our pure aesthetic enjoyment, where we successfully bracket intentionality, but dwell in the realm of pure qualitative feeling.

B. The *Turīya* state is a self-certifying, self-illuminating state just as our phenomenal states are. When I sense the qualitative feel of redness, I appear redly, I am said to be in an incorrigible state.

C. Phenomenal consciousness is non-functional and non-demonstrable. It cannot be described in language properly and is amenable to ostensive definition only. Pure consciousness has also been described as undemonstrable, unthinkable and indescribable

Yet we should not consider the *Turīya* state of consciousness as phenomenal because it transcends all duality. It is said to be a seamless flow of experience without any experiencer, though it sounds like a misnomer. It cannot be construed as subjectivity for subjectivity is always related to a particular point of view. Pure consciousness has no point of view.

How then should we understand this state, vis-à-vis contemporary theories of consciousness? Thomas Nagel in his now classic essay "What is it like to be a bat?"[8] has raised a question, whether any sense can be made of experiences' having an objective character at all. Does it make any sense, in other words, to ask what my experiences are really like as opposed to how they appear to me? To quote from Nagel, "At present we are completely unequipped to think about the subjective character of experience without relying on the imaginative—without taking up the point of view of the experiential subject this should be regarded as a challenge to form new concepts and devise a new method—an objective phenomenology not dependent on empathy or imagination."

Nagel, though a naturalist at heart, dared to dream of an objective phenomenology. Of course, he confessed that he had no idea how to proceed. The *Turīya* state of consciousness may be the culminating point of that objective phenomenology. Pure consciousness transcends subjectivity and objectivity but serves as a ground for both. It is not linked with any point of view but is attainable by anybody through spiritual discipline, through praxis. In the pure experiential stream of consciousness, subjectivity merges with objectivity without remainder. It cannot even be said to be self-revealing (*svaprakāśa*) in the sense in which the term applies to the witness consciousness. It can at best be said that pure consciousness qua consciousness is essentially revealing in nature (*prakāśa-svarūpa*) and is therefore never devoid of this feature. When we experience different external objects or different internal states like pleasure and pain, etc., there is a witnessing consciousness giving unity to all our experience. Even when my 'I'-sense is given up, this detachment has to be performed in the background of a stream of consciousness. This stream or flow of consciousness acts as a permanent background of our conscious existence. It is permanent because there is no break in it. However, one may question the experiential nature of pure consciousness. If there is nothing to be experienced, nor is there an enjoyer of experience, how can there be any experience at all? Probably we should consider pure consciousness as the necessary logical presupposition of our conscious life.

What, in sum, then is the moral of the story? Both science and philosophy revolve round the representational conscious states. Pure consciousness is non-representational[9].

The moment we go beyond representation and step into the domain of the non-representational we are out of our depth. No discursive tool of analysis is adequate for knowing it. Therefore, the real hard problem of grasping the pure consciousness, of attaining *parāvidyā* remains 'forever undecidable' for the scientists and philosophers of rational persuasion.

NOTES

1. Though we have translated *'parā'* and *'aparā'* as the higher and the lower respectively, one should not read them as the superior and the inferior types of knowledge. *Parāvidyā* is so-called because it is conducive to the highest end of human beings, according to the tradition. *Aparāvidyā* is equally significant but does not lead to liberation. States with which these two types of knowledge are associated are phenomenologically different too.
2. Śaṁkara while commenting on this sloka wrote, '*anupraviṣṭam prakṛtaviṣayavikāravijñānaiḥ pracchannam-ityetat'*.
3. See, Bhattacharyya, K.C. *Studies in Philosophy,* vol. 1. Calcutta: Progressive Publishers. p. 162.
4. *Kaṭhopaniṣad,* 42/12.
5. Mohanty, J.N. 2001. "Advaita Vedanta as Philosophy and as Religion". *Explorations in Philosophy: Indian Philosophy.* Bina Gupta (ed.). New Delhi: Oxford University Press.
6. Chalmers, David. 1996. *The Conscious Mind.* Oxford: Oxford University Press.
7. Nelkin. 1994. "Subjectivity". *A Companion to the Philosophy of Mind.* Samuel Guttenplan, (ed.). Oxford: Blackwell.
8. *Philosophical Review,* vol. 83. 1974.
9. Citsukhācārya in his *Tattvapradīpikā* has defined *svaprakāśatva* as follows: *avedyatve sati aparoksavyavaharayogytva* meaning that *svaprakāśa* is revealed in the most direct manner, though it is not revealed through any representation, sensory or otherwise. And *Svaprakāśa* is that which can never be an object of consciousness. Pure consciousness can be said to be *svaprakāśa* in this sense and this is my justification for regarding it as non-representational.

CHAPTER 6

Philosophical Consciousness and Scientific Knowledge: Problem of their Interrelationship

Kireet Joshi

I

Cultural experience of the past and the present seems to suggest an important lesson for the future in regard to the way in which the pursuit of scientific knowledge, and that of philosophical consciousness, ought to be blended in a harmonious equilibrium or synthesized under the guidance of pursuits of deeper and higher dimensions of consciousness which have infrequently and so far inadequately affirmed themselves. For there are two great phenomena which have prevented in the long history of humankind durability of culture and solidarity of collective life, and these are tyranny and war or terrorism—local, regional and global. At the present juncture of humanity's journey, where pursuit of scientific knowledge has tended to marginalize philosophical consciousness and ignore or dismiss ethical and spiritual aspiration for knowledge and fulfilment, the evils of oppression and violence have been accentuated to such an extent that they threaten a global failure of humanity or even a widespread fear and calamity to earthy existence. The issue is thus so important that if a happier and freer future has to be secured, we need to understand at closer quarters the nature of pursuits of science and philosophy and their normative drives, idealities and possible harmonies.

The subject is vast, important and difficult, but we can suggest here only preliminary reflections.

II

We may begin with an elementary elucidation of the three terms—science, religion and philosophy. Science may be defined as a quest of knowledge, which lays a special emphasis on detailed processes of objects of knowledge in order to arrive at utmost precision, and the distinguishing methods of this quest are those of impartial observation, experimentation by working on falsifiable hypothesis, verification in the light of crucial instances and establishment of conclusions which are repeatable and which are also modifiable in the light of advancing quest.

Religion may also be looked upon as a quest of knowledge, but the object is to relate the human beings with something that lies beyond the realms of Matter, Life and Mind, and the distinguishing features of the methods are those of practice of beliefs, dogmas, rituals, ceremonies, prescribed acts and pursuits of social, ethical, and other institutional norms.

Philosophy is also a quest of knowledge, but it concentrates on the ultimate or intrinsic processes and substances so as to arrive at most general and universal features of the universe as a whole and even if that may transcend into what may be conceived as the original source of the Universe and Man. The quintessential element of philosophy is its search for meaning and significance of existence, temporal and even the supra-temporal, if such there maybe. The distinguishing features of the methods of philosophy are those of: (i) impartial and critical questioning of beliefs (religious or otherwise), presuppositions and conclusions (scientific or otherwise), and speculations on all the fundamentals of enquiry; and (ii) application of logical rigour in relating to all fundamental processes of the world and the underlying assumptions of thought and knowledge in an attempt to arrive at the most indubitable universal and essential conclusions, which even though not verifiable, may yet be found to be rationally incorrigible. Hence, it would be advisable to speak of philosophical consciousness rather than of philosophical knowledge.

Philosophy is often described as 'No Man's Land', since it falls outside the domain of science and religion—the two domains to which the entire humanity is related in one way or the other. Philosophy is something like science and something like religion, but it belongs to neither. It is, like science, a critical inquiry, an impartial inquiry, an inquiry that follows the rigour of logic. It is unlike science, because its attempt is to scale the highest heights to the study of the ultimate substance and its significance and value. Its main concern is with essence, not so much with processes or demands of processes in their minute precision. Unlike science, philosophy is satisfied with mere intellectual incorrigibility, even when verification in experience is provided for in regard to its conclusions. As a result, philosophy can freely examine critically the contentions and conclusions of science and there could develop also an elaborate philosophy of science. Philosophical inquiry can anticipate scientific discoveries; it can even provide guidelines or chalk out possible lines of inquiry for science. The conclusions of philosophy need not necessarily coincide with the conclusions of science; and yet the future developments of science may eventually come to substantiate the conclusions of philosophy. In the intermediate stages, therefore, there could be conflicts between philosophy and science, but since both are critical in their approach, these conflicts do not take serious proportions as has happened in regard to conflicts between science and religion. In recent times, however, science has influenced the entire domain of knowledge to such an extent that certain tendencies of scientific thought have come to refute the validity and justification of philosophy, or else, it has tended to provide only a subordinate role to philosophy and allowed it to exist only as a handmaiden of science. But whatever be the temporary phases or relationship between science and philosophy, the best way to establish a harmonious relationship between the two would be to allow philosophy its own unique position, its own special methods, and respect its conclusions and even utilise them as helpful guidelines for pursuits of science. At the same time, philosophy should admit that although its own methods or pure reason may arrive at rationally incorrigible conclusions, it should accept with humility the truth behind the assertion that what is intellectually incorrigible need not be scientifically or even ultimately conclusive, particularly when its conclusions collide with higher levels of experience which lie beyond the level of Reason.

In India, there has been a tradition that philosophical conclusions, however, convincing they be intellectually, must also be shown to be confirmed by the deliverance of spiritual experiences. Therefore, except the materialistic school of Cārvāka, all systems of Indian philosophy provide for a special room where philosophical conclusions are shown to be supported by spiritual experience either as they are obtained directly or as they are obtained through the records of *Śruti.* On account of this reason, as also on account of the fact that philosophy did not attempt to prescribe to science its own conclusions and respected the experiential and experimental character of science and its conclusions, there was hardly any conflict between science and philosophy. In the West, the conflict between science and philosophy has, in recent times, come into some kind of sharpness, and philosophy has also come to be increasingly discredited. This is mainly because certain tendencies in pure philosophy came to be a battleground of conflicting philosophical positions, each claiming some kind of incorrigibility and yet not admitting that the quarrel could probably be settled by verification in experience. It may also be added that there have arisen trends in philosophy in recent times which are themselves anti-rational and anti-philosophical and which plead for the supremacy of science or for the supremacy of deeper claims of experience in existentialism or in the philosophy of Will as against Reason as illustrated in trends of pragmatism or in trends of the revolutionary trends for Action.

Philosophy, science and theology have some kind of relationship, which needs to be brought out. Theology is normally connected with a specific religion and it attempts to defend the basic doctrines of that religion in terms of rationality. Theology consists of speculations on all matters, which constitute the subject matter of philosophy. But its tendency is, even though critical, ultimately supportive of the doctrines of a particular religion. Theology tends to support and defend dogma and develops a theory of Reason and Revelation and advocates supremacy of Revelation, even though that revelation has assumed the form of unquestionable dogma. Philosophy, on the other hand, appeals to human reason, and even when it develops a theory of Reason and Revelation, and even of the superiority of revelation, it refuses the authority of dogma, whether that of tradition or that of revelation. If it accepts the superiority of Revelation to Reason, it accepts it only on the basis of repeatable experience, which would verify the contents of revelation.

Science aims at and provides *definite* knowledge; dogma which claims to be unquestionable and yet which claims definite knowledge belongs to theology. Philosophy is a field of all the questions of deepest interest to speculative mind, which science cannot answer, or which science as yet within its present limits has not been able to answer. These questions relate to ontology and cosmology; but philosophy also raises the questions that relate to axiology and discusses the questions of value, purpose, goal and normative standards that should govern the quest of the *summum bonum.* Even the questions such as that of the distinction between knowledge and wisdom, for which no answer can be found in the laboratory, are dealt with by philosophy.

Science and philosophy have tended to oppose religions and theology, and this conflict arises from the sharpness with which theology or religion is defined as necessarily tied up with dogmatic belief. Historically, it is true that, in the West, science and religion have clashed with each other, and this clash rests on the claim that science is rational, empirical and progressive, while religion is supra-rational or anti-rational, dogmatic and conservative. It is also a fact that science and scientists came to be persecuted in the West, particularly at the commencement of Renaissance, by the Church. Even now, that conflict has not ceased, though scientists are no more persecuted by the authorities who uphold any dogmatic belief.

Evidently, science and religion must remain in perpetual conflict, if religion continues to uphold unquestionable dogma as the source of the knowledge of the truth and science continues to uphold that rationality and empiricism are the only sources of the knowledge of truth. This conflict is further complicated by the fact that although science provides definitive knowledge and science tells us what we can know, the disconcerting fact is that what we can know is little and what we cannot know by science relates to many things of great importance. The modern trends in knowledge have confirmed that axiological questions which science can never attempt to investigate or answer are indispensable if the right direction of human journey is to be determined and guided on the ground of definitive and ascertainable knowledge. If science cannot answer these questions, humanity must turn irresistibly to that which claims to answer these questions or to discover new means of knowledge by which these questions can be answered.

Sometimes, a compromise is effected. It is contented that in matters of the empirical world, rationality and science must be resorted to, but in respect of axiological questions, religion must be resorted to, even though religion maybe anti-rational or supra-rational or dogmatic. But this compromise seems to be opposed to the inexorable demands of the quest of knowledge. It has been contended that it is not good either to forget the questions that ontology and axiology ask, or to persuade ourselves with the religionists that we have found indubitable answers to them. In the same line of argument, it is, therefore, advocated that the best thing is to teach people how to live without certainty, and yet without being paralysed. But even this counsel does not eventually succeed. There is, therefore, a legitimate pressure to re-examine interrelationship between science, philosophy and religion and to consider whether all of them can be refashioned in such a way that the conflict among them can be resolved.

III

Fortunately, there are new trends in all these new fields, which need to be welcomed. The word 'religion' has come to be redefined in some quarters. A distinction is being made between religion and religionism, where the latter connotes dogmatic assertion of a particular religion or religious creed and the former connotes the quintessential nature of religion that is common among all religions which emphasises living contact or experience of the individual in his or her encounter with the totality of the universe or that which lies beyond the universe. Swami Vivekananda, for example, constantly spoke of religion as experiential in character and contended that religion is a matter of experience, a matter of knowledge and a matter of verifiable and repeatable knowledge. He even expounded at length different systems of Yoga and declared that Yoga is veritably a science *par excellence*—a science relating to those domains, which the modern science leaves out of its purview. Rabindranath Tagore also spoke of Religion of Man, which also seeks to underline the experiential aspect of religion. Religion of humanism is another aspect, which has developed in recent times, which wants to install man and his holistic search of knowledge and fulfilment as the central concern. Śri Aurobindo has spoken of spiritual religion of humanity as the hope of the future, a religion that is non-dogmatic, that is entirely removed from religionism and devoted to the Yogic pursuit of knowledge and action in their integrality.

There is also a powerful trend in recent times to bring about a resolution of conflict among religions because this conflict hurts even those who want to follow religion but are sceptical when different religions give conflicting answers to the deepest questions regarding the meaning and value of life. Here again, attempts are being made to develop attitudes of equal respect to all religions or to discover common elements of all religions that present to humanity a path of axiological development, which might be free from the disabling conflicts among religions. As an idealist position, many have tended to adopt this trend, but exclusivism of religious beliefs is so strong that it is doubtful whether and on what lines religions can come together. And even if they come together, the question will be whether this unity or synthesis or harmony of religions will be reconcilable with science. The question is also gaining importance as to whether philosophy will be able to play any important role, and, if so, whether while playing this role, philosophical standpoints of today will need to undergo a major change.

It seems fortunate that in the present web of emerging trends in science, philosophy and religion, Yoga has emerged; for Yoga has specific characteristics which bring it closest to science, philosophy and religion and has yet the potentiality of going beyond all of them so as to provide to humanity a new mode of knowledge whereby world-knowledge, soul-knowledge and God-knowledge can all be integrated.

The methods of Yoga can be pursued without recourse to any dogma and they require the same rigour as science insists, namely, observation, experimentation, and verification by repeatable experience. Yoga can be looked upon as the experiential basis for philosophical speculations and conclusions, and if rightly used, Yoga can be a bridge between philosophy and science.

But how far these tasks can be accomplished will depend upon one central issue. Modern science has so far tended to concentrate on the knowledge of Matter or on life and mind as embodied in Matter. It has also tended to develop those methods, which have proved successful in studies where empirical observation and measurement are feasible. It is evident that the domains which philosophy, religion and Yoga deal with centrally transcend Matter and the boundaries of embodied life and mind; the question is whether science would consent to extend its inquiry into these new domains, and if so, with what methods. The present scientific methods insist on empirical verification, measurement and objectivity. The question is whether science would consent to develop new methods where the domains of inquiry themselves are supra-physical, which escape the boundaries of empiricism, measurability and physical objectivism. Indeed, it seems rational to admit that to insist on physical proofs of what is claimed to be supra-physical is illegitimate. But are there, it maybe asked, appropriate methods of investigating the supra-physical which can give guarantee against subjective bias, subjective interference and lapse into unquestionable but erroneous beliefs? Yoga claims that it has developed methods, which can deal with the supra-physical as rigorously and as objectively as modern science deals with physical phenomena. Yoga claims that its methods can deal both with the physical and supra-physical, and, if needed and encouraged it could develop an integral science of both the physical and supra-physical and their interrelationship.

This is where we stand today in regard to the issues that are confronting the contemporary scientists, philosophers and advocates of religions and Yoga. In the spirit of inquiry, all the emerging trends need to be taken into account, and one could repeat the fundamental spirit of science which is to explore knowledge and to reject all the dogmas, even though some dogmas have come to be built in science itself.

CHAPTER 7

Developing a Science for Consciousness: Philosophical Underpinnings

A. K. Mukhopadhyay

"The history of science is the autobiography of consciousness"—J. Andrew Ross

Developing a Science for Consciousness requires some essential philosophical underpinnings without which the attempt rarely brings any success. This presentation is meant to highlight and share those intellectual realms with the colleagues engaged in developing a Science for Consciousness. The presentation is divided into ten parts. In Part I three possible relationships amongst Science, Philosophy and Consciousness have been discussed. Part II leads towards a science for consciousness along with some historical events relevant in the context. It also elaborates on what do we mean by science, different forms of science and finally the limitations of science including recent observations by which the boundary of science seems to be porous. This part also highlights the points why the scientists are not so far successful in developing a science for consciousness. Part III focuses on the established schools of philosophy, which have direct bearings in developing a science for consciousness. Part IV goes on elaborating nine different viewpoints on a science for consciousness, and crystallizes the viewpoint of a pragmatic consciousness-scientist. It offers a five-plane model of nature and their relevance in yoga and naturopathy. Finally it draws a connection between philosophy of nature and social philosophy in the context of two menaces of a civil society namely Corruption and Terrorism. Part V describes the characteristics of a science for consciousness and elaborates on how does science for consciousness differ from Theology and Science in its present form. Part VI offers five concrete suggestions for the scientists and philosophers of science engaged in developing a science for consciousness. Part VII reviews the three very basic, different views on how we become aware of our surroundings and of our thoughts and feelings. In part VIII, the modalities of reconciliation of Brain-bound and Brain-independent consciousness have been discussed. An emphasis has been laid on the modes of communication within Nature at the level and in the context of cortico-supracortical interaction. Part IX suggests Nanoune models for both Brain-bound and Brain-independent consciousness. Part X focuses on the future of Neuroscience in the context of continued evolution of brain and suggests evolution of a 'new brain' over the triune brain.

I

INTERRELATIONSHIP OF SCIENCE, PHILOSOPHY AND CONSCIOUSNESS

Scientists are concerned with facts, the philosophers with truths and the spiritualists prefer enlightenment to facts or truths

Though all facts are not truth, in essence a scientist, a philosopher and a spiritualist all seek Truth in their respective plane of working. While an ordinary scientist feels satisfied with sensory/empirical truth, an ordinary philosopher feels accomplished in the course of successfully handling perceptual, cognitive, intellectual and logical truth. An extraordinary philosopher or an extraordinary scientist aspires for intuitive truth and dives into the deeper plane of nature. The spiritualist does not feel accomplished till he gets enlightenment which is accompanied by revealed truth. In developing the science for consciousness, we need in one person a spiritualist, a philosopher and a scientist. And, we need plenty of them.

With this background, while every discipline has been seeking truth, maybe being confined to their respective terrain of play, the interrelationship of Consciousness, Philosophy and Science could be narrated best in the following three ways.

1. Consciousness, Philosophy and Science Bear an Ontological Relationship

Where the science ends, philosophy begins. Where philosophy falls silent, the experience of the domain of consciousness begins. While philosophy transcends but also includes science, consciousness transcends and also includes philosophy. When one's philosophy is correct, science automatically and spontaneously follows the suit. On the other hand, the hard core scientific data tightens the loophole of a loose philosophy. When one's consciousness works in harmony with universal, transuniversal, inter-universal consciousness, one's philosophy rolls on a unique tract. The correct philosophical pursuit leads to the opportunity for entering the domain of consciousness. Consciousness feeds philosophy, and through philosophy it feeds science as well.

Consciousness has a component that is inscrutable and non-negotiable. This part of consciousness is not amenable to either philosophy or science. It is this property of consciousness that offers it the supreme ontological status. Science can explore only nature while Philosophy explores both nature and consciousness. In this sense, philosophy occupies an ontologically higher status than science.

2. Philosophy and Science are Two Different Facets having their Common Origin in Consciousness

Here, though consciousness forms the terrace, the relationship between Philosophy and Science is not considered vertical. Both science and philosophy have a common origin in consciousness. However, they are horizontally related through a boundary that states that this is science and that is philosophy. Science deals with sensory, measurable, objective experience. Philosophy deals with subjective, non-measurable feelings.

Philosophy and Science are usually used as tools to explore consciousness. In turn, consciousness strengthens both the tools. What is not adequately emphasized in this context is the role the experience plays. Within the experience all three could be accommodated. 'Experience' results from the concurrence of Reasoning (Cerebral cortex), Feelings (Limbic system) and Instinct (Thalamo-reticular system of brain). The experience may be a sensory experience, an extrasensory experience like clairvoyance or non-sensory experience of phenomena, particularly of elementary phenomena like, Love, Sex, Ego, Life and Death. All are supposed to be relevant in this context.

3. Consciousness, Philosophy and Science are Related as a Causally Interacting Triangle

Here, no single discipline can claim its primacy over the others. Each one of them is causally created by others and in turn influences their causal existence. All are equally important. However, all three are taken as the products of the brain and they interact within the brain. Consciousness, science and philosophy all appear brain-bound. The all-important experience is the result of state-specific activity of the brain. In fact, the state-specific consciousness in the brain is responsible for the birth of state-specific philosophical principles or a scientist's research hypothesis. Scientific process operates through causally interacting triangle of 'Data-Theory-Control beliefs'[1] system. In this sense, when one tries to find out the exact relationship of the three, one is to look into the information processing and the state of responsivity of the brain.

Situation where the Man-made Boundary of Convenience Dissolves. Is there any occasion when Consciousness, Philosophy and Science lose their respective identity? Certainly! It happens in the course of experiencing elementary phenomena which puts Science, Philosophy and Consciousness in their proper perspectives. The identity of each and their differences dissolve while one addresses the existential issues, when one is thrown into life and death situation (elementary phenomena). The man-made boundaries of convenience differentiating Science, Philosophy and Consciousness get dissolved while one is subjected to near-death experience, transcendental death experience, transformational death experience and the experience of getting re-born in the same body ('born again' experience). In this phase, the unmediated and direct experience crystallizes as wisdom rather than as knowledge or information. Later, we may dissect this wisdom into knowledge, information or their supporting data and classify them under convenient boundary of science, philosophy and consciousness while in some other time it seems that the wisdom cannot be tailored to suit any boundary.

The practice of any and each of these three, in its true spirit, is effective enough to get through the realization that within 'science' there is a philosophy, within the philosophy there is a science and embedded within consciousness are both science and philosophy.

The Credibility of Science and Philosophy. The credibility of science lies in its (i) reproducibility and (ii) objectivity. Its data and result are open to public scrutiny. Although 'objectivity' in science gets replaced in insightful philosophy by inter-subjective sharing, the reproducibility of science is retained in philosophy in a different form. The same philosophical principles continue to be pursued from teachers to students, from the seers to his followers, from the master to his disciples through independent revelation and realization. In this sense there is a 'science' within the philosophical exploration of consciousness. The scientific rigor, as it is called, is usually observed in those philosophical principles which are derived from the experience of consciousness.

II

(Major portion of Part II has been developed over the lectures delivered at the University of Pune on *The Limits of Science* in October, 2001 and at Jawaharlal Nehru University, Delhi, on *Science for Consciousness*, in December, 2001)

DEVELOPMENT OF IDEAS TOWARDS A SCIENCE FOR CONSCIOUSNESS

In the last decade of the nineteenth century, it was Swami Vivekananda from India who unequivocally expressed and affirmed that a Science for Consciousness could be developed. However, neither the science was prepared at that point of time for this venture, nor was it so focussed, as it seems now.

In the first quarter of the twentieth century, two landmark observations were made. One was on the mystical front by the accomplished Indian mystics. The other was on the science front by the accomplished western quantum mechanists. Quantum physicists from the West identified the 'measurement' problem in quantum mechanics. They became aware of the fact that observer's consciousness does influence the process of observation and creates problem in measurement. This was the first blow to an objective and positivistic practice of science. More or less at the same period of time the visionaries like, Akhandamandaleshwar Sri Sri Swami Swarupananda Paramahansa Dev, Sri Aurobindo (and later Pundit Gopi Krishna) from India unequivocally expressed that emergence of a new human species as embodiment of higher consciousness is on the card of nature's mechanics. The former observation in the discipline of science could be visualized as a stepping stone for the scientists to enter the domain of consciousness. The later revelation may be utilized as the springboard for the humanity to join the adventure in consciousness. In the effort to connect these two important landmarks in human pursuit of knowledge, a Science for Consciousness comes in demand.

Then followed two World Wars. In the 1930s, for the purposes of investigation of formal deduction, machines and formal computation were defined. During the time of Second World War the discovery of mathematical theory of computation made an ineffable inroads in the scientific culture. Since then the scientists from a couple of related disciplines got interested in the study of mind. Probably, the mind works like a computer! It is this assumption which made the scientists to think that a science of mind might exist which can be investigated. Since then many advancements towards this direction have been made in the field of multidisciplinary cognitive science. New Age Movement in

America in 1960-70s, which brought down 'spirit' in young minds, followed the 'cognitive revolution' of post-war years. Transpersonal movement was also born during this period. By that time many renowned scientists had been changing their focus of attention on research on consciousness. At the classical neurophysiology level also, two Nobel neurophysiologists, Sir John C. Eccles and Roger Sperry made significant contributions in neurophysiology of Consciousness. Eccles and Popper's celebrated book, *The Self and its Brain*[2], threw an emphatic indication that the brain belongs to 'self'. "Structure and Significance of Consciousness Revolution" by Sperry[3] is a well-reviewed article published in *The Journal of Mind and Behavior Bulletin* in 1987. Two other Nobel scientists, Francis Crick and Gerald Edelman took active interest in the field of consciousness and published papers and wrote books on this subject. *Astonishing Hypothesis*[4] of Crick has highlighted the reductionist's approach. Consciousness can be explained by the sum total activities of the neurons in the brain. Evolutionary Biologist Edelman's latest title *A Universe of Consciousness*[5] (2001) has just come out of the press. Similarly, from the stream of physics, Nobel celebrities like Brian D. Josephson and many other physicists like, David Bohm, Henry Stapp, Material scientist like William Tiller[6] and the Mathematicians like, Roger Penrose[7] have all shown a leaning of physical science towards consciousness. Robert Jahn from the University of Princeton, USA, and his colleagues have documented in their several publications (e.g.[8]), "the unique capacity of consciousness to precipitate anomalous behavior of a variety of physical systems and processes."

In USA, the Centre is being set up for consciousness study in the University of Arizona. Tucson conference on *Towards Science of Consciousness,* held every two years since 1994, has offered a reliable tent for all those who are engaged in exploration of consciousness. The annual conferences of Association for Scientific Study of Consciousness (ASSC) have attracted scientists and the philosophers of science from all over the world. There has been a peer reviewed multidisciplinary *Journal of Consciousness Study,* an outcome of Tucson conference, being published regularly since 1994. Similarly, the outcome of ASSC conference is another journal, *Consciousness and Cognition.*

Today there are about fifty Science and Religion Centres all over the world (with their illustrious web sites) to address this issue. Scientific & Medical Network, UK, Centre for Frontier Science in the Temple University, Fetzer Institute, Institute of Noetic Science and The John Templeton Foundation of USA are worth mentioning in this context. For our Indian friends here to know, our neighbour, Pakistan, has a registered society working on Science Religion issue. In Aligarh, India, there is a Muslim Association for Advancement of Science (MAAS) working on consciousness and Islam. Recently, Government of India has been in the process of setting up of Departments of Consciousness Study and Yogic Sciences in ten Government Universities. Indian Council of Philosophical Research has been made a nodal organization by Government of India for networking consciousness research throughout the country. During such exciting point of time, I am privileged to deliver this lecture on the philosophical underpinnings as required for developing a Science for Consciousness.

WHAT IS SCIENCE?

The word science is derived from Latin word *scientia*. It is a noun formed from the present participle of the verb *scire*, meaning know. The word science also has a Greek root where science is the *means to split*, to break up. Basically, science deals with knowledge, the process of acquisition of knowledge (epistemology) and the levels or domains of knowledge (ontology). The way Albert Einstein defines science, even logic and philosophy can be included within the realm of science. "Science is the attempt to make the chaotic diversity of our sense-experience correspond to a logically uniform system of thought." (Einstein, 1950). He, however, remained confined to sense-experience only. Extrasensory or 'non-sensory' experiences do not come into the picture in his definition. Science, as presently understood, is the knowledge gained systematically by human beings through observation and experimentation. The process of 'sciencing' steps through (i) identification of problem, (ii) collection of basic available information, (iii) working out a research hypothesis, (iv) designing experimentation, (v) observation, (vi) analysis of data to draw conclusion, and finally (vii) generalization of the conclusion, if possible. Finally, we must remember that "Science never proves but merely probes." (Gregory Bateson).

There is also a caution. "When most people say 'scientist', they mean 'technician'. A technician is a highly trained person whose job is to apply known techniques and principles. He deals with the known. A scientist is a person who seeks to know the true nature of physical reality. He deals with the unknown." (Gary Zukav).[9]

Scientific community, like any other social community, works with a self-preservational tendency. The endeavor of science has four dimensions as pointed out by Alan Wallace. The science itself, scientific realism (the philosophy on which the methods of science work), scientific materialism (the metaphysical principles which the science can not afford to leave) and scientism (the dogmatic dimension of scientific knowledge and truth). Scientific materialism and scientism fall within the spectrum of scientific fundamentalism or scientific vigilantism. This could be well correlated with the psychology of the scientists. Scientism is often born out of an "arrogant, autocratic, 'almighty' 'I', a battered, besieged and bothered 'Me' and a clutching, captive, clasping 'Mine' of the scientists."

DIFFERENT FORMS OF SCIENCE

Science deals with relationship between facts. Scientific discovery is essentially the discovery of a new relationship. Depending on the nature of relationship there are four[10] kinds of science. *Orthodox science* is confined to ordinary facts in ordinary relationship. The ordinary fact described in an extraordinary relationship makes it a *Para-science* (e.g. parapsychology). Extraordinary facts (e.g. seeing a white crow) in ordinary relationship makes it a *Cryptoscience*. When extraordinary facts are described to be in extraordinary relationship it makes a *Paracrypto science* (e.g. observing a new star through telescope which violates the existing laws of astrophysics).

Quasi-science is a subject that deals with relationship that seems to be scientific but still definite proof is lacking since no experimental verification is available. Astrology belongs to this category.

Premature science is a science that is 'ahead of time'. Since it is premature it is weak to thrive. Its arrival ahead of time makes it difficult to be understood by the contemporaries. Alfred Wegener's continental drift theory and Mandel's discovery of rules of heredity are two examples that were proposed much ahead of their time.

Pseudoscience or junk science claims a relationship that can be proved incorrect by applying scientific methodology. Since it depends on anecdotal evidence and there is a tendency of generalization from one single example, it lacks the scientific rigor. In its preposterous presentation, one identifies the presenter either as a fool or as naive. Therefore, so far as the institution of science is concerned, pseudoscience does not have any place within it.

THE LIMITS AND BOUNDARIES OF PRESENT SCIENCE

Science works within a framework that sets its limits and boundaries. Present science works within certain limits and does not favour to cross its boundaries.

The limiting constants[11] in the framework of present science are (i) The constant of Einstein (the velocity of light), (ii) Planck's constant and (iii) Entropy barrier. It is difficult for an explorer to document, describe and publish in the mainstream science journal something that does not work under the umbrella of these three constants. Nothing can move faster than light is the dictum of Einstein and it sets the limit for classical mechanics and its extension in Relativity. There is always a gap between the observer and the observed and, the energy is made up of discrete quanta are the basics of quantum mechanics. This leads us to Planck's constant which sets the limits for describing the events confined to the quantum plane of nature. Cybernetics works under the umbrella of entropy barrier. Information exchange across this barrier is strictly prohibited. Einstein's constant excludes the possibility of simultaneity of events, Planck's constant excludes continuity of events, and Entropy barrier excludes the possibility of identity of events.

What are the different boundaries the present science seeks to conform with? The present science limits its question to What? Where?, When? and How? The science at its present stage does not allow persuasion of the questions like Why? and Who? The present science is not ready to acknowledge any proposition, ideas, or thinking that is teleological. It works within the framework of the Universe and is uncomfortable to perceive or conceive the existence of multiple universe(s), the Multiverse. The present science is limited by and limited to cerebral cortex only. Transcortical or supracortical phenomena are anomalies for present science. Finally the present science does not wish to 'see through' the phenomenon of Death. Beyond death nothing exists for science. However, there are phenomena now documented, which seem to transcend the space-time boundary of present framework and points towards something 'transcendental'.

POROSITY OF THE BOUNDARY OR TRANSCENDENCE!

There is an opinion against using the term 'transcendental' in science. For those who hold such view, it may be indicated that the boundary we are used to in science is porous. There are some remarkable conceptual advances and some notable observations made in the realm of science which transcend boundaries or indicate the existence of a porous boundary. We are aware that three great theories of physics have been facing three great 'problems' today. Theory of Relativity is confronted with the problem of space-time singularities. Quantum theory has been facing the problem of measurement and the Quantum-field theory suffers from the problem of infinities. However, these problems indicate that the boundary of science is porous and the reality does extend beyond the present framework. The scientists get the glimpses of something transcendental, something beyond space time, something which opens up to the infinity. Nonlocal communication dissolving the barrier of space, the dynamic aspect of the spatial nonlocality, may be called type I nonlocal communication, challenges Einstein's constant, while nonlocal communication dissolving the barrier of time, the dynamic aspect of the temporal nonlocality, may be called type II nonlocal communication, breaks loose the barrier of time and is a challenge for Planck's constant. Nonlocal communication type III, if it exists, dissolves the barrier of both space and time, transcends the realm of causal intricacies and is a challenge for entropy barrier.

We can readily mention a few more areas, which demand extension of the present framework of Science. Namely, they are the findings of the cold fusion experiment, zero point energy (ZPE), infinite dilution of water and retention of memory, over-unity devices and Unidentifiable Flying Object (UFO), which are often debunked by scientific fundamentalism. Nevertheless, these phenomena excite scientific imagination towards an extended framework of science. Other similar phenomena that take us beyond the boundary are the possible existence of magnetic monopole, magnetic current and existence of inverted space time (William Tiller)[12] domain.

The concept of existence of multiple universe(s) has been highlighted in *Conquering the Brain*[13] and *The Millennium Bridge*[14]. The idea is under exploration by cosmologists and astrophysicists. There is an opinion that at the beginning, at the time of random fluctuations, near infinite number of universe(s) were existing in potentia, in probability mode, out of which 10^{223} or more came into actualities. Those who believe in Anthropic Principle add, out of these 10^{223} universe(s) at least one, i.e., ours, succeeded to acquire the essential requirements for emergence and sustenance of life. In addressing such issue, the scientists cannot afford to remain confined to the universal laws only. They are to look for the laws which the universe abide by. The concept of multiple universe(s) forming a system, *The Multiversity*, remains an open-ended theory[15].

WHY DO WE AT ALL NEED A SCIENCE FOR CONSCIOUSNESS?

Following Descartes, Kant and Hegel, science and secularity have been recognized as two important features of western 'Modernity'. In the context of religion and spirituality, nothing could be more secular than consciousness. On the more, science deals with knowledge that works. Knowledge that works is the source of power. That's why for last three centuries there has been an incredible growth of science. Today science appears more powerful than philosophy, religion, or theology. By its appeal to rational intellect, by its power of taming emotion and by its ability to probe deeper knowledge, science has gained legitimacy in the various cultures of human societies. Each one of the members of the community, when confronted with a new fact, information or knowledge, therefore, asks is it scientific? The question comes in their mind spontaneously and, here lies the strength of science. This tendency to relate anything with science has been amalgamated with the culture and the society.

A mystical view of consciousness, a spiritual doctrine on consciousness or a subjective expression on consciousness, therefore, gains Rationality, Legitimacy and Power when conforms to the rules of science. The Science for Consciousness, however, has been evolving out of several felt needs in the domain of Humanity, in the domain of Spirit and in the domain of Science itself.[16]

Felt Need in the Sphere of Science

We have pointed out some of the areas where the scientists while doing science experience the glimpse of nature that is beyond their present framework. At the bottom line, in spite of spectacular achievements in technology and several conceptual breakthroughs, science is muddled with scientism in one hand, and unexplained heaps of anomalies on the other. Attending those anomalies is a great challenge to the scientific endeavor. In the course of exploration of anomalies/exceptions, the hidden laws of nature get exposed. Besides, for the benefit of human kind engineering vacuum, tapping the zero-point energy are necessary imperatives. There is upcoming discipline of complementary and alternative medicine which at places works better than the modern conventional medicine. Science is required to account for and explain its mechanism. It has been suggested to work under the principle of inter-convertibility of energy, field, form, information, and life.[17] The picture is expected to gain clarity once we make an effort to develop a Science for Consciousness.

Felt Need in the Sphere of Humanity

Humanity with its elevated awareness for almost everything possible and impossible, probable and improbable feels for a scientific exposition of their religious and cultural belief system, longs for a scientific explanation of the extraordinary phenomena in nature and desires to have a scientific foundation of their spiritual evolution. They feel this is the only way they can come out of stale categories of mental organization, can look beyond the death trap and get prepared for a new leap to emerge as a new species on this planet.

The Felt Need of the Spirit

The felt need of the spirit to develop a science of its own is understandable when we find so many accomplished mystics, *Gurus*, spiritual leaders working as 'transformer' for the humanity, as if the spirit itself now wants to liberate it from the matter, as if it wants to come out of the bondage which are of its own make, as if it desires to overcome the uncertainties which are its own creation.

Therefore, the science for its own reason, the humanity for its own requirement and the spirit for its own obligation seem to be in need of a Science for Consciousness. Emilios Bouratinos of Ekali, Greece, has said, very rightly, "if there is need for consciousness to be investigated by a science that is finest of its kind, there equally is a need for science to be assessed by a consciousness that is the most alert possible. How consciousness treats science and society tomorrow will depend on how science and society treat consciousness today."

WHY SCIENTISTS SO FAR ARE NOT SUCCESSFUL IN DEVELOPING A SCIENCE FOR CONSCIOUSNESS?

In spite of amazing progress across the conceptual horizons and also on the technological fronts, there are five important reasons[18] which can account for why the scientists are not so far successful in their endeavor in developing a Science for Consciousness. The reasons could be summarized as follows.

1. While science remains a human enterprise most of the scientists are prisoners of their **a**rrogant, **a**damant and **a**lmighty 'I', **b**esieged, **b**attered and **b**othered 'Me' and a **c**lutching, **c**linging, **c**lasping 'Mine'. Knowing this it is not difficult to explain the abundance around of scientism and scientific materialism. The 'dwelling' in consciousness transforms the investigators to have an **a**ctualized 'I', **b**uoyant 'Me' and **c**ompassionate 'Mine'. American Neurologist James Austin describes this as **ABC** of the problem in his work *Zen and the Brain*[19]. The attempt to develop a Science for Consciousness demands for personal transformation of the scientists resolving the problem of *'I-Me-Mine'*, a triangular guard within the core of the 'self' of any human being and so also of a scientist. Are we prepared for this personal transformation?

2. Science occupies the objective realm while Consciousness deals with the subjective. It is almost impossible to express some of the profound subjective (First person's perspective) experiences into objective (Third person's) perspective. To put it into Second person's perspective is not often easier either. Here one gets stuck with another triangular guard made by They-You-Me! Probably it represents a lower version of the causally interacting triangle of World-*Brahaman*-Self as found in Upaniṣadic non-dualism. It also reminds us of the causally interacting triangle of Data-Theory-Control Beliefs system[20] in any scientific process. One is expected to go through an inside-out (and outside-in) phenomenon while penetrating through this triangular guard. This is supposed to happen when one crosses the boundary of the system under investigation. Are we equipped with for taking up this severe strain?

3. The present science works within the boundary of the universe that is in turn determined by the boundary of cerebral cortex. Most of the scientists find it difficult to accept the existence of multiple universe(s). Multiple universe(s) is an open-ended theory for cosmology and astrophysics. The parallel of it in the discipline of neuroscience is the

theory of *supracortical consciousness.* To have an 'open brain' engaged in transcortical holographic and/or nonlocal communication without any compromise with the integrity of the brain is equivalent of dealing with multiple universe(s) in a system of the Multiversity. This no-boundary concept demands a radical revision of the framework on which the present science works. Are we ready for this?

4. As pointed out earlier, the present science has been working under the umbrella of three inviolable constants. Einstein's constant excludes simultaneity of events; Planck's constant excludes continuity of events; Entropy barrier excludes the possibility of identity of events. It seems that these three constants guard the *Cosmological Pleasure Triangle* (CPT) of the deepest recess of nature! In the domain of *nature of consciousness,* the events are quite often simultaneous, continuous and even identical. Therefore, it is likely that the nature beyond these three constants is the *Nature* of all natures, *Mother Nature.* As fire cannot be studied dissociating from its burning properties, similarly consciousness cannot be explored leaving behind its nature, Mother Nature, which could also be described as the kinetic facet, mobile pole, and executive front of consciousness. Mother Nature-Consciousness may thus be visualized as a 'biune' model of the Ultimate Reality. The task ahead is, therefore, to have an access into this nature of consciousness and to find out as how to 'perforate' this CPT? *Ānanda,* the divine ecstasy, the root of all consciousness is seemingly experienced only thereafter!

5. All of these four reasons spring from one single reason. The scientists do not wish to *see through* the phenomenon of 'Death'. For them death is the end of all existence. It is the final terminus for all endeavors of mankind. All enquiries stop at the doorstep of death. Death has been traditionally visualized as metaphysical issue and never as an issue for science. Are the scientists ready to account for the whole spectrum of death, which includes not only near-death experience but also transcendental death experience, transformational death experience and the experience of being reborn in the same body?

ARE THESE THREE CONSTANTS OF PRESENT SCIENCE MANOEUVRABLE?

Planck's constant, Einstein's constant (velocity of light) and Entropy barrier guard the conventional scientists from the view of that could be stated as the deepest recess of nature, Nature of all natures or, Mother Nature.

However, if one looks at the originators of these constant, may be Einstein or Planck—they are amazingly philosophic! The originator's mind/consciousness have been working from a plane that is beyond these constants. What does it mean? It means human consciousness naturally transcends these constants which are so valuable for the mechanistic worldview the same human being proposes. Therefore, when one has resolved to develop a Science for Consciousness, this very fact is to be taken into account. To put it in another way, unless science transcends the boundary created by the scientist there is little scope for the progress of science. In the present context it is to develop a Science for Consciousness.

Further, 'nonlocality' which has been accepted in Physics as an issue, throws unambiguous challenge for these constants. Einstein's constant excludes simultaneity of events. Nonlocal communication type I remains a challenge for this framework of looking at the mechanics of nature. Planck's constant excludes continuity of events and it is uncomfortable with Nonlocal communication type II. Finally, Nonlocal communication type III questions the inviolability of the Entropy barrier.

It brings us to a very important philosophical question. Do we reach God (here consciousness) through 'gaps' in the rules of nature or through the rules of nature? It reminds me of Bertrand Russell's famous witticism that, "Sir Arthur Eddington deduces religion from the fact that atoms do not obey the laws of mathematics. Sir James Jeans deduces it from the fact that they do."

I like to respond to it as under. During *Ascent*, 'gaps' are the ways to God. During *Descent*, God usually communicates through the rules and the constants. Here lies the importance of these honorable constants. These constants are to be looked from a different perspective should we wish to develop a Science for Consciousness.

I do not think that these constants can ever be 'ignored'. These 'constants' may be regarded as the 'guards' of the king. Their duty is to keep the king free from the mundane worldly affairs. One can reach the king only through the gaps between the guards. The king himself often may ask the guards to allow you to go in. Remember that the guards are the guards of the king. Therefore you cannot 'bribe' them. You can not take advantage of their sleepy state because they never sleep. You can please them by your behavior when they themselves may be interested to let you in and may try to have an ear of the king for you. There is also possibility when the king himself creates a 'situation' that all his guards fall asleep and the desired 'devotee' enters the palace with an absolute ease. This story may probably explain the mechanics of *Ascent* in relation to these constants. In the course of *Descent*, the king usually sends his message through his messenger, through his organization, through his network those by themselves are considered amazing personality, beautiful organization and charming network! However, as the king enjoys absolute freedom, he can also quietly send a messenger to you to give you the relevant message. In my works, *Conquering the Brain*[21] and *The Millennium Bridge*[22], I refer those as phenomenal hands of Mother Nature. There is one more exceptional situation. There are some persons who are considered King's own persons, those who can go in and come out at any time even inside the king's bedroom. In the context of mythology, the king's person is *Nārad. Rad* in Sanskrit means 'stop'. Nobody and none can stop him and that is why he is *Nārada.* In the context of cosmology and particle physics those could be 'Neutrinos'. Even eight kilometers deep within the earth where experiments on bombardment of proton are carried out, the scientists can get rid of all particles but neutrinos. These innocuous, neutral and omnipresent particles are of two kinds; left-handed and right-handed. The former can alter the 'weak force' of nature (R. D. Klauber[23]) and then through Electro-Weak interaction may probably influence the electromagnetic waves. Then the world network vibrates with the king's message.

III

ESTABLISHED SCHOOLS OF PHILOSOPHY DEALING WITH SCIENCE FOR CONSCIOUSNESS

"For every psychological term in English, there are four in Greek and forty in Sanskrit."
—A. K. Coomaraswamy

From the time immemorial, human beings have struggled to describe the relationship between matter and consciousness, insentient and the sentient, objective and the subjective. The formulation of this relationship has been variously structured as Dualism, Monism, Idealism, Realism etc. In this section, we would prefer to choose only those schools of philosophy, which have direct bearing on developing a Science for Consciousness.

First, we would briefly discuss the contribution and limitation of traditional approaches. This will be followed by highlighting three schools of philosophy having western roots which could be of some help in developing a Science for Consciousness. Discussing their inadequacy, we would explore from the rich spiritual heritage of India three Indian Schools of Philosophy which have concentrated on 'self'/soul-consciousness-world relationship. At the end, we would also consider an important physicalist's view on Science for Consciousness.

CONTRIBUTION AND LIMITATION OF THE TRADITIONAL APPROACH

We are familiar with Dualism. From India, Mādhvacārya (1238-1317) was the most profound advocate of dualistic philosophy in *Bhakti-Vedānta.* It is the refined and directed emotion, the devotion, which is considered as the vehicle of communication between the two, the soul and the God, *Jivātman* and *Paramātman,* Brain-bound consciousness and Brain-independent consciousness. However, in the West it was made emotionless substance-dualism, made famous by Rene Descartes, which has reigned over the civilization in general and science in particular for more than 300 years. When matter and consciousness are two distinct entities, the most important difficulty in this dualistic approach is how to account for the interaction of two kinds of substance? Similarly, with the 'idea' that consciousness is the ground of everything (Idealistic Monism), one cannot get along easily with any of the processes in nature, except probably that consciousness collapses probabilities into actualities by recognition and choice. In addition, the idealism is unable to overcome the Godelian constrain imposed in its deductive reasoning. Materialistic monism faces its difficulty when confronted with the issue of emergence, how sentience can emerge from otherwise wholly insentient matter? Double aspect theory of Spinoza, where consciousness and matter are two aspects of one entity also discounts the important process of evolution. The Realism pronounces the existence of a Reality that is independent of our observation or any effort in explaining or measuring it. Realism, however, is an important precondition for a theorist to formulate his theory. The process philosophy (of Alfred N. Whitehead[24]) emphasizes on the existence of the 'process' in the relationship between 'matter' and 'consciousness', which brings credential for cōnsideration of this philosophy in the process of 'sciencing' of consciousness.

THREE PHILOSOPHIES HAVING WESTERN ROOTS IN ADDRESSING CONSCIOUSNESS

Three philosophical schools with western roots, which attempt to bridge Science and Consciousness are (i) Systems Holism (Jan Smuts), (ii) Perennial Philosophy (Aldous Huxley) and (iii) the philosophy of Goethean Science (named after German scientist and poet Johann W. von Goethe, 1749-1832). Systems theory is based on holography—the whole is represented in every fragment, part, or point of the system. Transcendental essence is hierarchically immanent—is the dictum of Perennial Philosophy. Instead of reducing pluralism to a commonality, the Goethean science prefers to derive multiplicity from a pre-existing reality and Goethean phenomenology advocates an inside-out and outside-in phenomenon in the process of describing reality. All three schools are relevant in developing a Science for Consciousness, although each has its respective limitation. Systems Holism is limited by its 'boundary' problem, also called the problem of 'vertical depth'. The 'transcendental' element of Perennial Philosophy poses the problem of subjectivity in science. Inside-out and outside-in phenomenon of Goethean science is still to account for death phenomenon. All three schools are seen alien to 'me' and 'I'. None of these three philosophies addresses the issue of 'self'.

THE SPIRITUAL HERITAGE OF INDIA IN ADDRESSING THIS ISSUE

India has more than five thousand years of heritage in addressing this profound issue. Sāṁkhya philosophy of the sage Kapil is common to Buddhist, Jain and Hindu spirituality. It is based on dualistic philosophy of *Puruṣa* and *Prakṛti* (Consciousness and Nature respectively) and has its own version of twentyfour categories that make up the universe of mind and matter. *Anekāntavāda* of Jainism, universal compassion and total commitment to the process of enlightenment of Buddhism, *Nyāya-Vaiśeṣika* of Gotama (and Vācaspati Mishra in modern age), *Prajñāpāramitā* of Nāgārjuna and *Advaita Śāivism* of Kashmir offer tools of proven excellency to address various issues in this field. Finally, comes the oldest Vedāntic and Upaniṣadic epistemology that says, 'to know, one must be'.

SCIENCE-FRIENDLY PHILOSOPHY FROM INDIA NON-DUALISM, *ADVAITA-ŚAIVISM* AND THE *AKHAṆḌA* PHILOSOPHY

Three schools of philosophy from India are not merely useful but those are also science-friendly. The present science and the three schools of philosophy with western roots have to reconcile with these three eventually if they wish to establish an equation between scientific rationale and spiritual abstraction. These are the philosophy of Non-dualism, *Advaita-Śaivism* and the *Akhaṇḍa* philosophy. We would discuss Non-dualism and the *Akhaṇḍa* philosophy below. The third one, *Advaita-Śaivism*, originated in Kashmir, India, would be mentioned in the text as and when the proper context is built up.

Non-Dualism

Non-dualism makes a beginning with the 'self' but makes a refreshing departure from all other philosophies concerned with 'self' (particularly the 'self' of self-organizing system and the 'self' of Dualism) by stating that the 'self' is nothing but an indivisible spark of unconditional consciousness. The division or illusion is in the existence of mind. Mind is the cause of dualism. It is mind which cuts consciousness into two. Once mind vanishes (*monolay, mononāś*), there is consciousness only. *'Aham Brahamāsmi'*. 'I am He'. *'Ana-ul-Haq'*. Five different schools of Nondualism offer various expositions on Self (soul)-Brahman-World relationship. These five recognized schools of Advaita philosophy are *Dvaita-advaita* (Śri Nimbarka), *Acinta-Bhedābhed Advaita* (Śri Kṛshṇa Caitanya), *Śuddhādvaita* (Sri Vallabhācārya), *Viśiṣṭādvaita* (Sri Rāmānuja), and *Kevālādvaita* (Śri Śaṁkarācārya). Of these five schools, four are anthropomorphic meaning, all four hold respective personal gods as *Brahaman.* Only one, that is *Kevālādvaita* of Śri Śaṁkarācārya, expounds on nonanthromorphic non-dualism.

One assumption which is prevalent in non-dualistic tradition is that once one has left the base-camp of dualism or high above camps of various anthromorphic non-dualisms and has managed to mount the highest peak of the Absolute, it is never possible to come back or dismount again. This assumption, however, underestimates plasticity, potential, and evolving capacity of the human brain. If it were not possible to dismount from the non-anthromorphic non-dualism, then how does one explain Ācārya Śaṁkar himself performing idol worship, of course in a different context? In the recent past, we have observed this 'two way' getting personified in Śri Rāmakrishṇa Paramahaṁsa and in Akhandamandaleshwar Sri Sri Swami Swarupananda Paramahansa Dev.

The Akhanḍa Philosophy

The *Akhanḍa* state of the brain works without this assumption of irreversibility of the pathway from dualism to non-dualism and from anthromorphic non-dualism to non-anthromorphic non-dualism. It seems possible that the path from dualism to non-dualism and from anthromorphic non-dualism to non-anthromorphic non-dualism is an 'one way' to mount! However, there are ways to dismount again and it is possible to remount the peak whenever it is demanded.

In this sense, the *Akhanḍa* state of the Being indicates a much more mature and flexible state of the brain. It could be made possible through evolutionary progress of the brain. It becomes possible when the human brain has tasted the experience of every individual position and has acquired the ability of having freedom from any territorial imprisonment without loosing the capacity to enjoy the richness of every territory and always understanding the proper context. This positioning of the brain is unique to the Akhanḍa philosophy.

The Akhaṇḍa philosophy accepts an individual indivisible from the Whole. It deals with the divisions of the Indivisible (*A-khaṇḍa* 'in-divisible) with deft and dexterity. The divisions of the Indivisible are different from the parts of the 'whole' of systems holism. The 'whole' of systems holism excludes anything which could be transcendental while the 'Indivisible' of the Akhaṇḍa philosophy holds Consciousness-Mother Nature as irreducible constant. All other constants in nature work under them. The strength of the Akhaṇḍa philosophy lies in its acknowledging the existence of multiple universe,—the Multiverse. This worldview accepts pluralism at the highest intellectually comprehensible level. Multiple Universe(s) form a system, the Multiversity (cf., Systems Holism). It is comparable to Many-world/Parallel universe theory in Astrophysics.

The *Akhaṇḍa* is the First-Person-Universal swimming comfortably in the Interuniversal Essence. The potential of an individual can, therefore, according to Akhaṇḍa philosophy, eventually unfold to the hierarchical level of a universe. In this process, in the course of transcension (cf., Perennial philosophy) of the boundary of the universe there lies an experience of an inside-out and outside-in phenomenon (cf., Goethean Science) when one's nature *becomes* Mother Nature and the Being is realized as the personification of consciousness. The *Akhaṇḍa* remains continuously within a process (cf. the Process philosophy of Whitehead). He is even seen to swim comfortably in the Interuniversal Essence while experiencing an unfolding of the nested hierarchy of Being (Sri Aurobindo). The Akhaṇḍa philosophy is thus a neo-Vedāntin (may also be called post-Vedāntic and neo-modern) philosophy. In one hand it takes care of five different forms of non-dualism and on the other hand it reconciles Systems Holism, Perennial Philosophy and Goethean Science. The conceptual assimilation of the Multiversity dissolves the uniqueness of the universe we inhabit almost the same way Copernican Revolution demolished the unique position of the Earth in the cosmos. In astronomical scale, the *Akhaṇḍa* world view is therefore the highest and biggest comprehensible view, the human kind has ever made.

The Parallels between Vedāntic Aphorism and Quantum Realism

There are numerous parallels between Quantum Realism and Vedāntic/Upaniṣadic Aphorism. Where do all lead us? Fritjof Capra brought the first of its kind to the notice of people interested in it. However, almost all quantum doyens familiar with Upaniṣads, have expressed about the existence of these parallels not in their scientific papers but in their philosophical writings. Recently, Swami Jitatmānanda[25], a senior monk of Ramakrishna order and the President, Ramakrishna Ashrama, Rajkot, has brought out these parallels extremely well. Science has been telling what Vedānta has already declared. Whatever may be one's approach the ultimate truth would be One.

What is next? Would we stop now? Has the goal been reached? Probably not! To prove or justify that Vedāntic philosophy is of the 'highest' order could not be our final goal! Non-anthromorphic non-dualism of Vedānta does occupy the highest platform of human knowledge and knowable Truth. It is absolutely the 'highest'. There is not even a shred of doubt. It exemplifies Indian glory, pride, and joy. That the physical science independently has reached this stage to draw such conclusion or confirm the Vedāntic aphorism is a matter of incredible accomplishment for the science too. However, should Vedāntic philosophy stand at the highest platform, the question that knocks at the door is as follows. Does it have the capability of transforming present science? Could it initiate creative emergence in scientific endeavor? Could it throw light where the scientists are still groping in the dark? Swami Vivekānanda, about a century back, has offered us an emphatic 'yes' in this context. To go into this matter we require introspection by both scientists and spiritualists!

AN IMPORTANT PHYSICALISTS' VIEW MULTI-REVOLUTIONS VIEW ON MIND-BODY PROBLEM

In the October, 2001 issue of *Journal of Consciousness Studies,* Robert Van Gulick[26] describes twenty five options for addressing Mind-Matter problems from physicalist's point of view. There are ten versions of Reductions and ten versions of Emergence. The rest five have been grouped under 'others'. In this group of 'others' the last one is Multi-Revolutions view, held by Roger Penrose, Colin McGinn and Michael Lockwood. Van Gulick articulates their view as follows:

> The persistently mysterious nature of the psycho-physical gap gives good reason to believe that we need new ways of conceptualizing and understanding both the nature of the mental and the nature of the physical. Our inability to solve the puzzle of their link results from the inadequacy of both sides of the equations. McGinn, for example, claims that expanding the link would require both a better understanding of what he calls the hidden nature of consciousness (1991) and a radically different conception of physical space (1995). Lockwood (1989) finds the concept of matter itself deeply problematic and argues for what might be regarded as a dual aspect view in which matter and mind are closely integrated at the fundamental level. ...Penrose finds existing attempts to explain consciousness in terms of physical or algorithmic processes doomed to failure for reasons concerned with mathematical limits of formal system; he is equally dissatisfied with the present attempts to integrate our physical theories of the very small and the very large at the interface of quantum mechanics and general relativity. He optimistically hopes for a joint revolution that would address and resolve both puzzles.

The issue they have raised has already been addressed in *The Millennium Bridge*[27] where, the whole spectrum of nature has been divided into five planes. This has been discussed at the end of Part IV and in Part VI of this presentation.

IV

(Major portion of Part IV has been developed from a lecture delivered at Jawaharlal Nehru University, New Delhi, and from an informal presentation in Indian Council of Philosophical Research, New Delhi, in December, 2001 on the topic *Science for Consciousness*)

THE SCIENCE FOR CONSCIOUSNESS: NINE DIFFERENT VIEWPOINTS

We all know the story of the blind men and the elephant.
Nobody is wrong but offers a grotesque and an incomplete description of the reality.

With this background knowledge of limits of science and the problems in philosophy if one happens to meet people belonging to different disciplines that are known to seek knowledge on consciousness, one comes across different viewpoints on developing the Science for Consciousness. Consciousness is understood ordinarily as "an awareness of surrounding, awareness of 'self' and awareness of one's own thoughts and feelings". It is a consensus view from the meanings given in various English dictionaries. However, in the context of developing a Science for Consciousness, the whole gamut of culture, religion, background education and scientific grooming, folk-belief, mystical experiences and 'visions' all appear as cloud in the sky. We will discuss nine such viewpoints of which seven views have been stated earlier elsewhere.[28]

Transcendental Spiritualist's View

Most of the transcendentalists hold the view that consciousness is ever-transcendental and would always remains so. It is inscrutable, non-negotiable, and unexplorable. Therefore it is futile for the scientists even to make an attempt to develop a Science for Consciousness. Transcendental entity can never be brought down to non-transcendental level.

The view has some similarities with that of mystery-mongers. Consciousness is ever mysterious and therefore it would be a failure from the very start to develop a Science for Consciousness. The approach is called Fortean approach.

Some transcendentalists often exhibit an anti-scientific attitude when they emphasize that consciousness holds the secret of the universe. It is not explainable by rules of science at present. However, science one day may find some explanation for it. Even if the science does not find it, it does not matter and we need not be bothered about it. It is this last statement which makes the attitude anti-scientific.

Orthodox Scientist's View

Orthodox scientist who works on experiment-observation-inference principle, on the other hand, is of the view that science investigates nature, not consciousness. Therefore, consciousness does not come under purview of science. Consciousness is the domain of philosophers, mystics, or the spiritualists. The approach is that of *denial*, not even acknowledging an existence which can be investigated.

Look at another aspect of it. In the *Macmillan Dictionary of Psychology*[29] the concluding remarks of the entry under 'consciousness' is, "Nothing worth reading has been written on it." (1989)

Mystic's View

The mystics rely on their direct experience that is not mediated by any known means. They claim that Science for Consciousness already exists. The Science for Consciousness could be found in most ancient religious scripture of Hindus, i.e., in the Vedānta or in Upaniṣad. It can also be found in mystical tradition of Sufi, Buddhism, Judaism, and Christianity. The real problem faced by the present seekers is a language problem. The Science for Consciousness has been documented in a language different from that of modern science. Once someone, a philologist, or an etymologist explores the metaphysical meaning embedded in the mythological/spiritual symbols, appropriate research hypothesis will not be difficult to formulate. However, to understand that language, personal readiness/preparedness of the scientist is mandatory. Science for Consciousness could be explored by only those who 'dwell' in consciousness. The epistemology here is not merely 'participatory'. It is 'dwelling in'. It necessitates personal transformation of the scientists. Academic qualifications or university degrees are irrelevant here. Having experienced this transformation at least to some extent, the scientist may get the glimpse of five principles in the mystical science of consciousness.

(i) There is a Reality, which exists beyond material/sensory world, which is *a priori* as well as immanent, which is not within the reach of ordinary human brain.

(ii) This Reality is approachable by any one of us. The journey begins with a 'discontinuity'. One enters the terrain of elementary phenomena alone and only alone. One distinguishes 'self' from its conditioned properties (ego, etc.). In the course of the journey, the *'self' is* stripped of elementary phenomena. One experiences complete death experience which includes near-death experience, transcendental death experience and transformational death experience. The worldly journey ends with a 'surrender' to that Reality.

(iii) That Reality also approaches each one of us through the Grace Phenomenon. Most of the time it is mediated through a *teacher.* It can happen independent of a teacher, when one's brain is elevated to the *State of Grace.*

(iv) The experience of that Reality comes as Direct, Unmediated, Unmitigated (cf., Nonlocal communication in the language of science).

(v) It is possible to have a unitary experience with that Reality. This consummation is called Supreme Consummation that marks the beginning of a new life. One feels reborn in the same body with a new assignment. One starts dwelling in that Reality. There is Choice, Freedom, Ease, *Ānanda* and New Creation. The experienced one becomes an *Akhaṇḍa*—an individual indivisible from the Whole.

The Science for Consciousness, according to the accomplished mystics, revolves around the science of 'self'. If the scientist, therefore, can find out the relationship between this 'self' and the brain, (cf.: Eccles and Popper's highly esteemed work, *The Self and its Brain*[30]), then a bridge could be built up between the neuroscience and the Science for Consciousness.

Pantheist's View

Consciousness has a transcendental and an immanent aspect. The transcendentalist stresses only on the transcendental aspect of it while pantheists lay stress on the latter. "*Brahman* is the only real. World is unreal. *Brahman* is the world", said Raman Maharshi. From this paradoxical expression, the transcendentalist picks up the first sentence and the pantheist stresses on the last. According to this view consciousness is everywhere. Consciousness is everything. Where then is a need for the scientist to build up a Science for Consciousness? In the ocean where does one build the bridge? Or, what does one connect, from where to what? While the transcendentalist collapses the hierarchy on the higher (deeper) side, the pantheists collapse it on the lower side.

Skeptic's View

Skeptic's approach is neither Fortean nor denial. In response to a new claim, the skeptic first expresses his ignorance, subsequently starts genuine doubting (doubting is not denial) and finally, emphasizes on further enquiry, investigation and exploration.

In spite of being shown evidence after evidence there remains a group of skeptics who prefer to remain ever skeptical. They may be labeled as 'pseudoskeptic' in the words of Marcello Truzzi[31], or 'pathological skeptic' in the words of Ed Storms, or 'organized skeptic' in the words of L. David Leiter. David Leiter in the *Journal of Scientific Exploration*[32], hypothesizes on the origin of this organized skepticism to be some kind of wound at the deeper level of psyche inflicted during their formative phase of life.

Skepticism, however, has a legitimate place in science particularly when it is combined with open-mindedness. It helps add the most essential component, the 'rigor', in science. Here we would consider such true skeptic's view.

Can consciousness be researched? A million-dollar question! An entity that is *a priori*, could at best be found, reached out or merged into. Worst, it could be missed. When we miss it, does it prevent the scientists in painting a complete worldview? If we do not recognize it, does it affect our fulfillment as human being?

Once we accept consciousness as all pervading, then we are all within it. Being within it, how can we do research on it? It is a subjective experience and is therefore better left to be explored by the mystics. Science deals with which are objective. It describes things or phenomena in third person's perspective in a measurable or quantifiable way. "What can not be measured is not scientific," said Galileo and that were the beginning of a positivistic science. "Science is measurement and measurement is science," repeated Marie Curie. Positivistic science got further consolidated. With positivism in the core, the precision limit of present scientific instrument for resolution of space today is 10^{-15} cm. Maximum temporal resolution is expressed as thousandth of a millisecond. However, if consciousness is trans-temporal and trans-spatial then does it not stand far beyond the scope of science in its present form? One may take help of reasoning or logic while trying to bridge the gaps. However, have we not heard from the accomplished mystics that the reasoning stops at some stage of their exploration of consciousness and a terrain of silence is sandwiched between the domain of reason and the domain of consciousness? From both mystical and scientific point of view, therefore, consciousness can not be brought down to third person's perspective that is measurable and objective.

If so, what is the consciousness research all about? The question like what is consciousness appears to be fruitless to pursue in science. On the other hand, the skeptic suggests, if one re-frames the research question on consciousness it may become possible to address the issue in a different way. For example, does consciousness have a mechanics? Does it work? Is it anyway causally related to events or phenomena we observe in day to day practice? If it is independent of events or phenomena, how can it have influence on them? The questions like these seem amenable to science.

Consciousness in Social Scientist's Perspective

There can be no development of individual's consciousness ignoring the social context of it. One can see this in Freud's 'unconscious' directing behaviour of an individual towards his/her family/societal partner/colleague. Also this can be seen in Carl Jung's 'collective unconscious' as the fountain of social inspiration and in possibility of world revolution hidden within the unsatisfied consciousness of the proletariat of Karl Max.

Deep ecology and depth psychology are intimately connected. We are loved and we too love. We are conditioned and groomed by the society for a conditioned existence (e.g. as doctor, a philosopher, a scientist or a businessman) which is the basis of our 'ego' and for which we too are cautious about other's existence. We also live with a desire to perpetuate our ideals, values, tradition through our followers, disciples, students or genetic descendents, a manifestation of the basic instinct 'sex'. We are moved or perturbed by the birth or death of another member of our family or society. We too, as individual, when fallen in this life and death situation may look at it as most precarious. May the situation act as a turning point in our behavioural response!

Therefore, if one distills from the pluralistic transnational ocean of culture, five sparkling pearls that come out are Love, Sex, Ego, Life and Death. These are the five 'elements' of subjectivity, five private facets of 'self' and also are constituents of elementary phenomenology (in contrast to the surface phenomenology of classical and quantum worlds or the depth phenomenology in the realm of mind, soul, consciousness). Phenomenological integration in the brain integrates the phenomenal experience of these five. Depth psychology and deep ecology could be seen converging on this 'Five in one'. The early stage of *Tantra sādhanā* is practically aimed at reaching this point of social, cultural and civilizational distillate. The journey to the deeper plane of consciousness begins thereafter.

Consciousness in Natural Scientist's Perspective

If consciousness was not a part and parcel of nature how a nature, which sculpts actualities from plentitude of possibilities, could be so parsimonious, Hamiltonian, total action-conservationist and is able to demonstrate a spectrum of degrees of freedom/constraint in spite of being totally mutable! According to natural scientists, consciousness is a part and parcel of nature, intimately residing within it, as well as hiding in the deepest recess of nature. (cf. the immanent and transcendental properties of consciousness in perennial philosopher's view). Deepest recess of nature, according to them, could be found beyond computationlism where a living organism makes choice that often does not depend on algorithmic prespecification. Godel's Theorem appears as a 'death blow' to the formal system and formal logic and the naturalist started looking for source of life beyond Godelitis. Consciousness, therefore, according to natural scientists, could be explored in every plane or terrain of nature. Consciousness, thus defined, is brain-independent, independent of our brain-trapped consciousness. Nevertheless, the two are never mutually exclusive.

Life Scientist and Evolutionary Scientist's View

A conscious unicellular organism probes its environment by movement. In multicellular organism 'receptors' are left on the surface of the organism to sense and probe the environment. Neurons appeared sometime around 700 million years ago in a biological organism, and a rudimentary 'brain' much later. And, why to talk about animal kingdom! Scientist J. C. Bose[33] from India first documented evidence that plants are also conscious. Recently it has been shown by various experimental studies (for example on desert shrub *Ambrosia dumosa*[34] that the roots of a plant can recognize the roots of its fellow competing for nutrients in the same source of environment, a kind of 'self' non-self distinction!). Many persons involved deeply in agriculture, not necessarily a scientist, believe that it is possible to communicate with plants to keep them healthy and make them more productive. Life and evolutionary scientists, therefore, think at the very basic level that investigation of life and evolution are well within the purview of science. If we know the rules governing the emergence of life and the rules for the process of evolution, we are near to the causal mode of consciousness. Even our emotional response, according to them, is a result of evolutionary programme within. The advanced thinkers in the line of evolutionary biology look at the human being as a 'transitional being', who embodies one of the numerous phases of evolving consciousness on this planet. Millions of years have passed to evolve into this phase from a mass of protoplasm. The process is likely to culminate by making the human being as an embodiment of a higher consciousness. Emergence of a new species is on the nature's card. One finds, in this process, not only a Great Network of Being (Alfred North Whitehead[35]) but also a mechanism for unfolding of a Nested Hierarchy of Being (Sri Aurobindo). Evolution is, therefore, a play of consciousness and if the scientists explore the principles and mechanics of evolution and emergence of life, they get clues how does consciousness work.

Consciousness Scientist's Perspective

We would elaborate on this point a little further.

The Essential Background: Consciousness scientists are those who come form the background of a rich scientific culture (high 'Intelligence Quotient', IQ). They are aware of the recent developments in neuroscience, cognitive science, quantum physics, vacuum physics, particle physics, astrophysics, information technology, nonlocal communication, and the science of life and evolution. They know the 'limits' of present science and the problems in different schools of philosophy. They are expected not merely to be interested in but also to be emotionally involved (high 'Emotional Quotient', EQ) in exploration of consciousness. Moreover, the most important, they should have direct experiences of consciousness, which are rich and profound. This helps their personality to acquire one-pointedness (high 'Consciousness Quotient', CQ) and integrity (high 'Spiritual Quotient', SQ) over their already high 'Emotional Quotient' (EQ) and 'Intelligence Quotient' (IQ).

From this background it seems logical for them to consider that consciousness has a mechanics (causal mode) which could be connected with the causal modes in quantum and classical worlds.

Qualifications Desirable for Becoming a Consciousness Scientist: It would be certainly better if he knows a little bit of philology and etymology so that he can translate the myth, metaphor and symbol of different cultures into the language of science. As familiarity with Internet surfing for review of recent literature helps him to remain thorough in modern knowledge, so knowing Sanskrit would be an additional advantage for him to dig into the world's most ancient wisdom documented in Upaniṣads.

Look at how and why the present science occupies a supreme worldly position in the context of knowledge? It is because of the hard work of some open-minded scientists who are sensitive and intellectually honest, who have made their conclusion based on evidence and who do have deep reverence for nature (manifested as humility, awe, and wonderment). While the same scientists engage themselves in exploration of the deeper terrain of nature related to consciousness, two additional qualifications appear mandatory. These are:

(i) A readiness for personal transformation

(ii) A reverence for value system in Nature's mechanics.

For, in a Science for Consciousness, a balance is necessarily to be struck between capabilities of Science and the values and ethics, for the entire humanity.

Finally, last but not the least, his sufficient acquaintance with the modern research methodology, clinical epidemiology, with special reference to research on 'quality' makes him fully armed to join the adventure in consciousness.

Characteristics of a Consciousness Scientist: A consciousness scientist having direct experience of consciousness works at two levels. The first level includes intuition, illumination, and revelation that result in discovery and invention. At the second level, the intellectual level, he gets engaged in empirical validation of the intuitive/revealed truth. The capacity to integrate these two levels characterizes a consciousness scientist. He understands the connection that overarches Myth, Metaphysics and Science[36]. Besides, a consciousness scientist by nature would be a creative scientist. Whether he is a theorist or an experimentalist does not matter! A creative scientist is he who dissects, breaks, deconstructs, synthesizes and rebuilds. He creates new research hypothesis, puts the existing facts in a new context, digs out new meaning of available information, designs new experiment and innovates new technology, uses available resources for a new purpose. He is, therefore, not only an inventor, but also a challenger, an entrepreneur. When confronted with infinite complexity that is too difficult to comprehend he applies his masterstroke, the simplification, to simplify the matter again. There is always a refreshing newness in his presentation. However, as a creative scientist he suffers from several discontinuities. For him, Thomas Kuhn's[37] cautioning note is very appropriate. "Like artist, creative scientists must be able to tolerate crisis and occasionally be able to live in a world out of joint." He is also aware of Bernard Barber[38], who pointed out that contrary facts or ideas are routinely and inevitably resisted at first by scientific community.

Consciousness Scientist's View: The first question a consciousness scientist is confronted with whether this Science for Consciousness would develop from a new position or would be an extension of present science. Here, he agrees with what Werner Heisenberg once said. "For Christopher Columbus, it must have been the most difficult decision to leave all known land and sail so far west that the storage on board would not allow him to return. In a similar way, completely new land in science can not be discovered unless one is prepared to leave at a certain point the foundation on which traditional science is based and try to jump into emptiness."

Therefore, the Science for Consciousness is likely to develop from its own position and would extend into related disciplines of science to enrich them. Every discipline of science works under umbrella of a specific constant (mentioned earlier). In the Science for Consciousness, consciousness is the only constant and all other honorable previously identified constants are considered landmarks in hierarchy of nature.

The consciousness scientist takes a pragmatic note of all views expressed above and exhibits a multiprong composite approach. He takes the cue from the skeptic and formulates a research hypothesis that consciousness has a causal aspect, mobile facet, kinetic pole, executive front to participate in its mechanics. And, this aspect, this facet, this kinetic pole and executive front of consciousness may have connections with the lesser depths of nature. The scientists explore *nature*, not consciousness. While consciousness may be non-negotiable, inscrutable, unexplorable, its kinetic pole may not be so! If we can extend the spectrum of nature from physical nature to nature of consciousness, then there is no problem for science to explore this nature of consciousness under purview of science. Nature of consciousness may be called the Nature of all natures or *Mother Nature.* Consciousness-Mother Nature forms a 'biune' model of the Ultimate Reality (cf: *Parama Śiva* of *Advaita Śaivism* of Kashmir).

Science falls silent when confronted with phenomenon of death. Death is one of the phenomena in the elementary terrain of nature. This terrain of elementary nature and the plane of Mother Nature are the pieces missing from the whole jigsaw puzzle. Consciousness and Nature form a spectrum that for understanding can be divided into five planes[39]. This division is based on the presence or absence of perceived uncertainty in an observer-dependent reality and then on the levels/kind of uncertainty (see Part V). Every plane is independent of others but is also connected with each other. Connections are used at the time of necessity. The causal mode or the mechanics of every plane is run by a specific currency. The inter-convertibility of currency across these five planes is one of the key research frontiers in exploration of nature. This five-plane scheme of nature and consciousness (Pentaune model) fulfils the demand raised by Multi-revolutions theory of

Penrose McGinn and Lockhood. How? This scheme extends the plane of matter from the quantum world to the terrain of elementary phenomena and scales the plane of Mother Nature out of consciousness. The plane of Mother Nature and the terrain of elementary phenomena connect the plane of consciousness with the world of quantum.

Consciousness scientist does not work with the assumption that consciousness is skull bound or brain bound. Unification of brain-bound consciousness and brain-independent consciousness through self-consciousness remains the goal of his search. The hard core scientists, the physicists in particular, who first identified this 'consciousness' as an influencing factor in their observation of behavior of quantum particles, however, have been allured by the brain-dependent consciousness. However, to a consciousness scientist, consciousness is a ground reality and can also be brain-independent. Our working consciousness is brain-bound,—a kind of consciousness imprisoned in the 'case' of the brain, a kind of consciousness entangled by the shackles of the brain, a kind of consciousness which can work only using the mechanics of the brain. However, there exists consciousness that is 'free' and totally independent of our brain. This consciousness can be explored quite independent of recording what happens in the brain. In other words, consciousness can be explored totally independent of Neuroscience. This brain-independent consciousness could be explored by exploring different planes of nature as mentioned above. On the other hand, the brain-bound consciousness and the brain-independent consciousness can be connected (initially mystically) by self-consciousness, the awareness of 'self'. Increasing awareness of the existence of brain-independent consciousness by the members of the humanity is an indicator of the beginning of the era of supracortical consciousness. Like The Multiversity, Supracortical consciousness is also an open-ended theory[40].

The present human brain is a 'crowning achievement of the process of evolution', says Stephen J. Gould. However, to a consciousness scientist, the process appears to be in its infancy and is far from complete. The process in all likelihood would continue to evolve till the brain, the most complex conglomerate of matters in the entire universe, becomes comfortable with consciousness inside and outside it.

Finally, a consciousness scientist does not confuse epistemology for ontology. Consciousness, ontologically placed, is inscrutable and non-negotiable. Consciousness, epistemologically seen, has a mechanics that possibly could be connected with the quantum and classical mechanics. Consciousness along with Mother Nature (Planes V and IV) is responsible for depth phenomenology of will, intention, 'self', 'soul', purpose etc. This depth phenomenology of Consciousness-Mother Nature commands over the surface phenomenology of classical and quantum worlds Nature (Planes I and II) through the mechanics of elementary phenomenology (Plane III, which deals with life and death situation). For a consciousness scientist, the values are adored as the rules of the game of Nature and Consciousness. To go from one plane of nature to another these rules are to be learnt and practiced with a sportsman's spirit and without any fault. The clarity of knowledge about ontology of consciousness, epistemology of consciousness, phenomenology of consciousness and axiology of consciousness offers him a unique ability to swim comfortably in the ocean of consciousness.

PLANES OF NATURE, YOGA AND NATUROPATHY

Recently there has been a lot of activities world over on yoga research with an objective to reconfirm the ancient wisdom through modern research methodology. The research in yoga may be visualized as exploration *of* consciousness *by* consciousness *for* consciousness. The passage is spread over the entire spectrum of nature. That is perhaps the reason, yoga and naturopathy have been put under one central council by Government of India (Central Council for Research on Yoga and Naturopathy in New Delhi). Should we visualize nature as having a stratified and nested hierarchy and yoga as the process of journey of 'self' and its brain through all its five planes, it becomes easier to understand yoga and to do research on it. Similarly, when one understands the mechanics of nature in her different planes, the respective currency through which these mechanics are run and finally the probable mechanism of inter-convertibility of different currencies, it becomes easier for the researcher to formulate his research hypothesis. It may be for validation of the effect of nature-therapy or to postulate its mechanism. For example, the research hypothesis could be related to plane I of nature with the action of a plant alkaloid or hormone. It may relate plane II of nature and the effect of retained memory following infinite dilution. It could as well relate the plane III of nature and the mechanism of action of deep psychotherapy, or the plane IV of nature and the science in '*pranic*' healing, '*mantra*' therapy and transplantation of soul.

A CONNECTION BETWEEN PHILOSOPHY OF NATURE AND SOCIAL PHILOSOPHY

Whether this five-plane ('Pentaune' model) model of Nature and Consciousness could be of any use to understand the genesis of two menaces of human civilization namely, Corruption and Terrorism?

I guess, yes! The 'Self' and its brain have the amazing capacity to travel through the entire spectrum of nature and consciousness. An evolving brain integrates the experience of the journey. However, faults do take place.

Passage from Plane I to Plane II with lack of integration or, passage from Plane II to Plane I with breakdown of integration results in Financial/Energy corruption.

Passage from Plane II to Plane III with lack of integration or, passage from Plane III to Plane II with breakdown of integration can result in System corruption.

Passage from Plane III to Plane IV with lack of integration or, passage from Plane IV to Plane III with breakdown of integration can result in Terrorism. To a Terrorist, life and death mean the same and one. It is to achieve a purpose that he thinks is right. Life and death are the events in Plane III while purpose in this model is decided in Plane IV.

The model assumes that lack of integration or breakdown of integration is the cause of 'disease'/ailment/sickness. It also asserts that the mastermind for corruption (and terror) starts at the highest level although the recruitment of working hands occurs exploiting intolerance, jealousy, greed and the poverty of common mortals.

According to the infrastructure of the brain the manifestation of the terrorism differs. It may be manifested as political terrorism, cultural terrorism, and even terrorism in the endeavor of 'sciencing' (Scientific terrorism!).

V

(Major portion of this Part V has been developed over an interactive session on *Consciousness* at the University of Allahabad, organized by National Brain Research Centre, India, in October, 2000)

CHARACTERISTICS OF THE SCIENCE FOR CONSCIOUSNESS

The outcome of exploring Consciousness is always a refreshing newness

The Science for Consciousness is expected to be accommodative. It would resolve several paradoxes. Finally, it would be creative.

It would definitely accommodate the essence of different views on Science for Consciousness expressed above. In the process, it would take care of orthodox science, parascience and cryptoscience. In the Science for Consciousness one would come across ordinary facts in extraordinary relationship or extraordinary facts in ordinary relationship or even extraordinary facts in extraordinary relationship. It would honour epistemological pluralism. The mytho-poetic epistemology of Homeric age, the epistemology through 'all-pervading' *Logos* in the Greco-Roman cycle, theology as epistemology in the medieval age, mechanistic epistemology of post-Galileo era, the evolutionary epistemology encouraged in the post-Darwinian age[41] and finally the 'participatory' and 'dwelling in' epistemology of present age would find their place in the science of consciousness. We would also expect to see here a reconciliation of epistemology and hermeneutics. The effort would integrate Science, Humanity and the Spirit.

The developing Science for Consciousness is expected to resolve several paradoxes. The important ones of those are the paradox of subjectivity and objectivity and the paradox in relationship of brain-bound and brain-independent consciousness. In reconciling these two pair of paradoxes it would account for different types of existential uncertainties and even death.

The hallmarks for Science of Consciousness are creative emergence and new creation. New relationship in a new context for a new purpose is the fruit of pursuing a Science for Consciousness. It offers a new meaning to life.

HOW DOES SCIENCE FOR CONSCIOUSNESS DIFFER FROM THEOLOGY?

Theology has often been confused with science since it justifies and seeks rationale for a religion. While science limits itself to description, the religion ponders on prescription and the theology engages itself in justification. Unlike in Science for Consciousness, most of the theologies hold one personality or a scripture as an inviolable constant. This is not challengeable. On the other hand, in Science for Consciousness it is otherwise. The ideas, assumptions, conclusions are all open to public scrutiny. This all happens because most of the theologies work within a boundary. Science for Consciousness does not! Science for Consciousness welcomes and encourages attempts for verification. Inter-subjective agrreability and organic objectivity are features of Science for Consciousness. The cardinal validation criterion here is reproducibility.

DIFFERENCE BETWEEN THEOLOGY AND THE SCIENCE FOR CONSCIOUSNESS

	Most of the Theologies	**Science for Consciousness**
1	One personality or a holy scripture is held as an inviolable constant	No such constant
2	Works within a boundary	Prefers to have no boundary
3	Ideas, assumptions, conclusion are almost closed to public scrutiny	Ideas, assumptions, conclusion are open to scrutiny at appropriate level of expertise
4	Most of them do not acknowledge attempts for verification	Welcomes and encourages attempts for verification

HOW DOES A SCIENCE FOR CONSCIOUSNESS DIFFER FROM THE SCIENCE IN ITS PRESENT FORM?

Although Science for Consciousness is inclusive of science of matter and energy, it would be certainly different from the science of the 'rigid', 'compact', and 'dry' part of nature in the sense that it has to reconcile 'subjective' with 'objective', 'experiential' with 'experimental', values and aesthetics with form and structure. The process of this sciencing of the 'softer', 'wooly', 'wet' portion of nature, therefore, cannot remain independent of humanity and the science of 'self'. Unlike science in its present form, this new science would honour epistemological pluralism and is likely to strike a balance between epistemology and hermeneutics. In contrast to present science, ontological primacy and ontological relationship of various issues occupy most important position in Science for Consciousness. Reproducibility, although, remains the cornerstone for both forms of science, shared subjectivity, inter-subjective aggreability and inverted subjectivity (organic objectivity) would enter into the criteria for verification of Science for Consciousness. Conscious experience could be verified in a *sui generis* fashion. The currency of mechanics for present science does not include causal currency, which, however, remains most significant in the mechanics of consciousness. Inviolable constants under which present science works are the constants laid down by Einstein (velocity of light), Max Planck (Planck's constant), and Entropy barrier. In a Science for Consciousness, consciousness itself is the only constant. All other constants are flux in nature. Present science speaks in a language that is primarily left hemispheric. Quantification and measurability are considered a must there. Therefore, this is always positivistic. Science for Consciousness

DIFFERENCES BETWEEN PRESENT SCIENCE AND THE SCIENCE FOR CONSCIOUSNESS

Characteristics	Present Science	Science for Consciousness
1. Spectrum	Independent of Humanity. Keeps distance from Phenomenology	Inclusive of Humanity and Phenomenology
2. Deals with	'rigid', 'compact', 'dry' part of nature	'softer', 'wooly', 'wet' part of nature
3. Validation Criteria	(i) Reproducibility (ii) Objectivity	(i) Reproducibility (ii) Subjective sharing, Inter-subjective aggreability and Inverted subjectivity (organic objectivity) (iii) Verifiable in *sui generis* fashion
4. Epistemology	Epistemology is Dualistic/ Reductionistic	Honours epistemological pluralism. Epistemology is Non-dualistic/ Participatory/ Dwelling-in
&		
Hermeneutics	Little room for Hermeneutics	Likely to reconcile Epistemology with hermeneutics
5. Relevance of Ontology	Ontological issues are not important	Ontological primacy of issues and their interrelationship are most important
6. Inviolable Constant	Einstein's constant, Planck's constant, Entropy Barrier	Consciousness itself is inviolable constant. All other constants are flux in nature
7. Currency of Mechanics	Matter/Energy/Force Field/ Information	Includes causal currency and 'life', in addition to other currencies
8. Language	Primarily left-hemispheric	Bi-hemispheric language (e.g. language of *Vedānta, Gītā*)
9. Dimension of work	Primarily horizontal and limited vertical	Addresses vertical dimension, taking care of horizontal dimensions as well
10. Uncertainty & Boundary	'Helpless' in handling uncertainties Always seeks a boundary	Integrates uncertainties A science with 'no boundary'

speaks in a bihemispheric language. Integrated hemispheric transversion (where the left hemisphere behaves like right and right hemisphere as left) followed by an inversion of neuraxis (cerebral cortex is not only a perceiver but acts also as 'receptor') prepares the brain for expressing in a poetic language ('divine' rhyme) characterized by incredible clarity and profoundness (e.g., hymn of Vedas). Finally, present science works primarily in horizontal and rarely in vertical dimension which when it does, do it in a very limited manner. It also seeks a boundary without which it feels uncomfortable. The Science for

Consciousness, on the other hand, courageously addresses vertical dimension. It remains always open and loves to deal with profound uncertainties, the very characteristic of a system with no permanent boundary.

VI

FIVE IMPORTANT SUGGESTIONS FOR THE SCIENTISTS AND THE PHILOSOPHERS OF SCIENCE ENGAGED IN DEVELOPING A SCIENCE FOR CONSCIOUSNESS

Taking stock of why we failed leaves us composed. The sense of precarious and uncertain situation on the background of this composition initiates an ingenious step for learning

The limits of present science have been discussed and so also the problems in philosophy. The picture has been extended wherever possible. This section highlights what we are supposed to do if we are serious about developing a Science for Consciousness. Five suggestions[42] are offered in this context.

1. To Look Beyond the Constants set by Einstein, Max Planck, and Entropy barrier

The question is how? By exploring nonlocal communication Type I, II, and III. Nonlocal communication type I dissolves the barrier of space, type II dissolves that of time and type III of both space and time and transcends the intricacies of causality Documentation of nonlocal communications type I, and II, and proposition of existence of nonlocal communication type III pose challenge for velocity of light, Planck's constant and entropy barrier respectively.

Three constants under umbrella of which the present science works	The discipline of Science	Excludes possibility of	Challenged by the phenomenon of
1. Einstein's constant	The classical and Relativistic physics	Simultaneity of events	Nonlocal communication, Type I, dissolving 'space'
2. Planck's constant	The quantum physics	Continuity of events	Nonlocal communication, Type II, dissolving 'time'
3. Entropy barrier	Cybernetics	Identity of events	Nonlocal communication, Type III, dissolving 'space', 'time' and causal intricacies

2. To Learn to See through Death

The question is how? The scientists are already familiar with near-death experience. They are required to explore transcendental death experience, transformational death experience and experience of being reborn within the same body (born again). These profound experiences could be recorded in both first person's and third person's perspectives. For near-death experience, it has already been done. For other three phases too it is not impossible to do so. When the brain passes through the entire spectrum of death terrain, creative emergence becomes abundant. This may help to discover the missing pieces of the puzzle.

In this context, *Sāvitrī*[43] of Sri Aurobindo could be a very useful text that could offer guidelines for the scientists to conduct research in this direction. At the cell biology level, study of 'apoptosis' and the mechanics of 'malignant transformation' could be excellent models for unraveling the mystery of death and its transcension. In the discipline of Astrophysics, the path extends from black hole to white hole.

3. To Begin Exploration of Uncertainties at Various Levels

There is no uncertainty or indeterminism perceived in classical world (Plane I) in observation of conjugal properties of an object. In the quantum world (Plane II) uncertainty is observed during measurement between two observable conjugal properties of an object. At the terrain of formation of a black hole (Plane III), perceived uncertainty is observed between properties and the very existence of the object. The fusion of quantum language (Q-Language) and metaphysical language (M-Language) begins as one enters Plane III. At the level of the boundary of the universe (Plane IV), perceived uncertainty in observation could be recorded between 'existence' and 'no-existence', between 'Presence' and 'Absence'. At the level of the *Multiverse* (Plane V), perceived uncertainty plays between 'nonexistence' and 'a new existence', between 'Absence' and a 'New Presence'. Consciousness, I mean Unconditional Consciousness (Plane V) as a perceived reality, either does not exist or it exists as a Reality that is something new, novel, not hither-to-known.

These four levels of uncertainty depict four different depths of nature. On the basis of presence or absence of the perceived uncertainty for an observer-dependent reality and then on different levels/kinds/degrees of uncertainty, the total spectrum of nature in this scheme has been divided into five planes namely, classical world (Plane I), quantum world (Plane II), terrain of elementary phenomena like, life and death (black hole formation etc.) (Plane III), plane of Mother Nature (Plane IV) and plane of Unconditional Consciousness (Plane V).

Uncertainty is an issue of Science. It can be measured. For uncertainty at the level of quantum world, the famous equation of Heisenberg stands as follows.

$$\Delta Q \times \Delta P \textit{ is of the order of } h/2\pi$$

(where Q is the uncertainty about velocity and P is the uncertainty about position of an electron and h is Planck's constant, a definite number 6.63×10^{-27} erg. Sec.).

For an observer-dependent reality if one tries to measure other three uncertainties of three consecutive planes, their equations may be written as follows.

Δ *Conditioned* properties x ΔExistence *is of the order of* Mother Nature
(Mother Nature, the executive front of consciousness, is the only constant here)

Δ Existence x Δ Non-existence *is of the order of* Mother Nature-Consciousness
(The deep aspect of Mother's plane is indivisible from consciousness)

Δ Non-existence x Δ A new existence *is of the order of* Consciousness
(This is the plane of pure consciousness, non-negotiable, inscrutable)

Since these last three uncertainties are not measurable, the equation for planes III, IV or V appears absurd. This type of equation seems to be the products of brain incompletely surrendered to Unconditionality. With total active conscious surrender, the uncertainty itself suffers existential crisis. An equation of surrender replaces the equation of uncertainties. The results are illuminating. All measurements then appear trivial, a fabrication of the act of illusion or *Māyā* (compare the similarity in etymology of *māyā* and measurement). Which can be measured is called *māyā*. Or, only the *māyā* part is measurable. However, even without the desire or the capability of measurement, the feelings of uncertainty persist for sometime. Since the Plane IV is visualized as the plane where 'Purpose' is determined and the Plane V as the Plane for 'Will', uncertainty here, if any, appears to be a willful and purposeful illusion created by Consciousness-Mother Nature. As one continues to dwell within the Plane IV and Plane V, an equation of surrender is seen to grow. Concomitant feeding of relevant information clears most of the uncertainties and doubts.

Uncertainties are stemmed by an informationally open system by means of biologization of relevant information at appropriate levels. If there are four levels of uncertainty there should be four levels of quality of information. It amounts to extension of currency of conventional 'information' vertically further, or deeper within. There may be some special type of information like, qualified information, or a vital information that can change the life situation (live-information).

4. To Look Beyond and Cross the Boundary of the Universe

But how? It is the most difficult job for a seeker, explorer, or an experimenter of consciousness. It demands inside to be out and outside to be in. The only way to survive in this process is to surrender, surrender of properties, surrender of clothing of 'self'. It would be an active and total surrender to Unconditionality. Multiple universe(s) would be visible only then! The physics in these parallel universe(s) could be different in almost every respect, be it force, charge, mass or dimension. The cosmology and the astrophysics are required to invent new equations of relationship. Our universe is then no longer unique for its space, time or purpose. The centrality of the universe is no longer there. The central position is occupied by the Essence of the Multiversity.

While Zero-point Energy Paradigm (ZPE-Paradigm), proposed by some of the eminent physicists (e.g., H. Puthoff from Institute for Advanced Study, Austin, Texas), can lead us to the level of intergalactic space, the view of multiple universe centers us on the Essence of the Multiversity.

Assimilation of the concept of the Multiversity dissolves the uniqueness of the universe we inhabit almost the same way Copernican Revolution demolished the unique position of the Earth in the cosmos.

5. Finally we are to Reconcile and Connect Brain-bound Consciousness with the Brain-independent Consciousness

For consciousness there is no plural. Consciousness is singular, homogenous and indivisible. Heterogeneity is introduced by the presence of the brain or a brain-like structure that is engaged in dealing with the problems of consciousness. Consciousness works through the brain to produce conscious experience and to generate a sense of an experiencer, the One who experiences. It also works through nature's mechanics to produce natural phenomena and offers the possibility of (?) a cosmic/supracosmic existence (which people might have called God!). The same and one consciousness which is seen to work with the nature also works through the mechanics of the brain to result in conscious experience and the Being as the experiencer. The same and one consciousness, as seen in the brain, also works outside the brain through the mechanics of nature to produce natural phenomena and the existence of a cosmic/supracosmic Being (as God). The two terms, brain-bound and brain-independent consciousness, therefore, appear for the sake of description. Nevertheless, it is an important distinction. Consciousness as we understand ordinarily (as an awareness of surrounding, awareness of 'self' and awareness of one's own thoughts and feelings) and conscious experiences are relevant in the context of the brain. It is a recognized frontier for neuroscience. On the other hand the working mode of consciousness with nature are relevant in the context of phenomenology of the world, universe, multiverse (multiple universes) etc. It is a frontier for both the philosophers of science and the scientists. When consciousness works in concurrence with the working modes of the brain, one experiences it as brain-bound, brain-trapped, brain-confined consciousness. This is the same consciousness in nature that has been working in our brain to result in conscious experiences. When a mystic or a scientist of nature describes its presence in Nature and its working with Nature, it is described as working independent of the brain, independent of the presence or the absence of any brain anywhere, any time. One cannot call this anything but consciousness since it is the same consciousness of the brain that has been working with the nature quite independent of our existence or independent of any interpretation by the brain. This consciousness is not only brain-independent but also it works quite independent of the universe, the habitat for us. Big bang, in this sense, may be the just one of the stories of birth of one universe we live in.

VII

MECHANISM OF GENERATION OF 'AWARENESS' IN THE BRAIN: A GLIMPSE OF BRAIN-BOUND CONSCIOUSNESS

Whether consciousness emerges out of neuronal activity in the brain or consciousness uses this material (neural) infrastructure for manifestation of its own purpose is not conclusively known. The scientists favor the former view while the mystics and the spiritualists prefer the later. Let us have a glimpse of this consciousness within the brain.

In the splendur and grandeur of consciousness research, most of us are so enamoured by the so called 'higher' states of consciousness that we often afford to ignore the basic issue like, how we become aware of our surroundings or of our own thoughts and feelings. How and when the processing in the brain are brought to the threshold of conscious perception?

Is there any unconscious perception in the brain? The answer that crystallizes from the evidence of recent empirical research is all in affirmative. Are the consequences of unconscious perception anyway different from those of conscious perception? Yes, asserts Philip Merikle and Meredyth Daneman. They differ in cognitive and affective consequences. There is also difference in the duration of influence (? memory) of unconsciously and consciously perceived stimuli[44].

How these unconscious activities in the brain reach the level of conscious perception was an enigma till 1990. However, recent researches in neurophysiology and electrophysiology of neurons with electrocorticogram and basic electrophysiological recording of activities of cortical and deeper neurons along with the help of advanced technology like, PET and fMNR, have thrown some light on this mechanism of generation of 'awareness' in the brain.

Let me summarize the viewpoints of three eminent contributors in this field.

1. Karl H. Pribram[45]

Karl Pribram is one neuroscientist who introduces a holographic metaphor in the information processing of brain and genesis of awareness out of it. He finds content-addressable holographic like memory expressed in the language of the brain. His experimental research on monkeys and chimpanzees and clinical research on neurologically challenged persons suggests that the brain processes information in hierarchically located three-tier systems. Those are independent but interconnected with each other both in the sense of 'relational hierarchy' (working below upwards) and 'compositional hierarchy' (working above downwards). At the base there are automatic processing for reflexes with minimum synaptic delay and probabilities. He stresses on the existence of two other types of brain mechanism, one for referential or semantic processing and the other for conscious (which he calls episodic execution) processing. The former involves parieto-temporal lobe and the latter involves more anterior part of the brain namely fronto-limbic area and anterior temporal lobe. This three-tier processing system is self-regulated. Delay and probabilities are introduced more and more as the brain recruits the hierarchically placed higher circuitry. Conscious circuitry is eventually accessed with temporal course of events, may be with continuity of sensory stimulation and/or, by its lateral augmentation and/or, by central intervention.

2. Rodney Cotterill[46]

According to Cotterill, the complex phenomenon of generation of awareness is not merely dependent on the inputs from the sensory apparatus for perception, as was previously believed. It requires mandatory engagement of the subconscious proprioception from the muscle spindles, motor planning in the pre-motor area of frontal lobe and inputs from anterior cingulate gyrus (on apprehension of 'fear' or 'danger'). Interaction between thalamic intralaminar nuclei with other thalamic nuclei contributes to the emotional tone of consciousness.

Instead of breaking down the behavioral process into perception, cognition and action, the preference in Cotterill's view is to accept the composite picture of 'awareness' where perception and a kind of readiness for action are implicit in cognition. This is in complete consonance with the view 'Cognition Reclaimed', expressed in November/December, 1999 issue of *Journal of Consciousness Study.*

3. J. McFadden[47]

McFadden's theory on consciousness has been developed on the level of very basic neurophysics. According to his conscious electromagnetic information (*cemi*) field theory, 100 billion electrically active neurons generate an endogenous em field and a concomitant information field within the brain. And in this context, the brain processing can be bifurcated into two types:

(i) processing which is insensitive to endogenous electromagnetic field within the brain;

(ii) processing which is sensitive to endogenous electromagnetic field within the brain.

All former type of processing is unconscious processing and the latter comes under category of conscious processing. McFadden asserts,"The key to consciousness is not the presence of em fields, but their ability to transmit information to motor neurons.... Agents that disrupts the interaction between the brain's em field and neurons will induce unconsciousness."

"Although all neurons generate em fields," he continues, "natural selection has optimized the neurons firing capability and information-processing activity of only that fraction of the brain's em field that has contributed positively to host survival. Those em fields that have not contributed to host survival would have been invisible to natural selection and thereby remained unstructured and unlikely to influence motor neuron firing pattern."

Are these three views from classical neurophysiological point sufficient for explaining the genesis of 'awareness' in the brain? Probably not! Quantum physicists, the scientists from Neural network, Artificial Intelligence and Expert System groups, have their own stories to tell.

VIII

RECONCILIATION OF BRAIN-BOUND AND BRAIN-INDEPENDENT CONSCIOUSNESS

"When the great innovation appears, it will seem muddled and strange.
It will be only half understood by its discoverer and a mystery to everyone else.
For any idea that does not appear bizarre at first, there is no hope."

—Niels Bohr

Reconciliation of brain-bound consciousness and brain-independent consciousness is an important task ahead. It seems difficult but is not impossible! At present, five ways could be envisaged, which might be of some help to the consciousness scientist.

1. Understanding death while alive

It is a common religious belief that brain-bound consciousness and brain-independent consciousness get reconciled following death. However, it is not impossible to achieve it in one's own life, while one is alive. Reconciliation of brain-bound and brain-independent consciousness happens in life when one stems the tide of 'death', 'discontinuity' and 'uncertainty', while one sees 'life' as an extended reprieve from 'death'.

Four phases could be discernible while one sees through the phenomenon of death. Those are: near-death experience, transcendental death experience, transformational death experience and the experience of being reborn in the same body. I have already made an effort to describe these phases in the context of brain dynamics in the first chapter of *Conquering the Brain*[48], titled 'Experiencing death phenomena. Let the concept of death die.' All could have their neurological correlates. I am engaged in working on that. Hypothalamic 'spill-over', inter-hemispheric transversion and 'spill-over', shaking-up of the vertical neuraxis in the Triune brain and unification of brain-bound consciousness with brain-independent consciousness followed by the inversion of the neuraxis could be the respective gross neurological approximates of four phases of death. Sri Aurobindo, probably the most accomplished yogi in this context, experienced and expressed the whole spectrum of death including the experience of being reborn several times within an ever-transforming body in *Sāvitrī*[49] which could be a very useful text for the scientists to conduct research in delineating planes which one comes across during transcension of death while alive.

What could be this phenomenon of death in the language of the scientists who are engaged in exploration of nature of death? Death here could be seen as loss of existential properties, felt as an experience of *nothingness* (in the context of sensation, pleasure), *emptiness* (in the context of space), *stillness* (in the context of time) and *silence* (in the context of cause).

However,

"Not all silence is absence of cause,
Not all stillness is absence of time,
Not all emptiness is subatomic void,
Not all nothingness is absence of rhyme."

"There is silence which broods cause!
There is stillness, which generates time with pause!
There is void from which the universe is born
Ananda shines when nothingness is torn."

—Conquering the Brain, p 200

The exploration of death requires understanding of voids of different kinds, different ontological levels of uncertainty, different types of nonlocal communication, different qualitative levels of 'information' and the Brain-phenomena when the brain is challenged with death.

How does the brain handle this 'death phenomenon'? By developing new integration within it, by means of biologization of relevant information at appropriate level and thereby overcoming various depths of uncertainty.

2. Exploration of Quantum Discontinuity and Subsequent Uncertainties at Different Ontological Levels

Death has long been considered a metaphysical issue. However, discontinuity is not merely a metaphysical issue. It is a scientific issue as well. Uncertainty has been recognized as an issue for science by quantum scientists. That quantum description of nature seems to be an incomplete one is self-evident from the fact that quantum mechanics cannot and does not describe phenomena that are supposed to occur in-between quanta. Those are the phenomena at the depth of quantum discontinuity embedded within nature in between two 'discrete' states of particle/wave-package of energy behaving in a quantum way. While the mystics explore consciousness penetrating through the 'gap' (both in 'space' and 'time') separating two 'thoughts', the scientists engaged in consciousness research are to penetrate in between the two quantum states of a quantum existence. There they are to confront with uncertainties that are altogether different from Heisenberg's uncertainty. To measure those uncertainties and to learn how to overcome those uncertainties are the right kind of endeavour to delve into the domain of consciousness, which is independent of brain. For astrophysicists, the path extends from black hole to white hole.

3. Exploration of 'Mind'

The philosophers may prefer to attend the problem in a different way. If consciousness is singular, how can it be two? What is this dualism about? What communicates with what? Is our formulation of the problem correct? Answer to all these questions could be found with the introduction of the concept of 'mind'. It is mind which cuts consciousness into two. Destruction of mind, i.e., *mono-loy* or *mono-nash*, is said to be the beginning of experience of conscious. In monistic experience, consciousness is one and only one. As soon as dualism appears, the mind comes in between. Mind could be defined as the organ of communication between two conscious systems. Mind is a part of both nature and consciousness. At the extreme end mind, like nature, is also connected with consciousness. An effort has been made in the first chapter of *Conquering the Brain*[50] to explore this mind. A model of mind, consisting of three 'voids' with two intervening tunnels, has been made to look further into this problem. It may therefore be stated that the brain-dependent consciousness and the brain-independent consciousness communicate through their respective nature that includes 'mind' in the core.

4. Exploration of Modes of Communication between Intracerebral and Extracerebral Consciousness

The scientists again may pick up the thread here by looking at the nature inside the brain and the nature outside the brain. It is the nature inside the brain, which communicates with the nature outside the brain. What could be the route of such communication? Conventional sensory route or something unconventional like transcranial and transcerebral communication! Since 1985, in all of my presentations[51], I have been mentioning that the apical dendrites of the cerebral cortical neurons in general and their sensitive spines in particular, are responsible for communication between within and outside (outside the cranium) the brain. The apical dendrites come from the pyramidal neurons of the cerebral cortex. These neurons constitute about sixty to seventy percent of all cells of cerebral cortex and have two groups of dendrites, the basal small dendrites and one long, straight, stout, apical dendrite which intertwines with others to form a dentritic mat over the surface of the cortex. This dendritic mat formed at the topmost layer of cerebral cortex forms a very sensitive membrane where electrical dipoles are found in constantly shifting dynamics. In the evolutionary journey of the brain, the dendritic mat emerges as a crucial structure to play an important role in establishing cortico-supracortical communication. The possible modus operandi of this communication may be listed as follows. It would be easier to discuss this interaction in relation to the planes of the nature.

In the classical plane of nature (Plane I), (i) scalar field interaction remains a possible way of communication between this superficial dendritic mat of cerebral cortex and the nature outside. (ii) Secondly, one seriously has to consider the electromagnetic field within the brain, over the cortex and outside the meninges, skull and scalp. As an extension of this interaction one may like to go to the deeper level of brain for transcranial magnetic interaction between inside and outside of brain. Glial cells, I think, have the potential to get involved in this interaction.

In the quantum plane of nature (Plane II), there are three possible ways of communication. (i) Bose-Einstein condensation at the level of the spines of the apical dendrites of the cortical neurons, (ii) the quantum events at the perineural and synaptic spaces of the brain working in dynamic communication with 'quantum sea' of nature outside the brain, and (iii) the brain behaving as a macro-quantum object and communicating nonlocally (type I). One is required to consider the interaction amongst many-body quantum systems (MBQS) in the brain, in the context of existing suggestions in physics (Jain, 2002)[52] regarding cross over from fermionic to bosonic behaviour and vice versa.

In the Plane III of nature, there are seemingly three ways of communications as well. (i) Brain, behaving as a macro-quantum object and nonlocal communication type II may prevail. (ii) There could be 'information' exchange between 'inside' and 'outside' of the brain. The brain becomes supposedly 'open' informationally while voyaging through plane III of nature. Conscious electromagnetic information (cemi) field theory of Johnjoe McFadden (2002)[53] is worth exploring in this connection. This theory "identifies consciousness with only that component of brain e m field that is capable of downloading its information to motor neurones". The theory, although, does not imagine any supracortical extension in its present form, bears the potential, in my opinion, for helping exploration of the issue of cortico-supracortical communication through the possible inter-conversion of energy, field, information and causal currency has been discussed in the *Millennium Bridge*[54]. As McFadden has been exploring consciousness that is brain-trapped, he is justified to be emphatic in his theory to exclude any possibility of communication between extracranial electromagnetic field and intracerebral electromagnetic field. I am of the opinion that he is right for all ordinary circumstances, for the phenomena in Plane I and may be in Plane II. If outside information continuously bombards the brain one can imagine the chaos and the subsequent 'pathos' the brain has to combat with. However, there could be situations when extracranial electromagnetic field and intracerebral electromagnetic field do communicate, precisely in those situations which bear evolutionary potential, namely Love, Sex, Ego, Life and Death i.e., Plane III phenomena. (iii) Finally, the omnipresent neutrinos, in connivance with the 'weak force' of nature, may successfully bombard on the photon-phonon signaling system of neurons of the brain while the brain voyages through Plane III. Neutrinos, photon, phonon and conformon are, in my text (*Conquering the Brain*[55] and *Millennium Bridge*[56]), phenomenal hands of Mother Nature. Neutrinos that have been ceaselessly bombarding on the brain can get a hand of photon/ phonon transduction system in the neuronal membrane. Left-handed neutrinos can influence Weak Force (Klauber, R. D[57]) and through Electro-weak interaction they may influence the electromagnetic field where photon and phonon form the substratum.

In Plane IV, one additional way of communication between brain-bound and brain-independent consciousness could be nonlocal communication type III.

These are the nine suggested mechanisms for an 'open' brain depicting nine ways of communication between the natures of brain-bound and brain-independent consciousness.

The Crux of the Problem in 'Sciencing' Supracortical Consciousness: The crux of the problem for a scientist in exploring supracortical consciousness is to show that a specific pattern of some kind of physical (or nonphysical) force/energy/field, effective outside the cranium can act transcranially through the scalp, skull and meninges and lead to some kind of subjective experience expressed as 'Love'. Any subjective experience is generally produced following a sensory activity in the brain. For example, when the light falls on retina or a sound strikes the organ of corti in the ear or the smell of a rose stimulates the olfactory epithelium etc. Subjective experience often is generated independent of sensory stimulation, even without the presence of any sensory stimulation, as a direct effect of 'thought' as shown by recent PET and SPECT studies. The question is, could the subjective experience be produced by any specific pattern of some kind of force/energy/field acting on the cerebral cortex from outside the cranium? In other words, this is to show whether the cerebral cortex can have properties of 'receptor'! The 'receptor', in such case, would be for transcranial physical/nonphysical force/energy/field. If no known physical force is found to be involved, could it be an action of some nonphysical force/energy/field? If it is a nonphysical force/energy/field in nature, then at the present stage it seems to be only speculative. Should nonphysical force/energy/field exist, there could be two possible ways of this interaction. The first one includes a nonphysical-physical connection (transformation), following which the physical force acts on the cerebral cortex. Here, the receptor in the cerebral cortex would be meant for physical force/energy/field only. As a second possibility, the nonphysical force is supposed to act directly on the cerebral cortex without prior transformation into physical force/energy/field. The receptor on the cerebral cortex in this case is meant for non-physical force/energy/field only.

Nonphysical force/energy/field meant here may be the part of nonlocal communications of various types, or may be of some kind of ontologically higher level of information. Physical force/energy/field could be electromagnetic force/energy/field, weak force, and/or gravity. Walter Freeman (1999)[58], Susan Pockett (2000 and 2002)[59] and Johnjoe McFadden (2002)[60] have already made the case for electromagnetic field, although none of them has thought of any supracortical relevance of their respective theory.

The connection between physical and non-physical could be established by tracing Neutrino, Photon, Phonon and Conformon respectively through Neutrino equivalent of consciousness (Neut-E-Consc.), Photon equivalent of consciousness (Phot-E-Consc.), Phonon equivalent of consciousness (Phon-E-Consc.) and Conformon equivalent of consciousness (Conf-E-Consc.) as suggested in *Conquering the Brain*[61] and in *The Millennium Bridge*[62].

Distinguishing Supracortical Consciousness from Supracortical Phenomena: It would be better if we distinguish supracortical consciousness from supracortical phenomena.[63] Manifestation of supracortical consciousness is a subjective experience of Love, objectively manifested as creativity. For supracortical phenomena it is not so. It is usually a remote sensing, clairvoyance, clairaudience, etc. In the course of experience of both supracortical phenomena and supracortical consciousness the 'receptor' property of cerebral cortex is involved. Both of them appear inexhaustible within cortical limits (for examples, till the neurotransmitters are exhausted in case of focal epileptic fit, or the brain fails to retain its integrity during a sensory hallucination). However, in supracortical phenomena, usually the 'windows' of the brain (the sensory/motor association areas) are involved. The brain as a whole is never involved. Supracortical consciousness, on the other hand, is an outcome of integrated global response from the brain, although it originates from the vortex of the cerebral cortex. Besides, at the extreme end of the experience of supracortical phenomena the integrity of the brain may be threatened. The mechanisms of supracortical phenomena and supracortical consciousness are also suggested to be different. Nonlocal communication type I (dissolving the barrier of space) or type II (dissolving the barrier of time) might be involved in supracortical phenomena. Nonlocal communication type III that dissolves both the barriers of space and time and transcends the intricacies of causality, has been suggested to be the mechanism to effect supracortical consciousness.

5. The Mystic's way of Reconciliation. Using Self-consciousness as a Tool

In the process of reconciliation of brain-bound and brain-independent consciousness, the mystics might have a unique option. He uses self-consciousness as a tool in this endeavour.

Self-consciousness, as told, is the first step of nature in her attempt to free consciousness from the shackles of the brain, from the confines of neural entanglement, from the cage of neural networking. The mystic, although, begins with classical 'self' he relies more on the 'quantum self'. In the course of this onward journey for the search for more and more freedom, the 'self' sheds off its 'classical' properties and then also the quantum properties. In Plane III, it gets de-conditioned from elementary phenomena. Radical transformation occurs in Plane IV. In the process, self's nature becomes Mother Nature and the 'self' is realized as consciousness.

There is another way the mystics use self-consciousness as tool. Self-consciousness is used as *witness consciousness.* It begins with observations of the contents of consciousness, the external contents and then the internal contents. The process is graduated to a higher level when observation of the observer starts. The self starts observing the observer. In each step upward, it observes the observer in the downstream and continues to do so till eventually his back touches the unconditional consciousness. Then follows an about turn. The self becomes face to face with its origin.

In both the procedures, there are two important processes worth mentioning here. The first is the process of *Surrender.* An active, conscious, one-pointed and total surrender to the Unconditionality is the beginning of real reconciliation. The second is the Grace phenomenon.[64] During all these efforts made by 'self', the brain gets elevated to the State of Grace and the omnipresent Grace could get hold of the brain to result in Supreme Consummation.

The Boundary Issue Brings Us Back to the Very Basic: The crux of the problem in reconciliation of brain-bound consciousness with the brain-independent consciousness, however, could also be stated as some unique philosophical or scientific issues. For example, how the Infinite gets confined into a finite system? Or, how a finite system could be connected with the Infinite? Or, how a system can behave in both finite and infinite ways simultaneously?

It would be fruitful to look, in this context, into the working mode of *Prāṇa. Prāṇa* could be simultaneously finite and infinite. Ordinarily meaning, it is breathing, the act of respiration. Traced to the subtlety, it goes to the 'pace maker' neurons of Apneustic center, Pneumotaxic center, Inspiratory center, and Expiratory centers at the brainstem. Mystically perceived, it goes back to the generation of spontaneity, the '*Prāṇa*' in nature. *Prāṇa* is an expression in metaphysical language (M-language)! What could be representation of *Prāṇa* in quantum language (Q-language)? I often sense a major role of neutrinos in this representation. Neutrinos[65] are probably able to connect a photon-phonon-conformon operated finite system with the domain of the Infinite.

Communication of a finite system with the Infinity would be certainly nonlocal. Then, the questions can be framed in the following ways. How does local communication reconcile with nonlocal communication? Or, how nonlocal communication becomes ultimately able to deliver the message to a locally communicating system? For the new physics it is an attractive frontier of research.

When a finite system communicates with the Infinity, the interesting process that begins is Evolution. In the process of evolution locality and nonlocality work together and the finite system is seen to communicate with the Infinity. Today's human being is the outcome of such process continuing over millions of years. The only organ of the human being where evolution is yet to be completed is the brain. Brain is an organ that acts locally and can communicate nonlocally. And here, we require again focusing on neuroscience.

'Chaos' in the Brain and Supracortical Consciousness: It is Lorente de No, a student of Raman y Cajal, who in 1929 first demonstrated the presence of an axo-dendritic feedback loop in the neuron by Golgi staining. Lorente could not publish this paper because of strong opposition from his teacher. The paper was published in 1934 after Cajal died. This observation initiated a totally new era for the growth of neural assembly, neural network and self-organization concept in the brain. Interestingly the brain, today, is known to have all three types of *attractors* namely, Point attractor, Cyclic attractor and Chaotic attractor with their respective 'attractor basin' of functioning.

Sit quietly and observe the bubbles of thought arising on the canvas of mind. Are these outcomes of spontaneous neuronal firing from a chaotic pool? Observe the spurt of confusing and purposeless movements of a puppy or a kitten left of its own. Are these movement results of chaotic firings from the cortical motor neurons? Watch out the hysterical outburst of emotion of the wife of a police officer implicated in a murder? Could it be an uncensored limbic chaos expressed while reasons fail to act? Look at the seizure of a patient suffering from epilepsy, may be grand mal, petit mal, psychomotor or temporal lobe epilepsy! Do these involuntary spontaneous outbursts result from a deliberate escape of the neuronal chaotic processes from a normally existing censoring mechanism! These are important issues which the chaos-scientists are busy in addressing.

How is the 'order' brought out of the seemingly chaotic activity in the network of spontaneously firing of millions of cortical and limbic neurons? Intervention by 'consciousness' could be a possible mechanism. However, how consciousness does remain an important issue in connecting consciousness with chaos. The feed forward and feed back loops in the cortical neuropil are not closed loops. The loops remain 'open' at the level of the neuro-neuronal junctions (chemical synapses, electrical synapses and tight junctions). And possibly, those junctions are the meeting ground for the classical fields inside the brain and the classical fields outside the brain, the quantum world inside the brain and the quantum world outside the brain, the informational fields inside the brain and the informational fields outside the brain. Therefore, 'chaos' in the brain seems compatible with the existence of supracortical consciousness. And, who knows with supracortical consciousness embodied in the brain, the 'chaos' there may look completely different (as source of new creation) from what it appears now.

IX

NINE PLANES OF CONSCIOUSNESS. BRAIN-BOUND OR BRAIN-INDEPENDENT

"Every truth passes through three stages before it is recognized. In the first, it is ridiculed. In the second, it is opposed. In the third, it is regarded as self-evident."

—Arthur Schopenhauer

In this section we would present Nanoune model for both Brain-bound and Brain-independent consciousness.[66]

Nanoune Model for Brain-bound Consciousness

Let us describe now nine planes of the brain-bound consciousness and conscious experience. Consciousness in relation to the brain is responsible for conscious experience and generation of a sense of an experiencer.

Consciousness uses different modes of the brain to produce conscious experience. The brain usually works in six modes. The first three are in the modes of brainstem, limbic system, and the cerebral cortex (the Triune brain). The next three milestones have been proposed in my works.[67] Those are in supracortical mode.

Brainstem-cortical mode results in experience of brainstem consciousness by which one becomes awake, alert, and oriented. Limbico-cortical mode results in experience of limbic system consciousness, a motivation-guided consciousness to seek pleasure and avoid the unpleasant. In the cortico-cortical mode there is experience of cortical consciousness characterized by unitary experience and the ability to discriminate, analyze, reason out and judge.

The brain can also work in supracortical mode. There are three successive ontological milestones of the Being in this direction namely supracortical being, supracortical godhead and supracortical autonomy. Consciousness in supracortical direction is characterized by its apparent 'inexhaustibility' within cortical limits and is manifested as 'Love' which could be identified as sacrifice for the beloved. Whatever love and sacrifice one observes in day to day practice could be because of successful expedition of supracortical consciousness through numerous obscurities of the infrastructure of the nervous system. Another manifestation of supracortical consciouness is creativity, creative emergence and new creation. The next ontological milestone is supracortical godhead. There are two additional characteristic features expressed in such personality. Those are 'magnetic' attractability and a super-intellect or spiritual intelligence. Lord Krișṇa or Lord Rāma's (God-figures in Hindu mythology) station of the being was probably in this platform. The apparently final milestone is that of a supracortical autonomy where the whole of the brain behaves as an automatic and autonomic instrument of the 'Divine'. In the manifest personality of this state of consciousness two added features are personification of 'eternal yea' and 'melting love'. The person has no option but to love profoundly and to affirm forever. Multiple universe(s)/Many world theory is a reality in this stage of the Being. In India, such elevated or evolved personality has been traditionally regarded as *Sadguru*. Ramkrishna Paramahansa, Guru Nanak, Ramana Maharshi and Sri Aurobindo are some of the rare examples of the Being in such station of existence.

In all these existence of the Being, consciousness remains brain-bound. One can call this brain-bound consciousness as *Jīvātman*. In the English language, it is *'soul'*. According to the station of the being, the person could be described as a 'captive' soul or a 'great' soul etc. There is another interesting thing to note here that has already happened in the relationship between brain and consciousness. This is the emergence of self-consciousness. It has manifested following consolidation of cortical consciousness in the Triune brain. Emergence of self-consciousness is the first attempt of consciousness to free itself from the shackles of the brain. Sir John C. Eccles and Karl Popper were absolutely precise to put a title in their celebrated book, *The Self and its Brain* where it is meant that the brain belongs to 'self'! This 'self', in its absoluteness may be what the *Vedāntins* might have called *Ātman*. Brain-independent consciousness in this sense, is non-anthromorphic nondual consciousness that the Vedāntins might have called *Paramātman*.

The 'self' may identify itself with any of the six modes of the brain. According to the station of self-consciousness one gets *a chain of Being*, may be compared with the Great chain (or nest) of Being. The Great chain (or nest) of Being in perspective of neuropsychology starts from Brainstem being, Limbic being, Cortical being and leads to Supracortical being, Supracortical godhead and Supracortical autonomy.

It seems clear that as the 'self' moves higher through the ontological ladder, the gap between the brain-bound consciousness and the brain-independent consciousness becomes narrower. They attempt to reach a point of singularity. The experiences of *Jīvātman, Ātman,* and *Paramātman* are, therefore, additional experiences independent of Being-experience occurring at six ontological levels. In this sense one gets 6 + 3 = 9 kinds of conscious experience in the total spectrum. This is a 'Nanoune' model in the spectrum of conscious experience, experiencer, and the brain-bound consciousness.

Nanoune Model for Brain-independent Consciousness

We have already discussed the Pentaune model of nature and consciousness. However, the classical plane of the Pentaune model of nature does not form the rock bottom of nature. There is a huge 'unconscious' underneath it. The scientists are not yet sure of these unconscious planes in the nature. One becomes more certain of unconscious processing in nature by observing unconscious processing within the brain. Taking the 'cue' from the unconscious processing inside the brain, the 'unconscious' underneath the classical conscious world could be described as having four distinct planes corresponding to four planes overlying it. Respectively those are the plane of fringe consciousness, the plane of implicit perception and memory, the plane of fringe unconscious and rock bottom unconscious. These four unconscious planes have their respective mechanics too. The Science for Consciousness in the third millennium is to account for each of these nine mechanics (Nanoune model i.e. nine inseparable planes of Nature and consciousness) as nine divisions of the In-divisible (*A-khaṇda*) consciousness.

Are these two Nanoune Models Independent or Connected?

The Nanoune model of consciousness and conscious experience inside the brain and the Nanoune model of the mechanics of Nature and Consciousness outside the brain are not mutually exclusive. Sometimes I wonder that the characteristics of personalities like, Supracortical being, Supracortical godhead and Supracortical autonomy (*Sadguru*) could be accomplished by an evolving brain integrating the respective uncertainty of different planes of nature by the process of biologization/systemization of relevant information.

Exploration of the functions of the brain by traditional methods (SPECT, PET, fMNR, MEG, EEG etc.) at the classical plane seems more rewarding in the context of brain's unconscious processing. However, those could also be used to measure and record the representation of super-conscious planes at the classical level. Exploration of inter-convertibility of Energy, Field, Form, Information, Causal currency and Life remains the key in establishing the mutual interdependence of the two models.

A Simpler Nanoune Model for Researchers of Consciousness

This exploration takes the simpler route starting from where we stand to reach the state of content-free consciousness. Next, it confronts 'death phenomenon' in its entirety to reach Mother Nature's domain. Finally, the stream and the ocean, the sparkling and the origin become One. To begin with, there is (i) discontinuous stream of conscious experience on the background of a 'self'. (ii) Self-consciousness offers the ownership to these experiences. By practice, one is able to experience (iii) content-free consciousness. Transcension of the voids/death terrain follows. It passes through. (iv) Near-death experience, (v) Transcendental death experience, (vi) Transformation death experience, culminating in the (vii) Experience of getting re-born within the same body. Phase (vii) is not possible till one gains access to (viii) plane of Mother Nature which is nothing but the nature of consciousness. Unconditional consciousness forms the plane (ix) in this model.

CONTENTLESS CONSCIOUSNESS, TRANSCENDENTAL CONSCIOUSNESS, BRAIN-INDEPENDENT CONSCIOUSNESS AND SUPRACORTICAL CONSCIOUSNESS

The western philosophers (e.g. Jonathan Shear from Virginia Commonwealth University, USA, also Associate editor, *Journal of Consciousness Studies*) and the scientists (e.g. John G.

Taylor[68], Department of Mathematics, King's College, London and James Austin, Professor of Neurology and the author of *Zen and the Brain*[69]) have recently laid emphasis on the empirical existence of *contentless consciousness*, the consciousness which is free of intentional contents. Simply, it is devoid of any content originated internally or externally.

When consciousness is devoid of externally originated contents, it still may be full of internally originated contents as it happens during dreamy (REM) sleep. In dreamless (NREM) sleep, internally originated contents are also absent from consciousness. Dreamless sleep consciousness could be an example of contentless consciousness. Everyone experiences this during dreamless sleep. With practice of meditation, it is possible to remain 'awake' while one's brain has been passing through the state of dreamless sleep. The experience of contentless consciousness is, therefore, an experience equivalent of deep (dreamless) sleep while one is awake. I do not think, there is anything transcendental in it. However, this may be considered an extraordinary personal accomplishment when one gains the ability to experience it in full-awake condition. It can also be regarded as an achievement for science to demonstrate its existence empirically. Finally, it is the stepping stone for experiencing transcendental consciousness.

What is transcendental consciousness then? It is an experience past the complete passage through 'death', while one is alive. While experience of contentless consciousness may be described as an experience of dreamless sleep in the awakened state, the experience of transcendental consciousness would require a transit through death while one is alive. To understand/realize the phenomenon of transcension is, therefore, to understand/realize the phenomenon of death in its entirety.

Therefore, as long as one follows *Maṇḍūkya Upaniṣad,* to understand wakeful consciousness (*jāgrata*), dream consciousness (*swapna*) and dreamless consciousness (*susupti*), one is through and all right with first three states of consciousness. However, while one sojourns from the third state to the 'fourth state' (*Turīya*) of consciousness, one requires a practical transcension of 'death', the boundaries of space, time and purpose. All accomplished mystics who have experienced this fourth state of consciousness, have experienced it following complete transcension of death, the 'great void' of nothingness, emptiness, stillness and silence.

On the more, contentless consciousness, in the context of the view of above-mentioned scientists and philosophers, is a brain-bound consciousness. Transcendental consciousness may present as contentless too. However, the contentless consciousness, par se, is not transcendental. Brain-independent consciousness is an example of transcendental consciousness.

Here is another paradox. Brain-independent consciousness could be identified within the brain in the context of dynamics of the brain. Brain-trapped consciousness could be, on the other hand, far from the structure of the brain.

When one experiences transcendental (brain-independent) consciousness paradoxically by the brain itself, the process of 'transformation' of the underlying psycho-somatic apparatus begins. The first milestone of experience in this direction has been designated as the experience of supracortical consciousness.

Subjective Awareness, Objective Awareness and Supracortical Consciousness

Awareness may be 'subjective' or 'objective'. For example, my twelve-year-old daughter can sing beautifully a French music without feeling any of the meaning conveyed in its rhyming words. She is objectively aware of the song, correct pronunciation, and its rhyme. She is capable of playing with it without any trace of subjectivity in the interaction.

Karl Pribram[70], in a different context, suggests existence of two kinds of awareness, 'egocentric' and 'allocentric', having two different 'brain mechanisms' for them. Egocentric awareness is episodic, executive and involves more anterior part of the brain, the fronto-limbic system. Allocentric awareness is referential, semantic and involves more posterior part of the brain, parieto-temporal or temporo-occipital (in case of visual perception) region. Both mechanisms, although can act independently, are interconnected and one can influence the other. Two mechanisms, he speculates may be dissociated in cases of 'blindsight' where the patient shows unconscious vision-guided behavior.

The term blindsight was coined by Weiskrantz[71] in 1974, stating that there is denial of acknowledged awareness although the patient retain the ability to detect, localize and discriminate visual stimuli presented in his blind field. This develops following a lesion in the visual sensory cortex in the occipital lobe. The lesion is usually unilateral. Blindsight, however, is not the only case of dissociation of two kinds of awareness. Pribram[72] often sites the example of a case of history of 'Neglect' where the patient is unaware of having her left arm although she is able to use it, unconsciously for everyday purpose. This develops following a lesion in the light temporo-parietal cortex as confirmed by E.E.G. Carlo A Marzi[73] distinguishes two types of blindsight, normal and abnormal. In normal blindsight, the person is without any demonstrable organic brain lesion.

Subjective and objective awareness are found disconnected while one has been undergoing a death-terrain experience. Narratives from the patients who underwent Near-death experience reveal that the patient was aware of what all had been happening in the surroundings without any subjective experience of pain or discomfort in his organ or in the body.

This dissociation of subjective and objective awareness could also be seen in case of experience of supracortical consciousness in its early formative stage. Supracortical consciousness is characterized by its inexhaustibility within cortical limits. It is manifested by subjective experience of Love and Divinity. Its objective manifestation is creativity. In the early stage, it is possible for a person to experience Divinity and Love without any visible objective parameter of creativity. On the other hand, one may be inexhaustibly creative, for example, linking concepts, connecting ideas, joining different categories, and building up new context, new meaning or even judging high level creativity without any subjective experience of Love or Divinity.

Probably, the mechanism synchronizing and harmonizing two neural mechanics of subjective and objective awareness goes out of run following supracortical opening and it is regained and consolidated with supracortical consciousness gradually getting embodied in the brain.

X

TOWARDS A NEW EVOLUTIONARY ACCOMPLISHMENT

"Are you God?" they asked the Buddha.
"No", he replied.
"Are you an angel then?" "No."
"A saint?" "No."
"Then what are you?"
Replied the Buddha, "I am awake."

—Huston Smith

Awakening is the first step for evolution. Human consciousness is nothing but an awareness of 'difference in the process of making' (Hegel). And practically, "nothing in biology makes sense except in the light of evolution", asserted Dobzhansky.

The important question ponders, could this nine plane model either of brain-confined or brain-independent consciousness or a composite one be achieved and perfected by the present state of the Triune Brain (of P. D. MacLean)? Probably not! Are we then not taking adequate care of an evolutionary imperative hidden in the brain?

The brain is structurally a polylithic organ. Vertically it has three evolutionary components namely, the reptilian brain, the mammalian brain and the human brain. The present brain is, therefore, vertically a triune structure. Horizontally it also consists of two hemispheres, the left hemisphere and the right hemisphere, evolved and differentiated on cultural pressure (lateralization). The brain is the only organ of the body where one can recognize landmarks for both vertical and horizontal growth. And, this process of evolution has not stopped for the brain. Why? Because, the brain is also an organ where 'locality' and 'nonlocality' embrace, where nonlocal communication could be demonstrated by a locally acting system. And, evolution is the hallmark of the system where nonlocal communication can effect on a locally communicating system. If it is so, would we then eventually land up to own a new brain? Probably yes!

Julian Huxley is known to have looked for 'A Science of Human Possibilities'. Possibly at the farthest reaches of exploration of this science, we would develop a *Brain* of the Brain over the cerebral cortex which would usher a transition of present *homo sapiens* to future *homo spiritualis*! The first tangible milestone in this direction is an awareness that could be recorded as *supracortical consciousness*. To become aware of the brain-independent consciousness paradoxically by the brain-trapped consciousness is the beginning of supracortical journey. The first step for this is to take off from the cerebral cortex and to look up! And here, again quite paradoxically, we require focusing on Neuroscience in the context of profound spiritual experiences.

AWAKENED STATE AND EVOLUTION

What did this awakened state mean to Buddha? Who knows! Unless one becomes Buddha how does one know of it? The problem lies here! However, we are free to go through an 'imagery' here.

Buddha is awake! He is certainly alert and oriented (brain-stem consciousness). His motivation is streamlined for this awakened state (limbic system consciousness). His 'self' is awake intellectually, judgmentally (cortical consciousness). He is inexhaustibly awake (supracortical consciousness). He is awake in daytime, awake at night, awake round the clock, awake in all seasons, awake in sufferings and awake in pleasure! He is awake throughout the axiological stairs of values, the rules of nature, the mechanics of the cosmos. He is awake in phenomenological jungle. His awakened state is so impressive that any fortunate one who has seen of it, heard of it or has honestly imagined of it, gets 'magnetically' attracted towards him (supracortical Godhead status of Buddha). His awakened state is literally 'transforming' for all those brains, which are capable of sensing it, cognizing it, intending it (supracortical Godhead). He is awake in his full autonomy as an observer and is awake to participate in the play of creative cosmos. Being awake, he reaches the fountainhead of the creative cosmos (supracortical autonomy).

In this awakened state, the consciousness within the brain gains mastery over the entire spectrum of nature (cf. Darwinian concept of nature remains confined to classical plane only). The brain is classically poised from the base level of sensation to that of highest level of volition and 'free will', from the base camp of primitive reflexes to the highest echelon of cognitive probing, from the level of the muscle spindle to the level of premotor area of frontal lobe and anterior cingulate gyrus (to express in the language of Rodney Cotterill[74]). Astonishingly, there is also classical-quantum correspondence (may be at the level of 40-60 Hz oscillators in the brain)! Brain is seen to behave as a 'marco-quantum' organ, which seems open to nonlocal communication. The 'Quantum Sea' outside the brain and the 'quantum streams' inside the brain are in the state of equipoise. The brain is steady and ready to combat 'death' phenomenon. It is awake to see through the entire terrain of 'death'/ 'discontinuity'/'uncertainties'. The brain appears informationally 'open'. It is 'awake' for acquisition of some 'new', vital, life changing information (information which is 'alive') to help the mankind to come out of their present imprisonment. The electromagnetic field of the classical brain which can download information to its motor neurons (to express in the language of McFadden[75]) may be able to exchange information related to the outside electromagnetic field. The brain is 'awake' to realize the 'magnetic monopole' of nature (Mother Nature's plane) in brain dynamics. The brain is poised to participate in the dynamics of creative inter-universal Essence.

In this stage, it is certainly difficult for anyone to imagine what could be the impact of such extraordinary experience on the brain itself, on the body itself! Embodiment of such experience, certainly, will have a life-changing effect.

Profound Spiritual Experience and Evolution

Profound experiences of 'supracosmic'/ 'supracortical' consciousness, even for once, have life-changing, transforming, even paradigmogenic potential. This is in contrast to the experience of 'ego'-losing, 'ecstatic' altered state of consciousness of psychedelic origin even when it is experienced repeatedly The former experiences initiate a life-changing process of evolution in the brain by which one gains ability to modulate his/her old reflexes and acquires new reflexes ("*raison d'être* of consciousness is reflex modification and acquisition of new reflexes."—Rodney Cotterill).

I visualize the whole scenario in the following way.

In the course of exploration of consciousness while the 'self', as it is understood in worldly measures, journeys to establish identity with the universal/transuniversal/ interuniversal consciousness, there happens a serious reorientation of the structures and the functions of the brain. Structurally polylithic brain starts behaving as a functional monolith. The brain starts behaving as a macro-quantum object and participates in nonlocal communication, type I, II and III. I have proposed in my works[76] of three kinds of synchronization resulting from such a situation. Those are (i) synchronization of left and right hemispheres, (ii) synchronization of three vertical components of the brain, and (iii) synchronization of inside and outside of the brain.

Darwinian theory of natural selection speaks of selection pressure confined to classical plane of nature. Also, Darwin was silent on consciousness. However, the evolution we are concerned with would be a conscious evolution of the brain journeying through classical, quantum and elemental planes of nature under the respective selection pressure of different kind of uncertainties to secure a station within the plane of Mother Nature (Plane IV of nature). This station of brain could be described as the *State of Grace*[77]. To perceive and experience the *'Grace'* the brain is required to be elevated to the *State of Grace*[78]. In the *State of Grace*, three kinds of synchronization as mentioned above, are supposed to be in near-completion phase. In such extraordinary state[79], in the course of information processing and responsivity of brain, one finds little hemispherical bias. Stair-asynchrony is conspicuous by its absence. There is complete synchronization of the inside and the outside of the brain as well. In this state, while the brain remains in the 'State of Grace', the omnipresent, omniscient Grace can capture the brain to use it as a transmissive organ of Mother Nature. This is 'Supreme Consummation' (Sri Aurobindo).

> In the abyss of deep blue the sempiternal light is lit. The destined human cerebral cortex faces Infinity's finite front. Hidden asymmetries in the external cosmos are complemented by reciprocal asymmetries in the neurobiology. In cyclic symmetry and in metric plane, the quivering limbs of the cosmic facet embrace the virgin vibration of the dreamy chords of the living biological corpse. The undying love of cosmic integration center impregnates the passionate heart beat of biological integration center.
>
> —*Conquering the Brain*, p 17.

Supreme consummation initiates opening up of *chakras*, the integration centres. And the most important, it initiates a new brain formation.

Two most undifferentiated structures of brain, the reticular system and the cerebral cortex are called into sustained action along with the most undifferentiated cells within the brain—the stem cells. The reticular system takes part in delineation of integration centers within the central nervous system. Integration centers, in the yogic terminology, have been called *chakras.* The cerebral cortex re-orients its neurons for the brain to behave in a macro-quantum way. In the course of profound spiritual experience, it is suggested that the stem cells engage in 'renewal' of certain cortical structures and may participate in formation of a new brain over the vortex of the cerebral cortex (supracortical brain)[80]. The most potent stimulus for initiating this lasting change in the brain remains supreme consummation.

CONCLUDING OBSERVATIONS

Unlike Supreme Consummation which is a rare event, partial consummation of brain-bound consciousness and brain-independent consciousness is not an uncommon phenomenon. Thanks to the observers of nonlocal communication of various types and the state of maturity of human brain! The humanity seems to be on the threshold of a new formation. Therefore, this period is not only exciting but is also critical. In this critical and exciting period of Time, it would be rewarding to assess our glorious civilizational Past, developments, discoveries and phenomenology of the Present and to make use of those to build up a sustainable Future.

The study of consciousness, with special reference to its ontological, epistemological, phenomenological and axiological aspects, appears essential for this purpose. The inner space and the outer space, brain-bound consciousness and brain-independent consciousness, surface and depth phenomenology, organization within and civilization without are equally important in this context. Explorations of the phenomenon of 'death' while alive, which helps in letting the inside become out and outside become in, is expected to minimize their differences. The planes above 'classical' consciousness (super-conscious planes) and the planes underneath it (unconscious planes) could be placed in proper perspectives in the context of classical consciousness only thereafter.

We have drawn 'The Big Picture' necessary for developing a Science for Consciousness. The whole project seems to be a multidisciplinary adventure in a mega scale which is expected to crystallize into a New and unique Worldview / Paradigm which would be able to accommodate Humanity Science and Spirit and integrate Consciousness Philosophy and Science. Concluding comment, therefore, concurs with what has been stated in the opening paragraph of this paper. What we need is in one person a spiritualist, a philosopher and a scientist. And, we need plenty of such beings. We have, therefore, undertaken a never-ending project!

NOTES

1. Wolterstorff N. 1984. *Reason within the Bounds of Religion.* 2nd. enlarged edition. Grand Rapids: Edermans. pp. 67-68.
2. Popper, K.R., Eccles, J.C. 1977. *The Self and its Brain.* Springer International.

3. Sperry, R.W. 1987. "Structure and Significance of the Consciousness Revolution'. *The Journal of Mind and Behavior,* 8(1). pp. 37-66.
4. Crick, F.H.C. 1994. *The Astonishing Hypothesis—The Scientific Search for the Soul.* London: Simon and Schuster.
5. Edelman, G.M. 2001. *A Universe of Consciousness.* Indianapolis, USA: Library of Science.
6. Tiller, W.A. 1997. *Science and Human Transformation.* USA: Pavior. pp. 54-100. See also, Tiller, W.A. et al. 2001. *Conscious Acts of Creation.* USA: Pavior.
7. Penrose, R. 1994. *Shadows of the Mind.* USA: Oxford University Press.
8. Jahn, R.G., Dunne, B.J. 1988. *Margins of Reality: The Role of Consciousness in the Physical World.* New York: Harcourt Brace Jovanovich. See also, Jahn and Dunne. 1997. "Science of the Subjective". *Journal of Scientific Exploration, 11.* pp. 201-224; Jahn and Dunne. 2001. "A Modular Model of Mind/Matter Manifestations (M^5)". *Journal of Scientific Exploration,* 15. pp. 299-329.
9. Zukav, G. 1979. *The Dancing Wu Li Masters.* Toronto, New York, London etc.: Bantam Books. p. 36.
10. Truzzi, M. 1990. "Reflections on the Reception of the Unconventional Claims in Science". Reported by Simona Solovey. *Frontier Perspectives,* 1(2). pp. 12-15, 25.
11. Mukhopadhyay, A.K. 1995. *Conquering the Brain. Towards the Essence of Multiversity and the Akhanda Paradigm.* New Delhi: Conscious Publications. See also, Mukhopadhyay, A.K. 2000. *The Millennium Bridge. Towards the Mechanics of Consciousness and the Akhanda Paradigm.* New Delhi: Conscious Publications. Mukhopadhyay, A.K. 2002. "Science for Consciousness. Five Reasons for Failure and Five Ways to make it a Success". *Frontier Perspectives,* 11(1). pp. 33-35.
12. Tiller. pp. 54-100. See also, Tiller et al.
13. Mukhopadhyay. *Conquering the Brain.* pp. 62-73.
14. Mukhopadhyay. *The Millennium Bridge.* p. 199.
15. Mukhopadhyay. *Conquering the Brain. See also,* Mukhopadhyay. *The Millennium Bridge,* p. 201.
16. Mukhopadhyay. *The Millennium Bridge.* pp. 4-7
17. Ibid. p. 90.
18. Mukhopadhyay. *Science for Consciousness.* pp. 33-35.
19. Austin, J.H. *1998. Zen and the Brain.* Massachusetts, USA: The MIT Press. pp. 43-47.
20. Wolterstorff pp. 67-68.
21. Mukhopadhyay. *Conquering the Brain.* pp. 116-119.
22. Mukhopadhyay. *The Millennium Bridge.* pp. 99-100.
23. Klauber, R.D. 2000. "Modem Physics and Subtle Realms: Not Mutually Exclusive". *Journal of Scientific Exploration,* 14(2). pp. 275-279.
24. Whitehead, A.N. 1979. "Process and Reality: A Essay in Cosmology". Corrected edition. DR. Griffin and D.W. Sherburne (ed.). New York: Free Press.
25. Swami Jitatmananda. 1998. *Prophet who first reconciled Vedanta and Science. Swami Vivekanada Prophet and Pathfinder.* 3rd. edition. Rajkot: Shri Ramakrishna Ashram.
26. Gulick, V.R. 2001. "Reduction, Emergence and Other Options on the Mind/Body Problem. A Philosophic Overview". *Journal of Consciousness Studies,* 8(9-10). pp. 1-34.
27. Mukhopadhyay. *The Millennium Bridge.* pp. 41-50
28. Mukhopadhyay, A.K. 2003. "Science for Consciousness. How it is expected to be?" *Applied Philosophy.* R.P. Singh (ed.). New Delhi: OM Publications. pp. 151-181.
29. Sutherland, S. 1989. *The Macmillan Dictionary of Psychology.* London: The Macmillan Press.
30. Popper and Eccles.
31. Truzzi. pp. 12-15, 25.
32. Leiter, David L. *2002.* "The Pathology of Organized Skepticism". *Journal of Scientific Exploration,* 16(1). pp. 125-128.
33. Geddes, P. 1920. *The Life and Work of Sir Jagdis C. Bose.* London: Longmans, Green & Company.
34. Mahall, Bruce E., Callaway, Ragan M. 1990. *Root Communication among Desert Shrubs.* Proceedings of the National Academy of Science, 88. pp. 874-876.
35. Whitehead, A.N. 1979. *Process and Reality: An Essay in Cosmology,* Corrected edition. D.R. Griffin and D.W. Sherburne (ed.). New York: Free Press.
36. Chattopadhyaya, D.P. 2002. "Myth, Metaphysics and Science". *Consciousness Series,* 1. New Delhi: Indian Council of Philosophical Research.
37. Kuhn, T.S. 1970. *The Structure of Scientific Revolution.* 2nd. enlarged edition. Chicago: University of Chicago Press.

38. Barber, B. 1961. "Resistance by Scientists to Scientific Discovery". *Science*, 134. pp. 596-602.
39. Mukhopadhyay. *The Millennium Bridge.* pp. 41-50.
40. Mukhopadhyay. *Conquering the Brain.* See also, Mukhopadhyay. *The Millennium Bridge.* pp. 200-201
41. Skolimowski, H. 1996. 'The Participatory Universe and its new Methodology". *Frontier Perspectives,* 5(2). pp. 16-23.
42. Mukhopadhyay. 2002. *Frontier Perspectives,* 11(1). pp. 33-35.
43. Sri Aurobindo. 1990. "Savitri". *Sri Aurobindo,* vol. 27, *28.* Birth Centenary edition. Pondicherry: Pondicherry Ashram.
44. Merikle, P.M., Daneman, M. 1998. "Psychological Investigations of Unconscious Perception". *Journal of Consciousness Studies,* 5(1). pp. 5-18.
45. Pribram, K. H. 1991. *Brain and Perception: Holonomy and Structure in Figural Processing.* New Jersey: Lawrence Erlbaum Associates.
46. Cotterill Rodney, M.J. 1997. "On the Mechanism of Consciousness". *Journal of Consciousness Study,* 4(3). pp. 231-247.
47. McFadden, J. 2002. "Synchronous Firing and its Influence on the Brain's Electromagnetic Field. Evidence for an Electromagnetic Field Theory of Consciousness". *Journal of Consciousness Study,* 9(4). pp. 23-50.
48. Mukhopadhyay. *Conquering the Brain.* pp. 3-25.
49. Sri Aurobindo.
50. Mukhopadhyay. *Conquering the Brain.* pp. 17-20.
51. Mukhopadhyay, A.K. 1985. *Frontiers of Research for Human Biologists.* New Delhi: Conscious Publications. pp. 1-6. See also, Mukhopadhyay, A.K. 1989. "Consciousness—From Behavioral Neurologists' Horizon". *Journal of Indian Council of Philosophical Research,* VI(3). pp. 49-55.
52. Jain, Y. S. 2002. "Unification of the Physic of Interacting Bosons and Fermions through (q, -q) Pair Correlation". *Journal of Scientific Exploration,* 16(1). p. 117-124. See also, Jain, Y.S. 2002. "Microscopic Theory of a System of Interacting Bosons: A Unifying New Approach". *Journal of Scientific Exploration,* 16(1). pp. 77-115.
53. McFadden. pp. 23-50.
54. Mukhopadhyay. *The Millennium Bridge.* p. 90.
55. Mukhopadhyay. *Conquering the Brain.* pp. 116-119.
56. Mukhopadhyay. *The Millennium Bridge.* pp. 99-100.
57. Klauber. pp. 275-279.
58. Freeman, W.J. 1999. *How Brains Make Up Their Minds.* London: Weidenfeld & Nicholson.
59. Pockett, S. 2000. *The Nature of Consciousness: A Hypothesis.* Lincoln, NE: luniverse Ltd. See also, Pockett, S. 2002. "Difficulties with the Electromagnetic Field Theory of Consciousness". *Journal of Consciousness Studies,* 9(4). pp. 51-56.
60. McFadden. pp. 23-50.
61. Mukhopadhyay. *Conquering the Brain.* p. 116-119.
62. Mukhopadhyay. *The Millennium Bridge.* p. 99-100
63. Mukhopadhyay. *Frontiers of Research* pp. 1-6 See also, Mukhopadhyay. IJPR. 1989. VI(3), pp. 49-55.
64. Mukhopadhyay. *Conquering the Brain.* pp. 241-249.
65. Mukhopadhyay. *The Millennium Bridge.* pp. 166-169 See also, Klauber. pp. 275-279.
66. Mukhopadhyay, A.K. 2003. "The 'Pentaune' and the 'Nanoune' Models for the Mechanics of Nature and Consciousness". *Philosophy and Science: An Explanatory Approach to Consciousness.* Kolkata: Ramakrishna Mission Institute of Culture. pp. 347-372.
67. Mukhopadhyay. *Conquering the Brain.* See also, Mukhopadhyay. *The Millennium Bridge.* Mukhopadhyay. *Frontiers of Research.* Mukhopadhyay. IJPR. 1989. VI(3), pp. 49-55.
68. Taylor, J.G. 2002. "From Matter to Mind". *Journal of Consciousness Studies,* 9(4). pp. 3-22. See also, Taylor, J.G. 2002. "Paying Attention to Consciousness". *Trends in Cognitive Sciences,* 6(5). pp. 206-210.
69. Austin. pp. 43-47.
70. Pribram, K.H. 1999. 'Brain and the Composition of Conscious Experience. Of Deep and Surface Structure; Frames of Reference; Episode and Executive; Models and Monitors". *Journal of Consciousness Studies,* 6(5). pp. 19-42.
71. Sanders, M.D. et al. 1974. "Blindsight': Vision in a Field Defect". *Lancet,* 1(7860) April 20. pp. 707-708.
72. Pribram. *Brain and the Composition of Conscious Experience.* pp. 19-42.
73. Marzi, C.A. 1999. "Why is Blindsight Blind?" *Journal of Consciousness Study,* 6(5). pp. 12-18.
74. Cotterill. pp. 231-247.

75. McFadden. pp. 23-50.
76. Mukhopadhyay. *Conquering the Brain.* pp. 95-105. See also, Mukhopadhyay. *The Millennium Bridge.*
77. Mukhopadhyay. *Conquering the Brain,* pp. 241-249.
78. Ibid. p. 246.
79. Ibid.
80. Mukhopadhyay. *The Millennium Bridge,* pp. 136-151.

CHAPTER 8

Is Science Alone Likely to Unravel the Mystery of Consciousness?

P.N. Tandon

INTRODUCTION

Consciousness is one of the very few subjects which since antiquity has attracted the interest of the devotees of such diverse disciplines as religion, philosophy, psychology, neurobiology and, more recently, cognitive science, mathematics, physics, computer science, artificial intelligence and neural network. Historically the dominant intellectual force of a given era provided its own interpretation of this highest attribute of human evolution. Notwithstanding this intense intellectual activity through the ages, even today there is a lack of consensus on its nature, its definition, its evolutionary significance, leave aside its biological basis. One of the reasons for this failure is that till recently there were hardly any efforts to bring together at one forum the followers of these diverse disciplines at least to hear each other's views, hypothesis and concepts. Its study remained confined to religious seers and later philosophers for several millennia. It was not till the emergence of psychology and neurology beginning towards the end of the nineteenth century that it attracted the attention of bio-scientists. Interestingly enough the later parts of the twentieth century has witnessed an ever increasing number of some outstanding physical scientists getting attracted to the field of consciousness study. However, even today there is a paucity of inter-disciplinary interaction of the type planned for this seminar.

I

THE SCIENTIFIC QUESTIONS

Fully conscious of the difficulties of such interaction primarily because of a lack of commonly accepted definition of consciousness let me first outline the boundary conditions used for my presentation. This is necessary since I believe that much of the confusion and debate on consciousness arises as a result of the word being used differently by different individuals, even those belonging to the same discipline. Just to give a few examples : William James (1892) the father of American psychology said, "consciousness is not a thing but a process." He added that everyone knows what consciousness is until he tries to define it. While *Chambers Everyday Dictionary* defines consciousness as the totality of mental states and processes (precepitons, feelings, thoughts), mind in its widest sense, awareness, the working state of mind, it defines mind as faculty by which we think, the whole spiritual nature, memory, intention. The *Oxford English Dictionary*, (unabridged, second edition) gives eight definitions of 'consciousness' and twelve definitions of 'conscious'. In general in English language the words consciousness and mind are used interchangeably. Fisch Bach (1952) stated, "Mind is often equated with consciousness, a subjective sense of awareness" and yet he goes on to elaborate, "there is more to mind than consciousness or cerebral cortex." Schrodinger (1967) felt that, "consciousness is in many ways still a pre-scientific concept with multiple inconsistent meanings, included are such disparate elements as perception, attention, volition, self-awareness and memory." He repeatedly used the terms consciousness and mind as equivalent and goes on to state, "Mind has three aspects, i.e., knowing, feeling and willing". Many such examples can be quoted. (Those interested may refer to a compilation of some of these in the *Proceedings of the Round Table on Consciousness* published by the National Brain Research Centre 2000).

For the purpose of this discussion a conscious human being is one who is aware of the environment (as perceived through the various sense organs) as well as of self (subjective feelings) and is endowed with the capability of acting voluntarily. Consciousness is what perceives, emotes and acts out life. Fully realizing that epistimically consciousness is subjective, in clinical practice its evaluation is directed to elicit the presence of the above attributes. Mind, a term often used as synonymous with consciousness, refers to the mental processes involved in interpreting the sensory inputs and planning the response. This no doubt involves attributes like attention, discrimination, memory, feeling, emotions, precepts, concepts, etc. Fully realizing that many philosophers would be unwilling to accept these definitions, which may constitute the initial ground for debate, it may be mentioned that I have failed to find a definition universally acceptable even to the philosophers. It would thus be clear that this limited definition does not seem to take into consideration such commonly accepted attributes of human mind like inspiration, intuition insight and creativity.

As a neurosurgeon dealing with human brain, one's major preoccupation was evaluating and preserving the most sensitive index, its global integrity as manifested by the state of consciousness. From a purely clinical standpoint an all encompassing definition of consciousness, was less important to us, than to be able to assess its various states through its various attributes—awareness of self and environment on one hand and ability for volitional activity on the other. We no doubt knew that consciousness involved the ability of perception, memory, thought, emotion, intuition and creativity. Our professional background prevented us from paying much heed to subjects like parapsychology, out of body experience, mystic consciousness, or the so-called pure consciousness. It is not surprising then that throughout my professional life, along with my colleagues, I was involved in a variety of studies trying to unravel the patho-physiological correlates of various states of consciousness, establish diagnostic and prognostic criteria, and look for clinical syndromes which may throw some light on its possible neural correlates.

Nearly ten years ago having selected consciousness as the subject from my Presidential Address to the Indian National Science Academy, I attempted to summarise our decades of experience and at the same time explore the wisdom of others from diverse fields like physiology, psychology, physical sciences as well as philosophers. As a result it became obvious to me that there was more to consciousness than what we dealt with as clinicians, hence the title of my address, which sounded odd to many of my colleagues, "Consciousness: Clinical and Beyond". (Tandon 1993)

The debate no doubt is confounded not only because of a lack of definition but the prevailing linguistic and philosophical difficulties. For some consciousness and mind are interchangeable terms, while others like *Taittirīyopaniṣad* classify consciousness into different planes like the physical consciousness *(annamayakoṣa),* the psychic consciousness *(Manomayakoṣa)* the intuitive consciousness *(vijñanamayakoṣa)* and the beautitudinous consciousness *(ānandamayakoṣa). Abhidhammaṭhasangha,* a Buddhist treatise described 52 different modalities of consciousness which include feeling *(vedanā),* perception *(sannā),* volition (*śaṅkhara*), focused attention *(manaśikara),* decision *(adhimoṅkkha),* effort *(viriya)* and intention *(chanda).* A host of terminologies have been used to describe a variety of states of consciousness like being *(sat),* consciousness *(cit)* and bliss *(ānanda)* or awake *(jāgṛiti),* dreaming *(swapna),* deep sleep *(susupti)* and non-dual or thoughtless *(turīya).* In addition there are discussions and debates on subjects like the subconscious, the transcendental, the mystic, the spiritual and the ultimate pure consciousness or *Brahman.* (A somewhat more elaborate historical perspective is provided in author's paper, "Concepts of Consciousness: Brain-Mind Relationship in Decade of the Brain").

While most neurologists and psychologists would agree with Hughlings Jackson (1931) that "consciousness is a varying quantity, that is, we are from moment to moment differently conscious", but the difficulty arises while attempting to define the boundary conditions. Psychic states like Freud's subconscious, vedantic *turīya,* or the pathological ones like the global amnesia, hypnosis or post-epileptic automatism are difficult to account for, others like "mystic consciousness", "the cosmic consciousness", the mind of *"Gaia"* complicate any rational dialogue between philosophers, psychologists, neurological, cognitive and physical scientists. Yet a common meeting ground between all these groups would be essential at least to chart a future course of investigations, if one ever hopes to resolve the mystery of this most complex human attribute.

I am confident that there are many distinguished scholars amongst the participants of this seminar who can throw more light on these philosophical concepts. However, my plea would be to explore the significance of these concepts in the light of the voluminous empirical observations that have been made during the last couple of decades.

For the neuroscientists the basic question has been to test the hypothesis whether consciousness is the function of the brain. If so, is there a seat of consciousness in the brain? Alternatively what aspects of brain activity gives rise to consciousness. In other words to explore brain-mind relationship empirically?

II

NEUROSCIENCE APPROACHES TO STUDY CONSCIOUSNESS

Not unexpectedly most such approaches have been conditioned by the prevailing paradigm of scientific studies in general, i.e., a reductionist approach. Till recently most such studies were based on clinical observations on patients with brain disorders like epilepsy or focal damage due to injury or pathological lesions. As a result it was observed that discrete functions like motor activity, sensory perception, speech, memory, even emotions, were 'localized' to discrete regions of the brain. It was on the basis of such observations that Hippocrates, the Greek physician-philosopher proclaimed, "Men ought to know that from the brain and from the brain only, arise our pleasure, joys, laughter and tears. Through it in particular we think, see, hear and distinguish the ugly from the beautiful, the bad from the good, the pleasant from the unpleasant." Several millennia later Hughlings Jackson proposed the precise somatotopic localization of motor and sensory functions in the pre-and post-central gyrus of the opposite hemisphere and Broca, followed by Wernicke identified the speech areas in the left hemisphere of the right handed individuals. The concept of localization of various functions found a strong support in the work of Wilder Penfield and his colleagues at the Montreal Neurological Institute. They systematically explored the brain of conscious cooperative patients undergoing surgery for epilepsy under local anesthesia using gentle electrical stimulation. It was during such operations that he chanced to re-activate "the permanent record of the stream of consciousness" of a past experience from the temporal lobe of a few patients. Limited to the duration of electrical stimulation, the patient 're-lived' all that he had been aware of in that earlier experience, a record of which was laid down initially. To quote Penfield & Perot (1963): "The conclusion is inescapable that some, if not all, of these evoked responses represent activation of a neural mechanism that keep record of current experience. There is activation too of the emotional tone or feeling that belonged to the original experience. The responses have that basic element of reference to the past that one associates with memory. But their vividness or wealth of detail and the sense of immediacy that goes with them serves to set them apart from the ordinary process of recollection which rarely displays such qualities." These observations suddently aroused hopes that the seat of consciousness is soon going to be discovered. Around the same time, Milner (1958), Penfield and Milner (1958), Scoville and Correll (1973) studied patients with bilateral lesions of the hippocampus and hippocampal gyrus (a part of the temporal lobe) which had resulted in specific pattern of memory loss. This led them to suggest that "the capacity to record the daily current of conscious experience may be lost in such cases." The observations were considered to have "thrown welcome light on the location of some portion at least of the ganglionic record of current experience." Were we nearing solving the mystery of consciousness? Thus by now it had become possible to trace the neural substrate involved in sensory perception, voluntary movements and some of the higher mental functions like memory, arousal and sleep.

Notwithstanding all these and many other observations, Sperry (1966) eloquently pointed out that "the inner sensations, feelings, percepts, concepts, mental images or the like cannot be weighed or measured, photographed or spectrographed or chromatographed or otherwise recorded or dealt with by any known scientific methodology." Much to the surprise and concern of his colleagues when Penfield (1975) at the end of his scientific life sat down to finally analyse his life-long contributions to understanding human brain as recorded in a book, *The Mystery of Mind* concluded thus: "For my own part, after years of striving to explain the mind on the basis of brain action alone, I have come to the conclusion that it is simpler (and far easier to be logical) if one adopts the hypothesis that our being does consist of two fundamental elements." And "the mind is aware of what is going on. The mind reasons and makes new decisions. It understands. It acts as though endowed with an energy of its own. It can make decisions and put them into effect by calling upon various brain mechanisms. It does this by activating neurone mechanisms." In the end, "The certainity, to my mind is this : When we come to understanding man, we will see that the nature of mind and the mind's energy is simple and easily comprehensible."

It is interesting to note that around this time Penfield was not alone in this dilemma. George Wald (1979) felt that "consciousness is not part of universe of space and time, of observable and measurable quantities." Troubled by the difficulties of explaning mind on the basis of known laws of physics, Schröinger (1967) was motivated to write in his book, *What is life? Mind and Matter*, that "other laws of physics hitherto unknown, which however, once they have been revealed, will form part of the science of self and mind." Prof. Kothari (1980) talking of atom and self argued that "Atom or brain belongs to the external objective world of space, time, matter and energy. Self or mind belongs to the internal subjective world. The subjective (mental) world is not describable in terms of space-time and matter-energy concepts, self or mind therefore lies outside natural science." Prolonged personal discussions between Eccles, a Noble Laureate in neurophysiology, and Popper, a renowned philosopher, made the former conclude, "Hitherto it has been impossible to develop any neurophysiological theory that explains how a diversity of brain events comes to be synthesized so that there is a unified conscious experience of a global or gestalt character. The experienced unity comes not from a neurophysiological synthesis, but from the proposed integrating character of the self-conscious mind" (Popper Eccles, 1977). This is not the place to discuss the views of large number of distinguished scientists and philosophers of this era like Brodal, Cobb, Hebb, Jasper Fodor, Scoville, Sherrington, Skinner, Symonds, Wigner, or Waddington to name just a few. Their views have been summarized elsewhere (Tandon 1993). Suffice it to say that it resulted in competing groups of theorists: Behaviourist, Mentalists, Functionalists, Panpsychists, Parallelists, Emergent Materialists, in addition to the earlier Monists, Dualists and Mystics.

III

RECENT ADVANCES IN STUDY OF BRAIN FUNCTIONS

The last couple of decades have witnessed the emergence of a host of new techniques like computerized axial tomography (CT) and magnetic resonance imaging (MRI) which visualize the structural details of the brain non-invasively. Similarly positron emission tomography (PET Scan), functional magnetic resonance imaging (FMRI), single photon emission computerized tomography (SPECT) provide images of vascular and metabolic changes associated with function of a given region of the brain. Recording of event related evoked potentials (ERP) or magneto-encephalography (MEG) provide real time changes in the electrical or magnetic activity while a subject is participating in a mental task. A combination of results thus obtained gives a remarkable picture of spatial and temporal distribution of activity associated with a range of psychic functions like perception, memory, attention, thought, emotion, intentionality and volition, etc., all attributes of the global function of consciousness. It is this ability that has prompted a host of scientists to proclaim the possibility of assigning "anatomic specificity of the embodiment of mind" (Raichle 1992, Frackowiak 1998, Churchland 1999). A similar sentiment was expressed by Francis Crick, who proposed that, "all aspects of mind, including its most puzzling attribute—consciousness or awareness—are likely to be explainable in more materialistic way as the behaviour of large sets of interacting neurons (Crick and Koch 1992). Frackowiak (1998) said, "We live in an age when people are increasingly accepting the proposition that our emotional, intellectual and indeed biological lives are determined uniquely by our brains. ...it can be claimed at present that changes in the brain activity associated with pure thought, emotion and cognitive process are readily and reproducibly measurable." Or, Patricia Smith Churchland (1999) says, "Neuroscience can reveal the physical mechanisms subserving psychological functions...that awareness is some pattern of activity in neurons."

To add to this growing literature a recent book by Neuberg, D'Aquiti and Rice (2001)—*Why God Won't Go Away: Brain Science and the Biology of Belief*—provides enough material on the neurophysiology of mystical experiences. SPECT studies on Buddhist monks and Franciscan nuns made them claim that they have "uncovered solid evidence that the mystical experiences of (their) subjects—the altered states of mind they described as the absorption of the self into something larger—were not the results of emotional mistakes or simple wishful thinking, but were associated instead with a series of observable neurological events." Steven Rose, (1999) in his book, *From Brains to Consciousness? Essays on the New Sciences of the Mind* writes, "Questions which for most of humanity's existence have been the province of philosophy and religion are now the stuff of day-to-day laboratory experiment."

Thus, there seems to be increasing realization among many scientists like Gerald Edelman, Nick Herbert, Patricia Churchland, Toamassio Poggio and philosophers like John Searle, Daniel Donnett, Karl Popper and Ned Block that study of consciousness (or mind) is not impervious to science.

Further support for this optimism is provided by a variety of ingenious studies, on both animals and humans alike, which have elaborated the molecular basis of many attributes of mental activity. Thus, neurobiological basis of memory, learning, psychic dependence (addiction), joy, sorrow and rage has been explored not only at the biochemical but in some cases, even at the level of genes. Those interested in these aspects may refer to reviews by Chalmers (1996), Dennett (1996), Warner and Szubka (1994), Milner and Rugg (1992), Block et al (1999), Crick 1994, Daedalus (1998), Llinas and Churchland (1996), Rose (1999), *Philosophical Transaction: The Royal Society* (1998), Searle (1992), Damasio (1999), *Proceedings of Tucson Conference* (1998), Donald (2001).

The recent imaging and physiological techniques have greatly enhanced our understanding of the primary sensory and motor functions. To take the example of visual perception, one of the most extensively studied sensory system, it has now been possible to identify the neural substrate involved in detection of the various subsets of visual perception, e.g., detection and orientation of lines, colour, distance of the object from the observer, movement, etc. It has now been shown that certain groups of neurons are involved in processing of the appearance of the full face or in its various profiles while others deal with emotional expression of the face (Jeeves 1991). In short there are at least three dozen different areas in the brain contributing to visual perceptions. Similarly, the neuronal circuits involved in specific features of other sensations or motor activity have been worked out.

Moving from these 'simple' functions to more complex ones, a great deal is already known about the neural substrate of the so-called higher mental functions—like attention, memory, emotion, judgement, etc. Thus, voluminous scientific literature based on neuro-imaging studies on human subjects, electrophysiological studies on behaviourally active animals and molecular and genetic studies on cell and tissue cultures has accumulated during the last decade. It is impossible to summarise all this information, but suffice it to say that reproducible evidence establishes the role specific regions of the brain play in these well-recognized subsets of the unitary function of consciousness.

It will, thus, be observed that on the basis of the existing knowledge there is enough evidence to state that the brain plays an important role, in maintenance and manifestation of consciousness as defined above. It is obvious that the brain can sense the environment, categorize patterns out of a multiplicity of signals, select the relevant information from the noise, store it in memory, retrieve this knowledge when required, formulate and execute voluntary response be it muscular, verbal or emotional. The repeated demonstration of consistent pattern of local brain activation during defined mental activity now provides objective evidence of involvement of the brain in these functions, which is difficult to refute. Such measurements bring investigations of thought, consciousness, emotions and similar functions into the realm of 'hard' scientific enquiry.

In addition to these studies on normal volunteers, a host of others with well defined lesions in the brain have been subjected to detailed investigations combining the study of cognitive functions with modern imaging techniques. Thus studies on subjects on blind sight, phantom limb, binocular rivalry, gestalt switching have provided new insights on the question of self and non-self.

IV

DISCUSSION

Notwithstanding all this progress, it is also obvious that consciousness could not be ascribed to be the function of any specific region of the brain. The fact that damage to a small area in the brainstem can produce unconsciousness, should not imply that brainstem is the seat of consciousness. As mentioned above diverse regions of the brain participate in the process, which ultimately results in the unitary experience of consciousness. Thus, even if we accept that the unequivocal demonstrations of consistent patterns of local brain activation (or inhibition) during defined mental activity is a proof of consciousness being a function of the brain, a number of questions remain unanswered. The first one is that demonstration of alteration in the activity of a given region of the brain as revealed by the various techniques mentioned above does not necessarily imply causality. Even more elusive is the explanation of how the widely distributed neuronal activity is integrated to provide a unitary experience of self-awareness or consciousness. Whether this is the function of a specific region, or neuronal circuits (the so-called reverberating thalamo-cortical circuits as hypothesized by Crick or Edelman), or coherence of specific frequencies (Gamma oscillations as postulated by Rodriguez et al 1999) or a modification of the synaptic activity remains unresolved. This dilemma has been discussed at some length by William Uttal (2001) in a recent book, *The New Phrenology: The Limits of Localizing Cognitive Processes in the Brain.* He raises three questions:

1) Can the mind be sub-divided into components, modules or parts ?
2) Does the brain operate as an equipotential mass or is it divisible into interacting but separable functional units ?
3) Can these components—assuming they exist in some valid psychobiological sense—be assigned to localized portions of the brain ?

He concludes that while most neuroscientists would today answer yes on all counts, but when it comes to details one runs into so many 'limits and constraints' that the reply might as well be 'no'.

Thus neuroscientists today know how the brain processed vision, hearing, memory and emotions but does not know what it is like to see, hear, remember or feel happy or sad. The knowledge of the brain thus does not seem to yield complete knowledge of conscious experience. This is what philosophers like Chalmers call the 'Hard Problem' of consciousness, i.e., the question how physical processes in the brain give rise to subjective experience. Similarly, others argue that the exhaustive compilation of all the scientific data adds up to correlates of mental state, but "the detailed observations of living matter thus leads not to mind but simply to the details of living matter." To take it further the nay sayers question, "The understanding of how living matter generates the sense of self that is the hall-mark of a conscious mind—the sense that the images in my mind are mine and are formed in my perspective—is simply not possible." It is arguments like these, hard for me to comprehend, that make us turn to philosophers for a better understanding and direction for future research.

Notwithstanding all the progress made in neurosciences in recent years, some vital questions remain unanswered.

Do we accept a commonly propounded argument that consciousness is a subjective phenomenon, hence not amenable to empirical study, or the behaviourists' view popularized by Skinner who questioned the very reality of anything like mind or consciousness? In view of the objection that the indirect demonstration of changes in the brain in association with certain mental states cannot resolve the philosophical debate between physical determinism and occasionalism, should one continue to persue this line of investigations? Should we accept the fatalistic attitude of many scientists who proclaimed consciousness wholly impervious to science or beyond science, not explainable on the basis of currently known principles of physics including quantum mechanism or being an energy of a kind not yet described ? Or uncritically believe the proclaimations of many philosophers who argue that any explanation of consciousness or the mind based on physicalism must be necessarily untenable. In this respect I am greatly encouraged by the writings of Daniel Donnett, Ned Block and John Searle, specially the last who have very coherently argued consciousness is a biological phemenon like any other and it can be investigated neurobiologically. In that event there would not be any need for such a seminar. Notwithstanding these difficulties, and recognizing that philosophy interprets rather than generates new knowledge, I take this opportunity to suggest that so much new information has recently been generated that this is an opportune time to review the current philosophical concepts in the light of these observations. This may at the same time help the scientists to plan future investigations based on the new hypothesis thus formulated.

CHAPTER 9

Is Philosophical Doctrine of Consciousness Obsolete?

N.S.S. Raman

The recent advances in knowledge both in philosophy and the sciences (both physical and life sciences), have not been appreciated fully by the philosophers in this country. Even in European countries and the United States, philosophers are still adhering to the ideas and conceptions prevalent in the early half of twentieth century. It takes some time for new philosophical and scientific ideas to make an impact, and even methods of approach have been somewhat slow in changing from age to age. Fortunately, now there has been no total indifference to the developments in the sciences, though we are somewhat slow in understanding and appreciating the changes in their methods, goals and applications. Philosophers in India, used as they are to a three-thousand-year old tradition, are somewhat hesitant about absorbing new ideas and methods. The philosophical systems of the West which they are still fond of, no longer hold their ground in the West, and these include not only transcendental idealism, but also later trends like positivism, logical analysis, existentialism, Marxism, etc. Most Indian thinkers are too fond of the Advaita Vedānta (which to them is both philosophy and religion) to be interested in anything else. The fondness which many Indian philosophers had in Marxism has faded away because of the ideological and social failure of that kind of philosophy. One can apply the Toynbeean model to the history of philosophy too; there are trends in it, which have their rise, periods of prosperity, decline and fall, when they encounter stronger intellectual currents from outside.

I

The philosophical doctrine of consciousness has had a longer history than other trends of thought, and does not seem to be fading away, in spite of attacks on it from the field of psychology and the life sciences. In Indian thought, the concept of consciousness has had a much longer history than in the West. It has even become a part of our heritage. Beginning from the Upaniṣads till today, Indian philosophers are deeply involved in a study of consciousness, without ever having defined what it means. The interest in consciousness in Europe is only as old as the philosophy of Immanuel Kant. Earlier to Kant, European philosophers had been writing a great deal about reason, experience etc. Leibniz did speak of consciousness, but only as the tendency to confer self-identity by the monads on themselves, in order to distinguish them from other monads. The Greeks were not interested in the problem of consciousness, and Burnet is perhaps right in saying that the early Greek *Weltanschauung* is naturalistic, till the time of Socrates and Plato. Socrates, Plato, Aristotle and their successors did not talk of consciousness.

It is necessary to go into the reason why the idea of consciousness suddenly became important in early nineteenth century European philosophy. Immanuel Kant had in his first *Critique* posed the questions: How is knowledge possible? How are mathematics and science possible? among other questions about knowledge. This naturally led to questions about the nature of our awareness of the physical world and of ourselves. The question, 'How are we aware of the world' was synonymous with 'How are we conscious of the world?' Kant dissected the knowing process and found as its constituents, space and time (which he called forms of *Anschauung* (simply translated as perception, though N. Kemp Smith translates this term as 'intuition'), causal relationships (which could be reduced to temporal relationships), categories of understanding (Kant gave a list of 12 categories, in distinction from Aristotle who had given a much larger number of categories) and a few other notions like ideas of pure reason, amphibolies of reflection etc. Thus to define and explain such a simple thing as 'awareness' Kant had given what Nietzsche later called 'rainbow of concepts' and Bertrand Russell would have applied 'Occam's razor' to eliminate such a wide variety of redundant concepts to explain the simple fact of our being aware of the world. The elaborate development of the consciousness-idea in later German philosophy was called 'German moonshine' by the American philosopher, George Santayana, early in twentieth century.

The Indian philosophers too have had their share of this conceptual extravagance. Following on the aphoristic statements in the Upaniṣads like *prajñānam brahma, ayamātmā brahma, tattvamasi, sarvaṃ khalu idaṃ brahma* etc. (which are called *mahāvākyas* or great sayings), the Advaitins create a very wide network of metaphysical concepts, all centred around *prajñāna* (also called *vijñāna,* especially by the Yogacara Buddhists), which term is translated as 'consciousness'. Strangely, while Kant included impressions through sense-experience from without as a part of consciousness, Śaṁkara and the Advaitins who preceded him by several centuries exclude sense-perception from consciousness, which they claim to be the ultimate reality or something which constitutes ultimate reality. Perceptual experience on the other hand, is only an appearance.

Transcendental idealists are so called perhaps because they set up a sphere 'transcending' the empirical or experiential world as the ultimate reality. This super-sensible world is of the character of identity of thought with reality as Hegel and the German successors of Hegel (e.g. Lotze and Cohen) believed. Bradley identifies reality with experience, in the authentic British way, but does distinguish between the empirical' and the 'transcendental' like G.W.F. Hegel. Bradley thus avoids reference to 'consciousness' and if at all he mentions it, he identifies it with a sum total of sense-experience.

Kant had indeed introduced a Copernican revolution into philosophy, by shifting its attention from the external world to consciousness, which belonged to the sphere of the subjective. Prior to Kant, Descartes too had succeeded in turning our attention from the external world to the self, to the 'I' (which Kant had called the 'bare form without content', as Descartes did not say anything about this 'I'). The Cartesian 'I' remains a vague thing but Husserl in the early part of twentieth century in his famous work, *Cartesian Meditations,* attempts to give the Cartesian 'I' a content. He identifies it as the transcendental ego, which is no more a bare form. While Kant put the ego outside consciousness, Husserl brings this ego within consciousness, something which is no longer to be identified among the 'things in themselves', unknown and unknowable. The Cartesian certainty about the self had earlier been questioned by the British empiricists, particularly by Hume, whose statement has now become very famous:

> For my part, when I enter most intimately into what I call myself, I always stumble on some particular perception or other, of heat or cold, light or shade, love or hatred, pain or pleasure, and can never observe anything but the perception.

This means that what I call the 'I' or self-consciousness is reciprocal with the consciousness of the object. As Kant would have called it by highly technically-sounding expressions, 'the synthetic unity of consciousness' is reciprocal with the 'synthetic unity of apperception'. The Kantian jargon obfuscates what essentially is a simple fact: I can never be aware of myself, unless I am at the same time aware of the objective world. If all my senses were absent (i.e. if I am deaf, blind, insensitive to touch, smell and taste, I am not aware of the external world, and also, I am not aware of myself). Awareness (which is made synonymous with 'consciousness') provides the clue to the reality of the external world and also of my own being. Berkeley had introduced this view, but only in a naive way. He had not attempted, as Kant does to examine the nature of what he called *percipi;* he had not tried to understand the process of knowing intimately, as Kant did later. Ancient Indian philosophers belonging to the Advaita school, however, employ their acute analytical vision to understand consciousness in as minute a detail as Kant or the later Hegelians do or as the 'sensationalists' like Ernst Mach and Alexander Bain do. 'Consciousness' is deprived of much of its halo, if we also include sense-data within it. The difficulty about consciousness arises only when we keep it apart from perception and regard the latter as something unworthy of being considered a part of reality, as the Advaita Vedāntins and some Hegelians seem to do. It would be better for philosophy if we eliminate the distinction between appearance and reality, or between phenomena and noumena (to use Kantian terminology) or between *vyāvahārika* and *pāramārthika* (to borrow the Advaita characterization of the two fields of knowing).

II

The early phases of the phenomenological movement in Europe were very much involved in a conception of consciousness. The first stage of phenomenology (i.e. with reference to the pre-Husserlian philosophers like Carl Stumpf, and F. Brentano) tried to interpret 'phenomenology' as descriptive psychology, and Husserl himself in his first important work, *The Philosophy of Arithmetic,* was accused by G. Frege (in a review of this book) of psychologism. Mathematical ideas and concepts cannot be interpreted with any reference to psychology, as they are independent of the knowing mind, even as Plato's 'ideas' are. Thus, Husserl had to veer himself to this point of view, when he in his next major work,

Logical Investigations undertook a detailed criticism of psychologism in the first section of that book, in a very comprehensive manner. Hence phenomenology which started as a descriptive psychology, gave place to that as a descriptive study of consciousness, which again was transformed by Husserl into a descriptive study of 'essences' (*Wesenschau,* as he called it). The world of essences constitutes a realm independent of consciousness. These essences have the same reality which Plato conferred on the world of forms, having independence both epistemologically and ontologically, of the knowing subject. One sees this freedom conferred also on moral values, which are not dependent on consciousness. Nicolai Hartmann developes his philosophy of moral experience on these Platonic lines, making moral values ontologically independent of the knowing mind.

Phenomenology of essences is a break from the earlier phenomenology as a descriptive study of consciousness. The progress from phenomenology of *essences* to phenomenology of *language* is a further step in contemporary philosophy that rids it of any reference to consciousness, which seems to have now become obsolete, as it does not serve any useful purpose in philosophical discourse.

C.D. Broad has remarked that mentalism is irrefutable, because in rejecting the reality of the mind, we are rejecting ourselves, thus reinforcing the Cartesian position that the doubter cannot be doubted. Thus the idea of consciousness might come again and again in the history of philosophy, into the forefront. But freed from its psychologistic connotations, 'consciousness' is transformed into a realm of concepts and their logical relationships that one becomes aware of through language. Here phenomenology of essences is transformed into a phenomenology of language, into hermeneutics. Language is indeed primary to consciousness, because it is through language that we become aware of things in an infinitely pluralistic world of objects and their relations, sense-perception providing us barely with the data of consciousness. In the creative realm of human culture, it is sometimes amazing as to what one does with mere words. Creativity is something that the bare idea of consciousness cannot explain.

III

Thus if there is anything basic and central to our thinking and experience, it is language. We have to pose an important question here: Is thinking possible at all without language? All cognition involves identifying objects by their name; so do all relationships between objects. All events or happenings and all activity involves expression through language. Even a Robinson Crusoe cannot do without the use of language, because even when he is in reverie, i.e. enjoying his own thoughts in meditation, he has to do so in language. In brief, no experience, no thinking or contemplation and no activity is possible without language. Heidegger has indeed declared: Language is the house of being. In interpreting and understanding language at various levels of human activity, one has to fall back on one's consciousness, and through it, on language. Consciousness has become obsolete as the basic structure of reality, because it has been replaced by a more fundamental fact behind all experience language. Thus phenomenology as a study of consciousness has been replaced by phenomenology of language, by hermeneutics, i.e. by the language of being and experience, by interpretation and translation for the purpose of communication, for dialogue and discourse in the various spheres of human activity–science, philosophy, religious experience and the arts.

Unlike the vague and fictitious concepts of 'consciousness', language can be grasped as a reality. It is a unity, i.e. something that unites all the successive moments. It is also involved in a logical process that binds all terms in the objective world. It is realized that it is memory that confers unity to various points in time, the past, the present and the future, and objects of memory are expressed in and through language. A mere idea of consciousness cannot express memory. Thus what we have called consciousness in traditional philosophy can be reduced to four parts: a) physiological processes in the brain which make us aware of the world outside through b) sense perception c) memory or the capacity of the mind to store images, ideas or thoughts and to recall them when necessary and to give meaning to them through d) language. One may note in this connection that the analytical philosophers recognize only two kinds of meaning and truth: a) that which is verifiable by sense-experience and b) *a priori* truths of logic and mathematics. Both these can be reduced to language, but the analytical philosophers do not explain how awareness arises and why mind is selective in its responses to objects. Besides, in their definition of language, they ignore the infinite varieties in the use of language, including its creative character. We cannot also put aside as 'emotive' meanings conveyed and created through the various languages used as artistic media.

IV

To sum up: the philosophical concept of consciousness seems to have become obsolete for the following reasons:

1. The idea of consciousness is vague and cannot be defined except by equating it with awareness, which is both empirical (i.e. pertains to sense impressions) and related to the inner processes of the mind.
2. As defined by the idealists, it was too psychologistic; phenomenologists pass from the psychological to the logical, i.e., they attempted to shift the emphasis from the purely subjective states of mind to objective categories and logical relationships, which are *a priori.* Here their ultimate reduction to logic and language becomes unavoidable, rendering the concept of 'consciousness' infructuous and redundant.
3. Hence in the attempt to discover the final principles of our awareness of the universe (i.e. of our consciousness of the objective world), and of ourselves, which is the starting-point of all reflection and speculation, philosophers have stumbled upon language in its multifarious forms, as the basis of all enquiry. And it is the ability to create and use languages that distinguishes man as a living organism from other animals.
4. In Indian philosophy, the Advaita Vedāntins and the *Vijñanavādi* Buddhists posit a universal consciousness (*Brahman, Ālayavijñāna*), somewhat similar in import to Hegelian conception of Absolute Consciousness, but they are not able to

define or describe it and even to give a hint of what it is like, and end up by declaring that it is inscrutable and inexpressible. Or they resort to a series of metaphors, *ālaya* itself being one such metaphor.

Ultimately it appears as though we have to accept Nietzsche's almost prophetic vision of philosophy of the future:

> What then is truth? A flexible army of metaphors, metonymies, anthropomorphisms, in short a sum of human relations, which have been poetically and rhetorically intensified, transformed, bejewelled and which after long usage seems to a people to be fixed, canonical and binding.[1]

Consciousness is one such metaphor; it is like a crucible into which all contents of sense-experience and thought fall, to be mixed and synthesized to give us knowledge. Or is it like a screen (somewhat similar to Locke's *tabula rasa*) on which all data given by sense-experience is organized? Philosophy has found it unavoidable to use these metaphors. Can we possibly escape these metaphors, which are rooted in fiction? Is it possible to discover a principle, an ultimate truth beyond these metaphors?

V

It is in the very nature of science that it has to be free from any form of subjective bias, and be objective in its quest for knowledge. The question of the nature and functions of human consciousness is therefore irrelevant to it. Like the scientists, philosophers also have been busy in their attempts to discover a basis for our knowledge of the external world. Many philosophers today might be tempted to accept the following definition of philosophy given by a leading American analytical philosopher:

> Philosophy takes the conceptual systems developed by scientists, mathematician, art critics, moralists, theologians *et al*, as its subject matter, and seeks to explain and clarify what has to be explained and clarified about such systems in order to render them fully comprehensible.[2]

While reading the above definition about philosophy and its functions, one is happy that there is no reference at all to the traditional role of philosophy as a quest for truth and reality or to a quest after *mokṣa* or liberation as in Indian philosophy. But even when J.J. Katz (in the above statement) speaks of conceptual systems, he does not specifically mention what makes us construct such systems. He does not tell us what enables the scientists, mathematicians etc. to construct such systems. Sure enough, as a positivist, he would use the terms 'logic' and 'language' as exact and scientific, and would reject such 'fictions' as mind, consciousness etc. as unacceptable. But even as late as in the middle of twentieth century, some-scientist-philosophers (e.g. Eddington & James Jeans) fall back on consciousness as the basis of all scientific knowledge and a few others (e.g. Weizaecker) attempt to discover Kantian foundations for scientific knowledge.

But unnoticed by philosophers, in recent years scientists have revolutionized conceptions about the world of living beings. Earlier in the middle of twentieth century, biologists had tried to discover some hidden principle behind the evolution of intelligent life.

Indian philosophy did speak of consciousness, sub-consciousness, dream consciousness and even super-consciousness all different stages in the coherence of consciousness. Yoga psychology also contributed to our knowledge about the mind of man, but all Indian philosophers got bogged down in propagating a religious goal, *mokṣa* for various disciplines, including the sciences. Even scientific treatises on medicine, mathematics etc. start with *mokṣa* as their ideal, as the goal of their enquiry.

As regards consciousness, self-consciousness, etc., we should be clear about these terms, before embarking on speculations or discourses about them, and traditional psychologists are as vague as philosophers. Yoga philosophy does talk about *citta* (which is often rendered into English as consciousness) but Yoga philosophers do not attempt to find out what it is.

VI

At the level of science certain revolutionary changes in knowledge of the external world have taken place. Perhaps more momentous are the changes in biological sciences in the latter half of twentieth century. We are slowly discovering the nature of life and are able in the laboratory to 'clone' or duplicate the natural forms of life, including that of man. The human being has not been 'cloned' as yet, but scientists are not troubled by such possibilities and the dangers they pose to man's uniqueness or individuality. The problems of consciousness or any other epistemological concepts do not in any way affect their enquiries. Some scientists influenced by philosophy, as we have already pointed out, attempted to reduce all knowledge to consciousness, but in general it may be stated that it is not one of the problems of scientific knowledge. Strictly speaking, scientists would deviate from their tasks and goals, if they get involved in philosophical puzzles.

Biologists, it has to be noticed, have no use for the concept of consciousness. Even those dealing with human physiology and anatomy have seldom used the term consciousness, though psychiatrists and anesthetists do. The former use the term with reference to aberrations in a patient's awareness and his responses to the objects of awareness. The latter are barely concerned with consciousness only when they can create insensitivity to pain by the application of anesthetic techniques and not with the nature of consciousness itself. Psychologists have positively discarded the concept of consciousness. It was pointed out fifty years ago, that psychology first lost its soul, then its mind and finally its consciousness.

Revolutionary changes have taken place in the field of genetics and in the understanding of the human organism. Consciousness maybe quite advanced in the human person as the most developed among the living species, with five strong sense-organs, sharp memory and above all ability to express and communicate through spoken and written language, and also through other symbols, both artistic and scientific. He has the additional ability to use tools and to create them. Awareness starts at the rudimentary level, with the reptiles having only 2 senses. The mammals have all the senses, and the philosopher Bosanquet even spoke of a 'dog's system of logic'. This means that most animals have some form or degree of awareness (or consciousness). We have witnessed some outstanding achievements in unraveling the 'secrets' of the living world, and genetics has greatly helped us in this task within a short period of a hundred years (the very name 'genetics' having come into vogue only early in the twentieth century) and in quick succession, we have unravelled many facts about man's biological person, so much so that man is in a position to duplicate himself (or to 'clone' him), taking over , as some scientists boast, the work of God. In such a situation, it would be inconsistent with scientific progress, if we hold on to archaic concepts like 'spirit', 'mind' and 'consciousness', which have lost their relevance in the context of recent advances in knowledge, both scientific and philosophical.

It is, however, realized that in affirming the reality of what he calls 'consciousness', man seeks some form of self-assertion in a multitude of things in the universe, both living and non-living. Such a self-justification as a form of humanism is necessary, because it is obvious that man as a creator of a colourful world of symbols, including language, stands alone in the world.

NOTES

1. Nietzsche on "Truth and Falsity in an extramural sense" (*Ueber Wahrheit und Luge im ausserlichen Sinne*) 1870-73. *Gesamtausgabe* (Collected Works) Vol. III, 2.0.
2. Katz, J.J. 1962. *Philosophy of Language*. New York: Harper & Row. p. 2.

II
Science and its Larger Perspective

CHAPTER 10

Subjective and Objective in Knowledge

Ramakant Sinari

When Kant, for the first time in the history of epistemology, used the principle of Copernicus to explain how our knowledge of the world is determined by the constitution of our subjectivity, he bequeathed to subsequent philosophers, and particularly to phenomenologists, the task of defining the boundaries of the human mind vis-à-vis things in the world. Kant tried to prove that our experience of the world is governed by the categorical structure of our mind. The act of knowing conforms to the 'stuff' human mind is made of, i.e., to the constitutive principles of our faculty of knowing. The organizing norms of our reason shape the way we know whatever we know. The problem (which in fact arose with Plato's theory of knowledge) regarding the connection between the idea and the object, the 'understood' and the perceived, the thing as it appears and the thing-in-itself, was given by Kant a new status by placing the subjectivity of the knower at the centre of the whole process of knowledge.

Since Kant, the distinction between the subjective and the objective has remained the cornerstone of epistemologies. Science strives to discover the laws of the objective—its goal is to state the 'truth' about the objective structure of the universe. The most important assumption of science is what is called scientific empiricism, that is, the assumption that objective knowledge is the only valid kind of knowledge, for it is definitive, exact, unambiguous, and mathematically determinable. So, in order to know a thing reliably, it must be objectified, i.e., it must be posited outside by the knowing mind. The ultimate design of all sciences is to build up a single system in which the totality of phenomena, actual and possible, would cohere in accordance with the tacit laws of logic. Science keeps out of its consideration the elements that could belong to subjectivity. Its promise is to know the universe purely objectively and neutrally, to reach reality as it is.

The main thesis of Kant's *The Critique of Pure Reason* leans towards subjectivism and demonstrates human mind's inherent incapacity to reach phenomena-as-they-are. To know something, according to Kant, is to place it within a certain a *priori* frame of mind, to bring it under the 'categories of understanding', and by that very process construct it against the mind's natural endowments. Thus, the knowing subject is unable to leave off the epistemic enclosure within which he resides and leap out to the essence of the known. He apprehends the world as it is given to him in his innate conceptual setting and not as it in itself is. Things in their absolute objectivity, that is, things-as-they-are, are called by Kant noumena or things-in-themselves. It can be said that, for him, our knowledge of the world is not, really speaking, the knowledge of the world-in-itself but rather the knowledge of the way or modes by which we perform the act of knowing. Kant's subjectivism is the first forceful attempt to suggest that the scientist's faith (and indeed the metaphysician's too) that conclusive knowledge of the universe or Reality is attainable, is based on a kind of naivete.

Kant, like Husserl, the founder of phenomenology after him, was convinced beyond doubt that in the act of knowledge the mechanism of subjectivity must be regarded as most relevant. Not only does subjectivity organize the impressions given to senses by means of the *a priori* categories constituting it (the categories of unity, totality, quality, quantity, necessity, relation, negation, existence, modality, etc.), but it must also be said that without them no experience would be possible. The revolution Copernicus had caused in astronomy, with his hypothesis that the movement of the heavenly bodies is not just passively witnessed by the earth but that the latter too has its own independent movement, seems to have anticipated Kant's breakthrough in philosophy. Copernicus had made the earth's motion a central factor in the explanation of the scheme of heavenly bodies; Kant made the constitution of the knowing mind the pivot around which knowledge takes place and is systematized.

The subjective and the objective are like two poles implicit in all knowledge. They are the ontological extremities into which almost every knowledge situation is analysable. In empirical knowledge, more than in personal, introspective, or self-knowledge, the subject-pole posits the object 'there'. This merely means that the knowing mind intuits this 'object there' as having an autonomous being which it can study, describe, control, or change. Thus science has to trust that the knower is capable of discovering the laws that govern the universe, that is, the subject-pole, by applying the principles of reason, would one day succeed in establishing a system or hierarchy of systems ready to explain why the object-pole is as it is and how it would behave in the altered circumstances. For the purpose of scientific knowledge, the knowing mind and the knowable or known world are two fundamental substances into which reality itself is divided. The statement of the laws regulating the conduct of them both, and the development of an absolutely valid intellectual picture of their total operation are the ultimate programme of science.

Ordinarily it is not the function of science to doubt the objectivity of the universe. In natural sciences, for example, the reality of the physical and biological world is assumed—the world is believed to be there for its disclosure to the rational mind. Through the methods of observation, analysis, hypothesization and verification, researchers in these sciences aim at unfolding the 'mystery' of the universe. Thus, if the objective existence of the phenomena observed is questioned, that is, if the presupposition that events outside us follow a certain order or uniformity and occur independent of the factors constituting the act of observation, is doubted, scientific explanation would cease to have any 'real' reference. The very logic of natural sciences demands our unbiased registering of what goes on there 'outside'. The scientific attitude is to 'throw out' anything that it researches on and claims to know. To a scientist, reality is an organization of uniformities whose knowledge, inasmuch as it is contained inside descriptive or causal statements free from subjective nuances, must be taken as the truth.

Actually the very possibility of scientific knowledge, like that of common sense knowledge, is due to its reliance on naive realism. The assumption that the structure of the universe is self-governed, and fully knowable, runs underneath both scientific and common sense attitudes. That is why both these ways of knowledge are object-anchored, object-organizing, and, in their application in the actual world, object-mastering. By their very objectivist commitment, the scientific theories do not take into account the agencies that influence the knowing mind in its encounter with what is offered to it.

Now whatever may be its ultimate metaphysical standing, in any knowledge situation it is subjectivity that confers a meaning on the known object. In fact, unless a thing enters into the range of human subjectivity, it would not stand out as experienced. As Husserl, for whom the direction of Kant's philosophy was of great significance, has pointed out, the unique characteristic of subjectivity is its intentionality, i.e., its directedness towards whatever is given to it. This 'given' need not be empirically based. Husserl maintained that every experience harbours in itself a meaning of some kind, or, at times, several meanings, in accordance with which it emerges before consciousness as real. The peculiar nature of the object of knowledge is that it is something 'meant' to the knower, lies outside him, and is there because of him. Without this curious 'meaning' or 'beholding' function of the subject, or his intentionality, there would not be anything registered as known. Knowledge, in its essence, is an act of intuiting meanings whose organization and association-with-objects-outside is one of the most perplexing acts of our consciousness.

It was Franz Brentano who was mainly instrumental in developing the idea of intentionality in philosophy. The idea was later on taken up by Husserl and forms the main theme in the study of consciousness in phenomenology to our day. Brentano meant to point out the distinction between the mental and the physical phenomena and thought that mental phenomena, unlike physical phenomena, are distinguishable on the ground of their being intentional and having 'intentional relations'. In his epoch-making work, *Psychology from the Empirical Standpoint,* Brentano argued that while non-mental objects do not relate themselves to anything outside them it is the mental entity (the human mind) that necessarily related itself to some object or other, some content or other, which need not be empirically placed. Brentano says that in perception something is perceived, in judgement something is judged, in an affirmation something is affirmed, in desire something is desired, in hate something is hated. The subjective side of the experience of perception, judgement, affirmation, desire, etc., was all that Brentano and after him Husserl and other phenomenologists and existentialists were concerned with.

No inquiry into science can afford to overlook the fact that in our act of comprehending the world pure objectivity is a chimera. On the face of it, it might seem that in scientific observation the constitution of the observing mind is hardly a relevant determinant. A scientific statement is generally looked upon as an absolutely impersonal description of the state of affairs available in the world. Whoever may make such a statement, science maintains, the statement can be tested and seen as either mirroring or not mirroring reality as it is.

Scientific laws are thus recognized as logical entities corresponding to the perceived, 'public', material entities. Sciences like physics, chemistry and biology claim to show how, by the use of the techniques of analysis, measurement, experimentation, and proof, an objective, materialist explanation of the whole empirical domain is possible. With one of the strongest defences in our time of what he calls 'epistemology without the knowing mind', Mario Bunge argues in favour of objectivity in scientific knowledge thus:

> ... (an item of knowledge) is objective because, and to the extent that, there are animals capable of acquiring it and putting it to the test with the help of criteria independent of personal factors such as authority or firmness of conviction. The degree of objectivity of a proposition maybe estimated by virtue of the rules of the knowledge game, such as those of logic and empirical testing.[1]

> The sciences that study physical objects, or things, are the factual sciences... These disciplines try to find the laws of such subjects, in particular their laws of change, such as equations of motion, field equations, chemical reaction equations, social mobility matrices, and historical trends... The law statements that factual scientists are after tell us what the really possible states of things are as well as what the really possible changes of state (i.e., events or processes) of concrete objects are.[2]

Nevertheless, such an objectivism, although consistent with the conduct of scientific research and continuously supported by the spectacular progress it has made, is hard to stand in the face of what can be called the rise of the human individual or human subjectivity in the entire gamut of knowledge.

All scientific knowledge is basically the creation of man. For an impression to pass off as knowledge, it must appear within the field of our awareness. Human consciousness, or its intentionality, runs into objects, so to say, and focuses on them against the background of an infinite number of other objects. While it stays preoccupied with a particular object, the objects environing it linger on and vacillate as indistinct but ready to come into the zone of the known. Indeed, these environing objects may never become distinct and fixed before consciousness; on the other hand, they may eventually disappear into total obscurity, into some unfathomable spatial openness along the nexus between the knower's self and the world. The subjective idealists are serious when they argue that since, metaphysically speaking, it is our subjectivity in which ideas and their interrelations dwell, we should say that the world corresponding to them is in us, i.e., it is our own creation.

What must be emphasized is that the subject-pole encounters the given (a thing, an event, an idea, an impression) in a certain manner, or from its own peculiar vantage point. By granting the world a sense, a form, or pattern, and by selecting a definite aspect of it in observation, man apperceives and anticipates the very ontology of the world. It is perhaps in this sense that Thomas Nagel posits the origin of the 'point of view' as the unignorable riddle in our experience. He writes:[3]

> It is difficult to understand what could be meant by the *objective* character of our experience, apart from the particular point of view from which its subject apprehends it. (Italics original).

> The problem is not just that when I look at the Mona Lisa, my visual experience has a certain quality, no trace of which is to be found by someone looking into my brain. For even if he did observe there a tiny image of the Mona Lisa, he would have no reason to identify it with experience.

Hence, in the whole intercourse between man and the world, or between subjectivity and objectivity, unless what is given in experience satisfies what can be called the 'existential conditions' inherent in the whole structure of the experiencer's individuality, it would not be comprehended. The world, it would be appropriate to say, represents the uncovering of the ontological project of man.[4]

In fact when we go deep into the very anatomy of knowledge and raise questions like 'how does one know that one knows?' 'How does the mind *see* that the knowledge of something given to it is certain or clear?' 'How can we account for the gap between subject-pole and the object-pole?' 'What is the origin of the manner the subject-pole views the object-pole?' and perhaps the most germane question of all, i.e., 'What is the state of consciousness of a philosophical inquirer who steps behind the two poles of knowledge and watches their interaction?' we begin to realize the mystery of consciousness itself.

But natural sciences do not concentrate on the mechanism of knowledge, except by way of finding out it physiological co-relates. Since their design is to formulate laws that could account for the origin, the evolution, and the future condition of the entire universe, they take for granted that the laws of knowledge do not fall inside their preview. For them to explain the 'why' and the 'how' of knowledge is to determine the mechanics of the human brain, which, according to them, is nothing but a highly complex configuration of neuronal networks.

Because of the most dependable predictive ability and the resultant control natural sciences have come to command with all kinds of spatio-temporal events, it is no wonder that their method is today valued as the most promising one. And this is despite the fact that quantum theorists in recent times have spoken about the important role consciousness plays in the study of the entire realm of physical reality. The atomic uncertainty and the unpredictability in nature quantum theory has emphasized are based on the capriciousness with which material particles, such as electrons, behave without any rhyme or reason. While Niels Bohr pioneered this thought, Albert Einstein insisted on demonstrating that 'God does not play dice' and that therefore uncertainty and unpredictability we attribute to the atomic units of a system is largely due to our ignorance. Science therefore adheres to the presupposition that if all the factors pertinent to a system are known, we could anticipate every move within that system. For Einstein, nature as a system is fully predictable.

In social sciences, which basically attempts at understanding man and his life in society, the researchers consider the application of the scientific method as incumbent on them. Social scientists today conduct the study of the human or social material seemingly as objectively as the natural scientists treat physical objects. They look for laws of 'behaviour' of the humans—thus, their nickname 'behavioural scientists'—that would explain everything concerning the individual-society interaction.

There is no doubt that the immense credibility that the natural sciences have acquired, and the fantastic marvels that they have made possible in the spheres of their application, are largely due to their method of approaching the complexity of the universe. One cannot but admire the wealth of welfare and good they have generated for mankind by enabling it to develop technologies for facilitating its adjustment to the forces of nature. The ground they have prepared in space technology for the penetration of man into the solar system surely contains the possibility of a permanent solution to the rapidly depleting resources of the planet Earth. And all this is obviously the result of their trust in the possibility of objective knowledge, i.e., their assumption that all phenomena are basically material, that they are causally determined, and that, therefore, the logic comprising analysis, quantification, measurement and experimentation must be applied to them indiscriminately.

The celebrators of the view, sweeping in its scope, that any happening in the universe is fully reducible to a determinable pattern of change in the material structure of the universe, and that, as soon as this pattern in explained in terms of the laws governing it, other happenings in its set could accurately be predicted, is called by Karl Popper 'scientific determinism'.[5] The main thrust of this view is that there is no mystery about anything in the universe, including human phenomena, once we come to know the physical, the chemical and the biological constituents of it and the laws governing them. Subjectivity, the freedom of the human self, the spontaneity and creativity of the mind, even the uniqueness one experiences about his or her being in the world, are all translatable into, according to this view, material or neuronal configurations of the brain. The Cartesian dualism is thrown overboard. Hobbes had said that the basic condition of all organic, as of inorganic bodies, is one of motion, i.e., collision, conflict, and war. For Newton, the laws of motion are central to all happenings and it is these laws that can be shown to explain them. Laplace believed that the world is reducible to corpuscles interacting among themselves according to the laws of Newtonian dynamics; and Marx and Watson did not see anything in the mental reality of man which does not have, for its equivalent, man's bodily behaviour.

The use of scientific laws, that is, for instance, the laws in physics, chemistry, biology, neurology, etc., to determine 'human' events, has reached a stage when any reference to the subjective, to our 'inner space' is regarded as unwarranted. Efforts of the behavioural scientists to reduce humans and human societies to mathematically mappable systems of behaviour are made unrestrainedly. The assumption is that human beings are complexes of behavioural processes, conglomerations of definite hereditary and environmental factors, and, therefore, fully accountable by means of what B.F. Skinner anticipates as 'science of behaviour (adopting) the strategy of physics and biology'.[6] So, to understand men, scientists assert, is to look upon them as schemes of interactions between the organisms that they are and their environment, to evolve a mathematical model of their total existence. Like physics and chemistry and biology and neurology, social sciences promise to provide a complete model of man-as-a-machine.

The behavioural, empirical interpretation of human existence is objectivist—it ignores the subjective, the creative, and the existential at its core. The well-known policy of modern science is that it either claims to guarantee the conclusive explainability (in theory, if not in practice) of almost every phenomenon in the universe, or, if something does not fit into its compass, refuses to recognise its relevance. The phenomena, whose very legitimacy science thus rejects, usually have a base in the psychic, the intentional, the transcendental, or the inward.

The empirical study of man, conducted by behavioural scientists, is in tune with the emulation on their part of the natural scientists. The account of phenomena, with their anchorage in the inwardness of man which these studies may possibly refer to, is necessarily in terms of well-established natural laws. Such an account, stated in the language of cause-effect relationship, promises to provide us with an exhaustive chart indicating the actual and possible human responses to different stimuli. Thus, the empirical-analytic-positivist approach to subjectivity, to the 'inside' of man, is in every respect identical with the approach of the natural sciences to the structure of the universe.

If taken strictly on the ground of its effectiveness, the empirical-analytic-positivist explanations of man's behaviour patterns may seem to be flawless. This is because of the materialist and determinist character of such explanations. They make it a point not to construct untestable or transempirical hypotheses and not to confirm any statement unless it reflects observed or observable facts. So what has been regarded for centuries, as the ontological foundation of human reality is here understood through the categories of human behaviour. Our direct and most authentic experiences like feelings, self-knowledge, self-identity, mental acts, meaning-intuition, which are the 'stuff' constituting our subjectivity, are not looked upon as the primordial facets of our being, but rather as a variety of compounded behaviour expressions. In the process, man's subjectivity—that is, his 'inner space', or the act of trascendence that he fundamentally is—is lost.

We have already said that, however objective an understanding of the world science may claim to have reached, there is necessarily in this understanding an expression of consciousness's unique act of intuiting and organizing meanings. It is this act that both Kant and Husserl recognized as constituting the essence of man. It is because of man's presence in the world that all meanings, theories and explanations originate. The knowing consciousness *sees* the world to be there, builds up meanings and theories and explanations around what it sees, and develops the technique of controlling it. From the beginning of history, man has not only shown curiosity with regard to his environment but he has also, almost instinctively, applied whatever knowledge he could gain for changing it. In this sense, man has always been teleological and subjectivist in his encounter with the world.

One of the shortcomings of the very methodology of natural and behavioural sciences is that their investigation is strictly confined to the causes of phenomena. Any thinking about the purpose, the goal, the *raison d'être* of human activity is supposed to fall outside their investigation. However, it is in the planning of science, in its practice for changing the situation on the globe to man's advantage, that scientists cannot afford to forego the question of human subjectivity—human aspirations, hopes, desires, and projects concerning the collective well-being of mankind. In fact, the whole history of scientific-technological civilization represents mankind's decision to pursue certain values, a definite way of life, to seek the fulfilment of its inmate passions. Thus, if man is to attain the fullest realization of his spirit, it is necessary that he not only control his environment, and gain supremacy over the anti-survival forces, but also he be aware of the inner dimension of his self.

There is no technique by which the width of human subjectivity can be completely mapped out. It is a domain in which imagination, insights, intuitions, decisions, and one's

Weltanschauung spring up before they take a concrete shape in one's life, conduct, and in one's attitude towards others. The sphere of subjectivity is too elusive to be captured inside language. It is of the nature of a wholesome feeling of one's being real and absolutely unrestrained in one's inner space. In fact, the very sense of being human that lies underneath our experience of living in the world, is rooted deeply in our subjectivity. Subjectivity is the core of my existence, in the sense that within my inner self I am aware of my personal identity, my unique reality, and my freedom to manipulate my own thoughts, feelings, volitions, attitudes, and so on. The aim of what might be termed as the ontology of the inner man should be to verbalise this transempirical reality at the heart of our existence.[7]

The kind of reach we have to our inside is unlike any intellectual encounter we have with objects and other persons. The most significant characteristic of human consciousness is to intuit itself as the pivot of all that 'goes on' in and out of it. Consciousness is in freedom, it is freedom, for all mental acts are seen to arise in it wholly spontaneously as if they flow out of its open and elusive being. These acts are, of course, occasioned by what may seem to be objectively operating stimuli. I find myself as the seat of all that 'happens' to me—psychological and bodily processes, I own my impressions, I am an open awareness a priori. I am an authority with regard to my inside in the sense that I can transcend what I am, have a bird's-eye view of what I am. Śaṁkara, the famous Indian metaphysician of the eighth century A.D., and Husserl and Sartre in our own time, have stressed this when they say that consciousness, as a self-seeing 'act', constantly oscillates between the transcendental and the phenomenal, the pre-reflective and the reflective, and, almost out of its own inertia, reveals to itself that it is a world-experiencer. The world-experience is strangely intertwined with the subjectivity of the experiences.

The subjective parameter essential to all knowledge situations is most picturesquely brought out by Thomas Nagel in his widely-acclaimed paper, "What is it like to be a bat?." Nagel's argument is that subjective parameter of our knowledge is not analysable in terms of any explanatory system of functional states 'since these could be ascribed to robots or automata that behaved like people though they experienced nothing.'[8] Nagel further remarks that the subjective experience of anyone is not realizable by any onlooker unless the latter is able to reach the inner self of the former. There is an unbridgeable gap, Nagel asserts, between the perceiver and the perceived, with the result that the subjectivity of the perceived other is a domain forever closed to the perceiver.

Something must be said at this stage concerning the manner in which Jean-Paul Sartre develops the notion of subjectivity (called by him significantly the '*pour-soi*'). Sartre's model of human consciousness is two-pronged. He uses the terms '*pour-soi*' and '*en-soi*' to suggest that the former as subjectivity and the latter as objectivity are so interrelated that they appear to be two poles of the same mental activity. The *pour-soi* is man as the free manipulator of experience, the intentional interpreter, and reality is directly perceived by everyone as a movement between the empirical and the trans-empirical horizons of one's own consciousness. The *pour-soi* carries the peculiar sense of 'I-within-myself'—it is a reality directed towards itself, can make and unmake itself, is capable of giving meaning to itself, can circumvent itself, can solidify itself as ego-consciousness from its primordial pre-reflective, transcendental expanse. The objective (*en-soi*), on the other hand, is the world 'outside' the *pour-soi* and derives its meaning from it. For Sartre, the *pour-soi* and the *en-soi* are conjoined to each other and therefore neither of them can exist without the other. The *pour-soi* is the observer and the interpreter of the *en-soi*. There would actually be no meanings, no knowledge edifices, no artistic creations, no perspectives, had there not been *pour-soi* at their foundation. In Sartre's works, the term '*pour-soi*' carries the flavour of that core reality within us that is self-directed, self-made, self-seen in the sense that man or human consciousness has to be conceived as that basic flow or outburst from which the world (as the *en-soi*) is put into an epistemological or theoretical system.

The experience of freedom is deeply involved in the uniqueness one feels in being a subject. Subjectivity is elusive, self-defining, self-asserting, self-positing; it is a sphere where, as Nagel has pointed out, the subject is totally absorbed within himself or herself and cannot open himself up to the grasp of the other as the other would open up to the grasp of himself. This is the reason why Nagel talks of subjectivity as entailing a 'point of view'. An individual's point of view is something mysteriously anchored in the way he or she looks at the world, at his own or her own station in life, the singular perspective he or she forms and uses as a prism for understanding himself-in-the-world.

The twentieth-century scientific-technological culture which is the embodiment of objective knowledge has compelled a total change in our approach to the human individual: the human individual is regarded as a function, a mere 'one of them', as one not with an *ātman* (the ontological subject) or a human face. Today, the language with which an individual is described is function-based—he is defined as a producer, a consumer, an employer or an employee, an executive, a clerk, a statesman, a banker, and, perhaps the last of all, a human subject or a person.

Hindu ātmalogy[9] has one central message valid for all times and that is that man's empirical, objectively-studied consciousness is not the final domain of his total fulfilment. What ancient Indian seers insisted on is the deepening of subjectivity as a *sine qua non* of all our knowledge endeavours. From the level of *ātman*-awareness, the worldly, objective enterprises of ours could be seen as not an end-in-itself but as an instrument leading us to an experience of total being. A certain value system, humanistic in its essence and therefore comprising the values of brotherhood, compassion for the sufferer, selflessness, an openness of outlook and perception, a developmental paradigm having for its dimension the inner world of the other, is expected to evolve from the reflection of the self on itself. *Mokṣa* in Indian thought must be interpreted as an experience giving rise to such a value system.

The Hindu *Weltanschauung* is transcendence-oriented. The principal concern it embodies is the capturing of the meaning of individual's existence so that he is able to rebuild his relationship with the world and with his fellowmen. While the application of science and technology is speedily transforming man's lifestyle and confirming his mastery over his environment, basic existential questions are still asked as poignantly as they were being asked over centuries. What is human destiny? How could man attain perfection? How could the catastrophe, feared to arise out of the struggle for supremacy among the developed countries in the world be avoided? What would be the shape of the scientific-technological civilization fifty years hence?

The positivist-behaviourist-mechanist method, whose bedrock is the objective explanation of things in the world, has no reach to the transcendental openness of human consciousness, to the self's nostalgia to experience being. Human reality, being at the foundation of all organized knowledge, objectification, acts of communication, and models of explanation, is the most unpredictable and self-constructing phenomenon the cosmic process has thrown up. Being a ceaseless flux, an abode of epistemic possibilities very few of which are actually materialised in rational knowledge, our subjectivity is an outward-inward movement having no exactly markable boundaries. Thus, its precise characterization is impossible: it sees and posits the world in certain ways, constantly generates new meanings and projects them onto existence, and figures as consistently dynamic in its act of self-expression. Scientific explanation of things in the world, rational schemes, systems, theories, models, etc., are such a project designed by subjectivity. To account for the *raison d'être* and ultimate validity of scientific explanations, it would be necessary to plough deep into the inner structure of *ātman,* to take consciousness to the zero point and to compass consciousness in its acts of building meanings, systems and values. This is the central task which philosophical anthropology, complemented by phenomenology, hermeneutics, critical theory, and structuralism, can fruitfully undertake. It is a paradox built-in into ātmalogy (just as it is built-in into philosophical anthropology) that for comprehending the meaning of his life and for re-structuring his relationship to the world and others man must explore his 'inside', his self, but it is this very inside that eludes itself, paradoxically, from his intellectual grasp and language.

NOTES

1. Bungo, Mario. 1981. *Scientific Materialism.* New York: Reidel Publishing Co. pp. 152-53.
2. Ibid., pp. 162-63.
3. Nagel, Thomas. 1982. "What is it Like to be a Bat?" *The Mind's I.* Douglas Hofstadter and Daniel Dennett (ed.). London: Penguin Books. pp. 391-403.
4. See, Laing, R.D. 1965. *The Divided Self.* Middlesex: Penguin Books. pp. 19-20.
5. Popper, Karl. 1982. *The Open Universe: An Argument for Indeterminism.* London: Hutchinson & Co. pp. 29-33.
6. Skinner, B.F. 1973. *Beyond Freedom and Dignity.* London: Penguin Books. pp. 180-81.
7. For the development of this point, see Sinari, Ramakant. 1990. "Science, Technology and the Hindu 'Weltanschauung'". *The Technological Civilization and Indian Society.* B.D. Nag Chaudhuri (ed.). Shimla: IIAS. pp. 10-19.
8. Nagel, Thomas. pp. 391-403.
9. This word, coined by me some years ago, should denote, like the word 'phenomenology', the ego-exploring technique in Indian philosophics. The function of ātmalogy is to direct consciousness to 'bracket' the objective itself, to intensify its self-transcending process, and to put it in a position to observe its own 'roots' as it were. See, Sinari, Ramakant. 1970. *The Structure of Indian Thought.* Springfield, Ill.: Charles C. Thomas. pp. 11-12.

CHAPTER 11

A New Vision of Puruṣārthas and Quantum Entaglement

Raja Ramanna

It is well known that the four *'puruṣārthas'* summarize the value systems of the Vedic period. They have been there for a very long time and have received many an interpretation, each one of them equally profound, corresponding to the sociology of the period. The values as generally understood and interpreted are: (1) the importance of material well-being, economics, *Artha,* (2) creative pleasure, sex and entertainment, *Kāma,* (3) order of the established universe, both material and moral, *Dharma,* and, finally, (4) salvation leading to perfection, *Mokṣa.*

The four words, though they are not of equal importance, classify concisely the whole range human phenomena and seem to have an everlasting value over the ages. We look at them again in this second millennium to reflect on the various changes that have taken place in the present globally interacting civilization. The economic problems (*artha*) and the cultural impact through TV and internet programmes (*kāma*) are making deep inroads into our lives even in the remotest of villages of India. In modifying our views on *dharma,* we have to ponder over the usefulness of religion and culture, in the light of new capabilities that include not only the progress of science and its impact on better health and longevity but also on matters that lead to destruction of cities and the killing of people on a massive scale. The final question, will the new revolution in thinking permit a Utopia (*mokṣa*) of some sort in the millenniums to come?

The state the world finds itself is so absurdly strange that a group of terrorists are able to destroy not only the great towers of the city of New York, but directly or indirectly even shake up the financial structure of the whole world. Is our socio-financial system so fragile that it can be shaken to its very roots in institutions whose financial powers are such that billions of dollars are a matter of daily transactions? Perhaps financial instability has nothing to do with terrorism and comes about in reverse from overconcentration of wealth in one place and an overproduction of goods, not necessarily wanted by the public, but forced on them by high pressure techniques. It is a kind of competitive *artha,* and many economists believe it is the only way of creating wealth. In principle, *artha* as defined in the *puruṣārtha* is for fulfilling a basic need for higher order needs of the mind and not for share market speculation.

The second *puruṣārtha* refers to another basic need of mankind, e.g., love, sex and entertainment. The temples of Khajuraho have all this frozen beautifully on stone and give the true meaning of *kāma.* But the wonderful invention of the TV and internet is being used to project crude pornography and the classical arts are being made to look as pornographic as possible to suit modern tastes. It is not clear whether suffering is a part of *kāma* or *dharma.* Some people enjoy it and some believe suffering is a necessary path to *mokṣa.*

Many a scientist has complained that hours spent by them in developing the mathematics, the software, etc., required for information transfer is being used to project cheap entertainment rather than quality material to commensurate with the complex software developed for the purpose. While it is not possible to protect all scientific developments from misuse, one can in principle develop a community to appreciate the worth of the discoveries of science and technology and use it appropriately. This is possible through the third *purṣārtha,* viz., *dharma.*

The word *dharma* is difficult of translation and is used with many meanings, but for a Hindu and Buddhist the integrated meaning is clear. To others it may seem too diffuse and only confuse them. *Dharma* can mean religion, justice, charity, duty, observance, right. It can be practised by individuals or collectively. The collective *dharma* of the many sometimes remains an undefined and unattainable abstraction. The failure of the '*Dharma* of the many' is described in great magnificence in the *Mahābhārata,* whereas individual *dharma* is meant to lead to the fourth *purṣārtha,* i.e., *mokṣa* whose meaning extends from salvation to perfection.

The collective approach to *dharma* is the path to *mokṣa,* better understood as Utopia, and is dependent on the two earlier *puruṣārthas, artha* and *kāma.* Both these are closely related to the existing sociology, and present day sociology is heavily dependent on modern technology and, eventually, science. An appeal to God will not stop the use of weapons of mass destruction. It is only the mass action of *dharma* that can do it. Such action can come from yoga or as indications of science show, that terrorism and its manifestations either in war or peace results from feeding of wrong information to the brain and through an all round whipping up of hysteria. Those us who can recall World War II, and in recent times the Cold War and the Afghan War, will not forget the use of the hysterical side using religion (Talibanism), racism (Nazism), ethnic hate (Casteism) etc., to build up terror. It is good to recall the impression of what looked like a miracle when Mahatma Gandhi, through his personal *dharma,* was able to convince the capabilities of non-violent methods to the Frontier Leader, Khan Abdul Gaffar Khan, a leader from a most fierce tribe along the Indo-Afghan border, the Pashtuns. All this was disturbed by the Partition and, in reaction, a most destructive uprising known as Talibanism has come about in its various forms. We see in this how an appropriate *dharma* of an individual, derived by years of *sādhanā* can spread to a wider circle of people to show a path leading to *mokṣa.*

Finally, the question. Can modern science provide a method by which peoples' dharmic senses can be altered. *Dharma* depends on our consciousness and the one human activity that we know that exists, but cannot be given a true meaning in terms of science, is consciousness. We now know more about cellular behavior, genes, neurons, etc., and their immense capability to cure genetically derived diseases. Much of the depraved form of *dharma* could be due to a diseased consciousness and be sufficiently infectious as to build up to mass hysteria. All this seems far fetched but we have reason to believe that while all religions speak of compassion and teach their adherents to follow this path of peace and kindness at an early age, violence as a group behaviour shows up at adolescence somewhat similar to a kind of schizophrenia.

We cannot survive without including the philosophy of science into our value system. We recall how the discoveries of Newton had a deep influence on western philosophy. Now that the philosophy of classical science has changed, the same is required of the interpretation of the third *puruṣārtha* to include the philosophy of Quantum Mechanics and the behavior of the living cell. Classical logic has been challenged by the Buddhists and Godel's theorem and we may have to accept causes for which there are no effects and effects for which there are no causes. Sometimes one feels that life itself seems to have come about without a cause and we have to create a path that leads us to *mokṣa*.

While the world has considered the possibilities of achieving *mokṣa* by disciplining the mind through religion, education, and other societal efforts we now have to consider what contributions Science can make to build a roadway to *mokṣa*. Chemical and biological method may lead us back to drug therapies which are known to lead to side-effects of a dangerous type. Perhaps the new discoveries in Quantum Mechanics may give a clue as to how to bring people together by the connections between *Cit* and *Acit* already imbedded in us. I refer to 'Quantum Entanglement'. Prof. Dipankar Home has studied this quantum effect deeply. The results he has arrived at are quite startling. The objection that was raised by Einstein against Quantum Mechanics, has now become a real effect and has been proved to be true. A spooky connection binds us all together. Though originally the entanglement was all about the entanglement between photons, Home has shown that we can have other types of entanglements of significance dealing with macroscopic matter. Entanglement can indeed lead to *mokṣa* of the many.

APPENDIX

If on the y axis **all** the possible causes in some number order is listed and on the x axis all the effects in a similar manner, we will get the matrix as shown below. If for each effect we put all the causes for the required effect 1's and for those not required 0's, we get a matrix of 1's and zeros.

Causes 1 2 3 4 5 6 7 8————n————————to infinity
Effects 2 0
3 1
4 1
5 0
6 1
7 1
8 0 etc
*
*
to infinity.

Here the diagonal numbers 10110110 ————,could represent an **effect** since it has 1's at the required **causes**. If however we look for an effect with numbers all different from the diagonal formed by putting a 0 where there was a 1 and a 1 where there was a 0,which in this case it will become 01101001———etc. This last combination will never be found among the set of x's. If it happens to be a noticeable **effect** it cannot be due to any of the infinite causes that have been enumerated above. We can therefore have **effects** without **causes** and vice versa.

CHAPTER 12

Science, Philosophy and Consciousness: Reassessing the Connections in the Light of Quantum Theory

Ravi Gomatam
(a.k.a. Rasarāja dāsā)

I

INTRODUCTION

It is now widely perceived that certain developments in science hold new lessons for philosophy, not only with respect to the way philosophy has approached questions concerning the natural world (such as space, time or causality), but also with respect to questions that have been heretofore viewed as being solely philosophical or even theological. Here I refer specifically to the problem of consciousness.

Developments in a number of scientific fields in the last several decades, both experimental and theoretical, have made consideration of the nature and role of consciousness a central issue. For example, the causal basis for the appearance of an individual event in quantum experiments seems to be closely correlated with the free choices that conscious experimenters make. In contemporary neuroscience, there is a massive body of data providing neural correlates of consciousness, using techniques such as fMRI, PET and SPECT, that has laid the basis for a keen debate as to whether these correlations can be given a causal basis. In the field of artificial intelligence, the attempt to not only simulate but also actually construct a working human mind with a high order of intelligence using electronic computational machinery is closely connected to the issue of the nature of human consciousness.

However, the efforts to link the issue of human consciousness to the scientific data in these differing fields have so far run mainly in one direction: namely, to study consciousness in terms of our present understanding of matter as the sole ontological category. The philosophical basis for this materialistic monist approach was laid, curiously enough, by the Cartesian move to treat mind/consciousness and matter as two different ontological categories (*res cogitans* and *res extensa,* respectively). True, Descartes considered mind/consciousness to be fundamentally different from, and thus not reducible to, matter.[1]

Nevertheless, Descartes' dualism made modern reductionistic science possible, since his dualism equally meant that matter is also independent of mind. It is this flip side of the Cartesian dualism that drove the subsequent course of science, the main question being whether such an ontologically independent matter can also be rendered epistemologically independent, i.e., studied independent of mind.[2] It was concluded early on that as long as matter can be studied in terms of its primary properties, the resulting knowledge, even if it be our knowledge of matter (and thus enmeshed in the first-person perspective), could be treated for all practical purposes as objective knowledge. Thus, the Cartesian dualism that underpins modern science was and is a methodological dualism. Western science has otherwise retained ontological monism as the basis for its explanations.

It is therefore not surprising that contemporary attempts to make a connection between science and consciousness have run mostly in the direction of accounting for consciousness in terms of matter. These attempts can be called the matter-based study of consciousness. It remains to be seen whether such an approach can truly remain objective. For, in all such attempts, consciousness has remained irreducible,[3] such that we seem to have so far neither the desired naturalized account of consciousness, nor fundamentally new pragmatic scientific applications through the contemporary field of 'consciousness studies.'

In this paper, I sketch the possibility of launching an alternative approach that I shall call the consciousness-based study of matter. The proposed approach will not be to study consciousness itself or even the interaction between consciousness and matter (thus avoiding the vexing mind-body problem), but rather to get deeper insights about the nature of matter that can be applied within the empirical sciences. It thus has the potential to be more scientific (being essentially a study of matter) than the present matter-based study of consciousness.[4] Although it might seem counterintuitive at first, only dualism can aid the objective study of matter, imprisoned as we are by the first-person perspective. As already pointed out, it is by adopting dualism as a methodological tool that the very possibility of an objective study of matter was opened up by Descartes. In this paper we shall argue for enlarging the scope of Cartesian dualism to advance the objective study of matter. In this connection I will be drawing upon a particular strand of dualism from the Indian Vedāntic tradition called the *acintya bheda-abheda Vedānta,* developed in detail by Sri Chaitanya and his principal students during the fifteenth and sixteenth centuries. Of particular interest for us would be its sub-school of Bhāgavata Sāṁkhya, which holds that many functions we tend to associate only with consciousness—such as thinking, feeling, intelligence, etc.—are necessary but not sufficient characteristics of consciousness, such that they can also be associated with purely material systems, provided that we enlarge our conception of matter beyond the Cartesian confines.

I shall try to lay the basis for the plausibility, and even a need, for such an alternative approach by examining the connections among contemporary physics, philosophy, and consciousness in three parts. In the first part, I shall discuss in detail the foundational ideas in empirical philosophy and empirical science with particular regard to realism, and argue why, despite the common appellation "empirical", the two have little in common at present. This would explain how empirical science has been able to make progress thus far by essentially ignoring empirical philosophy's concerns.

In the second part, I shall argue that the implications of quantum theory are such that the project of scientific realism along classical (i.e., pre-quantum) lines has run aground in a way that involves not a causal role for consciousness (as sometimes held), but rather a role for philosophy within physics, a role that did not exist in the pre-quantum era.

In the third and concluding part of the paper, I shall propose how this understanding of the situation in quantum theory opens the possibility for relating traditional Indian philosophy, particularly the system of Bhāgavata Sāṁkhya, to the concerns of empirical science, in terms of the need to develop another non-Cartesian conception of matter at the macroscopic or observational level. Thus, during the course of the paper we will be analyzing the relations among philosophy, science, and consciousness, both conceptually and from an ancient civilizational perspective.

II

SETTING UP THE TERMINOLOGY

I begin by distinguishing among three types of object concepts: common-sense object concepts, mathematical object concepts, and physical object concepts. They occur respectively in common-sense thinking, mathematics, and physics.

Corresponding to these three kinds of objects, I identify three kinds of conceptual worlds, namely the phenomenal world, which is directly given in experience by definition; the mathematical world, which is entirely ideal; and the physical world, which is indirectly given in experience. Adopting a realist attitude, I additionally postulate the existence of the external world, which is different from all of these three conceptual worlds (see Figure 1).

All three object-concepts mentioned above, *qua* concepts, are equally abstract. However, common-sense object-concepts, being embodied in ordinary language, are directly coordinated to sense experiences and hence can be given an ostensive definition. In this sense, they are empirically the least abstract.

Mathematical object concepts, on the other hand, cannot be coordinated to experience at all, even if mathematicians often use ordinary language words such as 'space' to talk of the mathematical world. For example, consider the 'Hilbert space', which is the set of all functions that map from R(4) to C(2) and satisfy a 'square-integrability' condition. This set is a very abstract 'space', and we do not expect to be able to visualize it in terms of any notion we associate with the word 'space' in common-sense thinking. Nor can the objects of this abstract Hilbert space, called the Ψ functions, be visualized in common-sense terms, i.e., be given an ostensive definition. Thus, the mathematical concepts are relatively the most abstract, again empirically speaking.

Concepts of physics are in-between. I shall refer to them as 'physical concepts'. Being basically mathematical concepts and therefore essentially formal, they too cannot be directly coordinated to sense experiences and given an ostensive definition. Yet the physicist empirically interprets the theory in which these physical concepts play a role, by interpreting the solutions to the mathematical equations of the formalism as numbers that will appear as readings in appropriately calibrated metres. When subsequently these

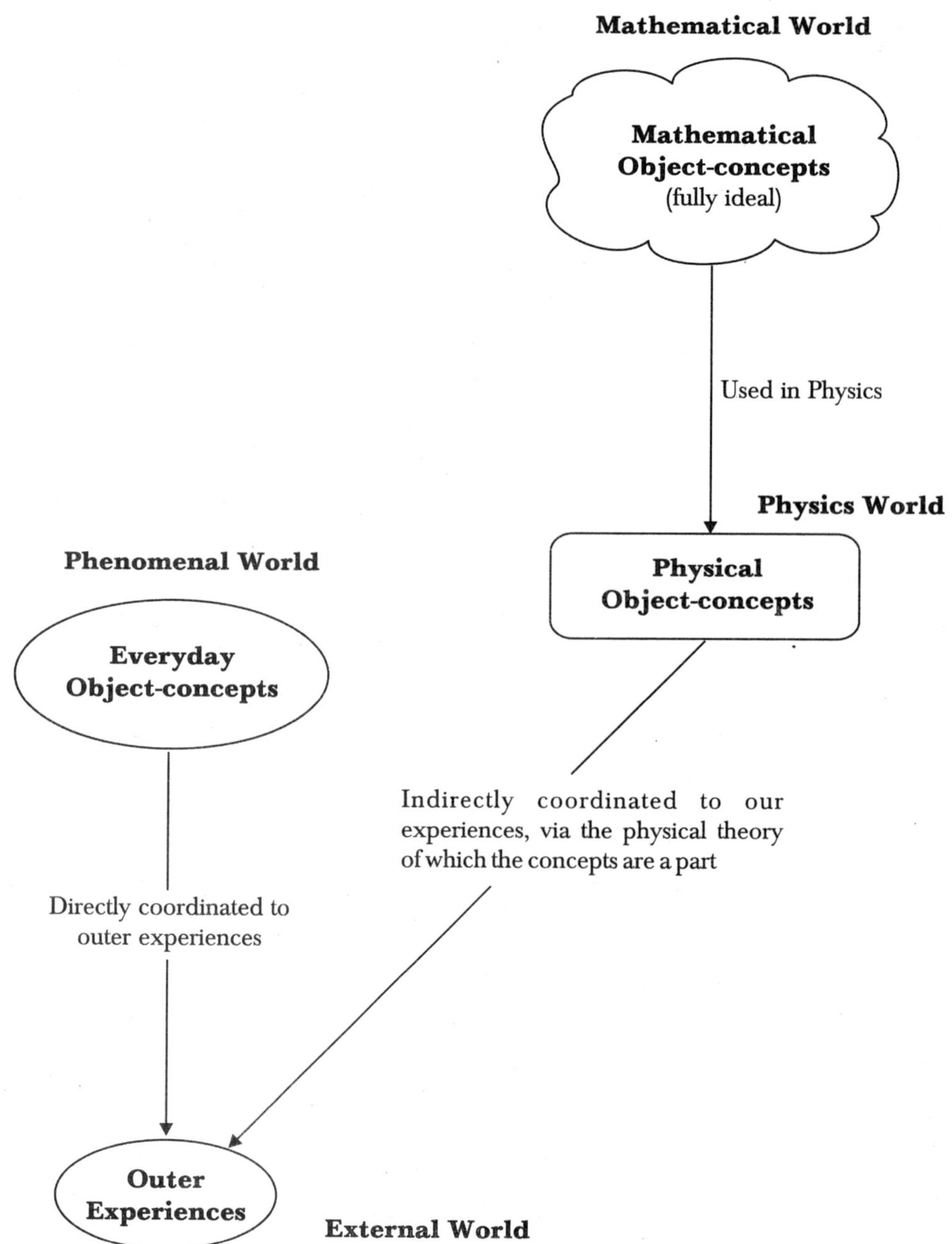

FIGURE 1: DIFFERENT CONCEPTUAL WORLDS AND THEIR INTER-RELATIONSHIP

predictions are verified by performing actual experiments, at that point, the abstract physical concepts can be coordinated to sense experience. For example, although we do not expect to be able to directly point to an 'electron' in our experience, when a localized dot is interpreted as being caused by an electron, we can (and do) point to that dot and say, 'this' is an observed electron. The corresponding mathematical concepts become physical concepts, at this point. For example, in quantum theory, the same Hilbert space we mentioned before is interpreted as the physical space in which the quantum dynamics takes place, and its element, the Ψ function, now becomes a physical state.

Note that from the viewpoint of the terminology being developed in this paper, a 'table' would not be a physical object. Rather, it is a phenomenal object. I reserve the term 'physical' to refer to theoretical entities postulated by physics. As per the viewpoint being developed here, such 'physical objects' exist only in a 'physical world', which is an abstract, physico-mathematical world that is internal to each physical theory and hence could be different for different theories. Thus, the same phenomenal 'table' *qua* physical object would thought of physically as a 'point particle' in the physical world of classical mechanics, in terms of a 'world line' in the physical world of theory of relativity, or in terms of a 'wave function' in the physical world of quantum theory. The corresponding mathematics for each of these physical worlds is accordingly different too. I shall have to say more on the use of the word 'physical' in this special sense in later sections.

III

COMMON-SENSE REALISM

Einstein said, "Physics is nothing but a refinement of common-sense thinking."[5] Common-sense thinking is embodied in our ordinary language. Thus, our common-sense thinking is implicit in the way we describe our sense perceptions using ordinary language.

When we express our sense perceptions using ordinary language, we may speak of 'the table in front of us' and believe that we are referring to a table that exists in the external world. This attitude is known as 'naïve realism' and is characterized by the belief that the world we come to know in experience is the external world, as long as there are no errors in perception or other mitigating factors that question the veracity of our very experience. In so describing our outer experiences, i.e., experiences of the external world, ordinary language is functioning in what I shall call the realist mode or the *R*-mode (see Figure 2).

However, ordinary language also functions in another mode, which I shall call the phenomenal mode or the *P*-mode. The ordinary language statement 'I feel happy', for example, refers directly to our inner experience and therefore is in the *P*-mode. Similarly, when we say 'the sunset is beautiful', ordinary language is functioning in the *P*-mode, since the statement refers to our inner experiential content. To say ordinary language is functioning in the *P*-mode in the statement 'the sunset is beautiful' is not to take a stance on the aesthetic question of whether it is objectively possible for the sunset to be beautiful. Nor am I particularly concerned by whatever implication the *P*-mode statement 'the sunset

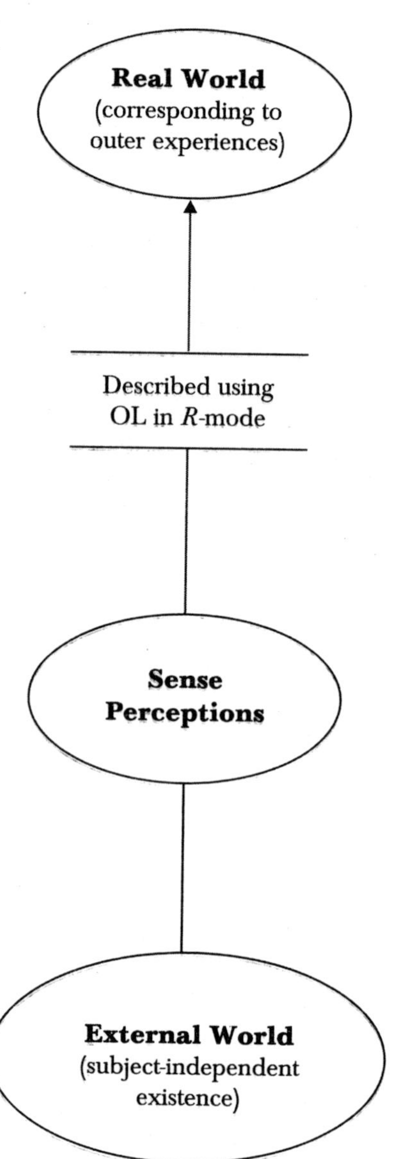

Naïve or common-sense realism
(a) believes that we directly comprehend the world as it is,
(b) that ordinary language (OL) can and must passively express this comprehension, and
(c) thus equates the known, or knowable real world with the external world
Legend: *R*-mode = Realist mode

FIGURE 2: NAÏVE REALISM

is beautiful' may have for the validity of the *R*-mode of ordinary language. As it will become clear below, my intention in introducing the distinction between the *P*-mode and *R*-mode of ordinary language is not to deny that the *P*-mode statements even with regard to inner experiences could imply *R*-mode ideas (after all, we could not have a veridical inner experience of a 'beautiful' sunset if there were not actually a sunset taking place in the world), but rather to pave the way for the discussion of a reverse point: that the start of modern empirical philosophy is characterized by the recognition that all statements concerning outer experiences in the *R*-mode imply the validity of the same statements in the *P*-mode first.

IV

PHILOSOPHICAL REALISM

The start of modern western philosophy[6] is characterized by Descartes' recognition that, logically speaking, even while describing outer experiences, ordinary language can be said to function only in the *P*-mode. Thus, even a statement of the sort 'I see a table in front of me' is to be taken, in the first instance, as a *P*-mode statement and referring to our experience. Empirical philosophy therefore views the common-sense naïve realist attitude —that ordinary language descriptions of outer experiences refer to objects in the external world—as an extrapolation that needs justification. The different schools of empiricism, such as skepticism, idealism and realism (as well as any number of other schools, such as operationalism, conventionalism, foundationalism, etc.) would respond differently to the question, of whether it is possible to justify treating ordinary language as functioning in the *R*-mode in such cases.

Since physics unavoidably involves realist praxis, and my plan is to examine the connection among philosophy, physics and consciousness, I shall focus on the attempts to justify realism (about the external world) within the analytical tradition. The first thesis of philosophical realism is that the subject-independent existence of an external world is a metaphysical presupposition, since the external world is not directly knowable as such. Given this presupposition, the next step is to postulate that the causal interaction of our senses with the objects of the external world gives rise not to sense perceptions but to semantically neutral sense impressions, which are then described by ordinary language (see Figure 3).

The distinction I draw between sense impressions and sense perceptions can be explicated as follows. In common-sense realism, if we report seeing a table in front of us, we assume that if we had merely looked, without saying anything, we still would be seeing a table. That is to say, the mere act of looking, i.e., letting our eyes causally interact with the world, results in perception, which already has cognitive meaning exactly the same as that of a subsequent ordinary language report ('I see a table in front of me'). The language simply enables us to transparently report what we see.

However, within philosophical realism as I espouse here, what we register when we merely look are 'sense impressions.' They do not have meaning, i.e., they are semantically

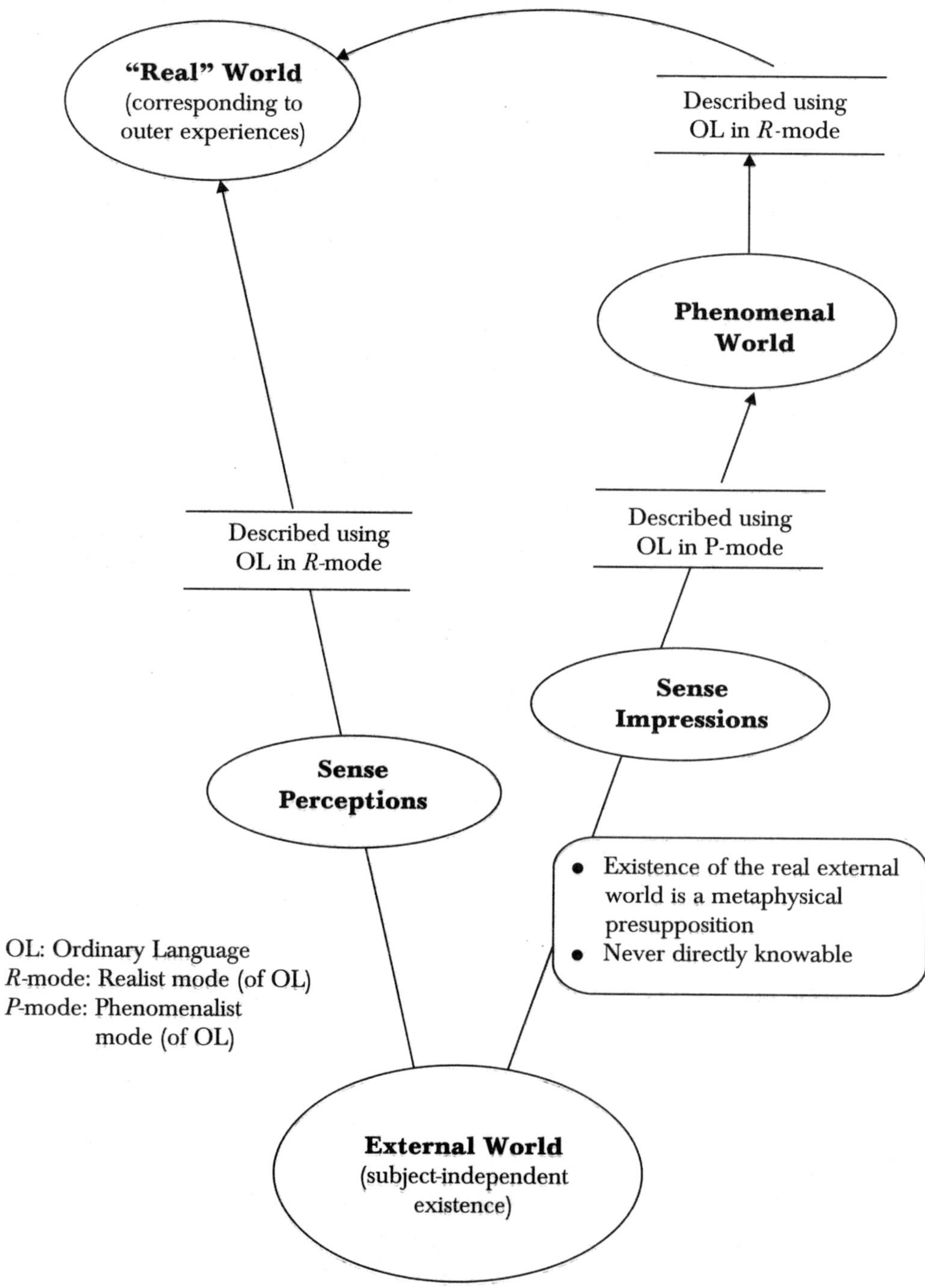

FIGURE 3: NAÏVE AND PHILOSOPHICAL REALISMS

neutral. In this sense, the interaction of our eyes with the world is no different from the interaction of a camera lens with an object. In either case, there is no cognitive act of perception yet.[7] However, when we do describe the sense impressions using ordinary language, the act of cognition is certainly completed, since we always talk of an actual experience. If so, somewhere between when the sense impressions are produced and when we state in ordinary language our experience, our act of cognition is consummated.

But where and how does this happen? Evidently, the problem of how we come to have an experience such as 'seeing a table' is very important for cognitive science.[8] However, ordinary language philosophers are concerned with another problem, namely that of analyzing what it means to *say* that we are seeing a table. In other words, ordinary language philosophers see the philosophical analysis of the problem of perception as an analysis of the common-sense intuitions behind the corresponding ordinary language statements. Although this may at first seem counterintuitive and an infertile exercise, we shall see later that it is not without its relevance because of the critical role that ordinary language plays in physics too (even though ordinary language philosophy developed independent of physics).

The immediate point is that, in describing our experience, ordinary language is functioning in the *P*-mode, and therefore the 'objects' referred to in our ordinary language statements, in the first instance, are not objects in the external world, but are only given in our experience. Indeed, philosophers refer to the objects given in our experience as phenomenal objects and take them to exist in the phenomenal world. Only via an act of further interpretation, philosophical realists would hold, do we transit from the *P*-mode to the *R*-mode to view our experiences as direct experiences of the external world.

In philosophical realism as I present it here, there exists an implicit distinction between the "real" world and the external world. The external world exists independent of us, in and of itself. The real world is what can be said to 'exist' when we realistically interpret our experiences using ordinary language in *R*-mode. Of course, the philosophical justification of the thesis of common-sense realism must eventually accept that the structure of the real world as given in our experience will correspond to the structure of the external world, but it is useful nevertheless to make the above distinction between real world and external world in philosophical realism.

Philosophical realism can then be defined as the project to justify the transition from the *P*-mode to the *R*-mode of ordinary language usage when describing our simple sense experiences. This project is already counterintuitive, since common-sense thinking takes the validity of this transition for granted. Moreover, even after centuries of effort, philosophy has failed to logically justify naïve realism. As a result, it is an open secret that this part of modern analytical philosophy, which sees problems in the *R*-mode use of ordinary language where common-sense usage sees none, has failed to be intuitively meaningful and accessible to the general public.

Precisely for the same reason empirical philosophical realism has also failed to excite the imagination of the physicist, since physicists too simply assume, both in the classical and quantum domains, the validity of the present *R*-mode of ordinary language in describing the laboratory events. If this assumption were to ever become questionable within physics, then philosophical realism would become relevant to physics. Since this is a crucial point to the theme of this paper, I shall investigate in some detail scientific realism in physics in the next few sections, contrasting it with naïve and philosophical realisms.

V

SCIENTIFIC REALISM

Scientific realism in physics holds that empirically correct theories in physics succeed because they provide a true description of the relevant part of the external world. This naïve view of scientific realism has its origins in classical mechanics and is thus very compatible with it.

A quick account of the details of this naïve view of scientific realism might run as follows: Scientists would accept they freely create a purely conceptual model of the external world out of their own imagination to account for sense phenomena. However, they would argue, unlike other forms of explanation—philosophical or religious, for instance—scientific explanations based on such conceptual models are required to have testable empirical consequences. A scientific theory is accepted if and only if all its testable predictions are shown to be true through appropriate experiments. Once a theory is shown to be empirically true and technological applications are made based on its correct predictions, it follows that its description of the underlying world must be true. How else could the predictions be true and the machines work? Thus, naïve scientific realism is the claim that scientists construct a true model of the external world. Such a model, of course, can and will change from theory to theory. Scientists will replace an older scientific model by a newer one—for strictly empirical reasons—but this need not mean that present models are passing fictions. Rather, science builds a true model of the external world by a series of approximations, each of which has demonstrable empirical validity and truth content.

The key conviction underlying this naive view of scientific realism is that if a theory in physics makes a correct prediction, then the 'physical' state of the system at the point of observation is a real state. That is, it is a state that existed in nature prior to and independent of our observation. Indeed, the assumption here is that because the physical state is real, the theory makes the right prediction. In this view, our observation just passively reveals information about a state pre-existing in nature.

However, quantum theory startlingly unseats this classical intuition and indicates that the opposite is true: namely, the physical theory predictively succeeds only because the physical state of the observed system could not have existed in nature prior to the actual measurement.[9] In other words, quantum theory seems to force us to distinguish between the ontological state and the observed state of a system (and hence the external world and the observed world). What we observe is a state that we can attribute to the system only in the context of that observation. This is the origin of the usual, popular statement that in quantum theory our observation creates the reality we observe.

Does quantum theory say anything about the unobservable real state of the world? Yes. This state is the 'superposed' state. However, an observation upon this state will always produce an 'eigenstate' that is different from this superposed state. Any connection we might wish to make between the unobservable real (i.e., superposed) state and the observed eigenstate (say, how does the eigenstate appear from the superposed state?) must be justified.[10]

Quite apart from the deep problems that this situation has posed in quantum theory, we can at once notice the similarity of the form of the above implication of quantum theory and the contention of empirical philosophy, namely, that what we can know is only an observed or phenomenal world, which is different from the real world and that any connection we make between the two requires justification.

Indeed, since the inception of quantum theory (nearly a century ago, with the invention of the quantum postulate by Planck to account for the observed 'blackbody radiation'), it has been recognized that quantum theory has irrevocably invalidated our classical (i.e., pre-quantum) notions of scientific realism. As a result, there has been a search for a proper understanding of the non-classical view of the world given by quantum theory. In order to truly understand how quantum theory is non-classical, we may do well to first properly comprehend the elements of the scientific realism in the classical era in greater detail, so we can accurately judge which part of this classical realism has failed in quantum theory.

Accordingly, I now furnish an account of the realist praxis in classical physics in terms of a 'scientific method' (see Figure 4). It is not my claim that physicists actually and always follow this 'method' in the stated sequence. As Einstein correctly noted, the physicist does not stick to one epistemological perspective (even that of realism) at all points during the development of a theory. For the physicist, empirical correctness is the major criterion, and whatever route takes him there is the one he must take.

> No sooner has the epistemologist, who is seeking a clear system, fought his way through to such a system, then he is inclined to interpret the thought-content of science in the sense of his system and to reject whatever does not fit into his system. The scientist, however, cannot afford to carry his striving for epistemological systematic that far. He accepts gratefully the epistemological conceptual analysis; but the external conditions, which are set for him by the facts of experience, do not permit him to let himself be too much restricted in the construction of his conceptual world by the adherence to an epistemological system. He therefore must appear to the epistemologist as a type of unscrupulous opportunist: He appears as *realist* insofar as he seeks to describe a world independent of acts of perception; as *idealist* insofar as he looks upon the concepts and theories as the free inventions of human spirit (not logically derivable from what is empirically given); as *positivist* insofar as he considers his concepts and theories justified *only* to the extent which they furnish a logical representation of relations among sensory experiences. He may even appear as *Platonist* or *Pythagorean* insofar as he considers the view point of logical simplicity as an indispensable and effective tool of his research.
>
> (Einstein, 1949, p. 684, italics in the original)

Nevertheless, I offer the following construction of the scientific method for the limited purpose of aiding the task at hand, namely an analysis of the connections among physics, philosophy and common-sense thinking. I do believe, however, that the method portrayed

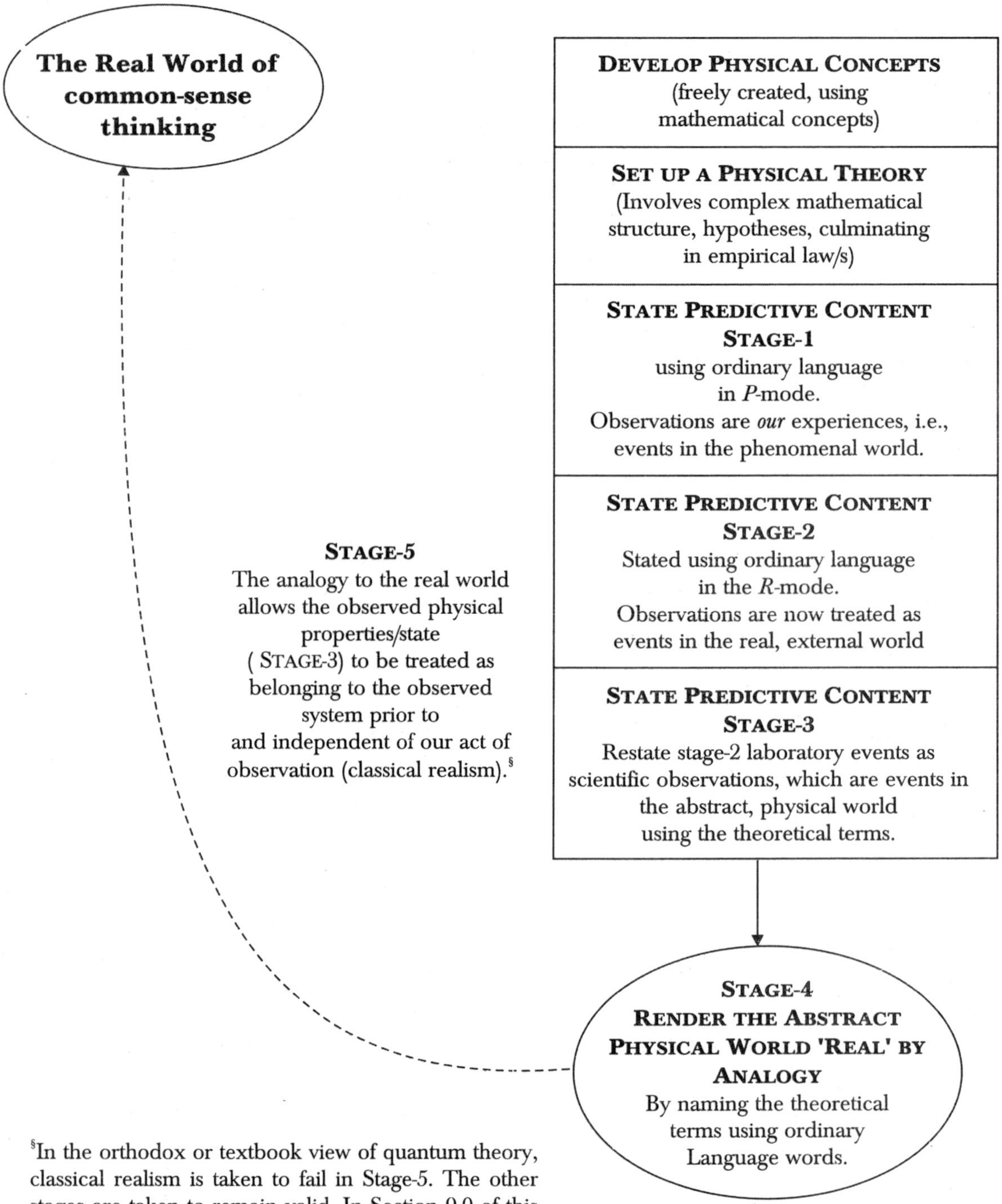

The Real World of common-sense thinking

DEVELOP PHYSICAL CONCEPTS
(freely created, using mathematical concepts)

SET UP A PHYSICAL THEORY
(Involves complex mathematical structure, hypotheses, culminating in empirical law/s)

STATE PREDICTIVE CONTENT
STAGE-1
using ordinary language in *P*-mode.
Observations are *our* experiences, i.e., events in the phenomenal world.

STATE PREDICTIVE CONTENT
STAGE-2
Stated using ordinary language in the *R*-mode.
Observations are now treated as events in the real, external world

STATE PREDICTIVE CONTENT
STAGE-3
Restate stage-2 laboratory events as scientific observations, which are events in the abstract, physical world using the theoretical terms.

STAGE-4
RENDER THE ABSTRACT PHYSICAL WORLD 'REAL' BY ANALOGY
By naming the theoretical terms using ordinary Language words.

STAGE-5
The analogy to the real world allows the observed physical properties/state (STAGE-3) to be treated as belonging to the observed system prior to and independent of our act of observation (classical realism).[§]

[§]In the orthodox or textbook view of quantum theory, classical realism is taken to fail in Stage-5. The other stages are taken to remain valid. In Section 9.0 of this paper, we make the proposal that Stage-2 through Stage 5 might *all* fail in quantum theory.

FIGURE 4: CLASSICAL SCIENTIFIC REALISM

here accurately takes into account the diverse elements of the praxis of physicists in general, even if the stated order is not always maintained.

The conception of the 'scientific method' illustrated schematically in Figure 4 consists of the following steps:

(1) Given a problem, say accounting for certain data, the physicist begins with certain intuitions about the underlying causal processes in the external world. This intuition is direct in some sense.[11]

(2) Based on these intuitions, the physicist uses mathematical concepts to 'freely create' (Einstein's phrase) 'physical concepts' which are different from the original mathematical concepts because they now express the intuitions of the physicist regarding the external world.[12]

(3) The physicist then develops hypotheses that govern relations among these concepts.

(4) Based on these hypotheses, and via complicated steps of physical and empirical reasoning, the physicist develops a physical formalism (with mathematical equations) whose solutions are real numbers which will appear as pointer readings on appropriately calibrated meters as a result of a laboratory procedure called measurement, involving both state preparation and observation. These laboratory events—pointer readings, detector clicks, magnetically recorded data, etc.—are the predictive content of the physical theory, which are expressed differently in different stages.

(5) **Stage 1:** The above predictive content is expressed using ordinary language in the *P*-mode. The laboratory events now are our simple sense experiences occurring in the phenomenal world (Machian sensationism).

(6) If the Stage 1 predictions are found to be correct (by performing actual experiments), then the theory is empirically verified. One now adopts further interpretive steps to move toward scientific realism.

(7) **Stage 2:** The predictive content of the physical theory is now re-expressed using ordinary language assuming the validity of the *R*-mode that drives common-sense thinking, to interpret the predictions of Stage 1 as objective events in the real world.[13]

(8) Thus, an observation statement of the form 'the meter needle is pointing to +1', which would be a statement about our experience at Stage 1, would now be a statement about the state of a real meter in the real world which existed in the world prior to our observation. Evidently, the observations now take place in the real world of everyday thinking.

(9) **Stage 3:** The predictive content of the physical theory is now restated using the formal terms of the physical theory (forming the vocabulary of the theoretical language). The observations of Stage 2 are now scientific observations. Thus, the observation 'meter needle is pointing to +1' is now a measurement of the value of a property, such as 'the property corresponding to observable x has been measured to have an eigenvalue of +1' at the point of this observation.

(10) These scientific observations take place evidently in the abstract, formal world of physics. This 'physical world' would be different for different physical theories.

For example, the dynamics of Newtonian mechanics takes place in the physical world housed in the abstract, mathematical Euclidean space. The physical world of relativity theory is the abstract, mathematical Riemannian 4-dimensional manifold. The physical world of quantum theory is the abstract, complex, Hilbert space.

(11) **Stage 4:** The motivation to treat the abstract physical world as 'real' is supplied by naming the various formal terms using words of ordinary language in *R*-mode. The scientific observation of Stage 3 is now restated to give it a realistic flavor. Thus, the observation of Stage 3 would now be restated as 'the electron was observed to be at the top slit' (corresponding to the value +1 on the meter needle), or that 'the electron's spin was measured to be in the up direction along the z-axis.'

(12) **Stage 5:** Because the physical world is shown to be 'real', the value measured for the physical property under observation at step 8 would now be treated as having belonged to the observed system prior to the observation.[14]

For now, the important point is that the restating of the scientific observations (initially stated using ordinary language in *P*-mode) using the theoretical terms named using ordinary language words enables the physicists to communicate the felt 'reality' of the abstract, non-sensible, physical world in terms of our only source of knowledge of the real, namely the common-sense notions of the real world of everyday experience. The ordinary language words play only a suggestive or evocative role, since the identity between the physical object and the common-sense object corresponding to its name is never perfect, only an *idealization.* Therefore, though the ordinary language words enable one to visualize the formal physical world in terms of common-sense space and time pictures, one accords the mathematical formalism itself the primacy in determining the true meaning of these terms. Thus, we conclude that the physical world is rendered real only by analogy to the real world of common-sense thinking. This analogical mode of visualization is needed because the real objects of common-sense thinking are directly coordinated to sense experience, whereas it is the physical theory as a whole that is directly coordinated to experience, and the physical objects which are part of the theory are coordinated to our sense experiences only indirectly.

If the physical world is entirely conceptual, how can the physicists talk of an electron interacting with a macroscopic detector, since the latter would be an object in the lived world? I propose that any such reference the physicist makes is not to a particular (i.e., this or that) detector, but any detector in the generic sense. Thus, the macroscopic detectors that inhabit the physical world (i.e., the world of physics, in which the physicist analyzes and interprets the experiment) are not the common-sense objects (i.e., the specific detectors that the physicists handle in the laboratory), but the corresponding *universals.* This renders the physical world fully conceptual, despite housing both formal entities such as particles or waves and laboratory equipment (since these are all now universals). In this way we can understand that despite the physicists' references to abstract physical entities interacting with detectors, the whole account of the experiment by the physicist refers to happenings in a conceptual physical world, not the real or external world. As we shall presently see, this description meets the happenings in the real world only at the interface of our experiences. In other words, the physicist himself provides the over-arching connection between the physical world and the world of observations.

We can now see why the physicist, while analyzing the experiments as performed in the 'real' world, i.e., the laboratory, nevertheless is able to interpret the same laboratory event *qua* our simple sense experience as different physical events under different theories. The same sense experience, say a meter needle pointing to +1, would be interpreted by the physicist in one theory as (say) the current being measured as one ampere by the meter, or the spin of an electron being 'up' in another theory. This possibility exists because, while the observation in Stage 1 (of Figure 4) is a sensible event in the phenomenal world, the interpreted scientific observation is an event occurring in the physical world.[15]

The distinction between the phenomenal and the physical becomes even more explicit when we consider that the same physical theory could allow us to make two measurements corresponding to two different properties (involving two different experimental arrangements) and come up with the same sense experience (i.e., a laboratory event such as 'a meter needle pointing to +1'). This possibility ordinarily does not exist in common-sense thinking, treated as a theory.[16]

To summarize, physics in particular and science in general constructs only an abstract world, which is a conceptual grid that helps us to impose an order upon a certain range of sense experiences, and put this order to practical use. Scientific realism is the claim that this conceptual world is every bit as 'real' as the external world by drawing analogies via ordinary language between the two worlds. To say the physical world is 'real' is not to say it is a model of the external world, but only that we can visualize the abstract, conceptual 'physical world' using ordinary language terms in much the same way we visualize the external world as "real" in common-sense thinking.

VI

EMPIRICAL SCIENCE AND COMMON-SENSE THINKING

We have suggested that common-sense thinking embodied in ordinary language enters physics in two stages:

(1) To describe the laboratory events *qua* our simple sense experiences (Stage 2 in Figure 4)

(2) To name the theoretical terms using ordinary language words to understand the physical content of the theory (Stage 4 in Figure 4)

Despite the growing abstraction of the formal physical theories, the possibility for making the connection between physical theory and common-sense thinking at Stage 4 remains crucial for understanding the physical theories realistically.

Thus, if it is true that science progresses by often superceding our common-sense thinking at Stage 2, it is equally true that science cannot but return to make connection with common-sense language at Stage 4 to ground scientific realism. In Stage 2, our common-sense analysis of the laboratory events might suggest one picture of the processes in the external world[17] underlying the observed phenomena, while the scientific account of the same phenomena in terms of the processes in the world of physics might be different. For example, from the observations of the sun's relative position in the sky, we might conclude in our common-sense thinking that in the external world, the sun is rotating around the earth. Now, in the Copernican model the same observations of the relative positions of the sun at various times of day are predicted by constructing underlying processes in the conceptual world of physics wherein the 'earth' is presumed to go around the sun. But in such a physical model (developed in Stage 3), all we have are two point-particles (theoretical constructs) in relative motion, and we name one as 'earth' and the other as 'sun'. Thus, the earth and the sun *qua* physical objects exist in the conceptual world of physics, and are different from the earth and the sun qua objects of the external world with which we associate with the same observations in common-sense thinking. We can adapt a quip Russell used to emphasize the distinction between phenomenal and external world ('the sun I see is not the sun I see') to say, the sun physics describes is not the sun we see, to emphasize the distinction between the real world and the physical world or the world of physics. The sun around which the earth is taken to rotate in physics is a point-particle that is different from the sun we say rotates around the earth in the real or external world.

To give another example, let us say our observations are of the relative positions of 'a steel ball rolling down an inclined plane.' This statement concerns, in the first instance, the phenomenal steel ball. However, in common-sense thinking, we are inclined to assume that there is also a 'real' steel ball in the external world accounting for the perceived motions. Now, the same observations involving the phenomenal steel ball are predicted in Newtonian mechanics by postulating the motion of a point-particle that we would also name as 'steel ball.' Yet the point-particle that is named 'steel ball', whose motion in an abstract, Euclidean space classical mechanics describes, is an object of the physical world—whereas the real steel ball that common-sense speaks of is an object in the external world. In Newtonian mechanics, the point-particle 'steel ball' is usually taken to be a model of, and thus correspond to the real 'steel ball' in the real world.

Despite the success of this soothing correspondence realism, even classical mechanics need not be seen as explaining the motion of the steel ball in the real world. We saw that empirical philosophy makes a distinction between the *P*-mode and the *R*-mode of ordinary language. Thus, a statement of the type 'the steel ball is rolling down an inclined plane' would be regarded in the first instance as a *P*-mode statement in philosophy, which would connote an infinite succession of our individual experiences, each of which could be described as an individual experience of the sort 'a steel ball at this location.' Only by the subsequent assumption of naïve realism can we be said to regard the statement "the steel ball is at this location" as a statement about the location of a real steel ball in the real world, and the statement "the steel ball is rolling down an inclined plane" as a statement about the real motion of a real steel ball in the real world.

In tracing in detail the stages of scientific realist thinking, I have made the description of laboratory events using ordinary language in the *P*-mode as Stage 1. Machian sensationism stops with this stage, and regards the theoretical language of the formalism as reporting laboratory events *qua* our experiences. Upon this view, the physical law is no more than a shorthand way of connoting the succession of our experiences that arise when we carry out well-defined laboratory procedures involving both state-preparation and observation. But it won't do to stop with Stage 1 in conceiving the scientific method, which is essentially realistic. The mistake of Mach—one that all the great system builders in the western philosophical tradition have made—is to take a single essentially correct insight within a domain of study and use it to complete the understanding of the whole domain. Mach made this error with respect to science. Thus Einstein, who acknowledged that Mach's *History of Mechanics* had "exercised a profound influence upon me while I was a student", and that Mach's "epistemological position influenced me very greatly." Nonetheless, in his later years Einstein also emphasized that Mach's skepticism is essentially untenable. "Mach's system studies the existing relations between the givens of experience; for Mach, science is the totality of these relations. That point of view is horribly wrong; in short, what Mach has made is a catalogue, not a system." (Einstein quoted in Howard, 1993, p. 216) What I am doing in this part of the paper is to recognize Mach's essentially correct insight, namely that we must begin with the position that involves minimum assumptions, but add to that position, consciously recognizing the assumptions we add at each stage, to reach a realistic view of physics for the limited purpose of analyzing the connections among physics, philosophy and consciousness.

The potential advantage in recognizing the steps involved in scientific realism in such a detailed manner as above, even in the era of classical physics, is this: if ever our current range of naïve realist notions turns out to be inappropriate for a physical theory at the level of observation itself, (as I shall argue is the case with quantum theory), then instead of concluding that scientific realism has failed (as is the current fashion in interpreting quantum theory), we can examine whether there is another route to go from the *P*-mode to the *R*-mode in ordinary language to re-describe the laboratory events, a route which would be more quantum-compatible.

VII

MORE ON SCIENTIFIC REALISM

With respect to the phenomena accounted for by early mechanics, common-sense thinking directly presents the objective processes underlying these phenomena, since the two are identical. The experience of a (phenomenal) 'apple falling down' directly suggests the underlying objective process in the real world, namely that of a real apple falling down in the real world. However, with progress in science our observations no longer directly revealed a picture of the underlying objective processes in the external world. For example, by moving a coil within range of a magnet we can observe a movement in the needle of an ammeter appropriately connected. This observation does not directly suggest the objective process underlying the observation. Electromagnetic theory accounts for such observations by positing an abstract, conceptual physical entity called the 'field.' Physicists visualize this 'field' as a 'wave' (an ordinary language word with an associated picture) in an approximate or idealized manner.[18] The logical force of the scientific realism, in treating the field as a 'real' object within electromagnetic theory, comes then from the fact that we invoke our only notions of the 'real', i.e., the common-sense ones ('wave' in this case), to visualize the physical ideas by *analogy*. The physicists cannot logically demonstrate any correspondence between such visualization and the relevant causal processes in the external world, since we sense nothing about these causal processes beyond the meter readings. However, this absence of a logically demonstrable correspondence between the external world and the physical world is true even of early mechanics, strictly speaking. Newton himself recognized and emphasized this absence.

> I use the word 'attraction', 'impulse', or 'propensity' of any sort toward a centre, promiscuously and indifferently, one for another, considering those forces not physically but mathematically; whereof the reader is not to imagine that by those words I anywhere take upon me to define the kind or the manner of any action, the causes or the physical reason thereof, or that I attribute forces in a true and physical sense to certain centres (which are only mathematical points) when at any time I happen to speak of centres as attracting or as endued with attractive powers.
>
> (Newton, 1687, Definition VIII, pp. 5-6)

With further growth of physics, we are even guaranteed that there cannot be a direct correspondence between the external world and the physical world, as in relativity theory. Here too, we have simple phenomenal experiences of observed bending of the light from a star in the presence of the sun, a body of great mass, but no clue within common-sense thinking about the real processes taking place in the presumed space and time of the external world. The physical theory, however, explains it in terms of a physical world that is a 4-dimensional mathematical continuum. We are therefore certain that the physical world now is a total abstraction, even though it predicts the same experiences that we have in the phenomenal world, namely the bending of the light.

Even so, the most abstract 'physical' 4-dimensional continuum has been given a realistic flavor by naming it as a 4-dimensional space-time continuum. This is made possible by the consideration that if we cut the 4-dimensional continuum along a chosen plane (representing time), the remaining 3-dimensional surface can be regarded as space. Thus, an actual observation event could be regarded as taking place in space and time, even within relativity theory. Thus, to view the mathematical 4-dimensional Riemannian manifold as a 'space-time continuum' has some, even if only very tenuous, justification. It allows one to regard the physical world of relativity theory as 'real' in much the same way we regard the common-sense world of space and time as real, simply because the same words are used to name both. Nevertheless, the move to name the freely-created theoretical terms using ordinary language words evokes a sense of the real, not actual correspondence. This is true of physics at all stages of its development so far. Thus, Einstein could say, "I believe physics concerns the 'real', but I am not a realist".[19]

The need for compatibility with common-sense pictures of the real world marks the distinction between strictly mathematical theories and theories in physics which use mathematics. Pauli summed it up quite eloquently.

> It is true that these [scientific] laws and our ideas of reality which they presuppose are getting more and more abstract. But for a professional, it is useful to be

reminded that behind the technical and mathematical form of the thoughts underlying the laws of nature, there remains always the layer of everyday life with its ordinary language. Science is a systematic refinement of the concepts of everyday life revealing a deeper and, as we shall see, not directly visible reality behind the everyday reality of colored, noisy things. But it should not be forgotten either that this deeper reality would cease to be an object of physics, different from the objects of pure mathematics and pure speculation, if its links with the realities of everyday life were entirely disconnected.

(Pauli, 1994, p. 2)

Our proposal that a physical world is to be viewed as 'real' not solely by virtue of its predictive correctness, but also by demonstrating its visualizability (in terms of our notions of the real world in common-sense thinking) has the consequence that, if a theory were to be empirically successful but not properly amenable to visualization using ordinary language terms, physicists should be expected to regard our 'understanding' of the physical content of a theory to be incomplete. This indeed is the case with quantum theory. Quantum theory is predictively the most successful theory we have yet of the relevant phenomena. Yet its formal terms resist a neat, single picture of the world in ordinary language terms. We are forced to use mutually exclusive wave-particle pictures to visualize the physical picture underlying even a single observation.[20] Because such a visualization of quantum theory's formal terms is not fully self-consistent, despite its prodigious empirical success, scientists do regard our efforts to 'understand' quantum theory as incomplete.

The foregoing discussions should explain our focus on the analytical philosophical tradition in the West, and particularly ordinary language philosophy, to discuss the connection between philosophy and science. In science, ordinary language considerations are essential.

VIII

SCIENCE AND PHILOSOPHY—THE MISSING CONNECTION

To recapitulate, philosophical realism in ordinary language philosophy concerns justifying the transition from the *P*-mode to the *R*-mode in common-sense thinking. We have proposed that physics too, in its first stage, predicts the observations *qua* phenomenal experiences. Thus, an instrumental view of the physical theory has been taken to be the logically correct starting point for physics, just as, for empirical philosophy, a necessary starting point is to distinguish between the phenomenal world and the real world (or between the *P*-mode and the *R*-mode use of ordinary language). However, philosophy has struggled to justify the transition from *P*-mode to *R*-mode in common-sense thinking, whereas physics has assumed the validity of the *R*-mode of ordinary language when reporting the laboratory events in Stage 2 (Figure 4). Scientific realism wrestles with the subsequent step of justifying the transition from the *P*-mode of the theoretical language of formalism, which is used to predict the observations *qua* sense experiences (Stage 3), to the *R*-mode in treating the same observations as 'real' physical events, by naming the theoretical terms using ordinary language words (Stage 4). For this reason, the concerns of philosophical realism and scientific realism have been entirely different.

This difference, not often clearly stated in the literature, can serve to explain, though not altogether justify, why although Descartes' philosophy served to trigger the start of modern western science, physicists have come to regard philosophy as largely irrelevant for their realistic concerns. Philosophy conducts a logical analysis of experience described using ordinary language in relation to the external world. Physics conducts an ontological analysis of the same experience described using the theoretical language in relation to the abstract physical world.

One major response to alleviate this irrelevance of empirical philosophy to the concerns of empirical science came from the logical positivists in the early part of the twentieth century, who proposed to redo philosophy by letting philosophy follow science. Reichenbach, for example, contended that philosophy must be done in the context of theory justification in science, i.e., after a theory is invented by physicists, empirically tested and accepted by the scientists, not before or independent of science. Quine was to say more succinctly, "philosophy of science is philosophy enough."

However, the positivist response is only one possible response. Significantly, it is even inappropriate in the context of one major theory in science: quantum theory. I shall now argue that a full solution of the outstanding problem of understanding the physical meaning of quantum theory at the level of the quantum world is centrally connected with the proper solution of the philosophical problem of the relation between the *R*-mode and *P*-mode of ordinary language at the level of the macroscopic world. If so, philosophy would have to operate in the context of theory creation, not just theory justification, and 'doing philosophy' would become an essential part of 'doing science.'

IX

QUANTUM THEORY AND HUMAN EXPERIENCE

We have noted that a physical theory is connected to experience via several stages. We have also repeatedly stressed that the physical world, though essentially mathematical and therefore ideal, is rendered 'real' by evoking the image of the real world of common-sense thinking by naming the terms of the physical formalism using ordinary language-words.

In quantum mechanics we saw that we have had to pay a much higher price to make such a connection between the formal terms and ordinary-language-based, common-sense thinking. We are forced to employ a wave-particle duality. At this level, the problem would seem to be a conflict between the ontological quantum physical picture and common-sense thinking. Indeed, this is how quantum theory is invariably presented. True, this is acute enough. However, I shall presently argue that the real problem in quantum theory may well be far more acute. In quantum theory, ordinary language can function only in the *P*-mode while describing the observations, and thus the usual assumption of the validity of the classical *R*-mode of ordinary language even at the level of the observations breaks down.

Consider the standard two-slit experiment. The electron can go through one of the two holes and thus have one of two possible 'positions' if observed close to the two-slit screen. Indeed, if we place two detectors close to each slit, we find that only one of them always clicks. However, either observation should not be regarded as revealing the position of the electron in the pre-quantum or classical sense, since in a three-slit experiment, the same electron in the same prepared quantum state would have one of three positions. In other words, even so simple a property as that corresponding to the x-observable in quantum mechanics could not be regarded in any straightforward manner as a 'position' in the classical sense of an absolute location in space, even at the point of an actual observation, since the observed position is due as much to the details of the experimental arrangement under which the quantum object is observed (the number of slits in the screen, in this case) as due to the electron itself.

Bohr is well-known for emphasizing this quantum inseparability.

> The finite magnitude of the quantum of action prevents altogether a sharp distinction being made between a phenomenon and the agency by which it is observed, a distinction which underlies the customary concept of observation and, therefore, forms the basis of the classical ideas of motion.
>
> (Bohr, 1934, pp. 11-12)

However, we must inquire as to what exactly is the implication of this inseparability for our understanding of the nature of quantum physical properties. David Bohm puts it as follows:

> The properties of position and momentum are not only incompletely defined and opposing potentialities, but also in a very accurate description, they cannot be regarded as belonging to the electron alone; for the realization of these potentialities depends just as much on the systems with which it interacts as on the electron itself.
>
> (Bohm, 1951, p. 620)

In the above passage, Bohm only speaks of the mutual contribution of the observed system and observing agency to actualize the measured value of a quantum mechanical property. This is indeed the orthodox view. However, we have seen above that in a more crucial sense, the experimental arrangement contributes to even *defining* the quantum mechanical property, even one apparently as simple in conception as 'position'. It is a great merit of Bohr that he recognized and emphasized that quantum theory poses a problem as much to the classical definition of properties, as to the classical notion of measurement. Bohr thus proposed that the observed system and the observing arrangement together weave a single inseparable epistemic whole at the point of an observation.

> In the description of atomic phenomena, the quantum postulate presents us with the task of developing a 'complementarity' theory the consistency of which can be judged only by weighing the possibilities of definition and observation... properties in quantum theory being definable and observable only through their interaction with other systems...
>
> (Bohr, 1934, pp. 55, 57)

> In any interaction, implied by the quantum, the measuring instruments and the atomic objects are inseparably entailed in the phenomena... We are concerned here with a general epistemological lesson...
>
> (Bohr, 1957, p. 89)

> An independent reality in the ordinary physical sense can neither be ascribed to the phenomena nor to the agencies of observation.
>
> (Bohr, 1957, p. 54)

In terms of the terminology introduced in this paper, Bohr's conclusion that we cannot treat the observations as referring to the real states of even the macroscopic measuring devices means that ordinary language can function only in *P*-mode to describe the laboratory events as our experiences.[21] Nothing more can be said about the predictions of quantum theory.[22] Any attempt to invoke the usual *R*-mode of ordinary language to speak of an underlying real state of even just the macroscopic measuring instrument is logically inadmissible within quantum theory, due to the inseparability principle.

The scientific method outlined in section 5 allows us to spell out the reasoning behind the above conclusion in some detail. Let us say we have an observation experience, 'the meter needle is pointing to +1.' In a classical theory, such as electromagnetism, the observation experience might be interpreted as, say, the measurement of a current of 1 Ampere. Such an interpretation would emerge in the following sequence (as per the conception of the scientific realism given in Figure 4):

Stage 1: Treat the observation as our experience. Ordinary language is functioning in *P*-mode.

Stage 2: Treat the observation as an event in the external world. Ordinary language is functioning in the *R*-mode. There is a real meter in the world whose needle is pointing at +1.

Stage 3: The observation (of Stage 2) corresponds to measuring the magnitude of a physical quantity represented (say) by *I* in the theory. (Scientific observation using formal terms)

Stage 4: The observation (of Stage 3) is a measurement of *current.* (Scientific observation restated, with the formal terms named using ordinary language words).

Stage 5: The current of 1 Ampere was flowing in the circuit prior to the observation.

Let us say that in an experiment involving quantum theory, we have the *same* observation experience, 'the meter needle is pointing to +1.' Let us say the physicist interprets it as a measurement of the spin of an electron. That is a Stage 4 interpretation of the observation experience. This implies that Stage 1 through Stage 4 all hold in quantum theory. Indeed, as already noted, the textbook interpretation holds that only Stage 5 would fail, i.e., the conclusion that the spin of the electron was +1 *prior* to the observation is invalid.

However, if one adopts the 'inseparability hypothesis' as discussed above, all we have are Stage-1 observation experiences, and we cannot even proceed to Stage 2 and talk about an independent state of even the macroscopic measuring device at the point of an observation. Upon this view, Stages 2 through 5 would all fail in quantum theory. In saying this we do not mean to deny the validity of the current common-sense realism in its own domain, i.e., at the level of everyday thinking, independent of science. Independent of quantum theory, we can continue to interpret the observation experience as indicating the real state of the needle of a real meter in the real world that existed prior to our observation. However, if one wants to render the observation experience (of Stage 1) as a scientific observation *within* quantum theory, then due to (our reading of) the quantum inseparability, even Stage 2 of classical scientific realism fails. Reason: just as the state of the observed system cannot be separated from the observation, because the electron and the measuring device form a single epistemic whole, neither can the state of the measuring device be separated from the observation, for the same reason. Hence, we are (logically) prevented from using the observation experience to talk about a pre-existing real state for either the electron or the measuring device. I have called this the 'observation problem', to distinguish it from the usual measurement problem. I have argued elsewhere that the observation problem is logically prior to the measurement problem, and that a solution to the former could avoid the latter altogether (see, Gomatam, 1999, 2003a, 2003b).

Solving the 'observation problem' would evidently require us to revise our conception of the nature of a 'real' object at the macroscopic level so we can go from the *P*-mode of ordinary language to the *R*-mode of ordinary language at Stage 2 in a non-classical and quantum-compatible way. That is to say, a revision to our notions of reality would have to occur at the macroscopic level before we can hope to realistically interpret the quantum physical properties at the microscopic level at Stage 3 and Stage 4.

Of course, the current praxis of physicists is to shrug off the above pointed-out inseparability problem as it occurs at the level of interpreting the observation itself (at Stage 2), and simply assume the validity of the current classical *R*-mode of ordinary language to interpret the observation experience as indicating a pre-existing state of the macroscopic device (how else could we understand an observation experience of the sort "the meter needle pointing to +1"). Then they notice that Stage 5, however, fails in quantum theory (i.e., the observed state of the microscopic electron could not have existed prior to the observation) and thus physicists battle with the problem of measurement and hence the physical understanding of quantum theory. [23]

In our opinion, this approach is the result of viewing the current classical-physics-compatible common-sense thinking as unalterably given to us at the level of experience, and hence as the only mode of common-sense thinking possible. Even Bohr, despite his keen insight that quantum theory indicates an epistemic inseparability at the level of observation, held this restrictive attitude.

> As our knowledge becomes wider, we must always be prepared, therefore, to expect alterations in the points of view best suited for the ordering of our experience. In this connection we must remember, above all, that, as a matter of course, all new experience makes its appearance within the frame of our customary points of view and forms of perception.
>
> (Bohr, 1927, p.1)

It is not necessary to stay stuck in this box. We could conceivably try to identify an alternate range of common-sense concepts (and associated forms of perception) to describe the observation *qua* sense experiences, using ordinary language concepts that are more quantum-compatible (see Gomatam, 1999 in this regard). Even if we accept that the classical range of common-sense object notions and their corresponding states are the only ones we can use to interpret the observations with respect to macroscopic measuring devices, the move to treat so simple a sense experience as 'meter needle pointing to +1' as referring to an independent state of the measuring device requires justification within quantum theory. Thus, quantum physics and empirical philosophy stand closely connected, unlike in the era of classical physics.

Western philosophy has still not been able to provide a rigorous justification for going over from *P*-mode to the classical *R*-mode of ordinary language in ordinary thinking. With quantum theory, the problem gets more compounded, since quantum formalism disallows even the simple idea of 'position' in the current classical *R*-mode sense. If so, we are faced with nothing less than the twin task of finding a quantum-compatible version of *R*-mode thinking in ordinary language, and then justifying the transition from *P*-mode to this new *R*-mode, in order to realistically interpret the observation experience at Stage 2 in quantum theory.

Doing only philosophy of science, western empirical philosophers working in the foundations of quantum theory have so far remained satisfied with interpreting the measurement problem that the physicists have created in the first place by retaining the quasi-classical notion of 'position'. Based on the discussion above, it is appropriate to ask whether it is possible to discover an alternative range of concepts in common-sense thinking regarding the states of macroscopic objects (and their properties) that could provide an alternative and quantum-compatible way of relating the *P*-mode of ordinary language to the *R*-mode in common-sense thinking, so that the physicists can consider interpreting the very observational content of quantum theory in a new light.

Any such revision to common-sense notions about the states of macroscopic objects can also be expected to revise the very notion of matter we presently have at the level of common-sense thinking, identified by Descartes as *res extensa.* Interestingly, ancient Indian philosophical thought, it seems, can bring in a new resource precisely at this point.

X

MODERN PHYSICS AND ANCIENT INDIAN THOUGHT— A POSSIBLE NEW CONNECTION?

Descartes defined matter as being characterized solely by its extension. However, in common-sense thinking as well as in classical physics, this extension is averaged out as a single location, say, the center of center of gravity. Thus, absolute location is fundamental to the classical, Cartesian conception of matter. Indeed, in all classical theories, absolute position is the most basic observation in physics.

We have seen that such a notion of absolute location, however, is incompatible with the quantum formalism. Indeed, in the standard approach to quantum theory, the ontological quantum object in a state of 'superposition' does not have a well-defined position.[24] Thus, quantum physicists would happily accept that the Cartesian notion of matter as res extensa has failed in quantum theory. Nevertheless, physicists have managed to retain the classical idea of absolute location as the basic observation in quantum physics via the Born's rule, according to which the square of the wave function yields the probability for the quantum object to be found in an actual observation in one of many classical locations, i.e., one of many narrow regions. Such a quasi-classical or quasi-Cartesian approach has brought success in practical applications of quantum formalism, but equally, it has failed to bring clarity about the ontological quantum conception of matter itself.

In such a situation, it is easy to see why many attempts to clarify the quantum ontological situation connect quantum theory directly to consciousness.[25] If the physical reality described by quantum mechanics at the ontological level could not be of the classical Cartesian extended substance, and if the Cartesian system allows for only one other category, namely mind, it follows that the reality described by quantum mechanics must pertain to mind.

However, this might be too quick a jump. What if there are other notions of matter, besides *res extensa*, which Descartes may have lumped together under the label of mind or 'consciousness'? In that case, what would seem indicated as a nexus with consciousness may well turn out to be a another level of matter that is in-between *res extensa* and consciousness. This may still not solve the 'consciousness-matter' interaction problem (or the mind-body problem), but at least it might open the way for an objective interpretation of matter that goes past the classical concept of matter without directly bringing in a role for non-physical consciousness.

Indeed, within the Vedic tradition of India, consciousness (*cit*) and matter (*acit*) are not the only two ontological categories. Many other levels of matter are also identified. For example, in the *Bhagavad Gītā*:

> Earth, water, fire, air, ether, mind, intelligence and false ego—all together these eight constitute My separated material energies.
>
> (Prabhupādā, 1969, Ch. 8, Text 4)

The Sāṁkhya system, delineated in great detail in Srimad Bhāgavatam Ṗrabhupādā, (1971 see III.26), holds that the basic ontological categories include Supreme Purusha, Time and the plurality of conscious *jivās*, and primordial matter (*pradāna*), and identifies within *pradāna* twenty-five further levels of matter: *mahat tatvā* (the principal manifested state of matter); polluted consciousness; false ego; intelligence; mind; the five knowledge-gathering senses; the five working senses; five *tanmātrā* (the elemental essences) and the five *bhutā* (the basic sensible elements).

Could the description offered of any of these different levels of matter in Bhāgavata Sāṁkhya correspond to matter as described by quantum formalism via the superposed state? If the answer turns out to be a yes, then it would be in line with my thesis that the problem with the Cartesian 'cut' between mind and matter, or subject and object, is not that quantum theory denies the very feasibility of such a cut, but rather that the Cartesian cut is not deep enough. If there could be many levels of matter besides *res extensa*, then it would be the case that they have been swept under the rubric of 'mind' in the simplistic Cartesian dualism. Bhāgavata Sāṁkhya suggests that there could be a more structured dualism, in which, despite identifying consciousness as fundamentally different from matter, more of what we now regard as functions of consciousness—activities of intelligence, mind, qualia, etc.—can be reconceived as necessary but insufficient conditions for ascribing consciousness to a system. In principle, such functions of consciousness could be present in a material system without the system being thereby conscious.

Within this approach, the task of unraveling the physical picture behind quantum theory would involve developing models of the deep structure of consciousness. The empirical relevance of such models for science, in the first instance, would not be in terms of how far they could help us understand consciousness itself, but how far they contribute to developing newer conceptions of matter that can be applied within science to further our objective study of matter. In the case of quantum theory, this would mean that such models of consciousness should not only offer an alternative, non-extensional concept of matter at the macroscopic, observational level, but also enable us to describe the observations in a alternate *R*-mode of ordinary language and thereby rename and reinterpret the theoretical terms of the quantum formalism. That would be one feature of a consciousness-based approach to the study of matter, in contrast to the matter-based approach to the study of consciousness that presently holds sway within modern science. It would be beyond the scope of the present paper to further elaborate on the ongoing work in this direction, in developing the connection between the conception of different forms of matter in Bhagavata Sāṁkhya and alternate R-modes of ordinary language. However, the mere fact that in this paper such an approach to the study of matter has been shown to be capable of meaningfully bearing upon the connections among science, philosophy and consciousness underscores its inherent possibilities.

APPENDIX A

We present a simple technical argument due to Peres (1984, p. 644) as to why quantum theory seems to entail the view that measurement creates what is observed.

The total angular momentum L for a particle is given by

$$L^2 = l(l+1)\hbar \text{ where } l = \tfrac{1}{2}, \tfrac{3}{2}, \tfrac{5}{2} \ldots \qquad [1]$$

The angular momentum component L_i in any chosen direction x, y or z (L_x, L_y or L_z) is given by the formula

$$L_i = m\hbar \text{ where } -l < m < +l \qquad [2]$$

Suppose we performed a measurement corresponding to the total angular momentum observable L and obtained result corresponding to l ˙$3/2$. The total angular momentum L^2 would then have the value $15/4$ (by eq. [1]).

If we measure one of the angular momentum components, say L_x, the result will always turn out to be $\pm\tfrac{1}{2} or \pm\tfrac{3}{2}$ (by eq. [2]). Can we say that L_x really had one of these values before the measurement, but we just did not know which one? In that case, L_x^2 would *always* have objectively one of the values, $\tfrac{1}{4} or \tfrac{9}{4}$, and likewise L_y^2 and L_z^2. However, it is impossible to combine the values $\tfrac{1}{4} and \tfrac{9}{4}$ to fulfill $L_x^2 + L_y^2 + L_z^2 = \tfrac{15}{4}$.

We are therefore led to the conclusion that L_x is forced into one of the two values, $\pm\frac{1}{2}, \pm\frac{3}{2}$ by the act of measurement; that these values did not exist in some 'objective reality' prior to the measurement, but are created by it.

NOTES

1. Descartes did *not* distinguish among consciousness, mind and intelligence. For example, in the following passage, he conflates the three: "To speak accurately, I am not more than a thing that thinks, that is to say a *mind or a soul or an understanding or a reason*, terms whose significance was entirely unknown to me before." (151-152, First Meditations, italics mine)
2. Indeed, one could say that even Descartes' own aim was to analyze the conditions under which such an 'objective study of matter' independent of mind, i.e., physics, is possible. After submitting his "Meditations" to the dean and doctors of the sacred faculty of theology in Paris, Descartes wrote to his friend Father Mersenne privately "...and I want to say, just between us, that these six "Meditations" contain all the fundamental ideas of my physics. But please keep this quiet, because if they knew it, the Aristotelians would be very reluctant to accept my views." (Palmer 1991, p. 65)
3. For a good discussion of the problems in this regard, see Harnad, S. 2000. "Correlation vs. Causality How/Why the Mind-Body Problem is Hard," *J. Consciousness Studies*, **7**(4):54-61; Chalmers, D.J. 1997. *The Conscious Mind: In search of a Fundamental Theory*. Oxford University Press.
4. I have used the term 'consciousness' here (instead of mind) specifically because the distinction between consciousness and mind (as well as other levels of matter) that is made in ancient Indian philosophical thought will be an important point for discussion later in the paper.
5. For the purposes of this paper, I shall consider only that range of common-sense thinking that is in relation to the external world (Figure 1).
6. I restrict myself in this paper only to a consideration of the analytical tradition of western philosophy, and in particular to a sub-field called "ordinary language philosophy". Similarly, in discussing science in this paper, I shall restrict myself to physics.
7. Obviously, this point applies to our other four sense modalities as well.
8. While it is most likely correct to hold that semantically-neutral sense impressions are all we have to start with, recent experiments in psychology of perception seem to show that stages may be involved in perception between the formation of sense impressions and eventual ordinary language description of experience. Such a conclusion is also in line with the Bhāgavata Śāṁkhya model I shall be discussing in the penultimate section, since Bhāgavata Śāṁkhya distinguishes between organs of perception (such eyes, nose etc.) and corresponding *senses* of perception (such as sense of sight, sense of smell etc.), the senses being a 'higher' level of matter than the organs. See, *Bhagavad Gītā*, 3.42 in this regard: "The working senses are superior to dull matter; mind is higher than the senses; intelligence is still higher than the mind; and the conscious soul is even higher than the intelligence."
9. See Appendix A for an explanation of the technical basis for this statement.
10. Justifying this connection is the essence of the famous, as yet unresolved 'measurement problem' in quantum mechanics.
11. "The cornerstone of science's own structure [is] the direct perception by consciousness of the existence of external reality.... Now that is something which the skeptic questions in regard to religion; but it is the same in regard to science." (Planck, 1931, p. 218)
12. Sometimes, the physicist even creates the needed new mathematics first. Newton's invention of calculus is the first and famous example of it. Heisenberg too created matrices (although mathematicians had already invented matrices; Heisenberg simply didn't know about them). In modern times, the work of Witten and others in string theory also have led to much advancement in pure mathematics. As to why mathematical concepts at all are used in physics, we shall merely take their use in current praxis as a fact. Wigner questioned "the unreasonable effectiveness of mathematics in physics." The ideas in this paper do contain one possible answer to this question.
13. We are separating Stage 1 and Stage 2, both to account for Mach's essentially correct basic insight, and to enable us to see in a later section how quantum theory may require, precisely at this Stage 2, a non-classical move.

14. The reader would recognize that we had previously mentioned that this assumption holds in classical physics, but not in quantum physics. However, our detailed analysis can aid us to check whether some other classical prejudice fails antecedently. Indeed, later we will be proposing that the antecedent classical prejudice to fail in quantum theory is in Stage 1 itself.
15. Thus we can understand Einstein's reported statement, "it is the theory which decides what is observable."
16. Kant, for example, did not see the need to distinguish between the phenomenal and physical, because science of his times did not need this distinction. My whole purpose in drawing out this distinction is to show, in subsequent sections, that the changes wrought to our physical understanding by quantum theory could be grasped better if we do not equate the phenomenal and physical even in understanding the pre-quantum or classical theories.
17. In this section, I do not differentiate between the real and the external world while discussing common-sense notions, since the distinction is not significant for the purposes of this section.
18. For example, a wave in common-sense thinking always requires a substantive medium, i.e. it be a wave of something, whereas the electromagnetic 'wave' is not a wave of any medium.
19. If the physical world can be said to be 'real' only in the limited sense of being capable of visualization by analogy to the real external world, and physical theories, despite their demonstrable pragmatic value in the external world, would fail to aid in our understanding of it, would such a limited scientific realism be satisfactory? Wouldn't a demonstration that science can also contribute to our increased understanding of the real, external world give a fuller credence to the stance of scientific realism, as well as more adequately respond to the social constructionist's critique of science? I believe the answer is yes, if one adopts a viewpoint called 'tandem realism,' in which common-sense thinking is expected to evolve, along with scientific thinking. I explore tandem realism in a forthcoming paper.
20. The popular idea that the individual quantum callea 'electron' or 'photon' (with respect to matter or radiation) appears as a particle in some experiments and as a wave in some other experiments is quite superficial. It is more accurate to say that in order to account for all aspects of even a single observation (both why a localized event takes place and why it takes place where it does) requires invoking both particle and wave pictures.
21. Bohr increasingly came to recognize this, even if none too clearly, during his long career in interpreting quantum theory. Whereas he titled his 1927 set of essays on the physical content of quantum theory as "Atomic Theory and Description of Nature", he titled his subsequent set of essays in 1954 as "Atomic Physics and Human Knowledge".
22. Thus Bohr: "The decisive point is that the physical content of quantum mechanics is exhausted by its power to formulate statistical laws governing observations obtained under conditions specified in plain language." (Bohr, 1963, p.12)
23. In some sense, this point also formed the nub of Einstein's difficulties with the standard response to quantum theory: "The 'macroscopic' and the 'microscopic' are so inter related that it appears impracticable to give up this program in the microscopic alone." (Einstein, 1969, p.673)
24. It is not the case that the state of superposition means that the electron is simultaneously present in more than location (in the classical sense of the word location) as is often popularly but loosely portrayed. If treated as a real state, 'superposition' indicates a 'smeared out' presence of a particle in a region that is of a fundamentally non-classical nature, formally characterized by complex-valued amplitudes whose real physical meaning is not yet fully understood.
25. See, among others, London, F. and Bauer, E. 1983. *Quantum Theory and Measurement,* J.A. Wheeler, W.H. Zurck. Princeton, New Jersey: Princeton University Press; Wigner, E.P. 1961. "Remarks on the Mind-body Question". *The Scientist Speculates,* I.J. Good (ed.). London: W. Heinemann; Goswami, A. 1993. *The Self-Aware Universe.* New York: Putnum Publishing group; Penrose, R. 1994. *Shadones of the Mind: A search for the Missing Science of Consciousness.* Oxford University Press; Stapp, p. 1993. *Mind, Matter, Quantum Mechanics.* Berlin, NY: Springer-verlag.

BIBLIOGRAPHY

1. Bohm, D. 1951. *Quantum Theory*. Englewood Cliffs, NJ: Prentice Hall.
2. Bohr, N. 1934. *Atomic Theory and Description of Nature.* (refer to 1961 edition). Cambridge University Press.
3. ———. 1957. *Atomic Physics and Human Knowledge.* New Delhi: John Wiley & Sons.
4. ———. 1963. *Essays 1958-1962 on Atomic Physics and Human Knowledge.* New York: Interscience Publishers.
5. Einstein, Albert. 1969. "Remarks to the Essays Appearing in this Collective Volume". *Albert Einstein: Philosopher-Scientist*, P. A. Schilpp (ed.). Illinois: Open Court; original work published 1949.
6. Gomatam, R. 1999. "Quantum Theory and the Observation Problem". *Journal of Consciousness Studies*, 6 (11-12), 1999. pp. 173-90; also at http://www.bvinst.edu/gomatam/pub-1999-01.htm.
7. ————. 2003. *Against 'Position'.* Paper read at the annual meeting of the Canadian Society for History and Philosophy of Science (CSHPS), May, Halifax, Canada; also at http://bvinst.edu/gomatam/pub-2003-01.htm
8. ————. 2003. *On Going past the Statistical Interpretation.* Paper proposal submitted to the international conference on "Quantum Theory: Reconsiderations of Foundations-2", June, Vaxjo University, Sweden; also at http://bvinst.edu/gomatam/pub-2003-02.htm
9. Howard, D. 1993. "Was Einstein Really a Realist?" *Perspectives on Science*, July. pp. 204-251.
10. Newton, Issac. 1687. *Sir Issac Newton's Mathematical Principles of Natural Philosophy and His System of the World*, A. Motte and F. Cajori (trans.). 1962. University of California Press.
11. Palmer, D. 1991. *Does the Center Hold?: An Introduction to Western Philosophy.* London & Toronto: Mayfield Publishing Company; 2001 paperback edition by McGraw-Hill Higher Education.
12. Pauli, W. 1994. *Writings on Physics and Philosophy.* Berlin: Springer-Verlag.
13. Planck, M. 1931. *Where is Science Going*? Woodbridge, CT: Ox Bow Press.
14. Peres, A. 1984. "What is a State Vector?" *American Journal of Physics*, 52(7), 644-650.
15. Prabhupada, A.C.B.S. 1969. *Bhagavad Gita As It Is.* Translation with commentary. New York: Macmillan.
16. ————. 1971. *Srimad Bhagavatam.* Translation with commentary in 18 vols. Los Angeles: BBT International.

CHAPTER 13

Facets of Quantum Entanglement

Dipankar Home

What is Quantum Entanglement? *How* does it give rise to the two mutually linked central foundational issues of Quantum Mechanics, viz. the *Quantum Measurement Problem* and *Quantum Nonlocality*? In *what* way does Quantum Nonlocality lead to applications in *Quantum Communications*, such as a scheme that has recently been discovered for transporting information which is not only *secure* against decoding but also *transfers* a quantum state (*teleportation*) to a distant location *without* sending any particle? The theoretical and experimental aspects related to these questions have, of late, attracted considerable interest. In this article a brief overview of the key conceptual ingredients of the relevant studies is given, without delving into much technicalities.

I

INTRODUCTION

In classical physics, if two systems interact for a while and then get spatially separated so that they do not interact any more, they are subsequently regarded as 'independent' of each other. However, if the systems and their interaction are all described quantum mechanically, this is *not* true. Once two quantum mechanical systems interact, their states become inevitably *entangled*; i.e., their 'joint state' is no longer a direct product of their individual states but is a 'superposition' of product states. More crucially, the entanglement *persists* irrespective of how large the spatial separation is between the systems. This results in a variety of counterintuitive manifestations of a 'mutual dependence' between the systems that have interacted only in the past. Schrodinger[1] regarded 'entanglement' as "not the one but rather the characteristic trait of quantum mechanics, the one that enforces its entire departure from classical lines of thought."

The full import of the above observation by Schrodinger has increasingly been recognised from the '80s due to a resurgence of interest in the foundational issues of quantum mechanics such as the quantum measurement problem and quantum nonlocality. Both these are no longer merely conceptual issues but have become amenable to experimental studies as well; the latter has even given rise to the possibility of practical applications for more secure and efficient methods of information transfer. In this article, while discussing the relevant basic issues, we will try only to convey a flavour of the type of studies that are being pursued. For more details, the appropriate references will be cited. We begin by mentioning what is formally meant by Quantum Entanglement.

Generally speaking, if H_1 and H_2 are Hilbert spaces of any two systems which may be spatially separated and noninteracting, quantum mechanics assigns to the entire system the Hilbert space $H = H_1 \otimes H_2$, that is the tensor product of the individual spaces for the two systems. An entangled state is one which is 'not' expressible 'in any basis' as a product of the separate individual states of the systems that are entangled. A typical example of an entangled state is the singlet state of a pair of spin ½ identical particles

$$|\psi\rangle = \frac{1}{\sqrt{2}}\left(|\uparrow\rangle_1 |\downarrow\rangle_2 - |\downarrow\rangle_1 |\uparrow\rangle_2\right) \qquad (1)$$

It is important to note that the concept of entanglement is applicable, in particular, in the context of an interaction between a system and a measuring apparatus. This is what gives rise to the Measurement Problem as discussed in the next section.

II

THE QUANTUM MEASUREMENT PROBLEM

This problem reveals a subtle inner inconsistency within the standard framework of quantum mechanics. Weinberg has called it "the most important puzzle in the interpretation of quantum mechanics" [2]. The underlying basic question is 'how' to ensure within the standard framework of quantum mechanics, the very occurrence of a 'definite individual outcome' in a single measurement. In quantum mechanics, the results of measurements can only be predicted probabilistically. Hence the statistical frequencies of outcomes are the quantities whose predictions can be verified by measurements, essentially on an 'ensemble' of identically prepared systems. Thus it is required to guarantee within the theory, the occurrence of individual outcomes whose collection enables us to test the computed probabilities. It is, in general, logically impermissible to speak of the probability of a particular outcome unless the 'definiteness' of that outcome and its 'distinguishability' from other outcomes in the ensemble can be ensured. Now, let's examine what happens in quantum mechanics.

A generic feature of all examples of measurements analyzed quantum mechanically, by including the measuring apparatus, is as follows. Consider a system initially in a state ψ ($\psi = a\psi_1 + b\psi_2$) which is a superposition of two states, say, y_1 and y_2 which are the eigenstates of a dynamical variable which is to be measured. The interaction of this system with a measuring device results in a final state of the form

$$\Psi = a\psi_1\Phi_1 + b\psi_2\Phi_2 \qquad (2)$$

where F_1 and F_2 are 'mutually orthogonal' and 'macroscopically distinguishable' states of the device (for a review of the various specific models of quantum theoretic treatment of measurements, see for example, Refs. [3, 4]). An ineluctable feature of the linear unitary quantum mechanical treatment of any measurement process is that the final state of a measured system coupled to a measuring apparatus is 'entangled' (nonfactorisable), given by Eq.(1). How this entanglement gives rise to the quantum measurement problem, is briefly explained below.[3]

First, note that because of the entangled nature of the wave function (2), *no separate* state can be ascribed to any apparatus. However, an outcome of a measurement is registered essentially by associating it with some property of the apparatus (like a pointer reading). But Eq.(2) represents a pure state. A pure state in quantum mechanics corresponds to an ensemble of 'identical' members. This means that according to Eq.(2), each member (in this case, a system coupled to an apparatus) of the 'postmeasurement ensemble' is described by the *same* wave function Y. Thus such an ensemble is 'homogeneous' whose members are 'indistinguishable'. On the other hand, all measurements culminate in a final ensemble of systems coupled to apparatuses, the latter in turn correspond to *different* outcomes. Thus such a postmeasurement ensemble is, in actuality, essentially 'heterogeneous'.

Now comes the punch-line. A heterogeneous ensemble is required to be represented by a 'mixed state' in quantum mechanics whereas, within the formalism of standard quantum mechanics, under *no* unitary time evolution a pure state can evolve into a mixed state 3-5. Then the question arises *how* to accommodate within quantum mechanics the occurrence of definite outcomes. Note that the 'definiteness' of an individual outcome necessarily implies that it is 'distinguishable' from other outcomes. Hence the distinguishability between different outcomes needs to be ensured within the theory—a feature that is not entailed by a final state of the form given by Eq.(2). In other words, there is *no* element in the quantum mechanical description of the postmeasurement state given by Eq.(2) which corresponds to a definite outcome of an individual measurement. This, in essence, is the Quantum Measurement Problem whose acuteness was highlighted by Schrodinger through his famous "Cat Paradox".[4]

The Measurement Paradox implies that it is inherently enigmatic in quantum mechanics to compute the probabilities of various outcomes when the very occurrence of an individual outcome is not ensured. One is often tempted to put this problem aside as nothing different from that in classical statistical mechanics. For example, one may refer to an apparent analogy between this and the purely classical problem of the tossing of a coin where because of the unknown and uncontrollable ingredients inherent in the specification of the relevant initial conditions, one can predict only that the probability for head/tail is 50%. Once, say, head is observed, the probability for head becomes 100%. There is, however, nothing problematic about this feature because the formal structure of classical mechanics ensures that, at least *in principle*, *if* the initial conditions *were* exactly known, an individual outcome for a single tossing is definitely *either* head *or* tail, *irrespective* of whether it is actually observed. On the other hand, in quantum theory a measurement gives rise to a superposition of various *possibilities* where the possibility of distinguishing an individual outcome from other possible outcomes is *not* allowed, even *in principle*.

For completeness, here one may add that the key point of the measurement paradox remains unaffected even if the initial state of the macroscopic apparatus is taken to be a mixture of different states rather than a pure state.[5] For simplicity, we've confined ourselves to assigning a pure initial state to the macroapparatus, instead of using a density operator description. The acuteness of this paradox makes one inclined to suspect, as Bell[6] puts it, the standard formulation of quantum theory is "intrinsically incomplete or ambiguous at a fundamental level." Various versions of the standard approach have tried to alleviate or minimize this paradox, but all those remain unsatisfactory. We shall now briefly comment on them and will also briefly mention some of the modern attempts to tackle this problem.

The Standard Solution and its Inadequacies

Bohr[7] did recognize that if a measuring device is described quantum mechanically, its interaction with a measured system cannot lead to a definite result in a single run of any give measurement. He sought to *avoid* this problem by simply *decreeing* that the interaction between an object and an apparatus is an "unanalyzable whole" and the apparatus "must be" described in classical terms.

An obvious criticism of this is Bohr makes the very concept of a 'measuring instrument' depend on an ill-defined limiting procedure of the 'cut' between quantum and classical domains. In expressing what Bohr calls 'a simple logical demand', he assumes by fiat that the composite system in a measurement process is composed of two distinct parts: the measured system and the measuring apparatus. However, there is no precise cirterion definable within standard quantum mechanics that delineates the borderline between the two. Is it that we merely find it convenient to consider some parts of the global system as parts of the instrument or is it determined *a priori* in a more physical way? Is it consistently possible within the framework of quantum mechanics to assign a classical description to the measuring apparatus? Such questions remain unanswered in Bohr's writings as well as in the advocacy of his position by others.[8]

We now turn to Heisenberg's position.[9] Heisenberg admitted: "It is not possible to decide, other than arbitrarily, what objects are to be considered as part of the observed system and what as part of the observer's apparatus." Once the macroscopic level is reached, Heisenberg conceded, a *cut* is necessary to avoid the problem of infinite regress in ensuring a definite outcome. However, he argued that it is of no practical importance where we put the split. As Bell put it, the Heisenberg dictum was to "put sufficiently much into the quantum system so that the inclusion of more would not significantly alter practical predictions." Though this recipe is useful, it is ambiguous *in* principle. There is no fundamental reason why the physics involved in measurements should differ from the way other physical interactions are described. Hence the very legitimacy of such a conceptual discontinuity, *not* so much its precise location, is what that matters. In other words, the founders of quantum mechanics consciously preferred not to tackle on this problem at a deeper level—a pragmatic standpoint perhaps justified in the years when quantum mechanics was in the formative stage.

Modern attempts towards the resolution of the Measurement Problem require to go beyond the standard framework of quantum mechanics by either modifying or enlarging the standard framework in an appropriate way so that the empirical validity of quantum mechanics is retained in the domains explored to date. Schemes to this end that have been formulated quantitatively are of two categories: (a) Approaches which leave the mathematical formalism of quantum mechanics unmodified but introduce new elements into the conceptual framework.[10] (b) Models which modify the mathematical formalism (by preserving the results of the standard formulation in their empirically verified domain) in order to provide a dynamical description of a measurement process in terms of an actual transition from a pure to a mixed state (the so-called "collapse of a wave function").[11] (c) Models which introduce the idea of "decoherence" induced by a strong interaction of a typical macro-measuring device with what is called an "environment" (which is modelled mathematically in an appropriate way) in order to account for the fact *why* we see only one outcome in a particular run and *not* a superposition of various outcomes.[12]

To what extent the above approaches can be experimentally discriminated or whether any of them can give rise to *testable predictions beyond* the standard framework of quantum mechanics is a challenging area of current investigations. Note that a key ingredient in any of the above approaches is the notion that a measurement outcome has a definite objective (observer-independent) reality in the sense that once actualised, it remains 'out there' so that the result can be inspected at any subsequent instant without perturbing it. This therefore requires a precise specification of at what stage a measurement result is recorded in a stable and discernible form. The schemes mentioned above use different *a priori* criteria for specifying this stage. An objective formulation of such a criterion amenable to empirical scrutiny is called for. On this question, some studies have been initiated to explore new directions by using biomolecular analogues of quantum measuring devices which could be of significance because biomolecules such as DNA occupy a strategic position between microscopic and macroscopic bodies.[13]

The line of study to probe the quantum measurement problem in an experimentally meaningful way that has been most substantially developed is the approach which was suggested by Leggett.[14] This seeks to test the basic idea of interference between 'macroscopically distinct' states of a 'macro-object' implied by the pure state of the form Eq.(2) which is a crucial ingredient in the Measurement Problem. Some recent fascinating experiments have tested the implications of the above idea in the context of a superposition of two macroscopic currents moving in clockwise and anticlockwise directions of a SQUID ring (superconducting quantum interference device) which is taken to be of a macroscopic dimension.[15] Such experiments promise to provide empirically relevant insights on the Measurement Problem. In particular, they could expose the inadequacy of the "decoherence" approach to the Measurement Problem.

We now turn to discussing how Entanglement is related to what is known as Quantum Nonlocality.

III

QUANTUM NONLOCALITY

The term quantum nonlocality appears in various guises in the literature. Broadly speaking, it denotes quantum mechanical *action* at a distance in a situation where a distant influence appears to be counterintuitive because of the absence of any classically describable form of physical mediation.

More precisely speaking, a nonlocal effect means affecting the "state" of an individual entity by any form of dynamical intervention in a faraway region such that no known physical influence can causally connect the occurrences in that region to the system in question. In the particular case of a 'spacelike separation', a nonlocal effect entails 'superluminal' causal influence. We shall now discuss Bell's theorem which captures the essence of what is meant by quantum nonlocality in a precise quantitative way. It will be seen that such nonlocality hinges on properties of Entangled States for the spatially separated particles.

Bell's Theorem

In his famous paper of 1964, Bell[16] formulated a mathematical demonstration of an incompatibility between quantum theory and a general class of theories satisfying the locality condition. Different ways of proving Bell's theorem have been comprehensively discussed.[17] Here we shall discuss a very simple version of the proof in the deterministic case.

A typical example[18] used in such proofs pertains to two spin-1/2 particles (1 and 2) prepared in a singlet state, which is an entangled state given by Eq.(1). Particles fly apart from each other. Measurements of the components of spins $\vec{s}_1$ and $\vec{s}_2$ along two different directions are performed on these particles. For the particle 1, one measures *either* of the spin components A or A' where $A = 2\vec{a}.\vec{s}_1$ and $A' = 2a'.\vec{s}_1$ ($\vec{a},\vec{a}'$ are two unit vectors along different directions). The measured values of A, A' are ±1. Similarly, for any given particle 2, *either* of the two quantities B or B' is measured, where $B = 2\vec{b}.\vec{s}_2$ and $B' = 2\vec{b}'.\vec{s}_2$ (B, B' = ±1).

Now, consider the linear combination $AB + A'B + AB' - A'B'$. For any given pair of spatially separated 1 and 2 in the singlet state, one can measure only one of the product quantities $AB, A'B, AB', A'B'$. In each case, by construction, the answer will be either 1 or -1. The experiment consists in making measurements on a large number of such pairs, with the setting on one wing (particles 1) alternated between $\vec{a}$ and $\vec{a}'$, and that on the other wing (particles 2) between $\vec{b}$ and $\vec{b}'$. Thus a large number of measurements of each of the quantities $AB, A'B, AB'$ *and* $A'B'$ are performed. The final experimental data are the average values of these quantities which are denoted by $\langle AB\rangle, \langle A'B\rangle, \langle AB'\rangle$ and $\langle A'B'\rangle$.

Assumptions

A. An individual outcome of a particular measurement of any observable of a particle is definite and *not* affected by changing parameters or by what outcome is obtained by measurement in a region which is "sufficiently separated" from the entity in question (locality condition at the level of individual events).

B. The randomly chosen sample of pairs on which one happens to measure a quantity such as AB is typical of the entire ensemble (the principle of induction).

The assumption **A** implies that for each particle there is a definite result for any observable which we "would" get if we measure the observable in question and that this result is not influenced in any way by measurements in a distant region of spacetime. Let us now see how the above suppositions lead to a testable constraint on the correlation functions, *without* any input from quantum mechanics.

Considering the example of a pair of spin-1/2 particles (1 and 2) in a singlet state, the assumption **A** implies that one can associate definite measured values with *both* the spin components $A(+1 or -1)$ and $A'(+1 or -1)$ for each particle 1, which are independent of whether B *or* B' is measured on the particle 2. Similarly, for a particle 2, there are definite measured values of B and B' which are independent of whether A *or* A' is measured. Consequently, *each* particle pair has either a value 1 or -1 of *each* of the measured quantities $AB, A'B, AB'$ *and* $A'B'$. It is then easy to see that for *each* of the 16 different cases corresponding to the possible choices ±1 for each of A, A', B, B' separately

$$AB + AB' + AB' - AB' = \pm 2 \qquad (3)$$

Note that it is crucial for the validity of (3) that both the occurrences of, say, A in the expression (3) have the *same* value; similarly for A', B *and* B' (the locality condition).

Summing (3) over the entire ensemble of pairs and taking the average

$$|\langle AB\rangle + \langle AB'\rangle + \langle A'B\rangle - \langle A'B'\rangle| \leq 2 \qquad (4)$$

By virtue of the assumption **B** we can then identify the averages $\langle AB\rangle, \langle AB'\rangle$, ... with the experimentally measured values of these quantities. Thus we have a *verifiable prediction* involving the measurable quantities given by the Inequality (4) (known as *Bell's inequality*) which is a direct consequence of the locality condition.

It is rather straightforward to see that the above inequality is violated by the quantum mechanical results for, say, the singlet state for which $\langle AB\rangle = -\vec{a}.\vec{b} = -\cos\theta$. The *maximum violation* occurs when all the directions are coplanar, with the $(\vec{a}', \vec{b}')$ angle equal to 135° and the three others to 45°. Then the left-hand side of Bell's inequality (4) is $2.(2)^{1/2}$.

If one takes $\vec{a}=\vec{b}$ with $\vec{a}$ and $\vec{b}$ at an angle q on each side, then $\vec{a}.\vec{b}'=\vec{a}'.\vec{b}=\cos\theta$ and $\vec{a}'.\vec{b}'=\cos 2\theta$. The left-hand side of Bell's inequality becomes $|-2-2\cos\theta.(1-\cos\theta)|$ which exceeds 2 for any q ˙90´.

The significance of Bell's theorem lies in entailing that, irrespective of the specifics of any causal model, no causal theory satisfying the locality condition can be fully *consistent* with the formalism of quantum mechanics—a classic "no-go theorem". Thus it is an empirically decidable issue whether the idea of *local causality* is tenable vis-a-vis quantum mechanics. This is rather a rare instance where by appealing to experiments pertaining to the *statistical* properties of ensembles one is able to draw conclusions regarding assumptions about the *causal* description of individual events. Not surprisingly, Gottfried and Mermin 34 have commented, "Bell's theorem has now achieved a level of popular acclaim exceeded by few theorems in the history of science."

There are three possible responses to Bell's theorem:

(a) One may be inclined to give up the assumption **A.** It would then mean giving up the causal description at an event-by-event level. Such a decree could have been an acceptable solution to the dilemma posed by Bell's theorem, but for the Quantum Measurement Problem. This paradox, as discussed in Section 2, suggests that within the framework of the standard formalism of quantum mechanics, there is no way of escaping the Measurement Problem *unless* one gives up the assumption that y provides a 'complete description' of the state of an individual entity. This in turn implies the necessity of using the 'supplementary' or 'hidden variables' in order to specify the state of an individual microsystem. In other words, *unless* one is willing to modify the formalism itself, the assumption of an underlying causal description is unavoidable, given the acuteness of the Quantum Measurement Problem.

(b) Now, if one grants the necessity of a causal model of quantum mechanics because of the Measurement Problem, the remaining alternative is to interpret Bell's theorem as implying that *any* viable causal model of quantum mechanics must necessarily be *nonlocal.* This, however, raises tricky questions as to what extent the Lorentz invariance is compatible with such putative nonlocal influences at the level of 'individual quantum events'. This aspect is being probed in depth by many.[20]

(c) Some suspect that if careful experiments are actually done by plugging all possible loopholes then Bell's inequality will always be satisfied. But this would mean falsifying the standard quantum predictions under those conditions. Although the experiments to date, all using photons, have shown the violation of Bell's inequality, certain technical loopholes remain due to the available low detection efficiencies (~50%) of the detectors for photons in the visible range.[21] Experiments testing Bell's inequality are yet to be done with material objects. Recently, a generic scheme for this purpose which is applicable for both fermions and bosons, as well as for macro-molecules such as bucky-balls (C_{60} molecules for which self-interference experiment has already been done[22]), has been suggested using the "indistinguishability" property of identical quantum objects.[23] An entangled spin-state of two caesium gas samples (each comprising 10^{12} atoms) has also recently been produced[24].

A loophole-free fully decisive experimental refutation of Bell's inequality has a nontrivial implication for even those who would refuse to entertain any consideration about the "causal individual description" of quantum mechanics. The empirical validity of quantum correlation functions in the situations where Bell's inequality is violated implies an 'irreducible quantum nonseparability for macroscopic' separations. This is a repudiation of the cherished notion of "divisibility by thought"; viz. the principle that any composite extended system can be regarded as composed of elements which are localized in separated regions so that the knowledge of the full Hamiltonian function and of the values of the relevant physical quantities associated with each one of the constituents will yield an exhaustive knowledge of the composite system as a whole.

A general form of the correlated two-particle wave function violating Bell's inequality is given by

$$\Psi = \sum_i c_i \phi_i \eta_1 \qquad (5)$$

where f_i , h_i are mutually orthogonal states of the particles 1 and 2 respectively. It can be proved that using any correlated state of the form (4), Bell's inequality is violated by quantum correlations if one chooses the observable appropriately.[25]

Note that the knowledge of the total wave function of the form (5) does not enable us to ascribe an 'individual wave function' to each of the subsystems; in other words, the many-particle system in a pure state (5) has to be regarded as a single whole even after the particles cease to interact.

IV

QUANTUM COMMUNICATIONS

In this Section we briefly discuss one of the striking effects that have been discovered relating to the emerging area of Quantum Communications.

Quantum Teleportation

Suppose a two-level quantum system (henceforth called "qubit") is in a state

$$|\psi\rangle = a|0\rangle + b|1\rangle \qquad (6)$$

where the mutually orthogonal states $|1\rangle, |0\rangle$ span a two-dimensional Hilbert space. This qubit is initially given to, say, Alice who has no information about the state, except knowing that it is a qubit. Her task is to send all the information encoded in such a state to a distant location (Bob) without physically transporting her system in a way which is secure against eavesdropping. Since she has no *a priori* information about the state, she can neither get any information about the state without distributing it nor she can produce copies of this state so that she can determine the state by measurements on an ensemble (the latter is not possible because of the no-cloning theorem[26]). Therefore, Alice has no way of telling Bob what the state is. However, there is a way out which has been discovered by Bennett *et al.*[27] The scheme for this purpose operates by letting Alice and Bob share a singlet state of two particles A and B

$$\psi_{AB} = \frac{1}{2}(|01||10\rangle)_{AB} \qquad (7)$$

where $|01\rangle_{AB} = |0\rangle_A|1\rangle_B$, $|10\rangle_{AB} = |1\rangle_A|0\rangle_B$. Denoting the state of the unknown qubit by the index Q, the initial state of the three particles Q, A, B is given by

$$(a|0\rangle + b|1\rangle)_Q \frac{1}{\sqrt{2}}(|01\rangle - |10\rangle)_{AB} \qquad (8)$$

This state maybe rewritten as

$$(|01\rangle-|10\rangle)_{QA}(-a|0\rangle-b|1\rangle)_B + \frac{1}{\sqrt{2}}(|01\rangle+|10\rangle)_{QA}(-a|0\rangle+b|1\rangle)_B + \frac{1}{\sqrt{2}}(|00\rangle-|11\rangle)_{QA}(b|0\rangle+a|1\rangle)_B$$
$$+ \frac{1}{\sqrt{2}}(|00\rangle+|11\rangle)_{QA}(b|0\rangle-a|1\rangle)_B \qquad (9)$$

The next ingredient in this scheme is that Alice performs a projection-valued joint measurement on Q and A with respect to the Bell-basis of states (such states are used to study Bell's inequality) which are given by

$$\psi_\mu = \frac{1}{\sqrt{2}}\left(|01\rangle_{QA}\, \mu|10\rangle_{QA}\right) \qquad (10)$$

$$\psi_\mu = \frac{1}{\sqrt{2}}\left(|00\rangle_{QA}\, \mu|11\rangle_{QA}\right) \qquad (11)$$

Subsequently, she telephones Bob and tells him the outcome of her above measurement. Bob then applies a unitary operation (operator) on his qubit according to the following table:

Result of Alice's 'measurement'	Bob's 'unitary operation'
$\psi-$	I
$\psi+$	σ_z
$\phi-$	σ_x
$\phi+$	$i\sigma_y$

In each of these cases, Bob ends up with the state $|\psi\rangle$ which is the original states (6) Alice had.

In the above scheme, quantum nonlocal correlations embodied in the joint wave function (7) of A and B, in conjunction with the Bell-basis measurement on Q and A lead to a disentanglement of the entangled state (7) in such a way that B is endowed with the state that Q originally had. In order to actually implement the above scheme, performing the Bell-basis measurement on two independent particles is a formidable experimental challenge which has been overcome by a number of experiments using photons.[28] Teleporting states of massive objects remains the next important goal. For this, entanglement of massive objects needs to be prepared.

Note that the teleported quantum information encoded in the state does not travel materially from Alice to Bob. All that travel materially is the message about Alice's measurement result, which tells Bob how to process his particle but carries no information about Alice's state itself.

In one out of four cases, Alice is lucky with her measurement, and Bob's particle immediately becomes an identical replica of Alice's original. Then it might seem as if information has travelled instantly from Alice to Bob. Yet this strange feature cannot be used to send usable information instantaneously, because Bob has no way of knowing that his particle is already an identical replica. Only when he learns the result of Alice's Bell-state measurement, which is transmitted to him via classical means, can he exploit the information in the teleported quantum state. Suppose he tries to guess in which cases the teleportation was instantly successful. He will be wrong 75% of the time, and moreover, he will not know which guesses were correct. If he uses his particles based on such guesses, the results will be the same as if he had taken a beam of particles with random distribution of $|1\rangle, |0\rangle$ states. Thus, even the "spooky" instantaneous action at a distance implied by quantum mechanics fails to send any usable information faster than the speed of light.

CONCLUDING REMARKS

Quantum Mechanics is a great deal more than a theory; it is a whole new way of looking at the world. This realization has been deepened because of the recent studies on Quantum Entanglement. Not only fresh conceptual insights have been obtained regarding the puzzles associated with the Quantum Measurement Problem and Nonlocality, a number of alternative models of Quantum Mechanics other than the standard "Copenhagen Interpretation" have been substantially formulated. As to what extent such models can be empirically discriminated from the Standard Interpretation remains an intriguing question which is being actively probed. It is, however, clear that experimental works related to the measurement paradox are becoming progressively more sophisticated and will eventually advance into the areas of macro and biosystems subjected to quantum mechanics, thereby playing a possible role in testing the Alternative Models. Not surprisingly, this whole enterprise has been called "Experimental Metaphysics".[29]

As far as the emerging exciting area of practical applications of Quantum Entanglement for finding effective means of transfering, storing and processing of information is concerned, in this article, we've only briefly mentioned Quantum Communications in the context of Teleportation.[30]

Finally, it may be said that the exploïtation of the weird properties of entangled states is only in its infancy and there could be surprises in the offing which are now difficult to guess.

NOTES

1. Schrodinger, E. 1935. *Cambridge Philosophical Society,* 31(555).
2. Weinberg, S. 1933. *Dreams of a Final Theory.* London: Vintage. p. 64.
3. For a detailed exposition see, for example, Peres, A. 1993. *Quantum Theory—Concepts and Methods.* Dordrecht: Kluwer Academy. pp. 373-429. See also, Home, D. 1997. *Conceptual Foundations of Quantum Physics—an Overview from Modern Perspective.* New York: Plenum Press. pp. 67-68; d'Espsgnat, B. 1994. *Veiled Reality—an Analysis of Present—Day Quantum Mechanical Concepts.* Wesley, Reading: Addison. pp. 138-85; Bell, J.S. 1987. *Speakable and Unspeakable Quantum Mechanics.* Cambridge: Cambridge

University Press. pp. 119-127; Leggett, A.J. 1987. *Quantum Implications.* B.J. Hiley and D.Peat (ed.). London: Routledge & Kegan Paul. pp. 85-104; Leggett, A.J. 1986. *Lessons in Quantum Theory.* J. de Boer, E. Dal and O. Ulfbeck (ed.). Amsterdam: Elsevier. p. 47.

4. Schrodinger.
5. Wigner, E.P. 1963. *American Journal of Physics,* 31(6).
6. Home. pp. 67-68.
7. Bohr, N. 1948. *Dialectica,* 2(312).
8. For a review see, for example, Murdoch, D. 1987. *Niels Bohr's Philosophy of Physics.* Cambridge: Cambridge University Press.
9. Heisenberg, W. 1930. *Physical Principles of Quantum Theory.* Chicago: University of Chicago Press; reprinted Dover, New York. p. 64.
10. Holland, P. 1993. *The Quantum Theory of Motion.* Cambridge: Cambridge University Press. See also, Bohm, D. and Hiley, B.J. 1993. *The Undivided Universe.* London: Routledge.
11. Ghirardi, G.C. Rimini, A. and Weber, T. 1986. D34 (470). Pearle, P. 1989. A39 (2277). See also, Ghirardi, Rimini et al. 1990: A42 (1057). Diosi, L. 1989. A40 (1165). Ghirardi. 1995. *Fundamental Problems in Quantum Theory.* D.M. Greeberger and A. Zeilenger (ed.). New York: Annals of New York Academy of Sciences. pp. 506-523; Ghirardi, G.C. and Grassi, R 1996. *Bohmian Mechanics and Quantum Theory: An Appraisal.* J.T. Cushing, A. Fine and S. Goldstein (ed.). Dordrecht: Kluwer. pp. 353-377; Penrose, R. 1996. *General Relations and Gravitation,* 28 (581).
12. Joos, E. and Zeh, H.D. 1985. *Physics,* B59 (223). Zurek, W.H. 1991. *Physics Today,* 44(36) October. See also, Omnes, R. 1994. *The Interpretation of Quantum Mechanics.* Princeton: Princeton University Press; Omnes. 1999. *Understanding Quantum Mechanics.* Princeton: Princeton University Press.
13. Shimony, A. 1989. *Philosophical Consequences of Quantum Theory.* J.T. Cushing and E. McMullin (ed.). Notre Dame: University of Notre Dame. p. 61. See also, Home, D. and Chattopadhyaya, R. 1996. 76 (2836). Shimony, A. 1998. *Quantum Measurement: Beyond Paradox.* R.A. Healey and G. Hellman. Minneapolis: University of Minnesota Press. McFadden, J. and Al-Khalili, J. 1999. *Biosystems,* 50 (203).
14. Leggett, AJ. 1980. 69 (80). See also, Leggett, A.J. and Garg, A 1985. 54 (857). Leggett, A.J. 1998. *Quantum Measurement: Beyond Paradox.* Healey and Hellman (ed.).
15. Van der Wall, C.H. et al. 2000. *Science,* 290 (773). See also, Freidman, J.R. et al. 2002. *Nature,* 406 (43).Vion, D. et al. In print.
16. Bell, J.S. 1964. *Physics,* 1 (195). Reprinted in, *Speakable and Unspeakable in Quantum Mechanics.* p. 14.
17. See for example, Greenberger, D.M., Home, M.A. and Zeilinger, A. 1989. *Bell's Theorem, Quantum Theory and Conceptions of the Universe. M.* Kafatos (ed.). Dordrecht, Netherlands: Kluwer. pp. 73-76; Greenberger et al. 1990. *American Journal of Physics,* 58 (1131). Mermin, N.D. 1990. *American Journal of Physics,* 58 (731). Hardy. L. 1992. 68 (2981). Hardy, L. 1993. 71 (1665). Cabello. A. 2001. 86 (1911). Cabello. A. 2001. 87 (010403-1).
18. This example was first suggested by Bohm, D. 1951. *Quantum Theory.* Englewood Cliffs, NJ: Prentice-Hall. p. 614.
19. Gottfried, K. and Mermin, N.D. 2000. *Quantum Reflections.* J. Ellis and D. Amati (ed.). Cambridge: Cambridge University Press. pp. 186-192.
20. Mauldin, T. 1994. *Quantum Non Locality and Relativity.* Oxford: Blackwell.
21. For a review, see for example, Home. pp. 224-228; Shimony, A. 2000. *Quantum Reflections.* J. Ellis and D. Amati (ed.). pp. 136-164.
22. Arndt, M., Nairz. O. et al. 1999. *Nature,* 401 (680).
23. Home, D. and Bose, S. 2002. 154 (201).
24. Julsgaard, B., Kozhekin, A. and Polzik, E.S. 2001. *Nature,* 413 (400).
25. Gisin, N. 1991.154 (201).
26. Wootters, W.K. and Zurek, W.H. 1982. *Nature,* 299 (802).
27. Bennett, C.H., Brassard, G. et al. 1993. 70 (1895).
28. Weinfurter, H. and Zeilinger, A. 1997. *Nature,* 390 (575). London. Bouwmeester, D., Pan, J.W. et al. 1998. *Nature,* 394 (840). Hardy, L. and Popescu, S. 1998. 80 (1121). Weinfurter, H. and Zeilinger, A. 1998. *Nature,* 394 (840). London. Kible, H.J. and Polzik, E. S. 1998. *Science,* 282 (706).
29. Ibid.
30. For an overview of the experimental status, see for example, the review by Zeilinger, A. 1999. 71 (S288).
31. For in-depth accounts of the present status of studies on such areas, including *Quantum Cryptography and Quantum Computation, see for example,* Nielson, M.A. and Chuang, I.L. 2000. *Quantum Computation and Quantum Information.* Cambridge: Cambridge University Press.; Bouwmeester, D., Ekert, A. and Zeilinger, A. (ed.). 2000. *The Physics of Quantum Information.* Verlag: Springer.

CHAPTER 14

A Rational Critique of Standard Quantum Theory: Overview, Popper's Trail and New Results

C.S. Unnikrishnan

We examine the tension between the general rational structure of physical theories and some essential concepts like nonlocality and acausal indeterminism in quantum theory. Some consequences of attributing a link between the mathematical machinery of standard quantum theory and the physical reality in space and time are examined. In particular, we examine the predictions from standard quantum theory for the properties of a particle that is not disturbed by a real measurement, but whose properties could be deduced from measurement on another correlated particle separated far away from the first. Taking two different mathematically correct routes for this prediction yield two contradictory results. Therefore, standard quantum theory seems to be inconsistent as a theory of phenomena in space and time. This inconsistency is traced to the concept of wave-function collapse in standard quantum theory. Our results are rooted in the logical and natural extension of criticisms of standard quantum theory by Einstein and Popper. Some guesses regarding the features of a future theory are discussed at the end.

I

MOTIVATIONS

I have chosen to direct certain firm criticism on the standard quantum theory for several reasons. (a) There are several indications that the standard quantum theory is complete only in an abstract mathematical space and seems drastically incomplete as a theory of phenomena in real space-time. (b) Almost everyone who pioneered and nurtured the theory could never defend the theory as the 'end of the road' regarding its conceptual features, interpretations and its link to the real physical world. (c) Once out of its shell of abstract mathematical space, standard quantum theory includes the necessity of instantaneous action at a distance, a feature which, in my opinion, is a highly irrational feature in conflict with the spirit of special relativity. Therefore, it is in conflict with a large part of the physical worldview that we have developed starting on another line of logical rational enquiry. (d) There is no experimental proof that there is indeed instantaneous action at a distance.

The nonlocal features of the quantum theory arise in the standard interpretation due to the need for the theory to connect up to the real world physical phenomena. In other words, the mathematical formalism of the standard quantum theory by itself does not necessitate action at a distance till the theory tries to incorporate a description of act of measurements. This brings in a sort of discontinuity that is essential, but not understood yet. Just to stress the logical and rational difficulties encountered while building up the theory of the microscopic world, I may point out the contrast with the other good theory that we have—the general theory of relativity and gravitation. It was essentially conceived, built and interpreted by one individual, whereas the present quantum theory is the result of the efforts of scores of exceptional minds, and still everybody except the instrumentalists, who are anyway strong conformists, are in doubt regarding its interpretations. My criticisms arise in a 'determined effort to understand'.

Another motivation for taking up such a study is the impressive and well-reasoned critique by Popper of the interpretation of the wave-function in quantum mechanics—what he termed as the great quantum muddle. This concerns the issue of identifying a qualifier satisfied by an individual element of an ensemble with the individual itself. This, according to Popper, is the source of a serious confusion in quantum theory, and it is the source of wrongly attributing an intrinsic wave nature to particles. This is a very interesting and deep issue. Understanding this clearly would lead to a deeper and confusion-free understanding of topics such as the uncertainty principle, complementarity and wave-particle duality.

Finally, there is also a strong desire to understand the relation between elements that could be compatible with the notion of 'inseparable' and unified, and those that are local and causal. There is a tension between inseparability on one hand and locality and causality on the other, in the language of quantum physics, whereas such a tension is perhaps absent in our philosophical discussions on these concepts. It is interesting to note that the spookiness associated with quantum theory originates in its use of the 'superposition of the opposites (alternatives)'. This is also the source of concepts like uncertainty principle and complementarity principle. The interpretation that emerges from my study is different from what is popular in standard quantum theory where locality and causality are rejected when contrasted against the inherent inseparability of wave-functions. Our attempt is to reconcile the two opposing notions by going deeper than the level superficially suggested by the mathematical structure of quantum theory. The final result of this attempt will be important for the pure physical theory since even apparent incompatibility between two fundamental theories of physics is not a desirable feature for a consistent description of the physical world. This is also a very important aspect for the individual exploring the physical universe since the worldview that emerges from the exploration always has it roots and interpretation in terms of his cultural, philosophical and linguistic backgrounds where such a strong tension between inseparability of the whole and the local causal flow of events do not seem to exist.

II

DEFINITIONS

Before we proceed we should try to agree on some definitions.

Standard quantum theory = The mathematical formalism (Schrodinger equation, Operator algebra etc.) + the Born statistical interpretation for connecting the square of the wave function to the probability density + the instantaneous change in the wave-function or 'state' that occurs as a result of a measurement on any physical system.

The first two aspects allow the calculation of the probabilities for the observations of specific values of observables, and also allow a consistent interpretation in terms of the agreement of the statistical predictions of the quantum theory and the observed statistical averages of values of observables. It seems worth stressing at this point that the standard quantum theory has only statistical predictions, and individual events are described in terms of probabilities. Yet, it is fundamentally different from the statistical theory of phenomena of chance, a dice-game, for example.

The last aspect in the definition of the standard quantum theory is called the collapse of the wave-function, or the state reduction. This becomes necessary in the theory to calculate any quantity after a measurement has been performed. After every measurement, the 'weight' of each elemental state that make up the total quantum state (the probability amplitude) needs to be renormalized depending on the result of the measurement for calculations to proceed for making another statistical prediction. Therefore, the feature of wave-function collapse and renormalization is an essential part of the mathematical machinery of quantum mechanics, even though it is not accommodated naturally by the fundamental equation of the theory—the Schrodinger equation. Another way of saying this is that the change in the wave-function or the state after a measurement is abrupt, and does not conform to the smooth evolution described by the differential equation (The Schrodinger equation). Note that according to Popper, the difficulty arises from assigning a physical link between the wave-function and the physical object (particle), and somehow calling the wave-function as a physical aspect of the individual particle. We should also realize that such an interpretation seems to be forced on us from experimental situations and this needs further study to see whether there could be a consistent interpretation that avoids the "quantum muddle".

There are many physicists who think that everything is all right with quantum mechanics as a theory, and they think of quantum mechanics as a set of rules to calculate statistical averages of measurable quantities. At that level quantum mechanics is not a theory of phenomena in real space-time, and do not have a description or answer to even very simple questions (Typical response of the quantum physicists high on the Copenhagen interpretation is to admonish anybody asking simple questions about physical reality). Also, issues like nonlocality do not even come into discussion for any theory that is confined to some abstract space.

Locality: An act of observation or measurement at one location does not in any way influence the factual physical situation or the experimental results at another location that is spatially (space-like) separated from the first. This definition is due to Einstein.[1] The definition of locality follows from the spirit of special relativity, and essentially defines what is technically called Einstein locality. Almost the entire community of quantum physicists maintain the view that Einstein locality is violated in standard quantum mechanics—a view forced on them due to the adherence to the standard interpretation. We will show beyond doubt that this view is incorrect, and that quantum theory that violate Einstein locality is inconsistent.

III

SCOPE OF THIS DISCUSSION

I will present some remarks on standard quantum theory discussed by Einstein, to bring out an interpretational issue of quantum theory—whether the quantum theory is a statistical theory describing only ensembles (as any statistical theory) or is it a description of individual microscopic systems. Einstein's repeated assertion was that it was a statistical theory, and therefore incomplete. Then, there is scope for another theory, yet to be invented, that might describe reality objectively and possibly nonstatistically.

I will then go on to a criticism by Popper, again asserting that quantum mechanics is a theory of statistical ensembles, and therefore uncertainty principle represents mere scatter relations and has no implication to limits of measurability on single quantum systems. He advanced his arguments as a critique of the Copenhagen interpretation.

I will take Popper's argument and advance it further to an interesting logical and rational conclusion where it turns out that quantum theory, as a theory of events in real space and time, might be an inconsistent theory! This might be a surprising conclusion for many, but as far as I can see this conclusion is inevitable, and therefore the present quantum theory cannot be the final theory. To clarify, I should add right here that the mathematical formalism of the present quantum theory might be complete in itself, in the sense that any future theory might have the same mathematical structure at its base. But as a description of single quantum systems, and phenomena in real space and time, the present theory is inadequate. This is also a very exciting conclusion since that leaves tremendous scope for looking for a new theory.

IV

THE CRITIQUE

Einstein had often remarked that the wave-function description of quantum phenomena was incomplete and that it was in fact a description of a statistical ensemble, contrary to the standard view that it was also the description of single quantum systems.

This maybe compared with classical mechanics that has a description of single particles in space and time. Quantum theory describes an ensemble and it is essentially a statistical theory. The Schrodinger wave function allows only a statistical description, through the Born interpretation.

Let us look at some experimental situations to clarify this point.

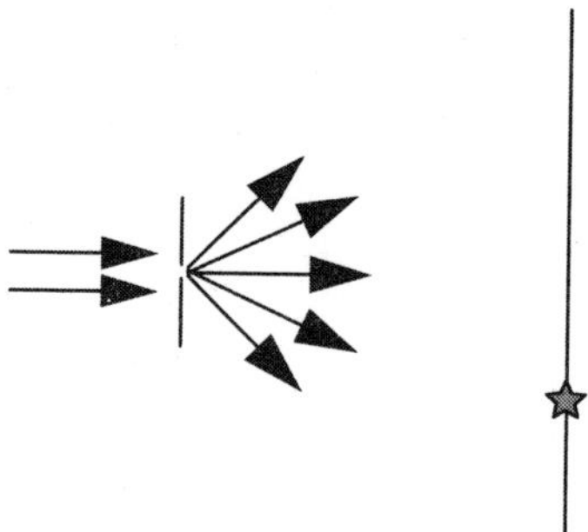

Fig. 1

A stream of quantum particles is passing through a narrow slit. The quantum description and the uncertainty principle predict that the momentum of each particle after passing through the slit is unpredictable, and falls in a range of possible momenta. The wave-function starts spreading after the slit. A detection at the screen is an individual event. In the quantum description, the wave-function is spread out almost uniformly over the screen just before a detection. Therefore, the wave-function has to *spontaneously localize* after detection to a small region where the detection took place. Any sensible theory of phenomena in space-time has the right to ask where the detected entity was just before the detection. Since the entity existed before it entered the slit, and since it entered the slit, it must have existed till it reached the screen. But quantum theory has to deny this existence itself within the theory, since between the slit and the screen the wave-function has the character of spreading, and cannot in a sensible way represent anything localized. On the other hand, if anyone insists that the wave-function somehow represents the particle it will lead to absurdities like a spreading charge (again the quantum muddle). So the only consistent interpretation is that wave-function squared is the probability of finding the particle at any time in that region, and quantum mechanics cannot give answers to any other question.

To clarify, Quantum Mechanics (QM) is able to calculate precisely what is the probability of observing any observable for this system—and these predictions agree well with observations. But there are several questions that you can sensibly ask in a world of experience that has no answer within the quantum theory, and Einstein's point was that this situation is similar to the situation in any statistical theory like statistical mechanics.

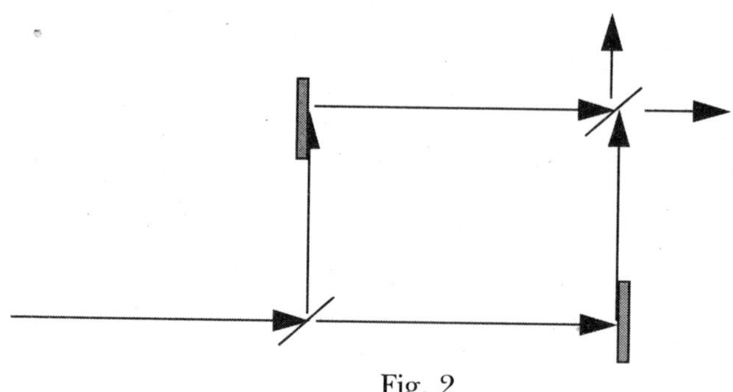

Fig. 2

There is another experiment that I want to discuss that brings out this point more clearly. This experiment also reveals why there is a problem with a mere statistical interpretation.

We start our experiment with a beam of particles—photons or electrons or whatever. Then there is a splitter. Quantum theory predicts that the probability of finding a single particle is 50%. If we consider a massive microscopic particle like the electron or an atom, all of physics we know and think correctly tells us that the particle cannot split at the beam splitter. The mathematical description of quantum mechanics says that the wave-function splits, when the experimental situation is represented in an abstract space. If that is the case, when you suddenly put a detector in one of the paths, you may or may not detect the particle—probability of success being 50%. If you detected, then standard quantum theory says that the entity representing the other path (the wave-function) vanishes instantaneously. There is no experimental proof for this, but that is what QM says. Thus there are nonlocal effects in QM. At first glance it might seem that the statistical interpretation is the only consistent interpretation here, especially if we want to avoid the strange nonlocality.

Now, it is not possible to get away from nonlocality by saying that the split takes place in an abstract mathematical space, since *even for a single particle* we can affect the result of a measurement after the second beam splitter on top right (where an interference pattern is detectable due to the two combined beams) by moving *either* of the mirrors, while making sure that the particle itself did not reflect on the mirror! So any rational theory will have to admit that there is something that splits at the beam splitter. It is not an abstract quantity, since it is something that can be affected by moving a mirror, and it embodies all the responses of the particle to external fields. But it is not the particle itself.

This simple experiment actually shows that neither a statistical interpretation nor the standard interpretation is appropriate. For, if the statistical interpretation is correct, then how is that we are able to affect single particle by moving either mirror? There must be something in both paths though energy, charge etc. cannot be split at the beam splitter. If the standard quantum theory was right, on the other hand, then we are faced with nonlocality. We may agree to accept nonlocality and instantaneous changes during measurements as plausible, though it is not in harmony with the rest of the physics we know of, and may try to proceed further. It turns out that this view cannot be maintained since it clashes with empirical tests. That is where Popper's ideas have become relevant.

Popper had stressed several times that the Copenhagens interpretation of quantum mechanics was contradicted by conceivable experiments.[2] In particular, the uncertainty relations are merely scatter relations between conjugate observables and do not imply that the two quantities cannot be measured for any system accurately and simultaneously. Let me illustrate this point briefly, since it is a similar experiment that will be used later to arrive at the conclusion that the standard quantum theory is inconsistent.

Consider the following experimental configuration where pairs of particles are correlated such that their total momentum is zero. Classically they will propagate in opposite directions. Quantum mechanically also the measured values of momenta for the two particles should add up to a small value, depending on the initial state. A measurement of transverse position on one particle using a slit (position A in Fig. 3) determines its position accurately, say, within the width of a slit used to localize the particle, and then disturbs its momentum according to the uncertainty principle. Since the total momentum at the instant of measurement is close to zero, knowledge acquired in the first measurement can be used to predict where the second particle will be detected. Quantum mechanics gives a precise prediction for where to keep a slit such that the second particle will surely pass through. In other words, and in the language of quantum mechanics, localizing the first particle also localizes the second particle without a real measurement.

Then the question can be asked: does the indirect 'measurement' of the position of the second particle disturb its momentum? Popper argued that it would not. Therefore, there are instances where the position can be determined without disturbing the subsequent momentum, clearly violating, according to Popper, the Copenhagen interpretation of the uncertainty relations. In Popper's words, "I wish to suggest a crucial experiment to *test* whether knowledge alone is sufficient to create 'uncertainty' and, with it, scatter (as contended under the Copenhagen interpretation), or whether it is the physical situation that is responsible for the scatter".[3] The reasons why Popper's criticism against the entire Copenhagen interpretation is not valid are subtle[4] (*and probably not even valid*), and are related to the Copenhagen view that the quantum system consisting of two particles are not to be seen as two separate quantum systems even when they are separated well in space. However, the usual criticism by the follower of the standard quantum theory that Popper's experiment was flawed originates in a complete misunderstanding of the central point in Popper's argument. In fact, anybody who cares to reformulate what Popper said (the quotation above, for example) mathematically would be able to see the depth of his insight and the essential correctness of the main point. We do not discuss this aspect here in detail. Instead we merely note that Popper had successfully devised a thought experiment that shows that the Copenhagen interpretation of the meaning of the uncertainty relation was not correct if the particles could be viewed as separated physical systems with independent realities. In such a view, the uncertainty relations are mere scatter relations, obtained as a statistical average over many trials of the same experiment.

Despite this clarification of the uncertainty relation, we see that QM cannot be treated as merely a statistical theory. Then what does it represent in real space and time? Can we say that it is a complete description of microscopic phenomena in space and time, though there is nonlocality and instantaneous action at a distance?

My next step is to show that this interpretation also fails miserably—if we take the present interpretation seriously and proceed to analyse an experiment that involves two particles, then we arrive at a contradiction. That means that the standard interpretation rooted in the Copenhagen view is inconsistent. But to see this inconsistency clearly and rigorously we need to take one step more than what Popper did.

The standard quantum theory deals with physical situations where the description is in terms of a *superposition*—a sum of two abstract quantities, each of which when squared represents the probabilities of independent outcomes in a measurement (Then the probabilities for certain measurements also contain a "cross-term", which the essence of quantum phenomena like particle interference). Such a superposition then *abruptly becomes a single term after a measurement.*

If the particle can be in two states, say (UP) or (DOWN), then the "state" of the particle can also be a sum of the state representing (UP) and the state representing (DOWN), whereas in a classical system only *one* of the two possibilities can be a valid state. For two particles together, a more interesting superposition called an entangled state is allowed.

It is represented approximately as (1-UP, 2-DOWN) + (1-DOWN, 2-UP), with the meaning for measurement that if the particle 1 is found in state UP, the second one will definitely be found in state DOWN and vice versa (Such a state can be created by breaking up a system with zero total angular momentum or spin). But each particle taken separately is not even in a superposed state of UP and DOWN. Individually they have no state at all! Together they have a definite state. We are able to say what they are not, but not what they are.

So, *taken individually each particle has no definite state*—whatever direction you take, it can give either (UP) or (DOWN) with equal probability. States of this kind—a superposition of multiparticle states in which individual particles have no definite state—are called entangled states. They cannot be written as a simple joint state where each particle has *some* definite state. Now the interesting thing is that a measurement on *just one* particle uniquely determines the state of both particles separately! For, suppose that we measure the first particle to be in the (UP) state, then necessarily the second has to be in the (DOWN) state, since total spin is zero. So the superposition turns abruptly, after a measurement on just one particle, to a single term where the states of both particles are fixed. This will happen in the standard theory however far the two particles are from each other. So, here we see how there is nonlocality built into standard quantum theory provided we say that the mathematical description actually corresponds to *some* physical reality for each particle in space. Before measurement we have a situation where both particles did not have any definite state. A measurement on one forces the other into a definite state even if the unmeasured one is light years away!

Having established that standard theory has this seemingly irrational feature, we proceed to show that there are situations where accepting such a feature lead to an inconsistency of the theory.

Consider a situation where two particles are generated from a single source such that the restriction now is on the momentum—total momentum is zero. Then both particles will classically shoot off in opposite directions. Quantum mechanically the description is in terms of a superposition with neither particle having definite momentum till a measurement is made. If a slit is put on one side, once in a while a particle might pass through. When a particle comes through, its transverse position is well determined to be within the size of the slit, and that is a measurement and localization. Since the particles are correlated, measurement on one completely determines the value of the same observable for the other particle. So, if position of first particle is measured, standard quantum mechanics asserts that the real position of the second particle gets determined instantaneously. Same conclusion applies for momentum, but both cannot be simultaneously determined.

Such an experiment was discussed both by Popper, and earlier by Einstein (with B. Podolsky and N. Rosen) to criticize standard quantum theory. (Some relevant paragraphs from a letter from Einstein to Popper explaining his criticism that the wave-function description is incomplete are reproduced in the appendix. Later, Einstein discussed the same experiment in a paper in *Dialectica* in which he clearly established that *the notion of locality and the description in terms of wave-function in quantum mechanics are contradictory*). There have been many criticisms of Popper's original proposal, and most of them miss the central point of the paper and criticise certain technical issues that in fact can be solved without altering the main argument. Some of them make the point that Popper did not understand what the Copenhagen interpretation was. (Max Born accuses Einstein of a similar shortcoming in the commentary to the 'Born-Einstein letters'—that 'Einstein's reflections resulted from his inadequate knowledge of quantum mechanics'. But if one reads Born's description of what Einstein was trying to say, it becomes immediately clear that it was Born who inadequately understood Einstein's criticism and concern). Popper surely made the point that uncertainty relations were statistical scatter relations and therefore single quantum systems admit a measurement of two conjugate observables with arbitrary accuracy. Whether the Copenhagen interpretation allows this or not depends very much on the interpretation of the Copenhagen interpretation itself! What could be said without doubt is that both Popper and Einstein gave great importance to objective physical reality as a primary requirement. Einstein also stressed the need for locality, and in later years Popper also strongly advocated the need to preserve locality (absence of instantaneous influences). We now take one leap further from the critique by Einstein and Popper and arrive at the unambiguous conclusion that standard quantum theory might be inconsistent.

V

THE INCONSISTENCY OF STANDARD QUANTUM THEORY

Assume that standard quantum theory is correct and consistent. We consider the entangled, correlated two-particle system discussed earlier. It is a simple matter within the mathematics of standard quantum theory to calculate the correlation of the two particles for the same kind of observable, say their position. Then it has a definite prediction for where the second particle will be found *if* the first particle is localized at some position at some time T. The prediction is that the second particle will in fact be found close to the line passing through the source and the slit that localizes the first particle. (This is a consequence of the physical constraint that the momenta should add up to nearly zero). I have marked this location in figure 3 by a small black square on the right to indicate where the second particle would be found at the time T when the first particle was localized. Instead of calculating the position where the second particle would be localized at time T, we could also calculate the position where it would be found at a later time T + t, if we do not care to look at the second particle at time T. The answer is simple—it will be found close to the line joining the source and the slit, but displaced further down along this line. Again, this follows from the momentum conservation, the initial momentum being nearly zero. This is also indicated in the figure 3. The important point is that *the answer is calculated in a single step, without assuming that the measurement on the first particle has affected the state of the second particle at the instant of this measurement.* In fact, this calculation does not even ask any question about the state of the particle after the first measurement—it simply answers *where the second particle would be found if measured* at time T + t.

But, suppose we do this calculation in a two-step process, using standard quantum theory. First we ask what is the state of the second particle after the first measurement. Quantum theory gives a simple answer to this question. This answer is well known from the famous EPR paper, and that is that the state of the second particle is identical to that of a localized particle, similar to that of the first particle itself. Mathematically it is an approximation to the delta function since a position measurement on one particle reveals the position of both particles in a correlated system. (It is easy to realize that this is what Popper meant by 'knowledge' without a measurement in his critique of the Copenhagen interpretation). If this is correct, then the subsequent *evolution of both particles should be similar, since their states (wave-functions) are similar.* In particular, the subsequent momenta of both particles will not be predictable according to the uncertainty principle. This can be directly tested for the particle on which the real measurement was made. It will show the usual 'diffraction' after the localizing slit. Since the second particle is localized according to the standard quantum theory, even without a real measurement, it should also show diffraction, since this depends only on the quantum state. The probability for detecting the particle away from the line joining the slit and the source becomes significant, and in fact, the narrower the slit, the smaller the probability that the particle will be detected along this line. Clearly this means that *if we wait sufficiently long, the probability that the second particle will be detected close to the line decreases drastically, contrary to the prediction from the direct calculation of the correlation.* Thus we have arrived at two contradictory predictions from standard quantum mechanics.[5] This is testable experimentally, and the test is identical to the experiment that was proposed by Popper for criticising the uncertainty principle itself.

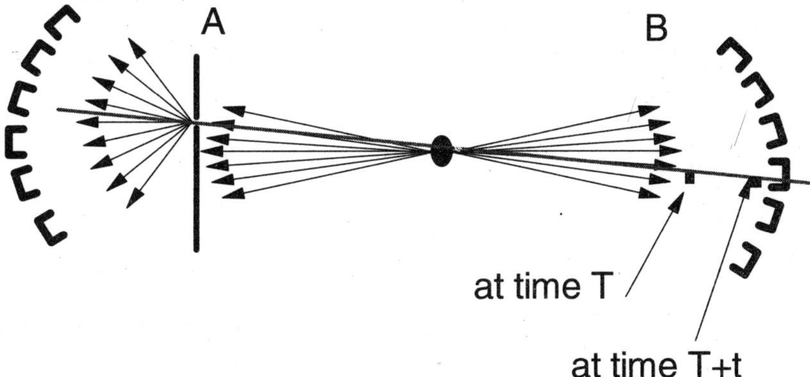

Fig. 3

An experiment of this sort was done by Kim and Shih at Maryland in which it was found that the evolution of the two particles is actually different.[6] They set up an experiment that approximates the Popper's proposal well, and measured the momentum spread for particle that has been localized using a narrow slit, and also for the entangled companion particle that did not face such a slit during its propagation. While the momentum spread for the particle that passed the slit agreed with the quantum mechanical expectation from applying the uncertainty principle, the spread in momentum for the second particle was only about 0.3 times the expectation from uncertainty principle, and essentially remained at a value consistent with that of an unlocalized particle. Only the particle on which the real measurement was done was seen to show the characteristic spreading expected after a real localization.

The experimental results seem to show that the second particle is indeed detected closer to the line joining the slit and the source than what would be expected if the second particle were localized (or nonlocally collapsed to a definite position state) as a result of the position measurement on the first particle. This is an unambiguous empirical proof that standard quantum theory that incorporates instantaneous wave-function collapse is inconsistent and should be replaced by a consistent theory. There are other quantum optical experiments that can illustrate the inconsistency of standard quantum theory. I have discussed one of these employing photons, an extension of Popper's experiment for the variables 'Energy and Time of arrival' of the particles instead of their position and momenta, elsewhere.[7]

VI

SOME COMMENTS ON BELL'S THEOREM

One may wonder how all this will fit in with the Bell's theorem and the apparent demonstration by experiments that there is indeed some quantum nonlocal influence. It is important to realize that the only conclusion from these experiments that test the Bell's inequalities is that the measured correlations violate the Bell's inequalities and show a larger correlation than what is calculated according the prescription of a local hidden variable theory. The measured correlations also agree with the prediction of standard quantum theory. Since the local hidden variable theory is supposedly built on the assumptions of Einstein locality and reality, the general belief is that these experiments prove a violation of these requirements. According to the standard view, reality is not tenable since experiments agree with the quantum mechanical prediction and quantum mechanics explicitly deny any physical reality before measurement. Einstein locality is violated because neither of the particles has any state before the first measurement, and *both* acquire definite states after just one measurement.

But, a close examination of Bell's theorem and local hidden variable theory will convince anyone that they were attempts to reproduce quantum phenomena using purely classical concepts relevant to particles. There is a complete denial of any wave aspects in the description. It is as if one could hope to reproduce quantum phenomena using a large number of unknown, hidden, influences locally acting on entities resembling tossed coins. Clearly there is no surprise that such an attempt failed miserably, since the primary quality associated with quantum phenomena was the notion of some kind of wave aspect. In fact, the Bell's theorem uses a correlation function that fails to recognize the importance of the wave aspect, and goes one step backwards from even classical optics.[8] In other words, Bell's theorem could be restated as the impossibility to reduce quantum probabilities to coin tossing probabilities even with arbitrarily large number of classical hidden variables.

SUMMARY

We have explored certain testable consequences of the standard quantum theory following well-known criticisms of the theory by Einstein and Popper. There are situations in the standard quantum theory where there are conflicting predictions for the statistical results for the same experimental configuration. This shows that the standard quantum theory that incorporates the concept of state reduction on measurement (wave-function collapse) is inconsistent. Einstein locality is valid in quantum phenomena, contrary to the conclusion that is implied by the standard quantum theory. Standard quantum theory is not the final theory of the microscopic world.

Any assertion at this stage regarding the features of a future theory would be speculative, and therefore, I will avoid it. It is not clear whether a consistent theory of microscopic physics could be constructed that has features close to our macro-experience and notions of reality, determinism, cause and effect relationships, and locality (absence of instantaneous action at a distance). It seems to me that all these are fundamental notions applicable to both the macroscopic and microscopic world in some way, and we have not yet arrived at the correct representations of the microscopic physical world. Even if we have succeeded in a representation, we certainly have not understood the interpretation. This situation is temporary and I expect that we will have a more *satisfactory* theory. One aspect that maybe absent in such a theory, as I strongly feel, is determinism in the usual sense. The indeterminism and randomness in quantum phenomena might be arising in a cause that can take random values, but unobservable even in principle. It is conceivable that all relational quantities and probabilities are correctly reproduced under such a situation, yet containing an essential and uncontrollable, but *comprehensible indeterminism*. This seems possible if we examine the unique features, especially the unobservable called the phase, of the concept of the wave-function carefully. Only relative phases are observable, and this allows the possibility of correctly determining definite relative behaviour while leaving the possibility of random individual behaviour open. Thus Einstein's God does not play dice, but the quantum world observable by us is chancy. Understanding this, in my opinion, is the key to the new interpretation of quantum mechanics.

APPENDIX

Excerpts from Einstein's letter to Popper (reproduced in 'Logic of Scientific Discovery') explaining his view that the wave-function description is incomplete.

"Should we regard the wave-function whose time dependent changes are, according to Shrodinger equation, deterministic, as a *complete* description of physical reality, and should we therefore regard the (insufficiently known) interference with the system from without as alone responsible for the fact that our predictions have a merely statistical character?

The answer at which we arrive is the wave-function should not be regarded as a complete description of the physical state of the system.

We consider a composite system, consisting of the partial systems A and B which interact for a short time only.

We assume that we know the wave-function of the composite system *before* the interaction—a collision of two free particles, for example—has taken place. Then Schrodinger equation will give us the wave-function for the composite system *after* the interaction.

Assume that now (after the interaction) an optimal measurement is carried out upon the partial system A, which maybe done in various ways, however depending on the variables which one wants to measure precisely—for example, the momentum or the position co-ordinate. Quantum mechanics will then give us the wave-function for the partial system B, and it will give us *various wave-functions that differ, according to the kind of measurement which we have chosen to carry out upon A.*

Now it is unreasonable to assume that the physical state of B may depend upon some measurement carried out upon a system A which by now is separated from B (so that it no longer interacts with B); and this means that the two different wave-functions belong to one and the same physical state of B. Since a *complete* description of a physical state must necessarily be an *unambiguous* description (apart from superficialities such as units, choice of the co-ordinates etc.) it is therefore not possible to regard the wave-function as the *complete* description of the state of the system."

NOTES

1. Einstein, A., Podolsky, B., and Rosen, N. 1935. "Can the Quantum Mechanical Description of Reality Considered Complete?" *Physical Review* 47, 777.
2. Popper, K.R. 1992. *Quantum Theory and the Schism in Physics.* London: Routledge.
3. Ibid.
4. Unnikrishnan, C.S. 2000. "Popper's Experiment, Uncertainty Principle, Signal Locality and Momentum Conservation". *Foundations of Physics Letter* 13, 197.
5. Unnikrishnan, C.S. 2002. "Is the Quantum Mechanical Description of Physical Reality Complete? Proposed Resolution of the EPR Puzzle". *Foundations of Physics Letters,* 15, 1.
6. Kim, Y.H. and Shih, Y. 1999. "Experimental Realization of Popper's Experiment: Violation of the Uncertainty Principle?" *Foundations of Physics,* 29, 1849.
7. Unnikrishnan, C.S. 2002. "An Experiment that proves the absence of Non-locality in Quantum Mechanics". *Quant-ph/*0206190.
8. Unnikrishnan, C.S. "Is the Quantum Mechanical Description of Physical reality Complete?

CHAPTER 15

Springs of Scientific Creativity

R.A. Mashelkar

I

Science is an exploration of the nature of reality, both inside and outside us. The emphasis here is on things which are quantifiable and measurable, theories which can be tested and demonstrated and facts which can be observed and verified by others.

What is the origin of the word 'creativity'? Referring to the *Oxford English Dictionary*, we find that the word 'creativity' was not coined until 1875, when it was used to refer to poetic imagination. But let me begin by saying that science itself has something intrinsically poetic. Indeed science has been considered to be a meeting place of two kinds of poetry: the poetry of action and the poetry of thought.

That science admits aesthetic criteria just like the arts, is something that has been expressed by a number of great scientists and mathematicians. The quest for beauty in science has found excellent expression in the writings of our own astrophysicist, Chandrasekhar. While examining the question as to the extent to which the quest for beauty is an aim in the pursuit of science, Chandrasekhar quotes Poincare: "The scientist does not study nature because it is useful to do so. He studies it because he takes pleasure in it; and he takes pleasure in it because it is beautiful. I mean the intimate beauty which comes from the harmonious order of its parts and which a pure intelligence can grasp... It is because simplicity and vastness are both beautiful that we seek by preference simple facts and vast facts; that we take delight, now in following the giant courses of the stars, now in scrutinizing with a microscope that prodigious smallness which is also a vastness, and, now in seeking in geological ages the traces of the past that attracts us because of its remoteness".

The place of beauty in mathematical equations has been explained by Dirac a long time ago, but we cannot limit beauty to equations alone. There is beauty in the architecture of molecules and materials as well as in the pathways of transformations. There is beauty even in the way science works and developes.

The scientist who develops a theory or designs an experiment, is no less creative than an artist who produces a painting or sculpture. Artists and scientists share certain common motivations. These include, among other things, a desire to make a positive contribution to the welfare of humanity as well as a sensitivity to aesthetics in their work, although their criteria for 'beauty' maybe quite different. Philosopher L.L. Whyte observed that "both science and art have to do with ordered complexity." Both artists and scientists seek a sense of order in the natural world. Scientists and artists are driven by a strong desire to interpret nature or the natural world. Nature has been one of the main sources of artistic inspiration for as long as humans have made art, an example being the paintings on cave walls, which were perhaps the first instance of the interweaving of art and science. These paintings of animals, weapons, and other images of the hunt—demonstrate that even primitive humans had a drive to interpret and depict their experience of the physical world.

While their activities may differ, scientists and artists share one essential component in their work. In the words of physiologist A.L.Copley: "What is common to both art and science is the creative process and the synthetic thinking in both human endeavors." Both are noted for a certain impatience or uneasiness with the conventional demands of social interaction, preferring to toil in comparative solitude in the sanctuary of the studio or the lab.

Imagination plays a vital part in both science and art, but in science it has certain constraints. As stated by Feynman, "whatever we are allowed to imagine in science has to be consistent with everything else that we know. The problem of creating something which is new, but which is consistent with everything which has been seen before, is one of extreme difficulty." At the same time, the difficulty with science is often not with the new ideas, but in escaping the old ones. A certain amount of irreverence is essential for creative pursuit in science, which is the case in the art also.

The thinking man has always had a compulsive occupation with unfettered intellectual explorations to satisfy his philosophical urges. Science is one of those urges. In social science usage, the term 'Science' denotes the systematic, objective study of empirical phenomena and the resultant bodies of knowledge. According to this definition, many disciplines related to social sciences should also come under Science. Science as a human activity is itself a subject of social science investigation. One must admit, therefore, that as an intellectual effort, science cannot be regarded as something apart. It is an important part of our culture. Science permeates our thinking today and it would be incorrect to completely separate it from what we normally refer to as humanities and social sciences. Natural science does not simply describe or explain Nature. It is a part of an interplay between Nature and man. As Heisenberg stated: "Science describes Nature as exposed to our method of questioning."

Let us first turn to understanding the springs of scientific creativity in this 'Man of the Century' as the *Time* magazine put it, namely, Albert Einstein. Three types of approaches have been used to understand what it is that takes to make a genius like Albert Einstein. In the first, an assumption is made that genius is to be understood in terms of neural mechanisms within the brain or through other, more general biological processes. This view links intelligence, creativity, and IQ scores to genetic factors. The second is the attempt to objectify the concept of creativity by devising inventories and instruments closely related to IQ score tests for predicting creativity. Such efforts have been singular failures. A third approach focuses on the accounts of the conscious thought processes that led to the creative act. The most famous of these studies in which Einstein himself participated were Jacques Hadamard's *The Psychology of Invention in the Mathematical Field* and Max Wertheimer's *Productive Thinking.*

It was interesting to note that long before he wrote scientific papers, Einstein was Einstein—already at the age of three, playing silently, resisting verbal language and refusing thereby to accept an externally imposed authority in names and rules. Once Einstein himself said: "For me it is not dubious that our thinking goes on for the most part without use of signs (words) and beyond that to a considerable degree unconsciously. For how, otherwise should it happen that sometimes we 'wonder' quite spontaneously about some experience?" Our inner voice or inner pictures are probably more like *summaries* of thinking. By that time, the process, which occurs at some deep level, is completed. It is clear that even if we elucidated every chemical reaction on the brain and traced every neuron, and even if by artificial stimulation of individual neurons we were able to induce specific thoughts, thinking would remain an enigma.

It has been generally agreed that Einstein's genius can be characterized by three qualities: curiosity, intuition, and concentration. He had a childlike curiosity. It was almost as if he were wearing special glasses to make all that was irrelevant invisible. Second, Einstein had an unerring intuition for what the right question should be. Sometimes he was so sure of himself that in the face of seemingly contrary evidence, he had even rejected the results of experimental tests at variance with his own conclusions. Third, Einstein could concentrate on a problem with uncommon zeal. Most people might give up after days or months or even years at a time. Not Einstein. After 1920, his commitment to developing a unified field theory, a single theory of explaining all physical interactions, was unshakable. His concentration was such that even near death in 1955, his ever-present pad and pen were nearby so that he could continue working on his field equations.

Lct me now turn to one of the greatest experimental scientists that the world has known and that is Michael Faraday. He was gifted with extraordinary imagination and experimental creativity. He made monumental contributions to chemistry, physics and materials science and engineering. Most interestingly, Faraday was not spoiled by formal education; he was self-taught. He left school at the age of thirteen and started his career as an errand boy, then as a bookbinder, and rose to become one of the greatest scientific giants.

We always speak of sporadic bouts of inspiration and creativity among both scientists and artists. But Faraday proved to be an exception. Faraday's productivity was out of this world! In a single year he did so much more than what great scientists do in a lifetime. Just look at the year 1833. From his laboratory notebooks, one sees that he discovered fused-salt electrolysis in February 1833 and identified superionic conductivity in silver and other halides the same month. In early November, he did some work on catalytic activity of platinum and, on November 22, he worked on the separation of gases such as ethylene and carbon dioxide. On November 25, Faraday carried out investigations on the wettability of solids such as quartz. In mid-December, he worked on the equivalence of electricity from various sources and, later that month, carried out studies that led to the laws of electrolysis. On December 24, he did experiments on chemical changes brought about by the passage of electricity through moltern tin chloride. On December 26, he did an important experiment on the decomposition of lead halides and other salts. There was no entry for the December 25, obviously, because it was Christmas Day!

Let us turn to our own Srinivasa Rāmānujan. He was a mathematician so great that his name transcends jealousies, the one superlatively great mathematician whom India has produced in the last thousand years. His leaps of intuition confound mathematicians even today, several decades after his death. His papers are still plumbed for their secrets. For five years, walled off from India by the war, Rāmānujan would remain in strange, cold, distant England, fashioning, through twenty-one major papers, an enduring mathematical legacy. There is a very touching story about Rāmānujan's stay in England.

Rāmānujan's notebooks have acquired a legendary status now. The first of the published *Notebooks* was prepared when he left Pachaiyappa's College in 1907. Only over the course of years, and subsequent editions, did those early, haphazard scribblings evolve into the published *Notebooks* that today sustain a varitable cottage industry of mathematicians devoted to their study.

Both Faraday and Rāmānujan did not have a formal education in its entirety which we consider so crucial for becoming a world class scientist today. In 1807, a hundred years before Ramanujan was to fail his F.A. exam for the last time and experience India's educational system in all its oppressive rigidity, William Thackeray had written:

> It is very proper that in England, a good share of the produce of the earth should be appropriated to support certain families in affluence, to produce senators, sages and heroes for the service and defense of the state; but in India that haughty spirit, independence and deep thought which the possession of great wealth sometimes gives ought to be suppressed. They are directly averse to our power and interest. We do not want generals, statesmen and legislators; we want industrious husbandmen.

If Thackeray's sentiments mirrored British educational policy in India, no better evidence for it could be found than Rāmānujan, for whom college might have seemed aimed at suppressing 'haughty spirit, independence, and deep thought'. Indeed, Indian higher education's failure to nurture one of such undoubted, but idiosyncratic, gifts could serve as textbook example of how bureaucratic systems, policies, and rules really do matter. People, as individuals, appreciated and respected Rāmānujan; but the system failed to find a place for him. It was designed, after all, to churn out bright, well-rounded young men who could help their British masters run the country, not the 'restless and ambitious spirits' Thackeray warned against.

Sadly, during 1904 to 1909, Rāmānujan floundered—mostly out of school, without a degree, without a job, without contact with other mathematicians. Paradoxically, the hardship and intellectual isolation spurred his independent thinking and honed his talents. His academic failure forced him to develop unconventionally, free of the social straitjacket that might have constrained his progress to well-worn paths. There was something divine about Rāmānujan's work. Rāmānujan spoke with such enthusiasm about the philosophical implications of his work that sometimes one felt he would have been better pleased to have succeeded in establishing his philosophical theories than in supplying rigorous proofs of his mathematical conjectures. Rāmānujan would build a theory of reality around Zero and Infinity, though his friends never quite figured out what he was getting at. Zero, it seemed, represented Absolute Reality. Infinity, was the myriad manifestations of that Reality. The mathematical product of infinity into zero was not one number, but all numbers, each of which corresponded to individual acts of creation. In the West, there was an old debate as to whether mathematical reality was made by mathematicians or, existing independently, was merely discovered by them. To Rāmānujan, each new theorem was one more piece of the Infinite unfathomed. Rāmānujan told a friend, "An equation for me has no meaning unless it expresses a thought of God."

Complexity and heterogeneity are also major barriers to recognising problems. The genius of Newton was in recognizing that a ball thrown in the air and a planet circling the sun are 'the same' with respect to gravity. He made the further crucial abstraction of treating his objects as point masses, reducing the complexity to a minimum.

The ability to see what everyone else sees but thinks of what no one else thinks is the hallmark of a great scientist. Everyone saw that the sea was blue, but only Sir C.V. Raman thought of what no one else thought. While describing his own experiments on board the ship, Raman writes:

> Observations made in this way in the deeper waters of the Mediterranean and Red Sea showed that the colour, so far from being impoverished by suppression of sky-reflection, was wonderfully improved thereby... It was abundantly clear from the observations that the blue colour of the deep sea is a distinct phenomenon in itself, and not merely an effect due to reflected skylight. When the surface-reflections are suppressed the hue of the water is of such fullness and saturation that the bluest sky in comparison with it seems a dull grey... The question is: What is it that diffracts the light and makes its passage visible? An interesting possibility that should be considered is that the diffracting particles, may at least in part, be the molecules of the water themselves.

This ability to see what no one else could see brought Sir C.V. Raman the distinction of becoming the only Indian scientist to win a Nobel Prize in the twentieth century for the work done in India.

II

INDIAN CHALLENGE

Let me now turn the focus on India and Indian science. Since the Indus Valley Civilization of about 5,000 years ago, scientific thought and innovative ideas have been part of the Indian culture, and the basis of its civilization, throughout its history. Our great achievements include remarkable town planning, the use of standardized burnt bricks for dwelling houses, interlinked drainage system, wheel-turned ceramics, solid-wheeled carts and copper-bronze craftsmanship that one finds in the excavations; also the dockyard to Lothal, regarded as the largest maritime structure ever built by a bronze-age community. The discovery of zero and the decimal-place value system by Indians possibly dates back to the Vedic period (c. 1500 B.C.)—the later pioneering work in algebra and trigonometry, and some in geometry, the atomic nature of matter; the work in medicine, which not only aimed at the cure of diseases but even more at the preservation of health; the advances in surgery including laparotomy, lithotomy and plastic surgery; the iron pillar at Delhi, which testifies to the achievements in metallurgy some 1,500 years ago. One truly feels inspired.

Science based on observation and empirical methods is to be found in the practice of many ancient civilizations including Indian—in fact, China and India could not have become great civilizations without a fair amount of science and technology—and that science is as much a part of Indian heritage as the greatly extolled mystical tradition.

It is clear that Indian civilization over a period was characterized by scientific thought, capabilities and techniques, at levels certainly contemporary with anywhere else in the work, and in many cases more advanced. However, when the Scientific and Industrial Revolutions took place in the West a few hundred years ago, there was a period of stagnation in India because of developments in society leading to a highly feudalistic structure and internecine strife. Lack of development over this period was the result of a hierarchical approach, irrational subjective thinking, and build up of superstitions and superficial ritualism. The earlier great traditions were allowed to decay. It was in this state of its society that India came under colonial domination. During the colonial British period, development in science and technology did take place, but basically to cater to the requirements of the then existing government.

The real Indian awakening in modern science took place through the efforts of a large number of outstanding Indians, who worked over the three quarters of the century prior to Indian Independence. They include names such as Sir C.V. Raman, J.C. Bose, S.N. Bose, P. Mahalanobis and so on—a spectacular array of thinkers. These were the products of the ferment in Indian society which motivated the freedom struggle. They were greatly influenced by interaction with western liberal thought, and through information on the great new developments in science that were taking place in Europe, following the scientific and industrial revolutions.

A question that is often raised is if the Indians had the questioning attitude and made such major contributions to science and technology, especially upto about 1200 A.D., then why did they fail to build on these further? Various socio-political and historical circumstances would have been responsible for India's failure to build on this base. Opinions differ and they could be debated, but the factors that are often discussed include the Indian culture perceiving the world as "*Māyā*" or illusion and no interest in worldly pursuits, rigid caste system that led to the separation of the head and the heart (with Brahmins exclusively doing the theoretical studies and practical art and crafts left to other castes), suppression of the scientific spirit, conflict between science and religion, tendency to accommodate conflicting opposites, handicap of oral traditions, etc.

Even in the area of technology, when we had a lead, we lost it. An interesting example is provided by the relative expertise of the British and the Indians in rocket technology round 1800 A.D. The Mysore rockets of this period (1799) were much more advanced than what the British had seen or known. The British at Seringapatanam had suffered more from the rockets than from the shells or any other weapons used by Tipu's forces. A vigorous programme on rockets was immediately started in Britain. Several rocket cases were collected and returned to Britain for analysis; experiments were made with a number of black powder formulas, and specifications were worked out for their composition; Newton's laws were applied to understand rocket behavior; appropriate designs were made; standardized construction details were worked out; improved production techniques introduced; suitable products developed, tested and systematically evaluated; tactics for their use were also studied. The development was chiefly the work of William Congreve.

With the Industrial Revolution, engineering science had emerged as a pursuit in Britain and then in Europe. This was something about which the Indians of the eighteenth century had no idea or knowledge. Indeed, India remained untouched by the vast transformation that Britain and the rest of the Europe were experiencing; production here still remained a craft whereas, in Britain, it was rapidly becoming an industry backed by scientific research and development. Therefore, though there were products of Indian technology in the second half of the eighteenth century that were still superior to those available anywhere else in the world, e.g. high quality iron and steel, India soon got left behind.

III

NEW OPPORTUNITIES

What is the opportunity for Indian science in the emerging century? I feel it lies in our recognizing three different domains of knowledge and synergising and unifying them. Let me explain: As scientists, we focus rather narrowly only on science and technology-based knowledge, which is established through the rigorous methodology of science. But there are two other domains of knowledge, which we have kept away from. One is the so called 'parallel', indigenous', 'traditional' or 'civilizational' knowledge system. These systems belong to societies in the developing world, that have nurtured and refined systems of knowledge of their own, relating to such diverse domains as geology, ecology, agriculture, and health etc., our Ayurvedic medicinal systems being one such domain. They were, as yet, neglected by modern science but not any more so. New bridges between the modern and the traditional are being built. CSIR's pioneering partnership with Arya Vaidyashala of Kottakal is an example of the benefits of blending the modern science and the traditional knowledge. But this is only a small step, we have miles to go.

Indigenous knowledge systems must be sustained through active support to the societies that are keepers of this knowledge, be they villagers or tribes, their ways of life, their languages, their social organization and the environment in which they live. We need innovative ways of preventing the erosion of such knowledge, which usually vanishes with people. Equally importantly, we need an in-depth analysis of the parallelism of insights between the indigenous knowledge systems, on the one hand, and certain areas of modern science concerned with fundamental aspects, on the other. Our university education and research needs to shift the search light on this important issue, which it has neglected so far.

The third knowledge system is the knowledge systems of the spiritual world. Here again, the tools of modern science are giving us deep insights. For example, quantum physics is leading to inquiry into consciousness, computational advances are leading to inquiry into human intelligence, advances in neuro-sciences are leading to inquiry into the working of a human mind.

The new millennium Universal Knowledge System will have to be a beautiful confluence of these three knowledge systems. I feel confident that India will lead in interpreting, creating, synergising and enhancing these knowledge systems and that the foundation of the new millennium Indian knowledge society will be based on this Universal Knowledge System.

CHAPTER 16

Germination and Legitimation of Science

D.P. Chattopadhyaya

I

BIRTH OF SCIENCE

One can easily think of another title for this presentation: **LIRTH AND ACCEPTABILITY OF SCIENCE.** Science is not born either in library or in laboratory. Science is not peculiar either to head or to heart. Mother of science is the experience of limitless *possibilities*, not limited necessities. In making science possible both heart and head, library and laboratory, spontaneity and creativity contribute and are at work. This is not to deny the traditional wisdom hidden in the maxim: necessity is the mother of invention. The limit of the implication of the maxim is clear when one points out that though sub-human animals have their numerous necessities but have no science in the received sense. Science as an institution is peculiar to humanity.[1]

Unless the humanistic *essence* of science is properly understood, one is likely to be misled by its non-essential characteristics like mathematical language, quantitative approach, proof, emphasis on causality, laboratory experiments, theory and test and similar other things. Each one of the so-called defining characteristics of science, if not suitably qualified and contextually situated, turns out to be misleading.

The origin of mathematics, whether of arithmetic or geometry, is difficult to trace reliably. For the beginnings of the subject are much older than the art of writing. But it can be safely assumed that even the pre-historic man was interested in, and conscious of, spatial designs and relationships which were rooted in his aesthetic feeling and the enjoyment of beauty of *form*. Every philosopher and mathematician agrees that form is the heart of mathematics. But few realize that form is first felt *within* and then sought to be depicted outside in symbols like number, line, triangle and circle.

It is imperative to recall that geometry, like counting, had its origin in primitive ritualistic practices. For example, *sulvasūtras,* or rules of the cord, had been the earliest geometrical results found in India. Herodotus tells us that the ancient Egyptian rulers used to divide the land of the country among its inhabitants. If the river Nile used to carry away any portion of man's land, the King used to send surveyors to examine and determine by measurement the exact extent of the loss. From this practice, Herodotus concludes, geometry appeared in Egypt and wherefrom it passed into Greece. It is an accepted view that the civilizations of China and India are of far greater antiquity than those of Greece and Rome. While the former go back to the Potamic Age, the latter were of the Thalassic

Age. The oldest mathematical documents from China, *Chou Pei Suan Ching* (c. 1200 B.C.) seem to refer to the use of the gnomon in studying the circular paths of the heavenly bodies and the book is concerned with astronomical calculations.

II

FEELING OF WONDER AND THE QUESTIONING SPIRIT

The point to be mainly noted here is this: science is born of the feeling of wonder. The German philosopher-scientist, Kant, speaks of two things, astronomical laws and the moral laws, which stir his feeling most. The search for astronomical laws, governing the starry heavens above our head, and the moral laws within us, pertaining to our free will is rooted in a strange feeling, seeking the orderliness obtained in nature and culture.

It is not surprising that the forces which are at work immediately within and around human existence naturally attract our first attention. Therefore, among the most primitive and common sciences found in all civilizations are mathematics, medicine and morality or spirituality. Both causes and cures of human diseases are found in their environment. It is well known that climatic conditions have much to do with the kinds of physiological diseases and psychological disorders which we undergo. All forms of life—vital, plant, animal and human—are environed by similar or comparable conditions and that accounts for the similarity of disease patterns, for example, of different tropical countries and temperate countries. This is evident from the indigenous systems of medical knowledge, works of authors like Caraka, Śuśrūta, Galen and Isocrates. The Hindu medical system is traced to the *Atharvaveda* and the two main works on the subject, *Caraka-Saṁhitā* and *Śuśrūta-Saṁhitā* are based on extensive experience and intensive reflection.[2] The ancient Hindus speak of 1,120 types of diseases. The Indian *Materia Medica* was extensive and consisted mainly of vegetable drugs extracted from indigenous plants. Caraka knew of 500 medicinal plants and *Śuśrūta* of 760. Both of them, it seems, followed a long tradition and had intimate familiarity both with the subject of their study and the antiquity of the concerned branch of knowledge. In the ancient medical systems, both in East and West, there was a heavy dose of philosophy. Caraka, for example, was deeply influenced by the Sāṁkhya-Yoga system of philosophy.

The same maybe said of both Hippocrates and Galen. In the Graeco-Roman world their knowledge proved extremely influential and both of them were following and extending a very old tradition. Galen was a Hippocratic in sciences like anatomy and physiology, and Aristotelian in his philosophical inclination. Galen, primarily a medical philosopher, interpreted, among other things, works of Plato, Aristotle and Epicurus. Before the mechanical medical philosophy of Harvey came into vogue in the seventeenth century, the twin influences of Hippocrates and Galen, reflective of the Mediterranean temper and teleology, proved very long-lasting. Similar findings are there in the history of mathematical astronomy in India (by Pingree, Thibaut and Subbarayappa), Egyptian astronomy (by Neugebauer and Parker), Mathematics and Astronomy in Mesopotamia (by B. L. van der Waerden and A. Sachs) and Maya Mexican Numeration, Computation and Calendrical

Astronomy (by Lounsbury, Zimmermann, Thompson and others). Needham's scholarly and comparative work on astronomy in China, India and West Asia also needs to be recalled in this connection.[3]

Euro-centric writers like David Pingree think that Indian astronomical works had always been borrowed from others, viz., (a) Mesopotamia via Iran (fifth century B.C.); (b) from Mesopotamia via Greece (second century A.D.); (c) from Greece directly (fourth century A.D.); (d) from Iran (tenth to eighteenth centuries A.D.) and (e) the Copernican model from England (nineteenth century). But this view has been recently contested and rejected by some European and Indian writers like R. Billard, Subhash Kak and Subbarayappa who show that Indian astronomical tradition had much originality both in its impetus and execution.

III

ON TWO ERRORS: INDUCTIVISM VS. DEDUCTIVISM AND EXPERIENCE VS. EXPERIMENT

Scientific enquiry has often been a victim of two serious errors. The first is the unexamined belief that it is from the experience of the particulars, through a sort of inductive method, the scientist infers general truths of laws.[4] The second is the supposed 'dichotomy between experiment and experience'.[5]

Reflective consciousness reveals that man does not, rather cannot, experience any particular thing as such. To his experience everything appears as a particularization or exemplification of some or other general truth. Human experience because of its native spontaneity always views everything *as* instances of a general truth of law. This transcendental orientation of the human mind is natural, not metaphysical (in the pejorative sense).

It is interesting to recall, in this connection, that in the Indian tradition of thought there is no fundamental division between induction and deduction. The basic structure of inference, *anuman,* has in it both universal (*vyāpti*) and particular (*udāharaṇ)* components. These two components cannot be sharply demarcated. Even the distinction that is drawn between them in the analytic mode of human thought is embedded in a synthetic whole. Synthesizing tendency of the human mind is rooted in the spontaneity, spontaneous creativity.

The pre-reflective scientist often thinks that experimental activities are autonomous in character. The untenability of this presupposition can be brought out in very many ways. Experiment, to start with, is not undertaken for its own sake. Every experiment is an experiment-*for*, experiment for establishing or disestablishing a hypothesis, some or other proclaimed truth. Secondly, experience and experiment differ not in kind but only in degree. In terms of experiments the scientist tries to show the precision and exactitude of his view. Experiment is nothing but experience under controlled conditions. Here arises the third point to be noted in the context of experience-experiment relationship. All the efforts—mechanical, mental and measuremental—purported to draw a sharp line of demarcation between experience and experiment are doomed to fail. This is because the very process of controlling has an irremovable influence on the findings of the controller, in this case experimental scientist. The observer and the observed are entangled. The user of an instrument, the use of it and the object on which it is used are somehow inseparably related. This issue of entanglement, a fall-out of Quantum Mechanics as cosmology, is yet to be controverted and rejected.[6]

The more important point to remember here is the true nature of experience itself. The empiricist view of experience, which highlights external stimulus or excitement for causing experience in us, misses the basic issue. It fails to see the internal incitement of human consciousness which makes human senses prepared to receive and interpret which comes from outside. In the context of understanding experience the main word to be reckoned with is incitement and *in*look, not *ex*citement and outlook. The modern biologists ask us to believe that millions of years yearnings for, and exposure to, light account for the development of visual organ in animals and humans. Even now sub-human animals' visual ability to experience the wide spectrum of colours, compared to the human ability, is very limited. The fact that human organs, both of information and action, are more gifted and enabling than those of other animals is to be explained by the *drive* of consciousness towards the outer world rather than by causal impositions of the environment. Even if it is recognized, and I think it should be, that human life and its development are due mainly to two factors, genetic and environmental, we are obliged to accept the primacy of the internal endowment. In other words, genetic endowment is the latent disposition of the will power inherent in human consciousness.

Unfortunately, many of the modern philosophers of science, forgetful of the mind's initiative in extending Nature, endow the latter with the causal power to impress its structure on the human mind. Some philosophers of science like Kant, who under the Newtonian influence, are otherwise causalist and mechanical in their surface approach, duly recognize the truth that scientific adventure is triggered off by the mind's will to map Nature, together with its complex structures and sub-structures. On its own Nature has nothing to tell us about itself. The truths about Nature's structures, available in the forms of theories and laws, are gradually disclosed to us only in response to our questionings and queries. Man asks and Nature responds. It is not the other way round as the mechanical causalist asks us to believe in the name of science. Viewed in this way, Nature and Culture are not antithetical. Reviewed in this way, Nature is both a part of natural science and of human culture.

IV

SCIENCE AS WILL-TO-DISCOVER THE SECRETS OF LIFE AND NATURE

Science, rightly understood, is more in the nature of invitation from the truth lying ahead than that of causal invasion from behind. The signal of the secret invitation emanating from truth is addressed to, and understood best by, the gifted scientist. No rules of thumb are there to tell us how the structure of truth in the forms of law and theory is grasped by the interested scientists and missed by the uninitiated laity.[7]

Though the birth of science lies hidden in the womb of hypothesis, imaginations and intuitions, its official establishment, recognition or acceptance, however provisional they maybe, is subject to certain rules or norms. At the germinal point science may appear mysterious but at the terminal point it seems to be visible, public and convincing. Because of this variance and alteration between the birth, growth and establishment of the developing science, the professional philosophers of science, often under the influence of Reichenbach draw an important distinction between "the context of discovery" and "the context of justification." While from the end of discovery science appears to be mysterious, it is claimed to be demystified at the end of justification.

The so-called context of discovery, as said above, consists of hypothesis, speculative exploration, imagination and intuitive apprehension. Without hypothesis experiments and observations make no sense. Both experiment and observation are purpose-oriented, the purpose being scientific truth-discovery. Hypothesis is prompted by the researchers of well-informed mental background. Good hypothesis does not fall from the heaven's blue. It is required to be doubly disciplined, firstly by the accepted and respectable scientific truths and secondly, it must have the *possibilities* built in it for being fair to facts for which it is being invoked.[8]

The second component of discovery, i.e., imagination, has been praised by so many working scientists. For example, Tyndall, referring to Faraday, writes that "imagination becomes the chief architect of physical theory" only when it accurately works on experiment and observation. Referring to Newton he observes, "Newton's passage from falling of an apple to a falling moon was an act of the prepared imagination."[9] It is true that there is no guarantee that imagination will surely and certainly take the scientist to the goal of truth. Imagination may fail but even the failed imaginations are instructive. Because they narrow down the range of possibilities and thus help the scientist to reach his goal of truth. Somewhat in a similar vein Max Planck writes: "Again and again the imaginary plan on which one attempts to build up order breaks down and then we must try another. This imaginative vision and faith in the ultimate success are indispensable. The pure rationalist has no place here." The visualization of thought, pictorial representation of truth and the forms of mental images have helped many scientists to get to their solicited truth. It is said of Maxwell that he developed the habit of forming mental picture of every problem and of its *possible* solution. Many other scientists have emphasized how imagination, rather than logic, succeeds in penetrating the secrets of Nature. The general laws which relate and explain the facts and processes of Nature found in physics and mathematics are due to imagination and intuition. Supporting this view, Einstein writes: "There is no logical way to the discovery of the elemental laws of Nature. There is only the way of intuition, which is helped by a feeling for the order lying behind the appearance."[10]

It is true that the word "intuition" is not free from ambiguity. Its synonyms are numerous, viz., second sight, insight, inspiration, sub-conscious perception and *a priori* knowledge. The lives and works of many great scientists show how important scientific ideas dawned on them suddenly when they were not at all prepared for the same. For example, Poincare writes : "One day, as I was walking on the cliff the idea came to me... with...characteristics of conciseness, suddenness and immediate certainty, that arithmetical transformation of indefinite ternary quadratic forms are identical with those of non-Euclidian geometry."[11] A closely comparable problematic experience of the mathematician Gauss is related by Hadamard. Gauss had been trying, unsuccessfully, for years but, then, he tells us, "Finally two days ago I succeeded...like a sudden flash of lightning, the riddle happened to be solved. I cannot myself say what was the conducting thread which connected what I previously knew with what made my success possible."

While it is true that the logical map of intuition cannot be drawn, some clarificatory comments on the subject seem to be in order. Neither a common man nor a scientist has in his *present* focus of attention all that he has in different layers of his mind. Sub-conscious, conscious and super-conscious are among the recognized levels of consciousness. In between the said levels there are several other levels. Within every level there are many sub-levels. What is more, the concerned person can never be clearly aware of the complex and changing connections between the contents available, at least in principle, within the said levels and sub-levels of consciousness. Para-psychological and Yogic experiences bring to our notice many phenomena which are not readily amenable to the known laws of psychology and known rules of logic. The cases of many prodigal children are available confirming that extraordinary gifts, mathematical, scientific, musical and poetic, at an unbelievably young age have been actually attained and displayed. From the immortality of soul, transmitted heredity to unrecorded environmental influences have often been cited as possible explanations of this range of extraordinary phenomena.

Whatever maybe the case, it is undeniable that human consciousness has in it so many hidden possibilities which cannot be readily summoned for either remembrance or use. At the same time, it seems from the cases cited above that the scientists who are historically credited with great discoveries had been found to be in deep engagement over a long time with the concerned subjects in their problematic form. Negatively speaking, it maybe pointed out that, ordinarily speaking, great mathematicians or physicists are not found to have authored masterpieces in literature or poetry or in the areas with which they did not have deep acquaintance or engagement.

V

FROM CONTEXT OF DISCOVERY TO CONTEXT OF JUSTIFICATION

While the context of discovery is visited by so many indefinite but instructive imponderables, the context of justification is beset with deeply disturbing uncertainties. There was a time when both scientists and philosophers of science were inclined to believe that while the context of discovery is very nebulous, the context of justification is very concrete. But a closer look into such concepts as justification, confirmation, verification, falsification and their cognates have brought out the weakness, if not paradox, in most of these concepts. At one stage it was thought that it is only induction which needs justification, later on it has been realized that even deduction needs justification. The question arises: What about the truth-claim of the justificatory principles themselves? Do they need higher-order justificatory principles? Or, must we think that these principles are themselves self-justified? This notion of self-justification, it is clear, hinges on the acceptability of intuition as the indubitably valid source of knowledge.

In the heydays of logical positivism most scientists and philosophers of science used to talk in terms of the 'principle of verification'. The idea was that this is the bedrock principle of scientific justification. Subsequently, it was pointed out that the universal laws of science, because of the 'universality' or open-endedness of their scope, can never be conclusively verified. Realizing the validity of the criticism, some philosophers of science came forward and offered an alternative principle which was known as 'the principle of falsification' or disconfirmation. Closer scrutiny revealed that if the verifiability principle cannot verify the 'universal statements' of laws and theories, the falsifiability principle fails to test the truth-claim of 'existential statements'. Analytic epistemologists soon found out that verifiers, falsifiers, basic statements and ilk had to be taken as true without question in order to make sense of the principles of verification and falsification. This was hardly scientific or rational.

This created an unforeseen impasse in the context of justification. In scientific systems or theoretical structures, as we all know, we had two main types of statements, universal and existential. If the universal statements are unverifiable and the existential ones are unfalsifiable, then what happens to the systems or structures of science. The response was two-fold. Some writers on the subject pleaded for a less ambitious criterion for determining the truth-claim of scientific statements and they found it in 'testability'. They felt that testability is free from the vitiating infirmities of verifiability and falsifiability. But even this modest or much watered-down criterion of truth also attracted criticism soon. The final upshot appeared to be that scientific statements are 'not' specially privileged and that, like other factual statements, they can never be entirely free from the possibility of error. In other words, the consensus emerged around the 'fallibilistic' character of all types of sciences factual and even formal. The time-honoured form/fact, analytic/synthetic distinct started crumbling. The strong defenders of the special respectability thesis of scientific knowledge felt disappointed. The very aristocracy of the cognitive claim of science was at stake.

The second response has been further moderate and low-keyed. It says the criterion for determining the scientific truth-claim should be something like precisifiability or improvability, not verifiability or falsifiability. This new formulation of the scientific truth-claim emphasizes that in every factual discourse our aim should be only to precisify our statements in the light of both factual findings and logical scrutiny. Collaterally, it has been pointed out that the strong provability requirement, be it inductive, deductive or even axiomatic, is difficult, if not impossible, to satisfy.

The implication of all these radical views was unmistakable. Even the mathematical form of scientific knowledge was at peril. The mathematical science which in nineteenth century was praised as the perfect science, as infallible and true in any possible world, has not only lost during the twentieth century its claim to truth, but was also soiled by the conflict between the foundational schools. Different schools of foundationalism, formalism, logicism and intuitionism came forward to repair the damaged reputation of mathematics. But, it seems, every attempt of every school, turned out to be unsuccessful.

Hilbert in his paper, "The Foundation of Mathematics" (1927), claims that his version of proof theory is free from all blemishes attached to the claims of other foundationalist schools. But in quick succession appeared some very influential views contesting this claim of Hilbert. For example, Eric T. Bell writes, "experience has taught most mathematicians what looks solid and satisfactory to one mathematical generation stands a fair chance of dissolving into cobwebs under the steadier scrutiny of the next." The more severe blow was yet to come from Goedel's paper (1931), "On Formally Undecidable Propositions *of Principia Mathematica and Related Systems"*. Both the consistency and completeness claims of mathematical systems came under the heavy gunfire of Goedel. This created an unprecedented problem for the justificationists of science, in general and all mathematical foundationalists, in particular. Dismayed by this disastrous development Hermann Weyl, famous physicist-mathematician, observed that God exists because mathematics is consistent and the devil exists because we cannot prove that consistency. Bertrand Russell himself confessed in 1950s that his attempt to provide foundations for mathematics have failed. Similar negative view was expressed earlier by his collaborator, Whitehead. It will not be out of place to quote an interesting passage from Morris Kline's book, *Mathematics: The Loss of Certainty*[12].

> The developments in the century bearing on the foundations of mathematics are best summarized in a story. On the banks of the Rhine, a beautiful castle had been standing for centuries. In the cellar of the castle, an intricate network of webbing had been constructed by industrious spiders who lived there. One day a strong wind sprang up and destroyed the web. Frantically the spiders worked to repair the damage. They thought it was their webbing that was holding up the castle.

My approach may appear unduly pessimist to many, particularly those who are uncritically committed to the infallibility of science. Personally speaking, I have deep respect for science as a mode of knowledge and I claim to be a realist and fair to the recorded facts of history, scientific biographies and autobiographies. I am fallibilist-realist in science.[13]

Idealism and realism, skepticism and fallibilism and their cognates give us a split and misleading picture of science. In order to get to a sane and humane view of science we must look backward, inward and forward. The views of past masters, or *ācāryas*, as available from history or *paramparā*, must be first taken into account. And we should be honestly convinced that ours is not the first or only generation of wise men informed of the deep truths about life and the nature of reality.

Our insight and inlook are enough to convince us that within the short span of our life we are obliged to unlearn, learn and relearn many things. Simultaneously we keep on yearning for the hitherto unknown answers to our many questions.

The questionability and corrigibility of the current views of science and philosophy are hinted at and anticipated by such well-known principles like one and the same thing maybe "experientially real but transcendentally ideal", "*jagat-prapañca,* though real, is sublatable or supersedable", "*saṁsār* is *nirvaṇ* and *nirvaṇ* is *saṁsār* ", "shadows do have their reality", and "dream objects are real in a way". Great names from science and philosophy may be easily cited in support of the referred to views.

In our search for scientific truths we must not allow ourselves to be unduly influenced by the extensive and pre-reflective use of key words like "skepticism" and "*jijñāsā*". Following the Indian tradition, one can well say, "without *jijñāsā* we cannot hope to have *jñān*" or "without *Brahmajijñāsā* one cannot realize *Brahman*". The Greek root of the English word "skepticism", ordinarily used in a derogatory sense, is "*skepsis*" which itself sounds rather positive in character, meaning *search* or *jijñāsā*.

It is in this context that we are strongly advised to bear in mind the importance of language in the contexts both of discovery and justification.

NOTES

1. For my earlier views on the subject the reader may see, Chattopadhyaya, D.P. 1967. *Individuals and Societies*. Calcutta: Allied Publishers. (2nd edition, 1975. Calcutta: Scientific Book Agency); Chattopadhyaya, D. P. 1976. *Individuals and Worlds: Essays in Anthropological Rationalism*. Delhi: Oxford University Press.
2. Pande, G. C. (ed.). 1999. *The Dawn of Indian Civilization, upto 600 BC*. Delhi: Centre for Studies in Civilizations & Munshiram Manoharlal. Ch. 27 by P.V. Sharma.
3. Gillispie, Charles Coulston, (ed.). 1981. *Dictionary of Scientific Biography*, vol. 15. New York: Charles Scribner's Sons.
4. Popper, Karl R. 1959. *The Logic of Scientific Discovery*. London: Hutchinson; see also, Carnap, Rudolf. 1966. *Philosophical Foundations of Physics*. New York: Basic Books.
5. Chattopadhyaya, D.P. 1966. *Interdisciplinary Studies in Science, Technology, Philosophy and Culture*. Project of History of Indian Science, Philosophy and Culture & Delhi: Munshiram Manoharlal. See, in particular, "Human Experience and Scientific Experiment". pp. 31–77.
6. Mehra Jagdish and Rechenberg, Helmut. 2001. *The Historical Development of Quantum Theory*, vol. 6. New York: Springer.
7. Chattopadhyaya, D.P. 1996. "Science, Technology and Their Human Roots" in (5) above.
8. Suppe, Frederick. 1977. *The Structure of Scientific Theories*, 2nd edition. Illinois: University of Illinois.
9. Tyndall, J. 1868. *Faraday as a Discoverer*. London: Longmans, Green and Company.
10. Einstein, Albert. 1933. *Where is Science Going?* Max Planck (trans.). London: James Murphy, George Allen and Unwin. Preface.
11. Poincare, H. 1914. *Science and Method*. London: Thomas Nelson and Sons.
12. Kline, Morris. 1980. *Mathematics: The Loss of Certainty*. Oxford: Oxford University Press.
13. Chattopadhyaya, D.P. 1991. *Induction, Probability and Skepticism*. New York: State University of New York (SUNY) Press; Indian Reprint, 1992. Delhi: Sri Guru Publishers (India Book Centre). See also, Chattopadhyaya, D.P. 1990. *Historiography of Science*. Athens, USA: Ohio University Press; Indian Reprint, 1991. Delhi: Motilal Banarasidass.

CHAPTER 17

Till Science Transcends the Scientist: Role of Human Factor in Science

Rajesh Kochhar

Most people would baulk at a phrase like 'literature (or music) and culture' on the ground that the first term is already contained in the second. But they would uncritically accept a construction like 'science and culture'. The reason probably is this. Like a poet or a painter, a scientist is also culturally anchored; but there is a difference. When scientists discover fundamental laws, uncover patterns in nature or establish linkages among seemingly disparate phenomena, they do so on behalf of the whole humanity. Their work in fact transcends even humanity in the sense that laws of nature as discovered on the earth will be recognized as such by scientists working elsewhere in the universe even though one cannot even imagine what the cultural setting of these extraterrestrial scientists would be.

In other disciplines, creative work remains the property of its creator. Science, however, aims to liberate itself from the scientist. For a scientific theory, hypothesis or model to become established, be accepted as received wisdom and treated as textbook material, its author's name must cease to be proprietory and become merely descriptive instead. Till such time as science transcends the scientist, human factors like values, judgements, foibles, idiosyncracies, prejudices and biases play a role, but not afterwards.

It is notable that controversies in science are not settled by the contestants but by time. Timescales needed to establish theories are longer than those associated with individual scientists. At any point in time, science raises questions that cannot be answered by the scientists of the day. It is on such questions that scientists take positions. The issues are settled not because one set of scientists succeeds in convincing the other, but because new evidence accumulates and slowly the issues resolve themselves. The controversies however do serve an important scientific function. They bring the issues into sharper focus and encourage further observations/experiments.

An important question that needs to be addressed is this: When the existing evidence is not adequate to choose between two competing models or hypotheses, what are the arguments proffered by the adherents of each side in support of their point of view, and how these arguments influence the future course of development. We can illustrate the above points with the help of some examples, drawn from astronomy and cosmology. In 1920 two leading astronomers of the day, Harlow Shapley and Heber D Curtis, participated in a 'great debate' on the scale of the universe. The debate raised a number of important questions: Was the galaxy bigger than hitherto assumed? Yes. Was the sun at the centre of our galaxy? No. Was our galaxy the only one in the universe, or were there others like it? [It was one among many].

"In the debate, both participants supported their conclusions with formidable arrays of observational data that they themselves had secured. Both had carefully scrutinized observations by others and checked their results. Written statements were prepared by both men and exchanged before the meeting. Each had made minor revisions after reading his opponent's views, but neither found it possible to accept the others principal conclusions."[1] Significantly, "nor were other astronomers able to decide definitely between the two points of view."[2] The debate provides "a glimpse into the reasoning processes of eminent scientists engaged in a great controversy for which the evidence on both sides is fragmentary and partly faulty. This debate illustrates forcefully how tricky it is to pick one's way through the treacherous ground that characterizes research in the frontiers of science."[3] The scientific issues involved in the debate were resolved over a period of two decades when the frontiers of knowledge got progressively pushed further.

Three decades later there erupted another controversy, this time on the origin of the universe. Did the universe begin by exploding from a hot dense state ('big bang'), or was it without a beginning ('steady state'). (Interestingly, the now standard technical term big bang cosmology with the same initials as British Broadcasting Corporation, was coined rather pejoratively, in 1948, by Fred Hoyle.) The steady state model was finally proved wrong by the detection in 1965 of the three degree kelvin microwave background radiation, which proved that the universe was hotter in the past. While the controversy lasted, it brought into focus philosophical postulates (Was there need for a 'perfect cosmological principle'?) as well as questions of methodology (What constitutes Popperian testability in areas such as cosmology?). How do proponents of a theory respond to its rejection? Max Planck, the founder of quantum physics, held a rather extreme view. "An important scientific innovation rarely makes its way by gradually winning over and converting its opponents. What does happen is that its opponents gradually die out, and that the growing generation is familiarised with the ideas from the beginning."

While it is true that many propounders stick to their views till their physical or intellectual death, there are any number of examples where the proponents of a view have willingly abandoned it when new evidence to the contrary came along. In one respect however Planck was right, that is, about the growing generation. Even though attempts are still on to salvage steady-state model, the new generation of researchers is being brought up on the standard big-bang. (I was once told by an American academic that his pro-steady state proposal was turned down by funding agencies on the ground that younger generation should not be involved it it. An otherwise well-respected American astronomer was refused telescope time for his non-standard observational programme, and moved over to Germany, a reversal of the historic scientific traffic.)

Human factor has played a role in the case of mathematical theories as well. Einstein himself intervened in his entirely self-consisted gravitational theory, erroneously called General Theory of Relativity (GTR), by introducing an arbitrary term to prevent the theory from permitting expansion of universe which he thought was unphysical. Once the universe was observationally shown to be expanding, sensibly the theory was left alone to speak for itself. The Nazi attempts to brand GTR as Jewish science were short-lived, for two reasons. First, the well-known failure of Newtonian gravitation to explain Mercury's orbit had already created a slot for an improved theory, even if nobody had any clue as to what the new theory would look like. More importantly, within four years of its enunciation, a prediction by GTR (bending of starlight by sun) was experimentally verified.

Einstein was fortunate that the verifiability of his theory was within the capabilities of the technology of the day. Subramanya Chandrasekhar was not so lucky. He was the first to apply Theory of Special Relativity to problems of stellar evolution. His mathematically rigorous work on the white dwarf stars, which essentially predicted the existence of black holes, was ridiculed by Sir Arthur Eddington, the then most influential astronomer in Europe. With a haughtiness one associates with Viceroys rather than scientists, he declared: "I think there should be a law of nature to prevent a star from behaving in this absurd manner." Sir Arthur was blinded by his self-righteousness; the others by the glare of his personality.[4] It was not that one hypothesis was competing with another. It was an exact mathematical theory that was pitted against refusal to listen. Eventually, the discovery of the pulsar stars and quasar galaxies vindicated Chandrasekhar. Interestingly, though Chandrasekhar won a number of academic awards for his subsequent researches, it was only in 1974 that an award citation referred to his pathbreaking white dwarf work. Eddington's prejudice had delayed the development of relativistic astrophysics by forty years! Ironically, a film on white dwarfs recently made by BBC was titled 'Absurd Stars' and showed a photograph of Sir Arthur rather than Chandrasekhar, making light of the former's prejudice. Therefore, the journey of a scientific theory from its enunciation till its enshrinement in textbooks is often a long one. It is in the interim period that human factors come into play.

NOTES

1. Struve, O. and Zebergs, V. 1962. *Astronomy of the 20th Century*. New York: Macnultan. p. 416.
2. Ibid. p. 444.
3. Shu, F. 1982. *The Physical Universe. An Introduction to Astronomy*. Mill Valley: University Science Books. p. 286.
4. Struve and Zebergs.

BIBLIOGRAPHY

1. Kochhar, Rajesh. 1995. "Transcending the Limits: Chandrasekhar's Stellar Contribution". *Times of India*, 19 October.
2. Shu, F. 1982. *The Physical Universe. An Introduction to Astronomy*. Mill Valley: University Science Books.
3. Struve, O. and Zebergs, V. 1962. *Astronomy of the 20th Century*. New York: Macnultan.

CHAPTER 18

Logic of Metaphors and Scientific Discovery

A.V. Afonso

The present paper attempts to understand the close links between metaphors and scientific discovery. Metaphors, which were looked upon as intrusions and aberrations in relation to precise language of science, are now posed as the essential part of the scientific enterprise. The attempt here is to show how metaphors are part of logic of discovery to the extent of being theory-constitutive. Further, the growth and progress of science seem to be essentially linked with the capacity of scientists to use metaphors to break away from the established structures of thought and allow revolutionary changes.

Although Hans Reichenbach, Karl Popper and C. G. Hempel expressed reservations regarding the possibility of logic of discovery, an inquiry into the 'language' of 'discovery' reveals structures that go beyond the 'creative intuition' of Popper or 'unconscious inferences' of Reichenbach. N. R. Hanson, while proposing 'retroactive inferences' which sought to introduce logic in the creative scientific discoveries, fell prey to psychologism. It is for the same reason that Hanson is said to have failed to distinguish between 'logic of generation' and 'logic of evaluation'. One may doubt whether such a distinction results in problems and difficulties to the understanding of scientific discoveries and the consequent 'progress' of science.

Mary Tiles, for instance, while arguing that science 'progresses' by 'correcting concepts' pointed out that the progress of science is neither exclusively linked with the analysis of the context of discovery nor the analysis of the context of justification. Petruska-Madej and Van Peuerson have found the distinction between the two contexts (discovery and justification) as irrelevant to the debate regarding scientific realism. Martin C. Curd redirected the debate when he argued that the two logics are not concerned with things but theories. He distinguished between 'logic of prior assessment' (LPA) and 'logic of theory generation' (LTG), as two aspects of 'period of theory generation' (PTG), the "time beginning at the moment when a scientist (or research group) first begins thinking seriously about a problem and ending when the theory... is written down in a form suitable, say for publication in a scientific journal." (Curd, 1989:418)

Inherent to the controversy of logic of discovery versus logic of justification; or logic of discovery and logic of justification is the question whether the linguistic expressions employed can overcome the psychologism inherent in the discourse. In other words, when the scientist cannot describe in logical terms a discovery of scientific theory, one need not look for 'irrational elements' for its justification. Instead, one should investigate into the linguistic enterprise of science and the linguistic capacity of scientists to 'manipulate' language to 'correct' and 'extend' concepts.

Theoretically, most significant use of language is to 'create' a world capable of being meaningfully communicated to others. The resultant linguistic expressions may not have strict identity of meanings. At one level, for instance in general discourse, such an identity is neither envisaged nor verifiable. Besides, what is verifiable at one level is axiomatic at another. And in spite of a possibility that what is axiomatic at level one maybe verifiable at level two and vice-versa, communication does not suffer and science 'progresses'. 'Metaphors' function as such linguistic expressions that are both theory constitutive and capable of making 'scientific progress' possible. An inquiry into 'what is a 'metaphor' in science?' and 'what role it plays in the growth of knowledge?' will compel us to investigate into the nature of 'metaphor' as a linguistic tool capable of 'creative' insights that makes it possible for us to go beyond the 'givens'. In fact, there seems to be no other way to 'go beyond' and 'extend concepts' except though metaphors.

Everyday language is full of metaphors and any dictionary will set aside our doubts regarding most of our words as straightforward and literal. That there are actually 'dead' or 'frozen' metaphors in our daily language can be illustrated from a single example. Consider the verb 'run'. In its simplest and most basic sense it designates a human (and animal) activity. But through metaphorical extension it comes to be applied to objects that lie outside its basic reference class, such as rivers. The term began with a more limited scope or extension, and when people first talked of rivers running it must have sounded bizarre. When the metaphor was green and fresh it might well have been objected, on the ground that rivers cannot run—they have no legs. This is a banal example of so-called frozen (or dead) metaphor. Once metaphor freezes (or dies) it becomes an ordinary part of our literal vocabulary. So it comes about that rivers run, taps run and fences run, and they 'run' in a way which has generalised the meaning of this expression. With apologies to Gilbert Ryle, there is no categorical mistake in the use of the term.

Metaphors in everyday discourse are 'invisible' as we understand them immediately as if they are literals. Metaphors are 'conceived' and 'grasped' as easily as ordinary literal vocabulary. There has never been a problem of understanding metaphors. The problem is at one level, to explain *how* we understand them and at another level how they are constitutive of semantic evolution. Linguistic philosophers have in recent studies recognized the centrality of metaphors in general explanation of language and communication, and more particularly the role metaphors play in the semantic evolution. Similarly, that metaphors have an inalienable role in creating (sic. generating) new meanings is accepted by the philosophers of language. Metaphor is the primary tool with which an individual moves from the cognitively 'givens' (concepts available in the speaker's immediate vicinity) to the world beyond. Although 'metaphorical generalization' may be restricted to the simplest form of metaphorical application, metaphorical processes have a larger role to play in the human creative processes. In fact, the primitive linguistic resources of natural language employed to represent sensible objects and expression for basic activities, transcend these limited roles to express abstract thought and elements so well defined in Karl Popper's World 3. Consequently, one may conclude that metaphors function as 'fundamental mechanism' with which we extend and refine language; and ascribe new sense to the world as an expression of creative insights of the author.

Another important aspect of metaphors that needs consideration is the distinction between 'live' and 'dead' metaphor on the one hand and between these two and 'dormant' metaphor. 'Dead' metaphor is just an ordinary part of our literal vocabulary and we fail to recognize or regard it as metaphor. 'Dormant' metaphors are metaphors that we use without ever considering them to be metaphors—it is only when pointed out that we recognize them as metaphors. These types of metaphors are approaching 'death' and soon they are recognized as literals. Again, there are some who believe in 'paraphrase thesis, namely, that everything which can be stated metaphorically can be restated literally. The fact however remains that 'something' in the metaphorical expression will remain unstressed or uncaptured in the paraphrase. It is not those aesthetic or affective aspects of the metaphor that we are concerned about but descriptive and cognitive contents. Further, the cognitive role that metaphor plays cannot be exhausted by the literal use of language. Paraphrases are supplied *ex post facto* (retrospectively) and surely cannot provide us the significant 'insights' that metaphors provide in making unfamiliar situations familiar. As Wittgenstein states: "Metaphor is a ladder of cognitive ascent which can be kicked away after the vista it has exposed is revealed." (1961, 6.54)

The 'interaction' view of metaphor enables us to understand the role of metaphors in 'discovery'. Further, distinct subjects of a metaphorical statement (namely, primary-secondary or principal-secondary or literal-frame) are such that the 'secondary' term must be a system with reference to a thing (primary). Further, a metaphor projects upon the primary subject associated implications that are predictable of the secondary subject. This predication or attribution is selective, as the speaker either emphasises or suppresses some features of the secondary subject while applying to the primary subject. And finally, one notices a three-fold 'interaction' between primary and secondary subjects. First, reference to primary subject 'incites' the hearer to select some property of the secondary subject. Secondly, it compels him to 'construct a parallel implication-complex' that allows understanding of the primary subject. And finally, the process brings about reciprocal changes in the secondary subject on the basis of the new constructs.

Although the very notion of 'interaction' is itself metaphorical, the position ensures a 'dynamic' conception of metaphor. The mutual interaction between the 'primary' and the 'secondary' subjects can be used to account for evolution of the concept articulating both the past and the future from the standpoint of the present. The notions 'primary-secondary', 'literal-frame' must be seen not from the chronological point of view in relation to history of mankind, but chronological in relation to individual's epistemic framework. It is in this context that one can say that interaction view accounts for the understanding of metaphor as a creative process.

T.S. Kuhn, Richard Boyd and others further developed Max Black's linguistic insights into the realm of science when they recognised the use of metaphors in science as theory-constitutive. There is a class of metaphors whose presence is obvious in the development and articulation of theories in relatively mature sciences. Richard Boyd referred to their function as that of cathachresis. Metaphors possess many characteristics, such as 'open-ended', 'imprecise', etc. But the eventual explication of 'similarities' (sic. metaphors) depend upon the success of scientific research. And to claim that the metaphors in science will ever remain imprecise, as Boyd argues, is based on a mistaken understanding of precision in science.

Philosophers of science recognise distinct type of roles for metaphors in science. Some metaphors are purely exegetical in the sense that their function is to explicate a theory. There are metaphors that are simultaneously pedagogical and insightful, in the sense that without these metaphors a scientist would not have been able to express the theoretical insights into the nature and the theory formulated thereof. Finally, there are those metaphors which scientists use in expressing theoretical presuppositions and claims for which adequate literal paraphrase is not available. It is these metaphors that are said to be 'theory-constitutive'.

Some may question the existence of such theory-constitutive metaphors. They may even argue that such metaphors are pre-theoretical as they lack the 'explicitness' or 'precision' attributed to scientific theories. What type of 'explicitness' or 'precision' is expected of new and developing sciences such as cognitive psychology and computer sciences, has never been articulated. What one observes is that metaphors employed by these new sciences are theory-constitutive to these disciplines as there are no literal paraphrases representing their theoretical claims.

Literary metaphors (when used for the first time) have their 'home' in the original work of the author, and when used by others, have reference to their original use. But this 'implicit to the original use' loses its exactness when metaphors are used in science to convey meaning that hitherto was not known to exist. Their use is pedagogical as well as insightful, in the sense it affords to break new grounds, create new language, express new and hitherto unknown relations. These metaphors, in due course of time when accepted by the community of scientists become concepts. And as concepts, they feature not in one literary work or the other, but through the work of an entire generation or more of scientists. Linguistic expressions, which were hitherto known as metaphors and hence imprecise, are now treated as concepts, precise and theory-constitutive.

Richard Boyd and others recognise the use of theory-constitutive metaphors only in relatively young or immature sciences. But analysis of language of most mature sciences such as physics, show greater use of 'theory-constitutive' metaphors, than in other sciences. Advanced sciences make greater use of 'theory-constitutive' metaphors to break new grounds, develop new frameworks, articulate new insights as the existing vocabulary and linguistic expressions seem to limit their conceptual articulation. 'Theory-constitutive' metaphors provide one (if not the only one) and the best strategy for accommodation of language to discover and describe the undiscovered causal features of the world.

"Science progresses by correcting concepts," argued Mary Tiles while offering a commulative model of scientific progress as alternative to Kuhnian 'incommensurable alternative'. Mary Tiles recognised three dimensions of science: the empirical, theoretical and metaphysical. The empirical dimension concerns itself with the concepts that are empirically developed in a scientific context and are often taken for granted. Scientific investigations are never given purely empirically, as one has to accommodate and incorporate changes occurring in the non-empirical (theoretical and metaphysical) dimensions of science. This accounts for the non-empirical framework determining what kind of thing or phenomena it is investigating. If the existing linguistic expressions can account for both the empirical dimension and non-empirical one, science continues to work within the existing framework—it only adds or subtracts scientific knowledge by the 'in built mechanisms' it has developed. But if the existing framework cannot account for both the empirical and non-empirical dimensions of the scientific concept, 'metaphors will have to be used', resulting in a new dimension. This new dimension, though initially alien to the theoretical dimension, in due course of time when scrutinised in the light of newly developed explanatory ideals, results in correction of concepts. It is by this increased coordination and unification of the initially radically different theoretical dimension, that science progresses.

E. Pietruska-Madej, while arguing for a logic of discovery, pointed out that anti-psychologism is the root-cause of nihilistic attitude. She tried to answer a series of questions: Why does science sometimes manage to ignore insights of genius only to rediscover them years later? Why does it at other times explode a series of simultaneous discoveries? How should we account for 'premature' discoveries that fail? How can we distinguish between discovery in subjective psychological sense and scientific discovery proper? Her answer is: "There is some internal logical determination in science by which science proceeds from established knowledge to new elements of knowledge, and that there comes into play something like a 'logical necessity' conducive to a new discovery. [Further] ... for a given discovery, and that so long as it science is not 'mature' enough for this (discovery) even the most ingenious ideas are doomed to be regarded as irrelevant for scientific progress ... (and finally) when the stage is reached the discovery is 'inevitable' resulting in something 'several scientists may make the discovery simultaneously." (Pietruska-Madej, 1985:12). The three concepts (logical necessity, maturity and inevitability) that Pietruska-Madej claim to account for a newly discovered idea, maybe better understood with reference to the development of language of science and its acceptance by the community. The absence of 'metaphors' both for exegetical purpose and insights, seems to account for why 'discoveries' or 'new ideas' fail to catch the imagination of the scientific community. They have to 'wait' for appropriate period when adequate linguistic expressions or metaphors are available.

Metaphor is a tool of discovery, providing a way of imposing or discovering structure within novel or unfamiliar situations. And the results of such a discovery (*ex post facto*) attempted to be paraphrased (in non-metaphorical terms) leads to an essential component of development of language and consequently, cognitive development including the development of scientific concepts. It is not only language that would be duller and unable to develop its complex and powerful resources of 'generalisation' and 'abstraction' without the resources of metaphor but scientists would be cognitively hampered in their conceptual generalisation without the tool of metaphor to transcend the existing modes of thinking. A more detailed inquiry into the above will provide better understanding of progress in science and alleged 'paradigm shifts'.

BIBLIOGRAPHY

1. Black, Max. 1979. "More about Metaphor". *Metaphor and Thought.* Andrew Ortony (ed.). Cambridge: Cambridge University Press.
2. Boyd, Richard. 1979. "Metaphor and Theory of Change: What is "Metaphor" a Metaphor for?" *Metaphor and Thought.* Andrew Ortony (ed.). Cambridge: Cambridge University Press.
3. Curd, Martin. 1989. "The Logic of Discovery: An Analysis of Three Approaches". *Readings in Philosophy of Science.* B. A. Brody and R. E. Grandy (ed.). N.J.: Prentice-Hall.
4. Hanson, N. R. 1958. *Pattern of Discovery.* Cambridge: Cambridge University Press.
5. Pietruska-Madej, E. 1985. "Should Philosophers of Science Consider Scientific Discovery?" *Ratio,* 27(1): 7-18.
6. Popper, K. R. 1965. *Logic of Discovery.* London: Hutchinson and Co.
7. Tiles, Mary. 1985. "Correcting Concepts". *Ratio,* 27(1):19-36.
8. Van Peuerson, G. A. 1989. "Discovery as the Context of any Scientific Justification". *Man and World,* 27:471-484.
9. Wittgenstein, Ludwig. 1961. *Tractatus Logico-Philosophicus.* D.F. Pears and B.F. McGuiness (trans). London: Routledge & Kegan Paul.

III
Interplay of Science on Consciousness

CHAPTER 19

Model-makers versus Algorisers: Some Thoughts on the Indian Half of the Needham Question

Roddam Narasimha

Much debate has taken place on the famous question raised by Needham regarding "the failure of China and India to give rise to distinctively modern science while being ahead of Europe for fourteen previous centuries..." A variety of explanations have been offered in India for the failure mentioned in the above quote. These explanations have ranged from a (alleged) preference for idealist philosophies and an inward looking, other-worldly culture, to the prevalence of a rigidly stratified social system, etc. It is argued in the paper that while there is some truth in many of the explanations that have been offered, they are in the final analysis, not truly convincing for three major reasons: (a) the philosophical systems of India are very diverse, (b) at the end of the first millennium the sciences in India were in a relatively strong position in the civilized world of the day, and had indeed become very influential, and (c) (as the quote above from Needham admits) India (and China) were in fact ahead of Europe for fourteen centuries before the European scientific revolution and there is no evidence that the explanations offered were not operative in that long period.

The proposal in the paper is that it would be more useful to approach the question by looking at what happened in Europe in the sixteenth century and later as the manifestation of a European miracle. In order to understand the roots of this miracle it is important to study earlier developments in Europe, say during the twelfth to fifteenth centuries. It is now well known that several eastern inventions travelled to the West during and after the Crusades. Among these were a variety of technologies from China, and the new numeral and mathematical inventions that went from India (both through creative West Asian intermediaries). The renowned mathematician Hermann Weyl wrote in 1929: "Occidental mathematics has in past centuries broken away from the Greek view and followed a course which seems to have originated in India and which has been transmitted, with additions, to us by the Arabs; in it the concept of number appears as logically prior to the concepts of geometry." Indeed the history of mathematics in India can be interpreted as indicating the occurrence of a mathematical revolution heralded by Āryabhaṭa and leading in the next several centuries to the development of the Indian numeral system, algebra, techniques for solving both linear and quadratic indeterminate equations, and the germs of the calculus. These new mathematical techniques travelled West over the course of centuries and appear to have played a decisive role in the mathematization of science that was such an essential ingredient of the European scientific revolution—in ways that still have to be more completely studied.

The Needham question then rephrases itself to ask why the Indian mathematical revolution did not lead to a corresponding 'distinctively modern' scientific one. One reason could be that it was not accompanied by the generation of new technologies—or their absorption from elsewhere (e.g. China). (Quite possibly no economic or political need was felt for them in India at the time.) But there appears to have been another fundamental philosophical reason, illustrated by the totally different approaches to science taken in classical Greece and classical India. By a detailed comparison of two texts in geometry (the Indian *śulva-sūtras* and the Greek Euclid) and in astronomy (Ptolemy and Āryabhaṭa), it is proposed that, in a useful over-simplification, the Greek approach may be thought of as that of axiomatizers and model-makers and the Indian approach as that of pattern-seekers and algorisers. The style of the Indian intellectual approach indicates a deep suspicion of axioms and models, but great ingenuity in handling numbers and discerning patterns (for example in the motion of heavenly bodies). It is suggested that the European scientific revolution, which may be traced to Copernicus, Galileo and Newton, came about in part because of a powerful fusion of the ideas of model-making and algorithms. It is also argued that while the distrust of universal axioms and models in Indian logical systems appears to have been philosophically justified, and may be said to have been vindicated by twentieth century developments in quantum mechanics and logic (e.g. wave-particle duality, Gödel's theorems, deterministic chaos), the use of a somewhat less fastidious approach in Europe towards understanding nature led to an unreasonably and unexpectedly spectacular successes in the development of science there.

We can say that European model-making could not progress without the mathematical tools whose roots can be traced to India, and similarly that Indian science could not progress without the model-making abilities of the West. The distrust of models, while not philosophically unjustified, has turned out to be historically expensive for India.

It is widely accepted that a spectacular scientific revolution occurred in the Europe of the sixteenth to seventeenth centuries, and spread to North America and Asia. (For our purposes here, a 'revolution' in a system is a change that takes place in a time relatively short compared to the time scales of change in that system before the revolution.) Then followed the Industrial Revolution in eighteenth century Europe, and this also diffused across the globe in later centuries. The first effects of these revolutions on India were historically painful: they led to the decimation of the famed textile and metallurgical industries of the country, accompanied by a European political domination that was supported—indeed often driven—by superior military and civil technologies. Raja Rammohan Roy was among the first Indians to have realized that the rapid expansion and consolidation of British power by early nineteenth century was not an isolated success, but that it represented the advent of a new cultural force based on novel knowledge systems.

Roy went to England (in 1830) because 'He longed to see...the country of the Lockes, of the Bacons, of the Newtons, of the Hampdons and of the Watts'; and elsewhere he spoke of the 'perfection of the mechanical arts' in England, and even advocated the settlement of Europeans in India to help introduce their knowledge into the country. The questions that he raised for himself then have since concerned the growing community of scientists and engineers as well as political and social leaders all over the East.

The issue of the new knowledge systems that arose in Europe has now acquired a remarkable intellectual and philosophical dimension, following the monumental work of Joseph Needham on science and technology in ancient China. Needham has carefully documented the extensive technological achievements of the Chinese civilization, often pre-dating western developments by centuries. It is enough to note here that, among the inventions of the Chinese were not only paper, the printing press, gun-powder and compass, but also rockets, the (clock) escapement mechanism, silk, etc. After a meticulous survey of these instances of eastern inventiveness, Needham pointed out:

> With the appearance on the scene of intensive studies of mathematics, science, technology and medicine in the great non-European civilizations, debate is likely to sharpen, for the failure of China and India to give rise to distinctively modern science while being ahead of Europe for fourteen previous centuries is going to take some explaining.

There have been very stimulating surveys of Indian science and technology too in recent years, but nothing that even remotely matches the scale, scope and magnificence of Needham's effort. Nevertheless, as I have already mentioned, the question now associated with Needham's name has plagued many Indian scientists and leaders, and there have also been efforts to explain, or analyse, why the scientific and industrial revolutions did not (or even could not) take place in India. One favourite explanation, going back to P.C. Ray, the great chemist, is based on the inequities of the caste system. The Marxist philosopher Debiprasad Chattopadhyaya, while claiming that the world's first natural scientist was Uddālaka Aruṇi who appears in the *Chāndogya Upaniṣad*, went on to argue that Indian idealist philosophies created an intellectual climate inimical to the growth of modern science.

As an aside, it is interesting to note that Needham finds it so easy to make the parenthetical assertion about the great eastern civilizations having been ahead of Europe for so long; late British colonial historians would of course have been shocked by the assertion, and so, I suspect, would the considerable number of modern Indians brought up on the view of the likes of Macaulay and Mill. Earlier European observers, on the other hand, would have found that Needham would have only been repeating a widely-held view of their own times.

A catalogue of various proposed explanations for the failure of India in giving rise to modern science appears in Box 1.

Box 1

POSSIBLE REASONS WHY THE SCIENCE AND TECHNOLOGY REVOLUTIONS DID NOT OCCUR IN INDIA

- 'Idealist', 'speculative' philosophies
- Inward-looking, other-worldly culture
- No 'Protestant ethic'
- Social rigidity, caste system, lack of professional mobility, no cross-fertilization of ideas
- Weakness in observation, data-keeping
- Relative insularity: no foreign travel
- Civilizational complacency
- Oral traditions, resistance to documentation, closed education systems
- Inadequate public patronage
- Conflict between science and religion
- Inherent cultural tendency to live with contradictions

While there is some truth in many of the explanations listed above, there are serious difficulties as well. A major one is that these explanations do not recognize the diversity of Indian civilization, including its philosophies. Thus, while one may argue that Vedāntic philosophy is idealistic or speculative, it must be remembered that there were many philosophical systems in India: the Sāṁkhya, Nyāya or Vaiśeṣika cannot be accused of being anti-science. There was a vigorous materialist school as well (the Lokāyata). Similarly, while the impression persists everywhere in the world that Indian culture is inward-looking and other-worldly, we must remember that this could not have been true for the vast majority of the population. India is also the land of Kautilya's *Arthaśāstra* and Vātsyāyana's *Kāma-sūtra*, and Indian merchants have been entrepreneurial for thousands of years (from Indus Valley days). Similarly, while it is true that the Indian caste system has been there for centuries, survives to this day and has inhibited mutual reinforcement of science and technology, it has been less rigid than is often thought, and social stratification elsewhere in the world was not always more dynamic or flexible than here. As for relations between science and religion, there were clashes between 'rationalist' and 'conservative' views (e.g. Āryabhaṭa and Brahmagupta), but the conflict never reached the intensity of western violence (as it did e.g. when Bruno was burnt at the stake for his irreligious beliefs). Incidentally, while on this subject, we need to recall that the great star of the scientific revolution, Isaac Newton, spent far more time and wrote far more words on theology than he ever did on science.

The second difficulty with these explanations is that they ignore the presence of strong scientific traditions in India at different periods in our history. For example, the eleventh century Spanish-Arab astronomer Said al-Andalusi said, "Eight peoples have interested themselves in the sciences: the Hindus, the Persians, the Chaldeans, the Hebrews, the Greeks, the Romans, the Egyptians and the Arabs. The premier nation among these in the sciences is that of the Hindus." This comment was made only five centuries before the scientific revolution in Europe may be said to have begun. One could argue that *modern* science dates from the sixteenth and seventeenth centuries and that it represents such a fundamental historical departure that the pre-revolution position of science in India was rendered irrelevant. That however would be inconsistent with the view of many western scholars who insist that 'the Greeks invented science' (which for example is the sub-title of a recent essay by Lewis Wolpert in the well-known British magazine *Nature*). This statement could probably be justified if the scope of the word science is suitably restricted. Thus, is science systematized, consensible knowledge (as Indians and many other civilizations tend to think), or is science a quest for the ability to predict the behaviour of nature with the use of the fewest possible universal principles? If the former, science was certainly not invented in Greece; if it might have been the latter, then in periods when the quest for such intellectual minimalism begins to look unfruitful—as it must have done in the Europe of the Middle Ages—progress may become impossible. (And pre-Darwinian biology would not be science at all.) It seems certainly true that the Greeks had a special way of thinking about nature which characterizes their best scientific work. However, as we shall discuss below, the Greeks often got carried away by their philosophies and models. As Kitto remarks, "Greek philosophy sought for uniformity in the multiplicity of phenomena, and [this] desire. . . led to guess work and neglect of fact in the attempt to frame a comprehensive theory. . . ." As Daremberg says, "the philosophers tried to explain nature while shutting their eyes"[1].

The third difficulty is that for nearly 1,400 years after these fundamental developments in Greece, European science was by and large barren; no great advances—certainly in terms of fundamental ideas—were made in what in fact have come to be known as the Dark Ages (a period that incidentally was a Classical Age for India—in spite of all the 'reasons' listed in Box 1).

It must further be understood that the great eastern civilizations of India and China have survived for millennia, and for much of that time have been some of the most advanced and prosperous ones in the world.

The standard explanations may thus not be convincing, but the Needham question cannot be brushed under the rug. I would like to propose that it may be fruitful to approach the question from the opposite point of view. Namely, instead of asking why India and China did *not* give rise to modern science, we could ask how it happened that Europe *did* so. Given the long Dark Ages that Europe went through, it is in fact more appropriate to think of what happened there in the sixteenth century and later as the European miracle (just as we have in the last fifty years come to talk about the East Asian miracle, for example). What was it that triggered the great scientific revolution of the sixteenth century? To answer this question it is necessary to look at the period immediately preceding the birth of modern science. For example Paolo Rossi, in his book of the same name, by and large examines the period 1500-1700 A.D. (more precisely he dates the revolution as having occurred in the period of 160 years between the publication of *De Revolutionibus* by Copernicus in 1543 A.D. and of *Opticks* by Newton in 1704 A.D., p. 2). A far more interesting period to study from our point of view would be the three centuries preceding the revolution, namely 1200-1500 A.D.

One clue regarding the precursors of the revolution is to be found in a very interesting essay by Gombrich (*Daedulus* 1998 Winter: 193-205, *Eastern inventions and Western Response*), who says that "it was the western response to the technical inventions that reached Europe from the East that undermined and finally swept away the belief that, in Bacon's words, 'excluded all theory of Progress' ", and so led to the scientific revolution.

One fascinating piece of evidence that Gombrich provides is a book published in 1471 by Giovanni Tortelli. As a student of languages Tortelli was concerned with words in current use deriving from the Greek. His analysis showed that many words could not be traced to Greek roots and so presumably came from inventions unknown to the ancient world. Among such were spring-driven clocks, the marine compass, the bombard, stirrups, watermill, cotton, silk, candle, the organ, falconry, gilding and spectacles. In one of the paintings of the period, Gombrich points out, the numerous new inventions listed came mostly from China. These not only included the famous trio of compass, gun powder and printing but also silk, possibly the watermill, the escapement in the clock etc. Gombrich points out that there were two important things missing in the painted list: one was the paper on which the list was written (which came also from China), and the other the numerals that listed them (which came from India).

In 1620, Francis Bacon (who can be considered the patron-saint of the European scientific revolution) wrote:

> Consider the force and effect of inventions which are nowhere more conspicuous than in those three which were unknown to the ancients, namely printing, gunpowder and the magnet. For these three have changed the appearance and condition of the whole world, the first in letters, the second in warfare and the last in navigation, and from these there sprang innumerable changes so that no empire, sect or star appears to have exercised a greater power and influence on human affairs than these mechanical matters.

And where did those 'mechanical matters' come from? Here is what Samuel Purchas was writing, as late as 1625:

> Others, therefore, looke further unto the East, whence the Light of Sunne, and Arts, have seemed first to arise to our World; and will have Marco Polo the Venetian above three hundred yeeres since to have brought it out of Mangi (which we now call China) into Italy. True it is, that the most magnified Arts have there first been borne, Printing, Gunnes, and perhaps this also of the Compasse, which the Portugals at their first entry of the Indian Seas found amongst the More, together with Cards and Qudrants to observe both the Heavens and Earth.

It is therefore clear that in the centuries just preceding 1500 a large number of technical inventions came into Europe from the East, in particular from China (through West Asia). It is natural to speculate that the 'invention of invention' that occurred in Europe at this time must have been triggered and inspired by the technological flood from the East.

The second clue comes from mathematics. This is important, for one of the most striking features of the scientific revolution was the mathematization of science. Galileo used mathematics to describe his experimental findings; Newton named his great and epoch-making book *Principia Mathematica Philosophiae Naturalis*: the Mathematical Principles of Natural Philosophy. Where did this mathematics come from?

It is here appropriate to quote from the renowned Swiss mathematical physicist Hermann Weyl, who wrote in 1929, in the preface to his pioneering book on quantum mechanics and group theory, "Occidental mathematics has in past centuries broken away from the Greek view and followed a course which seems to have originated in India and which has been transmitted, with additions, to us by the Arabs; in it the concept of number appears as logically prior to the concepts of geometry." (He went on to say that, with the advent of group theory, the trend in mathematics was returning to the Greek standpoint.) Although the *Principia* is couched in the language of geometry, it appears that Newton did so because that was the 'proper' way to do it (he was clearly in the grip of Euclid-worship); he almost certainly derived many of his results by quite different methods, involving algebra and equations, tools that were clearly imported from India and West Asia—and, of course, subsequently greatly improved in Europe. The tortuous trajectory of the spread of the Indian numeral system and associated methods of calculation—through West Asia, Islamic Spain and Jewish scholars and merchants to Christian Europe—has been brilliantly described by Georges Ifrah.[2]

One can therefore argue that the long dark ages of Europe were broken only by the technical and mathematical inventions imported from the East. Europe came into contact with these through the violent conflict that took place with the Arabs during the Crusades. It is well known that at that time the Islamic adversaries of Christian Europe were the party more advanced in science. In fact Europe had often to rediscover some of its own Greek scientific heritage through translations that were more easily available in Arabic than in European languages—reminding one of what happened in India in the eighteenth and nineteenth centuries when British scholars were able to tell us more about Indian heritage in many areas than we Indians could remember ourselves.

Let us return to the question of what science really represents. Accepting for the present that science is systematized knowledge, it is clear from a reading of eastern and western scientific literature that, at the very least, there are strong differences between different civilizations in the style in which they accumulate that systematized knowledge. These differences do appear to reflect deep philosophical differences in the approach to knowledge.

To illustrate, let us compare two approaches to geometry. One comes from the *Śulva-sūtras* dating perhaps to seventh or eighth century B.C.E., and the other from Euclid (third century B.C.E.). The former is basically a manual of ritual geometry; its objective is to provide instructions on how to construct various fire altars that were part of Vedic sacrificial rites. Euclid on the other hand is a set of 'theorems' in geometry derived from a set of 'axioms'. Box 2 shows both the first page of the *Śulva-sūtras* and the set of five axioms from Euclid. The contrast cannot be stronger. The *Sūtras* start with a listing of the units of length measurement, and go on to make a variety of propositions, including the so-called theorem of Pythagoras (who came much later, in the sixth century B.C.E.). The result is stated in general terms, but (significantly, I believe: we shall return to this point) with explicit examples. No attempt is made to *prove* it; it is clearly considered a valid conclusion—a confident inference rather than a logical deduction. The *Sūtras* also consider the problem of how to construct a fire altar that is twice as large in area as a basic one. We know of course that this can be done by increasing the linear dimensions by $\sqrt{2}$, for which the *Sūtras* give the (excellent) approximate value of 1.414.

On the other hand Euclid begins by stating five axioms which he considers would be widely accepted and can provide a suitable basis for deducing, purely by logic, a variety of 'new' results. Euclid avoids introducing measures of distance or area: i.e. he is non-metric; but the *Sūtras* are metric from the word go. Euclid also states the theorem of Pythagoras, but derives it from the axioms that he accepts at the beginning of his book. The idea of $\sqrt{2}$ was a mystery to the Greeks, because it could not be expressed as a fraction. To the Indians on the other hand the question was one of finding an adequate approximation; there is no evidence that it caused any great intellectual agonization.

We might similarly compare the two great astronomers, Ptolemy (second century C.E.) and Āryabhaṭa (fifth century C.E.). Ptolemy proceeds once again with a basic physical model in mind. The model is geocentric, and the planets move in epicycles, that is to say they trace small circles whose centers themselves move on other, larger circles. (The circle was a perfect figure for the Greeks, and all celestial bodies had therefore to move on circles, or circles on circles. As an aside, I cannot resist the temptation to say that this kind of Hellenistic faith in 'perfection' persists in the West to this day, as e.g. when Dirac made the famous statement, ". . . it is more important to have beauty in one's equations than to have them fit experiment".) Space (which could not be empty, for the Greeks believed nature abhors vacuum) is a set of layered crystalline spherical shells each of which carries along one of the planets. (The shells had to be crystalline, or a transparent solid, because one had to be able to see through to the stars.) The universe is finite, and outside the last shell is a 'mover' who rotates the shells. With these and some other hypotheses, and by geometrical deduction appealing to Euclid for example, Ptolemy proceeds to derive a series of results on planetary motions. Now Āryabhaṭa also uses epicycles, but by splitting planetary motion into a slow mean and a rapid epicyclic fluctuation superposed over it. It is likely that the basic idea of epicyclic motion was borrowed from the Greeks, but the interesting point is that Āryabhaṭa does not speak of any underlying model at all. His book starts with a small introduction which describes a system by which he is going to express numbers and a listing of the numerical parameters (including the trigonometric sines) that go into the calculations, which form the bulk of the book. The values he chooses for the parameters are not justified in detail, but a series of instructions are provided on how to make calculations for prediction of planetary motions. [Such sets of instructions got to be called 'algorithms' following the Iranian mathematician Al-Khwarizmi (nineth century C.E.), who transmitted many Indian mathematical ideas, along with his own very significant additions, to West Asia.] In the process however several brilliant new mathematical ideas are introduced by Āryabhaṭa but his objective is to make the calculations straight-forward and rapid. We could say that he invented the subject of 'algorithmic astronomy', and proceeded to present its first exposition in 499 C.E.

Box 2

Baudhāsyana-Sulvasūtra[3]

1.1 The various constructions of sacrificial fires are now given.
1.2 We shall explain the methods of measuring areas of their (different) figures (drawn) on the ground.
1.3 Now the measure of an *aṅgula* 14 *anus* (grain of *Panicum milliaceum*); according to others, (it is) 34 *tilas* (*sesamum indicum*) placed broad side on. One small *pada* is 10 *aṅgulas* each; one *prādeśa; a* 12 *aṅgula*; one *pṛthā* and one *uttarayuga* 13 *aṅgula* each; one (big) *pada* 15 *aṅgula*...

1.12 The areas (of the squares) produced separately by the length and the breadth of a rectangle together equal the area (of the square) produced by the diagonal.
1.13 This is observed in rectangles having sides 3 and 4, 12 and 5, 15 and 8, 7 and 24, 12 and 35, 15 and 36.

Euclid's Five Postulates ('Axioms')

1. Given any two points, there is a straight line containing them.
2. Given any straight line segment, we can extend it indefinitely to both sides.
3. There is a circle with any given center and radius.
4. All right angles are equal.
5. Given straight line and any point not in it, there is exactly one straight line parallel to the given one and containing that point.

There are some conclusions we can draw from these comparisons. In the first place we realize that there appear to have been scientific contacts very early between Greece and India, but what was borrowed or taken was extremely selective. One fascinating puzzle is why India apparently borrowed the *idea* of epicycles (but not the details), whereas it totally ignored Euclid, who made no impact at all; in fact he was not translated into Sanskrit till the eighteenth century! I consider that this fact must be of fundamental significance, for Euclid has been virtually worshipped in the West: his *Elements* are next only to the Bible in readership over the centuries. Furthermore the Indian refusal to be impressed by Euclid survived centuries of Muslim rule in different parts of India, even though Islamic scholars were also admirers of Euclid. It almost looks as if the Indians took the view that (for example) the theorem of Pythagoras was a matter of observation and inference; I fancy that they did not think that its deduction from a set of axioms was either useful or interesting, because they were skeptical about the reliability of the axioms. Similarly, although Āryabhaṭa does not say so, it would seem that he would have had great reservations (in retrospect most justified) in accepting the physical model of Ptolemy; after all Indians had no philosophical problems with the concepts of infinity, surds, vacuum etc., as the Greeks did. On the other hand Āryabhaṭa finds the mathematical model very convenient in helping to make computations, and proceeds to devise very clever algorithms to carry out such calculations.

We may summarise the situation by saying that the Greek paradigm appears to have been axioms or models through logical deduction to theorem or result; the Indian approach seems to have been observation through algorithm to validated conclusion. Contrary to popular perceptions Indian astronomers were very good at observation; the parameters in Āryabhaṭa's algorithm were repeatedly fine-tuned over the centuries, as observation revealed discrepancies; so verification was very much a part of the Indian approach. We may also recall here the comment made in 1790 by the eighteenth century British mathematician John Playfair, then a well-known professor at Edinburgh, now remembered as the author of 'Playfair's Axiom'. (This formulated the notorious fifth axiom of Euclid in the form in which it is most widely used today, namely as it appears in Box 2.) Playfair was so impressed by the accuracy of Indian astronomical calculations that, in a review he published in 1790, he contemplated (but dismissed) the possibility that 'some ages ago there had arisen a Newton among the Brahmins . . . and a De La Grange . . .'; he preferred the explanation that accurate astronomical observations had been made in India as early as 3100 B.C.E.

Incidentally Āryabhaṭa had a profound influence on Indian astronomy, for almost as long as Ptolemy had on western astronomy. And we could say that, as far as astronomy and mathematics were concerned, there was a rapid change in India between the middle of the fifth century and of the seventh century, i.e. between Āryabhaṭa and Brahmagupta. If we accept the definition of revolution given earlier we can say that an algoristic or mathematical revolution occurred in India in those two centuries, or more precisely between the time of writing of the Āryabhaṭa (499 C.E.) and the *khaṅḍa-khādyaka* (665 C.E.) of Brahmagupta.

A strong belief in models has an interesting concomitant, namely the notion of fraud. The history of western science is shot through with the idea of theories and models and of fraud. Ptolemy himself has been accused of fraud; so in more recent times have Galileo, Newton, Mendel, Millikan and a great variety of other less well-known figures. I believe the reason for this can be traced to faith in two-valued logic, namely the idea that answers to questions have to be yes or no; models have to be true or false. (There is no fundamental reason to believe that models are unique; more than one model may at any time be able to explain a given set of observations, to some specified accuracy.) Scientists get carried away by their models, and often encounter a situation where there may be discrepancies between model and observation—in the crucial cases small but not negligible. (If the discrepancies are large the theory would of course be quickly rejected.) If the scientist falls in love with his model he is tempted to ignore some of those inconvenient observations that do not agree, as all the names mentioned above did at one time or the other. If on the other hand observation is the starting point and one has no great faith in any particular model, as the situation was in India, the question of fraud does not arise. Indian scientists, even classical ones, do not appear to have accused each other of fraud. This could not have been mere politeness, as they did make charges of ignorance or even stupidity (as Brahmagupta did on Āryabhaṭa, for example). We could say that fraud is the besetting sin of a model-making scientific culture.

All these issues are connected with the subject often called Logic. There were several schools of logic in India, but both Indian and western scholars have often said that there was no truly formal deductive logic in India. On the other hand Indian logic seems to have been more nearly related to inference. (To oversimplify matters somewhat, we could say that in the Indian view the only reliable axioms would themselves have to be the result of valid inference. The Indian insistence on providing examples in any syllogistic argument has been seen by some western scholars as superfluous and irrational, but the chief purpose of examples could well have been to keep the 'axioms' realistic. What example would Ptolemy have been able to give for his assumption of a crystalline spherical shell in the heavens?)

As time passes, it is not at all clear that this rather fastidious Indian position was either unjustified or inferior. The developments in physics and mathematics in the twentieth century would seem to vindicate the skeptical Indian philosophical position on two-valued logic. For example Heisenberg's uncertainty principle and the wave-particle duality of quantum mechanics would not at all be philosophically disturbing to a classical Indian mind. When Gödel's theorem was 'proved' in the 30s and showed how a system of deductive logic had to be incomplete, one can almost hear the applause he would receive from classical Indian logicians. I must of course hasten to add that this does not for a moment mean that ancient Indians had any inkling (let alone knowledge) of quantum mechanics or of the kind of fundamental inadequacies in deductive logic that were demonstrated by Gödel's technically complicated proof. All that one can say is that these twentieth century discoveries were philosophically acceptable, and even gratifyingly confirmatory, to a mind reared in Indian systems of thought.

From this point of view what a classical Indian logician would have found most disturbing is not the science of the twentieth century but that of three centuries earlier: namely the spectacular success of Newton in providing a physical-mathematical model that was algorizable and so often agreed with observation or experiment to a most remarkable degree in so many widely different situations. The power of Newtonian mechanics, both terrestrial and celestial, was considered amazing by his European contemporaries; in India it would have further been considered philosophically mysterious, puzzling and disturbing. The fact that one could go so far with just three laws of motion and the law of gravitation was something that I believe was the result of an enterprise that Indian scientists would not even have contemplated (although the *idea* of gravitation was present in earlier Indian work). We can say that Indian civilization paid its ultimate tribute to the genius of Newton when S. Chandrasekhar produced what can legitimately be considered a twentieth century *bhāṣya* on the *Principia.*

On the whole the Indian approach to scientific problems seems to have been severely practical. The classical Indian scientist would have applauded what some western scientists have recently said about models being 'useful lies' and mathematics being like botany; if they turned out to be more it would be astonishing. But then the fastidiousness of Indian philosophy and logic have been historically very expensive for the country.

This view leads to an interesting aside on modern Indian science. Science in India during the last hundred years or so has very largely followed the western style, and there have been many significant contributions. But model-making still does not appear to come naturally to us. From this point of view it would seem that the truly exceptional scientist in India was S. N. Bose, whose formulation of a new statistical model for the kind of particles that have now came to be known as Bosons was very much high science in the western spirit. (Paradoxically, though, the Bose model was really the outcome of a counting exercise—but based on what for the time were unusual rules.) But the very rarity of this kind of achievement shows the enduring power of culturally determined patterns of thought.

There is no time to go through other related arguments in detail, so let me summarise the position as I see it by stating a few paradoxes about Indian science.

- There have been few physical/mathematical models originating in India.
- The philosophical liberalism and pluralism of India did not give birth to a modern science here. (There is the alarming possibility that the pluralism was actually a hindrance, not a help.)
- Twentieth century physics not only did not produce philosophically disturbing thoughts in India but in fact may be said to have confirmed ancient Indian suspicions about the nature of logic and model-making.
- The Indian preference for inference over deductive logic seems ultimately to have been justified.
- The classical Indian scientific tradition is, if anything, over-pragmatic. Thus there was never any truly pure mathematics in India. There was brilliant mathematics, but this was usually inspired by astronomy, commerce or some similar application.

We must of course admire the power of a scientific approach that has led it to go back on some of its most cherished assumptions after four centuries of continuous achievement. We must at the same time also admire a set of philosophical views that, in spite of short-term losses, appear to have been fundamentally sound.

While the great mystery, therefore, is how Newtonian science got so far, using deductive logic on the basis of a model with four laws, we can also see that it was not completely successful: relativity and quantum mechanics upset the Newtonain apple-cart. It is now a common-place to say that science is only tentative; as the British physicist J J Thomson once said, science is policy, not creed. It may not be able—ever—to give us the truth, whatever that may be, but we must admit that it has been extraordinarily successful. Modern science seems to have acquired—perhaps by fortunate accident—the property that the great Buddhist philosopher Nāgārjuna called *prāpakatva*: i.e. it delivers what it promises; it may not be Truth, but it is honest.

I believe it is this characteristic of modern science that Einstein had in mind when he talked about how the greatest mystery about the world is that it is comprehensible; or when Wigner wondered at the 'unreasonable effectiveness of mathematics in the natural sciences'. Is it possible that the great pragmatic civilizations of the East misjudged how far the quest for truth might go based on what they considered shaky foundations? Were our rules of inference too stringent—our pursuit of Truth so demanding—that we missed the gains that could accrue from a less fastidious approach to knowledge, which (again mysteriously) turns out not only to be often 'correct', but also to lend itself to such systematic enlargement of its scope?

I want to conclude by saying that the view one takes may well depend on the physical and intellectual tools one has. If the phenomenon is too complex and complicated (e.g. biology, meteorology, social science), one may be forced to resort to data analysis to infer patterns, without the aid of axioms or models; if on the other hand the phenomena are simpler (physics, chemistry, aerospace science), it seems worthwhile to try to construct suitable minimalist models or to discover the most parsimonious set of axioms, and 'axiomatization' becomes a worthwhile goal. I presume modern science will go ahead pursuing both paths—it is, in the final analysis, a question of choice regarding the most appropriate strategies at any given point of time in our never-ending attempts to organize the reality of nature.

Till now I have scarcely mentioned the Industrial Revolution. There is not enough time to consider it separately, but we must note that the pioneers of this revolution, like Newcomen, Watt and Stephenson, were by and large not highly educated people. Nevertheless their own attitude was undoubtedly influenced to a considerable extent by the changed intellectual climate in England that followed the scientific revolution. To the extent that this revolution did not occur in the East, the chances that an industrial revolution would occur here were also lower.

However it must be clearly understood that, at the times we are speaking of, the East in general did not feel the need to change the prevailing global order, i.e. it represented status quo powers, whereas Europe was the economic underdog that wanted change. The reason for this was the relative prosperity of India, noted by the many foreign travellers who came here, and sung about in English poetry. Andre Gunder Frank has made a detailed study of India in the world economy between 1400 A.D. and 1750 A.D.[4] He notes that some eighty per cent of the world's GNP in the centuries before 1750 came from China, India and West Asia; indeed Europe at that time suffered from a chronic balance of payments problem. The core regions, especially of industrial production, were in China and India, which were also the primary centres of accumulation of capital in the world system. Europe was not a major economic force as far as eastern countries were concerned. The common global economic expansion that started around 1400 A.D. benefitted Asian countries earlier and more than it did the rest of the world. Interestingly the Europeans pursued policies in the seventeenth and eighteenth centuries that were very similar to those that Asian economies adopted around 1950: namely encouragement of import substitution and then of export promotion. However the introduction of labour-saving and power-generating technologies in Europe slowly began to favour West over East. Indeed the same Indian industries that were so strong till the middle of the eighteenth century, namely textiles, iron and steel etc., were virtually wiped out in the first few decades of the eighteenth century.

In summary I would like to suggest that, apart from the various factors that have been extensively discussed, there are two that played a major role in why the scientific and industrial revolutions did not take place in India.

First, from an economic point of view, the East in general was strong and prosperous, the status quo was comfortable and there was no great internal pressure to change the global order. India's 'tropical' productivity in agriculture was so high that land revenue was a sufficient source of income for government, i.e., we were largely (but not solely) a sun-and-water economy. So there was no great pressure to promote foreign trade, but in spite of this India's trade balance was in general favourable. Europe had to pay for Indian goods in silver because India would not accept anything else; and that silver came from the

Americas. Furthermore Indian rulers had no ambitions to subdue countries beyond their border lands, if only because our immediate neighbours on the other side had perforce to live in desert, high mountain or dense jungle. (The only attractive neighbourhood was South East Asia, where Indian influence did indeed spread in the second half of the first millennium.) To West Asians India must have seemed like a subcontintental oasis, to Europeans like a subcontinental hot house.

The second reason was that the Indian scientific and logical tradition was weak on devising physical/mathematical models for nature, in part because there appears to have been strong philosophical skepticism about the validity of such models. Although from a fundamental point of view this skepticism was not unjustified, in the three centuries between 1600 and 1900 it was discovered in Europe that spectacularly successful models could be devised. This effort in Europe would not have been possible without the injection of eastern inventions—major technical ones from China and brilliant mathematical ones from India, both through West Asia. These inventions were married to an old Greek faith in universal principles, also served up by West Asians, in a remarkable episode of cultural exchange and transfer. The resulting synthesis turned out to be unreasonably successful, and revived science in Europe after a long period of nearly 1500 years of utter stagnation.

What is the future? We could ask whether it may now be the turn of the East similarly to combine their ancient strengths with the successes of western scientific methods. This of course cannot be legislated, but will new strengths emerge as West-inspired science and technology spread in the East?

*An extended version of this article has appeared in Interdisciplinary Science Reviews 28: 54-66 (2003).

NOTES

1. Kitto, H.D.F. 1957. *The Greeks.* p. 190. Baltimore, Maryland, Penguin Books.
2. Ifrah, Georges. 1998. *The Universal History of Numbers.* London: Harvill Press.
3. Sen, S.N. and Bag, A.K. 1983. The *Śulbasūtras.* New Delhi: Indian National Academy.
4. Frank, Andre Gunder. 1966. *Economic and Political Weekly,* 27 July PS 50; *Re-Orient.* Vistaar Publications.

CHAPTER 20

Structure of Philosophical Knowledge: In Defence of the Metaphysics of First Principles

R.C. Pradhan

The present essay aims at re-examining the prospect of the metaphysics of first principles which occupies the centre-stage of philosophical inquiry. Philosophy has often been called the science of first principles precisely because there is the need of uncovering the first principles in the domain of human knowledge. The first principles are the presuppositions of human knowledge. It is because of the centrality of these presuppositions that they have been part of the world-views which philosophers have offered from time to time.

In this paper I will work out a framework for understanding the first principles which have been a matter of controversy throughout the ages. I will also suggest that the exact nature of the principles may differ but we cannot do without such principles. Metaphysics, whatever its form maybe, needs a set of first principles which are, by definition, non-empirical and transcendental.

I

PHILOSOPHICAL KNOWLEDGE: METHOD, LIMITS AND LEGITIMACY

The question which perplexes philosophers the most is the legitimacy of philosophy itself as a cognitive inquiry. So questions arise: Does philosophy discover a new domain of knowledge? If so, how does the domain of philosophical knowledge differ from that of scientific knowledge? The positive answer to these questions consists in the supposition that philosophy constitutes an independent and autonomous domain of knowledge which does not depend on the domain of scientific knowledge for its validation.

Philosophical knowledge is self-validated in the sense that it develops its own method of inquiry and criteria of justification. Philosophical explanations are meant only for clarifying the meaning and coherence of the philosophical truths rather than for testing them in the world because of the fact that philosophical knowledge, unlike scientific knowledge, is not accountable to the world in the sense that the philosophical truths are not derived from our experience of the world. Philosophical systems remain valid even if the philosophical concepts do not have matching correspondence with the world. The concepts like Form, Substance, Soul, Absolute, *Māyā, Brahman,* etc., do not directly apply to the empirical world as we find it. These concepts have evolved in course of the development of certain philosophical systems. Therefore, however remote these concepts may appear to be from our everyday experience of the world, they cannot be dispensed with while understanding the philosophical systems.

There are philosophical systems which come closer to science and common sense and have such concepts as Matter, Mind, Physical World, Life, Consciousness, etc., which seem to be closer to our empirical observations of the world. But none of them are empirical concepts because none of them are products of our experiential encounter with the world. Therefore, one can imagine that if the world which we experience in our everyday life changes, we may not be obliged to dispense with these philosophically loaded concepts. If, *ex hypothesi,* the universe stops functioning the way it functioned in the past, the philosophical concepts like Nature, World, Law, Causality, etc. will remain meaningful and perhaps coherent, even though they may not apply in the actual world because they could apply to some possible worlds. For example, the idea of immortality of man remains coherent even if there is not a single instance of an immortal human being in the actual world. Thus philosophical concepts remain coherent and meaningful irrespective of whether they are true and applicable in the actual world or not.

Philosophy, like logic and mathematics, is not directly derived from the world. It is because its theories are largely conceptual and therefore need no validation through experience of the world. The truths of logic and mathematics are established to be true *a priori* and are not dependent on the world for their truth or falsity. The truths of logic are tautologies which speak nothing about the world.[1] The truths of mathematics are no less conceptual in character, though Kant[2] argues, for transcendental reasons, that mathematical judgments are synthetic *a priori.* Even in the latter case mathematics is not accountable to the empirical world, that is, it is not dependent on the empirical world for its validation. It is another matter that the actual world responds favourably to our mathematical constructions.

Now one may say that philosophy is closer to the formal sciences in certain respects than to the natural sciences in its quest for truth. Like the formal systems, philosophical systems are also conceptual constructions. The philosophical truths are therefore bound to be conceptual and grammatical[3] in character. It is no wonder that philosophy provides conceptual schemes or maps of the possible worlds so as to make these worlds intelligible. In this sense, though the philosophical constructions are regarding the world, the philosophical constructions themselves remain largely indifferent to the actual world. That is, philosophical propositions are true whatever may happen to the actual world.

Philosophy provides worldviews which are the conceptual structures for understanding the universe around us. The worldviews are the ways the world is made intelligible to us. These worldviews are not dictated to us by the world, but are rather made available by the human mind for understanding the world. Human mind constructs the worldviews for its own benefit, that is, for making the world intelligible to us. There are multiple worldviews because human mind is creative and is interested in creating new ways of understanding the world. The worldviews, as I have indicated earlier, are not accountable to the world because there is no perfect match between the world and the worldviews. The worldviews are *about* the world but *are not thereby subject to the contingencies in the world.* The conceptual necessities created within a worldview are not justified by the facts in the world.[4]

The method of constructing a worldview or conceptual scheme is a matter of conceptual decision (or, in Wittgenstein's words, a grammatical decision[5]). It is not a scientific or empirical decision. Therefore the legitimacy of a worldview is dependent on the conceptual grounds which the philosophers offer. Philosophers are allowed to have conceptual preference in view of their own intellectual light or the light of reason, to use a Leibnizian phrase. That is why it is often said that philosophy is the gift of human reason.

II

REASON AS THE SOURCE OF METAPHYSICAL TRUTHS

A worldview is known for its conceptual coherence and logical consistency. Worldviews are therefore based on reason and the principles of logic When a worldview is offered, it is proposed to be a comprehensive account of the world. The worldviews are thus the metaphysical systems which provide different ways we can understand the world. Each metaphysical system offers a comprehensive system of thought about reality.

The metaphysicians provide reason for preference for one kind of worldview rather than another. Why the worldview$_1$ is preferred to worldview$_2$ depends on what conceptual simplicity the former provides. A worldview that makes the understanding of the world simpler is preferred to the worldview that makes it complex. Understanding of the world is a matter of intellectual necessity because in the conceptual scheme of the world alone have we such necessary statements as 'The world is spatio-temporal', 'The world is law-governed', and so on. These general law-like statements are metaphysically necessary because they constitute the framework for understanding the world. These truths are part of the worldview which metaphysics offers. They are necessary because they are derived from reason and are not the products of our everyday experience.

Metaphysical thinking is a way of discovering the basic structure of reality. It is the task of reason to decipher the essential or necessary structures which underlie the phenomena. The phenomena that are presented to us are subjected to philosophical analysis for making the essential structures evident to reason. That is the reason why philosophers have followed the lead of reason in discovering the truths regarding the necessary structures of the world.

The worldviews which philosophers offer present the basic structures of the world within a conceptual vocabulary. This vocabulary has to demarcate which of its statements are necessary and which of them are contingent. That is, it has to make a basic distinction between the necessary truths as distinguished from the contingent truths. For example, if we a take a system of metaphysics like that of Spinoza or Leibniz we can very well distinguish between what is necessary in the system and what is contingent. In either of these systems the truths regarding the substance are necessary while those regarding the modes of existence of things in the world are contingent. Thus philosophers have made a conscious effort to preserve necessity as a crucial component of the conceptual schemes. Metaphysics, in short, strives to preserve necessary truths in its conceptual scheme.

But now the question is: What is the source of this necessity? Is it language or reality which is the source of necessity? To this one of the answers has been that necessity is a matter of the linguistic description of the world and not of the world as such. That is, necessity is a matter of how we describe reality and not how reality is as such. Necessary truths of logic and mathematics have been taken by the proponents of this view as candidates for the necessary truths in language. The logical positivists who have boldly claimed that necessary truths are linguistic in character have argued that necessary truths are logical in nature and so are found only in language. There is no necessity, according to them, which is found in the world.[6]

The truths of logic and mathematics are necessary because of the fact that they are not derived from our experience of the world. Similarly, since the truths in metaphysics are not derived from the world, they are found to be necessary. That is, the metaphysician may claim that metaphysical truths are necessary because that is how the world is to be viewed. What the world is in itself is beyond the comprehension of the metaphysician. Kant, for example, has argued that necessity is mind-dependent for the reason that it is only the mind which decides which truths are necessary and which are not.[7] There is little that the world can contribute to this because, according to this view, necessary truths in metaphysics are prescribed by the human reason and not by the world.

However, there can be the opposite view that necessary truths of metaphysics are true of the world because the world as described in a conceptual scheme is the only world real for us. In that case metaphysical truths are necessary in the world as well because the world could not be otherwise than what the metaphysician prescribes. Thus there is a happy convergence of language and the world on what is to be taken as metaphysically necessary.

However, since there are different metaphysical systems claiming to provide different necessary structures of the world, it is imperative to know which metaphysical systems decipher the necessary structures correctly. The materialist, for example, may claim that the necessary structure of the world lies in the physical laws of the universe, whereas the idealist claims that the universe is necessarily mental and spiritual. It is now a matter of conceptual preference which metaphysical scheme is to be offered. The materialist is convinced that the laws of matter alone govern the phenomena of the universe. He is not ready to accept that matter itself maybe a phenomenon of a still deeper reality that is not material in nature.

Materialists[8] in general argue that the universe is governed by the mechanical laws and that consciousness and other mental phenomena are explainable through the laws of physics. This worldview is sufficient in explaining only the material phenomena and not others which cannot be reduced to the material phenomena. The only ground for offering this worldview is that there is a conceptual preference exercised by the metaphysician. He accepts one set of laws as fundamental and the rest as secondary to those laws. The idealist metaphysician, on the contrary, argues that the mental phenomena are fundamental and so need to be treated as necessary. He claims that since the metaphysical truths regarding the universe are discovered by mind , there cannot be anything more basic than mind itself.

Now, the choice between the two conflicting worldviews has to be based on reasoning and the conceptual preference based on logic. The preference cannot be arbitrary and irrational. It must be based on arguments as to why one system of metaphysics is preferable to another. Just as there is theory choice in science so also there is theory choice in metaphysics.[9] But while theory choice in science is guided by the theory's conformity with the world, metaphysical theory choice is solely guided by reason. It is through critical analysis that a metaphysical system is found to be more acceptable than another.

III

THE EXTERNAL AND INTERNAL QUESTIONS

Carnap's[10] distinction between the external and internal questions regarding the conceptual frameworks in science and mathematics needs to be sorted out in the present context. The distinction above referred to is between those questions which arise *about* a theory and those which arise *within* a theory. The former are about the choice of the theory and the grounds thereof, while the latter are about the things or entities which fall within the theory. Carnap's main argument is that philosophy raises only *external* questions and not *internal* questions because the external questions alone demand theory choice. These questions are such that we can adopt a theory only on the ground that they are relating to the language we adopt for describing reality. Language is a matter of choice and this freedom can be exercised only on the ground that theories are themselves languages of some sort.

Carnap's argument presupposes that there are multiple theories possible and that all are not equally acceptable. This leads Carnap to argue that theories are chosen not on empirical grounds but on the ground that they fulfill the demand of rationality. Besides, according to him, there is no metaphysical reason possible, or even intelligible, to support a particular theory against another theory. All theory choice is pragmatic[11] based on the rational utility of the theory.

Quine[12] rejects the above distinction on the ground that the internal questions are as much pragmatic as the external questions and that the internal questions can be collapsed into the external ones precisely on the ground that the theories and the things both belong to our conceptual vocabulary. Given this fact it is now imperative to see that for Quine there is no distinction between metaphysics and science because both are continuous with each other. Metaphysics is a more general science because it only elevates the scientific questions to a higher level of generality. However, metaphysics is as much a matter of theory choice as science itself. Quine's metaphor of Neurath's boat[13] is apt for showing that science and metaphysics both are conceptual constructions for negotiating with the world with our linguistic and conceptual tools.

The fact of the matter, however, is that there are rational constraints on our theory choice and this itself demands a space for reason and logic among our conceptual tools. So the matter of theory choice cannot be left open indefinitely. There must be a resting ground for our conceptual preference. This resting ground or foundation cannot be the language we choose because the language we choose must remain itself rationally grounded. This leads us to the Kantian considerations of the *a priori* acceptability of a system on the ground of human reason.

Kant opens up the possibility of a transcendental argument for accepting a metaphysical system. The transcendental metaphysics arises, not because metaphysical truths are concerning the choice of a theoretical framework, but because there are necessary truths in that system which cannot be accepted just pragmatically but rationally. In that case the whole idea of external and internal questions is dissolved and science and metaphysics are seen as two independent modes of thinking. Though there is theory choice in both, metaphysical theory choice is more fundamental making reason play a decisive role. A metaphysical system is chosen because it is rationally found to provide the necessary structure of reality.

IV

THE TRANSCENDENTAL ARGUMENT

What needs to be emphasized is the possibility of a transcendental argument for the necessary truths in metaphysics. The argument is not whether there are such truths in metaphysics but how they are possible. The Kantian answer is that such truths are the same as the synthetic *a priori* truths available in our conceptual scheme. The sentences like '2 + 2 = 4' and 'The world has a causal order' are such truths that are metaphysically necessary and they derive their necessity from the human reason itself. This Kantian derivation of the metaphysical truths from reason is valid on the ground that there is no way we can avoid the rational constraints on the metaphysical truths themselves. Metaphysics for Kant is a transcendental way to the truths which are necessary.

It is well known that Kant[14] does not accept metaphysics in the sense in which transcendental truths have no constraint at all. Such free floating truths regarding soul, God and the world have no validity because there are no constraints on them derived from reason. Metaphysics, for Kant, is constrained transcendentally to make truths amenable to reason and to be made available for understanding the empirical reality. Kant does not make metaphysics irrelevant to the world because, according to him, the necessary truths of metaphysics are the presuppositions of the phenomenal world.

According to Kant, metaphysical truths do not have the same status as the scientific statements regarding the world. For him, the metaphysical truths are transcendental while the scientific statements are empirical in nature. He opposes the empiricist move to dissolve metaphysics into science. Metaphysics is autonomous in that it delivers its own truths from a conceptual space of necessities. This space cannot be dissolved and disowned. Putnam[15] takes the empiricists to task for dissolving the space of necessities in their quest for symmetry between science and metaphysics and their anti-Kantian zeal to abolish synthetic *a priori* truths. The empiricists converted the necessary truths to linguistic truths thus making them ontologically free-floating. This led to the collapse of the Kantian project of first principles

The empiricists, more specifically the positivists, have done no service to science, the cause of which they espoused, because they have rejected the very possibility of science discovering the laws of the empirical world. If science itself is inductive and is based on the principle of verifiability, how can it explain how the laws of science operate in the universe which is largely inaccessible to empirical experience? The laws of the universe available to sense-experience are limited. Therefore verifiability of the scientific laws becomes an obstacle to scientific progress as science progresses through its intuitive understanding of the laws of the universe. It is also a fact that science itself demands a set of laws of logic and metaphysics which have no verifiability at all. The positivistic science is without a metaphysical foundation because it denies itself the advantage of the necessary truths which metaphysics provides.

V

METAPHYSICS AND THE LIMITS OF SCIENCE

Natural sciences themselves presuppose metaphysics because they need the idea of reality and its necessary structure for making their own discoveries available in a formal language. Empirical sciences have their limits in the fact that they presuppose rather than explain that there are scientific truths and that the truths are accessible to human reason. Besides, they presuppose the fact that the universe is rational in structure and that beyond the apparent chaos of the universe there is a rational order.[16] These presuppositions are metaphysical in character and are not subject to empirical verification. This shows that there are limits to the empiricist approach to science. Science itself presupposes what is non-empirical which is the ground of what is empirical.

What Kant and Husserl call 'transcendental'[17] is precisely that which is non-empirical and yet is the ground of the possibility of the empirical. In this sense there is a space of the non-empirical which cannot be dissolved by hard empiricism. The non-empirical is the domain of the laws of the reason which cannot be merely psychological laws. They are what are contributed by the human reason. They could aptly be called the synthetic *a priori* truths for the simple reason that they are not linguistic truths, nor are they the truths derived purely from experience. If there is a space for reason to articulate these truths, then they could be called metaphysically necessary truths.

The positivists' move to linguisticize necessary truths[18] fails for the reason that truths are truths and not linguistic entities and that they are not derivable from language as such. Language is the medium of truth and so cannot manufacture it. That is why Wittgenstein[19] holds that language has its limits and that, though grammar provides expression to the truths, the truths are not due to grammatical decisions. Grammar can take care of its rules but it cannot take care of what the grammatical rules are about. The truth that there is already a world which is presupposed by language is not a truth of grammar but something metaphysical. Similarly, that there is a self which thinks is not a matter of language and the world. It is transcendental[20].

The transcendental truths are the limits of language and the world. They are presupposed by language and the world. Hence science must accept these truths as belonging to metaphysics and not to the domain of the empirical. This is a Kantian legacy which can be disowned by science only at its own peril. Science as such is a rational inquiry and so it needs the metaphysical foundation in the human reason. This of course does not exclude its being rooted in the empirical experience.

VI

REASON, THE FIRST PRINCIPLES AND THE POSSIBILITY OF ALTERNATIVE METAPHYSICS

The idea of reason needs elaboration since there is no one definite meaning of 'reason' or of its cognate terms such as 'rational' and 'conceptual'. Reason stands for a set of activities which we may call acts of reasoning. These acts are governed by logic and its laws. Such acts therefore maybe called rational acts. The nature of these acts is such that they define rationality itself. Rationality characterizes human thoughts in general.

Science, like art and religion, is such a rational act. It is an elaborate act of knowing the world with the help of certain laws supposed to be true of the world. Thus science becomes a discipline of the reason in its search for ground-level laws to explain the phenomena of the world. It is a discipline which is accountable to reason and the world. Unlike art and religion, it is not bound to cultures and traditions. Culture is specific to time and history, while science transcends to a great extent the limits of local cultures. That is why science claims universality, while, on the contrary, art and religion are products of cultures.

Philosophy rises above science, on the one hand, and art and religion on the other because it provides a space for critical inquiry. It is accountable to reason and reason alone and so it can afford to be transcendental while science cannot. Science has to be rooted in human experience; so is the case with art and religion. But philosophy cannot be subservient to experience because it can critically analyze experience itself. Philosophy can examine the limits of experience. Thus philosophy inherits the reason's capacity to transcend its own categories through critical reflection.

Being transcendental is no misuse of reason because it has to be transcendental in order to be critical. And to be critical is to be analytical and probing by nature. Therefore reason searches for its own roots and its own laws of operation. These laws are the first principles which Aristotle, Kant, Hegel and many philosophers have talked about. These principles can be defined as those which are the primary sources of our knowledge of reality. They constitute the basic structure of human thought about reality. These basic laws of reason include the laws of logic as well as the laws of metaphysics.

In metaphysics the first principles are of a wide variety. There is no single set of metaphysical principles which could be called 'the principles of metaphysics'. Each metaphysical system has to search for its own first principles. The Aristotelian first principles are not the same as the Kantian ones. Similarly, the Kantian ones are different from the Hegelian and the Advaitic principles. Thus there are alternative sets of principles in metaphysics. And yet they are all derivable from reason. That is why there is rational and cognitive affinity among all metaphysics systems. They constitute one large family of metaphysical systems as distinguished from the family of scientific systems.

The opponents of metaphysics may argue that metaphysics itself is an illusory discipline and that the idea of first principles is equally illusory. They may say that reason has died with Hegel and that the enlightenment project of rationality itself is under scrutiny by postmodernism. There is a serious debate going on as to whether there is reason in the universal sense. The postmodernists like Foucault and Derrida have questioned the very idea of one universal reason which transcends time and history.[21] This has seriously undermined the enlightenment project of Descartes, Kant and Hegel.

The anti-metaphysical argument does not take into account the fact that reason itself is self-critical and therefore it cannot be called dead in the postmodernist thought which is known for its self-critical nature. The postmodernist attack on reason is a self-critical move of reason itself against its own dogmatic assertions about the metaphysics of the enlightenment. This may mean that the first principles typically associated with Descartes and Kant can be discarded. But the fact of the matter is that reason itself fights back against the postmodernist undermining of reason.

Reason cannot disown its prerogative to provide the first principles which guide all activities of man including science and religion. It cannot cease to philosophize because it cannot cease to be critical by raising fundamental questions about science and religion. This is the main reason why philosophy keeps itself open to fresh ideas and categories. That is why the first principles remain changing as the metaphysical systems change.

VII

REASON, HISTORY AND THE TRANSCENDENTAL PRINCIPLES

There has been a debate in recent years as to whether reason, if admitted, could be transcendental and ahistorical as Kant and Hegel have claimed it to be. According to D.P. Chattopadhyaya[22], human reason is rooted in time and history because it is shaped by the human life-world. The nature of the life-world is such that our rational activities including our philosophy and science are historical and human in nature in the ultimate analysis. Thus there is no conflict between reason and history. Both are part of the same life-world in which reason shapes its metaphysics and interprets the historical events and things in the world. Metaphysics provides the principles by which history and the world are themselves studied and made intelligible. Chattopadhyaya argues that the so-called transcendental reason cut off from history cannot be simply conceived.[23]

Now one can argue that there is no conflict between reason as it operates in its own domain and as it stands vīs-a-vīs history. No doubt reason is human and anthropological and therefore the human sciences are sociological in character. Besides, it cannot be denied that even metaphysics carries to some extent the human interest. Thus one can agree with Chattopadhyaya that the historical roots of human reason are self-evident, but it is not self-evident that reason cannot be transcendental. It can be argued that philosophy lays down how science and history are rational in nature. In this sense philosophy is transcendental as it is the source of the principles by which science and history can be understood.

The harmony between the historical and human, on the one hand, and the transcendental on the other is made possible by philosophy. It is philosophy which makes the two halves come together. To make one more prominent than the other can only jeopardize the balance between the ground-level thinking and the thinking of the higher type. Transcendental thinking does not disown the historical but appropriates it in its overarching framework. In this sense, the historical is comprehended within the metaphysical framework because history itself is without meaning without the active participation of reason in it.

The relation between the historical and the transcendental is preserved by Kant and Husserl and many other transcendental philosophers. This is evident in Kant's distinction between empirical realism and transcendental idealism in which the same reality is approached from two different but interconnected standpoints. It is not implied that only one standpoint is right, rather both together make one single frame of reference. Husserl also allows for the possibility of transcendental philosophy by keeping the two standpoints together. He has not denied the reality of the empirical world though his interest is in making the transcendental standpoint available. It is here that one can notice the fact that reason is not partial only to the transcendental; it is equally responsible towards the historical and the empirical. One can argue for the compatibility of the two standpoints by showing that the empirical itself demands the transcendental and vice versa. There cannot be any empirical domain without a corresponding transcendental domain.

My argument is that the transcendental use of reason is not an illegitimate move because in this use alone is reason free from the contingencies of the empirical world. It is also free to assess its own powers and also to discover the principles which govern the empirical world. This is the reason why metaphysics is a legitimate discipline of the reason as the domain of the first principles. The first principles are the essences which philosophy discovers in its critical understanding of the domain of the empirical reality. These essences are the reason's own discoveries which it attributes to reality.

NOTES

1. Wittgenstein. 1961. *Tractatus Logico-Philosophicus.* D.F.Pears and B.F.McGuinness (trans.). London: Routledge and Kegan Paul. 6.1-6.11.
2. Kant. 1929. *The Critique of Pure Reason.* N.K.Smith (trans.). St. Martin's Press: Macmillan, pp. 41-62.
3. Wittgenstein. 1953. *Philosophical Investigations.* G.E.M. Anscombe (trans.). Oxford: Basil Blackwell, Sect. 90.
4. Ibid., Sects. 371-372.
5. Ibid., Sect. 373.
6. Logical Positivists do make a distinction between logical necessity and factual necessity. It is the latter that is traceable to the world, but it is not necessity that is worth the name, according to them.
7. Kant is emphatic on the internal necessity derivable from reason rather than on necessity found in the world. The internal necessity is guaranteed by the structure of human thought.
8. Churchland, P. M. 1984. *Matter and Consciousness.* Cambridge and Mass.: MIT Press.
9. Popper, Karl. 1963. *Conjectures and Refutations.* London: Routledge and Kegan Paul. pp. 184-200.
10. Carnap, Rudolf. 1956. "Empiricism, Semantics and Ontology". *Meaning and Necessity,* 2nd Edition. Chicago: Chicago University Press.
11. Ibid.
12. Quine, W.V. 1960. *Word and Object.* Cambridge and Mass.: MIT Press. pp. 270-276.
13. Ibid.
14. Kant.
15. Putnam, Hilary. 1995. "Logical Positivism, the Kantian Tradition and the Bounds of Sense". *The Philosophy of P.F. Strawson,* P.K. Sen and R.R. Verma (ed.). New Delhi: ICPR.
16. Chattopadyaya, D.P. 1996. *Science, Technology, Philosophy and Culture.* New Delhi: PHISPC.
17. Husserl, Edmund. 1970. *Crisis of European Sciences and Transcendental Phenomenology.* D. Carr (trans.). Evanston: Northwestern University Press. pp. 97-100.
18. Ayer, A.J. 1936. *Language, Truth and Logic* London: Gollancz. pp. 96-115.
19. Wittgenstein. 1953. *Philosophical Investigations.* G. E.M. Anscombe (trans.). Oxford: Basil Blackwell, and his *Tractatus Logico-Philosophicus.*
20. Wittgenstein. *Tractatus Logico-Philosophicus.* 5.632-5.633.
21. Farrell, Frank B. 1994. *Subjectivity, Realism and Postmodernism-The Recovery of the World.* Cambridge: Cambridge University Press. pp. 245-278.
22. Chattopadhyaya, D.P. 1989. *Knowledge, Freedom and Language.* New Delhi: Motilal Banarasidass.
23. Ibid.

CHAPTER 21

Reappraisal of the Civilizational Question: Why the Scientific Revolution did not take place in China or India?

Prajit K. Basu

INTRODUCTION

History of science inextricably involves explanation. What is it that one explains in history of science? The phenomena to be explained may belong to specific episodes in history of science, e.g., why did Joseph Priestley refuse to accept and employ the Principle of Conservation of Mass unlike Antoine Lavoisier? Or, why did Isaac Newton work on alchemy for more than twenty years? Or, why did the scientists decide to accept Darwin's theory and not Lamarck's? Or, why are the Indian alchemical texts strewn with sexual metaphors? Or, why did Europe provide the material and cultural grounds for scientific revolutions in the seventeenth century? Sometimes the questions are formulated with the expression 'how' and not with a 'why'. How did Newton arrive at the force law? Or, how did Robert Millikan measure the charge of electrons? While the first of the how-questions is ambiguous in that it may ask for the details of Newton's arguments so that one can 'see' the conceptual development of the Force Law, the same question can also be answered by apparently delineating the social and economic roots of Newton's work as Borris Hessen had tried to do. The second how-question is more descriptive and the historians of science very often use the answer to this question in order to answer what they take to be a more well-formed question.

Thus the details of Millikan's experiment were employed by Peter Galison to argue for his thesis that there are 'constraints' in performing experiments and also in bringing about an 'end' to an experiment. I have not said much about the why-questions raised or about their general nature. I will have something to say about them and about the answers to the why-questions in the first section of this paper. Viewing history of science as an explanation is neither unusual nor new. Philosophers like Jospeh Agassi, Maurice Finocchiaro, as well as sociologists of science like David Bloor or Simon Schaffer, or Barry Barnes, or Steven Shapin, in fact the social constructivists maybe said to be looking at science in order to explain the phenomena known as science. The intellectual historians of science like Alexander Koyre or I. B. Cohen and others, I think, are no different in that they have attempted, although in a very different way from the social constructivists, to explain the historical episodes of science.

In this paper I first attempt to analyze the different ways the why-questions in history of science are raised. I try to show that the logic of why-questions demands that only a certain kind of answers be offered to these questions. The logical analysis also shows how several kinds of why-questions can be raised. In the civilizational context, why-question(s) that Joseph Needham posed will be briefly reviewed in the next section. In the third section, the background assumptions required to pose the civilizational question will be probed and it will be argued that the question is ill-posed and provides no historiographical insight. The explanatory schema it engenders is at best misleading. I conclude by outlining the problematics to be developed on a key background assumption, that of universality.

I

THE LOGIC OF WHY-QUESTION

In this section, I discuss the logic of why-question. In this I follow mainly the work of van Fraassen[1] and of Belnap[2]. The attempt is to bring out the important features of why-questions and of the answers to these questions. The discussion, in this section, will probably throw some light on the civilizational question that Joesph Needham raised when he asked,

> Why modern science, the new or experimental philosophy of the time of Galileo had arisen *only* in European culture and not in Chinese or Indian?[3]

This has been an important why-question which had attracted and perhaps still attracts the attention of many researchers in the area of science studies. A clarification of the why-question raised above maybe possible when the logical features of why-questions in general are brought to bear on the particular civilizational (or grand) question at hand.

The logic of why-question is somewhat well understood. The pragmatics of questions and answers shows us that a why-question, Q, expressed by an interrogative, in a given context, is determined by three conditions. First, there must be a topic, Pk, of the question. To take an example, 'Why did Joseph Priestley believe that charcoal is a source of phlogiston?' is a why-question. The topic of the question is that Jospeh Priestley believed that charcoal is a source of phlogiston.

Second, there must be a contrast class, X, of which the topic, Pk, is a member. The contrast class, X, can be depending upon the situation, of various kinds. It might be as simple as a class which has only two members: (1) Jospeh Priestley believed that charcoal is a source of phlogiston; and (2) Joseph Priestley did not believe that charcoal is a source of phlogiston. Or the contrast class, X, may have members like: (1) Joseph Priestley believed that charcoal is a source of phlogiston; (2) Joseph Priesetley believed that water is a source of phlogiston; and (3) Joseph Priestley believed that metal calces are source of phlogiston. These contrast classes maybe viewed as sometimes bearing the logical burden of the linguistic expression 'rather than'. To take an example, the following why-question: why did it snow rather than rain, seems to be amenable to the above-mentioned analysis. The topic, Pk, of the question, is that it snowed. The contrast class, X, has two members: (1) it snowed; and (2) it rained. I qualify the view by the expression 'sometimes', in part, due to the fact that it maybe hard to arrive at an answer, in some cases, which will imply the topic of the question and also show that the other members, of the contrast class, are false or unlikely.

Third, there is a relevance relation, R. A proposition A is called relevant to Q just in case A bears relation R to the couple (Pk, X). This relevance relation is important because it is possible to have why-questions with the same Pk, but different X, or with different Pk, but same X. And in each case, a proposition that is relevant to Pk with respect to X, will probably be different. A why-question presupposes, therefore:

(a) its topic, Pk, is true;
(b) in its contrast class, X, only its topic is true; and
(c) at least one of the propositions that bears its relevance relation to its topic and contrast class, is also true.

The first two presuppositions are called the central presuppositions. Now questions are not raised in vacuum. Hence, there is some background knowledge and information, K, in which the question *arises.* This background knowledge and information form a part of the context. It is this background which determines whether or not the question *arises.* Whether or not the question *arises,* depends on whether or not K implies the proposition that (Pk; and for all ik, not Pk), i.e., the central presuppositions above. Also K must not imply that (c) is false. This brings out the point that a why-question '*arises* in context'. The notion of implication is tricky and I keep it deliberately vague at this stage saying that the background theory provides us with the answer. Of course, there is also the question of evaluating the answer. Since there could be more than one answer, one must know how to evaluate one answer to be better than the other. I am not going to worry about that very much in this paper.

II

THE CIVILIZATIONAL QUESTION

In this section I discuss, again very briefly, how the civilizational question or the grand question was raised in different forms by Joseph Needham. This is done more to give textual support to how Needham actually perceived the grand question. This sets the stage for a critical evaluation of the research programme the grand question engenders. The problem of what to include in the expression 'modern science' and what to exclude is also reviewed.

Needham's formulation of the grand question has been many. One of the most often quoted is the following:

> Why did modern science, the mathematization of hypothesis about Nature, with all its implications for advanced technology, take its meteoric rise *only* in the West at the time of Galileo?[4]

Needham clarifies the issue somewhat more by listing some of the important aspects of modern science as it took root in the West...

> When we say that (modern) science developed only in Western Europe at the time of Galileo in the late Renaissance .... we mean, surely that it was there and then alone there developed the bases of the natural sciences, ... namely, the

> application of mathematical hypotheses to Nature, the full understanding and use of the experimental method, the distinction between primary and secondary qualities, the geometrisation of space, and the acceptance of the mechanical model of reality.[5]

He contrasts the new science with the sciences of the medieval period. He points out that the sciences of the medieval period were 'tied to their ethnic environment' and were informed by incommensurable or quasi-incommensurable discourses as 'it was very difficult if not impossible for the people of those different cultures to find any common basis of discourse'.[6]

It has been pointed out by Nathan Sivin that there is a second question that Needham adds and that it has a bearing on the fact that modern science had not developed in China. This question is:

> (W)hy, between the first century B.C. and the fifteenth century A.D., Chinese civilization was much *more* efficient than Occidental in applying human natural knowledge to practical human needs?[7] (italics his)

It is to be mentioned that Needham is committed to continuous progress in science. He says that there is 'incommensurability between the civilizations in arts'; but there is a clear increase in man's knowledge and power through the centuries...

> In any case within the field of natural knowledge we cannot but recognise an evolutionary development, a real progress, over the ages.[8]

If science is taken as a body of knowledge, then one may legitimately think or ask what are the landmarks in science qua signposts of knowledge? Needham seems to have given us some of the signposts. Clearly one question arises as to how does one decide which are the landmarks? Are these socially highlighted as landmarks? How does one circumscribe the 'social' here? Does it contain the sub-culture comprising of scientists, and the sub-culture comprising of the historians of science?

A nuanced response to identify these signposts of knowledge will be to situate the activity called science in a larger context. The context includes metaphysical, theological, and even political ideas of a milieu. How these ideas interacted among themselves told us a more interesting story about the genesis of a scientific idea or about the validation and subsequent acceptance of the idea or about the rejection of the idea and so on. I think that Joseph Needham's social history of science presupposed, if not also practiced, although in a more diluted way, this kind of historical investigation. That the Needhamian project presupposed the results of the intellectual historians' work cannot be doubted. The long quotation above explicating features of modern science or his recognition that Newton's Law of Inertia can be logically juxtaposed (if not related) to Jean Buridan's work, through the intermediate ideas of Galileo and Descartes, bear clear testimony to this view.

There is a third response possible to the question how to identify landmarks in science. That is to deny that the accepted ones as indeed the landmarks and search for a different set. This may not be bad tack to take since if one is trying to show that at every period, there might have been other possibilities the society could have adopted, and the hegemony of knowledge called science reasserted itself as a ruthless political force in every period, then the landmarks we should look for are those which were the best forms of dissent against science.

Last but not the least is the problematic issue of scientific revolution. Why call the happenings in the seventeenth century Europe scientific revolution? Was there really a scientific revolution? What was the scope of this revolution both in terms of the intellectual and temporal realms? David Lindberg argues that E. H. Butterfield and A. Koyre employed the term 'scientific revolution' to characterize the scientific events between 1300 A.D. and 1800 A.D.[9] It might be worthwhile to look at the issue again and see whether there is an aspect of rhetoric in this claim. Cohen's exhaustive and book length account shows how intractable the notion of 'scientific revolution' is.[10]

III

PLAUSIBILITY OF THE CIVILIZATIONAL QUESTION

In this section I employ the discussion on the logical features of why-questions to bear on the civilizational question discussed in the last section. I first try to show how one can raise the question in one sense. Next I consider Sivin's objection to the historiographical value of raising the question in light of certain deeply embedded assumptions. I point out how a plausible but incomplete response to the objection can be made, I end by outlining briefly the issue of 'universality' of science and its repercussion on the civilizational question.

The contrast class X, in the question: "Why did modern science, the mathematization of hypothesis about Nature, with all its implications for advanced technology, take its meteoric rise *only* in the West at the time of Galileo?" contains the member: modern science arose in China. It is possible to add other members in the contrast class, X, e.g., modern science arose in India, modern science arose in other civilizations. Putting it this way, the question assumes importance. What are the background assumptions in arriving at either of the above two contrast classes of this question? One of these has to be that science is universal. I shall look at this notion more critically later on. But assuming that science is universal, one infers that the modern science is what every civilization 'ought to have had'.[11] If that is so, and since most civilizations did not have modern science, then there must have been something that held these civilizations back from developing modern science. And now the historical investigation will be to identify those inhibiting features in cultures or civilizations which did not produce a Scientific Revolution or modern science. In this sense, the civilizational question does *arise.* However, I think that this way of posing the question is extremely problematic and, as Sivin points out, comparing...

> all of the scientific and engineering activity of one civilization with all that of another conceals more than it reveals. ....They tell us nothing at all about what we can expect to learn from one culture or the other.[12]

Sivin goes on to claim that all the traditions of science and technologies must be 'attentively studied if we want to understand the general relations through history and across the globe between science and culture, science and society, science and individual consciousness'.[13]

At this point, I digress a little to bring out one logical feature of the answer, to the why-question, being sought. A why-question of the form 'Why-Q rather than Q1?' maybe understood in various ways. First, the why-question above is actually a conjunction of two why-questions: (1) why-Q?; and (2) why-(not-Q1)? And answer to the first question maybe quite different as to what the answer to the second would be. Sivin views the grand question as a complex question and argues that once this complexity is foregrounded, the answers to the constituent questions may turn out to be different. At the least, the answers cannot be taken, *a priori*, to be the same. Sivin's argument points to a possible misconstrual on Needham's part as to what the grand question is all about and hence the answer to the same. I elaborate on that a bit now.

I mentioned above in Section I, that there are why-questions which are expressed with a linguistic expression 'rather than', e.g., why did it snow rather than rain. This kind of question assumes that there is a contrastive fact describing snowing to be the case rather than raining. This fact is not to be reduced to the following facts; it is snowing, and it is not raining. The contrastive fact requires an explanation. This explanation will invoke appealing to a fact which maybe viewed as causally efficacious in bringing about snowing. Needham's grand historiographical question attempts a similar kind of explanation. The factors to be identified should show that the presence of these factors, Ạk,. brought about the occurrence of modern science in Europe. The next step would be to show that similar factors did not obtain in any other civilizations. Added to these factors, the attempt would also be to identify factors, Ḅi,.that were causally inhibiting in the non-European civilizations. This second set of factors are required because Needham's grand question presupposes, as Sivin points out, that the "Chinese civilization had been much more effective than the Europeans....for fourteen centuries or so before the scientific revolution."[14]

Taking a cue from Sivin that the presupposition regarding Chinese civilization being more effective than the Europeans for fourteen centuries or so before the scientific revolution, I point out that this presupposition may work in one of two ways. First, the expression 'question Q1 is behind Q' may mean that Q1 is logically prior to Q. This may, in turn, mean that the answer to Q1 is logically prior to any answer to Q. It may also mean that background knowledge, K1, required to answer Q1 will not be sufficient to answer Q. And the background knowledge, K, required to answer Q must include K1. Second, the expression 'question Q1 is behind the question Q' may mean that Q1 is causally prior to Q. This may, in turn, mean that the question Q1 is raised first, and then Q is raised. It is Q1 which causes Q to be raised. Or the answer to Q1 causes Q to be raised. Or the answer to Q1 causes the answer to Q. Now, Needham perhaps assumed the first interpretation—the 'logically prior' interpretation. This is borne out to an extent by Needham's articulation of K1, the background knowledge required to answer Q1. Some of the factors, Ḅi,.involved in explaining Q1, were suggested as actively inhibiting causes in not bringing about modern science in China. Other factors, Ç̣j,. in K1 were employed to argue that China had a prominent and thriving scientific and technological tradition. And now the explanation for why the modern science did not occur in China looks formidable. It takes the form that the lack of Ạk,.presence of Ḅi,.despite Ç̣j. This explains one part of the central presuppositions (the second presupposition) of the question Q.

Logically speaking, Needham is right in one sense. This is because he is not looking for complete explanations of the two questions why-Q and why-(not-Q1). He is instead looking for contrastive facts, much like scientists do, which will explain the contrast. Sivin's criticism is not on the logical point. Sivin is right when he looks at the background knowledge within which the question is raised. If Chinese science is virtually impossible to understand for a European, then the demand that the Chinese civilization attain the scientific revolution of Europe at least needs explanation to justify its reasonableness. This is relevant for asking does the why-question actually *arise*? Needham is confident that one can draw a connecting path from the Chinese knowledge of nature, in the fourteenth century to the scientific knowledge generated in Europe, in the sixteenth century, in an unproblematic, cumulative way.

IV

THE PROBLEMS WITH THE CIVILIZATIONAL QUESTION

In this section, I pursue the problematics involving the Needham question. I first look at the background assumptions of the question in light of criticisms made by Sivin. Next I elaborate on the implications of the assumptions. I show that these assumptions are not a part of the socio-historical knowledge claims in the light of which the central presuppositions of the grand question are to be established. These are more like a set of meta-level assumptions. And questioning these assumptions leads to a weakening of the basis of raising the grand question.

Sivin points out that the western assumptions underscore the 'way of putting the problem'.[15] These assumptions include:

> The Scientific Revolution is what everybody *ought* to have had."[16] (My italics)

> Sivin goes on to say that it is not at all clear that...(S)cientific theory of a characteristically modern kind were what other societies yearned for before they became, in recent times, an urgent matter of survival amidst violent change.[17]

> Another assumption is that...civilizations which had the *potential* for a scientific revolution ought to have had the kind that transpired in the West and encompassed the sorts of institutional and social changes that are identified with modernization.[18] (My italics)

> Sivin argues that these assumptions are...linked to a belief that European civilization all along was somehow in touch with reality in a way no other civilization could be, and that its great share of world's wealth and power comes from some intrinsic fitness to inherit the earth that was there all along.[19]

> Sivin points out that there is also the assumption that...since modern science has so quickly and throroughly become international, it transcends European historical and philosophical biases, and is as universal, objective, and value-free as the Nature that it seeks to understand and manipulate.[20]

I now take up the first two assumptions and related beliefs. The assumption that modern science is universal is open to various interpretations and objections. I shall say very little about that at the end since this assumption deserves an examination in an entirely different setting.

I begin by taking a historical development pattern in the history of ideas in the area of science called motion. There are arguments to show that the Law of Inertia proposed by Newton could be seen to be a culmination of a progression of ideas starting with the 'impetus' theory of Jean Buridan, through Galileo's work and Descartes' mechanics. Suppose it is asked that why did this chain of ideas appear only in Europe. The assumption behind this question is that the logical 'progress' of ideas mentioned above is a part of the 'progress' in science or natural philosophy. It was achieved in Europe and not in any other civilization. Humans think and follow the inexorable logical progress of ideas. Humans have the ability to do that. When they fail, there must be reasons for such failure. The reasons must be located either in the inability of humans or in the counteracting causes operating within the culture or civilization.

The steps in the reasoning are interesting. Humans did X in culture Y. Therefore, humans *can* do X in any civilization. Therefore, humans ought to (have done or) do X in every civilization. This conclusion is supported by the assumption that every civilization must (or ought to) yearn for the same kind of knowledge and social/institutional arrangements that go with this generation of knowledge as the Europeans did. Several issues are worth mentioning here. First, the 'logical' progress that is mentioned in the history of ideas is seen as the only mode or the easiest mode or the dominant mode of progress. Second, the notion of 'can' is to be understood as logically possible or physically possible. This is especially so for those civilizations 'which had the potential for a scientific revolution".[21] It is this latter sense that Sivin wants to refute. Third, the notion of 'ought' seems to be a curious mixture of rational and moral ought. One employs a specific interpretation depending upon one's goal. In fact, Sivin's argument that some civilizations may not yearn for western science may be taken as a sign of moral inability on the part of the civilization in question for not realizing that modern science itself is a value. At the least, it will be a sign of rational inability in that one fails to see that pursuing modern science is worthwhile. And Europeans may be seen as both rationally and morally superior.

The explicit nature of the arguments may be reconstructed as follows:

P1: If a civilization rationally ought to have goals like achieving scientific revolution, then they rationally can have goals like achieving scientific revolution.

P2: If a civilization rationally can have goals like achieving scientific revolution, then they must have opted for those goals. (Empirically supported from the European example)

P3: Some civilizations did not opt for these goals.

Therefore, those civilizations are not rational in their pursuit of scientific knowledge.

Similarly, moral inferiority of a civilization can be inferred. Sivin challenges the empirical adequacy of the second premise in both arguments. He points out that there are no historical investigations to support that the Europeans *yearned* for modern science. Needhamian question arises because these conclusions about rational inferiority or moral inferiority tend to conflict with the assumptions that the civilizations like China 'which had the *potential* for a scientific revolution *ought* to have had the modern science'.[22] In the liberal tradition, when native intelligence or moral superiority of any specific civilization is questionable, the assumption that any civilization ought to have modern science begins to assert itself in formulating the grand question as well as the answer to that question in a certain way. It appeals to the socio-historic contingencies. It also allows for the possibility of looking elsewhere for the cause for the failure to bring about modern science. It appeals to socio-economic and structural aspects, of civilizations, which are adduced as explanans. This is one way the grand question and its answer (the kind Needham searched for) can be made meaningful. In fact, it would be hard for Needham or for that matter anyone to avoid the rational or moral superiority arguments as proposed above unless the assumptions of the liberal traditions are invoked.

I end this section by asking whether the socio-economic factors which Needham alluded to would satisfactorily answer the question. Thanks to Sivin, we begin to see this move also will not be successful. As mentioned in the last section, there is a set of positively contributing factors which are posited as causally efficacious in bringing about modern science in Europe. There is another set which enumerates the counter-acting causes for the failure of other civilizations in not being able to bring about modern science. Sivin shows with a wealth of examples that what was taken for a causally contributing factor for the effect in one place lacked the efficacy in another place.[23] Worse still, what was taken for a causally counter-acting factor in one place was seen to be not a counter-acting variable in another place.[24] Sivin rightly concludes that this positing of necessary causal conditions and counter-acting causes is fallacious and misleading. It is a kind of no-win situation for non-western civilizations. As a result, Sivin thinks that this kind of analysis must be given up and in fact this line of inquiry must be given up.

What is Sivin arguing against is perhaps what Steve Fuller calls an 'overdeterministic' account of the rise of modern science in Europe.[25] This overdeterminism underwrites a unilinear notion of progress in knowledge and science and civilization at large. It also underwrites a strong form of whiggism. The path of progress from the past to the present situation is delineated in terms of what is taken to be the 'progressive' present. The landmarks of the past are chosen appropriately to develop the seamless story of progress which is taken to be necessary and deviation from it being a sign of irrational human behaviour. I do not claim that whiggism of some form does not or cannot inform our historical endeavour. It seems that we cannot but be somewhat whiggish in that our present categories do influence what we look at in the past and how we look at them. However, this does not entail that a historian needs to commit to an 'overdeterministic' account of progress or development. Positing an 'underdeterministic' account of rise of modern science in Europe requires looking at how in Europe modern science developed without the attendant question why it did not develop somewhere else. This 'underdeterministic' strategy opens the possibility that science might have developed in other civilizations at some other times and also that science might not have developed in Europe. Not only that but also the possibility that modern science may not even flourish in Europe at a later time and may even decay, is a possibility under this strategy. It is unclear that Needham would take this route. For him knowledge is gathered in a cumulative fashion. And he believes that all civilizations can participate in this process today. His future looking project of all human civilizations participating in science on an equal basis tends to take the 'overdeterministic' position and yet his concern for the civilizations which did not produce scientific revolution forces him to search for historical contingencies and there lies the tension of the project and it informs his grand question and his attempt to answer the grand question in terms of socio-economic factors.

CONCLUSION

It appears that the why-question that Needham raised is not well formed. This is because its background assumptions do not allow the possibility of variation in modern science. It does not allow in its background knowledge the differences in the intellectual aspirations among different civilizations. This situation might have been entailed by the view that science is universal and as a result the why-question is ill-formed.

Turner has argued that the scientists while thinking about the history of their own disciplines are often committed to an unwritten assumption. This is as follows: "If the correct interpretation of the world is obvious to us (the present day scientists) now, it should have been obvious (to the scientists of the past) then, and only prejudice could have prevented them from seeing it."[26] The correct interpretation is the one which is prevalent now. It is accepted by the present day scientists that the correct interpretation of the world was not obvious to the scientists of the past. There are two responses that can be made at this point. One is to explain away why the scientists of the past did not accept the present day interpretation of the world as obvious. The explanation is offered by appealing to the prejudice of the scientists of the past. The moral failure of the scientists, qua human being, is then explained away either in terms of sociology or in terms of individual psychology.

The other response is to confront the problem differently by accepting that the conclusion of the argument is that the correct interpretation of the world is not obvious (even) to the present-day scientists now. This move opens up the possibility of investigating science as human enterprise where an apparent success is not explained by human rationality and intelligence, and an apparent failure is not explained by human moral and intellectual failure. This shows that there is a space in which the work of the scientists of the past need not be viewed as attempts to answer the same questions that the present-day scientists are raising. This, in turn, opens up the issue of universality of science. If it is possible that even within a culture/civilization, the intellectual communities were raising different questions across time, then it is equally likely that the intellectual communities in different civilizations could raise different questions across time and space. This is compatible with the principle that "There are many possible ways of knowing and studying the world and that science is just the particular way-of-knowing currently dominant in the western culture."[27] This possibility would begin to militate against the thesis that there is an essential continuity with the past and across cultures. Sivin argues that indeed was the case in many Chinese scholars' including Shen Kua's attempt to acquire knowledge. I quote in detail to bring out the issue clearly:

> Understanding is a matter of introspection. The questions we ask in divination are the ones we have tried to deal with reflectively but can't, because at the time

> our minds are too burdened for introspection to work. Divination techniques ritually manipulate passive material objects, yarrow stalks and so on, providing an external process or set of images on which to concentrate as a way round that blockage. In other words, prognostication draws indirectly, through ritual, on the power of self-examination.
>
> Access to one's personal future, whether by visionary foresight or by divination, is a perfectly natural phenomenon. It merges into the moral faculties, whose choices condition the future. It merges at the other end into the rational comprehension of the natural order as it is reflected in any authentic experience. Shen did not confuse introspection and observation, nor did he draw a clear line between them. Nor did he need to compare the importance of these two ways of knowing. What finally united the sciences, in other words, was the universal sysytem of knowledge—uniting intellection, imagination, and intuition—of which they constituted only a part.[28]

The modern western science claims its universality in an interesting way. In order to understand that profitably, I introduce very briefly Romila Thapar's work[29]. Thapar argues that the notion of 'universality' can be profitably understood in two ways—vertical universality and horizontal universality. She gives examples of the transition of early societies to agricultural societies and points out that many societies undergo this transition. Equally importantly these transitions happen discretely or in isolation. This kind of transition exemplifies vertical universality. Thapar, in contrast, insists that industrial revolution 'has a horizontal universality when it cuts across various societies'.[30] She holds that 'changes are encouraged' both 'by the internal dynamics of the society and as a result of diffusion and transmission'.[31]

The western modern science claims its universality in a 'vertical' sense. Assuming that modern science is a stage in the intellectual development in any human society, one concludes that this *ought* to have happened in every known society. If this did not happen in any particular society, then it requires explanation. And the explanation is given both in terms of citing favourable conditions that brought it about in one society, and in terms of inhibiting conditions that could not bring it about in another society. In the previous section we have seen the problematic nature of these conclusions and the repercussions of these on the civilizational question and the historiography engendered by that question.

The argument for the conclusion that modern science *ought* to have developed in all human civilizations is further supported by at least two claims. Modern scientific knowledge is value neutral and objective in the sense of being independent of human consciousness. Second, modern science spread across the non-western human societies. That this spread of modern science has taken place through colonisation and the fact that modern scientific knowledge perhaps is value-laden and non-objective begin to undermine the argument. And thus horizontal universality of modern science is suspect if not a myth.

In another way, Needham's question may seem to arise because one attempts to arrive at a set of causally efficacious as well as a set of causally inhibiting factors to explain why modern science took root in one civilization but did not in another. But identifications of these causes are difficult if not impossible if Sivin is right. The best one could hope for, therefore, is to treat the grand question as a heuristic one which could help elaborate the research programmes in history of science in Europe, and history of science in China without the evaluative extra baggage that Europe was and is in some way (rationally or morally) superior.

NOTES

1. van Fraassen, Bas C. 1980. *The Scientific Image.* Oxford: Clarendon Press. Chapter 5; see especially, pp. 141-6.
2. Belnap. Jr., N. D. quoted in ibid. p. 145.
3. Needham, J. 1969. *The Grand Titration.* London: George Allen and Unwin. p. 3.
4. Ibid., p. 16.
5. Ibid., pp. 14-15.
6. Ibid., p. 15.
7. Ibid., p. 190.
8. Needham, J. et al. 1980. *Science and Civilization in China.* Cambridge: Cambridge University Press. Vol. 5, Part 4, p. xxxv.
9. Lindberg, D. 1990. "Conceptions of the Scientific Revolution from Bacon to Butterfield". *Reappraisals of the Scientific Revolution.* D. Lindberg and R. S. Westman (ed.). Cambridge: Cambridge University Press. pp. 1-26.
10. Cohen, H. F. 1994. *The Scientific Revolution: A Historiographical Inquiry.* Chicago: The University of Chicago Press.
11. Sivin, N. 1984. "Why the Scientific Revolution did not take place in China—or didn't it?" *Transformation and Tradition in the Sciences.* E. Mendelshon (ed.). Cambridge: Cambridge University Press. pp. 531-554. See p. 537.
12. Ibid., p. 532.
13. Ibid.
14. Ibid., pp. 531-554.
15. Ibid., p. 537
16. Ibid.,
17. Ibid.
18. Ibid.
19. Ibid.
20. Ibid.
21. Sivin.
22. Ibid.
23. Ibid., pp. 540-2
24. Ibid.
25. Fuller, S. 1999. "Prolegomena to a World History of Science". *Situating the History of Science.* I. Habib and D. Raina (ed.). New Delhi: Oxford University Press. pp. 114-151.
26. Turner, J. R. G. 1990. "The History of Science and the Working Scientist". *Companion to the History of Modern Science.* London: Routledge. p. 25.
27. Cunningham, A. and Williams, P. 1993. "De-centring the 'big picture': The Origin of Modern Science and the Modern Origin of Science", *The British Journal for the History of Science,* 26 (1993), pp. 407-432. See p. 409.
28. Sivan, p. 536.
29. Thapar, R. 1999. "History of Science and the Oiukemene". *Situating the History of Science.* I. Habib and D. Raina (ed.). New Delhi: Oxford University Press. pp. 16-28.
30. Ibid., p. 18.
31. Ibid., p. 19.

CHAPTER 22

The Notion of Absolute (Whatever is *is of* the as well as *in* the Absolute) Śaṁkara, Kant and Hegel Lyotard, Derrida and Habermas

Raghwendra Pratap Singh

In this paper, I will try to expound and examine the nature and status of the notion of Absolute in the intellectual traditions of the East and the West. Couple of years back, I came across the book by Prof. Daya Krishna entitled *India's Intellectual Traditions: Attempts at Conceptual Reconstructions*[1]. At the same time, there was another book *The Western Intellectual Tradition*[2]. It was an experience going through these two books. I felt strongly about locating ourselves in our own intellectual tradition. More so, for over the last two decades, I have been teaching and guiding research students on different aspects of modern and postmodern western thinking. Bhartṛhari (fifth century A.D.), in his *Vākyapadīya*, at the end of the second book, has said, "What does he know who knows only his own tradition?" This was the period of confident India with collaborative and contending Buddhist, Jaina and different Brahmin schools of thought—the *Sampradāyas*—that have emerged, defined and established them. They were also interacting with China, with the Middle East and with all other civilized centers of learning.

So Bhartṛhari's statement that one has to know other traditions was quite relevant. But today, we have to say another thing—what does he know who does not know his own tradition? This tradition is in a bad way. This tradition is historically rooted in the 300 years of colonial India. The ideas of the dominant class—the Imperialist forces—became the ideas of the people under domination and subjugation—the colonial subjects. Even in the post-colonial India, under the garb of neo-imperialism, the same tradition continues. We have to be vigilant. A re-awakening to this effect came up during Indian Renaissance, which got its revival during the movement for the Independence of India with the revitalization of the Vedāntic thought. It has given rise to generations of intellectuals who have been trying to define India's intellectual traditions within and outside India. In the present paper, I am going to deal with the notion of Absolute in the Advaita Vedānta of Śaṁkara and the absolute idealism of G.W.F. Hegel. In my attempt to defend the Advaita Vedāntin position and thereby to supplement Hegel's Absolute, I would like to present some clarifications, annotations and summations which maybe useful for the limited end of an acquaintance with the Absolute in Śaṁkara, on the one hand, and that of Hegel on the other.

One of the fundamental reasons for comparing Śaṁkara with Hegel is that Hegel was fully aware of the Hindu religion and the Advaita Vedānta of Śaṁkara. Interestingly, Europe in the early nineteenth century took to classical Indian studies in a big way. The ethnic Croat Ivan FilipVesdin (1748-1806), better known under his monastic name Paulinus, a Sancro Bartholomaco, wrote the first published Sanskrit grammar *Sidharubam Seu Grammitica Samscṛdamica,* Rome 1790[3]. Every major university in Europe started developing a deep interest in Indology. With the efforts of German thinkers like J.W.von Goethe, J.G. Herder, A.W.von Schlegel, W.von Humbolt, special Sanskrit chairs were established at German Universities—in 1818 in Bonn, 1821 in Berlin, 1926 in Koenigsberg (now Kaliningrad in Russia). Hegel was appointed at the University of Jena in 1801. All young scholars in Europe during nineteenth century were doing Sanskrit. A galaxy of scholars in Europe were able to read and write in Sanskrit—Schiller, Schelling, Hegel, Schopenhauer, Nietzsche, Paul Duessen, Max Muller, Ferdinand de Saussure and so on. Under this intellectual atmosphere, a comparison between Śaṁkara and Hegel concerning the notion of Absolute can help us understand a similar problem in two cultural contexts.

I wish to divide my paper in four parts; Part-I, I will expound the nature and status of the Absolute in Advaita Vedānta and give a brief comparison between Śaṁkara and Kant on consciousness; in Part-II, I will discuss Hegel's notion of the Absolute and its dialectical appreciation by the thinking consciousness. Herein I will bring Kant's transcendental consciousness and the distinction between reason, understanding and sensibility. I'll also give a short comparison between Śaṁkara and Hegel on the notion of the Absolute; in Part-III, I will examine the basic charges levelled by Jean Francois Lyotard and Jacques Derrida on Hegel's notion of Absolute; in Part-IV, I will assimilate the arguments of the critical theorists like Adorno, Horkheimer, Marcuse and Habermas on the Enlightenment Rationality of Kant and the Absolute of Hegel. In the conclusion, I'll propose a dialectical dialogue between Śaṁkara, Kant and Hegel on the one hand and Lyotard, Derrida and Habermas on the other.

Dialectical dialogue is not the same as dialogue. A dialogue is always *dia-logos,* it is the view of the other *as the other* or the *contradiction,* which is the operative term. But a dialogue is possible only when both the speakers maintain a fundamental consensus, i.e. both the speakers (a) speak and (b) listen, (c) aim at truth, (d) understand each other's language, (e) understand each other's way of thinking, and (f) do not live in two worlds whose contents totally differ. In dialogue, we thus find two characteristic features; namely, consensus and contradiction. These are the two operative terms for the possibility and development of ideas under the method of dialogue. Absolute consensus is nothing but a dogma. Absolute contradiction leads us nowhere. It is only under certain degree of consensus that certain amount of contradiction is entertained and thinking is thus stimulated. We have several such illustrations in the Upaniṣads on the one hand and Socrates on the other. However, I am proposing a dialectical dialogue, which will not simply be dia-logued but multi-logued in order to appreciate the plurality of ethnic identity, cultural identity, linguistic identity, etc. Dialectical dialogue could further be used as a method to facilitate a dialogue between persons, identities, ethnicities, communities, cultures and civilizations. The subject matter for such a dialogue will centre on the notion of Absolute between two cultural contexts i.e.

East and West. This comparison does not imply detecting similarity and distinction, and cataloguing the resemblances between Śaṁkara and Hegel. Instead my attempt would be to show how the arguments of one philosopher pass into that of the other and this helps the growth of the philosophical heritage.

THE NOTION OF ABSOLUTE—AN OUTLINE

If we look at the history of the problem of the Ultimate Reality or the notion of Absolute, we find that there are three ways that we can approach this problem—the psychological, the theological and the cosmological. We can begin with our analysis into what goes on in our mind or the *antaḥkaraṇa* and try to find the absolute in us. Or we can begin with an estimation of the outside world and try to establish an absolute causality operating in nature. Or finally, we can resort to God as the ultimate unifying force between the inner world and the outer world. The Father of Modern Philosophy, René Descartes (1596-1650), in search of certainty in philosophy, started with a method of doubt regarding the outside world and arrives at the certainty of the *cogito*. From the *cogito*, says Descartes, we arrive at the conception of God, who is the cause of the *cogito*, and whom we must, therefore, regard as more perfect than the *cogito*. Finally, it is from God that he arrives at the world, which he had started by negating, by regarding as the creation of a demon. Opposed to Descartes, to the God-intoxicated philosopher, Spinoza (1632-1677), neither the mind nor the material reality is primary. To him, God is the be-all and the end-all of all things; it is self-conceived, self-existent and self-caused. Even Kant, to anticipate a later discussion, has subscribed to Rational Psychology, Rational Cosmology and Rational Theology. However, the way the Upaniṣads deal with the problem of Absolute is neither the Cartesian nor the Spinozistic. Śaṁkara, for instance, subordinated the world and the God to the self. In what follows, let me outline this problem.

Indian Perspective

The Vedic *ṛṣis* expressed their vision of the Absolute or the Ultimate Reality in the form of hymns, evoking responses at the varying levels of self-realization, worshipful devotion or ritual sacrifices. The Upaniṣadic saint tried to impart the knowledge of the Absolute to his pupil through the method of a dialogue. An example of this is found in the *Bṛihadāraṇyaka Upaniṣad* in the dialogue between the sage Yājñavalkya and his wife Maitreyi who asks him question about the way to realize the Absolute or the ultimate Truth. As the dialogue proceeds, Yājñavalkya convinces her that it is the *Ātman* or self that should be known, and when this knowledge is achieved, everything in the Universe is known, because there lies an identity between *Ātman* (self) and *Brahman* (the Ultimate Reality). The five *Mahāvākyas* or great teachings (literally, Great Sentences), express this vision from different *Upaniṣads* in the following:

1. *Prajñānām Brahma*, "Consciousness is *Brahman* (*Aitarīya Upaniṣad*, III. 1. 3.)
2. *Aham Brahmāsmi* "I am *Brahman*" (*Bṛhadāraṇyaka Upaniṣad*, iv. 3. 23)
   Aham eva idam sarvosmi "I indeed am this whole Universe."

3. *Tattvamasi* (That Thou art), (*Chāndogya Upaniṣad,* VI. 8.7.)
4. *Ayam Ātma Brahma* "This *Ātman* is *Brahman*" (*Chāndogya Upaniṣad,* iii, 10-14), *Taittirīya Upaniṣad, i. 5., Bṛhadāraṇyaka Upaniṣad,* II. 5. 19
5. *Sarvam Khalu Idam Brahma* "Everything is *Brahman*" (*Mundaka Upaniṣad, iii, 13. 1., Chāndogya Upaniṣad, III. 14.1)*

The *Mahāvākyas,* in brief, are the different paths for the realization of the Absolute. The statement '*Prajñānām Brahma*' directs the seeker to meditate on the *Chittsvarūpa* (Pure Consciousness form) of *Brahman,* leading to the merger of the individual consciousness in the Universal and the attainment of *Mukti* (liberation from worldly bondage) and the state of Supreme Bliss (*paramānanda*). '*Aham Brahmāsmi*' is an endeavor to make the pupil engage in deep meditation to realize the Absolute, in the '*Tattvamasi*' the teacher is trying to make his pupil realize that his innate Being is part of the Absolute, '*Ayam Ātma Brahman*' also accomplishes the same thing.

Western Perspective

In the Preface to the *Phenomenology of Spirit,* Hegel says: "The True is the whole. But the whole is nothing other than the essence consummating itself through its development. Of the absolute it must be said that it is essentially a result, that only in the end is it what it truly is; and that precisely in this consists its nature, *viz.*, to be actual subject, the spontaneous becoming of itself."[4]

And in his *Lectures on the Philosophy of Religion,* Hegel adds, "Philosophy is itself, in fact, worship (*Die philosophie ist der selbst Gottesdienst*); it is religion, for in the same way it renounces subjective notions and opinions in order to occupy itself with God...The object of religion as well as of philosophy is eternal truth in its objectivity, God and nothing but God and the explication of God...In philosophy, religion gets justification from thinking consciousness."[5]

This position of Hegel is in sharp reaction to what Kant has to say in the Preface to the First Edition of *Critique of Pure Reason:* "Human reason has this peculiar fate that in one species of its knowledge it is burdened by questions which, as prescribed by the very nature of reason itself, it is not able to ignore, but which, as transcending all its powers, it is also not able to answer."[6]

The central claim of Hegel's philosophy as against Kant is that we cannot speak of the Absolute without at the same time speaking of self-consciousness of human mind, nor fruitfully pursue that interrogation itself unless we conceive our activity in doing so as one sustained and made possible by the Absolute. This is perhaps the best part of Hegel's philosophy responsible for the origin and sustenance of the Absolute Spirit and its epistemological justification by the subjective spirit or the thinking consciousness. At the same time, there is no part of Hegel's philosophy except this, which the post-Hegelians, including the present-day Postmodern and Critical Theory Hegel scholars, are less willing to accept on its own terms.

I

ŚAṀKARA'S NOTION OF ABSOLUTE THE ULTIMATE PRINCIPLES OF KNOWLEDGE, VALIDITY AND THE LIMITS OF *PRAMĀṆAS*

Śaṁkara was a philosopher of One Thought and the same could be the claims of the Vedāntins like Rāmānuja and some others also. If I could bring, by way of illustrations only, two thinkers from the West, they are Hegel and Heidegger who have been regarded as philosophers of One Thought, i.e., Spirit (*Geist*) and Being respectively. Therefore, the first thing is that Śaṁkara is a philosopher of One Thought, i.e., *Brahmavādī.* I would like to explain the term *Brahman* before I go to elaborate the issues in and around it. The term *Brahman* has been derived from the root word *Bṛh,* which means "to grow". It means that wherever we have growth or development, we have *Brahman.* There are several examples, like, *annam Brahma, śabdam Brahma, rasam Brahma,* etc. Wherever there is orderliness, purposiveness, motion or creation of some specific form, there is the hidden presence of *Brahman.* The awareness, of the growth and the purposiveness, etc., involves the existence of a conscious being or *Ātman.* Growth and the awareness of the growth cannot be separated. Hence *Ātman* and *Brahman* are in perpetual unity. This has been the prime concern of Śaṁkara. I may go against the oft-repeated contention that Śaṁkara was a *Māyāvādī.* I would argue that the central doctrine of Śaṁkara is *Brahman* and *Ātman. Māyā* and *Advidyā* come only in the course of philosophical investigation that Śaṁkara undertakes. Secondly, Śaṁkara is traditionalist emphasizing openly on the tradition, i.e., *Sampradāya* and thus abandoning the claim of originality in his writings and preachings. The main inspiration for him comes from the Upaniṣads, the *Bhagavadagītā* and the *Brahmasūtras.*

Śaṁkara has made a distinction between the knower of a *Sampradāya* and the knower of *Śāṣtras.* One can know scripture, quote scripture but that does not mean that one is conversant with the tradition. Śaṁkara even goes to the extent of saying that a person, who is learned in *Śāṣtras,* is not acquainted with the tradition, such a person has to be ignored. This shows that tradition is very important for the study and interpretation of a text.

Śaṁkara has certainly been inspired by Gauḍapāda, his *paramgurū,* and the traditional method invoked by him. Śaṁkara makes use of the method is known as *Adhyāropa* (projection) and *Apavāda* (refutation)[7]. This is known to Vedāntins even before Gouḍapāda. Mandan Mishra in *Vimalsiddhi* has referred to this method. *Adhyāropa* is natural propensity of man to formulate a view of that which is observed. It precedes observation, because observation is not possible without *Adhyāropa.* Śaṁkara calls it by the name of *Adhyāṣa* and explains it in terms of being natural, beginningless and firmly established in common sense. What is Śaṁkara's prime interest in philosophy? Though Śaṁkara is a *Brahmavādī,* he is primarily interested in *jīva,* its existential problems and of the worldly life—*lokavyavahāra.* It is to find out what human being is, what he thinks and experiences as an agent of action involved in the day-to-day life and activity. Therefore, Śaṁkara looks at the Vedānta text in order to identify the causes of human problems and to make the way out to resolve human problems. Unlike other Vedāntins who started their thought with the interpretation of first *sūtra,* i.e., *Athāto Brahmajijñānṣā,* Śaṁkara does not go to this *sūtra* to start with. He begins with an introduction to the *sūtra* and his introduction is known as *Adhyāṣavākya.* To understand Śaṁkara's *advaita* is to understand the problem of *adhyāṣa. Adhyāṣa* provides a foundation to Śaṁkara's *Sūtrabhāṣya, Upaniṣad bhāṣya* and *Gītābhāṣya.*

How does Śaṁkara begin in the doctrine of *adhyāṣa?* The theory of *adhyāṣa* begins with day-to-day life and experience, a kind of *naiveté* of outlooks containing certain elements of truths and untruths. This is a kind of power of discrimination. Every proposition contains a truth content and a falsity content. So it is natural for every seeker of truth to undertake the work with critical evaluation. When he finds the view contains more untruths than truths, he rejects it and accepts another view, which has a greater degree of truth than the previous one. This rejection is known as *apavāda,* which literally means discordant view and that it does not accord with the reality any more. Advaita Vedānta maintains that there are views, which accord with the reality more adequately than others. Śaṁkara, for example, prefers, Sāṁkhya to Vaiśeṣika and some of his later followers prefer Śaktism to Śaivism.

Since Śaṁkara's prime concern is to understand *Ātman* and its relation to *Brahman,* let us dwell on this issue. Let us take chapter VI of the *Chāndogya Upaniṣad,* which discusses the most basic problems of Śaṁkara's metaphysics—the problem of *Brahman* and that of *Ātman,* which is the widest, the deepest, and the most fundamental problem. All other problems can be derived from this basic problem. We have a dialogue between the father Uddālaka and his son Śvetaketu. The Upaniṣad conceives the problem systematically. It makes a promissory statement and it is followed by certain examples drawn from the empirical life and then it formulates the grand thesis. Śvetaketu returns home after having a formal education for nearly about 21 years. Then father puts this question to Śvetaketu—Have you known that after knowing which everything else is known? This is traditionally known as 'from the knowledge of one to the knowledge of all', '*Ek vijñāna tu sarva vijñāna'.* This is the promissory statement that the Upaniṣad gives to us through the teacher Uddālaka. Śvetaketu says that he does not know that. He even goes to the extent of saying that perhaps his teacher did not know, because if he had known, he would have definitely told him (Śvetaketu). Then the illustrations are given from *empirical life.* Even *Brahmasūtra* begins with this. It begins with the need for an enquiry and it goes into causes of the world. So there is an empirical example. The person, who knows clay, knows that everything made of clay, is known to him, because clay is the *upādāna kāraṇa,* the material cause. The forms may change, the names may change, but what remains in all the objects made of clay is the clayness. All the modifications have certain names, certain forms, but in all these cases what is real is the cause. Then a grand thesis is formulated that the supreme reality that is the cause of the world is one—*Ekam eva advitīyam.* For Śaṁkara, it is enough to build up a metaphysical system out of this *grand thesis.* Śaṁkara's *Advaita* can be identified by four doctrines—there is the theory of *Nirguṇa Brahman,* there is a theory of *Vivarta,* there is the theory of *anirvaćanīya khyāti* and finally there is a doctrine of *Jīvan Mukti.* One can go from the first to the second, from both to the third and finally to the fourth. There is consistency in Śaṁkara's writings. There is coherence and comprehensiveness in Śaṁkara's *Advaita.* Śaṁkara begins his philosophy with the inquiry into the *pramāṇas, pramāṇa vichāra* to establish the metaphysical system. Śaṁkara says that existence and non-existence of a thing can only be established by means of *pramāṇa.* How do we know that something exists here or that something does not exist here? We know it only through *pramāṇa.* Śaṁkara starts with the world given in day-to-day life. To start with, Śaṁkara does not talk of the illusoriness of the world. In the *Sūtras,* Śaṁkara asks how do we decide that something is and something is not. If the world is proved by all the *pramāṇa,* we cannot say that it does not exist. But there is a *pramāṇa vyavasthā,* every *pramāṇa* operates in a particular area, it has its own subject matter. What one *pramāṇa* comprehends another *pramāṇa* cannot, just as what one sense organ comprehends another sense organ cannot. On the basis of *pramāṇa vyavasthā,* Śaṁkara repeatedly points out in his writings that there is absolutely no conflict between a Scripture on the one hand and other *pramāṇa* on the other. If *pratykṣa* has validity so far as empirical world is concerned, Scripture has validity to what is transcendental. Śaṁkara says that an object which has got certain quality (*guṇa*), generic feature (*jāti*) is involved in action (*karma*), has some kind of relation with something else (*sambandha*) or which has name and form (*nāma-rūpa*). That is all about empirical world. There is a complete breakdown of language in the case of supreme reality because it does not have *jāti, guṇa,* etc. It does not even have a name. These are simply the contextual forms that are required to convey what ordinarily cannot be conveyed. The *Sārirakabhāṣya* says that wherever there is orderliness, purposiveness, motion or creation of some specific form, there is hidden presence of *Brahman.* This can be explained only by *śruti,* other *pramāṇa* cannot explain it.

The first condition for objective knowledge, according to Śaṁkara, is (a) that an object should possess a generic unity with specific differences: "An object can be known only when it is differentiated from things other than itself" (*Evam hi tat jñānam bhavati yadānyebhyo nirdhā item)*[8]. We can identify an object only under the conditions in which we can differentiate the object from the rest of the objects. We can know a table, its size, its colour, etc. only if we distinguish it from the rest of the things. 'The category of Substance-attribute, therefore, implies for its application a plurality of things that should at the same time belong to the same genus' (*yadā hi tada viśeṣaṇasya arthavattvam*).[9] (b) The characteristics of an object, such as generic unity, specific qualities and actions, it is urged elsewhere, are the conditions of intelligible discourse" (*Tat anyāsamai upadestum sakyam jāti-guṇa-kriyā-viśeṣaṇaiḥ—Commentary on the Kenopaniṣada,* I, 3). Śaṁkara has also said, "Every word employed to denote a thing can do so only in so far as it is associated with certain *genus,* or a certain *act,* or a certain quality, or a certain mode of *relation.* The cow and horse imply genera, teacher and cook imply acts, white and black imply qualities, wealthy and cattle-owner imply possession".[10] In this case if one thing is distinguished by the other and therefore it is necessarily limited by the other, it must be remembered that both must belong to one class, they must be *ekajātīyani,* as Śaṁkara puts it. This is true for Śaṁkara as it is true for Descartes. The Cartesian distinction between the *cogito* and the unthought, though distinct as far as their attributes are concerned, yet somehow they are conceived under the common concept of 'substance'. Even Immanuel Kant could also formulate it in the form of Judgment, under Relation, specifically in the Disjunctive Relation-'Earth exists either through a blind chance, or through an inner necessity, or through an external cause'. These three possibilities mutually exclude each other but jointly somehow they give us complete knowledge. It is the category of 'community', which is operating here. Apart from this community, they could not be defined in antithetical and mutually conflicting terms. Vāćaspati Miśra has very clearly explained that all differences and conflicts would be impossible if their had been difference at their foundation. The judgment 'intellect is non-eternal', for instance, cannot conflict with the judgment, 'the soul is eternal' *(Na ca bhinnāsraya viruddhah- Brahmasūtra.)*.[11] Hence, conflicts can neither be foundationless (*anāsraya)* nor can they exist when there is difference at the very basis of the conflicting ideas or judgments *(bhinnāsraya)*. This requires an elaborate analysis of the nature and status of consciousness. Let me begin with consciousness.

On Consciousness

The intellectual expedition in the realm of consciousness is extremely complex and multifaceted. In the extensive field of philosophy, we come across consciousness as an ontological being, an epistemological subject, a moral agent, an aesthetic being, a psychological being, a Yogic subject and so on. It has moved the philosophical insight so persistently that the combined study of East and West has not solved the problem of consciousness, once and for all. Socrates, who shifted philosophic problems from physics to ethics, expressed it in the form of a command 'Know Thyself' at Delphi, and the ancient Hindu saints, sages and seers expressed the problem in the form of a forceful interrogation '*Koaham*?' Obviously, there is a philosophical unrest, anxiety and apprehension concerning consciousness. Let me begin with the description of consciousness in Śaṁkara.

The doctrine of consciousness has been discussed by the Upaniṣadic seers, not only in the *Māndūkya Upaniṣad* but also in the *Bṛhadāranyaka Upaniṣad,* in the famous dialogue between Yājñavalkya and King Janaka. There is also an in-depth study of consciousness in the commentaries by Gauḍapāda, Śaṁkara and others, down to Vivekananda and Sri Aurobindo. The discussion that we come across in *Māndūkya Upaniṣad* is very much complemented by all succeeding works of the kind. Here I will be basically concerned with Śaṁkara's analysis of consciousness. For Śaṅkara, to get into the problem of consciousness is to begin with the three states of consciousness—the *avasthātraya*—in the *Vedāntic* tradition. Whenever we come across the problem of consciousness, we not only have a reference to human being alone but also to *Brahman* which is *sat, ćit and ānanda*–particularly the *ćit svarūpa* of *Brahman.*

To being with the consciousness of the human being, we have to begin with the human body, i.e., the vital force, the senses, the *antahkaraṇa*—the internal organ, popularly known as Mind, endowed with *Buddhi,* of intellect, with *ahaṅkaraḥa*—the 'I'. Deeper than *ahaṅkarḥ,* the Vedāntins have an entity, i.e., consciousness, *cit, caitanya, sambrita* or the self. In the German idealist tradition, there is no such distinction between the ego, mind, spirit, self or consciousness. These terms have similar meanings. However, Husserl has drawn a distinction between Ego, *cogito* and *cogiteta.* These are tripartite stages involved in Husserl's phenomenology—descriptive stage, transcendental stage and egological stage. In the descriptive stage, issues are raised, everything around us is an object of consciousness. It is because of consciousness that we are aware of the objects or ideas and so on. What is so fundamental at this stage is that a distinction has been drawn between consciousness and the objects of consciousness. Husserl assigns several functions to consciousness; such as, consciousness objectivates, identifies, supplements, unifies, etc. Husserl has made a distinction between pure ego and empirical ego, between transcendental ego and the psychological ego. But there remains a fundamental difficulty, i.e. the distinction between consciousness, ego, mind, etc. have not been clearly defined in the German idealism including Husserl's phenomenology. But this problem no longer exists in the *Vedānta.* The functions that Husserl assigns to consciousness like objectifying, unifying, etc. are all the functions of *antahkaraṇa* under the witnessing act of consciousness in the *Vedānta* tradition. The *antahkaraṇa* is material and it requires the witnessing act of spiritual force, i.e., consciousness. The sense organs can work properly under the close relationship with the *antahkaraṇa,* which in turn has to be guided by the consciousness. In his commentary to *Brahmasūtra,* Śaṁkara refers to the I/Thou problem in the *Adhyāṣabhāṣa* i.e., *Asmat/Yusmat* problem, *asmat* is the self and *yusmat* is other than the self in which comes the mind, senses, body and things of the world. Any claim regarding affirmation or negation made for anything in the world presupposes evidence provided by the consciousness by means of the *pramāṇa.* Not only that even the ultimate presupposition of all *pramāṇa-* perception, inference, verbal testimony, is provided by consciousness but also given the consciousness, all *pramāṇas* operate, absence of consciousness, no *pramāṇa* can operate.

To understand *antaḥkaraṇa,* we have to go into the details of the three stages of consciousness—*Jāgrat, Svapna* and *Suśupti.* Related with these three stages of consciousness, there is the problem of *intentionality* and self-consciousness. One of the *Vedāntins,* Rāmānuja, for instance, regards these three states as double intentional: on the one hand, it is intentional towards the subject; on the other, it is intentional towards the objects. But the other *Vedāntins* including Śaṁkara believe that consciousness by its nature is not intentional, but it becomes intentional because of its association with the mind. In the *Māndūkya Upaniṣad,* at waking state consciousness is intentional; it is in relation to several objects and their mechanisms and operations. These objects in their properties and relationships act on our senses and the mind. Thus our consciousness becomes aware of the things. What is true of waking level is equally true at the dream level because in dream experience, consciousness encounters the objects. The *Māndūkya Upaniṣad* brings the association of consciousness with the mind, senses, body and things at the waking level; and the association of consciousness at the two levels, i.e., waking and the dreaming states. This also involves the knowledge situation, i.e., the *triputi jñāna*—the subject, the object and the means of knowledge. At waking level, there is knowledge-situation *prajñā,* which is outward, but at the dream level, the similar knowledge-situation is there but not the same knowledge-situation. Consciousness at waking level is called *vishwā,* at dream level it is called *taijasa,* and at deep sleep level or *suśupti* it is called *prajñā.* These are three different terms used for consciousness depending on its three involvements. At the level of deep sleep, we are not aware of the objects of the outside world, or anything internal, because mind as mind is not functioning at this level. At this level we do not have a knowledge-situation, we are free from all desires is what the Vth *Mantra* of *Māndūkya Upaniṣad* declares. Consciousness is uniformly present in all the three stages of experience.

The body and the senses are present at the waking level, but these are absent at the dream level, even the mind is absent at the deep sleep level, but consciousness is present at all the three levels of experience. Consciousness is the witness of all the three episodes. But consciousness as such cannot be known under the knowledge-situation just as tongue cannot taste itself. This is the fourth state, the nameless, i.e., *turīya.* It is the state where consciousness is left to itself, trans-empirical, trans-rational, trans-linguistic. At the most we can describe it negatively. There is no other than anything outside, no other than anything inside, is the way that *turīya* state is described in the VII *Mantra* of the *Māndūkya Upaniṣad.* Then question arises how does *turīya* state differ from the *suśupti* state? *Turīya* state could be a mystical state, through meditation, etc., which if one has it, one has it, one does not have it, one does not have it. It is *adṛistam, avyavahāryam, agrāhyam, alakṣaṇam, achintam, śāntam, śivam, advaitam,* etc. It is at this stage that *Ātman* is to be entirely identified with the *Brahman.* In other words, if I am the *Ātman* and *Ātman* is Absolute then, it follows syllogistically, that I am the Absolute. I am *Brahman. Aham Brahmāsmi.*

So far as the knowledge of self is concerned, there is an astonishing similarity between Śaṁkara and Kant. Kant has criticized Aristotle's formulation of categories like this: ' he simply picked them up as they came in his way'. Kant goes to give a systematic formulation of the categories. The common structure of consciousness, Kant designates as 'transcendental unity of self-consciousness'.[12] It consists of 'forms of intuition' (space and time) and 'forms of understanding' (the categories), which are not static forms but forms of operation that exist only in the act of apprehending and comprehending sensibility. The 'forms of intuition' synthesize the manifold of sensibility into spatio-temporal order and by virtue of the categories, they are brought to universal and necessary relations of cause and effect, substance, reciprocity and so on—'receptivity is thus combined with spontaneity'.[13] This entire complex is unified in the transcendental apperception, which relates all experience to the 'thinking ego'.[14] This is what Kant calls as beginningless, transcendental, original, synthetic unity of apperception. In the synthetic unity of apperception, according to Kant, I am conscious of myself not as I appear to myself, not as I am in myself, but only that I am. The 'I think' must be, Kant insists, capable of accompanying all my representations. But the 'I think' always remains unknown and unknowable by means of the categories because it cannot as such be given in representation. If we try to apply the categories to the 'I think', such categories as 'substance', 'existence', 'person', etc., we come across a series of paralogisms.[15]

This view of the self, developed by Kant, is very close to the Advaitic doctrine of *Ātman* developed by Śaṁkara. Kant has worked on the same position which had inspired Śaṁkara from the Upaniṣads 'How can you know that which is the knower of everything'. The categories of understanding can be applied to objects given in sensible intuitions. Generic unity, specific difference, act, quality, relation, etc., are supposed by Śaṁkara to be the ultimate conditions of knowledge. To these, he sometimes adds space, time, causality, and non-contradiction *(Deśa-kāla-nimitta-sampatti ravadhāsca- Śaṁkara Bhāṣya,* III, 2,3). Śaṁkara emphasizes that the categories are not applicable to the witnessing self. It was for the first time in European philosophy that a view of the self approximating to the Advaitic doctrine of the self was so clearly formulated. It goes to the credit of Kant to have conceived so clearly that the self is not to be identified with the individual self involved in the subject-object dualism, the self is the universal principle of the consciousness or thought which is the pure or the transcendental subject as distinguished from the empirical subject and that this subject cannot itself be known as an object of knowledge. Here the Kantian doctrine of self looks like Upaniṣadic view expressed in the words 'How can you know that which is the knower of everything'. The self cannot be dislodged from its pivotal position as a knower. It can never be shifted from the centre to the periphery, because in every attempt to do so, we shall be compelled to put it back again into the centre under the force of logical necessity. The upshot is that it will remain there in the centre and it can never be the knower and the known simultaneously. That which we must presuppose as the precondition of all knowledge cannot itself become an object of knowledge.

The basic purpose of Kant's critical philosophy is to present an effective solution to Hume's skepticism. The first *Critique* with the transcendental deduction of categories tries to 'justify the claims of science philosophically' or 'to provide a philosophical basis for physical science'. As opposed to this, the primary motive of Śaṁkara's philosophy is to emphasize the self-shining character of the pure *ćit*, and consequently, placing it far beyond the ambit of inference and reasoning. Kant appears to be more interested in the organization of the experience than in the agency that organizes it. But Śaṁkara shows much more interest in the revelatory consciousness than in the objects that are revealed.

II

HEGEL'S NOTION OF ABSOLUTE DOCTRINE OF SPIRIT-REASON, UNDERSTANDING, SENSE CERTAINTY & DIALECTIC

Hegel's Spirit is, above all, a doctrine about the relationship between thought and objective reality. Hegel means by speaking Spirit the mediation or middle point between the Idea (the categories and the Notion which are also known as the truth in the most absolute and objective form) and Nature (the sphere of external existence which the truth is 'about'). The term 'Idea' Hegel designates to the absolute truth. Nature is the term, which Hegel gives to that truth as we find it in the outward existence of the world. Spirit, however, is the mode of existence of the whole in which everything, which is known, is embodied in being. Idea and Nature are dialectical opposites, but spirit is the unity between them. Hegel's contention is that there is something, which is identical neither with the sphere of our thought nor with the objects of our thought. It is the *Geist* that imparts an intelligible form of both these spheres. Spirit is the active synthesis of our consciousness of the world, and what we are conscious of. This is Hegel's epistemological quest too. In epistemology, then, we are concerned with the object which we have with our consciousness of it. But this is of such a nature that the distinction between what exists 'for us' and what exists 'in itself' is not a distinction between what is available to us in consciousness and what is not. Both sides of distinction fall within the grasp of consciousness. In other words, the Kantian distinction between phenomena and thing-in-itself is not acceptable to Hegel. The basic question, for Hegel, is how in consciousness we are related to our objects, and when our object is our own consciousness, it is clear that there is no danger that our consciousness should have an existence 'in itself' which is in principle hidden from us and separate from that consciousness as it exists 'for us'.

In formulating his own position, Hegel applauds Kant's discovery of the 'transcendental consciousness' as the ultimate source of conceptual synthesis. He approves Kant's criticism that consciousness cannot be an object of sensibility and hence categories cannot be applied to it. But this is not, Hegel contends, because categories overstep their legitimate limits, but because soul is a living and active being, just as complex as it is self identically simple. In fact, its simplicity is just as indivisible whole that is constituted solely by the cohesion and inseparability of its diverse traits, aspects and activities. Kant's objections, according to Hegel, are valid but his reasons are wrong ones.

Hegel elucidates two aspects of Spirit, first that Spirit requires the distinction of subject and object, and second that Spirit overcomes the supposed distinction between subject and object. The first is the moment of estrangement and the second is its transcendence or enlargement. Spirit is, thus, the locus of both estrangement and enlargement. Hegel takes over the doctrine from Kant that consciousness is necessarily bipolar and it is part of Hegel's general espousal of the view that "rational awareness requires separation. Consciousness is only possible when the subject is set over against an object."[16]

First of all, we should recall that Hegel's *Encyclopaedia of the Philosophical Sciences-An Outline*, his most general presentation of the philosophic system, is divided into three parts:

I. Logic: the science of the Idea in and for itself.
II. The Philosophy of Nature: the science of the Idea in its otherness.
III. The Philosophy of Spirit: the science of the Idea comes back to itself out of that otherness.[17] (Section 18)

Since the philosophy of Spirit is followed by Logic and the philosophy of Nature, the philosophy of Spirit is concerned to show 'that' and 'how' spirit 'frees itself from nature, from its otherness'. All three moments of this 'movement'—anthropology, phenomenology and psychology—are concerned with this "notion of freeing itself",[18] but only the moment of psychology shows the 'reality' of reason: the anthropological moment of subjective spirit shows reason to be the goal of nature, and the phenomenological moment shows reason to be the goal of consciousness. But the goal of the psychological investigation of spirit is to show that reason is the element of subjective spirit, that reason is the active power of spirit. To develop Hegel's psychological investigation of spirit, we have to discuss three sources of knowledge—sense certainty, understanding and reason along with dialectic—with its features of contradiction and sublation—operating in it.

The opening arguments of the *Phenomenology of Spirit* are good illustrations of the procedure Hegel adopts. The notion of spirit with which Hegel begins is our ordinary consciousness of things and from there he takes us to the true perspective of spirit. The work is called 'phenomenology' because it deals with the way things appear for consciousness, or with the forms of consciousness. But 'appearance' here is not to be contrasted with 'reality'—which is most real, the absolute, is essentially self-appearance. Phenomenology is not a science of lesser things, which can be left behind but one way of ascending to absolute knowledge of making the absolute apparent.

The method Hegel adopts to appreciate the Absolute Truth is to start with 'ordinary consciousness' of things and does not introduce at this moment any thing from the activity of mind whatsoever. From this ordinary experience of things, Hegel proceeds through the stage of 'understanding' and finally comes to 'reason', which is no longer a prey to contradiction and holds it reconciled within itself.

Hegel accepts and further develops the distinction manifested in Kant's philosophy between 'understanding' and 'reason'. In Kant, 'reason' is never in immediate relation to an object. It is 'understanding', that holds sway in his epistemology. By 'understanding', Hegel means, the capacity of reflective interpretation, a capacity which unrelentingly separates identity from difference, particular from universal, one from many, form from content and so on, and allows neither to contaminate the other. The 'understanding', however, restricts itself to the finite, and its thinking is always finite thinking. Hegel often calls it 'finite reason'. Hegel also uses the expression 'isolated reflection' to the numberless polarities, which emerge out of the operation of 'understanding'. The distinction and precise determination of things in terms of identity and difference characteristic of 'understanding' depends upon negation. A thing is what it is just because and so far as it is not another thing. What it determines is what it excludes, and what it excludes defines what it is.

Now that which is negated issues itself in a result, brings with itself and carries in itself that from which it has emerged, sublated and preserved within it is although also cancelled in its original finite formulation. This state is higher than the original finite one and it holds within itself both the finite and its negation. The result is thus more concrete, more complete and comprehensive than the first abstract, finite and limited one.

Hegel here brings 'reason' to unify that which the 'understanding' has divided. 'Reason' shows that the function of 'understanding'—to define things in terms of their isolation—constitutes a process of abstraction. The function of 'reason' is to make manifest the 'concrete' relation in which an idea, concept or thing subsists. In the process of unifying the opposites, 'reason' negates the finite and its negation, and binds them together in mutual dependence so that they are revealed as moments of more inclusive whole. This wholeness in which the antagonisms are resolved Hegel terms 'the Absolute', 'the Truth' of which I have mentioned at the beginning of the paper. The mutual exclusion of finite and its negative are complimentary so that they are revealed as moments of a more inclusive whole. The whole, which is thus achieved, is rational through and through, because it is systematically ordered.

With this interpretation of sense-certainty, understanding, and reason, Hegel gives strikingly new interpretation of logic. Novelty consists in Hegel's attempt to incorporate dialectic into logic. It requires two lines of argument: the first showing that a given category is indispensable; the second showing that it leads us to a characterization of reality, which is somehow contradictory. Hegel, infact, fuses these together. This makes Hegel's logic fundamentally different from Kantian-Aristotelian tradition. The categories, in Kant's formulation, are valid if they were correctly formed and if their use was in conformity with the laws of thought and the rules of syllogism—no matter what the content to which they were applied. Contrary to this procedure, Hegel's Logic and with it his dialectic is always dynamic and expresses dynamics of objective reality as well.

The negative or contradictory character of the categories basically motivates Hegel's dialectic. As stated, Hegel's categories denote and deal with the reality, so the dialectical operation in reality is basically the dialectic operating in the formulation of the categories. There are two terms, which are operative in Hegel's dialectic. These are (i) contradiction, (ii) sublation or *aufheben*. In fact, these are not two separate terms but are mutually interdependent and under certain circumstances they pass into each other. Let me first explain Hegel's position on contradiction. In the *Science of Logic,* Hegel emphasises by saying: "...everything is inherently contradictory, and in the sense that this law in contrast to other expresses rather the truth and the essential nature of things. It is one of the fundamental prejudices of logic as hitherto understood and of ordinary thinking, that contradiction is not so characteristically essential and immanent a determination as identity. Nevertheless, if it were a question of grading the two determinations and they had to be kept separate, then contradiction would have to be taken as the profounder determination and more characteristic of essence. For, as against contradiction, identity is merely the determination of the simple immediate, of dead being; but contradiction is the root of all movement and vitality; it is only in so far as something has a contradiction within it that it moves, has an urge and activity."[19]

Contradiction, for Hegel, is internal to each term. That is why every term, whether a concept or a reality, develops. Hegel continues, "...internal self-movement proper, instinctive urge in general...is nothing else but the fact that something is, in one and the same respect, self contained and deficient, the negative of itself. Abstract self-identity is not as yet a livingness, but the positive, being in its own self a negativity, goes outside itself and undergoes alteration. Something is therefore alive only in so far as it contains contradiction within it and moreover is this power to hold and endure the contradiction within it."[20]

Hegel concludes near the end of the *Logic* that there is nothing, whether in actuality or in thought that is as simple and abstract as is commonly imagined. "Nothing exists as just brutally given and simply possessing one or two fully positive characteristics. Nothing exists that is just first and primary and on which other things depend, but they cannot really succeed in doing so unless they stay on the level of imaginative pictures. Imagining that such things exist is possible only as long as we are ignorant of what is actually present. What appears at first simple and immediate is actually complex and mediated."[21] Mediation (*Vermittlung*) and mediated (*Vermittlet*), and the opposites, immediacy (*Unvermittlung*) and immediate (*Unvermittelt*) are key terms through which Hegel explains not only contradiction but also sublation and dialectic. Let me clarify these terms.

To 'mediate' is to be in the middle, to connect two extremes. Everything, Hegel states, is mediated that nothing exists as 'immediate' first. In the *Logic,* 'mediation' will involve the gradual development of categories to a point where there is nothing that is posited as first and independent. In Hegel's dialectic, the thesis is always regarded as 'immediate' or as characterized by 'immediacy'. The second term, the anti-thesis, is 'mediate' or 'mediation'. The third term, the synthesis, is the merging of 'mediation' and emerging as a new 'immediacy'. And this process goes on.

The synthesis of a triad both abolishes and preserves the differences of the thesis and the antithesis. Hegel expresses this activity of the synthesis as *aufheben* or sublation, which is the other operative term of Hegel's dialectic. It maybe seen as manifesting three distinct but mutually interrelated moments. "First, it has the moment of 'transcendence', in which it goes beyond a 'limit' or 'boundary'; secondly it is 'negation' of this first negation, this 'limit', in which it is overcome or removed; and thirdly, it is the moment of 'preservation', in which what has been gone 'beyond' or transcended is brought again into a new relation."[22] These three moments of sublation, though distinct, form a unitary process of *Logic*, which is differentiated into its various components only for the purpose of helping as 'understanding' of the process itself. The very process by which a category is formulated and is intimately related to another is, at one and the same logical moment, the process by which it transcends its limited abstract self-identity, 'negates' that identity and emerges into a connected unity or nexus, in which it is preserved as an intrinsic part of some greater whole. The differences between the first and the second member of each triad are sublated by the third. This, however, does not require sufficient explanation and necessary substantiation. For this purpose, one may take up the categories of Being, Nothing and Becoming, and bring out the various ways in which dialectic is operating in the formulation of the categories of Being and Nothing, and their sublation in the category of Becoming. Herein operate two fundamental principles of Hegel's dialectic; namely, 'unity and struggle of opposites and negation of negation'. The same process is applicable to the rest of the Hegelian categories.

As a matter of fact, the more general and more abstract concept is always prior to the less general and less abstract. And this principle not only decides for Hegel that the first category is being, but also determines the order of the subsequent categories. Moreover, every logical deduction is essentially based on the principle that the subsequent must be contained in the antecedent. The breach of this principle of formal logic is what is called the fallacy of illicit process. There cannot be anything present in the conclusion, which is not present in the premises. This is really the old principle *ex nihilo nihil fit.* I will try to show that this is just as true of the Hegelian Logic as of the humble formal logic. The exclusion is not absolute, what is absolute is the mutual supplementation. The result of the supplementation is a growth, a development. This is a principle of Hegel's dialectic known as 'the negation of negation'. Just as Being is implicitly Becoming, so Becoming is implicitly the next synthesis. In the next synthesis, we find that Becoming expresses itself in the moment of a 'determinate being', which is further expressed as below:

(i) as determinateness, such as quality,

(ii) as determinateness transcended: quantity,

(iii) as quantity qualitatively determined: measure.

Quality, for Hegel, is the internal self-determination, which is identical with the being, which it determines. Quantity is a determination, which is external to what it determines. The combination of quality and quantity is found in what Hegel calls as measure. Quality, when fully developed through repulsion and attraction, passes into quantity and *vice-versa.* Hegel calls this unity as measure. It is the synthesis of the spheres of quality and quantity as the thesis and the antithesis respectively. With this synthesis we arrive at another principle of Hegel's dialectic known as 'the transition from quantitative changes to qualitative changes and *vice-versa.*'

We have so far explicated three laws of Hegel's dialectic; namely, (i) 'unity and struggle of opposites', (ii) 'negation of the negation', (iii) 'transition from quality to quantity, and *vice-versa*'. These three laws of dialectic are operating not only in the whole process of Hegel's deduction of categories, but also in the appreciation of the Absolute.

If, therefore, we understand by Hegel's dialectic as a gradual explication and development of the 'connectedness' of the categories of Logic, then dialectic is operating in our thought alone. But such a dialectical nexus of concepts is not itself sufficient to account for our knowledge of the objective reality. Dialectic must come out of thought and confront the world, which is given. That is to say, it must have a relation to the objective world of matter into which man daily finds himself thrown.

Hegel very clearly recognizes this fact and in the subheading 81 of the *Encyclopaedia of the Philosophical Sciences,* he writes, "Everything that surrounds us maybe viewed as an instance of Dialectic. We are aware that everything finite, instead of being stable and ultimate, is rather changeable and transient; and this is exactly what we mean by that Dialectic of the finite, by which the finite, as that which in itself is other than itself, is forced beyond its own immediate or natural being to turn suddenly into its opposite...All things, we say—that is, the finite world as such—are doomed; and in saying so, we have a vision of Dialectic as the universal and irresistible power before which nothing can stay however secure and stable it may deem itself. We find traces of its (Dialectic's) presence in each of the particular provinces and phases of the natural and the spiritual world. This moment the planet stands in this spot but implicitly it is the possibility of being otherwise the planet brings into existences dialectical...It is the same dynamic that lies at the root of every other natural process and as it were forces nature beyond itself."[23]

The above passage sufficiently demonstrates that the laws of dialectic are not only operating in our thought but are also the fundamental features of the change and development taking place in the material reality. So, the dialectic has this dual function to perform *viz.* to show that dialectic is operating in human thought and that simultaneously it is operating in the objective reality. But as an absolute idealist, Hegel regards the dialectic of thought as primary and the dialectic of reality as secondary, as an externalisation of the dialectic of thought. This is evident from the fact that Hegel first formulates the principles of dialectic in the sphere of Logic—the concepts and categories—and then introduces those laws of dialectic to the world outside. The laws of dialectic are the 'externalisation' of the spirit. This is another illustration of what Derrida calls Hegel's 'idealising mastery' because it is spirit that gives rise to the laws of dialectic.

With the above exposition of Hegel's doctrine of spirit and dialectic alongwith the related concepts like reason, understanding, sense-certainty, etc., it will be appropriate to come to Hegel's theory of sign more precisely. Hegel's semiology is situated in the first movement of spirit, i.e. subjective spirit that in general is formulated by Hegel in three phases.

1. *Subjective spirit*: the spirit's relation to itself, an only ideal totality of the idea. This is being—near—to itself in the form of only internal freedom.
2. *Objective spirit*: as a world to produce and produced in the forms of reality, not only ideality. Freedom here becomes an existing, present necessity.

3. *Absolute spirit*: the unity, that is *in itself and for itself*, of the objectivity of the spirit and of its ideality or its concept, the unity producing itself eternally, spirit in its absolute truth—absolute spirit. (Section 385).

To sum up Hegel's notion of the Absolute, we can say that Hegel's notion of Absolute is essentially embodied in his doctrine of spirit and the dialectic along with the onto-theological or onto-teleological synthesis. Hegel's *Aufhebung* depends on his doctrine of spirit in as much as it rests on dialectical principles and it is within human experience in the world—the phenomenology—that it begins to progress until it reaches the Absolute.

Śaṁkara and Hegel on Self-consciousness and the Absolute

In the Upaniṣadic philosophic thought, we come across a conflict among the metaphysicians; some regarding the Self as an entity entirely distinct from the Absolute, others regarding it as a part of the Absolute, and yet others regarding the Self and the Absolute as entirely identical. These constitute respectively the fundamental positions of the three great metaphysical schools—the dualistic, the quasi-monistic and the monistic. It is the monistic metaphysics, as already explained in the Part-I, which Śaṁkara has advocated and which has come very close to what Hegel has to say on the Absolute.

The *Chāndogya Upaniṣad* arrives at the conception of self-consciousness as constituting the Ultimate Reality. In *Taittirīya Upaniṣad* the identification of the Absolute with consciousness has been brought out like this—the Absolute is Existence, Consciousness and Infinity (S. 12. 9). In the *Aitarīya Upaniṣad*, we find, "of the gods, of the heaven, and the beings of the earth, whether produced from the eggs, or embryo, or sweat, or from the earth, everything that moves, or flies, or is stationary—Self-consciousness is eye of the world; it is self-consciousness which is Absolute." (S. 12.b.). With an extensive survey of the different approaches to the notion of Absolute and the Ultimate Reality, the *Upaniṣadic* seers have established Ultimate Reality firmly on self- consciousness. God to them is not God unless he is identical with self-consciousness. Existence is not existence if it does not mean self-consciousness. Reality is not reality if it does not express through out its structure the marks of pure self-consciousness. On the cognition of the Absolute, the *Taittirīya Upaniṣad* says: That, from which our speech turns back along with mind, being unable to comprehend its fullness, is the Ultimate Reality. *Kenopaniṣad* says: That where the eye is unable to go, where neither speech nor mind is able to reach—what conception can we have of it, except that it is beyond all that is known, and beyond all that is unknown. Śaṁkara and Hegel would agree with each other that the comprehension of Being as immanent in all other categories is the most fundamental category of all things. Śaṁkara in his *Commentary on the Chāndogya Upaniṣad* (vi,2, 1.) says, "Existence or Being, it is urged, is pure, subtle, indefinable, all-pervading, one, taintless, indivisible, knowledge." On the concept of Pure Being, Hegel has also to say the same thing: Pure Being is complete indeterminacy, absence of all qualities, a vacuity, an empty concept. Being is the most irrepressible category for both Hegel and Śaṁkara. Hegel's Absolute is the unity, which realizes itself in the differences, and it is not in which all differences are lost like that of Schelling. As already stated, Hegel too has to say the same thing like this: 'The True is the whole. But the whole is nothing other than the essence consummating itself through its development. Of the absolute it must be said that it is essentially a result, that only in the end is it what it truly is; and that precisely in this consists its nature, *viz.*, to be actual subject, the spontaneous becoming of itself'. And Hegel adds, 'Philosophy is itself, in fact, worship (*Die philosophie ist der selbst Gottesdienst*); it is religion, for in the same way it renounces subjective notions and opinions in order to occupy itself with God. The object of religion as well as of philosophy is eternal truth in its objectivity, God and nothing but God and the explication of God. In philosophy, religion gets justification from thinking consciousness.' For Hegel, nothing could be external to consciousness; but as consciousness exists through its opposition to the 'other' which it at the same time sublates and this process goes on until it reaches to the Absolute Unity.

Immediate experience is the very heart of Śaṁkara's absolutism, whereas Hegel would never accept pure immediacy in the Absolute. In Hegel's dialectic, the thesis is always regarded as 'immediate' or as characterized by 'immediacy'. The second term, the anti-thesis, is 'mediate' or 'mediation'. The third term, the synthesis, is the merging of 'mediation' and emerging as a new 'immediacy'. And this process goes on. The 'Absolute idea' in its final form is the 'free-subject', the Notion or *Begriff*. Its otherness or negation is the object. Both the *Begriff* and its otherness are constantly overwhelmed by the ontological conception of Hegel's Absolute idealism. Hegel's *Science of Logic* thus ends where it began with the category of Being and through all its mediations. But for Śaṁkara, Absolute is nothing if it is shorn of immediate experience.

This is the position of Absolute Monism. Whether this state of Absolute Monism is to be intellectually apprehended as Hegel does or expressed in self-realization as Śaṁkara does, both the ways are of the same spiritual pilgrimage.

III

MODERNITY AND POSTMODERNITY JACQUES DERRIDA AND JEAN-FRANCOIS LYOTARD *DIFFÉRANCE* AND CRITIQUE OF THE NOTION OF ABSOLUTE

Before I come to assess Derrida's reactions to Hegel's Absolute, I would like to furnish a brief note on the basic issues concerning modernity and postmodernity. Modernity breaks with the endless reiteration of traditional (classical) themes, topics and myths; and postmodernity operates at the places of closure in modernity, at the margins of what proclaims itself to be new and a break with tradition. To be modern means to search for new self-conscious expressive forms. To be postmodern is to marginalize, delimit, disseminate and decenter the primary and often secondary works of modernist inscriptions. It implies that the line of demarcation between modernity and postmodernity remains a matter of uncertainty because postmodernity operates at the edge of modernity.

In 1979 Jean-Francois Lyotard was assigned by the Canadian Government to compile, assess and critically evaluate the intellectual climate in the most advanced countries of the Western Europe and USA. In this study Lyotard, as a point of departure, uses the term 'postmodern' to describe that climate. In *Driftworks,* for example, Lyotard inveighs against modernist reason as the main instrument of repression and stresses the free play of both language and action that leads to 'plurality of singularities'.[24] He proceeds to analyze the changes and transformations that took place since the end of the nineteenth century in the fields of philosophy, science, literature, politics, art, etc. This he terms as 'the crisis of narratives'. These narratives are the reflections of the modernist conceptual framework in which a criterion or a standard or a legitimation with reference to its own system is designed. This could be an appeal to a Grand Narrative such as the Dialectic of Spirit (Hegel), Emancipation of the Rational Subject (Enlightenment Rationality of Kant) or the Working Subject (Marx). As against this, Lyotard defines postmodernity as 'incredulity towards metanarratives'. Any statement of conclusion needs to be placed in the context of validation criterion. Postmodernity is an end of the validation criterion. In *The Postmodern Condition: A Report on Knowledge,* Lyotard has emphasized on similar concern on developments in modern science, catastrophe theory, chaos theory and so on, all of which display, he thinks, the bankruptcy of traditional forms of epistemology.

Postmodernity could be defined as an 'attitude' or a 'mood' or a 'Movement'. Modernity could be defined as an 'ism'; i.e., 'a clear set of ideas' and a programme of action based on it. Postmodernity is not a systematic thing where you can develop concepts and relationships, precisely that is what the postmodernists are against. In modernity, everything is a system like 'foundationalism', 'essentialism', 'teleology', 'rationalism', 'freedom', 'logocentrism' and so on. I would like to dwell little more on the question of what is the relation of postmodernity to modernity? No postmodernist will say that postmodernity is a denial of modernity. They say, it is a reconstruction, a reinterpretation, and an attempt to give a new meaning to modernity. This is what the spokesman of postmodernity, Jean-Francois Lyotard says, "The whole idea of postmodernity is perhaps better rethought under the rubric of rewriting modernity."[25] Modern means something, which is not traditional, "To be modern is to break with the past and to search for new self-conscious expressive forms."[26] The transition from the tradition to the modernity consists in the fact that the centre shifted from 'religion to human reason'. The beginning of modernity can be traced to that intellectual fervor that spread in Europe from the middle of the eighteenth century. The French Revolution of 1789 was the high point in the spread of this intellectual-spiritual as well as political-economic-social ferment in western society. We have a long list of philosophers who are moderns, such as, Descartes, Bacon, Galileo, Newton, Hume, Kant, Hegel, Marx, Mill, Comte and so on. The basic philosophical quests in modernism are that 'man can be an interpreter of the world' (Bacon), an observer of nature through an instrument such as the telescope and the mathematical foundation of the world (Cartesian-Galilean mechanics), universal law of gravitation and the three laws of motion (Newton), 'understanding makes nature' (Kant), 'what is rational is actual and what is actual is rational' (Hegel), the point however is to change the world' (Marx)—in a nutshell, one can shape and control the world through science is what inaugurates the modern world-view. Behind that drive there lies an absolute confidence in the capacity of unaided and autonomous human reason to solve all puzzles and remove the veil of mystery from reality. Reason alone can make the objective reality under human control through science and technology.

The postmodernity, on the other hand, wants to ignore even the present, in order to make a creative leap into the future untamed by laws, norms and institutions which are dominating the modernist society. Postmodernity is certainly not anti-modern in the sense of being backward looking. It does not want to reinstate the norms of religion and tradition which modernism repudiated. Nor does it want to abide by the norms of modernity—especially the emphasis on system-prone thinking and logical rationality. The stalwarts of postmodernity are the irrationalism of Nietzsche, the structuralism of anthropologist Claude Levi-Strauss, the cultural semiologist Ronald Barthes, the psychoanalytic theorist Jacques Lacan, the poststructuralist Michel Foucault, the deconstructionist Jacques Derrida, Levinas, Richard Rorty, critical theorists like Max Horkheimer, Adorno, Marcuse, Jürgen Habermas and others, but each in his own way.

What is held to be common to the disparate thinkers of postmodernity is a belief, though it is expressed in various ways, that in the present-day intellectual climate, we are observing a general crisis of 'philosophy'. In other words, we are facing "a series of crises... in which older modes of defining, appropriating and recomposing the objects of artistic, philosophical, literary and social scientific languages are no longer credible and in which one common aspect is the dissolution of the very boundary between the language and its object".[27] Stephen White has suggested that what he calls 'postmodern problematic' consists of four interrelated phenomena: "the increasing incredulity towards metanarratives, the growing awareness of new problems wrought by societal rationalism, the explosion of new informational technologies and the emergence of new social movements".[28] Richard Rorty has brought the postmodern claim about knowledge, language and the world like this—the modernist assumption was that we had a 'glassy essence' that could be rationally perceived and interpreted through particular techniques and through which we could perceive the world but postmodernism smashes that glass.

Given the above, postmodernity is, of its very nature, 'philosophical'. Let us take, for example, one of the key areas of postmodern discourse regarding philosophy—the notion of Hegel's Absolute by Derrida.

Derrida's critique of Hegel's notion of Absolute and his idealism, and more specifically to the extent that he takes Hegel seriously, can be nowhere better viewed than in his treatment of Hegel's theory of representation and the sign. As stated by Derrida himself, "The problematic of the sign derives from a fundamental logocentrism, from a philosophy of consciousness or of the originary subject."[29] In his celebrated history of the notion of the sign in *Of Grammatology* as well as the shorter version presented in his interview with Julia Kristeva in *Positions,* Derrida attempts to show that the very concept of the sign has always depended on, or been determined by, that fundamental metaphysical opposition: the sensible and the intelligible. Derrida treats the sign work in various ways in order to show that the metaphysical tradition has always treated the sign as a transition or a bridge between presence in the form of the object (the sensible) and presence in the form of self-presence (the intelligible), Derrida views it as the time of referral which signifies self-presence; in the case of Hegel, to anticipate a later discussion, it is the self-presence of the absolute as subject, the subjective spirit, on which the theory of sign is located.

What is central to Derrida's reading of Hegel's doctrine of spirit, dialectic and the sign is that Derrida tries to retain the horizontal character of Hegel's notion of philosophy without its teleology. We have already given an elaborate account of Hegel's notion of Absolute in Part-II. Derrida tries to reject the teleology involved in such concepts as truth, spirit and dialectic, but he accepts the horizontal feature of these concepts. As a matter of fact, for Derrida, writing always leads to more writing, and more, and still more; just as history does not lead to Final Struggle, but to more history, and more, and still more. Notion of truth cannot lead us to Absolute Truth but to more truth, and more and still more. The vision of truth in the *Phenomenology* as stated above involves a development, which is dialectical whereas Derrida has a conception of development based on ruptures and mutations.

Derrida, however, rejects the aspects of continuity and development in the history of philosophy. In an interview in Paris in 1981, Derrida said, "...the relationship between the ancient and the modern is not simply that of the implicit and the explicit. We must avoid the temptations of supposing that what occurs today somehow pre-existed in a latent form, merely waiting to be unfolded or explicated. Such thinking also conceives history as an evolutionary development and excludes the crucial notions of rupture and mutation in history. My own conviction is that we must maintain two contradictory affirmations at the same time. On the one hand we affirm the existence of ruptures in history, and on the other we affirm that these ruptures produce gaps or faults (*failles*) in which the most hidden and forgotten archives can emerge and constantly recur and work through history..."[30] Derrida's historical writing is located in *différance* between past and present, determination and under-determination, in the space traced out and traversed by the supplement as excess, therefore between binary poles or on the 'fourth side' of the triangle. *Différance* in history has the effect, infact, of reopening the present to the past, situating each in terms of the other. Hegelianism, therefore, is historically situated, emerging at a particular time and place, but it should be read at the same time in terms of history because to write is to supply a context with all that is necessary for its operation as well as all that is necessary for its erasure, the reopening of context that would close down the question of the relation even as it works it, and protect the present from the past.

Besides Derrida, within postmodernism, Hegelian orientation that 'the true is the whole' is allegedly criticized by Lyotard as a 'terror' and the 'nostalgia' of the 'whole and the one' in philosophy. Lyotard's answer to Hegel's concept of reason as the unifying agency is "let us wage a war on totality."[31] Taking a clue from Hegel that the speculative philosophy if applied on physical sciences will lead to a "Road of doubt... road of despair... skepticism,"[32] Lyotard gives a final blow to Hegelianism, "the speculative apparatus maintains an ambiguous relation to knowledge. It shows that knowledge is only worthy of that name to the extent that it reduplicates itself ('lifts itself up', *bebt sich auf*, is sublated) by citing its own statements in a second-level discourse (autonomy) that functions to legitimate them. This is as much as to say that, in its immediacy, denotative discourse bearing on a certain referent (a living organism, a chemical property, a physical phenomenon, etc.) does not really know what it thinks it knows. Positive science is not a form of knowledge. And speculation feeds on its suppression. The Hegelian speculative narrative thus harbours a certain skepticism toward positive learning as Hegel himself admits."[33] Derrida also rejects Hegel's claim for rationality. He summarizes as "'myth of the presence' whether this takes the form of the immanent presence, presence of God, or of the world as a determinate entity, or of the self as an inner certainty. This 'theo-ontological tradition' refuses to consider the possibility that there is no such certainties, and even the language we use to talk about philosophy is riddled with distinctions and world that makes this myth avoidable."[34]

To develop Derrida's basic contention behind this position, we have to go to "The Pit and the Pyramid: Introduction to Hegel's Semiology" of the *Margins of Philosophy* wherein he presents a comprehensive and critical account of Hegel's theory of speech and writing. But this criticism has to be seen within the general strategy of transformation, displacement and reinscription at work in the Derridean project of grammatology. Derrida locates Hegel quite firmly within the history of the logocentric tradition and then with the help of his method of deconstruction, he not only 'differs' from Hegelianism but also 'defers' from that.

Derrida presents a detailed analysis of Hegel's theory of speech and writing-semiology—and he does so by focusing on two long remarks from *The Encyclopaedia of the Philosophical Sciences-An Outline.* Both remarks are found in the subchapter 'Imagination' in the Chapter 'Psychology' within 'Subjective Spirit.'[35] Derrida's critique of Hegel's semiology lies in criticising the primacy Hegel accords to psychology and it amounts to Derrida's most general criticism of modernism—the quest for subjectivity. Derrida takes it as a problematic, the fact that Hegel's theory of speech and writing—his semiology—falls with in the sphere of subjective spirit and more precisely within the area of psychology and not for instance, within anthropology or phenomenology—the two previous moments of subjective spirit.

Since Hegel's semiology is situated in the subjective spirit, and, since subjective spirit is finite and transitory, Derrida argues, "The sign indeed appears as a mode or determination of subjective and finite spirit as a mode of determination or transgression (*Ubersichhinausgehen*) of itself, a transition within transition, a transition of the transition."[36] This is another instance of Hegel's idealism or what Derrida calls the 'idealizing mastery' because Hegel's semiology does not provide a way out of itself but a return to itself of spirit. The 'idealizing mastery' consists, as Derrida suggests, in the Hegelian system as a whole: as a moment of intelligence (*Inteligenz*), representation makes the transition between intuition and thought explicit (Section 458, Addition). Representation (*Vorstellung*) distinguishes the activity of immediate intuition from the content intuited, transforming the sensible appearances which intuition has always mediated. Throughout all the moments of representation—recollection, imagination, memory—such transformative activity is present. Indeed, in the production of signs, or language generally, intelligence explicitly posits its imaginative activities. Since signs are external, they escape the provisional character of the consciousness, which produces them. Hegel says, "Intelligence...appears in taking up sensuous content and forming representations for itself out of this material it then gives its independent representations a definite determinate being (*einbestimmtes Dasein*)." (Section 458 Addition).

Hegel's idealism or the 'idealizing mastery' of semiology lies precisely at this point. Derrida has given an elaborate analysis of it. I would like to quote in full what Derrida claims in this regard, for it is the basis of his critique of Hegelian semiology. Derrida says, "The sign unites an 'independent representation' and an 'intuition', in other words, a concept (signified) and a sensory perception (signifier). But Hegel must immediately recognize a kind of separation, a disjoining which, by dislocating the 'intuition', opens the space and plays of signification. There is no longer in the signifying unity, in the welding of representation and intuition, an intuition like another. Doubtless, as in every intuition, a being is given, a thing is presented and is to be received in its simple presence...It is there, immediately insible, indubitable. But in so far as it is united to *Vorstellung* (to a representation), this presence becomes representation, a representation (in the sense of representing) of a representation (in the general sense of conceptual ideality) put in the place of something other, it becomes *etwas anaderes Varztellend:* here *Varstellen* and *represent* release and reassemble all their meanings at once."[37]

Due to logocentric preoccupation, Hegel's idealism gives rise to a strange 'intuition', as Derrida says, presents in the sign, which represents ideality—the ideality of a *Bedultung* or meaning. And as the unity of the signifying body and the signified ideality, the sign itself "becomes a kind for incarnation".[38] Thus, in general and most importantly for Derrida's project, "The opposition of the intelligible and the sensory condition the difference between the signified and the signifier, between the signifying intention (*bedeuten*), which is an animating activity, and the inert body of the signifier."[39] Derrida, therefore, notes that for Hegel, the proper and animated body of the signifier (the sign) is a tomb. "The body of the sign thus becomes the monument in which the soul will be enclosed, preserved, maintained, kept in maintenance, present, signified. At the heart of this monument the soul keeps itself alive but it needs the monument only to the extent that it is exposed-to death-in its living relation to its own body...The sign-the monument-of-life-in-death, the sepulcher of a soul... is the Pyramid."[40]

Hegelian production of signs of the use of language, according to Derrida, "is an interiorization of spirit relating itself to itself with its sight set on truth—'*with its sight* set'—conceived in its destination on the basis of truth toward which it is oriented."[41] Since in Hegel the movement of spirit is dialectical, Derrida's subsequent analysis in "The Pit and the Pyramid" shows Hegel's semiology founded on dialectic, "the resolution of the sign in the horizon of the non-sign, of the presence beyond the sign".[42] Since I have already explained Hegel's dialectic with its operative terms of contradiction and sublation along with its three principles, it will be appropriate to examine Derrida's criticism of Hegelian dialectic and with it, of course, Hegel's semiology.

Derrida subjects to a rigorous criticism and a reinterpretation of Hegel's term *Aufhebung* with its concepts of negativity and contradiction. As a matter of fact, Hegel's sign works on the basis of contradiction and the negative character of reality motivates his dialectic. Derrida carefully distinguishes his term *différance* from the Hegelian term 'difference' which is the same as contradiction; for difference, alleges Derrida, is determined in the *Science of Logic* "as contradiction (*Widerspruch*) only in order to resolve it, to interiorize it, to lift it up...into the self-presence of an onto-theological or onto-teleological synthesis."[43] As stated earlier, Hegel's idealism with its dialectic incorporates all the contradictory features in all the earlier philosophical systems. In other words, the novelty of Hegel's logic is that it incorporates dialectic into it. Therefore, Derrida says that

Hegel's idealism with its dialectic is, "A resolution of contradiction into a third term that comes in order to *aufheben,* to deny while raising up, while idealizing, while sublimating into an amanuensis inferiority (*Errinnerung*), while interring difference in a self presence."[44] *Aufhebung* is required to preserve the meaning of a sign and *Aufhebung* can only be understood in terms of difference, or contradiction, as negativity, or as a *Esenheit,* or essentiality as Hegel explains it in the *Science of Logic.*

Derrida examines Hegel's dialectic and the deduction of categories both thematically and methodologically. As a determination of reflection, contradiction (along with the categories of identity and difference) is treated thematically as a category of essence. But contradiction, as the structure of *Aufhebung,* suggests that the Hegelian method itself embodies contradiction. As a matter of fact, Hegel has divided *Science of Logic* into Objective Logic and Subjective Logic and the division may correspond to Kant's classification of Logic into General, Particular and Transcendental, in the Transcendental Analytic of the *Critique of Pure Reason.* What Kant calls as General and Particular Logic and the concepts he deduces from them is what Hegel calls as Subjective Logic. But whereas the concepts of General and Particular Logic, in Kant's analysis, are purely formal, abstracted from contents; for Hegel, the concepts of Subjective Logic have a content of their own, though not sensibly intuitable one. Moreover, what Hegel calls Objective Logic would partly correspond to Kant's Transcendental Logic. Partly, because whereas the concepts of Transcendental Logic are incapable to comprehend the thing-in itself, the Objective Logic denotes and deals not only with the appearance of a thing but also with the essence of a thing.

The deduction of categories from their *implicit* to their *explicit* phases in Hegel's *Logic* cannot be viewed on the basis of the phases themselves. The development from the category of Being to the category of Essence has to be explained in terms of the entire internal complexity. Each category provides this complexity and it is because of the complexity that it is further evolved. Each category is thus a logical function and can be explained in terms of its systematic meaning within the *Logic* as a whole. This leads to the thematic understanding of each category.

However, the *Logic* also requires three principles of development and these are quantitative changes lead to qualitative changes and *vice-versa,* unity and struggle of opposites and negation of negation. These are the principles of Hegelian dialectic, which elicit the logical function of each category. This, then, is the methodological understanding of Hegel's dialectic. But Derrida's focus on contradiction as the structure of *Aufhebung* suggests that Hegel's dialectical method itself embodies contradiction. Therefore, the distinction between thematic and methodological senses of contradiction is of crucial significance for Derrida's project. As Derrida describes *différance* (the process of differentiation), "It can no longer simply be subsumed by the generality for heterogeneous modes of conflictuality, or, if you will, of contradictions... To reduce difference to *différance* is to stay far behind in this debate."[45] Both Hegel's *Logic* and Derridean *différance* regard contradiction as an indispensable feature of human thought. Thought and reality would be meaningless, if thought comprehends reality outside its categories. Derrida draws a distinction between a merely 'logical contradiction' and 'a differentiated accounting of contradictions' and this can be appreciated if we stick to what I have spoken of as the thematic and the methodological senses of contradiction. *Différance* is the most operative term of Derrida's deconstruction. In *Of Grammatology*, Derrida has this to say about deconstruction, "A sowing that does not produce plants, but is simply infinitely repeated... a semination that is not insemination but dissemination, seed spilled in vain, an emission that can not return to its origins in the father."[46] In *Positions,* he remarks, "In the final analysis, dissemination means nothing and can not be reassembled into a definition..."[47] and therefore deconstruction is not a theory, not a position, not a critique, not a technique, "not a method and can not be transformed into one".[48] With deconstruction, Derrida tries to transcend the binary oppositions like truth and falsehood, reality and appearance, good and evil, etc. and dismantles these conceptual oppositions. Richard Kearney, in a Prefatory Note on Derrida, writes, "Derrida was working out his central notion of the irreducible structure of *différance* as it operates in human consciousness, temporality, history, and above all in the fundamental and overriding activity of writing (*L'e'criture*). By means of this concept of *différance*—a neologism meaning both 'to defer' and 'to differ'—, Derrida proposes to show how the major metaphysical definitions of Being as some timeless self-identity of presence (e.g. *logos*...), which dominated western philosophy from Plato to the present day, could ultimately be 'deconstructed'. Such deconstruction would show that in each instance difference *precedes* presence rather than the contrary..."[49] In *Positions,* Derrida writes, "...*différance* refers to the (active and passive) movement that consists in deferring by means of a delay, delegation, reprieve, referral, detour, postponement, reserving. In this sense, *differance* is not preceded by the originally and invisible unity of a present *possibility that* I could reserve, like an expenditure that I could put off calculatedly, or for the reasons of economy. What defers presence, on the contrary, is the very basis on which presence is announced or desired in what represents it, its sign, its trace..."[50]

To conclude this part, I can say that Hegel's semiology is essentially embodied in his doctrine of spirit and the dialectic along with the onto-theological or onto-teleological synthesis. However, in rejecting the presuppositions of modern philosophy, Derrida fails to offer a serious and constructive counter hypothesis to supplant the doctrines, which lie at the roots of the German Idealism. Derrida's method of 'deconstruction' means, like in guerrilla warfare, to attack quickly and run back, to puncture and parody, and to defuse through refusing to take a thesis seriously. Derrida has an intense distrust of metaphysics, including the metaphysics of self as the presupposition of the notion of Absolute. For Derrida, the job of philosophy is not to depend or account for the system, but to 'deconstruct' it. Consequently, Absolute has no substance, and Derrida tries to make up for it. Hegel's *Aufhebung,* despite the fact that it has the element of idealism with the doctrine of spirit, cannot however be reduced to Derridean symbol of an 'idealizing mastery', just as Hegel's semiology cannot be reduced to the logic of representation. Hegel's *Aufhebung* depends on his doctrine of spirit in as much as it rests on dialectical principles and it is within human experience in the world—the phenomenology—that it begins progress within the limits of meaning and explanation. This is modest in a way I don't think Derrida would reject.

IV

CRITICAL THEORY OF FRANKFURT SCHOOL CRITIQUE OF ENLIGHTENMENT RATIONALITY-HABERMAS

As maybe imagined, Kantianism and Hegelianism have made a great stir not only in the field of philosophy, but also in the fields of psychology, theology and socio-political philosophy. Postmodernity is a critique of enlightenment rationality. As a matter of fact, Kant is the philosopher of the enlightenment rationality and Hegel continues on the same line of thinking. A critique of enlightenment rationality implies a critique of Kant and Hegel. Among the Critical Theorists who strongly criticise Kant and Hegel are the Frankfurt scholars like Max Horkheimer (1895-1973), Theodor W. Adorno (1903-1969), Herbert Marcuse (1898-1979) and Jürgen Habermas (L.1929-). These critics, each in his own way, have attempted to go ahead of Kant and Hegel, either by offering emendation of Kantianism and Hegelianism or by making Kant and Hegel relevant in the changed intellectual climate in Europe and America. In what follows, I shall re-assess the basic charges levelled by the critical theory of the Frankfurt school, especially with reference to Jürgen Habermas—the second-generation critical theorist.

Habermas was recognized as a leading younger social theorist in post-war Germany. The most striking and impressive feature of Habermas' approach to the range and complexities of human inquiry is the way in which he weaves whatever he analyzes into coherent 'whole'. There is a 'unity' of vision that informs his work. To this extent he is greatly under the influence of Marx, the young Hegelians, Hegel, Schelling, Fichte and Kant. Even before Habermas became fully aware of the Critical Theory of the 1930s, he was recreating the experience and pathway followed by Horkheimer, Adorno, Marcuse and other members of the Frankfurt School. Recalling these intellectually formative years, Habermas has written, "In retrospect, I sometimes have the impression that a student can recreate a segment of the critical theory of the 1930s, if he systematically works his way from Kant through Hegel, including Schelling, and approaches Marx via Lukács."[51]

In *Knowledge and Human Interests* (1968 & English edition in 1971), Habermas outlines his first systematic philosophical exposition. His major theses were succinctly summarized in the inaugural address he gave at Frankfurt University (published as an Appendix to the book). In the Preface, Habermas announced, "I am undertaking a historically oriented attempt to reconstruct the prehistory of modern positivism with the systematic intention of analyzing the connections of knowledge and human interest. In following the process of dissolution of epistemology, which has left the philosophy of science in its place, one makes one's way over abandoned stages of reflection. Retreating this path from the perspective that looks back towards the point of departure may help to recover the forgotten experience of reflection. That we disavow reflection is positivism."[52]

By 1968 the positivist tradition, from Auguste Comte to logical positivist like A.J. Ayer, was already under severe attack. But one cannot underestimate the extent to which the positivistic thinking pervaded and dominated the intellectual and cultural life. Habermas, in this context, is speaking of 'positivism' in a broad encompassing manner. He wants to identify that tendency to which many philosophical schools have contributed. This formulation is very close to issues that preoccupied thinker of different philosophical positions. He has advanced a provocative interpretation of a movement of thought that encompassed Kant, Fichte, Hegel, Marx, Dilthey, Peirce, Nietzsche, Comte and Freud. But I would like to emphasize the point that at the roots of Habermas' philosophical formulation to reconstruct the prehistory of modern positivism, there lies an essentially Kantian paradigm of 'reason'. Habermas has derived from Kant that 'reason is self-reflective' or 'the self-reflection of reason upon the conditions of its employment'. This is the thrust of Kant's *Critiques*—where 'pure reason' can self-reflexively come to grasp the universal and necessary conditions for the very possibility of theoretical knowledge, i.e., synthetic *a priori* proposition; 'practical reason' can give rise to categorical imperatives and 'judgment' can provide aesthetic judgments. Further the 'critique' is the self-critique of reason where reason is both the subject and the object of critique. This is the emancipatory sense of self-critique and self-reflection. Kant's epistemological quest could be seen in the perspective of European Enlightenment. In December 1783, Kant wrote a small pamphlet entitled "Answer to the Question: What is Enlightenment?" And the answer was, "Enlightenment is the coming out of Man from his self-imposed immaturity. Immaturity is the incapacity to serve one's own understanding without direction *(Leitung)* from another. This immaturity is self-imposed: Reason languishes, not because it lacks understanding; what it lacks is resolution and courage; it is unwilling to serve itself without an external authority. Wise up! Wake up! Be bold! Take courage to serve your own understanding. This is therefore the motto of the Enlightenment."[53] The attempt to get rid of 'self-imposed immaturity' is both self-critique and self-reflection with the aim to attain emancipation. Emancipatory self-reflection is dependent on giving a rational reconstruction of the universal conditions for reason. To use the Kantian analogy, only when we understand the possibility, validity and limit of theoretical knowledge and the categorical imperatives does it become intelligible to specify what must be done to attain autonomy and emancipation.

The nature and status of human mind divided into three distinct faculties—pure reason, practical reason and judgment—was essentially Kantian and remained Kantian from historical perspective. Post Kantian philosophers especially Hegel has resolved, once and for all, the Kantian distinction. Before I come to Hegel's resolution of the Kantian 'reason', I would like to briefly discuss and recapitulate the socio-historical and philosophical background to Kantian distinction between pure reason, practical reason and the judgment. Late Dr. Paulos Mar Gregorios, in one of his lectures, has this to say: The basic thing about European enlightenment is an attempt to totally undermine the feudal system and to give a rationale to new bourgeoisie—that is where the enlightenment begins. Bourgeoisie means 'city dwellers', 'Burg' means 'city'. Bourgeoisie was a new class of people comprising of artisans, craftsmen, traders and others, just coming out around the seventeenth century as a result of the economic and social developments. They wanted in the first place to overthrow feudalism and to establish a new philosophical justification for the new class. The class is the new bourgeoisie—the citizens. In doing so, one thing became very clear as a historical fact. The old feudal system was so integrally related to the religion and it was very clear that as long as religion and feudal system work together, any attack on feudal system would not work. So in the European enlightenment, it was decided that religion as such should be put out. Even in the French Revolution, there were some people who were 'deists' believing that God started the whole thing, then He went away and everything goes on in accordance with the natural laws, that is, deists. Even Voltaire was like that. But others were strongly convinced that you cannot defeat feudalism unless you defeat the religion. The best example of that is Heinrich Heinz—the great German poet and writer. He said that in France you are able to beat religion but in Germany we are not because religion is so deeply rooted and unless we defeat this religious entrenchment, we cannot begin our task. This was one side of it. Voltaire was also influenced by this idea that religion was a reactionary force. Nehru himself was partly of the same point of view that religion was an obstacle to progress. If you want progress, not only should you attack religion but also put it aside.

Until enlightenment, the integrating intellectual principle was the belief in God. It was in theology that all human problems in experience were integrated. Now the enlightenment threw out that integrating principle—the religion as the matrix of thought process. In that place enlightenment put the human reason which could integrate everything. This was the basic change which European enlightenment brought. I myself do not subscribe to that theology as integrating element. But once you subscribe to enlightenment reason, you find that the integrating principle does not fully work. So you divide 'experience' into three compartments—science, ethics and art. In the new enlightenment thinking, technically it is human reason that reconciles the three. But that integration is very flimsy. It does not have adequate foundation. Immanuel Kant particularly was the one who was trying to distinguish between three kinds of reason—pure reason, practical reason and the judgment. In the one, you know the things (phenomena); in the other, you know how to act; in the third, you have to discern what is good. By making this separation, he held on the 'idea of reason', which was already divided in three compartments. European enlightenment has this problem that 'reason' as such is not able to fulfil the task of integrating everything. But the enlightenment was able to assert on the 'autonomy' and 'adulthood' (maturity). According to the evolutionary ideology, which was going through that time, humanity has been developing into three phases; one is the religious stage, the second stage is metaphysics. These two stages are the stages of 'immaturity' of humanity. Humanity becomes 'mature' when its knowledge becomes 'scientific' which is the third stage. Science is the mature form of human dealing with reality. Both religion and metaphysics belong to the 'childhood' of humanity. Maturity means repudiating religion and metaphysics. The positive thing is that it affirms humanity. In the eighteenth century, Immanuel Kant wrote, "What is Enlightenment?" In the pamphlet, he says, 'Enlightenment is the coming of the age of maturity throwing away all that belongs to childhood'. And why is humanity languishing because, it does not have the 'courage' to trust its own 'reason', it is too dependent on religion and metaphysics. So the enlightenment means that human being has to have the 'courage', to think boldly, to overthrow childishness. It was industrial revolution, which was coming out of feudal relationship and was trying to affirm human autonomy. Individual's dignity, freedom and rights are affirmed in enlightenment reason. If reason has to be criticized, it has to be criticized by reason alone. That is what we mean by critical reason.

Within this rather larger perspective that the reactions of Habermas could be reassessed. Like Kant and Hegel, Habermas takes the split between science, morals and art as the 'fundamental philosophical problem of modernity'. Habermas sees that Hegel "solves the problem of the self-assurance of modernity too well, because the philosophy of Absolute Spirit removes all importance from its own present age ...and deprives of its calling to self-critical renewal."[54] He sees the popularity of 'end of philosophy' thought as an over-reaction to this over-success.

Habermas thinks that we need not be restricted as Horkheimer and Adorno were, to mere socio-historical forms of social criticism. He views Horkheimer, Adorno and Foucault as working out new versions of 'the end of philosophy' "...no matter what name it (philosophy) appears now—whether as fundamental ontology, as critique, as negative dialectic, or genealogy—these pseudonyms are by no means disguises under which the traditional (i.e. Hegelian) form of philosophy lies serves as the drapery of philosophical concepts more likely serves as the cloak, for a scantily concealed of philosophy."[55]

Habermas' account of such 'end of philosophy' movements is offered as part of a more sweeping history of philosophy since Kant. He thinks that Kant was right to split 'reason' up into science, morality and art and that Hegel was right in accepting this as "the standard (*massgeblich*) interpretation of modernity."[56] He also thinks that Hegel was right in believing that "Kant does not perceive the ...formal divisions within culture ...as diremptions. Hence he ignores the need for unification that emerges with the separations evoked by the principle of subjectivity."[57] It maybe recalled that unification was the fundamental philosophical preoccupation for Hegel. In a very remarkable manner in his early fragments entitled *Glauben und wissen,* Hegel has said, "Unification and Being (*sein*) are equivalent; the copula 'is' in every proposition expresses a unification of subject and predicate, in other words, a Being."[58] In the process of unifying the opposites, 'reason', for Hegel, touches every part of reality; 'reason' sublates the finite and its negation, so that they are revealed as moments of a more inclusive whole. Habermas agrees with Hegel that there is a 'need for unification'. He wants to go back to Hegel and to start it again. He thinks that, "in order to avoid the disillusionment with the philosophy of subjectivity which produced Nietzsche and the two strands of post Neitzschean thought which he distinguishes and dislikes (the one leading to Foucault, and the other to Heidegger) we need to go back to the place where the young Hegel took the wrong turn; that was the place where he still held open to option of using the idea of uncoerced will formation in a communication community existing under constraints of co-operation as model for the reconciliation of a bifurcated civil society...it was the lack of a sense of rationality as *social* that was missing from the philosophy of subject which the older Hegel exemplified from which the 'end-of-philosophy' thinkers have never really escaped."[59]

Habermas thinks that the philosophical requirement is that 'the philosophy of the subject' gratified is as real as it was during Hegel's own time, and can perhaps be fulfilled by his (Habermas') own focus on a 'communicative community'. With Hegel's overemphasis on the *Geist,* philosophy has become 'an isolated monastery/sanctuary' in which an individual forms an isolated order of priests untroubled by how it goes with the world. This position has certainly come from Kant's 'three-sphere' picture of culture, which Hegel tries to resolve. On this latter view, Kant's attempt to deny knowledge to make room for faith (by inventing 'transcendental subjectivity' to serve as the function for the Copernican revolution) was provoked by an unnecessary worry about the spiritual significance or insignificance of modern science, "Like Habermas, Kant thinks that modern science has a theoretical dynamic, one which can be identified with (at least a portion of) the nature of rationality. Both think that by isolating and exhibiting his dynamic, but distinguishing it from other dynamics (e.g.,) practical reason or the emancipatory interest, one can keep the results of science without thereby disenchanting the world. Kant suggested that we need not let our knowledge of the world *qua* matter in motion get in the way of our moral sense. The same suggestion was also made by Hume and Reid, but unlike these pragmatical Scotchmen, Kant thought that he had to back up this suggestion with a story which would differentiate and 'place' the three great spheres into which culture must be divided."[60]

Despite being under the influence of Kantian paradigm, Habermas remains a critical theorist. One of Habermas' most basic and challenging thesis is that "we cannot even make sense of the concepts of meaning, understanding and interpretation unless we rationally evaluate the validity claims that are made by participants in these forms of life. We must be able to discriminate what participants themselves count as reasons for their actions, and this requires a performative attitude on our part where we assess what 'they' count as good reasons for action with reference to 'our' standards of rationality."[61] To illustrate it, we can say that we are essentially embodied beings. We are embodied in the family—the property, language and the value systems—, in the tribal community and in the ethnicity. At the sometime, we are able to transcend this infrastructure and bracket all judgments of the validity claims made by participants in a form of life. It is dialectic that lies at the centre of Habermas' critical theory. Habermas says, "A critical social science will not remain satisfied with this. It is concerned with going beyond this goal to determine when theoretical statements grasp invariant regularities of social action as such and when they express ideologically frozen relations of dependence that can in principle be transformed...thus the level of (non-reflective) consciousness which is one of the initial conditions of such laws, can be transformed. Of course, to this end, a critically mediated knowledge of law cannot through reflection alone render a law itself inoperative but can render it inapplicable. The methodological framework that determines the meaning of the validity of critical propositions of this category is established by the concept of self-reflection. The latter releases the subject from dependence on hypostatized powers. Self-reflection is determined by an emancipatory cognitive interest."[62]

Habermas' critical theory is a dialectical synthesis of the empirical-analytic and the historical—hermeneutic disciplines. It is a constant cognition and vigilant criticism and this process always goes on and never reaches to any finality. There are also issues and their criticism, further issues and further criticism; but there is no final issue and no final criticism. Habermas' synthesis comes into clear focus when we turn into the third type of cognitive interest: the emancipatory interest: "This interest is at once derivative and the most fundamental cognitive interest. If we reflect upon the forms of knowledge and the disciplines guided by the technical and practical interests, we realize that they contain an internal demand for open, free, non-coercive communication. The validity of knowledge claims in empirical-analytic sciences and the historical hermeneutics disciplines always allow of further testing, challenge and rational evaluation."[63]

Habermas agrees with Kant that there are basic structures, rules and categories that are presupposed by reason (Kant) and communicative action (Habermas). But he is skeptical of pure transcendental philosophy, which cannot transcend itself. Habermas takes the help from Hegelian dialectic, which can break with the legacy of pure *a priori* transcendental philosophy. It is this synthesis of Kantian *a priorism* and Hegelian dialectic that has given rise to Habermas' critical theory of communicative action.

Although the details of Habermas' communicative action are subtle, complex and controversial, we can sketch some of its basic features: "Communicative action is a distinctive type of social interaction—the type of action oriented to mutual understanding. It must be distinguished from other types of social action and non-social actions, which are oriented to 'success', to the efficient achievement of ends. These latter action-types exhibit the form of purposive rational action where we seek to achieve an end or goal by appropriate means."[64] Habermas elucidates "...the goal of coming to an understanding (*Verstanding*) is to bring about an agreement (*Einverstandis*) that terminates in the intersubjective mutuality of reciprocal understanding, shared knowledge, mutual trust and accord with one another. Agreement is based on recognition of the corresponding validity claims of comprehensibility, truth, truthfulness and rightness."[65] All communicative action takes place with two operative terms—consensus and disagreement. Habermas argues that anyone acting communicatively must, in performing a speech action, raise *universal validity* claims, and must suppose that such claims can be vindicated. As indicated in the above quotation, there are four types of validity claims—comprehensibility, truth, truthfulness (sincerity) and normative rightness. In most empirical situation, we resolve our conflicts and disagreements with these validity claims. But there may arise a situation where validity claims can breakdown or be challenged by one of the participants in the communicative context. To resolve a breakdown in communication, Habermas proposes to have a discourse and argumentation or dialogue where we explicitly seek to warrant the validity claims that have been called into question and replace it with a new model of validity claims, which could be higher, more comprehensive than the earlier one. And that there is no dispute about a validity claim beyond rational argumentation by the participants involved.

CONCLUSION

In the conclusion, I'll propose a dialectical dialogue. However, I cannot go into all the details of the dialectical dialogue. Nevertheless, I'll provide some of the features of it. Dialectic as developed by Kant and Hegel is theory loaded and an elevated concept. Its pre-theoretical surrogate is obtainable in Socrates' dialogues. Dialectical dialogue will incorporate, absorb, sublate and even transcend the features of dialogue and dialectic together along with Habermas' communicative action. It is dialectical in its formulation. It means that dialectical dialogue will incorporate all contradictions, oppositions and differences between one culture and another, and will try to transcend and sublate them, so that it becomes all-inclusive and can evolve a global culture. *One's* identity (linguistic, ethnic, cultural, etc.) could be identified and shaped only by means of a dialogue through its exposure to and experience of the *other's* identity of the same or the neighbouring culture. An identity is therefore identical within differences. This is the principle of the unity and the struggle of opposites. The being of an identity is being-with and being-in-contrast-with-other identities. Dialectical dialogue will address the problems not in abstraction like Kant and Hegel, but in terms of the social nexus, spatio-temporal frame, earthly existence, historical and actual life of human culture and civilization. Dialectical dialogue is dialogic in its comprehension, so that one's views can participate with those of the other. It will not simply be a dialogue, such binaries as East and West, Indian and Ionian, Oriental and Occidental; rather, it will be multi-logue which fits into the multipolarity of the world order. Multi-logue could be between one and many, between persons who are living and those who are not. "One can well imagine stimulated conversations also between the persons who are *all* dead. The historians, archaeologists and anthropologists are, in different ways, engaged in this sort of conversation and communication between the peoples and cultures, which have disappeared from the face of the earth. It is not without reason that the historians speak of *contemporaneity* of history, suggesting that the historians and the themes of their history, involving individuals and cultures of the past, are in a sense contemporaneous. To them the past is living, relives in their thought, and is not something dead."[66] It also could be used in the morals and the conceptions of good which are said to be relative to cultures, even large cultural identities—the cultural universals—have now disintegrated into smaller ones, i.e. multiculturalism or cultural pluralism. This forces us to go into the radical revision through multi-loguing, if not total rejection of the dialoguing East-West or Indo-European approaches on the notion of the Absolute.

NOTES

1. Krishna, Daya. 1987. *India's Intellectual Traditions: Attempts at Conceptual Reconstructions.* Motilal Banarasidass.
2. Bronowski, J. and Mazlish. 1975. *The Western Intellectual Tradition (From Leonardo to Hegel).* New York: Harper & Row Publishers.
3. Upadhyaya, Vachaspati. 2001. *Sanskrit Studies Abroad.* New Delhi: Shri LBSRSV. pp. 20-42.
4. Hegel. 1973. *Phenomenology of Spirit.* A.V. Miller (trans.). Oxford: Clarendon Press. Preface, p. 11.
5. Hegel. 1895. *Lectures on the Philosophy of Religion.* E.B. Speirs and J.B. Sanderson (trans.). London. Vol. III, p. 353.
6. Kant. 1973. *Critique of Pure Reason,* N.K. Smith (trans.). London: Macmillan Press Ltd. Preface, p. 7 (Hereafter CPR).
7. *Adhyāropapavadabhyam nisprapancam prapancyate.* Śaṁkara. 1970. *Pancikaranam.* Gujarat: Gujarati Printing Press. p. 1. I am also grateful to Professor R. Balasubramanian's lectures on Advaita Vedānta on 26 May, 2000, at India International Centre organized by Centre for Studies in Civilizations.
8. *Commentary on the Taittiriya Upaniṣad,* II, 1. Quoted in Mukherjee, A.C. 1943. *The Nature of Self.* Allahabad: The Indian Press Ltd. p. 154.
9. Ibid. p. 154-55.
10. Ibid. *Commentary on the Gītā,* XIII, 12. Ibid. p. 155.
11. Shastri, MM. A.K. (ed.). *Śankara Bhāsya with Nine Commentaries.* p. 821, p. 156.
12. Kant. *CPR.* A97. p. 130.
13. Ibid. p. 130.

14. Ibid. p. 143.
15. Ibid. p. 327.
16. Taylor, Charles. 1979. *Hegel and Modern Society.* London: Cambridge University Press. p. 26.
17. Hegel. 1977. *The Encyclopaedia of the Philosophical Sciences An Outline.* M.J. Petry (trans.). Dordrecht & Boston: D. Reidel Publishing Company. Section 445-60, pp. 103-208.
18. Ibid. p. 91.
19. Hegel. 1909. *Science of Logic.* A.V. Miller (trans.) London: Book II, p. 439.
20. Ibid. pp. 439-40.
21. Kolb, David. 1986. *Critique of Pure Modernity—Hegel, Heidegger and after.* Chicago: The University Press. p. 46.
22. George, Michael. 1984. "Marx's Hegelianism: an Exposition". *Hegel and Modern Philosophy.* David Lamb (ed.). London: Croon Helm. p. 123.
23. Hegel. 1892. *The Encyclopaedia of the Philosophical Sciences. W.* Wallace (trans.). Second revised edition. London. p. 150.
24. Lyotard, Jean Francois. 1982. *Driftworks.* New York: Semiotext. p. 15.
25. Lyotard, Jean Francois.1988. *"Reecrire La Modernite". L'Inhumain.* Paris: Galilee. p. 33-34.
26. Kearney, Richard. 1984. *Dialogues with Contemporary Continental Thinkers: The Phenomenological Heritage.* Manchester: Manchester University Press. pp. 112-113.
27. Boyne, R. and Rattansi, A. (ed.). 1990. *Postmodernism and Society.* London: Macmillan. p. 12.
28. White, S.K. 1991. *Political Theory and Postmodernism.* Cambridge: Cambridge University Press. p. 4.
29. Derrida, Jacques. 1981. "Positions", an interview with Jean-Louis Houdebine and Guy Scarpetta. *Positions.* Alan Bass (trans.). Chicago: University of Chicago Press. p. 43.
30. Kearney, Richard. *Dialogues with Contemporary Continental Thinkers,* etc. pp. 112-3.
31. Lyotard, Jean Francois. 1984. *The Postmodern Condition: A Report on Knowledge.* Geoff Beniengton and Brian Massumi. Manchester: Manchester University Press. pp. 81-2.
32. Hegel. *Phenomenology of Spirit.* Preface.
33. Lyotard. *The Postmodern Condition.* p. 38.
34. Solomon, R.C. 1988. *Continental Philosophy since 1750.* New York: Oxford University Press. p. 200.
35. Hegel. 1977. *The Encyclopaedia of the Philosophical Sciences.* M.J. Petry (trans.). Section 445-60, pp. 103-208.
36. Derrida, Jacques. 1982. *Margins of Philosophy.* Alan Bass (trans.). Chicago. University of Chicago Press. p. 74.
37. Ibid. p. 81.
38. Ibid. p. 82.
39. Ibid.
40. Ibid. pp. 82-83.
41. Ibid. pp. 80-81.
42. Ibid. p. 74.
43. Derrida. *Positions.* p. 44.
44. Derrida, Jacques. 1981. *Dissemination.* Barbara Johnson (trans.). Chicago: University of Chicago Press. pp. 269-70. This point has been forcefully argued in Gauche, Rodophe. 1986. *The Train of the Mirror: Derrida and the Philosophy of Reflection.* Cambridge, Massachusetts: Harvard University Press. See especially, pp. 102-40, & 204-40.
45. Derrida. *Positions.* p. 101.
46. Derrida, Jacques. 1978. *Of Grammatology.* Gayatri Chakravorty Spivak (trans.). Baltimore: John Hopkins University Press. p. LXV.
47. Derrida. *Positions.* p. 57.
48. Wood, David and Beransconi, Robert. 1988. *Derrida and Différance.* Evaton: Northwestern University Press. p. 3.
49. Kearney, Richard. *Dialogues with Contemporary Continental Thinkers,* etc. p. 114.
50. Derrida. *Positions.* p. 8.
51. Habermas, Jürgen. 1981. "The Dialectic Rationalization: an Interview with Jürgen Habermas". *Telos,* 40. Fall. p. 6.
52. Habermas, Jürgen. 1971. *Knowledge and Human Interests.* Boston. Preface, p. vii.
53. Singh R.P. 1997. *Philosophy: Modern and Postmodern.* Foreword by Paulos Mar Gregorios. New Delhi: Intellectual Publishing Company. p. vii.

54. Habermas, Jürgen. *Paris Lectures,* II. p. 28. Quotation from, Rorty, Richard. 1985. "Habermas and Lyotard on Postmodernity". *Habermas and Modernity.* R.J. Bernstein (ed.). Polity Press. p. 168.
55. Habermas, Jürgen. *Paris Lectures,* III. p. 3. Quotation from, "Habermas and Lyotard on Postmodernity". p. 166.
56. Ibid. I. p. 7.
57. Ibid. p. 17.
58. Hegel. T*heologische Jügendschriften,* p. 383. Translated and quoted by Marcuse, Herbert. 1941. *Reason and Revolution.* New York: Oxford University Press. p. 35.
59. Rorty, Richard. 1985. "Habermas and Lyotard on Postmodernity".
60. Ibid.
61. Ibid. p. 168.
62. Habermas. *Knowledge and Human Interests.* p. 310.
63. Bernstein. pp. 10-11.
64. Ibid. p. 18.
65. Habermas, Jürgen. 1974. "What is Universal Pragmatics?" *Communication and the Evaluation of Society.* Boston. p. 3.
66. Chattopadhyaya, D.P. 2001. "One, Two and Many: Many Perspectives". *Reason, Dialectic and Postmodern Philosophy: Indian and Western Perspectives.* R. P. Singh (ed.). Faridabad: Om Publications. p. 40.

CHAPTER 23

Reason and Tradition: Two Strands of Knowledge

Mahasweta Chaudhury

I

The aim of this paper is to make a distinction between traditional knowledge-system and what is known as modern western scientific tradition and then to make a claim on the basis of this distinction. The claim comes from a consideration of the post-modernist critique of science in capturing the other horn of the dilemma than the one held by these critics. The critique in question generally rejects the cognitive claim of modern science (Rationality,Universality, Truth, etc.,) reducing it to just another culture, nothing more than any other particular standpoint. An attempt has been made here to argue that instead of divesting science of its cognitive status (that would be intellectual hypocrisy) for its various failures, we can re-examine the issue of the distinction between traditional knowledge vis-a-vis scientific knowledge and confer cognitive status to traditional system as well so long it solves some cognitive problems as it has done for ages.

Science seems to be the typical rational model of knowledge and universal truth. Indeed there are differences between modern science and /or non-western knowledge and traditions, but that difference is historical and contingent. In all societies and all ages, science being a culture notwithstanding, a difference can be made between degrees of validity of beliefs /knowledge. To call non-modern or/and non-western traditions nothing but culture, is to deny history. Again although science is socially determined by various contingent social and cultural conditions for its actual course of research these are nothing but necessary conditions. The question of validity of belief and knowledge is independent of its history of genesis. It is also true that the focus of scientific research often ignores human cause and prioritise prestigious areas such as space research, nuclear science or quantum mechanics more than alleviation of human suffering. Focus of research is very important because it concerns lot of funding, expertise and time. For example, a common disease like malaria kills millions of people every year only in sub-Saharan Africa but much importance is *not* given to its research for an effective prophylactic which is affordable to most of the victims who are incidentally very poor.

On the other hand space research, super conductor or sophisticated military equipment get much more attention (and therefore much more funding). Moreover due to lack of transparency the actual scientific practice is often tyrannical. Indeed modern science has belied many of our hopes and aspirations with imbalance in its focus and priorities but that is due to science education and science policy. As a discipline science has nothing to do with its actual nature and political application. Notwithstanding all its wrong perception and values, scientific knowledge is still the only culture which expanded our horizon of knowledge of the world to an unprecedented extent. It also contains within its own tradition a self- correcting method of testability. This is because it contains the tests to tell us when a set of ideas is wrong or a theory is to be rejected. So even if scientific knowledge-system can be perceived as a kind of cultural tradition, we can still make a distinction between science and other cognitive systems. The norms by which that is done are not very far from the rationality model. Yet they capture the spirit of scientific enterprise in an acceptable form by common consensus.

Tradition and reason are supposed to be two opposite notions. In this connection it is important to distinguish between tradition and orthodoxy[1]. J.N Mohanty[2] has made an excellent distinction."Orthodoxy consists in fossilizing tradition into a lifeless, unchanging structure.Tradition as distinguished from orthodoxy, is a living process of creation and preservation of significations." Indeed when a tradition is alive and meaningful it does not need any coercive social process for its perpetuation; adherence to a living tradition is smooth and spontaneous. Only when it loses relevance and ready response from its followers does a culture becomes decadent and soon loses its natural appeal and needs coercive measures for its preservation, as found in many stages of civilizations of different societies. For example, in the middle ages Europe witnessed decadence of social and religious norms and thus resort to coercion and different types of persecution became rampant. In the East, specially in India there were periods of decadence when some tradition lost its creative growth and required orthodoxy to prove its purity. Being more ancient than its Occidental counterpart, eastern traditions were found to be more orthodox in comparison. Its long history seems to fossilize the traditions more rigidly than the comparatively less ancient western civilization. This point has been put very succinctly by Hajime Nakamura.[3] The moot point, however, is to define tradition and modernity in terms of rational criticism. Moreover all traditions are not necessarily anti-rational. So we should remember that the war should not be against all traditions, but only against orthodoxy which defies rationality and do not respond to new situations and challenges that were not faced by earlier traditions.

The dichotomy between tradition-modernity should be understood in its true perspective. If tradition means only obsolete, irrelevant and empty adherence to customary ideas and mores, then of course it is anti-modern. On the other hand, modernity is *not* accepting everything only because of novelty and rejecting everything that is old and traditional. This kind of perception will help us in understanding how some kind of dialogue is possible between the modern and the traditional, especially in connection with ancient culture and civilization like ours that has much to contribute to the general body of universal knowledge, including scientific thought. Of course it needs lot of steady and patient deliberations with an open mind and rational judgement. In this issue an interesting analysis has been done by Mohanty. In his view social and public philosophers like Gandhi, Aurobindo and Tagore have done the synthesis of these two distinct elements more fruitfully than academic philosophers. I shall come back to this point later in the context of Indian philosophical tradition and other traditions embedded in local cultures.

In historiography a distinction is drawn between intellectual history and sociological history. The first is internal and the second is external history. General historical account involves 'rational reconstruction' of how some events or ideas have grown. But any rational reconstruction requires a normative standard. Indeed the history of science and knowledge is richer than its rational reconstruction. There are always some empirical, sociological or psychological theories to explain the residual non-rational factors.

External history can only give an empirical account of the non-rational factors of growth of knowledge, while internal or rational history alone can provide a norm to do so; it tries to explain the growth of disembodied knowledge or concepts. The sociological / empirical factors are necessary components of the ideas/science but do not constitute its rationality. Rational history of knowledge and science is selective—it considers the legitimacy of the logical strength of ideas, theories or conceptual frameworks 'How, when, where or by whom'—the beliefs are held to be of secondary importance to an intellectual history of ideas.

Time and place are the two general dimensions of historical research. Periodization —dividing time into periods such as ancient, medieval and modern is an age-old convention, just as is the dichotomy of the East and the West. Moreover religion and philosophy/ science in contemporary vocabulary are very sharply demarcated. For a comprehensive history of ideas, however, these barriers seem arbitrary. In a study of concepts and theories one should cut across such traditional divisions, for it is possible that an idea or attitude held in occidental philosophy at a certain period finds a counterpart in an oriental philosophical thought, some times even in a religious tradition. Indeed certain intellectual problems are characteristics of certain stages in the history of culture. In different areas of the world similar (if not exactly the same) problems and ideas emerged at certain stages of cultural developments.

Hajime Nakamura[4] suggests that instead of speaking about 'East' and 'West' types of traditions we should speak of 'cultural areas,'in which some culturally advanced people have established its own cultural tradition in its own indigenous way. For example India, China and Japan are all 'eastern' traditions, but despite some partial points of similarity Japanese culture is radically different from that of India. West again is a heterogeneous amalgam of cultures. Greco-Judaic thought is different from say, Anglo-Saxon culture. It is to be noted that 'culture' here includes intellectual elements as well. The degree of cultural developments and diversity again is different in different Occidental traditions. The advancement, say of natural and mathematical sciences, in France and Germany are at a different level from that of Portugal and Spain. Logic and mathematical thought flourished in Poland and some other places more than many others.

The recognition of cultural factors in moulding scientific and philosophical ideas seems to lead to growing erosion in the sanctity of philosophical and scientific ideas and logical adjudication of ideas and theories seem to be meaningless to several philosophers besides a sociological analysis. Nakamura very rightly contested this standpoint and holds that each study by a specialist, after contextual treatment at some point must be placed in a comprehensive framework to make clear the significance of the total subject matter.That seems to be an enormous project. But in his colossal *History of Ideas* Nakamura himself has achieved a commendable height in that direction.

The view that comparative study of ideas and theories belonging to different systems of different age and society would not be meaningful, is right to the extent that each and every element of a conceptual system cannot be entirely compared to that of another system. But some elements of one can be fruitfully weighed against similar elements in another idea or a theory belonging to a different culture or philosophy. As Nakamura would put it, one such possible move would be to concentrate on a 'problem' approach rather than a "ism" approach. I would rather side with a slightly different expression of Popper that problems are more vital than theories, the latter only attempts or conjectures to solve some problems, theoretical as well as practical. In each stage of intellectual development, similar problems arise and responses or ways to solve them can be concentrated upon. New problems and ideas emerge from actual confrontation with problem situations and their tentative solution.

Divisions of periods and stages of development are only tentative, based on a rough estimate of common problems located by a later thinker or a school. The problems may be somewhat different but not entirely unknown to the ancients. Examples abound. A single instance is that of the problem of 'personal identity' which is a well-known traditional crux considered by both oriental and western philosophers, recognised by Locke as of substantial philosophic importance. In recent times many contemporary philosophers and cognitive scientists are engaged in research focussed on the problem of personal identity and mind body related issues. Theories of consciousness, time and space again are issues common among the ancients as well as the modern philosophers both in the East and the West.

Periodic categorisation has another misleading feature; the standard division into Ancient, Medieval and Modern often are associated with some rigid and often incorrect characteristics. First of all eastern civilization is much more ancient than its western counterpart. Therefore many concepts and cultural mores are differently accepted and legitimized in these different cultural areas. Eastern thinkers sometimes claim that there are no counterparts of their ancient ideas as these are deeply embedded in their culture. This is not entirely correct as parallels can be drawn from western tradition of similar periods, which can help us compare and contrast the two different traditions. Middle age there refers to a much earlier period (approximately from seventh-eighth to around fourteenth-fifteenth century) than medieval period (from twelve-thirteenth to seventeenth-eighteenth century) in say, Indian history. Apart from this problem of periodization there is another more serious problem which concerns characterising a certain period with some special feature.

The main thrust of my contention is to contest the tendency to stigmatise a certain period with a particular characteristic. The category 'Medieval' seems to carry a sense of mystic, anti-rational and anti-scientific thought compared to the pairing of 'Modern' with logical, rational and scientific approach. This kind of stereotyping is not only incorrect but also misleading. If we rummage through history of science, it would be evident that many scientific theories have actually originated from myths, fables and even from age-old superstitions.[5] The seed of the heliocentric theory was embedded in the ancient sun-worshipper's faith. It is interesting to note that in eastern religion and faith, sun occupied a central and reverential position long before the Copernican theory saw the light of day.

Many apparently unfounded legends gave birth to highly acceptable scientific theories in a later stage of intellectual development. Some cultural areas (societies or nation) again can lag behind some others during the same period. It is well known now that science was not unknown to the ancients. Old civilizations such as Greco-Roman or Indo-Chinese-Japanese have definitely shown rudiments of science with full-fledged theories although not exactly in the same terms as found in today's West-dominated scientific culture. Modern science involves a lot of hypothesis, imagination and extra logical factors. In fact modern sociologists of science tend to strip scientific enterprise of all acclaimed rationality and objectivity which are ascribed to it. Science in this view is nothing sacrosanct purporting to aim at truth and rationality. It is a social culture just like any other human endeavour. We shall come back to the issue in connection with modern sociologists of science.

As pointed out before, the most undesirable and misleading consequence of rigid periodic categorization is that it tends to attach some stigma with the categories. 'Medieval' thought, for example, seems to reek of irrationality and dogma, our ordinary use of language indicates this bias. 'Ancient' seems to mean antiquated, defunct or at least similar anti-progressive epithets. 'Modern' on the other hand, sounds progressive and is usually associated with all that is rational/logical and scientific, these kinds of associated meanings send wrong signals. If one studies the problem areas and theories of ancient thought-systems a substantial amount of it can be meaningfully reinterpreted in the light of ideas developed in other stages of scientific thought. What goes in the name of medieval philosophy again contains many impeccable arguments and vast amount of problems and theories worth a thorough re-examination. In fact recent spurt of research in these areas in the West confirms that point. Sophisticated comparative descriptions of various philosophical systems were not unknown in India at that time. *Sarvadarśana-saṁgraha* by Madhava (c1350) is one such masterpiece. It is true that before the advent of modern science religious supremacy reigned over free individualistic thought. In pre-modern era institutional authority dominated cultural life both in eastern and western societies. The negative dictum of "Thou shall not" predominated over "Thou shall" in social life. But social discouragement notwithstanding, free scientific thought was not completely weeded out. Otherwise great scientific theories would not have been possible. From Socrates to Galileo it is the same story of suppression and persecution but still the great ideas survived and were improved upon by posterity. We can remember the story of persecution of our own Kṣanā for her astronomical observations and mathematical calculations but still the scientific ideas survived and outlived social dogma of the time.

Again, if modernity implies emphasis on perception and reason as source of knowledge then it has been a part of Indian tradition of philosophy. If elaborate systems of grammar and language as well as theory of proposition and syntactical rules is any criterion, the same tradition exhibits sophistication of a high order.[6] Highly developed monism and realism are also to be found there.[7]

Moreover, otherworldliness and faith in supra natural/empirical existence were contested, like modern theories, by some 'atheist' systems of traditional Indian thought. Astronomy and mathematical sciences attained a considerable height in ancient India. Along with it aesthetics and logic (including the notion of class and the distinction of language and meta-language) were quite sophisticated. A comprehensive investigation of the great Asian traditions of China, Japan and India may indicate that the traditions were not unprepared for the advent of modern age. The same is true about any other ancient tradition, eastern as well as western.

Two kinds of knowledge can be distinguished: universal (reason, morality—monolithic truth) and particular (traditional, pluralistic, multi-culture/morality, truth and reason, immanent in the various traditions).

The first one is the norm of objective rational knowledge. Like truth, moral standard is also independent of the frameworks. Knowledge must be justified on good ground. Science is the paradigm of rationality. Reason is objective. Truth is one. Standard of validity is universal. Knowledge transcends the framework of culture, religion, language and other social conditions.

The universalist model of knowledge and rationality faces many internal problems in its pristine form as presented by the received view held by Carnap and many other philosophers and scientists in the earlier half of the twentieth century. The dissatisfaction found many responses in different directions. One direction took the form of rejection of the justificationist model of scientific knowledge, which amounts more or less to say that scientific knowledge is based on empirical evidences, therefore it can never be justified. In fact only trivial truth (like 'p is p') is verifiable/justifiable and it is apparent that these types of propositions are cognitively empty. Propositions that are cognitively rich, however, can never be justifiable. On the contrary more informative content makes them cognitively more rich and 'interesting' but at the same time more vulnerable to be falsified. As is well known, Karl Popper holds on to this type of critique of the justificationist model of scientific knowledge and at the same time argue for a non-justificationist but rational model of truth and knowledge

The other critical move in this respect is the total rejection of all kinds of attempts that distinguish between rational and irrational or true and false. Only a sociological analysis of scientific theories is carried out. In fact the distinction between scientific and non-scientific is blurred by these attempts. It is made also to argue that there is no such distinction. This move is generically known as sociology of knowledge as it attempts to give only a sociological analysis of scientific ideas and theories. It tries to reduce knowledge to only a kind of social culture which is no more than any other culture. Before going into an examination of the postmodernist critique of scientific knowledge, let us first examine some of the salient features of what is generally known as sociology of knowledge

II

SOCIOLOGY OF KNOWLEDGE

Kuhn in the sixties, and the sociologists of knowledge from the seventies, emphasised the cultural nature of science and social determination of knowledge. According to this view, science is nothing but a culture. There is no universal standard of truth and rationality. Anthropological research leads to a kind of relativism that espouses different standards and norms for accepting a belief. Rival paradigms determine different kinds of belief-systems in which a statement/belief would be rational if it is coherent with other beliefs of the system (example: "Black people are inferior", coheres with other beliefs in a racist society. "Lower caste people cannot marry a Brahmin" similarly would be rational in a caste-ridden Indian milieu). Rival paradigms or scientific theories similarly give rise to propositions, which follow from the paradigms (example: Copernican/Ptolemy or Euclidean/non-Euclidean geometry). The notion of truth and rationality thus is not absolute—but relative to a particular standard. No knowledge is thus universal; all knowledge is standard-specific, relevant only in a particular context. There is no universal norm to judge the absolute truth or rationality of knowledge. All epistemic standards are relative and determined by social conditions: one thing we should remember here—nobody would anymore subscribe to the naïve view that knowledge is absolute but that does not preclude the possibility that it is objective.

The proponents of relativism of various sorts put before us standards of mutual understanding and possibility of knowledge unrealistically high (not very much unlike the classical sceptics). And when we fail to meet those standards, they claim that understanding of those standards is impossible and therefore no cognitive status can be conferred upon any one of them. Karl Popper[8] is the greatest champion to explode what he calls 'the myth of the framework'. While he admits that there are different cultures including cognitive traditions and there is great deal of social factors influencing them, he does not think these factors are relevant for the validity of those traditions. It is also granted that it is very difficult to overcome the influence of the framework. It is not impossible, nevertheless, to overcome that difficulty by rational/critical discussion.

Unlike the relativists, Popper regards confrontation with different cultures as contributing to progress of knowledge resulting from what he calls 'culture clash'. History of western culture, science and civilization can authenticate this point.[9] Although he is an ardent admirer of tradition, at the same time, he is 'an almost orthodox admirer of unorthodoxy' and regards orthodoxy as the death of knowledge, for 'the growth of knowledge depends entirely on the existence of disagreement'. Indeed disagreement may lead to strife and even to violence, which is undesirable but it may also lead to mutual criticism and discussion, which are necessary ingredients of progress of knowledge. He cites the history of development of western science and philosophical ideas as a result of clash and confrontation of different frameworks. The strife of Greco-Roman civilization as well as their clashes with the Jewish, and other Middle Eastern civilizations brought forth advancement in knowledge. Progress in knowledge is also an indirect fallout of clashes with Germanic and Islamic invasions.

It is not very clear what Popper means by 'culture clash'. When it is conferred a positive role in the rise of Greek science, it seems he means that interaction with different traditions contribute to a better understanding of the world and its various problems. It also includes conceptually more rich ideas about nature, society and political and moral issues. Of course the most fundamental among these ideas is the idea of rationality. The tradition of rational and critical discussion shows the advent of democracy and the spirit of scientific tradition. Popper refers to the rise of Greek democracy as well as scientific ideas. We can similarly refer to the Indian tradition of *vāda, and vitandā,* mentioned in the

Nyāyasūtras and also the *nigraha-sthāna* or defeating situation in manuals. These methods determine win or defeat for a debating position in early Christian era. This tradition led to a gradual switch over to a rational and argument-based approach to solve intellectual and practical problems. His crusade against any form of relativism is well known, although he regards all knowledge as fallible and science only as a progress towards truth which may not be attained forever. However, Popper thinks rationality as the most fundamental idea related to our understanding of the world and thus gradually to the rise of science.

"In its application to the problem of understanding our world, and thus to the rise of science, rationality has components which are of about equal importance."[10] One of these two components in his view is poetic inventiveness or the invention of stories, which explain the world. It is rightly pointed out that in all cultures whenever there is some thing that needs explanation, people make conjectures, often wild conjectures, that created different kinds of myths about unknown powers to understand the world and the mysteries of human life which they cannot fully fathom.

It is true that this component is perhaps as old as human language itself and seems to be universally present in all traditions: "all tribes, all peoples have such explanatory stories, often in the form of fairy tales. It seems that the invention of explanations and explanatory stories is one of the basic functions of the human language."[11] The second component, which he thinks is comparatively modern, is found with the ancient Greeks, particularly with Anaximander, the second Ionian philosopher."It is the invention of criticism, of the critical discussion of the various explanatory myths, with the aim of consciously improving upon them."[12]

The main Greek example Popper gives of explanatory mythmaking on an elaborate scale is that of Hesiod's *Theogony,* which is a wild story of the origin, the deeds and the misdeeds of the Greek gods. In Indian mythologies we have comparable stories of relating natural phenomena with divine wrath or pleasure and even hierarchy among Gods along with their special characteristics to explain problems about human life and natural phenomena that we do not understand. Anaximander's break away from Thales' myth (that the earth needs some support for its stability) by maintaining that nothing is holding the earth—gradually made the bold idea of Copernicus possible and it even contains the seed of the idea of Newtonian forces. Examples abound in both Indian and other mythologies to indicate that traditional perception often led to some more reasonable explanation of the world and more critical understanding of the same.

Popper regards Anaximander's example of breaking away from the tradition of a support for the earth as a bold step to a more significant problem of the issue of the support and stability of earth. This initiates a new tradition—the critical tradition. There may be difference of opinion among historians and philosophers of science whether it can be called a 'critical tradition', but one thing is at least clear that a 'critical tradition (read scientific tradition) is constituted by adopting a method of criticising' a received story or given explanation and then going forward to a new, improved imaginative story which explains better but, by all means, is subject to further scrutiny or may be replaced by a better story or theory if you like. Undeniably this is the scientific method. Indeed lots of non-rational elements are there along with rational ideas in our attempts to understand the problems of the world. The sociologists of knowledge are right about it; they are also right in pointing out that it is a very difficult task to disentangle the non-rational from the rational elements of our understanding of the world. But from that difficulty we cannot conclude that the task is impossible.

Rational approach does not assume either infallibility or demonstrability of any idea or a theory. In my view the positive aspect of what Popper calls 'culture clash' is the growing recognition of other standpoints and perspectives. These may first seem to be very alien but a rational adjudication and understanding may reveal their worth. But mere recognition of alternative viewpoints does not also guarantee that these viewpoints are of the same value. Nor does it imply that none of them are more than reflective of a certain social/cultural condition. Translation or interpretation of other traditions is a great obstacle no doubt, and various cultural political factors are the main hindrances on the way. Historical events and contingent conditions such as colonization and imperialism are principal factors that made it difficult for the victors or the colonial powers to appreciate the meaning and value of the culture of the vanquished.

It is well recognised now that the indoctrination with western ideas is a major dogma that inhibit understanding of other traditions, say eastern traditions of understanding and attempts to solve similar problems. By this statement it is not intended to mean that all eastern ideas are of equal footing with comparable western ideas or that either of them is better or worse than the other. Each and every idea or theory is to be understood with reference to the context it is made and weighed individually for its value. For example Ptolemy's theory was consistent with the physical theory of the day and empirical observations, Copernican theory was eventually vindicated against it by the adequate physics of Newton. In this connection we can refer to Popper's concept of 'culture clash' and the possibility of inter-translatability of language (contra Quine) in principle, notwithstanding the fact that it is sometimes a very formidable task, given the actual cultural difference.

Moreover culture clash would lose some of its importance if "one of the clashing cultures regards itself as universally superior and even more so if it is so regarded by the other".[13] The reason for such loss is clear, if one of the cultural rivals becomes convinced of its inferiority, then the critical attitude is lost and hence no good consequence comes out of such intellectual confrontation which requires both the parties to be of similar strength. Moreover "whenever there was a major obstacle to overcome, it was as a rule the result of indoctrination with western ideas".[14] These two citations from Popper indicate his closeness to the sociological theory of knowledge in recognising the active role of social factors in theory-formation. His theory is often confused as a logical theory that does not take the socio-cultural factors into account. The only great difference lies in the recognition of these factors having relevance only with reference to the origin and nature of the theory or idea about the world and not about the rational validation of those ideas. Scientific tradition is different from all other traditions in offering a methodology to test the value of its ideas, which may very well turn out to be false/ invalid. It is by no means different from other traditions in leading to the realm of infallible or at least demonstrable knowledge about any empirical matter except trivial truth.

The moot point is not to equate reason with modernity alone or else the only alternative is not to banish reason from the realm of science because it is also a socially conditioned culture. On the other hand we may also consider some traditional idea and mode of reason to have the potential of good logical power. It is not, however, maintained that all systems of ideas are of equal strength as these are products of some social condition or other as the sociologists of knowledge presume.

Post Enlightenment liberalism has a big problem to face: how can Enlightenment universalism be abandoned and yet avoid a collapse into radical particularism which leaves liberalism as no more than one form of life amongst others with no privileged claim upon human reason? John Rawls and Richard Rorty have abandoned the pursuit of rational foundation for articulations and celebration of the confessedly particular ideas of a particular tradition, of 'certain ideas... latent in the public political culture of a democratic society.' Widespread reaction against the Enlightenment ideal, age of reason and liberal universalism, and a growing awareness of the tensions inscribed within multicultural societies give rise to a gradual break away from this ideal of truth and rationality. Sociologists of knowledge and science in recent times uphold that truth and rationality are not universal or one, they vary from one framework to another. Science seems to be the typical rational model of knowledge and universal truth which is generally the target of such attack. Thus Rorty's open and unapologetic grasping of the particularist horn of this dilemma has left him vulnerable to the charge that he ultimately lacks the courage of his lack of conviction, and is compelled covertly to invoke universal claims about human nature in support of his liberal allegiance. The moot point however is to override local beliefs and commitments in the name of logic and universal ethic and (particular) concept of respect, i.e., refrain from imposing principles on others that do not follow from their own belief-systems.

Notice that this debate is within the framework of a typical western scientific model. It does not include non-western or/and non-modern knowledge-systems. If we may call this latter kind 'traditional' knowledge, it may include both non-western type of knowledge and non-modern model which may still be prevalent in society where many people still live in traditional way. Ancient and vast countries like India, despite its enormous progress in science and technology still have a substantial population (like marginal farmers and forest-dwellers) who rely more on traditional wisdom than modern western science. Their standards, axioms and theories are different from the standardized universal knowledge like western science. Their standards, axioms and theories are different from that of other traditions. The reason for regarding them as alternative knowledge system is that the hypotheses are consistent with the axioms and other hypotheses of the system. In traditional Indian systems of knowledge (I am sure it is equally true about other ancient cultures such as Chinese, Egyptian, Mexican, etc.), there are full-fledged theories of the universe, astronomy, mathematics, medicine, agriculture and so on.

III

THE CASE OF INDIA

Basically there are two strands of knowledge: (1) The brahminical tradition of theoretical knowledge linked up with some philosophical system or other; (2) traditional local belief-systems that aim to solve practical problems rather than justifying a philosophical/ scientific theory.

The aim of any adequate theory of knowledge is to solve some problems and seek explanation for events unknown. All cognitive projects consist in attempts to answer some questions like 'how do I know that this is so and so? Or why this is so and so? Or else how to solve this problem?' If problem-solving is a feature of all epistemic projects it may either be purely theoretical, that is relating a theory or conjecture to a larger system of ideas or else solving some immediate problem, cognitive or merely practical (which does not necessarily excludes the possibility of being upgraded to a more serious idea). In that case many forms of traditional knowledge, no matter whether it is a part of an ontological theory or handed down by a local system of knowledge to the posterity, fulfils that requirement and cannot be denied an epistemic status.

With this consideration in mind it is not so clear that only universalist thesis is correct and the only form of valid knowledge since no non-trivial proposition can claim to be fully justifiable. If this point is granted then it is not so easy to dismiss various forms of local/ traditional knowledge by relegating it to a non-epistemic status, for after all these forms have reasonably handled various problems for ages and helped people of these traditions. I consider two vital problems, perpetuation of life and conservation of nature were handled if not solved quite successfully in India by both philosophical and local/traditional methods.

Examples of (1) Philosophical knowledge: different Vedas, Saṁhitā (the physical universe, astronomy, medical science, chemistry, logic and grammar, physical and mental health (yoga), etc. Examples of (2) Local knowledge of flora and fauna handed down from the ancestors, myths and legends, not necessarily related to a theoretical framework, but helpful guide for perpetuation of life and conservation of nature. Indeed, traditional livelihood rely heavily upon nature for its sustenance, but their need is not much unlike the modern commercial exploitation of nature which expedite denudation in a degree of destruction disproportionate in comparison with the degree of regeneration and growth. Some local beliefs/superstitions also helped conservation if we compare it with objective knowledge of modern science and technology. Examples abound in literature of traditional forms of knowledge aiding both perpetuation of human life and conservation of natural resources.

In pre-industrial time man was closer to nature in the sense of accepting it as such and interacting in a more direct way with no aggressive attitude towards it. In other words, there was a give and take relation with nature without more demands on it than the basic necessities. This attitude was prevalent in traditional India which was predominantly an agricultural society based on village communities and various mores rooted firmly on traditional values. The strong bonds of family and clan-sentiment led to respect nature in its diverse forms: rivers, mountains, plant and animals, with reverence and love. This attitude is regarded by intellectuals as animistic, i.e., attributing spirit or mind to inanimate objects. Instances of such respect for nature and other creatures are plenty, for example it was common practice in India not to milk cows for quite a while after calves are born, or not to tear leaves or pluck flowers or fruits from trees at night when they are supposed to 'sleep'.

All these attitudes are changed by the so-called epistemological conquest of nature by science, which claimed to 'know' and dominate nature so that the latter can serve human beings, by its enormous resource potentials. Even the problem of conservation of wild life was handled much more successfully here than it was done in the West. Given the long history of habitation in the Indian sub-continent the variety and number of wild animals is still reasonable despite mindless poaching and destruction for either game or for the motive of monetary gain. In comparison to that wolves became totally extinct in mid-nineteenth century England. In America wild buffaloes now belong to a rare species.[15] R. Sukumar argues that despite conflicts and confrontations between humans and wild life people in the sub-continent have dealt with wild animals such as 'rogue' elephants and man-eater tigers and other ferocious animals through the ages in a reasonably effective but tolerant way. Otherwise these animals would simply not have survived to this day. Especially if we consider the long history of settlement in our country and the large human population directly and indirectly dependent on forest for sustenance, it is evident that the problem of wild life has been satisfactorily tackled. Elsewhere people have solved their problem by simply wiping out an offending species.

As said before, during the nineteenth century wolf as a predator on sheep was completely exterminated in Great Britain. In the past religious or other taboos helped conservation in a more tolerant way than now. But we know that large mammals like elephants and tigers play an important role in an ecosystem by virtue of their large biomass or position at the summit of an intricate food web. Disappearance or depletion of such key species could lead to the disruption of ecosystem functioning, perhaps leading to extinction of other species as well.

Thus in less than three hundred years the symbiotic relation in which nature and man lived together for millenniums have been snapped by the onslaught of western science and colonialism. In this short period nature has been destroyed, depleted and exploited in an unprecedented degree which our five thousand year old civilization never witnessed before. The worst part of such conquest is that only a minority privileged class is benefited by it and the fruits of such exploitation never reach those who live nearest to nature and have drawn sustenance from nature for thousands of years. [16]

Apart from the specific account of exploitation of nature by the colonial power and at present the various governmental and non-governmental agencies, this kind of exploitation of nature in the name of industrial development, many ecologists think, is not only wrong but also myopic about its disastrous effect and future consequences. An ecologically rational man-nature system is one in which human and natural components stand in a symbiotic relationship. Besides this the rationale of the basic norm of "live and let live" corresponds to the norms of traditional philosophy to a norm of 'maximum fulfilment of life potentials' as J.S. Dryzeck[17] puts it. This norm implies norms of diversity, complexity (between man and nature, thus of structure and function) and of maximum symbiosis, that is arrangement of life forms and lifestyles with minimum negative interference with each other.

Another point we have to note is that the so-called natural classification also is socially determined: why for example, water hyacinth is to be destroyed while corn and sugarcane be protected? The reason is obvious that whatever is suitable for human consumption, and at least enjoyment (a rose or sandalwood), is to be preserved and the rest is to be destroyed or at least minimized to make room for human need fulfilment. The broken balance between man and nature thus creates an uneven and paradoxical picture.[18] Mukherjee maintains in similar vein with the modern trend of rational ecological principles that, "each community cannot appropriate more than its due place in the general ordering of life from which nothing can be obtained without influencing everything else. Working symbiotically, they represent interwoven threads of a complex web of life." No threads can be snapped or removed "without the whole garments of the life and nature and human society being disfigured."[19] The ecological knowledge and awareness of the new millennium echoes the old fashioned metaphors used by him almost seventy years ago to describe a hypothetical state of affairs which we face today.

The other reason to have discontent with universal scientific knowledge is that it is tyrannical in a certain sense. The sacrosanct model of scientific enterprise makes modern science as well as its practitioners hold a high status in the role of a neutral arbiter of truth and rationality, disregarding other alternative epistemological traditions. The disillusion with modern scientific model led some philosophers even to doubt the so-called ideals of knowledge for various contingent reasons which I have discussed elsewhere[20]. Indeed the problems related to the domineering role of science and technology cannot be overestimated. Feyerabends' fiery diatribe against science and scientists has many substantive points. It is time now to be aware that modern western science is engulfing other traditions. Even concepts and language are entrenched by it. Why for example, is western culture mainstream and other cultures 'alternative 'cultures? Surely eastern civilization has at least some claim to be temporally prior. The division into 'first world', 'third world' or 'developed' and 'developing' (a patronising change from 'underdeveloped') again is arbitrary and questionable.

The favourite example of the tyrannical nature of scientific knowledge is modern medical science where more transparency is desirable. It is also true that scientific research is guided more by political factors than human cause, but all these considerations at most indicate, that actual scientific enterprise has been often tyrannical, and not that there is something basically anti-democratic. I have also argued elsewhere that no protective measures (monitoring, supervising, etc., as suggested by Feyerabend) can help, for science itself is a free enterprise and scientists also are free individuals. So if there is any tyrannical element in any enterprise then it must be dealt with from within that very culture by methodological devices and transparency. Scientific research provides with lots of checks and balances from within the tradition. Therefore the actual state of scientific research cannot provide us with a reason to call it tyrannical. As said before modern science has been misused, and often assumed a domineering role but despite all these deficiencies it has been so far the most reliable cognitive tradition, for its methodological norms.

One point, however, has to be taken seriously regarding the value of other cognitive traditions which takes many basic values so far ignored by the universalistic attitude of modern science of sweeping all problems (and their solutions) under a standardised method and analysis. Many problems of a specific nature can be solved by some age-old ways more successfully than the standard methods of modern science. Feyerabend also pointed out a significant feature of most traditional methods which interferes in least degree with the area of investigation, be it human body (in case of medical treatment, or diagnosis) or other experiments as it is done in modern science. As mentioned before, most traditional methods are tolerant and least interfering in dealing with their subject matter or problem area

In traditional Indian agricultural system after each cultivation, for example, lands were not tilled for a long period, sometimes as long as a whole year. Unlike this custom, in modern scientific agriculture multi-crop system gradually robs the natural fertility of the soil leading to various problems including excessive use of chemical fertilisers which again causes or at least can cause harm to human and animal life.

Similarly cows were *not* milked for at least some months after a calf is born, unlike modern scientific dairy system where this kind of consideration is absent to make room for large scale production of milk and other dairy and poultry produces. Many herbal and other natural ingredients also were used as aphrodisiac as well as contraceptive without the hazard of harmful side effects. These are but a very few examples to show only the kind of way traditional knowledge operates. Some of these knowledge are merely part of the tradition handed down from customs and local knowledge, but there are many others which are not merely part of the tradition but can be related to some philosophical or ontological theories. The latter type of knowledge can therefore be called scientific because it is consistent with and follows from a general view of the universe.

Local knowledge, however, can be related to a philosophical theory. Or else it can degenerate into nothing but a mere local custom which still is not connected with other ideas or theories But the possibility can never be ruled out that an idea can be in principle related with some theory or other. The ancient way of sun worshipping, for example, led eventually to the heliocentric theory of the universe. The sacralisation of nature in similar way is a primitive way of respecting and understanding ecological problems and conservation principles.

As mentioned earlier in the discussion, J.N Mohanty's analysis[21] of the Indian scenario of modernity and tradition is worth mentioning in this connection. He rightly thinks that modernity and tradition are perfectly blended in Indian political thought and not so much in academic philosophy. This has been possible by linking theory with practice. The Gandhian model of combining ideology with practice is a good example. Mohanty thinks that the Gandhian ideas of decentralised village-centred economy and rejection of party politics in favour of direct and village centred politics has worked towards "modernisation of Indian tradition on the one hand and on the other, traditionalisation of western modernity for India." The modernisation is achieved by freeing the traditional society of its age-old concepts of 'otherworldliness' and fatalistic tendencies, which is mismatched with the modern ethos of work culture and individual enterprise. Traditionalisation of western modernity is achieved on the other hand by 'offering a moral critique of modernity, industrialisation and bureaucracy and advancing a set of norms to guide the political structure of bourgeois modernity'.[22] The idea of *dharma* (duty) plays a pivotal role in traditional Indian ethos although the concept is much maligned in the modern context and strayed far away from its original intention and purpose.

Gandhian notion of combining tradition and modernity is unfortunately perceived by many as irrelevant for current concept of liberal thought that emphasises competition rather than moral dimension as more important element in the advent of modernity in India. However, there are still some thinkers who hold that Gandhian concept can be remodelled in the context of modern India and is a better solution to resolve the riddle of combining tradition with modernity.[23] Rajni Kothari regards Gandhi as an "alternative to western Post-enlightenment thought and to its related ideology of developmentalism and on the other as representing the moral imperative of treating people as a source in the recovery of a humane order."[24] Mohanty thinks Kothari's interpretation can be seen as India's "own version of post-modern and post-secular society, with its own tradition of social pluralism (as distinct from the political pluralism of western democracies) and a new concept of unity and its high tolerance of ambiguity and scepticism."

Nandy, however, perceives Gandhi as the most 'creative critical-traditionalist' who accepts, combines and at the same time critically reviews both. He regards Gandhi's rhetoric and reference to traditional Indian myths as powerful instrument to overcome the dominant Eurocentric concepts in various areas. Some of these concepts are scientism (which has become the focus of criticism in the west much later), historical determinism (strongly critiqued and rejected by Popper) and technicism etc. These concepts attracted attention of many western philosophers. They recognised them as the root cause of much modern malaise that afflicts us in the present and would be aggravated in the future.

Gandhi rejected the historicist's dogma of historical inevitability of the future not very much unlike the Popperian critique of it without the latter's systematic arguments against the doctrine. Gandhian principle of local/partial reformation rather than wholesale social change also has an implicit cognitive import. It can be phrased as follows: the future is indeterministic and therefore not known or predictable; any holistic approach to social phenomena may have undesirable consequences. Therefore small scale social change at least cannot bring forth a great disaster even if it does not bring a great fortune or total change. Therefore small changes, political or economic are preferable to wholesale change like revolution on the social/political spheres and big capitalism on the economic front. Similar arguments are offered by Popper for his famous theory of 'piecemeal engineering' for social change which only is consistent with the rejection of historical determinism and emphasis on human fallibilism. Gandhi's view of local rather than total view of social change however is based on a moral basis of self-sufficiency, self-determination and self-criticism etc.

In an attempt to harmonise tradition and modernity one may hold a position that modern scientific knowledge is a stronger tradition and traditional local knowledge handed down by local practice needs protection. So long the universities were 'the repositories of modern scientific knowledge'. But as Ashish Nandy[25] maintains, modern scientific knowledge-system does not need as much protection as traditional knowledge-system, therefore future universities should act as legitimising authority for different types of these traditions before they are forgotten or at least dropped from practice. I completely agree with this stand and want to emphasise that by such endorsement it is not also claimed that all traditional knowledge can stand the test for acceptability. It is only argued that they should be given a fair chance to be tried along with modern science which is already on a much firmer ground. It is very well possible that much of traditional practices would not prove to be of much worth. But at the same time we cannot discount the possibility of retrieving something from the jumble of complicated social practices some of which at least may be counted as reasonable. After all, these traditions, for example as in India, have a long history of survival despite many unfavourable natural and social factors. Therefore these kinds of local knowledge need protection or at least patient hearing for a fair trial. This requirement does not by any means undermine the value of modern science but only demands a way to keep open the possibility of retrieving something from traditional local knowledge-system.

IV

SOCIAL DETERMINATION AND SOCIAL CONSTRUCTION OF KNOWLEDGE

Against the Universalist thesis, it is said that science is a kind of culture, so it is determined by social factors. A stronger position is that the facts science examines are not culture-independent, they are theory-specific objects, nothing but constructs of a particular scientific tradition. In recent discussions about anthropological universalism the notion of 'world-openness' is the main focus. Some philosophers think in the line of German philosophical-anthropological tradition that world-openness marks a transition from nature to culture. It can be argued first that this concept being ambiguous blurs important distinctions between openness to determination by cultural forces and capacity for self-determination.

Secondly, the use of the concept of either variant is compatible with radical cultural relativism, as it appears to allow for the deactivation of any universal biological dispositions.[26] It is claimed by Roughley in the 'Afterword', *Human Nature, A Conceptual Matrix,* that conceptions of the human enable the distinctions of four senses of the expression "human nature, the pre-givenness of properties and their essentiality for being human is one of the three ways: as conceptually, predicatively or axiologically central". It is argued that discussions of human nature need to be aware of the multiple reference of the term and to mark clearly which of the senses they are discussing. Particularly when the author wishes to argue that there are specific relationships between structuring role in theory construction in philosophical ethics, aesthetics and social sciences.

It is rightly claimed also that these roles are often unacknowledged or implicit. It can also be reasonably said that enlightenment ideal for reason and morality (science and the concept of good) stood for western expansion and colonialism. In a sense enlightenment becomes another name for empire or domination of western power over others. Roughley rightly adds, "exoticization of the non-western world is consequence of a historical force—the postcolonial celebration of the other—the mythic, the primitive (the ethnic), the non-western is deeply implicated in a system of global segregation." Without denying the importance of the actual impact and historical significance of the point made here it can still be argued that these historical consequences thereof does not show fundamental flaw of the rationality ideal but *only* its actual misapplication. The ideal is a general schema for what should be considered as good reason or good action, without making any further claim.

One can make a distinction 'between dialogue within a knowledge-community and between knowledge-communities.' (Zhao Tingyang argues that understanding other communities does not entail acceptance of them. Western epistemological community regards 'others' only as interesting and exotic, but do not accept them as equal alternatives.[27] Western universalism assumes that other systems of knowledge work in the same way. Tingyang claims that unlike western reason-based approach, Chinese philosophy emphasises appeal to the heart, practical negotiation, development of a reciprocal idea rather than logical argument characterises the latter. In this view "in a sense Universalism is Fundamentalism, a negation of the other."

One of the successful ways of understanding the other in the last decades is an anthropological epistemology, the contextualized local knowledge by the 'thick description', first recommended by Ryle as a philosophical task, and of the other culture as Geertz encourages. The epistemological turn from the universal knowledge to the local knowledge can provide us with more information of the other, but the problem of understanding the other still remains even in the 'ideal speech situation'. The so-called pluralism thus is only 'deconstruction' of universalism—a diluted version aiming at politically correct attitude to others. Tingyang thinks that an interactive reciprocal approach (like the Chinese way) aims at an appeal not to logic and reason but to 'heart', happiness rather than knowledge, is the more comprehensive way to understand epistemology. This sounds very similar to Feyerabendian clamour for ordinary reason and human happiness rather than scientific rationality and logic as the real goal of scientific epistemology. One point must be noted here, granting that it is difficult to understand other culture-based viewpoints we may also grant that understanding does not guarantee acceptance as Tingyang argues. But we may notice that whenever there was a major obstacle to overcome, it was generally a result of indoctrination with western ideas. Or it comes from at least dogmatic acceptance of some uncritical scientism amounting to nothing more than western ideology. This is no less a grave danger to critical thought (as Popper would have put it) than succumbing to age-old superstitions nurtured by orthodox traditions.

No one can deny the social factors for an idea or theory. As no theory can originate in a vacuum, social factors are always determinant, necessary conditions for a theory/ knowledge. An idea needs nurturing in a congenial atmosphere, otherwise it cannot thrive into a full-fledged theory/knowledge. Example: In ancient Indian mythologies and epics we find reference to objects like rocket/missile, flying saucer, aeroplane, amphibious vehicles, etc. But due to many contingent historical conditions like internal strife, invasions from outside over the ages, colonialism—these ideas are not first developed by the Indians but invented over the years by modern western science.

But social conditions are only necessary conditions for knowledge or rather for its origin. Knowledge/theory needs to be justified or legitimised by some logic or at least heuristics. That process transcends social/local factors. Such rationality is an accepted norm in a civil society. Its denial also has a dangerous moral corollary—any action by any social/cultural group can gain an approval by such sociological/local standard of rationality and good. The world has witnessed much destruction of humanity in the last century and also at present in the name of ideology. No sensible epistemological norm can dismiss it as only an alternative system of knowledge and ideas. Moreover, although there can be multicultural standards belonging to different traditions, the standards can be adjudicated by some reasonable norms of consensus.

CONCLUSION

The purpose of philosophical investigation is to help people make evaluation of their beliefs and actions using the most objective and least personal or idiosyncratic criteria that we possess. It can be done by articulating fundamental standards to utmost scrutiny and careful analysis. "Our understanding of basic epistemic and moral principles may be imperfect, but this fact provides no reason for describing every disagreement as merely a matter of personal history, societal position or cognitive taste."[28]

For India both the neo-Gandhian and the 'left' inclined post modernist critique of science and rationality has taken a peculiar turn faced with a consequence which is least desirable even for them. It denies the universality and objectivity of modern science, thus legitimising all local (traditional) knowledge to be at par with scientific knowledge.

This kind of epistemological populism does not help those in the non-western societies. On the contrary those who are in these countries need a strong and substantive equality in knowledge to combat various social inequalities prevalent there. We in India should realize the potential of the Enlightenment ideal which can defeat the various kinds of fundamentalism that is threatening the porous firmament of secularism in India. Both the neo Gandhian and the left inclined intellectuals share the post modernist and post colonial suspicion about reason and the Enlightenment, the only difference is the anti-essentialist stance of the latter. They agree on the cultural embeddedness of all ways of knowing which reduces modern science to a mere 'ethno-science' of the west. The whole project of 'alternative sciences' seems to have put the clock back on the hard-earned progress modern science has made in knowing how to know. Moreover the 'local' knowledge systems they speak of in connection with 'Indian modes' of knowledge are not consistent with each other and more often than not 'patently irrational, obscurantist and downright oppressive to the same subaltern on whose behalf these intellectuals claim to speak'.[29]

In a heterogeneous and multicultural society like India we cannot afford to dispense with the notion of reason and science which is basically the spirit of the Enlightenment and has become a much maligned target of the fashionable post colonial post modernist critiques. But in an open society that admits of a plurality of interests, identities and self chosen ends (at least our constitution promises that) it is important the public sphere and the norms of discourse is not guided or dominated by any one class interest. Public reason must be conceived of as a never ending critical debate among contending interests which can be judged through publicly testable experience, independently of the class/ caste /

gender identity of the arguer. This is the fundamental point of critical rationality in tune with the Enlightenment ideal which is indicted by various postmodernist critiques of modern science and epistemology. This ideal of rationality was not unknown to the architects of our Constitution. It is reflected by the way the rights and privileges of the individuals are enshrined equally in the constitution irrespective of caste and creed, gender and religion. Equality presupposes rationality, it ensures equal rights for everyone irrespective of all social differences.

The culturalist understanding of science and knowledge has diverted people's science movements into indigenist and economic critiques of imperialist and colonial science rather than a self- critique of dominant and oppressive traditions. Once one takes refuge to a local or 'standpoint' epistemology all kinds of superstition /prejudice shall find a way to claim justification. The various forms of social constructionist theories of knowledge and science can slide into irrationalism of different sorts that we fought against for a long time

It is possible to hold a variety of philosophical positions that incorporate account of rationality but is either realist, agnostic or anti-realist. No one anymore holds the naïve view that knowledge is certain or absolute and therefore universal. We can perfectly hold a rationalist position in epistemology with no more claim on its absoluteness. Thus traditional knowledge in its various forms can participate in the marketplace of knowledge. Moreover if problem-solving is a substantive part of any cognitive pursuit it will be difficult to dislodge various traditional forms of knowledge from making an epistemic claim so far there is no unreasonable demand also that all knowledge claims are at par. Surely we can make a distinction between different knowledge-claims which purportedly is being ignored by sociological analysts of knowledge. In whatever degree a theory/knowledge is well-entrenched, we know that it can be overthrown. What is possible however is to find meta-theories about how to grade or evaluate our epistemic claims using methods that are objective, not in any immutable sense but in the modest sense of an acceptable norm regardless of the personal histories or cultural locations of those using them.This innocuous looking requirement can respect traditional knowledge without sliding into irrationalism of various sorts from which we have just been emancipated.

NOTES

1. Karl Popper has made a distinction between tradition and orthodoxy and maintains that *'orthodoxy is the death of knowledge'.* See, Popper, Karl. *The Myth of the Framework.*
2. Mohanty, J.N. 1992. *Reason and Tradition in India.*
3. Nakamura, Hajime. 1992. *History of Ideas.*
4. Nakamura, Hajime. *A Comparative History of Ideas.*
5. For many such stories see, Koyre, Alexander. *From Closed World to the Infinite Universe.*
6. Matilal, B.K. 1999. *The Character of Logic in India.*
7. Mukhopadhyay, P.K. 1984. *Indian Realism: A Rigourous Descriptive Metaphysics.* As the title shows, this is an attempt to reinterpret Indian concepts of realism as well as Monism.
8. Popper, Karl.
9. Ibid. Section III.
10. Ibid. Section V.
11. Ibid. p. 29.

12. Ibid.
13. Ibid. Section IX.
14. Ibid.
15. Sukumar, R. "Wildlife—Human Conflict in India". *Social Ecology*. R.C. Guha (ed.).
16. For various accounts of such exploitation and resistance movements in India. See, Guha, R.C. (ed.). *Social Ecology*. See also, Guha, R.C. (ed.). *The Unquiet Woods.*
17. Dryzeck, J. S. *Rational Ecology.*
18. Radhakamal Mukherjee, a pioneer in ecological research in India has mentioned such examples of imbalance man have brought into nature. He says, "The plants which he (man) does not tolerate are called weeds." See, Mukherjee, Radhakamal. 1930. "An Ecological Approach to Sociology: Eco-contributions to Sociology". *The Sociological Review, vol. xxii* (4) October; reprinted in *Social Ecology.*
19. Ibid. p. 26.
20. Chaudhury, Mahasweta. 1999. "Tyranny in Disguise - Expert Knowledge and Human Interest." *Facets of Humanism.* Patnaik et al (ed.). New Delhi:
21. Mohanty, J.N. "Indian Thought: Between Tradition and Modernity". *Explorations in Philosophy.* Chapter 4.
22. Ibid. p. 61.
23. Rajni Kothari and Ashis Nandy are some of these thinkers who are trying to support the basic Gandhian principles in the context of modern problems.
24. Cited from, Mohanty. *Explorations in Philosophy;* Pantham, Thomas. *Political Theories and Social Reconstruction: A Critical Survey of Literature in India. I am indebted to J.N. Mohanty's own views and his reference to Pantham.*
25. Nandy, Ashis. 1996. "The Role of Future Universities". *Seminar,* June.
26. de Gruyter, Hawthorne. 2000. "Being Humans: Anthropological Universalism and Particularity". *Transdisciplinary Perspectives.* Neil Roughley (ed.).
27. Tingyang, Zhao. 2001. "Understanding and Acceptance". Paper presented on *Universal and Local Knowledge* seminar at Sorbonne, October 2001.
28. Coertge, Noretta. 1999. *"Review". British Journal of Philosophy of Science, 50.*
29. Nanda, Meera. *Breaking the Spell of Dharma.* p. 119.

BIBLIOGRAPHY

1. Bloor, David. 1976. *The Social Imagery of Science.*
2. ———. 1974."Popper's Mystification of Scientific Knowledge". *Science Studies, 4.*
3. Chaudhury, Mahasweta. 1999. "Tyranny in Disguise—Expert Knowledge and Human Interest." *Facets of Humanism.* Patnaik et al (ed.). New Delhi.
4. Coertge, Noretta. 1998. *A House Built on Sand: Exposing Postmodernist Myths about Science.* New York: Oxford University Press.
5. Collins, H.M. and Pinch, T.J. *1982. Frames of Meaning: The Social Construction of Extraordinary Science.* Routledge.
6. Feyerabend, Paul. 1987. *Farewell to Reason.* London.
7. ———. 1978. *Science in a Free Society.* Cambridge.
8. ———. 1991. *Three Dialogues on Knowledge.* Cambridge.
9. Gauss, G.F. 1996. *Jusificationary Liberalism: An Essay in Epistemology and Political Theory.* Oxford University Press.
10. Geertz, Clifford. 1983. *Local Knowledge.* New York: Basic Books.
11. ———. 1973. *An Interpretation of Culture.* New York: Basic Books.
12. Fernandez and Singer (ed.). 1995. *The Conditions of Reciprocal Understanding.* Chicago.
13. Hans, Kung and Karl-Josef, Kushel (ed.). 1993. *A Global Ethic: The Declaration of the Parliament of the World Religion.* USA: The Continuum Publishing Company.
14. Le Pichon, Alain. 1995. "The Sound of the Rain: Poetic Reason an Reciprocal Understanding". In Fernandez and Singer (ed.).
15. Mahajan, Gurpreet. 1995. "Cultural Embodiments and Histories: Towards Construction of Self'. *Crisis and Change in Contemporary India.* Upendra Baxi and Bhikhu Parekh (ed.). New Delhi: Sage.
16. Nagel, Thomas. 1986. *The View from Nowhere.* New York: Oxford University Press.

17. Nanda, Meera. 1998. "Epistemic Charity of Social Constructivist Theories of Science and Why the Third World must reject the Offer". In Noretta Coertge (ed.).
18. Popper, Karl. 1996. *The Myth of the Framework.* Notturno (ed.).
19. Rawls, John. 1971. *Theory of Justice.* Harvard.
20. Rorty, Richard. 1979. *Philosophy and the Mirror of Reason.*
21. ———. 1993. "Anti-Representation, Ethnocentrism and Liberalism". *Collective Papers.* Introduction.
22. de Gruyter, Hawthorne. 2000. "Being Humans: Anthropological Universalism and Particularity". *Transdisciplinany Perspectives.* Neil Roughley (ed.).
23. Sen, Amartya. 2000. "East and West: The Reach of Reason". *New York Review of Books.* July *20.*
24. Tingyang, Zhao. 2001. "Understanding and Acceptance". Paper presented on *Universal and Local Knowledge* seminar at Sorbonne, October 2001.

CHAPTER 24

Scientific Approaches to Consciousness Studies

B.V. Sreekantan

Most biologists have held that mental activities including consciousness are just physico-chemical activities of the brain. The neuroscientists have been able to map out in great detail these physico-chemical and electrical and electronic processes in the various cortices of the brain, in the billions of neurons that connect the cortices to various parts of the brain itself and to other organs of the human body and to the sensors like the eyes, ears, nose etc., which receive inputs from the outside world. They are trying to establish spatio-temporal correlates in terms of action potentials and neurotransmitter chemicals. If that is all there is to the functioning and definition of consciousness, then consciousness itself must be capable of being explained in terms of the more basic concepts of all sciences namely, in terms of concepts like mass, energy, space, time, force, causality and so on. However, experience tells us that while the electrical signals and the chemicals belong to one category of knowledge, sensations, feelings, cognition, insight, memory etc., which we associate with consciousness belong to an entirely different category that cannot be understood in terms of the above concepts only. The real problem of consciousness from the scientific point of view is to bridge this gap.

In the history of physical sciences, there have been many occasions when the scientists were faced with similar barriers. These were surmounted by (1) total modification of the prevalent concepts themselves, (2) recognizing the existence of an ultimate substratum that interconnects everything and whose activities are responsible, in the ultimate analysis, for all the happenings in the universe including creation of space, time, matter, force etc. and (3) emergence of new forms, effects from the coherent activities of the constituents. Typical examples of such instances will be presented and the need and relevance of similar transcendent approaches, of course, well within the framework of science, to the solution of the consciousness problem are discussed.

I

NEUROSCIENCES AND CONSCIOUSNESS

Most scientists, particularly biologists subscribe to the view that all mental activities including consciousness are just physico-chemical processes in the brain and in its accessories. This view is superbly exemplified by the hypothesis of Francis Crick,[1] which he calls the 'astonishing hypothesis' stated as follows:

> your joys, your sorrows, your memories and your ambitions, your sense of personal identity, your free will are all in fact no more than the behaviour of vast assembly of nerve cells and their associated molecules.

Following the anatomical studies that led to the identification of various cortices of the brain for particular functions, the neuroscientists in the past several decades have mapped out in great detail the physico-chemical, electrical and electronic processes that occur in the various cortices of the brain in the billions of neurons that connect to the sensors—the eyes, ears, nose, skin, etc., associated with particular perceptions, cognitions, memories, and so on. What is amazing is that though the different sensors respond to different physical inputs like light, sound, heat and pressure, the outputs of the sensors are all very similar electrical signals, the specific information being coded in the form of bursts, multiple neuron discharges and time sequence of single and multiple bursts and so on. These signals preferentially get aborted or are modulated further at the various synapses based on inputs from dendrites which connect to neighbouring neurons. The nature of final response depends on the particular cortex to which the neuronal information gets fed. The visual information becomes manifest if the neuronal pulses go to the visual cortex, the sound becomes manifest when the neuronal pulses from the ear go to the auditory cortex and so on. The crucial question that remains unanswered yet is: what is it that correlates all this information and gives meaning to whatever is happening? This, according to popular belief, is really the business of consciousness. Where is this consciousness located in the brain? And in what form?

Apart from cognition of the external world, the sights, the sounds, the textures, etc., consciousness also has to account for thoughts, memories and flashes of insight. There is no identification of specific regions of the brain that consciousness uses to perform these functions as well.

Essentially in all this we are dealing with two kinds of experiences as depicted in Table 1. During the simple act of observing a flower, the happenings in the brain can in practice be recorded with instruments of various kinds. In the other, mind (or consciousness) comes into play and no instrument has been designed so far to record the happenings. Even for the first, instruments alone will not suffice.

In Table 1, on the left hand side (A), there are terms like electrical signals, oscillations, chemicals etc. that have specific connotations which we learn in the process of schooling at various levels, and start attaching certain kind of reality to them. It is to be pointed out that these are actually representations of some things which are more basic and physical. For example, the electrical signal represents the flow of a certain quantity of electrical charge in a certain period of time in a certain location. These parameters are again related to more subtler realities as we shall see later on. Similar is the situation with the neurochemicals which are made of various elements, which in turn are made of fundamental particles like protons, neutrons and electrons. For certain purposes one can stop at the level of signals and chemicals. The question is whether we can stop at these gross levels for understanding what consciousness is.

TWO KINDS OF EXPERIENCES GENERATED IN THE INDIVIDUAL WHO LOOKS AT A ROSE FLOWER

A (Physicalism) What happens in the Brain and Its accessories?	B (Mentalism) What happens in the mind?
• Formation of 'image' of the flower in the retina.	• Distinctive perception and recognition of the flower as a rose.
• Activation of rods and cones in the retina's various layers.	• Evokes sense of beauty; smell of the rose flower.
• Generation of action potentials—electrical pulses.	• The colour of the flower.
• Transmission of pulses through axons in neurons.	• The softness and smoothness of petals on touching the same.
• Happenings in Synapses and Dendrites	• Appreciation of Symmetry, beauty and aroma.
• Releases of Neuro-transmitter chemicals at various locations.	• Earlier happy associations flood the mind.
• Activation of Cortices.	• Emotions triggered.
Basically: Electrical Signals oscillations, chemicals, time sequence. } in various locations	The mind is able to gauge the size, distance, shape and other physical characteristics as well.

TABLE 1

The terms on the right hand side (B) of the Table fall into an entirely different category. There we come across terms like beauty, fragrance, softness, etc. which we learn in the process of everyday living and through interaction with others. They cannot be described in terms of more fundamental entities. They cannot be quantified. They have a certain intensely personal (subjective) character about them. Some of these like joy, happiness etc. are triggered by past associations and memories of events and individuals. More than anything else, we read a certain 'meaning' to these. They are not just data as in the first case (A).

The crucial difference between (A) and (B) is that while (A) can happen even when one is unconscious, (B) can never happen when one is unconscious. Even if all the signals and chemicals are released in the brain and its accessories, (B) cannot happen if the person is in a unconscious state or when he is not paying attention—when the intentionality for registering the particular happening is not there. While for seeing a flower or registering its fragrance, (A) is necessary, (A) alone is not sufficient for (B) to happen. On the other hand (B) can happen in a different way—by thinking of the flower and recalling from memory, its fragrance.

Let us consider the reverse situation when the input is not from outside, but from within. If I "will" to get up, then the necessary instructions are sent to the relevant parts of my body and I stand up. What or Who is this I, that wills and how does the will get translated to all the mechanical actions of the body? Clearly I can "will" only when I am conscious.

In both these examples, the net result is some kind of 'action'. In the first case the source is physical and the action is mental and in the other the source is mental and the action is physical. In both cases, the action takes place is a certain space-time framework—the body and its surroundings and in a certain time sequence.

Is it possible at all to relate these two different kinds of experiences of the same event in any meaningful way? Clearly at the gross level they appear to be distinctly different and unconnected entities though the two experiences are the consequences of the same physical event, namely seeing and smelling a flower by the same individual. Can they be reconciled at a deeper fundamental level?

II

REALITY AND LEVELS OF EXPLANATION IN PHYSICAL SCIENCES

It has happened in the field of science, particularly in physics, that even the same event requires widely different concepts for explanation depending on the level and purpose for which the explanations are required. Let us examine a few typical examples of such cases.

Supposing I take a piece of stone and drop it from a certain height. It falls to the ground. Why? The standard school boy's answer is that the gravitational force between the stone and the earth is responsible for this. The stone is a solid and therefore does not change its shape while falling down, while it may break into smaller pieces when it hits the ground. This same phenomenon is explained by a chemist in a more elaborate way. He will say that the stone is a compound made of several elements like silicon, oxygen and other impurities and the molecules of these elements are made of atoms held together by electromagnetic forces. So when the stone falls it is an assembly of atoms falling down held together by these forces. An atomic-cum-nuclear scientist goes one step further and says that all these atoms are made of protons, neutrons and electrons bound together by nuclear forces and so what is happening when the stone is falling is that a bunch of protons, electrons and neutrons are all falling down together held by nuclear and electromagnetic forces. A fundamental particle physicist will go even further and say that the protons and neutrons are made of quarks held together by gluonic forces and it is the assembly of quarks, gluons and electrons that is falling.

What this shows is that though the gross phenomenon is just the falling of a stone, the realities are different at different levels of explanation. The reality goes on changing as we delve deeper and deeper into the structure of matter and nature of forces. Different levels of reality meet different purposes. An engineer designing a steel bridge does not have to go beyond the molecular structure of iron, while a pharmaceutical chemist designing a drug has to go to deeper levels. A nuclear engineer has to go to the nuclear levels for designing reactors and providing protection against radioactive emissions.

What we have considered so far is about the finer and finer constituents of matter. While we have made a reference to the various forces, we have not considered some of the intricacies involved. As the stone is falling, it is entering new regions of space. The electromagnetic, the nuclear and gluonic forces are not rigid bodies like rods that are permanently attached and move down with the particles they connect. According to present concepts of forces, their action is through the creation and absorption of virtual pairs of particles and anti-particles. So, strictly speaking, it is not only the bunch of quarks and electrons falling down, it is also the continuous creation and annihilation of virtual pairs of particles in the space between the falling particles. This highlights yet another intricate action that is going on which is very relevant to the act of the stone falling as one piece, but which is not apparent, at the gross levels. We normally treat the space as 'empty' of 'everything'. Actually this is not the case. Space is the repository of the ultimate constituents of all matter and forces, but existing in such a form that either by spontaneous fluctuation (which is one of the properties of this vacuum) or by the deposition of positive energy they can be made to manifest. For example, in the case of a hydrogen atom, the electromagnetic force between the proton and the electron is due to the continuous creation and annihilation of electrons and positrons created as virtual particle pairs by the mediating photons emitted by the charged particles. In the case of quark-quark forces the gluons are exchanged. Though the virtual pairs cannot be recorded by any instruments directly because of the extremely short time for their existence and the very short distance intervals in which they manifest, the effects of their production have been recorded (Lambshift, Casmir force etc.). What all this is telling us is that what meets the eye is very different from the plethora of many subtle phenomena taking place at deeper levels which are not only unseen, but unseeable.

In the above paragraphs, we have talked about force as due to exchange of virtual particles. This is a very different concept from the original ideas of force fields that were introduced in connection with gravitational, electric, magnetic and electromagnetic phenomena. The fields were introduced as mathematical concepts without defining what the physical contents of the field are. It was assumed that these are some vague properties of 'ether' which itself was supposed to be non-material something, not identifiable. For several centuries the ether concept held sway, but was finally replaced by the four dimensional space-time continuum by Einstein, as part of his special theory of relativity.

While quantum mechanics highlighted the properties of empty space in terms of its ultimate constituents (fundamental particles or fields representing them), the special and general theories of relativity brought out some other interesting aspects of space—connecting geometrical properties of space with matter and energy. The old common sense idea of time as absolute and same everywhere got a new twist in the special theory. Rate of flow of time became dependent on the velocity of the frame of reference and dilatated as the velocity of motion became higher. Space intervals contracted in the direction of motion. For certain purposes space and time could not be treated as separate characteristics, but had to be fused into a single concept of space-time continuum. The human experience of space is very different from the experience of time. Clearly they belong to different categories of experience. But according to the special theory they had to be merged. The special theory had more surprises in store. It combined energy and mass through the famous relation $E=mc^2$. Here again the concept of mass and the concept of energy, both anthropogenic in origin were certainly very different concepts and were introduced in different contexts. The most surprising of all was the equivalence of mass and curvature of space, established in the general theory of relativity. According to this, matter which is the most concrete of all our perceptions is just a geometrical property of space, in a sense topsy-turvying the old idea that empty space is there laid out for matter to occupy.

As is well-known the special theory of relativity was proposed by Einstein to account for the experimentally observed fact that the velocity of light was independent of the motion of the observer. Several unusual consequences that followed from the theory have been subsequently very well established experimentally. The bending of light around a massive object like the Sun predicted by the general theory of relativity was later verified by the observation at the time of a solar eclipse. The explosion of the atom bomb was clear indication of the equivalence of mass and energy.

It may be appropriate at this stage to state the revolutionary ideas that brought about a major change in the way of our thinking in science and also in philosophy, in the words of the masters themselves who brought about these revolutions.

Einstein: "Matter which we perceive is merely nothing but a great concentration of energy in very small regions. We may therefore regard matter as being constituted of space in which the field is intense. Field is the only reality."

Dirac: "All matter is created out of some imperceptible substratum. Nothing, unimaginable and undetectable. But it is a peculiar form of nothingness out of which all matter is created."

What these developments in the field of physics demonstrate is that many of the fundamental concepts like space, time, matter, radiation, energy taken over from common sense everyday ideas to science in its early days, have had to be radically transformed and even transcended[2] to be able to explain many new phenomena discovered especially in the twentieth century. These realizations of the fundamental connectivity of what appeared to be widely unconnected aspects of nature—electricity, magnetism, light, matter, gravitation—came about gradually and in different contexts, and with the application of more and more powerful tools for the exploration of nature—probing on the one hand extremely small intervals of space with high energy particles and with the ability to record happenings in extremely short intervals of time with sophisticated detector and electronic systems, and on the other, accessing the farthest reaches of the expanding universe and identifying entirely new kinds of celestial objects that revealed new features of the Universe. This new knowledge and the new physics is pointing towards a most important secret of nature as it were—that all this variety is a manifestation just of one substratum, a four dimensional space-time continuum according to theory of relativity and a quantum vacuum (Dirac vacuum) according to quantum mechanics, and theory of elementary particles and their interactions. How this substratum arose and how it was endowed with all the intrinsic properties necessary for these manifestations, science will, perhaps, never find answers. However, what science has been able to do is to specify the properties necessary from the point of being able to explain phenomena in the traditional scientific methodology of breaking down gross phenomena to finer and finer levels by the reductionistic method reinforced by experimental observations and theoretical constructions incorporating mathematical equations and their solutions and guided by conformity to laws and to constants of nature. However, several surprising features that unfolded in this endeavour are (i) occasional breakdown of laws was as, or more important on occasions to the emergence of new features (ii) these deviations were of a controlled nature (Heisenberg's principle of uncertainty) (iii) group behaviour was in some as yet inexplicable way depended on some individual parameters (spin dependent statistics) (iv) entirely new features emerged in assemblies (superconductivity, super fluidity, laser action, etc)—(v) 'Resonance' plays an extremely significant role in the explanation of many phenomena.

On the unification of space and time and the connection to gravity, Yu Vladimirov, et al[3] wrote: "Thus the curvature of space-time has a physical meaning. We have long got used to the fact that many things in this world are different aspects of the same entity. This was the case with mass and energy with inertial mass (resistence to force) and gravitational mass (gravitational charge) and now we see that the same is true of gravitational fields and geometrical properties of space time. Curvature is a geometrical entity whose components vary from point to point in any given system of co-ordinates. Thus curvature is a field in the mathematical sense of the word, and at the same time a manifestation of a physical gravitational field. The credit for this discovery goes to Einstein."

Further Yu Vladimorov, et al, continue: "... is there any difference between physics and geometry? The only reason we regard geometry as an independent physical reality is because we were educated in the spirit of Euclidean axioms. Think how absurd this viewpoint is: indeed our universe is whole and unique and its properties can all be learned only from experience. The geometry of the real world should be regarded as one of the experimental physical sciences and its assertions and predictions must always be verified through experience or practice. The axioms of geometry are, in fact, no more than a refined form of human experiences. To the question whether it is possible to construct a theory in which all the quantities have a geometrical interpretation the answer is "yes, the most elegant solution lies in the framework of higher dimension."

[Historically, it is interesting to note that William Clifford (1845-1879) had noted: (i) physical properties of matter and properties of curved spaces are related (ii) heat, light, electricity maybe related to changes in the curvature of space (iii) the electromagnetic field maybe related to geometry of space.]

III

ORIGIN OF THE UNIVERSE—CREATION OF SPACE, TIME AND MATTER

The Big Bang Theory of Creation of the Universe is one possible and at the moment the most popular theory of creation of the Universe. It spells out the intricate connections between widely different physical parameters in the light of all the developments in physics and astronomy in the twentieth century.

The Big Bang scenario and the first moments of the physical evolution of the universe is beautifully narrated by John Boslough[4] as follows: "Into a void, so absolute as to mock any human concept of emptiness, appeared a single point of raw potential. At the very instant of its creation, this point bearing all matter, all dimension, all energy, all time burst out spewing forth its contents. At the instant of its origin, all matter and all forces were indistinguishable from each other. As the universe expanded and cooled, matter and forces split again. Still in the billionth of a second in its history, the universe continued to fragment. Soon all the constituents of matter—what we now call quarks and leptons, assumed separate identities, falling into separate classes that have been joined again. The single force propelling the cataclysm also became fragmented and the different particles became associated forever with the new forces that were being created. Three of the fragmented forces are still at work inside the atom. The most powerful of these is the strong force that binds the constituents of the nucleus together—the quarks that make up the protons and the neutrons. One thousand times weaker is the electromagnetic force that keeps the electrons, a type of leptons, orbiting around the nucleus. This force makes atoms appear solid and also is responsible for radio and light waves. Another hundred times less powerful is the weak force that causes radioactive decay."

While the above describes the act of creation of matter and force in the first moments of the universe, Boslough[5] has a more graphic description of the whole creation of the universe including space, time, matter, space, galaxies, earth, life and people as follows:

> At first there was nothing—no time, no space, not even emptiness, only a void beyond voids, a place that was no place, without colour, without shape or substance, without passing a single moment or a prospect of eternity.
>
> From this pure nothingness sprang a speck of chaos, a seed seething with such raw energy that the thought capable of contemplating it has not yet been formed. Within this speck of vibrating energy still many times finer than an atom were the dimensions of time and space although these concepts were then meaningless. There was no now, then and will be; no here, no there. The infinitesimal cosmos began to expand. As it grew it cooled and its energy dissipated. Almost at once one of the forces ranging within it separated from the rest. Some pairs of particles capable of existing only in such extreme conditions flashed in and out of existence, colliding with each other in a shower of annihilation. Suddenly the infant cosmos erupted from subatomic proportions to the size of a cantaloupe. Within a second, it was as big as solar system a crucible of matter and energy denser than a star. Pure energized light blazed throughout the young universe. As it grew and cooled, flying particles began coalescing into larger structures of hydrogen atoms, which eventually swirled into immense clouds of billowing gas.
>
> Epochs passed. The universe expanded. Its blazing light faded into darkness. A million years, then a billion years came and went. All at once millions of stars began emerging from the swirling clouds of hydrogen gas. Galaxies appeared, then more stars, other worlds perhaps, Earth, Life and People.

This Big Bang theory is based on three critical experimental observations and a lot of information gathered from collision studies at high energy particle accelerators. The three crucial observations are (i) expansion of the universe, (ii) discovery of the universal 3^0k Microwave radiation and (iii) percentage ratio of Helium to Hydrogen in the universe as a whole. The creation scenario as a function of time from 10^{-43} sec to 20 billion years in the life time of the universe is shown in the figure taken from Boslough's book.

IV

CONSCIOUSNESS AND QUANTUM VACUUM

While the advances in theoretical elementary particle and nuclear physics and theoretical astrophysics and cosmology have helped us in formulating this Big Bang scenario—the creation of space, time, radiation, elementary particles, elements, compounds, stars, galaxies etc., what is missing is any hint even, of how and when inanimate matter became animate matter and how and when consciousness emerged. What is established beyond any shadow of doubt by biologists is that the constituents of animate matter at all levels from amoeba to man are made of the same elements as encountered in inanimate matter. No particular new element has been found unique to living matter though the organic molecules are very long chain molecules. Though it is more difficult to be categorical about the absence of any new forces unique to organisms, the biologists continue to work on the hypothesis that the same four physical forces operative in inanimate matter are the only ones in animate matter too.

It has to be pointed out in this context that the experience in the delineation and discovery of forces in the physical domain has depended on theoretical formulations and predictions followed by experimental effort costing enormous sums of money and involving construction of new facilities for carrying out these searches. In very recent years, there is considerable excitement over the possibility of yet another new force in addition to the four known forces, attributable to the detection of the 'dark energy' in the universe that is behind the faster expansion of the universe established by astronomical observations. Unfortunately, despite suggestions by Shelldrake and others about the possibility of new kinds of forces in the animate systems, no systematic efforts have been made in this direction, maybe because of the prejudice against the old concept of vitalism and vital forces. Since we do not know all the properties of quantum vacuum which is the reservoir of all forces, in principle it is not difficult to accommodate new forces. We have seen that the four known forces: gravitational, electromagnetic, nuclear and weak forces serve entirely different purposes. Yet another approach that is being advocated to explain consciousness is the systems approach which incorporates ideas of chaos, coherence, non-equilibrium nonlinear processes which has become popular in connection with phenomena that require group effort. In this class are phenomena which show the 'emergence' of new features which are not there in any manifest way in their constituents. Typical examples in the field of physical are superconductivity, superfluidity, laser action. These are mostly due to long distance phase couplings resulting from quantum coherence. In this kind of scenario consciousness is considered to arise resulting from the coherent firings of individual well separated neurons, the firing of individual neurons themselves being controlled by quantum coherence effects in the microtubules[7] of the neurons. In the ultimate analysis these again become processes in the universal substratum—quantum vacuum.

Finally, what this 'oneness'—the universal substratum, the space-time continuum, the quantum vacuum, has done is to point towards a way of resolving the trichotomy between the three entities involved in Consciousness, the experienced, the experience and the experiencer as just different manifestations of the same base level unity. What is interesting and perhaps significant is that similar insights of oneness (Urstoff, Brahman, Sunyata, Tao etc.) have been emphasized in several ancient philosophies (see Sreekantan[8]), of course following an entirely different line of approach—turning objectivity to subjectivity by exploring the inner halls of our experience.

NOTES

1. Crick, Francis. 1994. *The Astonishing Hypothesis.* London: Simon & Shuster.
2. Sreekantan, B.V. 2002. "Transcendences in Physics and their application to Consciousness." *Science and Metaphysics: A Discussion on Consciousness and Genetics.* NIAS Special Publication, 10-02. pp. 403-415.
3. Vladimirov, Yu, Mitskievich, N. and Horsky, J. 1987. *Space, Time and Gravitation.* Moscow: Mir Publication.
4. Boslough, John. 1992. *Masters of Time.* London: Phoenix-Orion Books Ltd.
5. Ibid.
6. Hameroff, Stuart R. 1994. "Quantum Coherence in Microtubules: A Neural Basis for Emergent Consciousness". *Journal of Consciousness Studies,* 1(1). pp. 91-118.
7. Sreekantan, B.V. 1995. *Modern Physics and Ancient Indian Philosophies: Science in the West and India.* Bombay, Delhi, Nagpur: Himalaya Publishing House. pp. 432-451.
8. Ibid. See also, Sreekantan, B.V. 1999. "Scientific Explanations and Consciousness". *Scientific and Philosophical Studies on Consciousness.* NIAS Special Publication, S-99. pp. 5-22.

CHAPTER 25

Is the Physical World Real and Deterministic?

Partha Ghose

I

CLASSICAL PHYSICS: ESTABLISHMENT OF REALISM AND DETERMINISM

The impact of the scientific revolution ushered in by Newtonian physics was so pervasive and deep that it changed man's thinking forever and influenced practically every branch of human knowledge. Newton was believed to have seen through God's mind. His was the new revelation, and his laws governed the universe. Although philosophers like Kant elucidated its epistemology, by and large scientists did not care much for such philosophical musings. Like Laplace they saw no need for an external agency like God. There was the great big universe 'out there' with the basic principles of its inner workings already revealed by Newton's daring insight. All that needed to be done was to work out the details.

This view was further bolstered in the nineteenth century by Maxwell's brilliant theoretical work that not only unified electricity and magnetism into a single entity but also led to the prediction that this unified entity was a continuous electromagnetic wave that could propagate through vacuum or empty space with the velocity of light. Electromagnetic radiation was soon experimentally produced and observed by Hertz and soon after by Sir J.C. Bose. This was the beginning of modern electrical engineering and wireless communication. Then came Darwin, finally banishing God altogether from the scene. Philosophy too was banished from scientific circles as idle speculation.

Physics at the end of the nineteenth century dealt with two different kinds of entities, (a) Newtonian particles and (b) Maxwellian waves (or radiation), both of which had a reality of their own that was independent of the human mind. The physical universe did not tolerate any human intervention. Freedom of the will was a mere human illusion. All observed arbitrariness and chaos were seen to arise from the limitations and inadequacy of the human mind. The Cartesian divide between mind and matter did not bother pragmatic scientists. The mind was tacitly believed not to be part of the physical universe. The physical universe behaved totally independent of the observer. It was a strictly rational, self-sufficient and deterministic system, an automaton. That was classical physics.

II

THE QUANTUM WORLD: REALISM AND DETERMINISM UNDERMINED

All this changed with the advent of Einstein's theory of relativity and quantum mechanics, particularly the latter, in the early part of the twentieth century. Step by step the classical ideas of realism, observer-independence and determinism started to crumble, giving way to quantum theory. The first step was most reluctantly and hesitatingly taken by Max Planck in 1900 when he introduced the idea of the quantum of energy. Matter was shown not to be able to absorb and emit energy continuously but only in discrete packets or quanta—matter was 'quantized', but not radiation. Then came Einstein's daring light-quantum hypothesis in 1905. He argued that fluctuations in the energy of black-body radiation satisfying Planck's radiation law indicated that radiation itself had a corpuscular character in addition to its wave-like character, and that the phenomenon of photoelectricity (emission of electrons by certain metals when irradiated) could be easily explained in all its details if this corpuscular nature of radiation was taken seriously. That was the beginning of *wave-particle duality*. The third step was taken by Neils Bohr in 1913 when he proposed his famous model of the atom. Bohr extended Planck's ideas and introduced the concept of discrete energy states in atoms, and showed how the observed discrete line spectrum of radiating atoms could be simply explained by the absorption and emission of radiation between pairs of these 'stationary' energy states. The fourth step was taken by Satyendra Nath Bose in 1924 when he extended Planck's method of quantizing matter to Maxwell's radiation, leading to a new form of statistics for Einstein's light-quanta, nowadays called photons. Now even radiation was 'quantized'. Einstein quickly applied Bose's method to monatomic gases and drew several dramatic conclusions.[1] One was that material particles should possess a wave-like character. Already in 1923 Lois de Broglie had come to the same conclusion starting from an entirely different hypothesis, namely that wave-particle duality ought to be a universal feature of nature and not a special characteristic of light. Einstein immediately drew everyone's attention to the papers by Bose and de Broglie. Matter waves were soon discovered[2], and the equation of motion for matter waves was written down by Schrodinger in 1926. That was the beginning of a new form of mechanics called 'wave mechanics' that replaced Newtonian mechanics for atomic and sub-atomic objects. Heisenberg more or less simultaneously proposed an equivalent form of mechanics called 'matrix mechanics'. The new mechanics with its two equivalent forms has come to be known as 'quantum mechanics' or simply quantum theory.

One of the key features of this new mechanics is Heisenberg's 'uncertainty principle' and the uncertainty relations. Stimulated by a remark of Einstein that 'it is only your theory that can tell you what you can observe', Heisenberg set about to show by a penetrating analysis of the new quantum theory that every observation of a quantum system involved an uncontrollable disturbance of the system, so that the outcome of the observation was essentially unpredictable. The complete set of possible outcomes appears as potentialities in the theory, and the individual outcomes occur essentially randomly as actualizations of these potentials. When a sufficiently large number of observations are carried out on exact replicas of the system (analogous to tossing a perfect coin many times), one can determine the probabilities of each individual outcome. In the case of the coin, one can in principle predict the outcome of each toss provided one knows precisely the initial conditions, i.e., exactly how the coin is tossed. This is not so in quantum theory. The theory precludes precise knowledge of the initial conditions in principle. It is therefore able to predict only the probabilities of the outcomes accurately. This immediately leads to the loss of both realism and determinism at the most fundamental level. Einstein was very skeptical. "Does God play dice with the world?" he used to ask.

III

QUANTUM PARADOXES

The situation was further accentuated in 1935 by the critical papers of Einstein, Podolsky and Rosen[3] and that of Schrodinger[4], highlighting certain 'unreasonable' features of quantum mechanics exemplified by the famous EPR paradox and the Schroedinger Cat paradox.

Einstein, Podolsky and Rosen started with the definition of three fundamental metaphysical concepts that they brought to bear on the conceptual structure of quantum theory. These are the concepts of *reality, separability* and *completeness.* They gave the following carefully honed definitions:

Reality Criterion

"If, without in any way disturbing a system, we can predict with certainty (i.e., with probability equal to unity) the value of a physical quantity, then there exists an element of physical reality corresponding to this physical quantity".

Separability Criterion

If two systems interact and then separate so that they are well outside each other's sphere of influence, "no real change can take place in the second system in consequence of anything that may be done to the first system".

Completeness Criterion

"Every element of the physical reality must have a counterpart in the physical theory."

Using these criteria, they showed that there are systems in quantum theory for which the criteria of reality and separability were valid but the quantum theoretic description of such systems was necessarily incomplete. Later, Einstein clarified the main issue of the paper by emphasizing that reality and separability could not be consistent with quantum theory.

Schrodinger came up with a different paradox that is equally important for understanding the conceptual structure of quantum theory. Here is how he introduced it: "A cat is penned in a steel chamber, along with the following diabolical device (which must be secured against direct interference by the cat): in a Geiger counter there is a tiny bit of radioactive substance, *so* small, that *perhaps* in the course of one hour one of the atoms decays, but also, with equal probability, perhaps none; if it happens, the counter tube discharges and through a relay releases a hammer which shatters a small flask of hydrocyanic acid. If one has left this entire system to itself for an hour, one would say that the cat still lives *if* meanwhile no atom has decayed. The first atomic decay would have poisoned it. The Y function of the entire system would express this by having in it the living and the dead cat (pardon the expresssion) mixed or smeared in equal parts."

Thus, "an indeterminacy originally restricted to the atomic domain becomes transformed into macroscopic indeterminacy, which can then be resolved by direct observation." The paradox lies in the fact that quantum and classical objects (like cats) behave essentially differently. Quantum objects have fundamental indeterminacies that classical objects do not have. Yet, quantum indeterminacies can be transferred to classical objects, and they mysteriously disappear only when someone looks at the objects! There is a mismatch between the classical and quantum worlds.

The skeptical role of two of these founding fathers of quantum theory spawned debates on the 'interpretation' of quantum theory, debates that are still raging in scientific and philosophical circles.

IV

HIDDEN VARIABLE THEORIES AND BELL'S THEOREM

Interpretative attempts to restore realism and determinism into physics by introducing "hidden variables" have not gone down well with the majority of physicists influenced by the Copenhagen school under the leadership of Niels Bohr (the Copenhagen Hegemony[5]). Hidden variable theories are of two types: 'contextual' and 'non-contextual'. A contextual theory is one in which the observable properties of a physical system depend on the context in which these properties are observed. Quantum theory is a contextual theory. For example, the wave and the particle characters of an atomic object usually appear in mutually exclusive experimental contexts. In a given experimental context one sees *either* its wave *or* its particle character. Thus, one has particles *or* waves. A non-contextual theory is one in which the properties of a physical system are independent of the experimental context. Classical physics is non-contextual. Theorems have been proved to show that all non-contextual hidden variable theories (with a Hilbert space of dimension greater than two) are incompatible with quantum theory, and therefore already experimentally falsified.

Hidden variable theories can also be either 'local' or 'nonlocal'. Locality is to be understood in the sense of EPR 'separability'. All hidden variable theories satisfy the EPR reality criterion. In 1964 John Bell[6] proved a theorem that showed that quantum theory implied correlations between physically separated systems that cannot be simulated by any local-realistic theory. All local-realistic hidden variable theories are therefore necessarily incompatible with quantum theory. Since then a number of experiments have been done that claim to have falsified local-realistic theories. Bell's theorem thus brought metaphysics within the realm of experiments: it showed, with the aid of experiments, that the world is not local-realistic. What if the world is real but nonlocal?

V

THE DE BROGLIE-BOHM THEORY

The only hidden variable theory that had defied all attempts at experimental falsification until recently is the de Broglie-Bohm theory[7] which is both contextual and nonlocal and therefore not eliminated by any theorem. An interesting aspect of this theory is the manner in which it interprets wave-particle duality. In contrast to the standard Copenhagen interpretation in terms of particles *or* waves, it implies particles *and* waves and is more in spirit with Einstein's original hypothesis. Standard quantum theory and the de Broglie-Bohm quantum theory therefore stand as equally possible and rival interpretations of the most comprehensive range of the most accurate empirical data gathered over the entire history of scientific development. Both of them are based on the same mathematical structure but are radically different and conceptually incompatible. The de Broglie-Bohm theory is a nonlocal realistic theory that does not renounce determinism. It is therefore sometimes referred to as the "causal theory". Although dice playing by God is thus eliminated and realism restored, Einstein did not approve of it because it achieved this feat at the cost of 'locality' which was to him sacrosanct. He called it a 'cheap' solution. On the other hand, Bohm considered 'nonlocality' together with contextuality to be the minimal conceptual departure from classical physics that atomic physics experiments seemed to require. Based on these concepts, he developed the notions of "quantum wholeness" and "implicate order".

The scientific community as a whole was not impressed by Bohm's ideas. Their judgement was based more on hearsay and a general dislike for anything that took away the mystical charm and radicalism of the Copenhagen interpretation than on an unbiased critical appraisal of the theoretical alternatives. James Cushing says in his book[8], "historical contingency was a crucial factor in the spread of the Copenhagen Hegemony and the exclusion of a causal theory." Bohm was known to be a Marxist, and this did not help matters in the United States during McCarthy's regime. He had to leave the United States. He was branded as a crank. It was John Bell who revived interest in his interpretation in a serious way through his famous theorem. Nevertheless, Bohm's theory continues to be ignored by the majority of physicists even today. For example, it is not taught in any university. Nevertheless, an increasing number of more philosophically oriented physicists have begun to take it seriously.[9]

Recently, however, even the de Broglie-Bohm theory (in its standard version) has been shown by the author to be incompatible with quantum mechanics in certain very special situations.[10] The main point of this demonstration is the concept of ergodicity. There is a well-known theorem that states that all quantum mechanical systems are ergodic. There is also a theorem in ergodic theory that states that the time and space averages of all observables are the same for ergodic systems. Another theorem in ergodic theory states that the time and space averages of at least one observable quantity must be different for non-ergodic systems. Now, it is possible to show that there are physical systems whose descriptions are non-ergodic in the de Broglie-Bohm theory but obviously ergodic in standard quantum theory. This proves the incompatibility of the standard version of the de Broglie-Bohm theory and quantum theory. A critical test to distinguish between these two theories based on these ideas was proposed[11] and has been carried out in a laboratory in Torino, Italy[12]. The results seem to favour standard quantum mechanics. Does that mean that the world is after all not real and deterministic? The answer seems to be yes, although it might still be possible to modify the standard version of the de Broglie-Bohm theory to make it compatible with quantum mechanics for every case.

NOTES

1. Ghosh, Partha. 1994. "Bose Statistics: A Historical Perspective". *S.N. Bose: the Man and his Work,* Part I. C.K. Majumdar et al (ed.). Calcutta: S.N. Bose National Centre for Basic Sciences. See also, Pais, A. 1982. *Subtle is the Lord.* Oxford: Oxford University Press.
2. Ghosh, Partha. 1999. *Testing Quantum Mechanics on New Ground.* Cambridge University Press.
3. Einstein, A., Podolski, B. and Rosen, N. 1935. *Physical Review,* 47 (777).
4. Schrodinger, E. 1935. Natui wissenschaften, 23, 807. 823, 844; *Proc. Camb. Phil. Society,* 31 (555).
5. Cushing, J.T. 1994. *Quantum Mechanics: Historical Contingency and the Copenhagen Hegemony.* Chicago, London: The University of Chicago Press.
6. Bell, J.S. 1964. *Physics,* 1 (195).
7. Bohm, D. and Hiley, B.J. 1993. *The Undivided Universe.* London: Routledge, Chapman & Hall.
8. Cushing.
9. Ibid.
10. Ghosh, Partha. *Quantum Physics,* 003126.
11. Ibid.
12. Birda, G. et al. *Quantum Physics,* 0206196.

IV
Traditional Linkage of Philosophy and Science

CHAPTER 26

Science, Spirituality and Philosophy: Their Distinct Domains and Complex Interplay in Society

T.R. Anantharaman

I

INTRODUCTION

As generally accepted by scientists and scholars of today, the first major and truly urban civilization of the human family struck roots some 9,000 years ago in the vast arid and semi-arid north-western regions of the Indian sub-continent, amidst the fertile valleys and basins of two great rivers, *Sindhu* (Indus) and *Saraswatī*, along with their many tributaries. Spread over a territory of more than 1.5 million square kilometers, this undoubtedly great civilization, now known as Harappan, Indus Valley or *Sindhu-Saraswatī*, grew from strength to strength and flourished in a spectacular fashion for nearly five millennia, roughly from 7000 to 2000 B.C. In its mature phase (2600-1900 B.C.), it featured planning and administration as well as technology and engineering skills of a high order, in fact of unbelievable sophistication for that pre-historic era. However, sometime before and after 2000 B.C., a series of unforeseen natural calamities viz., violent tectonic upheavals and powerful earthquakes, ravaged and devastated most of the affluent urban settlements developed by the Harappans over centuries of hard labour. Their life-giving river, the snow-fed and mighty *Saraswatī*, eulogized in glowing terms in the *Ṛg-Veda*, started declining, changed its course, dried up in stages and eventually disappeared altogether around 1800 B.C.. As a result, the Harappan landscape changed fast and dramatically. The glorious and centralized urban culture on the *Sindhu-Saraswatī* flood plains began to atrophy, breaking up gradually and giving way to a number or regional rural cultures.

As brought out over the last eight decades by numerous archaeological studies enriched with inputs from many scientific disciplines and recently also by the most modern remote sensing technology, the Harappan era was also characterized by many fascinating thought processes, apart from the numerous practical accomplishments which are quite visible on the ground even today. Fostering an oral tradition based on dialects, our forefathers seem to have made well over 5,000 years ago impressive forays into many domains of knowledge, both theoretical and applied, which our age has compartmentalized and deals with today under the broad heads of Science, Spirituality and Philosophy. As the story of this remarkable civilization is narrated to us by experts, we cannot but be dazzled by the immensity, grandeur and wide reach of this pre-historic civilization, its monumental buildings, impressive architecture, cultural uniformity, coordinated mass production, complex trade mechanisms, maritime trade channels, overland trade routes, mass transportation by caravans of pack oxen and intercultural contacts encompassing Mesopotamia, Bahrain, Oman, Afghanistan and Turkmenistan in the West. We are also struck by the steady development of what are known today as Sāṁkhya, Yoga and Mīmāṁsā philosophies and their decisive impact, through diverse spiritual-cum-religious practices and rituals, on the Harappan society. We are also impressed and fascinated by the gradual cultivation among the Harappan people of distinct cultural traits, some of which have endured for many millennia on our sub-continent and are quite visible even today in our socio-cultural milieu.

It becomes obvious from the foregoing that the Indian society of today, made up of over a billion people, offers the social scientist a complex, but definitely fertile field for the study and understanding of the mechanisms and processes involved in the nucleation and growth of different sectors or domains of knowledge.

II

SCIENCE AND SPIRITUALITY

Following the long era of dialects, Sanskrit seems to have emerged as the first-ever Indian language some time during the late Harappan phase (1900-1300 B.C.). The first-ever known composition in that language, namely the *Ṛg-Veda* marks the advent of the great Vedic tradition, which has had the deepest and the widest impact on the human mind among all the impressive intellectual edifices that have been raised on the Indian mental soil during the last four millennia. In the massive and many-splendoured Vedic Corpus made up of the four Vedas, *Ṛg, Yajur, Sāma* and *Atharva,* the concluding sections referred to as the Upaniṣads occupy a very special and exalted position. To quote the inspired and pregnant words written around 1920 by one of India's outstanding thinkers and writers of recent times, namely, Sri Aurobindo (1872–1950):

> The Upaniṣads are the supreme work of the Indian mind, the highest self-expression of its genius, its sublimest poetry, its greatest creation of the thought and word, not a literary or poetical masterpiece of the ordinary kind, but a large flood of spiritual revelation of the most direct and profound character. They are a record of the deepest spiritual experiences, documents of revelatory and intuitive philosophy of an inexhaustible light, power and largeness.

The early Upaniṣads, which are definitely pre-Buddhistic and may well be over 3,000 years old, deal clearly and unambiguously with the two distinct domains of knowledge, namely, *Parā Vidyā* or simply *Vidyā,* and *Aparā Vidyā* or simply *Avidyā,* which can be equated today with Spirituality and Science respectively. *Vidyā* is derived from the Sanskrit root "*Vid,* to know", exactly as the English word Science is derived from the Latin root *"Scire,* to know". As is generally accepted, both *Vidyā* and Science meant just knowledge originally. *Parā Vidyā* can be, and indeed has been, translated by many into English as Science of the Soul, Spirit or Self. It was Swami Vivekananda (1863-1902) who perhaps coined and used the word *Spirituality* for the first time, to refer to and explain *Parā Vidyā*. To quote from one of the Swamiji's memorable speeches delivered at Calcutta in 1893:

> There is one great truth that India has to teach the world because it is nowhere else. This is Spirituality, the Science of the Soul.— In this land of ours, the fountains of Spirituality are still there, but they will have to overflow and flood the world, to bring in new life and vitality to the nations, which are now almost borne down, half-killed and degraded, by political ambitions and social scheming.

Let us now turn to the oldest Upaniṣads to learn what they have to say about *Parā Vidyā* (Spirituality) and *Aparā Vidyā* (Science):

1. From *Mundaka Upaniṣad* (I.1.3,4 and 5)—

   "Respected Sir, by knowing which does all that is become known?"
   "There are two types of knowledge to be mastered—spirituality and science. Thus indeed have the knowers of *Brahman* told us."

   "Therein Spirituality is that by which the Imperishable is grasped. Science consists of the four Vedas, Phonetics, Ritual, Grammar, Etymology, Metrics and Astrology."

2. From *Īśāvāsya Upaniṣad* (9, 10 and 11)—

   "Those who worship at the altar of science only, enter blinding darkness; those immersed in spirituality only enter into *still more* blinding darkness."

   "Spirituality has its own distinct purpose; science has also its own, a different purpose. Thus we have heard from the brave explorers of both realms, as they analyzed these two for us."

   "One who masters spirituality and science, both together, conquers Death through science and tastes the Bliss of Immortality through spirituality."

3. From *Śvetāśvatara Upaniṣad* (V.1)—

   "Both spirituality and science exist hidden in the Imperishable and Infinite *Brahman*. Science is concerned with the perishable, while spirituality is concerned with the Imperishable. Different from the others is that one, who masters **both** (i.e., science and spirituality)."

4. From *Kathā Upaniṣad* (I.2. 4 and 5)—

   "Far apart are these, opposite and divergent in their paths, the one known as science and the other as spirituality."

   "Those who dwell in the world of science only, deeming themselves brave and learned, but actually bewildered, wander round stumbling helplessly, like blind men led by another blind person."

It follows from the foregoing that we have what the modern materials scientists call, an incoherent boundary between the realms, domains or sectors of science and spirituality. The latter two are entirely distinct from each other and there is no direct interaction between them. Man and Society definitely need both, but must appreciate their different natures, as elucidated in many a dialogue of the Upaniṣads.

SCIENTIFIC KNOWLEDGE	SPIRITUAL KNOWLEDGE
• Intellectual	Intuitive
• Experimental	Experiential
• Objective	Subjective
• Of the outer, material world	Of the inner, mental world
• *Vyāvahārika* (dealing with practical realities)	*Pāramārthika* (dealing with the Absolute Reality)
• Unique, objective intellectual formulation	Diverse, subjective intellectual frameworks
• *Laukika* (worldly, material)	*Ādhyātmika* (Other-worldly, spiritual)
• Emerges from an observational, active mind	Emerges from a meditative, quiet mind
• Amoral (neither moral nor immoral)	Source of Morality

III

THE DOMAIN OF PHILOSOPHY

To understand and appreciate the scope of philosophy in relation to science and spirituality, it is necessary first to grasp the inescapable fact that it is *buddhi*, the human intellect, that collects, codifies and communicates *all types of knowledge*. Starting with Sāṁkhya and Yoga, which are considered by many scholars to have preceded Mīmāṁsā and Vedānta based on the Vedas, the Indian tradition has all along highlighted the important role of *Citta* or *Antaḥkaraṇa*, the inner instrument of cognition and consciousness, in apprehending the vast continuum of knowledge. This subtle inner instrument is made up of three entities, namely, *Manas*, the emotional and instinctive entity, *Buddhi*, the thinking and discriminating entity, and *Ahaṁkāra*, the individual will and ego. Of these, *Buddhi* alone has the capacity to grasp, comprehend, experience or realise the Spirit or the Self, once it is cultivated and refined to attain its purest, sharpest and highest state through regular spiritual practices, as in the Yoga tradition. To quote again from the *Kathā Upaniṣad* (I.3.12):

> The Supreme is the secret Self in all existences and is normally invisible. Yet this Self is actually seen by the seers of the subtle through their sharp and subtle intellects.

The Sanskrit word, normally used to refer to philosophy in general and also to different systems of philosophy, is *Darśana*, which has many meanings like "seeing", "observing", "perceiving", "discerning", etc., that highlight the nature of the direct knowledge that can be acquired without intellectual activity or exertion. Thus the domain of philosophy, in fact any branch of the Liberal or Fine Arts, has a coherent boundary with *both* spirituality and science. Informed and enthused, to start with, by the available spiritual and scientific knowledge, the philosopher may also get further inspired and exalted by his spiritual experiences i.e., direct revelations of a transcendental nature. Thus the basic conditions or prerequisites for generating *new knowledge* get fulfilled and this knowledge gets nucleated and grows within the *Antaḥkaraṇa*, or the Mental Being of Man, to use the designation of Sri Aurobindo. However, the generation, formulation and communication of *any new* knowledge will be influenced and circumscribed, as in the case of purely spiritual knowledge, by the concerned originator's intellectual level and capacity, as also by the intellectual attainments of those to whom this knowledge is transmitted. In this context, one cannot but appreciate and admire the profundity of one of the earliest and most frequently quoted statements from the *Ṛg Veda* (I. 23.16):

> The Reality (of the spiritual or transcendental experience) is the same, but the learned persons put it across (to others) in many different ways.

One may thus view all types of knowledge, including philosophy which do not belong exclusively to the realm or category of either science or spirituality, as coming into existence because of the coherent boundaries they have with both these basic categories of knowledge. Drawing on both scientific and spiritual knowledge in different proportions, philosophy, as also any branch of Liberal or Fine Arts, acquires its own specific, hybrid identity through the fusion of its scientific and spiritual contents in the melting pot of the human *Antaḥkaraṇa.* The success in communication, as also propagation through organizations or institutions, of such knowledge will depend naturally on the personality, imagination and perseverance of the originator of this new knowledge. The success or otherwise will also be conditioned by many societal factors, particularly the intellectual background, receptivity, assimilation, enthusiastic response, missionary zeal, dedication etc. of those, to whom the new knowledge is transmitted.

IV

KNOWLEDGE AND SOCIETY

The interplay of different types or domains of knowledge in society is very complex and needs study and reflection in depth. The following sketch brings out in broad outline the impact of science and spirituality, the two basic domains of knowledge with an incoherent boundary between them, on human society through the interplay of their derivatives emerging through coherent boundaries as follows:

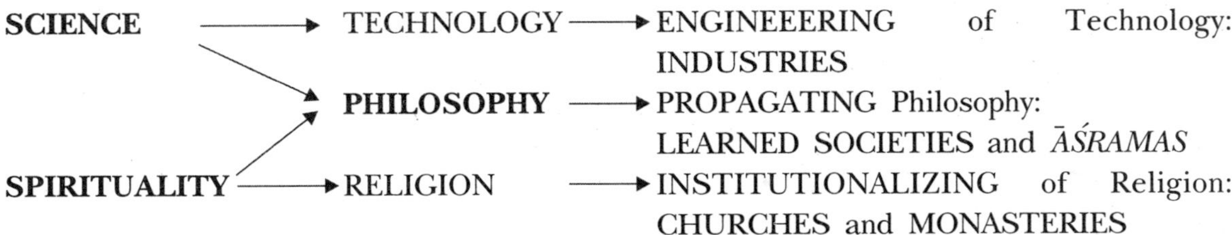

Taking science first, the vast spectrum of scientific knowledge, pure and applied, starts with science at one end, passes through technology in the middle and embraces engineering at the other extreme. The motivation behind science, at its best and purest, is the unquenchable thirst and relentless search for new knowledge through its well-established methodology of observation, experimentation, reasoning and inference. Absence of prejudice, avoidance of pre-conceived notions, eschewing of emotions, openness to others' views, global vision and complete freedom of thought have all come to be associated with the scientific quest. The use or abuse of the new knowledge obtained, considerations of material benefits for individuals, groups or nations and the possible application of new findings to satisfy one or more human, social, commercial or political needs simply do not figure in the domain of pure science. These latter belong to the domains of technology and engineering, which affect and influence social developments in a big way, both constructively and destructively.

Whenever studies and researches are concerned with the application of scientific knowledge to satisfy some need or aspiration of individuals, groups or societies, we enter into the realm of technology. The technologies developed in laboratories have to satisfy many requirements before engineering steps in to commercialize them on a large scale. The engineers are always on the look-out for appropriate technologies that are viable and economical, for which raw materials and capital inputs are available and the political climate is also favourable. Thus science, technology and engineering represent three distinct cultures and processes with their own bodies of knowledge or data bases and educational processes. To put it in a nutshell, the main base of science is *original* thinking, that of technology *innovative* thinking, and that of engineering *practical* thinking.

To cite one concrete example here from the glamorous field of nuclear or atomic research, it is science here when measurements are made to identify the nature and number of particles emitted during the break-up or fission of heavy nuclei like those of the metallic elements uranium and plutonium. It becomes technology when this scientific knowledge is applied to develop processes for power generation or nuclear explosion. We deal with engineering when the appropriate technologies are then made use of, or engineered, either to design and build atomic power stations to generate electricity or to set up industrial complexes to manufacture nuclear weapons for warfare and destruction. It is clear that moral or ethical considerations come up in the development and engineering of technologies, whereas science is amoral.

It is not generally appreciated that spirituality can also influence society through its own "technology" and "engineering"; only here the expressions "religion" and "institutionalizing" are appropriate to refer to these two derivatives of spiritual knowledge. When science and spirituality are combined together in the human mind to generate different systems of philosophy, we have to deal with the phenomena of Learned Societies or *Āśramas* "propagating" the concerned philosophical doctrines. One can clearly perceive this triune sequence in the lives and works of both the founders of great religions like Gautama Buddha (sixth century B.C.) and Jesus Christ (first century A.D.) and the originators of seminal philosophies like Sage Kapila (before 3000 B.C.?) and *Ācārya* Śaṁkara (seventh century A.D.?).

Looking into the inspiring life of Gautama Buddha as an example to illustrate the fascinating Saga of Spirituality, we learn from traditional accounts that Prince Siddhartha Gautama's supreme spiritual experience viz., attainment of the bliss of *Nirvāṇa* at the foot of the Bodhi tree in Bodh Gaya over 2,500 years ago, marked the culmination of a great and relentless spiritual quest that lasted for over seven years. When the Awakened One, the Buddha, desired out of compassion shortly thereafter to share his redeeming spiritual knowledge with his suffering fellow humans, he donned the robes, as it were, of the 'spiritual technologist' during his week-long trek to Sarnath near Varanasi, even as he developed the 'technology' of the Middle Way and Eight-fold Path to spiritual perfection. After setting the wheel of his *Dhamma* (Dharma, in Sanskrit) in motion, this great teacher makes a beginning to "engineer his new and well-tested technology" on a large scale, through the establishment of the *Saṅgha*, the Fellowship of Buddhist monks. Thus the *Buddha-Dhamma-Saṅgha* cycle takes full shape even during the lifetime of this spiritual giant, acclaimed as the 'Light of Asia'. Two centuries later, Emperor Ashoka becomes a devotee of the Buddha, accepts the *Dhamma* and gives his royal patronage to the *Saṅgha.* Thus Buddhism spread all over the world. All this is now history.

Today there is a great need to understand, appreciate and, if possible, control and guide the complex interplay of the awesome powers wielded by the above-referred six derivatives of science and spirituality. No doubt, we need all of them and would like to harness their potential for the peace and progress, health and happiness of the human family. Let us also remember at all times the undeniable fact that science and spirituality in their pure and pristine states constitute the foundation for all types and branches of knowledge. We have to accord these two a special, exalted and pre-eminent position in our society, particularly in our schools and colleges. The innocent human face with its rich promise of beauty and creativity at birth, gets often marred by ugliness and violence in later life, with scars and wrinkles caused by the many weaknesses of the human flesh. Such, unfortunately, is often the fate of the six derivatives of science and spirituality. Ethical overtones, questions of morality and immorality, judgements on the good and the bad and discussions on the creative and destructive, all these crop up in the operations and interplay of these many offsprings of the only two types of pristine knowledge. Let us become fully aware of the strengths and weaknesses of these many branches of the Tree of Knowledge and do all we can to add to their strengths and to cut down on their weaknesses. May we also be optimistic and entertain the hope at all times that the human family will produce time and again truly great scientists and towering spiritual leaders to provide the necessary course corrections and right guidance to society in its onward march towards a brighter and more glorious future!

CHAPTER 27

Science Approaches Vedanta

Swami Jitatmananda

I

INTRODUCTION

With Darwin's discovery that man came not from Adam and Eve but from apes, the entire theological edifice of orthodox Christianity was shaken to its foundations. In the later half of the nineteenth century western civilization was passing through a period of incertitude. A new life-giving philosophy of reason was yet to be born, while the old faith in a religion and an extra-cosmic God had lost credibility for the ever-growing number of rationalistic people. It was a time, as Vivekananda said, "when the sledge-hammer blows of modern antiquarian researches are pulverizing like masses of porcelain all sorts of antiquated orthodoxies, when religion in the West is only in the hands of the ignorant and the knowing one looks down with scorn upon anything belonging to religion."[1]

Swami Vivekananda, the first and the great exponent of Vedānta philosophy in modern times, knew fully well that traditional religious sentiments would not hold water with confirmed materialists and rationalists. What they wanted was reason. In his speech on 'The Absolute and Manifestation' delivered in London in 1896, Vivekananda declared openly: "Materialism prevails in Europe today. You may pray for the salvation of the modern skeptics, but they do not yield, they want reason. The salvation of Europe depends on a rationalistic religion, and Advaita—the non-duality, the oneness, the idea of the Impersonal God—is the only religion that can have any hold on any intellectual people. It comes whenever religion seems to disappear and irreligion seems to prevail and that is why it has taken ground in Europe and America."[2]

The main difficulty was the strait-jacket thinking of the scientists of those days who were almost totally reluctant to accept anything unless it came from their own stalwarts. In January 1896 Vivekananda openly exposed the scientific dogmatism of the West in his speech on microcosm delivered in New York: "When a great sage, a seer, or a prophet of old, who came face to face with the truth, says something, these modern men stand up and say, 'Oh, He was a fool!' But just use another name, 'Huxley says it or Tyndall', then it must be true, and they take it for granted. In place of ancient superstitions, in place of old Popes of religion they have installed modern Popes of science."[3]

The worship of scientific materialism was being safely conducted by the modern priests of science. It was a real struggle to make a dent in the adamantine walls of this great scientific bastion, which nineteenth century western thought had regarded as invincible and infallible. But Vivekananda did the great job by explaining Vedānta in the language of science on both sides of Atlantic.

Philosophy of Scientific Materialism

Newtonian science with its machine-like universe and a mechano-morphic God gradually brought a division between the universe, the automaton, and God, the ruling mechanic. A mechanical paradigm discourages any evolutionary purpose or free will of the individual, which only can inspire morality or ethics. Such a paradigm teaches one to submit to the rules and laws of a philosphy or a church, which asserts that God also runs the world in a perfect mechanical order. Positivism, a by-product of this mechano-morphic universe, was strongly advocated by science-philosophers like Ernst Mach. As a forerunner of logical positivism Mach said, "Science maybe regarded as a minimal problem consisting of the completest presentation of facts with the least possible expenditure of thought."[4] Mach also said, "Theoretical physicists should never use any idea in physics which cannot be given a precise, direct meaning through experimental operations."[5]

From the mechanistic paradigm, the objective external world of Matter emerged as the only object of scientific enquiring. 'Materialism' or acceptance of matter as the ultimate reality, and 'positivism' as the primary method of scientific investigaton emerged supreme.[6]

Science stood out distinctly separate from religion and philosophy, which were supposed to deal with the realms of mind and thought. Majority of scientists in the nineteenth century accepted what Rupert Sheldrake, the Cambridge scientist, calls the 'traditional monistic materialism', or 'material monism' and the "new religion of scientific materialism began a triumphant journey."[7]

Material monism stood triumphant on its primary cornerstones like strong objectivity, strict causal determinism, local cause and effect relation, and epiphenomenalism, which claims that matter produces consciousness.[8] With the rise of Relativity and Quantum Physics, material monism got the rudest shock from which it could not recover.

The tangible world of matter is bound on both microcosmic and macrocosmie sides by intangible realities.

More than a century ago Swami Vivekananda said: "Physics is bounded on both sides by metaphysics. So it is with reason—it starts from non-reason and ends with non-reason. If we push inquiry far enough in the world of perception, we must reach a plane beyond perception. Never can we give the reason for any fundamental principle."[9]

Relativity, Quantum mechanics, Particle physics, and Astrophysics, have opened an universe where our ordinary sense perception fails to work, and where only subtlest mathematics based on pure intuition can enter. Einstein's discovery was that the speed of light (C) is the only constant in this relative and changing universe. Max Planck's discovery of Planck's constant ($6.62 \text{ X } 10^{-34}$ Js) is a wonder. It is this constant which helps us to enter the microcosmic universe where the standard radius of the electron is 10^{-13} cm, and where sub-nuclear particles live only for a few particle seconds before changing into another type of sub-nuclear particle (one particle second is 10^{-23} second). It is on Planck's constant that Heinsberg's epoch-making equation of Uncertainty Principle ($\Delta Q \text{ X } \Delta P \geq h$), stands as a lighthouse in this micro-world of quantum mechanics. The three constants in physics—C (speed of light), H (Planck's constant), G (gravitational force) gave us the measurement of the smallest length (Planck length: $\sqrt{GH/c^3}$ or 10^{-35} meters) and the smallest time (Planck's time: $\sqrt{Gh/c^5}$ or 10^{-43} second).[10] The fundamental minimal energies are multiples of what is known as the Planck energy. The Planck's mass is ten billion (10^{19}) times that of a proton. It's about equal to the mass of a grain of dust or a collection of a million average bacteria.[11]

Astrophysics and Relativity have exposed a universe much vaster than we can imagine. Stephen Hawking and Penrose showed that the General Theory of Relativity predicts that Universe had a beginning and that Time is not an independently running eternal background from future to past (S.H.W. P-22). It is now calculated as 15 billion years old. According to Einstein's field equation its radius is 35 billion light years.[12]

This universe created after the big bang of a superdense supernova, probably a black hole (the historic world coined by John A. Wheeler) whose density was a trillion trillion trillion trillion trillion trillion (1 with 72 zeroes after it) tons per cubic inch (S.H.P. -23), is distintegrating since 15 billion years like splinters from a primeval explosion. Hubble calculated that the galaxies created afer Big Bang are moving away from one another with a velocity that is proportional to the distance that separats them. [V (Velocity of recession), D (distance between groups of galaxies), and H (the Hubble constant 11.8×10^{10} years). V = HXD.[13]] The galaxy in the Hydra cluster is moving away with a speed of 61,000 km per second.[14] According to John A. Wheeler our universe is filled with billions of galaxies spread over a "gigantic platform of superspace whose dimensions are not three or four but infinite."[15]

The immensity of our universe made Stephen Hawking admit, "We are such insignificant creatures on a minor planet of a very average star in the outer suburbs of one of a hundred thousand million galaxies." The impenetrable mystery of the universe which is beyond ordinary human comprehension, made Hawking refute, in his Boston Lecture on *Blackholes are White Hot,* Einstein's famous dictum "God does not play dice." Hawking proclaimed, "God not only plays dice but throws them where they cannot be seen."[16]

Transcending his own convictions that "the highest principles of our aspirations and judgements are given to us in the Judeo-Christian religious tradition'[17] Einstein became a "Cosmic man", and turned towards the mystical. He wrote:

> The most beautiful emotion we can experience is the mystical. It is the power of all true art and science. He to whom this emotion is a stranger is as good as dead. To know that what is impenetrable to us really exists, manifesting itself as the highest wisdom and the most radiant beauty, which our dull faculties can comprehend only in their most primitive forms—this knowledge, this feeling is at the center of true religiousness. In this sense and in this sense only I belong to the ranks of devoutly religious man.[18]

Do We Live in an Universe of Matter with 10 Dimensions and Imaginary Time?

Time, according to Newton, was an independent passive background. According to Einstein, Time is relative to space and space-time is curved in the presence of matter or energy.

Space-time is, therefore, a participant in the matter drama of this cosmic material universe. "It is a single universe", said Illya Prigogene.

How do you think of time when there were neither time nor space in the beginning of the Universe in a state of singularity. Hawking says: "To describe how quantum theory shapes time and space, it is helpful to introduce the idea of imaginary time. Imaginary time sounds like something from science fiction, but it is a well-defined mathematical concept: time measured in what are called imaginary number. Imaginary time predicts not only effects we have already observed but also effects we have not been able to measure yet nevertheless believe in for other reasons. So what is real and what is imaginary? Is the distinction just in our minds?"[19]

To understand the origin (past) and fate (future) of the universe, we need, according to Stephen Hawking, a quantum theory of gravity.[20] It proves that time is not infinite and that time had a beginning. A totally new kind of symmetry called supersymmetry was discovered in the 1970s that 'provides a natural physical mechanism to cancel the infinities arising from ground state fluctuations'. Supersymmetry is a feature of our modern mathematical models that can be described in various ways. One way is to say that *spacetime has extra dimensions besides the dimensions we experience.* These are called Grassmann dimensions. Sometimes the dimensions are 10 or 11. "6 or 7 dimensions are curled up so small that we don't notice them; we are only aware of the remaining 4 large and nearly flat dimensions", says Hawking, "I must say that personally, I have been reluctant to believe in extra dimensions. But as I am a positivist, the question, 'Do extra dimensions really exist?' has no meaning. All one can ask is whether mathematical models with extra dimensions provide a good description of the universe."[21] Why do we not see the extra dimensions of matter? Hawking explains that with extra dimensions working electron would not have been stable and matter and universe, as we know it, would also not be seen.

String Theory Works With Matter of 26 Dimensions

The old reductionist passion of discovering the fundamental building block of matter behind the material universe continues. The Quarks theory (that six quarks are the fundamentals of matter) failed to satisfy some basic questions. "What is the value of Quarks if they are permanently confined inside hadrons or heavy sub nuclear particles?" ask the physicists. Today, a group of physicists are trying, in one of the latest frontiers of physics, to explain the fundamentals of matter as made of "strings". The central idea of string theory is that entities such as electrons and quarks are actually linear, tiny 'strings'. Strings are the smallest conceivable element in the universe. One string is less than 10^{-30} cm in space. A typical atomic nucleus is about 10^{-13} cm across. So a nucleus is about a hundred million billion times bigger than the knots in the structure of space. It would take 10^{20} of these strips laid end to end, to stretch across the diameter of a proton.[22]

Advocates of string theory think of this theory as the possible "Theory of Everything" (TOE). In a reductionist way it hopes to reduce absolutely everything to string. But questions have started rising about the validity of this theory. In an article in *Scientific American* in 1986, one of the pioneers of strings theory, Michael Green of London, pointed out that with string theory details have come first. "We are still groping for a unifying insight into the logic of the theory. The occurrence of the massless graviton... appears accidental and somewhat mysterious", he said. What appeared to be the best versions of superstring theories, the ones in which gravitons seem to emerge naturally from the equations, "only work with matter of twenty-six dimensions." "Where are all the extra dimensions hidden?" asks Green.[23]

Despite his faith in the future success of the String theory, Brian Greene admits: "There will nevertheles be aspects of the universe that remain unexplained. Maybe we will have to accept that certain features of the universe as the way they are because of happenstance, accident, or divine choice."[24]

Quest for a Theory of Everything

The dream of a unified theory, the Holy Grail of modern physics for which Einstein started his race some sixty years ago, still haunts the physicists. It is a quest for a Theory of Everything or TOE, a grand unified theory, as dreamt by Stephen Hawking. It is the vision of a complete, consistent, unified theory in which all physical interactions are described by one set of equations. Today four separate theories are required to explain different features of the world—Newton's theory of gravity, Maxwell's equations of electromagnetism, Einstein's theory of relativity and the quantum theory to explain subatomic entities. The Theory of Everything 'dreamt of by physicists must accommodate all these four theories. The prospect of incorporating gravity into what the physicists would call a 'super-unified theory' was to, the twentieth century physicists, 'just around the corner' for well over a decade. That decade is over. Hawking's century is over. The "Theory of Everything" for which Hawking started his quest has not been achieved until today. Still the dream continues. All laws fail, all descriptions fail in a state beyond space and time, the boundary conditions, the state of singularity.

Nevertheless, scientists ask the ultimate question. In an interview with the author on 7.1.2000, at Princeton Residence, John A. Wheeler said that the ultimate question is 'How came existence?' 'What caused this Universe?' 'How did it spring to existence?' Hawking writes, "This was not a question that many scientists wanted to address. They tried to avoid it by maintaining that the origin of the universe did not lie within the realm of science but belonged to metaphysics or religion. In my opinion, this is not a position any true scientist should take. If the laws of science are suspended at the beginning of the universe, might not they fail at other times also? A law is not a law if it only holds sometimes. We must try to understand the beginning of the universe on the basis of science. It maybe a task beyond our powers, but we should at least make the attempt."

At his inauguration as Lucasian Professor at Cambridge, Stephen Hawking delivered a memorable lecture, entitled 'Is the End in Sight for Theoretical Physics?'. "Maybe the end is in sight for theoretical physicists, if not for theoretical physics," wrote Hawking's biographer. In an interview in *Newsweek* in 1988, Hawking said that after discovering 'a Theory of Everything there would still be lots to do', but physics would then be 'like mountaineering after Everest'.[25]

In an interview in Delhi (*Indian Express,* 16 January 2003) Roger Penrose said: "It will take centuries before we can reach the 'Theory of Everything', bcause everything includes first of all the consciousness—the mysterious knower of everything."

In an interview with physicist John A. Wheeler whose concept of 'Superspace' and 'Many-words interpretation' of quantum theory has considerably influenced the world of modern physics for the last thirty years, the interviewer Timothy Ferris mentions how Wheeler was dreaming of a drastic simplification about our knowledge of the universe. Sitting in his room and watching the river turning gold with rays of sunset, Wheeler said quietly: "We find the world strange, but what's strange is us. It seems to me that we don't yet read the message properly, but in time to come, we will see it in some single, simple sentence. As we say that sentence to each other we'll say, Oh, how beautiful'. How could we have missed, it, all that time?"[26]

Vivekananda predicted that modern science would touch its final destination as soon as it reached 'Unity'—that is, the knowledge that the microcosm contains in it the entire potentialities of the macrocosm. Wheeler's dream of a single, simple sentence explaining the strange, universe reminds us of the simple but profoundly powerful lines like, *Tat Twam Asi* (Thou art That) or *Aham-Brahmāsmi* (I am Brahman or Existence—Knowledge—Bliss Absolute). Both the sentences contain the cardinal principle of Vedānta—the microcosm contains the macrocosm. And Schrodinger declared *Ātman-Brahman* equation as the only solution to the problem of consciousness that has cropped in today's physics.[27]

Swami Vivekananda anticipated this culmination of western physics in the concepts of Vedānta as early as 1895 when the new physics of this century had not even been dreamt of. At the Thousand Island Park in New York he said: "Modern science has really made the foundations of religion strong. Though an atom is invisible, unthinkable, yet in it are the real power and potency of the universe. That is what the Vedāntist says of *Ātman.*"[28]

II

THE PHILOSOPHY OF VEDĀNTA

The philosophy of Vedānta is enshrined in the Upaniṣads which form the concluding (*anta*) portion of the Vedas (*veda*). The Vedānta philosophers were not merely intellectual cogitatiors. They were *mantra-draṣtās,* or seers of universal truths. They were the discoveres of the various universal principles, through the power of their intuition based on pure thought. Here are some truths on which Vedānta philosophy stands:

1. Everything living and non-living is interpenetrated by *Brahman,* the all-pervading consciousness (*Sarvam Khalu Idam Brahma—Chāndogya Upaniṣad*).
2. The finite has infinite as its background. The smallest contains the greatest (*Anoranian Mahto Mahīyān—Kathā Upaniṣad*).
   The individual soul (*Ātman*) is therefore indentified with the universal soul (*Brahman*) (*Aham Brahmasmi—Brihadāraṇyaka Upaniṣad*).
3. The universe is full of energy which is derived from One cosmic energy or *Prāṇa.*

4. It is a holistic universe where everything—matter-mind-energy, space and time, is fundamentally interconnected by a common background—the *Brahman* (*Mayi Sarvam Idam Protam Sūtre Manigana iva—Bhagavad Gītā*).
5. In this space-time-causation world of *Māyā* things can happen without any apparent or local cause (*Aghatanā-ghatanā pāṭiyasi Māyā*).
6. The external world which is transitory, therefore unreal, is created by our consciousness (*Driśyaḥ Dhivrittayah—Drik-Drśya-Viveka*). The physical world is not eternal but temporary, however long-lasting it maybe. The proton, the most stable matter in this universe also decays, and it has a half life of 10^{32} years. The stable background (*Brahman*) behind the mutable universe (*Jagat*) is real, says Vedānta—*Brahma Satya Jagat Mithyā*. *Brahman* is the eternity domain or the fifth dimension peeping through our 4th dimensional Universe. It is the Implicate order of David Bohm from which the Explicate order emerges. What is this Implicate order? Bohm says: It is that which is.
7. The ultimate Reality cannot be described by human language. Words and mind return failng to describe the Ultimate reality—says *Taittirīya Upaniṣad*—(*Yato Vāco Nivartante Aprāpya Manasa Saha.* "The letter killeth"—said St. Paul. The ultimate Reality can be describd, according to Vedānta only as "Not this, Not that" or *Neti, Neti.*

Intuition—the Common Basis of Science and Vedānta

How did Vedānta *Ṛṣis* discover the Universal truths without any laboratory or experiments? The *Śwetāswatara Upaniṣad* says the Ultimate Reality can be grasped by "pure heart, purified intellect and purified mind." (*Hṛida manīṣa mānasa Abhiclipto*). Again *Patañjali Vyās-bhāṣya* (*Yoga Sūtra* 44 Para 1) says that there are two kinds of intuitions. The first one is the empirical intuition (*Savicāra Prajñā*) which imposes forms of space, time, causation on real substance. The second is *Samādhi Prajñā* or *Nirvicāra Nirvikalpa Prajñā* which is a relationless intuition of Reality in which the subject is capable of perceiving the essence or truth beyond space, time and causality.[29] Einstein said, "I hold it true that pure thought can grasp reality as the ancient dreamed."[30]

The 'mystical overviews' or pure relationless intuition, which inspired Einstein, Stephen Hawking, or Heisenberg, were behind the discoveries of the fundamental principles of Vedānta. Ken Wilber explains how in eastern mystical experience intuition helps us to see Reality directly:

> In the mystical consciousness, Reality is apprehended directly and immediately, meaning without any mediation, any symbolic elaboration, any conceptualisation, or any abstractions; subject and object become one in a timeless and spaceless act that is beyond any and all forms of mediation.[31]

Primarily a theoretical physicist, Einstein found in the language of mathematics the vehicle of grasping the reality, which is supersensory. Physics is bound to transcend, as Einstein thought, 'the rattle of the senses'.[32] Einstein said, "But the creative principle resides in mathematics. In a certain sense, therefore, I hold it true that pure thought can grasp reality as the ancients dreamed."[33] With the help of this power of 'pure thought' or 'intuitive leap'. Einstein made strange postulates such as the equivalence of gravity and acceleration, the principle of invariance, time dilation, space-concentration, deflection of light by the gravitational field, etc. Most of these postulates later on got experimentally verified. Though he began as a positivist, Einstein became one of the most outstanding intuitive minds in human history. "If Einstein had remained a positivist, I doubt that he would have discovered general relativity", writes Heinz R. Pagels.[34]

The Japanese Nobel physicist Hideki Yukawa intuitively pedicted the existence of an unknown subatomic particle to account for the super-binding strength of the strong-interaction force, which hold the nucleus together. After twelve years of reserach the particle predicted was discovered in 1947 and it was called pimeson or PPIOM. Yukawa had been brought up in the Oriental tradition, which taught him the superiority of intuition over logic and experiments. In his book *Creativity and Intuition,* Yukawa writes, "A thorough-going rationalism eludes them (the Oriental and the Chinese)... in particular, the development of physics since the beginning of twentieth century has taken this kind of course. In this kind of course nothing can be done by logic alone. The only course is to perceive the intuitively and see through what is correct... the fact remains that in order to synthesize contradictions, it is necessarty first to survey the whole notion with intuition".

III

OMNIJECTIVE, NOT STRONG-OBJECTIVE UNIVERSE: HEISENBERG

The Universe exists as a mixture of the real and the unreal. (*satya—anṛite—mithuni Kritya*) said Śaṁkaracārya. The concept of Complimentarily has come into science today. Reductionist pride is gone. Max Bron felt that complimentarily of wave and particle dimensions of electron advocated by Niels Bohr is a historic contribution. Einstein already paved the way by the fusion of space and time into one space-time continuum, and of matter and energy into one entity by his $E=mc^2$. This complimentarily was again anticipated in the observer-observation participatory (or subjective + objective = omnijective) universe of quantum world by Heisenberg's Uncertainity Principle. And again the mind-body connection (or continuum) discovered by John Ecceles and Roger Sperry, established the complimentary co-existence of opposite dichotomies in science.

Is Matter Real?

The picture of electron turned to be statistical probability in an electron cloud. Louis De Broglie's electron-diffraction experiment showed that electrons also behave as waves. In fact the wave-particle duality puzzled scientists. Some of them termed all sub-atomic particles as '*wavicles*' (wave ¯particles). Max Bron completed the baffiling scene by finally declaring that electrons are not even real waves. They are, said Max Bron, "Probability waves" which is "a purely abstract... mathematical concept... in which we cannot enter." As if to add to the complexity of the new physics, Max Born showed that while the waves of a single electron can be represented in three-dimensional space, the waves of two electrons require a six-dimensional space, and three electrons a nine-dimensional space and so on *ad infinitum.*[35] *Wherefrom come those dimensions? Can our intellect* conceive of such a thing?

Matter: Real or Unreal?

With the emergence of Quantum physics, the vision of a solid matter-based universe began to turn hazy. Schrodinger asserted that "not only can an electron not be observed twice, but not even once, as the consistent application of Heiseberg's Uncertainty principle asserts." Movement of abstract, wave-like, almost unreal electrons and their occupying a position, and the possibility of one electron's simultaneous presence in many other places, baffled scientists. John A. Wheeler wrote of an interesting incident, when three great physicists were discussing about electrons.

> The professor at Copenhagen whom Niels Bohr most admired, who was his teacher and subsequent occupant of the house of honour that Bohr himself was to occupy, was Herald Hoffding. In an evening dialogue between Heisenberg and Bohr at that house of Honor about the uncertainty principle, Hoffding put his finger on the diagram between the double entrance slit and the terminating photographic plate and asked, "Where can the electron be said to be?" Bohr's reply is immortal: "To be? To be? To be? What does it mean, 'to be'?[36]

In a recent interview in Princeton University (held on 7 January 2000), John A. Wheeler told the author that the equation which impressed him most in modern times is an equation from Hamilton's algebra. This was applied, said Prof. Wheeler, by John D. Valera for the measurement of electron spin. The equation, $i = j^2 = k^2 = ijk = -1$, is part of Hamilton's algebra, and an extension of Complex numbers. It was during a moment of epiphany, a sudden revelation of truth, that Hamilton discovered this equation, which he called "the fundamental formula". Hamilton wrote about this discovery, which happened when he was walking along a royal canal and crossing a bridge.

> An electric current seemed to close and a spark flashed forth, the herald (as I foresaw immediately) of many long years to come of a definitely directed thought and work... I pulled out on the spot a pocket-book which still exists, and made an entry there and then. Nor could I resist the impulse unphilosophical as it may have been to cut with a knife on a stone of Brougham bridge, as we passed it, the fundamental formula with the symbols, i, j, k,: $i^2 = j^2 = k^2 = ijk = -1$ which contains the solution of the problem.[37]

The equation was applied by Irish physicist De Valera to electron's spin or rotation. It suggests that electron when measured in all its three dimensions—spin (i), momentum(j), and position (k), turns out to be –1. De Valera's –1 is not $\sqrt{-1}$ used by Physicist Pauli to define the spin of electron. A Calcutta physicist explains: "De Valeras' triple product ijk is equal to $(^{-i\sigma}x)$ $(^{-i\sigma}y)$ $(^{-i\sigma}z)$ in Pauli's notation and is also equal to –1 from the well-known property $^{\sigma}x^{\sigma}y^{\sigma}z = i$ of the Pauli operators".[38] While –1 is imaginary, $\sqrt{-1}$ can be philosophically interpreted as unreal. Is the objective world composed of electrons then fundamentally unreal? Advaita Vedānta says, "The phenomenal world is ultimately unreal. The stable background of this unreal world, *Brahman*, the Absolute Consciousness, alone is real—(*Brahma Satya Jagat Mithyā*)."

Nevertheless our objective world remains and persists. Why? Although each individual quantum maybe genuinely unpredictable, a collection of such events conforms to the statistical predictons of quantum mechanics. "It is the combination of contingency and intelligibility", writes philosopher Ian Barbour, "which prompts us to search for new and unexpected forms of rational order."[39]

IV

IS MATTER CONSCIOUS?

While Erwin Schrodinger described electron as standing waves, physicist Max Bron described electron as probability waves. This non-classical idea of electron as "Probability-waves" of Max Born, physicist Richard Fynmann tried to explain in his 1950 B.B.C. lectures.[40] When the electrons were sent through a double-slit experiment, the electrons started from their source as particles, and they reached the target screen as particles, but in between they behaved as waves, interfering with each other enhancing, or nullifying the intensity of movement. This is like some obedient school children who came our of their home as students and reached the school as obedient school students and yet in between they played and fought with each other as players in the fields on the roadside. No mechanical movement can explain this phenomenon known as *Quantum mechanical tunneling*. Are the electrons capable of conscious decisions? An electron particle when confronted with a big barrier, surmounts it by transforming itself into a wave, and then again moves as a particle. This is a phenomenon which only living organisms display. Physicist Heinz Pagels wrote: "This is rather weird and no ordinary idea of objectivity can accommodate it."[41] "Physicists found themselves dealing with energy," writes Gary Zukav in his popular book, *The Dancing Wu Li Masters*[42], "that somehow possessed information (which made it organic), and unaccountably presented itself in patterns (waves)." Illya Prigogine, the Nobel scientist, comments on his own book, *Order out of Chaos*: "This is the heart of the message ... in my book, matter is not inert. It is alive and active." Physicist Freeman Dyson of Princeton said:

> In other words mind is already inherent in electron and the process of human consciousness differ only in degree but not in kind from the processes of choice between Quantum states which we call "Chance" when they are made by electrons.[43]

Physicist Jack Sarfatti writes:

> I suspect that general relativity and quantum theory are simply two complementary aspects of a deeper theory that will involve a kind of cosmic consciousness as the key concept.[44]

Long before Max Bron appeard on the scene, in 1901 Indian biologist J.C. Bose demonstrated his epoch-making experiements of human like response in metals in the physics section of British Association at Bradford. Scientists saw with wonder the similar curves of human muscles and metals and plants, when they were responding to the effect of fatigue, depression and poisonous drugs. Bose's discovery conclusively proved that the same Consciousness pulsates in man, plants, and even metals in various ways. Bose summed up the essence of his findings.

> In many investigations on the action of forces on matter, I was amazed to find boundary lines vanishing and to discover points of contact emerging between the living and non-living.
>
> The physicist, the chemist and the biologist come in by different doors, each one in his own department of knowledge, and each comes to think that this is his special domain unconnected with that of any other. Hence has arisen our present division of phenomena into the worlds of inorganic, vegetal and sentient. This philosophical attitude of mind maybe denied. We must remember that all inquiries have as their goal the attainment of knolwedge in its entirety.[45]

Commenting on Bose's successful experiment, the then English metal scientist Sir Robert Austin admitted that he was happy to see that metals have life. The well-known Science Journal, *Nature*, commented that Bose's experiment proceed so smoothly and logically and yet it does not start from any place in the existing corpus of knowledge.[46]

Vedānta philosophy asserts through all the Upaniṣads that it is one Consciousness, which manifests through the myriads of entities within the universe, living or non living. *Sarvam Khalu Idam Brahma* (Everything in this Universe is *Brahman*: Existence—Consciousness—Bliss Absoltue) says, *Chāndogya Upaniṣad*. The *Īśa-Upaniṣad* asks us to see the One Supreme Consciousness in all things of this phenomenal universe (*Īśa Vaśyam Idam Sarvam Jat Kinca Jagatyam Jagat*).

Universe—a Sea of Energy: Energy Comes from Consciousness

Paul Dirac, in a new line of thinking, formulated the field concept of electron. In this new 'Quantum relativistic' model of sub-atomic physics, which is still the most successful, the primary concept is of 'Quantum field', that is, of a field of energy, which can take the form of quanta, or particles. "There is no place in this new kind of physics both for field and matter, for the field is the only reality," said Einstein.[47]

According to Uncertainty Principle, no electron or not even the smallest particle (which is also a field) can measue zero. The so-called empty space as a rule contains an enormous amount of waves. Waves are also particles and particles generally have mass, and mass is energy, according to Einstein's equation $E = mc^2$. The empty space emerged as an ocean of energy. Astronomer Hubble studied samples of space over the years and found that every cubic centimeter of empty space contains 10^{-24} gms of matter.[48] The total number of particles in the universe, as calculate by Edington is $N = 2 \times 136 \times 2^{256} = 10^{79}$ approx[49] and a cubic meter of so called empty space contains, besides other particles, 400 millions of photons.[50] According to Stephen Hawking, the gravitational field at the event horizon of a black hole is strong enough to do an astounding thing, turning the virtual particles, even those unfortunate ones with negative energy to real" particles.[51] The universe emerged as an ocean of energy which the physicists call the 'Dirac Sea' of energy.

This ocean of cosmic energy the Indians first conceived as *Adi Shakti*—the Primeval Cosmic Energy creating and sustaining the unvierse. Later Hinduism called this as *Kāli*. According to Vedānta, space is *Brahman* (*Kham brahma: Chāndogya Upaniṣad* 4.10.4). Cosmic energy is the ultimate truth (*Prāṇa vai Satyam: Bṛhadrāṇyaka Upaniṣad* 2.3.6). Empty space is the sea of continuous creation-destruction dance of Energy symbolized by Indian *Natarāja Śiva*, as Fritzof Capra has shown in his book *Tao of Physics*.[52]

Wherefrom does motion or energy come? A conscious being only has motion. Consciounsess is the root of all energy. *Bṛhadāraṇyaka Upaniṣad* calls the Ultimate Reality or Consciousness as '*Satyāsya Satyam*' (2:3:6) (The Truth behind the apparent truths of the phenomenal universe). It is Cosmic Consciousness, according to Vedānta, which is at the basis of Cosmic Energy. Hindus believe that *Kāli* creates, sustains and destroys, only in the presence of *Śhiva*—The Absolute Consciousness.

V

VEDĀNTA SAYS MIND SHAPES MATTER; SCIENCE SAYS MATTER SHAPES MIND: EPIPHENOMENON—WHICH IS TRUE?

Recent discoveries in medical science show that the power of thought can recreate our body. Nobel scientist Sir John Eccles told parapsychologists that our thoughts can move molecules. Eccles said that "the mind manages to move the atoms of hydrogen, carbon, oxygen, and the other particles in the brain's cells."

Dr. Herbert Spector of the *National Institute of Health* experimenting on a group of mice showed that thought could stimulate the immune system and thus strengthens the animals' defence against disease. A team at the University of Rochester later similarly experimented with rats and showed that the contrary is also possible. The two experiments proved that the body responds primarily to the thought and the ambience surrounding the living being.

In the 1970s the discovery of minute chemicals called neuro-transmitters have shown the power of thought on human body. These are 'communicator molecules', whereby the neurons of the brain can influence the rest of the body within 1/50th of a second and these spring into existence in the *amygdala* and *hypothalamus* region of the brain, with the least touch of thought. Along with this came the discovery of bio-chemicals called *endorphins* and *enkephalins*, which act as the body's natural painkillers. The word *endorphin* means 'internal morphine', and *enkephalin* means born 'inside the brain'. It is this *endorphine*, which helps a sick mother to enter into flames and save her burning child.

A positive news creates million of neuro-transmitters of happiness and strength, while a disastrous news of failure or loss nearly kills a strongman almost instanteously. By the mid-1980s, more than fifty such neuro-transmiters and neuro-peptides were known.

Dr. Cadence Pert, of the National Institute of Mental Health, USA thinks, that a biochemical like DNA or a neuro-transmiter belongs to the mind rather than the body because the entire mind-body system is a network of information.[53]

Placebo and Nocebo effects in medicine are well-known today. Even best medicine with doctor's negative words fail to cure, while only sugar pills with doctor's positive words can sometime cure.

Swami Vivekananda says:

> When the thought is joined to will, we call it power. That which strikes the sick person whom you are trying to help is not thought, but power.
>
> Although the power to overthrow poison maybe roused by medicine, it maybe more permanently roused by the force of thought. Imagination must hold to the thought of health and strength in order that in case of illness the memory of the ideal of health maybe roused and the particles re-arranged in the position into which they fell when healthy. The tendency of the body is then to follow the brain.

The best form of *Prāṇa,* however, is in the brain, manifesting itself as light of understanding. This light is under the guidance of thought.[54]

VI

CONSCIOUSNESS CREATES REALITY OUTSIDE

After the discovery of Heinsberg's Uncertainty Principle, the detached observer-scientist of classical physics is no more a detached observer of the classical physics, looking through the microscope at something separate from him. He is both the 'actor and 'participator' as physicists James Jeans and John A. Wheeler put it, in the great drama of existence. The subjective and objective have been fused into one *omnijective* reality, as Michel Talbot calls it in his book *Mysticism and New Physics.*

But quantum physics was heading towards another surprise. In Schrodinger's wave equation this omnijective reality ultimately appeared to be a creation of the subjective alone. Erwin Schrodinger's Wave equation opened a Pandora's box to scientists. In certain circumstances Schordinger's wave function predicted the behaviour of a given particle up to a point and then described two equally probable outcomes of the same particle. The two outcomes then branch into four, eight, sixteen, and so on to *ad infinitum* possibilities. In fact, the wave equation suggests 'an endlessly proliferating number of possibilities for the observed system (external reality) whether it is observed or not. It seemed that an electron, in Schrodinger's wave, can parade at the same instant, simultaneously in many forms, say as a saint or a sinner, a thief and a police. Schrodinger tried to explain this strange phenomenon through his *thought-experiment* known as *Schrodinger's Cat.* A live cat is thrown in a black box in the void. The box has got a mechanical device, which will eject one electron. If the electron touches the poisonous bulb inside the black box as a particle, the bulb will burst, the poison will come out and the cat will die. It the electron comes as a wave, the bulb will not burst, the poisonous gas will not come out, and the cat will not die.

Now the electron, which has been shot in this box in the void, develops Schrodinger's Schizophrenia, and it can move both as a wave and a particle at the same instant. The question now arises. What has happened to the cat?

The first answer from classical physics is simple. The old vanguards say that the cat is either alive or dead. It is useless to ask big philosophical questions. According to the Copenhagen interpretation of Quantum physics, nothing can be said until the box is opened and the reality is observed. One of the possibilities will emerge and the second possibility will collapse (Copenhagen Collapse) only after we observe it. Then only the final answer will be available.

The third interpretation is given by Graham, Hugh Everette and John A. Wheeler who interpreted that in Schrodinger's wave equation the wave function is the real thing. *All the possibilities that it represents are real and they all happen.* This is known as the *Many World Interpretation of Quantum Physics.* The interpretation has opened unprecedented possibilities of human creativity and higher evolution. We can see the world according to our states of consciousness. The cat is both alive and dead at the same time. It is dead for them who 'choose' to see it dead. It is alive for these who 'choose' to see it alive. Sinners like Magdalene or Āmrapali hated by the so called virtuous, became an object of hatred to commoners and at the same instant they became an object of compassion and care to the Buddha and Christ, and object of adoration and respect to Shri Ramakrishna. Physics had laid the rational foundation for these different visions of reality at the same moṃent. We create the world with our own ego, desires, mind and intellect.

According to Copenhagen interpretation of Quantum Mechanics, Schrodingers wave equation generates an endlessly proliferating number of possibilities. "According to the Everette-Wheeler-Graham theory, the same development generates *an endlesly proliferating different branches of reality,*" writes Michael Talbot.[55] "It might seem that if we cannot observe anything without changing what we observe, we should perhaps drop the idea that anything exists without our observing it," writes[56] physicist Fred Allan Wolf.

A similar conclusion was arrived in Vedānta philosophy a thousand years ago. *Dṛg Dṛśya Viveka,* a well-known Vedānta teatise, writes: *Dṛśyah dhi brttayah sakṣī dṛg eva na tu dṛśyate.* "All the scenes before us are projections of our intellect (activate by the presence of our consiousness). The only seer is the Self (the pure Consciusness) inside us. This Self cannot be seen because it is itself the Seer." (verse: 1) .Says the *Bṛhadrāṇyaka Upaniṣad* (1:5:9): 'Whatever is to be known is a form of the mind; because the mind is what is to be known.'

Today biology comes forward to endorse this idealistic view. In his book *The Astonishing Hypothesis,* Nobel biologist Francis Crick writes:

> My second general remark is that any one aspect of the visual information provided by your eyes is usually ambiguous. ... It is difficult for many people to accept that what they see is a symbolic interpretation of the world—it all seems so like "the real things."... Seeing involves active processes in your brain that lead to an explicit multilevel, symbolic interpretation of the visual scene.[57]

The same Vedānta text *Dṛg Dṛiśya Viveka* says: Exṭernal forms are objects of vision, and the organ of eye sees it. Again the organ of eye is the object of vision and the mind inside sees it (*Rūpam dṛiśam Locanam dṛik tat dṛiśyam dṛik tu mānasam.*)

Everette-Wheeler Interpretation makes the existence of parallel universes seem more and more real, and quantum physics opts for the view that the external reality is the creation of the observer's mind. Another interpretation suggested by physicist F.A. Wolf, is the *trans-actional interpretation* of Quantum Physics, which asserts that the future communicates with the present. In this interpretation, a physical system can actually appear to move from the present into the future, and backward through time from the future to the present.[58] *Kathā Upaniṣad* says: He, the Infinite Consciousness, is the ruler—controller of past and future, and therefore He is not afraid of anything (*Īśano bhūto bhavyaṣya tato na Vijugupsate*).

Nobel physicist Eugene Wigner, suggests that our consciousness alters the world by altering us. *It affects how we appraise the future.* And it does this by altering our own quantum wave functions. *It is our wills (our choice) that change those probable futures into an actual present.* Wigner discribes the process:

> It is the entering of an impression into our consciousness which ... modifies our appraisal ... for different impressions which we expect to receive in the future. It is at this point that the consciousness enters the theory unavoidably and unalterably.[59]

Wigner asserts that consciousness is the primary concept and that a mere materialistic approach to know external reality is not enough: "The principal argument against materialism is that thought processes and consciousness are primary concepts, that our knowledge of the exernal world is the content of our consciousness and that the consciousness, therefore, cannot be denied. On the contrary, logically, the exernal world could be denied—though it is not very practical to do so."[60]

Physics entered the domain of philosophy, with the undeniable supremacy of consciousness in determining the final outcome in quantum observation, and more importantly the rejection of the strong objectivity of classical science, so fondly cherished by Greek philosophers and Newtonian physics. Physicist Wolfgang Pauli told Heisenberg that this freedom from the old idea of an objective world running according to strict cause and effect relation, opened the door for the reconciliation of science and philosophy. Heisenberg wrote:

> ... it was precisely the idea of an objective world running its course in time and space according to strict causal laws that produced a sharp clash between science and the spiritual formulations of the various religions. If science goes beyond this strict view—and it had done just that with relativity theory and is likely to go even further with quantum theory—then the relationship between science and the contents religions try to express must change once again.[61]

The wave equation increasingly confirms that it is our mind-consciousness, which chooses the outcome of the observation. Since this outcome is our conscious experience, says physicist Amit Goswami in his book, *The Self-aware Universe*, it is equally true that, we choose our conscious experience—yet we remain unconscious of the underlying process. Many physicists view the selection process as random, an act of pure chance. This view provoked, according to Goswami, Einstein's protest that *God does not play dice.*[62] But if God does not play dice, asks Goswami, who or what selects the result of a single quantum measurement? De Cartes taught—*cogito—Ergo Sum—I think therefore I am.* After Aspect's experiment Dr. Goswami feels the new dictum should be—*Opto-Ergo Sum (I choose therefore I am).* Quantum Physics, as opposed to the strict cause and effect relation of old physics, allows free will to choose, and thereby encourages creativity and provides scope for evolution. According to the idealist interpretation of Vedānta, it is consciousness that chooses—but it is a non-local unitive consciousness, which works through the ego, intelligence and mind of human beings, says physicist Amit Gowsami.[63]

New truths emerging out of twentieth century scientific discoveries have pushed science from the domain of sense-bound matter to the realm of philosophy, and specially the philosophy of consciousness as discovered by Vedānta *Ṛṣis* some four thousand years ago.

VII

INTERFACE OF PHYSICS AND BIOLOGY: EMERGENCE OF HOLISTIC CONSCIOUSNESS ACTING ON MATTER: MIND SHAPES BODY

The new other-worldly foundation of matter, which is consciousness, emerges more powerfully in the interface of physics and biology. Scientists are trying to understand not what things are made of but how they are put together and function as integrated wholes, especially in living organisms. What is sought is not a Theory of Everything or TOE but a general Theory of Organization or TOO according to physicist Paul Davis.[64] The question, according to Paul Davis, is whether self-organizing systems "can be understood by the known laws of physics, or whether completely new fundamental principles are required." [65] The trend is towards ever-greater organizational complexity where things move not from order to chaos, as the traditional laws of Thermodynamics insist, but from order to higher order. This new movement of matter from order to higher order is according to Paul Davis, "a conspicuous feature of the universe." It is freqeuntly regarded as a puzzle because "it seems to go the wrong way from a thermodynamic point of view", says Paul Davis.[66]

Paul Davis says:

> If we accept that there exists a propensity in nature for matter and energy to undergo spontaneous transitions into new states of higher organizational structures, ... I have been at pains to argue that the steady unfolding or organized complexity in the universe is a fundamental property of nature.[67]
>
> ... The origin of life, the evolution of increasing biological complexity, and the development of the embryo form a single egg cell, all seem miraculous at first sight, and all remain largely unexplained.[68]

Cambridge Zoologist W. H. Thorpe speaks with the same conviction:

> The behaviour of large and complex aggregates of elementary particles, so it turns out, is not to be understood as a simple extrapolation of the properties of a few particles. Rather, at each level of complexity entirely new properties appear, and the understanding of these new pieces of behaviour requires

> research which is as fundamental as, or perhaps even more fundamental than, anything undertaken by the elementary particle physicists.[69]

Since the last sixty years biologists are trying to conceive of a single force-field in a living organism. In 1960s, F.S.C. Northop and Harold Saxton Burr postulated this field as the bio-gravitational field or the L-field.[70] Recently Rupert Sheldrake, a Cambridge scientist, has started building up, on the basis of some of his successful experiments, a similar idea of *morphic field.*

> The latest discoveries in physics have proved that particles of matter are fields of energy. "Yet this new vision of the physicists has so far had very little effect on the understanding of living organism", writes Rupert Sheldrake. "Quantum physics had dissolved atoms or subatomic particles into quantized fields of energy. Yet in the field of biological research much of the old atomistic way of thinking has persisted." The morphic fields of cells, tissues, organs, and living organism have, according to Sheldrake, so far been described "only in vague and general terms."[71]

The morphic-field or the energy-field in a living organism works in a way, which is strikingly different from a mere mechanical function. In fact they work in a holistic way. A branch of a tree, when planted, develops into a full-fledged tree. A sea urchin cut into two develops into a full sea urchin. A liver whose parts have been removed, develops into a full liver. Rupert Sheldrake writes: "The capacity to regenerate is, in fact, one of the most fundamental features of living organisms and any theory of life has to try to explain it... Process of regeneration reveals that in some sense organisms have a wholeness that is more than the sum of their parts; parts can be removed, and yet wholeness can be restored." And this holistic function of living organism has so far not been explained by the laws of physics. But new thoughts are emerging.

VIII

SPIRIT: THE FIFTH DIMENSION OF MATTER

Nobel physicist Winger speaks of his 'firm conviction of the existence of biotonic laws'. He asks: "Does the human body deviate from the laws of physics, as gleaned form the study of inanimate matter?" He goes on to give two reasons involving the nature of organic consciousness and argues that the laws that guide the growth and evolution of living organism are different from the laws of physics of matter. One reason is the supremely important role of consciousness in quantum mechanics. The second reason is the simple fact that in physics action tends to provoke reaction. This suggsts to Winger that, because matter can act on mind (e.g. in producing sensation) so too should mind be able to react on matter.[72] The Nobel-prize winning discoveries in Neurophysiology by Sir John Eccles and more recently by Roger Sperry of a non-physical consciousness, which transcends the physical brain-matter, but nevertheless works through the physical brain, are landmarks.

This fact that mind acts on matter is one of the most fascinating frontiers of science where physical laws becomes subservient to the functioning of organic consciousness.

Nobel scientist R.W. Sperry who has conducted extensive experiements on split-brain subjects, rejects reductionist explanations of mental phenomena which says all mental phenomena can be ultimately reduced to physical and chemical reactions. He argues instead for the existence of something like *downward causation.* It is technically known as emergent interactionism of consciousness on matter. Sperry asserts that higher-level entities possess laws and principles in their own right that cannot be reduced to lower-level laws. Speaking about cerebral function Sperry says,

> These large cerebral events as entities have their own dynamics and associated properties that causally determine their interactions. These top-level systems' properties supersede those to the various subsystems they embody.

Sperry explicitly states that '*mental forces or properties exert a regulative control influence in brain physiology*'. How does the 'mental force' exert a downward causality on physical brain matter? Sperry explains, "Once generated from neural events, the higher order mental patterns and programs have their own subjective qualities and progress, operate and interact by their own causal law and principles which are different from, and cannot be reduced to those of neurophysiology... The mental forces do not violate, disturb, or intervene in neuronal activities but they do supervene...Multilevel and interlevel causation is emphasized in addition to the one-level sequential causation traditionally dealt with."

Sperry talks of the lower-level entities becoming 'caught up' in the holistic pattern, just as a water droplet is caught up in a whirlpool and constrained to contribute cooperatively to the overal organized activity.[73]

Roger Sperry writes: "Consciousness pervades nearly all aspects of the human enterprise. Any basic revision in its conception, therefore, or in its role, or how it relates to the physical brain or to outside reality is bound to produce sweeping reverberations. An implied answer, for example, to just the one question. "Is consciousness mortal or immortal?" would have repercussions in all dimensions or levels of the social structure.

Subjective belief, in our new theory, is no longer a mere impotent epiphenomenona of brain activity. It becomes a powerful impelling force in its own right. From the standpoint of the brain's functional organization and cognitive processing, one can hardly overrate the commanding, central-control influence of the human belief system as a shaper of both individual and social behaviour."

Sperry belives that a universe with a supreme plan, spiritual values, purpose, and higher meaning, emerges out of a spiritually void, value-empty cosmos, governed throughtout by quantum physics.

"I no longer need to keep my religion and my science separate," because "banning consciousness from explanations of brain function rested, in fact, on an unrecognised logical oversight or shortcoming. As things stand, I no longer need to believe, as a scientist, that I and my world are governed solely from below upward through the "fundamental froces of physics" in a totally mindless and purposeless cosmos, indifferent to human concerns. In our new downward-control paradigm we are moved and surrounded in the modern world by higher, more-evolved vital, mental, cultural, and other social forces."[74]

Nobel scientist Alxis Carrel said: "Man is a material being, but belongs also to another world which extends beyond space-time". Hans Driesh, nineteenth century biologist thought of '*a fourth cause*', '*a trans-temporal factor*', 'which acted on the physical system but was not itself part of it.' He called it *entelechy*. British scientist J.G. Bennet offered the concept of a *fifth-dimension*, called *eternity-dimension* behind all fourth-dimensional matter-energy of the space-time world.

Vedānta says that this space-time unvierse of matter springs from the non-material souce of all creation—*Brahman*—which is Existence—Consciousness—Bliss Absolute.

Where is Consciousness?

Long before Sperry, Arthur Eddington spoke of the distinction between matter and consciousness: "... the distinction between ordinary matter and conscious matter is that in ordinary matters there is no correlation in the undermined parts of the behaviour of particles, whereas in Conscious matter correlation may occur."[75] In the same tune celebrated jeneticist J.B.S. Haldane declare: "Science must ultimately aim at gradually interpreting the physical world of matter and energy in terms of biological conception of organism." Another scientist echoed Haldane: "The notions of physics will have to be enriched, and their enrichment will come from biology."[76] Physicist Niels Bohr asks in the same tune how consciousness can be explained by physical and chemical laws:

> The word consciousness, applied to ourselves as well as to others, is indispensable when dealing with human situation. In view of all these how the claim of materialism, that "life could be explained by sophisticated combination of physical and chemical laws could so long be accpeted by scientists," asks Niels Bohr.[77]

Nobel scientist Geroge Wald regretted that scientists in general do not pay necessary attention to this dimension of modern science, namely, the 'Issue of Consciousness':

> Biologists tend to be embarrased by consciousness. As an attribute of some living organism, they feel that they should know about it and should indeed be in a position to straighten out physicists about it none of which has come their way. Hence the discomfort, the avoidance, or worse; talking ancillary mechanism that dodge the essential problem.
>
> If I say, with Eddington, to put the conclusion crudely the stuff of the world is mind-stuff, sceintists doubt it has a metaphysical ring." But, says Wald, if he speaks of equations of quantum mechanics, quantum electrodynamics, and quantum field theory, that sounds to the scientists like good, modern physics. "Yet what are those equations, indeed what is mathematcs, but mind-stuff? .... The mateiral universe, is then an Avatara, the materialisation of primal mind.[78]

Prof. Wald realized the importance of eastern philosophy in defining the role of a non-local consciousness, in our human life.

> A few years ago it occurred to me—albeit with some shock to my scientific sensibilities—that my two problems, that of a life breeding universe, and that of consciousness that can neither be identified nor located, might be brought together. But very quickly I realised that I was in excellent company. Not alone

> are rudiments of this kind of thought deeply embedded in millenia-old Eastern philosophies; it is stated explicitly or strongly implied in the writings of quite recent and some present physicists.[79]

The understanding of living structures as open system provided an important new perspective, but it did not solve the puzzle of the coexistence of stable structure and continuous change, or order and dissipation, until Ilya Prigogine formulated his theory of dissipative structures.[80] Prigogine combined 'dissipative' and 'structure' to express the two seemingly contradictory tendencies that coexist in all living systems.

A living organism is characterized by continual flow and change in its metabolism, involving thousands of chemical reactions. Chemical and thermal equilibrium exists when all these processes come to a halt. In other words, an organism in equilibrium is a dead organism.[81]

Prigogine wrties on this complimentarity of two seemingly opposite entities-dissipation like chaos and stillness: "Each great period of science has led to some model of nature. For classical science it was the clock; for nineteenth-century science, the period of the Industrial Revolution, it was an engine running down. What will be the symbol for us? In some of the most beautiful manifestations of sculpture, be it the dancing Shiva or in the miniature temples of Guerrero, there appears very clearly the search for a junction between stillness and motion, time arrested and time passing. We believe that this confrontation will give our period its uniquenss."[82]

Near equilibrium we find repetitive phenomena and universal laws. As we move away from equilibrium, we move from the universal to the unique, towards richness, and variety. This, of course, is a well-known characteristic of life.[83]

A bacterial cell synthesises 3,000 diferent kinds of proteins. Each protein may contain 100 amino acids. The cell requires only 10 seconds at 37°C to complete the synthesis of a protein. In 1969, the first laboratory synthesis of protein took several months, skilled chemists, expensive reagents, complete automated machines and hundreds of operations.[84]

The interface of physics and Biology has not only revealed an increasing importance of mind and consciousness but also brought a new renaissance of Consciousness in Science. Physicist Amit Goswami writes:

> I believe that such a massive movement of consciousness can be called a renaissance. Such transitional periods have occurred in many cultures and civilizations. The next such renaissance, which perhaps is a-birthing, will be a very speical one since, thanks to modern communications technology, humanity is now interconnected. The next renaissance will have worldwide reverberation; it will be a global renaissance of peace.[85]

Roger Penrose speaks about the brain functions—70 billion neurons or nerve cells operating in the upper brain cerebrum. Some have much more close relation to consciousness or conscious functioning. While 30 billion neurons working in the lower brain or cerebellum is often referred to as "just a computer" because of its entirely unconscious activity. Roger Penrose writes in the conclusion of a paper entitled: "Where Lies physics of the Mind?"—"One can agree that a universe governed by laws... that do not allow consciousness is no universe at all. I would say all mathematical description of a universe that has given so far must fail this criterion. It is only the phenomenon that can conjure a putative theoretical universe into actual existence"... For this, Penrose believes, attempts towards reduction of biology or physiology or neurology will not do. "It is rather Physics which will have to broaden its scope of study to be able to accommodate the complex functions of human brain in its conscious activities". Penrose writes, "I believe there is already an indication, within the mysterious development of Quantum Mechanics, that the concepts or mentality are a little closer to our understanding of the physical universe than it had been before, only a little closer.... Science has a long way to go."[86]

Bells Theorem: Science Moves Away from a Dualistic to a Holistic Universe

The Dualistic Universe of Newton where matter was separate from energy, matter was separate from matter and matter was separate from mind, began to crumble with the tremendous influence of the new discoveries of Relativity and Quantum Physics. Matter was found by Einstein to be only another form of energy in the famous equation 'E = MC^2. Not only that, extremely heavy matter was found in General Relativity, to be curving space. Space was found to be a new face of time in Einstein's space-time continuum.

Today we are forced to accept a universe where matter-energy-space have been connected together in a holistic way. "We live in a single universe", wrote Nobel chemist Illya Prigogine.

Physicists David Bohm, John Clauser and Freedman and finally Alain Aspect in Paris, who successfully experimented on Bell's Theorem proved that two similar photons (in the experiment with twin photon pairs) always and instantaneously communicate with each other. Even when the twin photons are theoretically speared by an astronomical distance (a distance that light takes several seconds to travel), the condition of one photon is immediately conveyed to its twin. How could instananeous communication between two distant objects be possible? Einstien's Theory of Relativity shows that 'faster than light' or 'super-luminal commnication' is not possible. According to Einstein, the fastest speed in this universe is the speed of light, which is 1,86,000 miles per second. How can two particles that are separated by a distance, for example, of 10 lakh miles, be connected instantaneously? Even the fastest communication speed will take at least 5 seconds to connect such paired particles. But the successful experiment of Bell's theorem has established the fact that superluminal, instantaneous connection is indeed possible. Alain Aspect, along with colleagues, Jean Dalibard and Gerard Roger, added in 1982 and 1985 the refinements necessary to make the results unequivocal. They found that the communication was '*almost instantaneous*'.

In 1980s when Paul Davis asked a few scientists in a B.B.C. brodcast definite questions on Aspects Experiment, the answer was evasive. In 1983 Nobel Physicist Brain Josephson commented on this that one part of the Universe could have knowledge of the other part under certain conditions. Einstein could not accept this non-local communication. He felt there must be some 'hidden variable' behind this non-local connection. Until today no such hidden variable has been discoverd. Eugene Winger suggests, "It is the consciousness of the scientist which is itself the hidden variable."[87] American physicist Henry Stapp in 1975 declared that Bell's theorem is the "most profound discovery of science". He asserted "our ordinary ideas about the world are somehow profoundly deficient even on the macrosopic level.[88] It is a holistic universe where matter floats like 'Quantum foam', as Wheeler calls it, on one single underlying order which Bohm calls the 'implicate order'.

Bohm wrote:

> The essential new quality implied by the quantum theory in non-locality i.e. that a system cannot be analysed whose basic properties do not depend upon the whole system... This leads to new notion of unbroken wholeness of the universe.[89]

This 'implicate order', according to David Bohm, is 'primary', 'self-existent', 'universal', and 'an unidentifiable totality'. This is the ground for both 'life-explicit' and 'inanimate matter', whose functioning go on in an 'unbroken and undivided totality'. This is *Brahman,* the substratum of all things, 'living' and 'non-living' described in the Upaniṣad. Bohm's idea of 'implicate order' is approaching the holistic worldview of Vedānta. The morphic field', located in a particular body, proposed by Sheldrake, is connected with a universal field, according to David Bohm. "Moreover," writes Bohm, "such a field could not be located anywhere... When the explicate order enfolds into implicate order, which does not have any space, all places and all time are, we might say, merged, so that what happens in one place will interpenetrate what happens in another place."[90]

Other physicists have come forward to defend the new holistic world view. Like an *Upaniṣadic Ṛṣi* another physicist Geofrey Chew wrote in 1996:

> According to quantum theory, even if we do not talk, even if we do not look at each other, you affect me, and I affect you... Your electron and my electron are only approximately distinguishable. In denying objectivity, quantum mechanics denies absoulte status to your individuality. The only individual is the entire universe.
>
> It was during his fifties, while I was applying Fermi's ideas to the structure of nuclear particles that I became aware that within every particle there is a sense in which every other particle resides. I was amazed that this essential aspect of quantum theory has not been emphasised by my teachers.[91]

According to Bell's theorem and Aspect's experiment, the discovery of non-local, and non-causal connection between two similar particles brings the concept of non-local, non-causal determination. Milic Kapek calls it "neodeterministic interpretation of contemporary microphysics". Gary Zukav calls it 'Super-determinism' far beyond ordinary determinism.[92] "According to Bohm, what happens in space-time is nevertheless detemined by what happens in a nonlocal reality beyond space-time", says Ruper Sheldrake.[93] Such new ideas worried many scientists rooted in old materialistic ideas. "The more the universe seems comprehensible, the more it seems meaningless," said the Nobel physicist Steven Weinberg at the conclusion of his popular book on cosmology. Physicist Amit Goswami comments: "We agree. Concepts such as non-local and untive consciousness and the idea of non-local collapse make the universe less comprehensible to the materilist scientist. These concepts also make the universe a lot more meaningful to everyone else."[94]

Psychologist Carl Jung coined the world *synchronicity* to describe meaningful coincidences that people sometimes experience, coincidences that occur without a cause except perhaps a common cause in the transcendent domain. Synchronistic phenomena prove the simultaneous occurrence of meaninfgul equivalences in heterogeneous, causally unrelated process.

Vedānta says that no communication is necessary between two particles at a space like distance as both are floating on the background of *one universal mind and one universal consciousness.* "I have interpenetrated this universe, like a thread connecting pearls," says Krișṇa in the *Gītā.* "O Gargī," says Yāgñavalkya, "that one universal imperishable consciousness has penetrated everything in this universe," (*By Upanișad 3/8/11*)." Know that *Ātman* which has interpenetrated the external and internal unvierse along with mind and vital energies. That is the way to immortality", says the *Mundaka Upanișad.* Vivekaṇanda exposes in 1897 this holistic vision of life in his Madras lecture on *Work Before Us:* "One atom in this universe cannot move without dragging the whole world along with it... The watchword and the essence have been preached in the days of yore when the Vedantic truth was first discovered, the solidarity of all life."

Through the discovery of a holistic universe, Science has created a rational foundation of human values. It is from the realisation of one single consciousness everywhere that sages have felt their inextricable interconnectedness with the rest of the universe. It is only after such realisation that true love, love for others, dawns. Then only ethics and morality are born. All ethics is based on the perception of the basic unity of all life. Then the higher man goes to live a holistic existence.

Vivekananda explained:

> Why should you do good to others? Because that is only the condition of life; thereby you expand beyond your little self, you live and grow. All narrowness, all contractions, all selfishness is simply slow suicide.[95]

The rational West is earnestly bent upon seeking out the rationally, the *raison d'etre* of all its philosophy and its ethics. Modern science with its discovery of a holistic universe has laid the rational foundation. Ethics cannot be derived from the mere sanction of any personage, however great and divine he may have been. Such an explanation of the authority of ethics appeals no more to the rational thinkers. They want something more than human sanction for ethical and moral codes to be binding; they want in the words of Vivekananda, "eternal principles of truth as the sanction of ethics."[96]

Vivekananda asserts that in order to reach real basis of morality or ethics one "must have the highest phiosophical and scientific conception.

Two highest eternal principles of life and unvierse stand out in the Vedānta Philosophy of the Upanișads.

(1) The Infinite is the background behind the finite (*Ātman = Brahman*)

(2) An esential Holistic Unity and interconnectedness is always there behind all apparently disparate realities of life and universe. (*Ekam Eva Advitīviyam*).

Both these truths today stand verified by modern science. Ethical values do not spring out of reason but from a higher level of consciousness which we call super-reason or intuition born of deep mystical insight into the true nature of reality around us. The same supra-rational background is termed by Plank as 'Divine Providence' and by Eddington as 'Unknown Background'. This source of higher scientific creativity is also the source of altruistic morality and ethics both for scientists and non-scientists. Vedanta calls this unknown background as *Sat* (Absolute Existence), *Cit* (Absolute Consciousness) and *Ānanda* (Absolute Bliss). But the supra-rational does not stand against reason. Says Vivekananda, "The superconscious transcends the reason but contradicts it never!" Just as the animal man with instinct matures into rational man, similarly by the process of concious effort rational man matures into intuitive and supra-rational man.

The discovery of truths through scientific investigation have often been inspired by some higher impulses which the scientists called 'God', divine providence' or 'Inner Light' etc. "Every advance in knowledge", said Max Planck, "brings us face to face with the mystery of our own being."[97]

IX

THE HOLISTIC PARADIGM: THE NEW PARADIGM OF SCIENCE

Aspect's experiments on Bell's Theorem where non-local consciousness communicates at a space-like distance, brings us nearer the Vedanta philosophy where a holistic consciousness interconnects the Universe of both sentient and insentient. There is a growing conviction that this discovery of a fundamental interconnectedness of the universe will stand further tests. Physicist Fritz of Capra says: "I believe the fundamental unity and the relatedness of the unvierse and the intrinsic dynamic nature of its phenomenon, the two basic elements of modern physics—will not be invalidated by future research."[98] In biology the same holistic pattern is emerging clearer. Nobel Scientist Francis Crick speaks of the multidimensional function of a nerve cell or Neuron. He writes: "One characteristic of a neuron is already fairly clear. A single neuron can fire at different rates and, to some extent, in different styles."[99] Karl Pribram's discoveries suggest the existence of one single Holographic consciousness working in human brian. "Brain is a hologram," Pribram concludes.[100]

Arthur Koestler coined a world, 'holon', to describe the sub-atomic particle, since each of them is inextricably connected with the rest of the universe. Each particle reflects the 'whole', as it were.[101] Physicist David Bohm has used this concept of holon in his new theory of 'Implicate Order'. The movement of a single particle, according to this theory, is connected with the movement of all the particles in the system. Bohm calls it 'holo-movement'. To establish his theory, says Fritzof Capra, Bohm has found it necessary to regard consciousness as an essential feature of the holo-movement and to take it into account explicitly in his theory.[102]

The "interconnectedness" between all entities of the universe, is described as an "ecological age" perception of reality. Everything is inferred to be in intimate touch with everything else. This suddenly popular concept, known as "ecophilosophy" and "New Age" thinking, apparently derives from developments in physics relating to Bell's Theorem.

Roger Sperry writes:

> The related, so-called New Age Movement of the past two decades, which has increasingly challenged Judeo-Christian and other traditions of western culture, I believed it also has its foundation in the consciousness revolution.

These new findings and connections have led to the creation of a new 'paradigm', a new set of values in the world of science. The old Cartesian or Newtonian paradigm of a dualistic world vision, of a 'schizophrenic culture' or division between mind and matter, between matter and matter, is today replaced by the new paradigm—the 'Holistic Paradigm', as Ken Wilber calls it. This 'Holistic Paradigm' is only another name of the monistic or advaitic (non-dualistic) philosophy of Vedānta in whose modern interpretation Vivekananda spoke of the Vedāntic idea of the unity of all beings in his speech on 'God in Everything', delivered in London in 1896.

"This is another great theme of the Vedānta, this oneness of life, this oneness of everything. We shall see how it demonstrates that all our misery comes through ignorance, and this ignorance is the obsession with manifoldness. The separation between man and man, between nation and nation, between earth and moon, between moon and sun. Out of this idea of separation comes all misery. But, the Vedānta says, this separaton, does not exist, it is not real. It is merely apparent, the limitations imposed by the five instruments of knowledge man is bound with the five sensory organs. In the heart of things, there is Unity still. And that Unity is God".[103]

Physicists Turn to Experience from Experiments

Speaking on 'The Spirit of Science' at the *Eranos Tagung* held in Ascona in 1946, Erwin Schrodinger spoke about the subject, the spirit inside us, which can not be understood by law of the objective world. He said: "... the spirit is to an eminent degree subject, and thus evades objective examination". In defence of this stance, Schrodinger quoted (in translation) the opening line of Śaṁkara's *Brahmasūtrabhāśya: Subject and object—the 'I' and the 'not-I—are in essence opposed to each other like light and darkness...*[104]

For Schrodinger, the phrase 'Science of Consciousness' is a mixture of contradictory elements of objectivity and subjectivity. Object can be *experimented* upon, subject has to be *experienced.* That is why Śaṁkara asserted the idea that the presence of one Absolute Consciousness is an act of direct mystical experience of *Aparokṣānubhūti.* "Religion is realizaton", says Swami Vivekananda. In Vedānta philosophy the realizaton of *I am the whole world* or *aham Brahmāsmi,* is the goal of human evolution. In western tradition philosophy is intellectural confirmation of an idea. In Indian tradition, phiosophy is the realization or vision of the idea (*Darśan*). All great philosophers of India spoke and preached only after themselves experiencing, and living the great principles, which they realized. Like an eastern mystic Schrodinger, declared:

> From the early great Upaniṣads the recognition Ātman = Brahman (the personal Self called the omnipresent, all-comprehending eternal Self) was in Indian thoughts considered far from being blasphemous to represent the quintessence

> of deepest insight into happenings of the world. The striving of all scholars of Vedānta was, after having learnt to pronounce with their lips, really to assimilate in their minds this grandest of all thoughts.[105]

With the same conviction in the Vedāntic philosophy, Schrodinger wrote as early as in 1924, when quantum physics just started its century-long journey.

> This life of yours which you are living is not merely a piece of this existence, but in certain sense the 'whole'... this, as we know, is what the Brahmins express in that sacred mystic formula which is yet so simple, so clear. *Tat Twam Asi.* This is you. Or again in such words as "I am in the east, I am in the west, I am below and above. I am this whole world."[106]

Schrodinger's idea—*to assimilate this grandest of all thoughts*—was, according to F.A. Wolf, prophetic. Wolf says: "I like to think of this statement, "I am this whole universe," as the initial postulate of quantum thinking". Like Schrodinger, Max Planck, the father of Quantum physics, raised similar questions in his book *Where is Science Going?* (London: George Allen and Unwin; 1903) in which, according to *Observer*, Planck could "transcend the limits of his own scientific work and enquire into the philosophical implicatons." (Book cover). He wrote:

> Science cannot solve the ultimate mystery of nature. And that is because in the last analysis we ourselves are part of nature and, therefore, trying to solve. Every advance in knowledge brings us face to face with the mystery of our own being. All great scientific discoveries are backed by ... a definite drang or fundamental urge, which seems to characterize the advance of physical science. In these cases, the movement has undoubtedly been from the relative to the Absolute.[107]

Physicist Paul Davis speaks of the impossibility of knowing the absolute since the absolute includes the knower also:

> We cannot know Cantor's Absolute, or any other Absolute, by rational means, for any Absolute, being a Unity and hence complete within itself, must include itself. And here we encounter once more the Godelian limits to rational thought—the mystery at end of the universe.[108]

The *Bṛhadāraṇyaka Upaniṣad* (2:4:14) asks, "How to know the knower" (*Vijñataram aure Kena Vijñaniat*)? Nobel Physicist Richard Feynman took a similar visionary flight like Schrodinger on higher imagination. Intuition made him see the Reality through broad mystic overview, and inspired him to wrote:

> Living things, masses of atoms, DNA, protein ... Dancing a pattern ever more intricate ... Out of the cradle onto the dry land ... Here it is standing ... Atoms with consciousness ... Matter with curiosity .... Sands at the sea ... Wonders at wondering ... I ... A universe of atoms ... An atom in the universe.[109]

Similarly another physicist Alan Wolf speaks like an Upaniṣadic mystic:

> A world without objectivity and locality would be a very subjective world. It would consist of one element: me. This is the world of the quantum solipsist. ... The

world of the quantum solipsist bears some resemblance to Descartes' "I think, therefore I am." A quantum solipsist says: I am the only reality. Everything out there is in my mind.[110]

Einstein spoke about his own discoveries as "the years of anxious searching in the dark, with their intense longing, their alternations of confidence and exhaustion, and final emergence into the light." His own turning away, from Mach's positivism to the 'intuitive leap' or 'Einstein's postulational method', turned him to search for the truth in the inner realm of mystic intuition free from the dogma of his own Jewish faith to which earlier he was genuinely committed.

As a scientist he spoke of the need of a "religious spiritualization of our understanding of life." He wrote: "It seems to me that science not only purifies the religious impulse of the dross of anthropomorphism, but also contributes to a religious spiritualization of our understanding of life." He became, as A.D. Reincourt pointed out, 'at heart an eastern monist, as most scientists who are religiously inclined."[111] Transcending his own convictions that "the highest principles of our aspirations and judgements are given to us in the Judeo-Christian religious tradition'.[112] Einstein became a "Cosmic man", and turned towards the mystical.

X

ERA III OF PHYSICS: A NEW REVOLUTION

Physics is poised, according to physicist Paul Davis, for a major revolution, not just rapid advances in tehnical details, but transformations of the very concepts upon which until today science is based. In physics such revolutions, according to Paul Davis, occurred twice before. The first was the systematic development of mechanics by Galileo and Newton. The second occurred with the theory of relativity and the quantum theory at the beginning of this century.

The third revolution, according to Paul Davis, has come with the interface of physics with biology. It is the discovery of steady unfolding of organisational complexity in the universe, especially in the self-organizing systems. Order leads to chaos, according to traditional mechanics of standard thermodynamics. In self-organising systems, on the contrary, Order leads to higher order and greater complexity. Symmetry leads not to broken symmetry but higher symmetry. "We have seen," writes Paul Davis, "how spontaneous self-organisation tends to occur in far-from-open, non-leaner systems with a high degree of feedback. Such systems, far-from being unusual, are actually the norm of nature." In self-organising systems like life-forms, it is consciousness and non-material thoguht that acts on matter and leads to higher order. Physics does not have any law to explain such phenomena. Arthur Peacock explains this with clarity: "Higher level concepts and theories often refer to genuine aspects of reality at their own level of description and we have to eschew any assumptions that only the so-called fundamental particles of modern physics are 'really real'."[113]

This third revolution was prophesised by John A. Wheeler in his lecture on the Mystery & Message of Quantum delivered to American Physical Society on 1 February 1984. Wheeler held out that the greatest task of modern physics will be to shift its foundation: "And how can the hard-won structure of hard science be moved over, solid as ever, onto this new and other-wordly foundation? Yet, despite all difficulties, and they are great, that must be the task and achievement of the coming Era III of physics."[114]

XI

THE HISTORIC QUANTUM REVOLUTION

The objective world started disappearing under the mounting pressure of quantum physics. The belief in the sure cause and effect relation was falsified with the emergence of uncertainty or indeterminacy in the sub-atomic world after Heisenberg's discovery of Uncertainty principle in 1927. Heisenberg himself studied eastern mysticism with Tagore in India, in order to find parallels of new discoveries in physics and the ideas of Eastern philosophy. He also wrote two books in order to illustrate how physics had to move towards philosophy after the discoveries in quantum physics—*Physics and Philosophy* and *Physics and Beyond.*

The far-reaching impact of the demolition of causality established by Heisenberg's Uncertainty Principle inspired Arthur Eddington to write: "... religion first became possible for a reasonable scientific man about the year 1927... If our expectation should prove well founded that 1927 has seen the final overthrow of strict causality by Heisenberg, Bohr, Born and others, the year will certainly rank as one of the greatest epochs in the development of scientific philosophy.[115] Since the Everett-Wheeler interpretation of Schrodinger's wave equation, Self-awareness or individual consciousness has gained upper hand. Quantum Physics had to accept the domain of non-physical mind or consciousness of the observer as an unavoidable factor in determining reality outside. The assumption that there exists, "out there", a real, objective reality, does not seem to exist without a perceiver of that reality. A simple particle, the electron which at times appears to be a electron cloud made up of an infinite number of possible electrons, "appear" as a single particle when and only when we observe one.[116] Consciousness and not matter, gives credibility to matter in the material world—this is the final thesis of physicist Amit Goswami. Commenting on Oregon physicist Amit Goswami's book on The Self-aware Universe, physicist Fred Alan Wolf writes: "Science seems to be signalling not only the end of a century but the end of science as we know it."[117]

In 1993 Ken Wibler wrote: "The quantum revolution was so cataclysmic...because it attacked not one or two conclusions of classical physics but the very cornerston...objective measurement to be the mark of absolute reality...because the measure and the measurer, the verified and the verifier, at this level are one and the same.[118] Physics have pushed scientists to the brink of metaphysics, and sometimes forced them to enter the domain of philosophy to find meaning of their own discoveries. Strangely, the metaphysics of this new physics has come nearer to the monistic (Advaitic) philosophy of Vedānta than any other philosophy available in the West. Commenting on these new dimensions of physics A.D. Reincourt writes in his book '*The Eye of Shiva*':

> A new spiritual vision is beginning to take shape under the spur of a most paradoxical alliance between new physics of the twentieth century and eastern, rather than western, mystical insight.
>
> The cardinal fact is that contemporary physics finds a remarkable echo in eastern and not western metaphysics; and that one of the prime elements of this conjunction is monistic and not monotheistic vision of underlying reality...(It is) perhaps the most outstanding cultural phenomenon of our times... In just a few decades scientific thought has moved light years away from the classical physics of nineteenth century.[119]

XII

SWAMI VIVEKANANDA'S CONTRIBUTION TOWARDS THE CONVERGENCE OF SCIENCE & VEDĀNTA

Swami Vivekananda anticipated this culmination of western physics in the concepts of Vedānta as early as 1895 when the new physics of this century had not even been dreamt of. At the Thousand Island Park in New York State he said:

> Modern science has really made the foundations of religion strong. That the whole universe is one is scientifically demonstrable. What the metaphysicians call 'being', the physicist call 'matter', but there is no real fight between the two, for both are one. Though an atom is invisible, unthinkable, yet in it are the real power and potency of the universe. That is what the Vedāntist says of *Ātman.*[120]

A hundred years ago Vivekananda declared in the West, "The senses cheat you day and night. Vedānta found that ages ago. Modern science is just discovering the same fact."[121] That is why Vivekananda's idea that relativity is space-time-causation was found by Michael Talbot to be a superior exposition of relativity than Herman Minkowiski's (also Einstein's) who failed to accept non-causality as a basic concept.

"Vivekananda further expresses a view that has become the backbone of Quantum Theory. There is no such thing as causality," writes Talbot.[122]

Vivekananda anticipated the holistic and mystical approach and hoped that modern science would take and turn from matter to the transcendental consciousness hidden in human beings, as the source of all existence.

> Religion is the science which learns the transcendental in nature through the transcendental in man. We know as yet little of man, consequently but little of the universe. When we know more of man, we shall probably know more of the universe. Man is the epitome of all things and all knolwedge is in him.[123]

Vedānta asserts that it is from pure consciousness that universe and life have emerged. Ken Wilber writes with the same conviction: "The highest level does not violate the principles of the lower. It simply is not exclusively bound or is explainable by them," writes, "The higher transcends but includes the lower and not vice-versa. Thus, life transcends but includes matter; mind transcends but includes life; souls transcends but include mind, and spirit transcends but includes soul."[124]

Vivekananda called Newton and Galileo 'prophets of physical science', and the Upaniṣadic *Ṛṣis* 'Prophets of spirituality', and declared that "the whole unvierse, mental and material ,will be fused into one".[125] He also prophesied that any branch of knowledge, even physics, when properly followed would reach the same conclusions, which the explorations into the psychic-spiritual world would ultimately reach.

It was Vivekananada's mission to bring the convergence of modern science and philosophy of Vedānta. "Science and religion will meet and shake hands," he said.[126] Again he pointed out that it is the philosophy of Advaita Vedānta, the idea of oneness, the fundamental unity of all existence, of mind and matter, of macrocosm and microcosm, which only can bring this convergence of science and Vedanta. He said: "Art, science, and religion are but three different ways to express a single truth. But in order to understand this we must have the theory of Advaita.[127]

And Vivekananda struggled a hundred years ago in a hundred different ways to interpret Advaita Vedānta in the rational language of modern science.

A.D. Reincourt writes in his well-known book '*The Eye of Shiva*' written on the convergence of Indian mysticism and modern physics: "Indian mysticism has evolved... as the science of physics itself leading towards an inevitable convergence of the two".[128]

CONCLUSION

A.D. Reincourt feels that this historic rationalistation of mysticism is due to the new interpretation of Vedānta by Sri Ramakrishna and Swami Vivekananda. He writes "Can a connection between the scientific and mystical frames of reference be established over and beyond a certain metaphysical parallelism? The answer lies perhaps in the fact that Indian mysticism, at least as far as its leading representatives are concerned, has evolved as much in the past hundred years as the science of physics itself, in a direction that points towards an inevitable convergence of the two. From its modern awakening with Sri Ramakrishna and Swami Vivekananda, eastern mysticism has begun to adapt its revelations to the entirely different cultural framework provided by science and technology, without in any way sacrificing what is valid in its traditional undestanding of the phenomenon itself.[129] A. D. Reincourt feels that this is "perhaps the most outstanding cultural phenomenon of our times."[130] Indian mysticism has evolved as the science of physics itself."[131]

The result of this confluence is '*Orientalisation of the West*', and more importantly 'a new planetary culture' in a holistic universe so powerfully confirmed by quantum physics. God has shifted His position from an extra terrestrial heaven to the inner realm of human psyche and this 'interiorisation of God' or Christ or Buddha within all of us, is inspiring humanity to search for happiness, peace, and fulfilment inside ourselves. Swami Vivekananda prophesied this convergence of modern science with monistic Vedānta and a consequent spiritualization of religion and civilization. "Civilization is the manifestation of divinity in man," Vivekananda declared to the western thinkers in his Harvard lecture in 1895. A.D. Reincourt finally concludes: "It might well be that mankind is now on the threshold of a psychological and physiological revolution of a magnitude that will overshadow all the social and political revolutions of our century, made possible by the seemingly incongruous, yet perfectly logical marriage betwen science and eastern mystical insights."[132]

NOTES

1. Swami Vivekananda. 1973. *Complete Works of Swami Vivekananda,* vol. 3. p. 110.
2. Ibid. 1976. vol. 2. p. 139.
3. Ibid. p. 218.
4. Quoted in, Wilson, Edward. 1978. *Or Human Nature.* Boston: Harvard University Press. p. 12.
5. Pagels, Heinz R. 1983. *The Cosmic Code.* Bantam. pp. 39-40.
6. Russel, Collin. 1893. *Science and Social Changes.* Macmillan. p. 244.
7. Sheldrake, Rupert. 1988. *The Presence of the Past.* New York: Times Books. p. 211.
8. Goswami, Amit. 1995. *The Self Aware Universe.* New York: Bantam. p. 17.
9. Swami Vivekananda. *Complete Works,* vol. 8. pp. 121-22.
10. Greene, Brian. 2000. *The Elegant Universe.* USA: Vintage Books. p. 130; Marshall, Paul. 1992. *The Living Mirror.* London: Samphire Press. p. 299.
11. Greene. p. 149.
12. Burnett, Lincoln. 1956. *The Universe and Dr. Einstein.* London: Comet Books Collins. pp. 101-02.
13. Marshall, Paul. 1992. *The Living Mirror.* Samphire Press. 213.
14. Narlikar, Dr. I.V. 1983. "The Exploding Universe". *Illustrated Weekly of India,* 6-12 November. p. 8.
15. Cited in, Smith, Huston. 1976. *The Forgotten Truth.* New York: Harper Collins Books. p. 102.
16. White, Michael and Gribbin, John. 1992. *Stephen Hawking.* Viking, pp. 166, 172-73.
17. Einstein, A. 1967. *My View.* Calcutta: Rupa. p. 65.
18. Weber, Rane (ed.) 1986. *Dialogue with Sages and Scientists.* Routledge & Kegan Paul. p. 203.
19. Hawking, Stephen. 2001. *The Universe in a Nutshell.* Bantam Press. p. 59.
20. Ibid. p. 43.
21. Ibid. p. 54.
22. White and Gribbin. p. 189.
23. Ibid. p. 261.
24. Greene. p. 385, 387.
25. White and Gribbin, pp. 252-53.
26. Wheeler, John A. 1983. Interview of Wheeler by Timothy Ferris. *The New York Times Magazine,* 23 June. p. 16.
27. Schrodinger. *My View of the World.* Cambridge: Chapter IV.
28. Swami Vivekananda. "Inspired Talks". *Complete Works,* vol. 7.
29. Seal, B.N. 1985. *Positive Science of Ancient Hindus.* Delhi: Motilal Benarasidass. p. 33-34.
30. Pagals. p. 24.
31. Davis, Paul. *Mind of God.* pp. 227-28.
32. Burnett. p. 118.
33. Quoted *in The Cosmic Code.* p. 24.
34. Ibid.
35. Reincourt, A.D. 1981. *The Eye of Shiva.* New York: William Morrow & Co. p. 25.
36. Wheeler, John A. Letter to Swami Jitatmananda on June 10, 1999. Department of Physics, Joseph Henry Lab. Princeton University.
37. Waerden, B. L. Vander, 1985. *A History of Algebra from al-Khawarizmi to Emmy Noether.* Springer Verger. pp. 177-190.
38. 2001. *Narendrapur Samachar,* Narendrapur, West Bengal, India.
39. Davis. *Mind of God.* p. 192.

40. Pagals. pp. 115-122.
41. Ibid.
42. Zukav, Gary. 1979. *The Dancing Wu Li Masters.* Toronto, New York, London etc.: William Marow Co. p. 90.
43. Dyson, Freeman. 1979. *Disturbing the Universe.* New York: Harper & Row. p. 249.
44. Talbot, Michael. 1981. *Mysticism and New Physics.* Bantam Books. p. 82.
45. Tompkin, Peter and Bard, Christopher. 1974. *The Secret Life of Plants.* USA: Penguin Books. pp. 81-86.
46. Ibid.
47. Capra, Fritzof. 1976. *Tao of Physics.* Fortune Y. Collin. pp. 220-21.
48. Brunette. pp. 101-02.
49. Marshall. p. 267.
50. Greene. p. 349.
51. Ferguson, Kitty. 1992. *Stephen Hawking.* Bantam Books. pp. 77-78.
52. Capra. pp. 257-59.
53. Chopra, Dr. Deepak. *Quantum Healing.* Bantam. pp. 65-222.
54. Swami Vivekananda. *Complete Works,* Vol. 1. p. 150, Vol. 6. p. 141, 129, 133.
55. Talbot. p. 38.
56. Wolf, F.A. *Taking the Quantum Leap.* p. 201.
57. Crick, Francis. 1994. *The Astonishing Hypothesis.* New York: Charles Scribners & Sons. pp. 28, 35.
58. Wolf p. 254.
59. Ibid.
60. Wigner, Eugene. 1967. *Symmetries and Reflections.* Indian Universities Press. p. 177.
61. Heisenberg, Werner. 1971. *Physics and Beyond.* New York: Harper & Row. p. 84.
62. Goswami. p. 174-75.
63. Ibid.
64. Davis, Paul. 1987. *The Cosmic Blueprint.* London: Heinemann. p. 138.
65. Ibid.
66. Ibid.
67. Ibid.
68. Ibid. p. 139.
69. Ibid.
70. Tompkins and Bard. p. 175.
71. Sheldrake. p. 119.
72. Davis. *The Cosmic Blueprint.* p. 147.
73. Ibid.
74. Sperry, Roger W. *Quoted in, C.L.* Mathew and R.A. Vargease (ed.). 1995. *Cosmic Beginning and Human Ends. Illinois:* Open Court. pp. 316, 324.
75. Reincourt. pp. 183-84.
76. Ibid.
77. Bohr, Niels. 1958. *Atomic Physics and Human Knowledge.* New York: Wiley. p. 52.
78. Wald, George. 1987. *Life and Mind in the Universe.* Paper submitted to NCERT Seminar, New Delhi. February.
79. Ibid.
80. Prigogine and Stengers. 1984. p. 86ff.
81. Capra, Fritzof. *The Web of Life.* pp. 175-176.
82. Prigogine and Stengers. pp. 22-23; Capra. p. 175.
83. Capra. p. 177.
84. Mukherji, S.K. 2000. IETE, *Technical Review,* issue no. December.
85. Goswami. p. 271.
86. Mukherji. 2002. *Technical Review,* no. 16, vol. 19. November-December.
87. Talbot. p. 33.
88. Zukav. pp. 306, 314.
89. Wolf p. 177.
90. Sheldrake. p. 306.
91. Chew, Geoffrey. 1996. *Prabuda Bharata English Monthly,* August. Mayavati Advaita Ashrama. p. 103.
92. Zukov. pp. 318-19.
93. Sheldrake. p. 306.

94. Goswami. p. 130.
95. Swami Vivekananda. *Complete Works*, vol. 7. p. 47.
96. Ibid. vol. 2. p 63.
97. Planck, Max. 1933. *Where is Science Going*. London: George Allen. p. 119, 218.
98. Wibler, Ken (ed.). 1992. *Holographic Paradigm and other Essays*. New York: Shambala. p. 51.
99. Crick.
100. Pribram, Karl. *Holographic Paradigm*. p. 7.
101. Capra. p. 43.
102. Ibid.
103. Swami Vivekananda. *Complete Works, vol.* 2. p. 125.
104. Nair, Ranjit (ed.). 2001. *Mind, Matter and Mystery*. New Delhi: Scientica Paperback. pp. 73-79.
105. Schrodinger. p. 92.
106. Wolf. pp. 182-87.
107. Planck. pp. 169 192, 193, 217
108. Davis, p. 231
109. Wolf. p. 227.
110. Ibid. p. 223.
111. Reincourt. p. 190.
112. Einstein. p. 65.
113. Davis. pp. 118, 138, 142.
114. Wolf. p. 174.
115. Reincourt. p. 32.
116. Goswami. p. 9.
117. Ibid. Introduction by Wolf.
118. Wilber, Ken. 1993. *Spectrum of Consciousness*. Illinois, USA.
119. Reincourt. pp. 7, 18, 40, 171, 114.
120. Swami Vivekananda. "Inspired Talks". *Complete Works,* vol. 7.
121. Ibid. p. 74.
122. Talbot. pp. 114-15.
123. Swami Vivekananda. *Complete Works,* vol. 8. pp. 20-21.
124. Wibler. p. 16.
125. Swami Vivekananda. *Complete Works,* vol. 6. p. 4.
126. Ibid. vol. 2. p. 140.
127. Ibid. vol.1. Introduction.
128. Reincourt. p. 15, 190.
129. Ibid.
130. Ibid. pp. 183-84.
131. Ibid. p. 23.
132. Ibid. pp. 196-97.

CHAPTER 28

Vedānga Astronomy and Mathematics

Subhash Kak

I

INTRODUCTION

Did the Indian and Babylonian astronomy evolve in isolation, was there mutual influence, or was one dependent on the other? Scholars have debated these questions for more than two centuries, and opinion has swung one way or the other with time. The similarities between the two systems that have been investigated are: the use of 30 divisions of the lunar month; the 360 divisions of the civil year; the 360 divisions of the circle; the length of the year; and the solar zodiac. Some have wondered if the Babylonian planetary tables might have played a role in the theories of the Siddhāntas.

I shall in this essay go over the essentials of the early Indian and Babylonian astronomy and summarize the latest views on the relationship between them. I shall show that the key ideas found in the Babylonian astronomy of 700 B.C. are already present in the Vedic texts, which even by the most conservative reckoning are older than that period. I shall also show that the solar zodiac (*rāśis*) was used in Vedic India and I shall present a plausible derivation of the symbols of the solar zodiac from the deities of the segments.

In view of the attested presence of the Indic people in the Mesopotamian region prior to 700 B.C., it is likely that if at all the two astronomies influenced each other, the dependence is of the Babylonian on the Indian. It is of course quite possible that the Babylonian innovations emerged independent of the earlier Indic methods.

The Indic presence in West Asia goes back to the second millennium B.C. in the ruling elites of the Hittites and the Mitanni in Turkey and Syria, and the Kassites in Mesopotamia. The Mitanni were joined in marriage to the Egyptian pharaohs during the second half of the second millennium and they appear to have influenced that region as well.[1] The Ugaritic list 33 gods, just like the count of Vedic gods.

Although the Kassites vanished from the scene by the close of the millennium, Indic groups remained in the general area for centuries, sustaining their culture by links through trade. Thus Sargon defeats one Bagdatti of Uisdis s in 716 B.C. The name Bagdatti (Skt. Bhagadatta) is Indic[2] and it cannot be Iranian because of the double 't'.

The Indo-Aryan presence in West Asia persisted until the time of the Persian Kings like Darius and Xerxes. It is attested by the famous *daiva* inscription in which Xerxes (ruled 486-465 B.C.) proclaims his suppression of the rebellion by the *daiva* worshipers of West Iran.

These Indic groups most likely served as intermediaries for the transmission of ideas of Vedic astronomy to the Babylonians and other groups in West Asia. Since we can clearly see a gap of several centuries in the adoption of certain ideas, one can determine the direction of transmission. The starting point of astronomical studies is the conception of the wheel of time of 360 parts. It permeates Vedic writing and belongs to second millennium or the third millennium B.C. or even earlier, and we see it used in Babylon only in the second part of first millennium B.C. Recent archaeological discoveries show that the Sarasvatī river ceased reaching the sea before 3000 B.C. and dried up in the sands of the western desert around 1900 B.C., but this river is praised as going from the mountain to the sea in the *Ṛgveda*. This is consistent with astronomical evidence indicating 3rd millennium epoch for the *Ṛgveda*.

II

WESTERN HISTORIES OF INDIAN ASTRONOMY

The early western studies of Indian texts duly noted the astronomical references to early epochs going back to three or four thousand B.C. As the Indian astronomical texts were studied it was discovered that the Indian methods were different from those used in other civilizations. The French astronomer M. Jean Sylvain Bailly in his classic *Traitẽ de l'Astronomie Indienne et Orientale* (1787) described the methods of the *Surya Siddhānta* and other texts and expressed his view that Indian astronomy was very ancient. Struck by the elegance and simplicity of its rules and its archaic features, Bailly believed that astronomy had originated in India and it was later transmitted to the Chaldeans in Babylon and to the Greeks.

As against this, John Bentley in 1799 in a study in the *Asiatick Researches* suggested that the parameters of the *Sūrya Siddhānta* were correct for 1091 A.D. But Bentley was criticized for failing to notice that the *Sūrya Siddhānta* had been revised using *bīja* corrections,[3] and therefore his arguments did not negate the central thesis of Bailly.

Meanwhile, in the next several decades Indian astronomy became a contested subject. Part of the difficulty arose from a misunderstanding of the Indian system due to the unfamiliar structure of its luni-solar system. Later, it became a hostage to the ideas that the Vedic people had come as invaders to India around 1500 B.C.,[4] and that Indians were otherworldly and uninterested in science and they lacked the tradition of observational astronomy until the medieval times.[5] The inconvenient astronomical dates were brushed aside as untrustworthy. It was argued that astronomical references in the texts either belonged to recent undatable layers or were late interpolations.[6]

As against this, Ebenezer Burgess, the translator of the *Sūrya Siddhānta*, writing in 1860, maintained that the evidence, although not conclusive, pointed to the Indians being the original inventors or discoverers of:[7] (i) the lunar and solar divisions of the zodiac, (ii) the primitive theory of epicycles, (iii) astrology, and (iv) names of the planets after gods.[8]

With the decipherment of the Babylonian astronomical tablets, it was thought that early Indian astronomy may represent lost Babylonian or Greek inspired systems.[9] But this leads to many difficulties, anticipated more than a hundred years earlier by Burgess, including the incongruity of the epochs involved. The only thing that one can do is to lump all the Indian texts that are prior to 500 B.C. together into a mass of uniform material, as has been proposed by Pingree.[10] But such a theory is considered absurd by Vedic scholars.

The *Vedāṅga Jyotiṣa*, a late Vedic text, belongs to the second millennium B.C. Although Śaṁkara Bālakṣṇa Dīkṣita's *Bhāratīya Jyotiṣa*,[11] published in the closing years of the nineteenth century, contained enough arguments against looking for any foreign basis to the *Vedāṅga Jyotiṣa*, the issue was reopened in the 1960s.[12] The basis behind rearticulation of an already disproven theory was the idea that "the origin of mathematical astronomy in India is just one element in a general transmission of Mesopotamian-Iranian cultural forms to northern India during the two centuries that antedated Alexander's conquest of the Achaemenid empire."[13]

Overwhelming evidence has since been furnished that disproves this theory,[14] but many people remain confused about the relationship between the two astronomy traditions. The idea that India did not have a tradition of observational astronomy was refuted convincingly by Roger Billard more than thirty years ago. In his book on Indian astronomy,[15] he showed that the parameters used in the various Siddhāntas actually belonged to the period at which they were created giving lie to the notion that they were based on some old tables transmitted from Mesopotamia or Greece. The distinguished historian of astronomy B.L. van der Waerden reviewed the ensuing controversy in a 1980 paper titled *Two Treatises on Indian Astronomy* where he evaluated the views of Billard and his opponent Pingree. He ruled thus:

> Billard's methods are sound, and his results shed new light on the chronology of Indian astronomical treatises and the accuracy of the underlying observations. We have also seen that Pingree's chronology is wrong in several cases. In one case, his error amounts to 500 years.[16]

For the pre-Siddhāntic period, the discovery of the astronomy of the *Ṛgveda*[17] establishes that the Indians were making careful observations in the Vedic period as well.

One might ask why should one even bother to revisit Pingree's thesis if it stands discredited. The reason to do so is that it provides a good context to compare Babylonian and Indian astronomy and examine their similarities and differences. It also provides a lesson in how bad method will lead to incongruous conclusions.

It is not my intention to replace Babylon by India as the source of astronomical knowledge. I believe that the idea of development in isolation is simplistic; there existed much interaction between the ancient civilizations. I also believe that the borrowings in the ancient world were at best of the general notions and the details of the astronomical system that arose had features which made each system unique. Rather than assign innovation to any specific group, we can at best speak of specific geographical areas in which, due to a variety of social, economic, and cultural reasons, some new ways of looking at the universe arose. Regarding the problem of astronomy, we cannot ignore the pre-Babylonian Indian literature just as we must not ignore the fact that in the mid-first millennium B.C. the Babylonians embarked on a notable period of careful astronomical records and the use of mathematical models.[18] The Babylonian astronomical tradition goes back to the second millennium B.C. or earlier but here we are concerned not with its remarkable tradition of careful observation but with the beginnings of mathematical astronomy which is ascribed to the middle first millennium.

The next section will introduce pre-*Vedāṅga Jyotiṣa* Indian astronomy which will be followed by an account of Babylonian astronomy so that the question of the relationship between *Vedāṅga Jyotiṣa* and Babylonian astronomy maybe investigated properly. Since the pre-*Vedāṅga* material belongs mainly to the Saṃhitās that are squarely in the second millennium B.C. or earlier epochs, it could not have been influenced by Babylonian astronomy. We will also use the evidence from the Brāhman as this also antedate the Babylonian material in the most conservative chronology.

Once we have understood the nature of this earlier astronomy, we will relate it to the *Vedāṅga Jyotiṣa* and the Babylonian astronomies.

III

PRE-VEDĀṄGA JYOTIṢA ASTRONOMY

Pre-*Vedāṅga Jyotiṣa* astronomy was described at some length in my essay titled "Astronomy and its Role in Vedic Culture" in volume 1 of the book[19] where the ritual basis of this science were sketched. It was shown that the organization of the Vedic texts and the altar ritual coded certain astronomical facts about the lunar and solar years. This showed that observational astronomy was a part of the tradition during the Vedic period itself. But we will not invoke this knowledge here and restrict ourselves to explicit statements from the Saṃhitās and the Brāhmaṇa literature.

The facts that emerge from the pre-*Vedāṅga* material include: knowledge of the duration of the year, concept of *tithi*, naming of ecliptic segments after gods, knowledge of solstices for ritual, the 27- and 12- segment divisions of the ecliptic, and the motions of the sun and the moon.

There were several traditions within the Vedic system. For example, the month was reckoned in one with the new moon, in another with the full moon.

Nakṣatras

Nakṣatras stand for stars, asterisms or segments of the ecliptic. The moon is conjoined with the 27 *nakṣatras* on successive nights in its passage around the earth; the actual cycle is of $27\frac{1}{3}$ days. Because of this extra one-third day, there is drift in the conjunctions that get corrected in three circuits. Also, the fact that the lunar year is shorter than the solar year by 11+ days implies a further drift through the *nakṣatras* that is corrected by the use of intercalary months.

The earliest lists of *nakṣatras* in the Vedic books begin with *Kṛttikās*, the Pleiades; much later lists dating from sixth century A.D. begin with *Aśvinī* when the vernal equinox occurred on the border of *Revatī* and *Aśvinī*. Assuming that the beginning of the list marked the same astronomical event, as is supported by other evidence, the earliest lists should belong to the third millennium B.C. or earlier. Each *nakṣatras* has a presiding deity (*Taittirīya Saṃhitā* 4.4.10). In the *Vedāṅga Jyotiṣa*, the names of the *nakṣatras* and the deity are used interchangeably. It seems reasonable to assume that such usage had sanction of the tradition.

Table 1 provides a list of the *nakṣatras*, the presiding deities, and the approximate epoch for the winter and summer solstice for a few selected *nakṣatras* that are relevant to this paper. It is noteworthy that the earliest Vedic texts provide us statements that recognize the movement of the solstices into new *nakṣatras*. This provides us a means to find approximate dates for these texts. Our identification of the *nakṣatras* has improved thanks to the work of Narahari Achar[20] who has used powerful new simulation software for sky maps that allows us to see the stars and the planets in the sky as the Vedic people saw them. Using this tool, he has shown that some previous identifications made without a proper allowance for the shift in the ecliptic due to precession be modified.

The *nakṣatras* in the *Vedāṅga Jyotiṣa* represent 27 equal parts of the ecliptic. This appears to have been an old tradition since the Saṃhitās (*Kāṭhaka* and *Taittirīya*) mention explicitly that *Soma* is wedded to all the *nakṣatras* and spends equal time with each. The stars of the *nakṣatras* are thus just a guide to determine the division of the ecliptic into equal parts. Each *nakṣatras* corresponds to $13\frac{1}{3}$ degrees.

The following is a list of the *nakṣatras* and their locations:

1. **Kṛttikā,** from the root *kṛt,* 'to cut.' These are the Pleiades, *n* Tauri. *Deity:* Agni
2. **Rohiṇī**, 'ruddy,' is α Tauri, Aldebaran. *Deity:* Prajāpati
3. **Mṛgaśīrṣa**, 'Deer's head,' *β* Tauri. *Deity:* Soma
4. **Ārdrā,** 'moist,' is *γ* Geminorum. (Previously it was thought to be Betelgeuse, *α* Orionis.) *Deity:* Rudra
5. **Punarvasū,** 'who give wealth again,' is the star Pollux, or *β* Geminorum. *Deity:* Aditi
6. **Tiṣya**, 'pleased,' or **Puṣya**, 'flowered,' refers to δ Cancri in the middle of the other stars of this constellation. *Deity:* Bṛhaspati
7. **Āśreṣā** or **Āśleṣā,** 'embracer,' represents *δ, ε, ζ,* Hydrae. *Deity:* Sarpāḥ.
8. **Maghā**, 'the bounties,' is the group of stars near Regulus, or α, η, γ, *ζ, μ, ε* Leonis. *Deity:* Pitarah.
9. Pūrvā **Phālgunī**, 'bright,' *δ* and θ Leonis. *Deity:* Aryaman (Bhaga)
10. **Uttarā Phālgunī**, 'bright,' *β* and 93 Leonis. *Deity:* Bhaga (Aryaman)
11. **Hasta,** 'hand.' The correct identification is *γ* Virginis. (Previously, the stars *δ, γ, ε, α, β,* in Corvus were assumed, but they are very far from the ecliptic and thus not correctly located for this *nakṣatra.*) *Deity:* Savitar
12. **Citrā**, 'bright.' This is Spica or *α* Virginis. *Deity:* Indra (Tvaṣṭṛ)
13. **Svātī**, 'self-bound,' or **Niṣṭyā**, is *π* Hydrae. (The previous identification of Arctutus or *α* Bootis is too far from the ecliptic.) *Deity:* Vāyu
14. **Viśākhā**, 'without branches.' The stars α_2 *β, σ* Librae. *Deity:* Indrāgni
15. **Anurādhā,** 'propitious,' 'what follows Rādhā.' These are the *β, δ, π* Scorpii. *Deity:* Mitra
16. **Rohiṇī**, 'ruddy', or **Jyeṣṭhā**, 'eldest.' This is Antares, a Scorpii. *Deity:* Indra (Varuṇa)

17. **Vicṛtau,** 'the two releasers,' or **Mūla,** 'root.' These are the stars from ε to λ, ν Scorpii. *Deity:* Pitaraḥ (Nirṛti)
18. **Pūrvā Āṣāḍhā,** 'unconquered,' δ, ε Sagittarii. *Deity:* Āpaḥ
19. **Uttarā Āṣāḍhā,** 'unconquered,' σ, ζ Sagittarii. *Deity:* Viśve devah.
    Abhijit, 'reaching victory.' The name refers to a satisfactory completion of the system of *nakṣatras.* The star is Vega, the brilliant α Lyrae. This is the star that does not occur in the lists which have only 27 *nakṣatras* on it. *Deity:* Brahmā
20. **Śroṇā,** 'lame,' or Śravaṇa, 'ear,' β Capricornus. (This is in place of Altair, a Aquillae.) *Deity: Viṣṇu*
21. **Śraviṣṭhā**, 'most famous.' Achar argues that it should be δ Capricornus rather than the previously thought β Delphini. It was later called **Dhaniṣṭhā,** 'most wealthy.' *Deity:* Vasavaḥ
22. **Śatabhiṣaj**, 'having a hundred physicians' is λ Aquarii and the stars around it. *Deity:* Indra (Varuṇa)
23. **Proṣṭhapadā**, 'feet of stool,' are the stars near a Pegasi. *Deity:* Aja Ekapād
24. **Uttare Proṣṭhapadā,** 'feet of stool,' and later **Bhadrapadā,** 'auspicious feet.' These are γ Pegasi and other nearby stars. *Deity:* Ahirbudhnya
25. **Revatī**, 'wealthy,' η Piscium. *Deity: Pūṣan*
26. **Aśvayujau**, 'the two horse-harnessers,' are the stars β and α Arietis. **Aśvinī** is a later name. *Deity:* Aśvinau
27. **Apabharaṇī**, 'the bearers,' are the group around δ Arietis. *Deity:* Yama

The antiquity of the *nakṣatra* system becomes clear when it is recognized that all the deity names occur in RV 5.51 (this insight is due to Narahari Achar[21]). This hymn by Svastyātreya Ātreya lists the deity names as:

Aśvin, Bhaga, Aditi, Pūṣan, Vāyu, Soma, Bṛhaspati, Sarvagaṇaḥ,
Viśve Devaḥ, Agni, Rudra, Mitra, Varuṇa, Indrāgni.

The *sarvagaṇaḥ*, the *gaṇaḥ* (groups) such as the Vasavaḥ, Pitaraḥ, Sarpaḥ (including Ahi and Aja), Apaḥ, and the Ādityagaṇaḥ (Dakṣa Prajāpati, Aryaman, Viṣṇu, Yama, Indra), complete the list. There is no doubt that the ecliptic is meant because the last verse of the hymn refers explicitly to the fidelity with which the sun and the moon move on their path, the ecliptic.

The division of the circle into 360 parts or 720 parts was also viewed from the point of view the *nakṣatras* by assigning 27 *upanakṣatras* to each *nakṣatra* (*Śatapatha Br.* 10.5.4.5). This constituted an excellent approximation because 27 × 27 = 729. In other words, imagining each *nakṣatra* to be further divided into 27 equal parts made it possible to conceptualize half a degree when examining the sky.

The identification of the *nakṣatras* is in consistent with their division into the two classes of *deva* and *yama nakṣatras* as in the *Taittirīya Brāhmaṇa* 1.5.2.7:

kṛttikāḥ prathamaṃ viśākhe uttamaṃ tāni devanakṣatrāṇi
anurādhāḥ prathamaṃ apabharaṇihyuttamaṃ tāni yamanakṣatrāṇi
yāni devanakṣatrāṇi tāni dakṣiṇena pariyanti
yāni yamanakṣatrāṇi tānyuttarāṇi iti.

Kṛttikās are the first and *Viśākhe* are the last; those are *deva nakṣatras. Anurādhās* are the first and *Apabharaṇī* is the last; those are the *yama nakṣatras.* The *deva nakṣatras* revolve from the south; the *yama nakṣatras* revolve from the north.

Kṛttikās to *Viśākhe* are the *deva nakṣatras* because they lie north of the equator, whereas the others are *yama nakṣatras* because they lie south of the equator. Since the *devas* are supposed to live in the north pole and *Yama* in the south pole, the *deva nakṣatras* revolve south of the abode of the *devas,* and the *yama nakṣatras* revolve north of the abode of *Yama.* This classification helps confirm the identification of the *nakṣatras.*

NAKṢATRAS WITH THEIR DEITY NAMES AND THE APPROXIMATE EPOCH OF WINTER SOLSTICE AND SPRING EQUNIOX AT THE MIDPOINT OF EACH SEGMENT

Num	*Nakṣatra*	*Deity*	*W. Solstice*	*S. Equinox*
1	Kṛttikā	Agni		2000 B.C.
2	Rohiṇī	Prajāpati		3000 B.C.
3	Mṛgaśīrṣa	Soma		4000 B.C.
4	Ārdrā	Rudra		5000 B.C.
5	Punarvasū	Aditi		6000 B.C.
6	Tiṣya or Puṣya	Bṛhaspati		
7	Āśreṣā or Āśleṣā	Sarpāḥ		
8	Maghā	Pitaraḥ		
9	Pūrvā Phālgunī	Aryaman		
10	Uttarā Phālgunī	Bhaga		
11	Hasta	Savitar		
12	Citrā	Indra		
13	Svātī or Niṣṭyā	Vāyu		
14	Viśākhā	Indrāgni		
15	Anurādhā	Mitra		
16	Rohiṇī	Indra		
17	Vicrṭau or Mūla	Pitaraḥ	2000 A.D.	
18	Pūrvā Āṣāḍhā	Āpaḥ	1000 A.D.	
19	Uttarā Āṣāḍhā	Viśve devaḥ	0 A.D.	
*	Abhijit	Brahmā		
20	Śroṇā or Śravaṇa	Viṣṇu	1000 B.C.	
21	Śraviṣṭhā or Dhaniṣṭhā	Vasavaḥ	2000 B.C.	
22	Śatabhiṣaj	Indra	3000 B.C.	
23	Proṣṭhapadā	Aja Ekapād	4000 B.C.	
24	Uttare Proṣṭhapadā	Ahirbudhnya	5000 B.C.	2000 A.D.
25	Revatī	Pūṣan	6000 B.C.	1000 A.D.
26	Aśvayujau	Aśvinau	7000 B.C.	0 AD
27	Apabharaṇī	Yama		1000 B.C.

TABLE 1

Abhijit, which comes between the nineteenth and the twentieth in the above list, does not occur in the list of the 27 in *Taittirīya Saṃhitā* or in *Vedāṅga Jyotiṣa. Maitrāyāṇī* and *Kāṭhaka Saṃhitās* and *Atharvaveda* contain lists with the 28 *nakṣatras*.

When the asterisms *Kṛttikā* and *Viśākhā* defined the spring and the autumn equinoxes, the asterisms *Maghā* and *Śraviṣṭhā* defined the summer and the winter solstices.

The Year and Solstices

There were two kinds of year in use. In one, the year was measured from one winter solstice to another; in the other, it was measured from one vernal equinox to another. Obviously, these years were solar and related to the seasons (tropical).

The wheel of time was defined to have a period of 360 parts. This number seems to have been chosen as the average of 354 days of the lunar year and the 366 days for the solar year.

In TS 6.5.3, it is said that the sun in its travels moves northward for six months and southward for six months. The *Brāhmaṇas* speak of ritual that follows the course of the year starting with the winter solstice. For example, the *Pañcaviṃśa Brāhmaṇa* describes *sattras* of periods of several days, as well as one year (PB 25.1), 12 years, 1000 days, and 100 years. In these types of ritual the number of days were recorded, providing a means of determining an accurate size of the solar year. The *sattra* of 100 years appears to refer to the centennial system of the *Saptarṣi* calendar.

The solstice day was probably determined by the noon-shadow of a vertical pole. The *Aitareya Brahmaṇa* speaks of the sun remaining stationary for about 21 days at its furthest point in the north (summer solstice) and likewise for its furthest point in the south (winter solstice). This indicates that the motion of the sun was not taken to be uniform all the time.

Months

The year was divided into 12 months which were defined with respect to the *nakṣatras*, and with respect to the movements of the moon. The *Taittirīya Saṃhitā* (TS) (4.4.11) gives a list of solar months:

Madhu, Mādhava (*Vasanta*, Spring), *Śukra, Śuci* (*Grīṣma*, Summer), *Nabha, Nabhasya* (*Varsā*, Rains), *Iṣa* and *Ūrja* (*Śardd*, autumn), *Sahas* and *Sahasya* (*Hemanta*, Winter), and *Tapa* and *Tapasya* (*Śiśir*, Deep Winter).

The listing of months by the season implies that parts of the ecliptic were associated with these 12 months. These months are also known by their *Āditya* names (Table *2*). These names vary from text to text, therefore, we are speaking of more than one tradition. It should be noted that different lists of names need not mean usage at different times.

Now we investigate if the *rāśi* names associated with the segments were a part of the Vedic tradition or if they were adopted later. In any adoption from Babylonia or Greece, one would not expect a fundamental continuity with the *nakṣatra* system. Taking the clue from the *Vedāṅga Jyotiṣa*, where the names of the *nakṣatras* and the deities are used interchangeably, we will investigate if the *rāśi* names are associated with the segment deities.

THE TWELVE MONTHS WITH THE *NAKṢATRA* NAMED AFTER AND ĀDITYAS NAMES
(FROM *VIṢṆU PURĀṆA*)

Month	*Nakṣatra*	*Āditya*
Caitra	Citrā	Viṣṇu
Vaiśākha	Viśākhā	Aryaman
Jyaiṣṭha	Jyeṣṭhā	Vivasvant
Āśāḍha	Āśāḍhās	Aṃśu
Śrāvaṇa	Sroṇa	Parjanya
Bhādrapada	Proṣṭhapadas	Varuṇa
Āśvayuja	Aśvinī	Indra
Kārtika	Kṛttikā	Dhātṛ
Mārgaśīrṣa	Mṛgaśiras	Mitra
Pauṣa	Tiṣya	Pūṣan
Māgha	Maghā	Bhaga
Phālguna	Phālgunī	Tvaṣṭā

TABLE 2

The *nakṣatras* names of the months each cover 30° of the arc, as against the $13\frac{1°}{3}$ of the lunar *nakṣatra* segment. Therefore, the extension of each month may stretch over up to three *nakṣatras* with corresponding deities. This will be seen in Figure 1 or in the list below. The choice made in Figure 1, where *Vaiśākha* begins with the the sun in the ending segment of *Aśvinī* and the moon at the mid-point of *Svātī* is the most likely assignment as it bunches the *Āśāḍhās* and the *Phālgunīs* in the right months, with the *Proṣṭhapadās* three-fourths correct and *Śroṇā* half-correct. The full-moon day of the lunar month will thus fall into the correct *nakṣatra.* Since the solar and the lunar months are not in synchrony, the mapping would tend to slip up to two *nakṣatras* signs until it is corrected by the use of the intercalary month. At worst, we get a sequence of *rāśis* which is out of step by one.

Vaiśākha = Svātī to Anurādhā = Vāyu, Indrāgni, Mitra
= Vṛṣa, Bull for Indra, e.g. RV 8.33; also Vāyu is sometimes identified with Indra and the two together called Indravāyū, and Vāyu is also associated with cow (RV 1.134)

Jyaiṣṭha = Anurādhā to Mūla = Mitra, Varuṇa, Pitaraḥ
= Mithuna, Gemini, from the cosmic embrace of Mitra and Varuṇa

Āśāḍha = Pūrva Āśāḍhā to Śroṇa = Āpaḥ, Viśve Devaḥ, Viṣṇu
= Karka, circle or Cancer, the sign of Viṣṇu's cakra (e.g. RV 1.1556)

Śrāvaṇa = Śroṇa to Śatabhiṣaj = Viṣṇu, Vasavaḥ, Indra
= Siṃha, Lion, after Indra as in RV 4.16.14

Bhādrapada = Śatabhiṣat to U. Proṣṭhapada = Indra, Aja Ekapāda, Ahirbudhnya
= Kanyā, Virgin, apparently from Aryaman in the opposite side of the zodiac who is the wooer of maidens, kanyā (RV 5.3.2)

Āśvina = U. Proṣṭhapada to Aśvayujau = Ahirbudhnya, Pūṣan, Aśvayujau
= Tulā, Libra, from the Āśvins who denote balance of pairs (e.g. RV 2.39, 5.78, 8.35)

Kārtika = Apabharaṇī to Rohiṇī = Yama, Agni, Prajāpati
= Ali (Vṛścika), Scorpion, from Kṛttika, to cut

Mārgaśīrṣa = Rohiṇī to Ārdrā = Prajāpati, Soma, Rudra
= Dhanuṣ, Archer, from the cosmic archer Rudra (RV 2.33, 5.42, 10.125)

Pauṣa = Ārdrā to Puṣya = Rudra, Aditi, Bṛhaspati
= Makara, Goat, Rudra placing goat-head on Prajāpati, and goat is the main animal sacrified at the ritual of which Bṛhaspati is the priest

Māgha = Puṣya to Maghā = Bṛhaspati, Sarpaḥ, Pitaraḥ
= Kumbha, Water-bearer, from the water-pot offerings to the pitaraḥ.

Phālguna = Phālgunīs to Hastā = Aryaman, Bhaga, Savitar
= Mīna, Fish, representing Bhaga (alluded to in RV 10.68)

Caitra = Hastā to Svātī = Savitar, Indra, Vāyu
= Meṣa, Ram, from Indra, see, e.g., RV 1.51

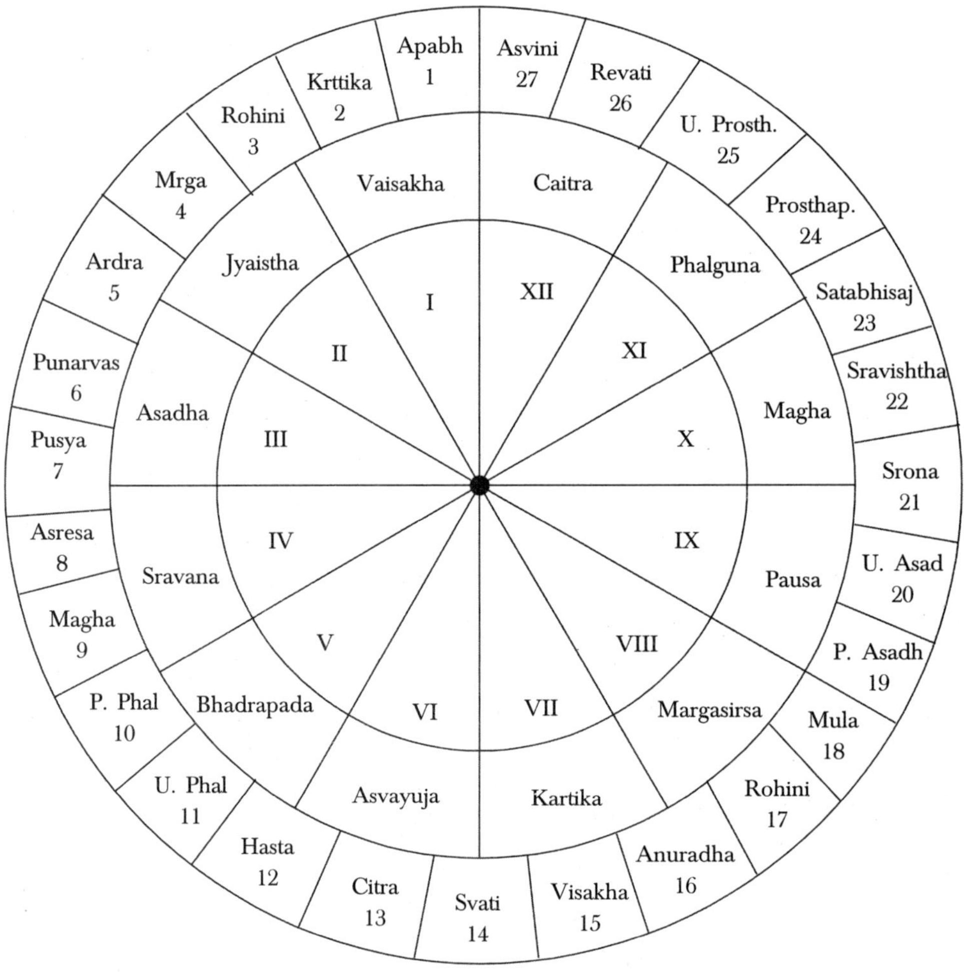

Figure 1
The 27-fold and 12-fold division of the ecliptic.
The first *rāśi* is *Vṛṣa* with the corresponding month of *Vaiśākha*

We observe that for most solar zodiac segments a plausible name emerges from the name of the deity. The choice of the symbols was also governed by another constraint. The Brāhmaṇa texts call the year as the sacrifice and associate different animals with it.[22] In the short sequence, these animals are goat, sheep, bull, horse, and man. Beginning with the goat-dragon at number 9 in the sequence starting with *Vaiśākha,* we have sheep at 12, bull at 1, horse (also another name for the sun in India) as the sun-disk at 3, and man as archer at 8.

IV

INTERCALATION

A system of intercalation of months (*adhikamāsa*) was used to bring the lunar year in synchrony with the solar year over a period of five years.

The use of the intercalary month (*adhikamāsa*) goes back to the *Ṛgveda* itself:

vedamāso dhṛtavrato dvādaśa prajāvataḥ
vedā ya upajāyate (RV 1.25.8)

Dhṛtavrata (*Varuṇa*) knew the twelve productive months; he also knew about the thirteenth additional month.

In the *Atharvaveda* (13.3.8), it is said:

ahorātraivimitaṃ triṃśadaṅgaṃ
trayodaṣaṃ māsaṃ yo nirmimīte (AV 13.3.8)

He who forms the thirteenth month containing thirty days and nights.

The names of the two intercalary months are given as *saṃsarpa* and *aṃhaspati* in the *Taittirīya Saṃhitā* 1.4.14.

There are several other similar references in the Saṃhitā literature to the various intercalary schems that were used to reconcile the lunar and solar years.

The Concept of Yuga

The *Ṛgveda* mentions *yuga* in what is most likely a five-year sense in RV 1.158.6. The names of two of these five years, *saṃvatsara* and *parivatsara* are to be found in RV 7.103.7. The *Vājasaneyi Saṃhitā* (27.45 and 30.16) and the *Taittirīya Saṃhitā* (5.5.7.1-3) give the names of all the five years. These names are: *saṃvatsara, parivatsara, idāvatvara, iduvatsara,* and *vatsara.*

The number five is fundamental to Vedic imagination. Thus there are five-layers of the altar, five breaths within man, five seasons, and five kinds of sacrifices. It was natural then to conceive of a five-year *yuga* as a basic period since larger *yugas* were known.

The use of the five year *yuga* is natural to do a basic synchronization of the lunar and the solar years. Longer periods are required for a more precise synchronization.

Circle of 360°

In *Ṛgveda* 1.164.11, mention is made of the 720 paired sons of the wheel of time which has twelve spokes. These 720 pairs are the 720 days and nights of the civil year. In RV 1.164.48 we are explicitly told of the 360 parts of the wheel of time.

dvādaśa pradhayaś cakram ekaṃ
trīṇi nabhyāni ka utaciketa
tasmin sākaṃ triśatā na śaṅkavo
arpitāḥ ṣaṣṭirna calācalāsaḥ (RV 1.164.48)

Twelve spokes, one wheel, three navels, who can comprehend this? In this there are 360 spokes put in like pegs which do not get loosened.

This means that the ecliptic, which is the wheel of time, is divided into 360 parts. Each of these parts is what is now known as a degree. The three navels appear to be the three different kinds of divisions of it: solar and lunar segments and days.

The division of the circle into four quadrants of 90 degrees each is described in another hymn:

caturbhiḥ sākaṃ navatiṃ ca nāmabhiś cakraṃ na vṛttaṃ vyatiḍr avīvipat (RV 1.155.6)

He, like a rounded wheel, hath in swift motion set his ninety racing steeds together with the four.

The division of the wheel of time into 360 parts occurs elsewhere as well. In *Śatapatha Br.* 10.5.4.4, it is stated that "360 regions encircle the sun on all sides."

The division into half a degree is very easy to identify in the sky. The radial size of the sun or moon is slightly more than this angular size, being exactly 60/113 degrees.[23]

Note, further, that the day is divided into 60 *nāḍikas* in the *Vedāṅga Jyotiṣa.* Since the day is to the year what the degree is to the circle, this means that the degree was further divided into 60 parts.

Various Divisions of the Ecliptic

One may argue that because the original list of 27 *nakṣatras* contains only 24 distinct names, these represent the 24 half months of the year. Later, to incorporate lunar conjunctions, the segments were expanded to describe the motions of the moon.

In the *Ṛgveda* (2.27), six *Ādityas* are listed which appear to be segments corresponding to the six seasons. The names given are: *Mitra, Aryaman, Bhaga, Varuṇa, Dakṣa, Aṃśa.*

This notion is supported by the fact that the ecliptic is also described in terms of the twelve *Ādityas* as in Table 3. In the *Śatapatha Brāhmaṇa* (6.1.2.8), *Prajāpati* is said to have "created the twelve *Ādityas,* and placed them in the sky." In *Śatapatha Br.* (11.6.3.8), it is stated that the *Ādityas* are the twelve months (*dvādaśa māsaḥ*). This means clearly a twelve part division of the circuit of the sun.

The correspondence between the 27-fold division and the 12-fold division of the ecliptic maybe seen in Figure 1.

Further division of the ecliptic is seen in the subdivision of each of the *rāśis* into 2, 3, 4, 7, 9, 10, 12, 16, 20, 24, 27, 30, 40, 45, 45, and 60 parts.

V

NAKṢATRAS AND CHRONOLOGY

The list beginning with *Kṛttikā* at the vernal equinox indicates that it was drawn up in the third millennium B.C. The legend of the decapitation of *Prajāpati* indicates a time when the year began with *Mṛgaśīṛsa* in the fifth millennium B.C. (Table 1). Scholars have also argued that a subsequent list began with *Rohini.* This reasoning is supported by the fact that there are two *Rohinis,* separated by fourteen *nakṣatras,* indicating that the two marked the beginning of the two half-years.

In addition to the chronological implications of the changes in the beginning of the *nakṣatra* lists, there are other references which indicate epochs that bring us down to the Common Era.

The moon rises at the time of sunset on *pūrṇimā,* the full moon day. It rises about 50 minutes later every night and at the end of the *Śivarātri* of the month, about two days before *amāvasyā,* it rises about an hour before sunrise. The crescent moon appears first above the horizon, followed by the rising sun. This looks like the sun as *Śiva* with the crescent moon adorning his head. This is the last appearance of the moon in the month before its reappearance on *śukla dvitīya.* These two days were likely used to determine the day of *amāvasya.*

Mahāśivarātri is the longest night of the year at the winter solstice. At present, this occurs on February 26 ± 15 days (this uncertainty arises from the manner in which the intercalary month operates), and when it was introduced (assuming a calendar similar to the present one), the epoch would have been December 22 ± 15 days. The difference of 66 days gives an epoch of 2600 B.C. ± 1100 years for the establishment of this festival.[24]

The *Kauṣītaki Br.* (19.3) mentions the occurrence of the winter solstice in the new moon of *Māgha* (*māghasyāmāvāsyāyām*). This corresponds to a range of 1800-900 B.C. based on the uncertainty related to the precise identification of the *Maghā nakṣatra* at that time.

The *Śatapatha Brāhmaṇa* (2.1.2.3) has a statement that points to an earlier epoch where it is stated that *Kṛttikā* never swerve from the east. This corresponds to 2950 B.C. The *Maitrayānīya Brāhmaṇa Upaniṣad* (6.14) refers to the winter solstice being at the mid-point of the *Śraviṣṭhā* segment and the summer solstice at the beginning of *Maghā.* This indicates 1660 B.C.

The *Vedāṅga Jyotiṣa* (*Yajur* 6-8) mentions that winter solstice was at the beginning of *Śraviṣṭhā* and the summer solstice at the mid-point of Aśleṣā. This corresponds to about 1350 B.C. if the *nakṣatra* is identified with β Delphini and to 1800 B.C. if it is identified with δ Capricornus, the more correct assignment.[25]

In TS 7.4.8 it is stated that the year begins with the full moon of *Phālgunī.* In the *Vedaṅga Jyotiṣa,* it begins with the full moon in *Maghā,* providing further evidence forming a consistent whole.

The *Śatapatha Brāhmaṇa* story of the marriage between the Seven Sages, the stars of the Ursa Major, and the *Kṛttikās* is elaborated in the Purāṇas where it is stated that the *ṛṣis* remain for a hundred years in each *nakṣatra.*

In other words, during the earliest times in India there existed a centennial calendar with a cycle of 2,700 years. Called the *Saptarṣi* calendar, it is still in use in several parts of India. Its current beginning is taken to be 3076 B.C., but the notices by the Greek historians Pliny and Arrian suggest that, during the Mauryan times, this calendar was taken to begin in 6676 B.C.

VI

BABYLONIAN ASTRONOMY

Our knowledge of Babylonian astronomy comes from three kinds of texts. In the first class are: (i) astronomical omens in the style of *Enūma Anu Enlil* ("when the gods Anu and Enlil") that go back to the second millennium B.C. in a series of 70 tablets; (ii) the two younger *Mul Apin* tablets which is more astronomical; (iii) royal reports on omens from 700 B.C. onwards.

The second class has astronomical diaries with excellent observations over the period 750 B.C. to A.D. 75. The third class has texts from the archives in Babylon and Uruk from the period of the last four or five centuries B.C. which deal with mathematical astronomy.

In late texts the ecliptic is divided into 12 zodiacal signs, each of length precisely 30 degrees. Aaboe has proposed[26] that the replacement of constellations by 30° segments took place in the fifth century B.C.

Babylonian mathematics is sexagesimal, that is, it uses a place-value system of base 60. This is considered one of the characteristic features of the Babylonian mathematical tradition.

The Babylonian year began with or after vernal equinox. The calendar is lunar with a new month beginning on the evening when the crescent of the new moon becomes visible for the first time. A month contains either 29 days (hollow) or 30 days (full). Since 12 lunar months add up to only 354 days, an intercalary month was occasionally introduced. Starting mid-fifth century, the intercalations followed the Metonic cycle where every group of 19 years contained seven years with intercalary months.

In the late texts the ecliptic is divided into 12 zodiacal signs, each of length precisely 30 degrees (*us*). The first list of stars which used the signs of the zodiac is dated to about 410 B.C.

The zodiacal signs have much overlap with the Indian ones, but they appear from nowhere. We cannot, for example, understand the basis of goat-fish, whereas the goat-headed *Prajāpati* is one of the key stories in Vedic lore. These signs do not belong to the same type. They include furrow, hired hand, and star. They could not have served as the model for the Indian zodiacal names or the Greek ones because of their haphazard nature. On the other hand, they could represent memory of an imperfectly communicated Indian tradition which was adapted into the Babylonian system. The Indic kingdoms in West Asia in the second millennium B.C. could have served as the intermediaries in such transmission.

THE ZODIAC SIGNS

Latin	*Babylonian*	*Greek*
Aries	hun, lu (hired hand)	Krios (ram)
Taurus	múl (star)	Tauros (bull)
Gemini	mash, mash-mash (twins)	Didymoi (twins)
Cancer	$alla_x$, kussu (?)	Karkinos (crab)
Leo	a (lion)	Leon (lion)
Virgo	absin (furrow)	Parthenos (virgin)
Libra	rĩn (balance)	Khelai (claws)
Scorpio	gĩr (scorpion)	Skorpios (scorpion)
Sagittarius	pa (name of a god)	Toxotes (archer)
Capricornus	máš (goat-fish)	Aigokeros (goat-horned)
Aquarius	gu (?)	Hydrokhoos (water-pourer)
Pisces	zib, zib-me (tails)	Ikhthyes (fishes)

Table 3

The Babylonians had two systems to place the signs on the ecliptic. In one, the summer solstice was at 8° in *kušu* (and the winter solstice in 8° in *máš*); in another system, the solstices were at 10° of their signs. They measured the moon and the planets from the ecliptic using a measure called *she,* equal to 1/72 of a degree.

They appear to have used two models for the sun's motion. In one, the sun's velocity changes suddenly; in another, it goes through a zig-zag change.

As far as planets are concerned, they calculated the dates of the instants the planet starts and ends its retrogression, the first visible heliacal rising, the last visible heliacal rising, and opposion. They also computed the position of the planet on the ecliptic at these instants. In the planetary theory, the synodic month is divided into 30 parts, which we now call *tithi* from its Indian usage.

In the Babylonian planetary models the concern is to compute the time and place of first stationary points. Two different theories to do this were proposed which have been reconstructed in recent decades.[27]

VII

BABYLONIAN ASTRONOMY AND THE *VEDĀṄGA JYOTIṢA*

The thesis that Babylonian astronomy may have led to Vedic astronomy was summarized in the following manner by David Pingree:[28]

> Babylonian astronomers were capable of devising intercalation-cycles in the seventh, sixth, and fifth centuries B.C., and there is evidence both in the Greek and in the cuneiform sources that they actually did so; and by the early fourth century B.C. they had certainly adopted the quite accurate nineteen-year cycle. It

is my suggestion that some knowledge of these attempts reached India, along with the specific astronomical material in the fifth or fourth century B.C. through Iranian intermediaries, whose influence is probably discernible in the year-length selected by Lagadha for the *Jyotiṣavedāṅga.* But the actual length of the *yuga,* five years, was presumably accepted by Lagadha because of its identity with a Vedic lustrum. Not having access to a series of extensive observations such as were available to the Babylonians, he probably was not completely aware of the crudeness of his system. And the acceptance of this cycle by Indians for a period of six or seven centuries or even more demonstrates among other things that they were not interested in performing the simplest acts of observational astronomy.

The specific items from Babylonian astronomy that Pingree believes were incorporated into the "later" Vedic astronomy are :

1. The ratio of 3:2 for the longest to the shortest day used after 700 B.C.
2. The use of a linear function to determine the length of daylight in intermediate months.
3. The use of the water-clock.
4. The concept of the *tithi* as the thirtieth part of the lunar month.
5. The use of two intercalary months in a period of 5 years.
6. The concept of a five-year *yuga.*

Each of these points has been answered by several historians. In particular, T.S. Kuppanna Śāstry wrote a much-acclaimed text on the *Vedāṅga Jyotiṣa* showing how the supports its dating of around 1300-1200 B.C., and now Achar has argued for its dating to about 1800 B.C. In fact, in his classic *Bhāratīya Jyotiṣa* (1896), S.B. Dīkṣita had already documented the Vedic roots of Vedic astronomy. More recently, Achar[29] has dealt with these questions at length in his paper on the Vedic origin of ancient mathematical astronomy in India.

Length of the Day

The proportion of 3:2 for the longest to the shortest day is correct for north-west India. On the other hand, the Babylonians until 700 B.C. or so used the incorrect proportion of 2:1. It is clear then that the Babylonians for a long time used a parameter which was completely incorrect. They must have, therefore, revised this parameter under the impulse of some outside influence.

In any event, the 3:2 proportion proves nothing because it is correct both for parts of India and Babylon. Its late usage in Babylonia points to the limitations of Babylonian observational astronomy before 700 B.C.

The Use of a Linear Function for Length of Day

The interpolation formula in the *Ṛgjyotiṣa,* verse 7, is:

$$d(x) = 12 + 2x/61$$

where *d is* the duration of day time in *muhūrtas* and *x* is the number of days that have elapsed since the winter solstice.

The use of this equation is natural when one considers the fact that the number of *muhūrtas* required for the winter solstice for the 3:2 proportion to hold is 12. This ensures that the length of day and night will be equal to 15 *muhurtas* each at the equinox.

The *Taittirīya Saṃhitā* 6.5.3.4 speaks clearly of the northern and southern movements of the sun: *ādityaḥṣaṇmāso dakṣiṇenaiti ṣaḍuttareṇa.*

The Brāhmaṇas count days starting from the winter solstice and the period assumed between the two solstices is 183 days. It is natural to adopt the equation given above with these conditions which are part of the old Vedic astronomical tradition. Use of it in either region does not imply borrowing because it is the most obvious function to use.

The Use of the Water Clock

The use of the water-clock occurs in the *Atharvaveda 19.53.3* in the expression:[30]

purṇah kumbho'dhi kalaahitah : A full vessel is placed upon kala (time).

The objective of this mantra is to exhort that "a full vessel be set up with reference to the [measurement of] time."

Since the *Atharvaveda* is prior to the period of Babylonian astronomy by any account, it shows that India used water-clocks. Babylonia may have had its own independent tradition of the use of water-clocks.

The Concept of tithi

The division of year into equal parts of 30 portions is to be found in several places in the Vedas and the subsequent ancillary texts.

In (RV 10.85.5), it is stated that the moon shapes the year. In *Taittirīya Brāhmaṇa* the correct technical sense of *tithi* is given at many places. For example, in 1.5.10, it is said that *candramā vai pañcadaśaḥ eṣa hi pañcadaśyāmapakṣīyate. pañcadaśyāmāpūryate,* "the moon wanes in fifteen, and waxes in fifteen days." In 3.10, the fifteen *tithis* of the waxing moon and fifteen *tithis* of the waning moon are named.

The idea of a *tithi* is abstract. There are only 27 moonrises in a month of 29.5 days. To divide it into 30 parts means that a *tithi* is smaller than a day. The reason it arose in India was due to its connection to *Soma* ritual.

The number 360 is fundamental to Vedic thought. It represents the equivalence between time and the subject. In *Āyurveda,* the number of bones of the developing fetus are taken to be 360.

Since all the six concepts were already in use in the Saṃhitās, in an epoch earlier than 1000 B.C. in the least, they could not have been learnt by the Indians from the Babylonians who came to use these concepts after 700 B.C.

CONCLUSIONS

The debate on the relationship between the *Vedāṅga* astronomy of India and that of Babylon became vitiated by the race and colonial theories of nineteenth century Indologists. Furthermore, their analysis was done using simplistic ideas about cultural interaction. They took knowledge to flow from one direction to another without recognizing that the reality was likely to have been complex and interaction bidirectional. Considering that a time range of several centuries was involved and interaction through intermediaries constituted a complex process, the answer to any question of borrowings and influence can only be complicated.

Our review of Indian astronomy shows that in the period of the early Vedic texts, that are definitely prior to 1000 B.C., the following facts were known:

- Vedic astronomy tracked the motion of the sun and the moon against the backdrop of the *nakṣatras.* The sky was divided into 12 segments (*Ādityas*) and 27 segments (lunar *nakṣatras*) where the *nakṣatra* and deity names were used interchangeably.
- Although the names of the solar zodiacal signs (*rāśis*) are seen first in the Siddhāntic texts, we see they can be derived from the deity names of the lunar *nakṣatra* segments. Given that the *nakṣatra* names are to be found in the Saṃhitās and the *rāśi* names are not in the Vedic books, one may conclude that the specific names were chosen sometime in the first millennium B.C., replacing the earlier *Āditya* names. But the solar signs were a very early component of Vedic astronomy, acknowledged in the *Ṛgvedic* hymn itself which speaks of the twelve division of the 360-part wheel of time.
- Astrology (*Jyotiṣa*) is a part of the earliest Vedic texts. Vedic ritual is associated with the time of the day, the *nakṣatras,* and the position of the moon. The year is divided into the *deva nakṣatras* and *yama nakṣatras* and this division is carried down to smaller scales, implying that certain time durations are more auspicious than others. The meanings of the *nakṣatras* (such as *Anurādhā,* "propitious," and *Punarvasu,* "giving wealth") provide us evidence that they had an astrological basis. Vedic *nakṣatras* are assigned different qualities and in the marriage ritual the astrologer recommended an auspicious time. *Taittirīya Brāhmaṇa* 3.1.4 lists the effects of propitiating the different *nakṣatras.*

  The fundamental notion in Vedic thought is the equivalence or connection *(bandhu)* amongst the *adhidaiva (devas* or stars), *adhibhūta* (beings), and *adhyātma* (spirit). These connections, between the astronomical, the terrestrial, the physiological and the psychological, represent the subtext without which the Vedas cannot be understood. These connections are usually stated in terms of vertical relationships, representing a recursive system; but they are also described horizontally across hierarchies where they represent metaphoric or structural parallels. Most often, the relationship is defined in terms of numbers or other characteristics. An example is the 360 bones of the infant—which later fuse into the *206* bones of the adult—and the 360 days of the year. Likewise, the tripartite division of the cosmos into earth, space, and sky is reflected in the tripartite psychological types.

The *bandhu* are the rationale for astrology. Indeed, they inform us that astrology was central to the world-view of the Indians.

- The use of the *tithi* system, the division of the lunar month into 30 parts, is closely connected to *Soma* worship, a uniquely Indian ritual. There is no such ritual connection with the *tithis* that we know of in the Babylonian context.

The evidence suggests that the Indian ideas of sacrifice, 12 divisions of the solar year, and the 30 divisions of the lunar month, and the zodiac reached Babylonia sometime in the early first millennium B.C. These new ideas, including the Indian ratio of 3:2 for the longest to shortest day of the year, triggered a new phase of careful observations in Babylonia which was to influence astronomy in a fundamental way.

But it is also possible that the Babylonian flowering was quite independent based on the presence of general ideas which were present in the lands across India to Greece. In any event, the borrowing was of the most general ideas, the actual methods were a continuation of local tradition. When we consider the details, we find the astronomical systems of India and Babylon (and also Greece) each have unique features.

Astrology was a part of the ancient world everywhere including Mesopotamia. But it appears that the solar zodiacal signs as we know them originated in India, where they have a relationship with the deities of the *naksatras.* They seem to have been later adopted in Babylonia in the middle of the first millennium B.C. and subsequently in Greece. But this does not mean that the practice of Vedic astrology was adopted by the Babylonians.

Subsequent to the establishment of the Indo-Greek states on the borders of India after Alexander, the interaction between Indian and Western astrology and astronomy entered a new phase. Increased political and trade interaction made it possible for texts to be exchanged.

NOTES

1. Kak, S. 2003. *Akhenaten, Surya and the Ṛgveda.* Louisiana State University. http://www.ece.lsu.edu/kak/akhena.pdf
2. Burrow, T. 1973. "The Proto-Indoaryans". *Journal of Royal Asiatic Society,* vol. 2. pp. 123-140. Burrow's ideas of proto-Indoaryans is not supported by current evidence.
3. Sen, S.N. 1985. "Surveys of Studies in European languages". *Indian Journal of History of Science,* vol. 20. pp. 49-121.
4. Leach, E. 1990. "Aryan Invasions over Four Millennia". *Culture Through Time, Anthropological Approaches.* E. Ohnuki-Tierney (ed.). Stanford. pp. 227-245. In this Leach, a distinguished anthropologist, suggests that racism was behind the idea of the Aryan invasion theory:

   Why do serious scholars persist in believing in the Aryan invasions? Why is this sort of thing attractive? Who finds it attractive? Why has the development of early Sanskrit come to be so dogmatically associated with an Aryan invasion?

   Where the Indo-European philologists are concerned, the invasion argument is tied in with their assumption that if a particular language is identified as having been used in a particular locality at a particular time, no attention need be paid to what was there before; the slate is wiped clean. Obviously, the easiest way to imagine this happening in real life is to have a military conquest that obliterates the previously existing population!

   The details of the theory fit in with this racist framework... Because of their commitment to a unilineal segmentary history of language development that needed to be mapped onto the ground, the philologists took it for granted that proto-Indo-Iranian was a language that had originated outside either India or Iran. Hence it followed that the text of the Rig Veda was in a language that was actually spoken by those who introduced this earliest form of Sanskrit into India. From this we derived the myth of the Aryan invasions. QED.

Leach's cry is in the face of the stubborn manner in which some scholars have persisted with the invasion model although it flies against archaeological, skeletal, and cultural evidence.

Shaffer, J. and Lichtenstein, D.L. 1995. "The Concept of Cultural Tradition and Paleoethnicity in South Asian Archaeology". *The Indo-Aryans of South Asia. G.* Erdosy (ed.). Berlin: Walter de Gruyter. For an overview of this general evidence see, Feurstein, G., Kak, S. and Fraley, D. 2001. *In Search of the Cradle of Civilization.* Wheaton: Quest Books. Kak, S. 2001; *The Wishing Tree.* New Delhi: Munshiram Manoharlal.

5. Pingree, D. 1981. "History of Mathematical Astronomy in India". *Dictionary of Scientific Biography.* C.S. Gillespie (ed.). New York: Charles Scribner's Sons. pp. 533-633. For a critique of such approach to India see, Dirks, N. 2001. *Castes of Mind.* Princeton: Princeton University Press. Say Dirks: "Orientalist generalizations to articulate the justifications for permanent colonial rule ... (using) the racialized language systems and conceits of late nineteenth century imperial world systems" led to a major revision in the western narratives on Indian science and society. He adds: "Colonialism was made possible, and then sustained and strengthened, as much by cultural technologies of rule as it was by the more obvious and brutal modes of conquest... Colonialism was itself a cultural project of control. Colonial knowledge both enabled conquest and was produced by it; in certain important ways, knowledge was what colonialism was all about."
6. Pingree suggests indirectly *(op cit)* that the *Ṛgvedic* hymns with the 360 divisions of the year must be dated around 500 B.C. because this knowledge arose in Babylonia! Elsewhere, Pingree in his "Astronomy in India" (Walker, C. 1996. *Astronomy before the Telescope.* New York: St. Martin's Press. p. 124.) suggests that the number 360 came from the Babylonian text *mul.apin* which in its present form is supposed to be no earlier than 1000 B.C. Pingree's suggestions that Indian text are a mass of undifferentiable material is incorrect. There is much material in the Indian textual tradition that has had no interpolations, such as Pāṇini's grammar and the *sūktas* of the Saṃhitās and other Vedic texts.
7. Burgess, E. (trans.). 1989 (1860). *The Sūrya Siddhānta.* Delhi: Motilal Banarasidass. For knowledge of planets in India in the third millennium B.C.
8. Kak, S. 1996. "Knowledge of the Planets in the Third Millennium B.C.". *Quarterly Journal of Royal Astronomical Society, vol.* 37, 709-715.
9. Pingree, D. 1973. "The Mesopotamian Origin of Early Indian Mathematical Astronomy", *Journal of History of Astronomy, vol.* 4, 1-12; Pingree, D. 1976. "The Recovery of Early Greek Astronomy from *India". Journal of History of Astronomy,* vol. 7, 109-123.
10. Pingree. *Dictionary of Scientific Biography.* This goes against linguistic, historical, and geographical evidence in the Vedic texts and would be rejected by any scholar of Indian literature. For details of the chronology of Indian texts, see Winternitz, M. 1972 (1927). *History of Indian Literature.* New Delhi: Orient Books. Winternitz believes that the beginning of the texts could not be pushed later than 2500 B.C. (see page 310 of volume 1).
11. Dīkṣita, S.B. 1963 (1896). *Bhāratīya Jyotiśśāstra.* Lucknow: Hindi Samiti.
12. Pingree, D. 1973. "Astronomy an Astrology in India and Iran". *Isis,* vol. 54. 229-246.
13. Pingree, D. "The Mesopotamian Origin of Early Indian Mathematical Astronomy". p. 10.
14. See for example, Achar, N. 1998. "On the Vedic Origin of the Ancient Mathematical Astronomy of India". *Journal of Studies on Ancient India,* vol. 1, 95-108.
15. Billard, Roger. 1971. *L'astronomie Indienne.* Paris: Publications de L'ecole Francaise d'extreme Orient.
16. Van der Waerden, B.L. 1980. "Two Treatise on Indian Astronomy". *Journal of History of Astronomy,* vol. 11, 50-58.
17. Kak, S. 2000. *The Astronomical Code of the Ṛgveda.* New Delhi: Munshiram Manoharlal; Kak, S. 2000. "Birth and Early Development of Indian Astronomy". *Astronomy Across Cultures: The History of Non-Western Astronomy.* H. Stein (ed.). Dordrecht: Kluwer Academic Publishers. pp. 303-340.
18. Neugenbauer, O. 1975. *A History of Ancient Mathematical Astronomy.* New York: Springer-Verlag. Aaboe, A. 2001. *Episodes from the Early History of Astronomy.* New York: Springer.
19. Pande, G.C. (ed.). 2000. *The Dawn of Indian Civilization.* New Delhi: Centre for Studies in Civilization.
20. Achar, N. 2000. "On the Identification of the Vedic nakṣatras". *Contemporary Views on Indian Civilization.* Bhudev Sharma (ed.). Proceedings of the WAVES conference, held in Hoboken, NJ. pp. 209-229.
21. Achar, N. 2000. "In search for nakṣatras in Ṛgveda". *Contemporary Views on Indian Civilization. Pp.* 200-208.

22. Kak, S. 2002. *The Aśvamedha: The Rite and its Logic.* Delhi: Motilal Banarasidass.
23. Kak. *The Astronomical Code of the Ṛgveda*
24. Abhyankar, K. D. 1988. "Uttarāyaṇa". *Scientific Heritage of India.* B. V. Subbarayappa and S.R.N. Murthy (ed.). Bangalore: The Mythic Society.
25. Kuppanna Sastry, T. S. 1985. *Vedāṅga Jyotiṣa of Lagadha.* New Delhi: Indian National Science Academy. the 1980 BC date for it is argued in Achar, N. 2000. "A Case for Revising the Date of Vedāṅga Jyotiṣa of Lagadha. *Indian Journal of History of Science, vol.* 35. pp. 173-183.
26. Aaboe. op. cit.
27. O. Neugebauer, op. cit.
28. Pingree. p. 9.
29. Achar.
30. Ibid.

ACKNOWLEDGEMENT

I am grateful to Narahari Achar and David Frawley for their advice and criticism.

CHAPTER 29

Some Aspects of Scientific Inquiry in Indian Tradition: Vijñāna, Pramāṇa and Vaiśeṣika

C. Ramanathan

Science as the empirical region of philosophy was conceived long ago in Indian tradition although science *per se* in the modern sense based on truth derived from experimentation hardly had any place in it. It is therefore difficult to find an equivalent for science in Sanskrit. Generally, the word *śāstra* is used to indicate science in a broader sense and there is, in the modern days, a tendency to use the word *vijñāna* in the sense of science. Almost all the works related to science are called Śāstra such as *vyākaraṇa śāstra, nāṭya śāstra, arthaśāstra, gajaśāstra and rasaśāstra.* Śāstra has an inherent sense of rule.[1] Significantly though they are included under *darśanas* quite often Nyāya and Vaiśeṣika are also called *śāstras*, besides Sāṁkhya and Yoga. The *Bhagavadgītā* is called *yoga-śāstra* which can be interpreted as "science of yoga.' Strangely, *Sarvadarśanasaṅgraha* includes even the *Rāmāyaṇa* and the *Mahābhārata* as *śāstras* although they are known as *kāvya* and *itihāsa* respectively. Nāgārjuna, the great exponent of Vijñānavāda understands the word *śāstra* as that which removes all enemies such as misery and saves one from bondage and rebirth. As an idealist Nāgārjuna interpreted the word conforming to the theory of Vijñānavāda which upholds the passage of intellect into spiritual experience. Thus the sense of *śāstra* appears to have acquired baffling proportions of meanings instead of limiting itself to science. It should be noted that the *śāstra* literature grew along with the theological literature of the Purāṇas and aesthetic literature of the Kāvyas. Medical works like *Carakasaṃhitā* and *Suśrutasaṃhitā* or astronomical works like *Āryabhaṭīya, Sūryasiddhānta, Līlāvatī* were, somehow, not referred to as Śāstras.

It is difficult to judge, in the absence of clear evidence, whether scientific inquiry existed during the Vedic days. All that one can say is that there was a remarkable curiosity to know nature which fascinated the primitive man. The mysticism of Vedic *ṛṣis*, however, yielded place to inquisitiveness during the *sūtra* period later on which is reflected in the theories of acquisition of knowledge through the *pramāṇas.* To the Vedic seers the whole creation was a mystery as a result of which some cosmoganic hymns emerged in the *Ṛgveda*, perhaps at a later date of its composition. The *Nāsadīya sūkta* relegates the gods to the second stage of creation. For the intutive vision of the seer some truths appeared in the passing. The seer of *Nāsadīya sūkta* imagines of a mysterious darkness which had enveloped all over before creation[2] which is comparable to the modern theory of "black hole' encompasing the whole universe.

As such cosmogonic problems have puzzled ancient Indian thinkers they puzzled many thinkers of the West also in the past. "One may consider problems of this kind;'

wrote Williams B. Drees, "What was god doing before he created the world? Rather than answering the question, the theologian Augustine of Hippo (400 A.D.) replied that the question is wrongly posed, as time is created together with material reality, rather than an uncreated universal background."[3]

Mysticism apart, investigation of useful things in life such as medicine yielded results. The *Atharvavedic* seers made experiments with some herbs and roots of medicinal value which opened up new horizons of medical knowledge.

As in Greece where debating on controversial subjects was held, debating was held in ancient India also. During the *Mahābhārata* period dialectics was one of the important tools to arrive at truth. Technical terms such as *Jalpa* (argument for victory) and *Vitaṇḍā* (destructive argument) are found in the *Mahābhārata*. This technique seems to have developed in Nyāyaśāstra further into several categories of which *tarka* is important. In fact, *tarka* became so important that *Tarkaśāstra* was eqated with Nyāya system itself. In other words, hypothetical reasoning or *tarka* gave a distinct identity to Nyāya among the schools of Indian Philosophy. But this technique of "ascertaining the real character of a thing unknown' (*avijñātatattvārtha*) by reasoning did not enter into the domain of scientific reasoning.

Despite the absence of scientific reasoning scientific theories based on observation and logical thinking were in circulation in Indian tradition as evidenced in Nyāya-Vaiśeṣika works. The following two illustrations give us a glimpse of scientific theories evolved out of observation. Vācaspati Miśra (nineth centurry A.D.) quotes, while refuting a Sāṁkhyan theory, an astronomical phenomena referred to by the Sāṁkhyans. This analogy must have been adopted by the Sāṁkhya school very early as it is the oldest school in Indian philosophy. The analogy is, "the moon which has no light of its own shines while the light of the sun falls on it; even so, *caitanya* gives light to the intellect, *buddhi,* and illuminates the object also."[4] As another instance, Udayana's remarks in *Kiraṇāvalī* that the movement of darkness as an optic illusion is noteworthy. He says, "Darkness appears wherever there is absence of light and one gets the illusion that it is moving."[5]

Vijñāna

The word *Vijñāna* is extensively used for denoting various meanings in Indian tradition including *Yoga* and *Tantra.* Amarakośa gives the meaning of *Vijñāna* as *Śāstra* (Science) and *Śilpa* (art).[6] But the primitive concept of *Vij ñāna* can be seen in the Upaniṣads and Buddhism which represent metaphysical idealism and subjective idealism respectively. The former therefore has a spiritual dimension while the latter, conceptual. We find in these a complete absence of or elimination of scientic thinking. In other words, there is incommensurability with scientific thinking as a metaphysical ideal cannot be analyzed as impressions of physical world and no experiment can prove it. As an Indian tradition which transcended scientific examination it represents "philosophical consciousness.' A brief examination of *Vijñāna* of the Upaniṣads and Vijñānavādins shows how, in Indian tradition, any scientific approach had no access to it.

Muṇḍakopaniṣad divides knowledge broadly into two categories, viz. *Parāvidyā* and *aparāvidyā i.e.* spiritual knowledge and non-spiritual knowledge. What is studied under scriptures and allied subjects is also included in non-spiritual knowledge indicating the superiority of the former over the latter. *Jñāna,* in general, is ordinary knowledge in the empirical sense equivalent to *buddhi* or intellect, whereas *Vijñāna* is used in the non-empirical sense. In some passages the Upaniṣads give the exalted place of *Brahman* himself to *Vijñāna.*[7] This corresponds to absolute philosophical consciousness or a state of self-realisation. *Vijñāna* is also called *Puruṣa.*[8] The cosmic *Puruṣa* of the *Ṛgveda* became *Puruṣa* who symbolised the life principle in man in the Upaniṣads. The word '*aupaniṣadapuruṣa*' is used in order to distinguish Vedic *Puruṣa* from the Upaniṣadic *Puruṣa. Vijñāna* is also associated with *Ātman* which is called '*Vijñānamaya,*' "bestowed with bliss.'[9] Śaṁkara quite often interprets the word *Vijñāna* as *buddhi* or intellect in the empirical sense as it is reflected in the *Tattirīyopaniṣad* and *Kaṭhopaniṣad.*[10] Śaṁkara explains '*Vijñāna*' specifically as 'inward experience as a consequence of spiritual knowledge'[11] which is the culmination of man's spiritual quest in contrast to *jñāna* which is empirical knowledge.

Vijñānavāda which believed in pure consciousness alone as reality again considered that the phenomenal world is momentary. '*Vijñāna* is unmanifest, infinite and liminous' according to a Pāli definition.[12] *Vijñānavāda* and Upaniṣadic *Vijñāna* have many things in common and it is believed, therefore that the Buddhist *Vijñāna* has its roots in the Upaniṣadic *Vijñāna.*[13] '*Vijñānavāda,*' argues Chandradhara Sharma, "cannot be considered subjectivism.... when the external world is declared to be unreal what is meant is that it does not exist independently outside consciousness.[14] *Vijñāna* can be absolute consciousness (*ālayavijñāna*) and individual consciousness (*pravṛtti-vijñāna*). "*Vijñāna* was not regarded," writes G.C. Pandey, "simply as a particular and transient phenomenon, but also as the original and pure consciousness which would be eternal and infinite on liberation. It is the empirical finite *Vijñāna* that is impermanent, not the original or ultimate condition."[15]

This duality of *Vijñāna* as seen in the Upaniṣads and Buddhism has an underlying idealism which represents "philosophical consciousness' and transcends the regions of science. *Vijñāna,* as we have seen, is basically a metaphysical concept and its post-Upaniṣadic ramifications show empirical dimensions. Later writers who adopted scientific approach to learning included subjects as music and business also under *Vijñāna.* But scientific knowledge had no access to the metaphysical regions of philosophical consciousness during the early period of Indian tradition as far as Upaniṣads and Buddhism are concerned.

Pramāṇa

While *Vijñāna* represents the metaphysical aspect of early Indian tradition *pramāṇa* represents the psychological aspect of post-Upaniṣadic Indian tradition. Two important schools emerged during the *sūtra* period (approx. second century B.C.); one went about examining the knowledge of the external world called '*pramāṇamīmāṃsā* and the other analysed all the objects of valid knowledge '*Padārthamīmāṃsā.*' The *pramāṇa* theory of knowledge engaged the attention of Indian thinkers for several centuries, a linkage which was sustained for at least fifteen centuries. When Nyāya and Vaiśeṣika theories got merged and the syncretic school evolved out of the two schools they became complementary to each other.

The advent of the *pramāṇa* concept opened new areas of definition of acquisition of knowledge. The perception of the physical world became the focal point of discussion among the schools before they formulated their doctrines. The whole contention of *pramāṇa* is that the physical world cannot be known without the aid of the *pramāṇa,* means of valid knowledge. The Nyāya system became the champion of *pramāṇa* theory that it came to be called as *Pramāṇaśāstra.* Vātsyāyana, the commentator on Gotama's *sūtras* succinctly declares, "Nyāya is an examination of objects through the means of *pramāṇa.*"[16] *Pramāṇa* could be a source of knowledge psychologically or logically and Nyāya was called *Ānvikṣikī,* a science in which valid cognition of objects was focused. "It is the science of an analytic and reflective knowledge of objects, subsequent to a less reflective and less analytical knowledge, in which the subject of knowledge is more receptive than critical."[17] It maybe relevant here to refer to what Einstein said on sense perception; "Sense perception," he said, "only gives information of this external world or physical reality indirectly and therefore we can only grasp the latter by speculative means."[18] However, Gangeśa Upadhyāya (eleventh century A.D.) who gave a new direction to Nyāya, defines right knowledge as, "True knowledge is that which informs us the existence of something in a place where it really exists, or which predicates of something a character really possessed by it.'[19]

Pratyakṣa, direct perception, is defined by Vātsyāyana as, perception consists in the functioning or action of the sense organ upon a particular object.'[20] This cognition results in the mental attitude of the person who accepts the object of perception or rejects it or is indifferent to it. This is called '*Pravṛttisāmarthya*'. The Nyāya system set out to analyse *pramāṇa* theory which had originated earlier as a product of synthesis by earlier philosophers. The search for truth of knowledge which perhaps emerged with the advent of Nyāya system became one of the focal points of discussion among many schools of philosophy, including Jainism and Buddhism, for many centuries. This intellectual exercise in Indian tradition on the theory of knowledge reflects a constant scientific search for truth about the external world and examination of right knowledge mainly at the psychological level.

Vaiśeṣikas

Besides the metaphysical and psychological realms of Indian thought there was a breakthrough in the scientific inquiry, albeit arbitrary, of the physical world by the Vaiśeṣika school. The Upaniṣads concept of name and form[21] *(nāma-rūpa)* attributed to the physical world became the focal point of study in the Vaiśeṣika in the perspective of its actual existence independent of consciousness. Vaiśeṣika calls all the objects of valid knowledge as categories of the physical world *(Padārtha)* which have the characteristics of existence, nameability and knowability.[22] The analysis of all the objects of knowledge was a daring exercise of Vaiśeṣika which aroused disputations of its theories by the exponents of other schools like Śaṁkara's *Advaita.* The most significant premise of Vaiśeṣika is the cognition of particularity of the elements which lies in the indivisible atom of the element which is also indestructible. This conception of atom was a clear product of scientific knowledge of an element in Kaṇāda's genius.

Kaṇāda (200 B.C.) declares that the distinction between the particular and the common lies in ones own discretionary power *(buddhi)*.[23] In other words, the physical features of the external world are recognised by the thinking mind and they are not conceptual constructs.

Another striking scientific knowledge reflected in the Vaiśeṣika is its recognition of motion in the objects in five kinds. According to the Vaiśeṣika physical motion is temporary and dynamic whereas quality is static and enduring. The five kinds of motion viz. upward motion *(utkṣepaṇa)*, downward motion *(avakṣepaṇa)*, contraction *(ākuñcana)*, expansion *(prasāraṇa)* and movement *(gamana)*, represent an attempt at scientific explanation of motion in general. That the quality such as colour of the object is inseparable as motion is in the object is also noteworthy. The division in Vaiśeṣika of the categories as entities and non-entitites also needs attention. They called *sattāsambandha* and *svātmasambandha* respectively. The substance, quality and action are related to being-hood whereas commonality, particularity and inherence are related to themselves. While the former lie in time and space the latter do not.[24]

Tendency *(Saṁskāra)* is stated to be of three kinds, viz. speed (*vega*), reminiscent impressions *(bhāvanā)* and elasticity *(sthitisthāpakatva)*. Of these speed and elasticity are properties only of corporeal objects.

Qualities such as weight or gravity (*gurutva*) and viscidity (*dravatva*) belong to the realm of science. The theory called '*Pīlupākavāda* where the chemical action on the atoms is conceived when an object is heated is a perfect scientific theory. But of all the scientific thoughts perhaps the atomic theory is the most impressive. As Mṛnalakanti Gangopadhyāya writes in his *Indian Atomism*, "With their serious methodology, invincible logic and strong common sense they (Nyāya-Vaiśeṣika) are best fitted to follow a scientific line of thought without any bias or hindrance."[25]

The treatment of the physical world by Vaiśeṣika reveals an undercurrent of scientific thought but conclusions are made conforming to contemporary concepts in such matters as evolution where divine will is mentioned. As a *darśana* it dispensed with formulation of scientific theories and its followers also dwelt on the limited areas of its postulates than exploiting them for independent scientific thought through the ages. Nevertheless, Vaiśeṣika attempts at an examination of the physical world and it is, as Radhakrishnan puts it, "more scientific than speculative, more analytic than synthetic.[26]"

It is believed that theism got into the system during the time of the Praśastapāda, the famous commentator on Vaiśeṣika sūtra (fifth century A.D.) but it did not dampen the scientific spirit of the system and remained in the persuit of knowledge of empirical world. "Science liberated from all exemplarism" said Descartes, "is indeed the work of man. But in the statement of its laws it cannot dispense with god."[27]

CONCLUSION

Although Vaiśeṣika is included among the *ṣaḍdarśanas* it bears characteristics of a scientific school. It maybe relevant to quote here what John Wisdom said, "Philosophic knowledge does not consist in acquiring knowledge of new facts but in acquiring new knowledge of facts, a passage via introspection from poor insight to good insight."[28]

There was no apparent conflict among the theories of *Vijñāna*, *Pramāṇa* and *Vaiśeṣika* as each of them set its own paradigms for speculation and as integral parts of Indian thought they became subjects of discussion for centuries in the history of Indian thought.

NOTES

1. शिष्यते अनेन इति शास्त्रम्।
   शास् with the suffix ष्ट्रन्.
2. तम आसीत्तमसा गूळमग्रे अप्रकेतम्। R.v. 1.129.3
3. William, Dress B. *Problems in Debates about Physics and Religion.* p. 199
4. तदिदं बुद्धितत्त्वं जडीकृततया इन्दुमण्डलमिव स्वयमप्रकाशं चैतन्यमार्तण्डलचछायापत्त्या प्रकाशते, प्रकाशयति च। Ṭīkā on Nyāya Sūtra.1.1.16
5. आवरकद्रव्ये गच्छति यत्र यत्र तेजसोऽसन्निधिः तत्र तत्र च्छायाग्रहणादन्यदेशतानिबन्धनो गतिभ्रम इव। Kiraṇāvalī (on number od dravyas).
6. विज्ञानं शिल्पशास्त्रयोः । Amarakośa 1.3.5
7. विज्ञानं आनन्दं ब्रह्म । BṛUp. 3.9.28
   विज्ञानं सर्वे देवा ब्रह्म ज्येष्ठमुपासते । Tai.Up. 2.1.5
8. मन्ता बोद्धा विज्ञानात्मा पुरुषः। Praśna Up. 4.9
   एष विज्ञानमयः पुरुष। Br.Up.2.1.17
9. स वा एष महानज आत्मा योऽयं विज्ञानमयः। Br.Up. 4.4.22
   कतम आत्मेति योऽयं विज्ञानमयः। Br.Up.4.3.7
10. विज्ञानसारथिस्तु मनः प्रग्रहवान् नरः। Kaṭhā.Up.4.3.7
    एवं विज्ञानमयमात्मानमुपसङ्क्रम्य एतमानन्दमयमात्मानं। Tai.Up.3.10
11. विज्ञायतेऽनेन कारणभूतं बुद्ध्यादि। Śaṅkara on Praśna 4.9
    ज्ञानं शास्त्रतः आचार्यतश्च आत्मादीनामवबोधः विज्ञानं विशेषतः तदनुभवः । Śaṁkara on B.G., 9.1
12. विज्ञानं आनिदर्शनं अनन्तं सर्वतोप्रभम् । (Sanskrit rendering of the Pāli sentence).
13. Pande, G.C. *Studies in Mahāyāna*, p. 102
14. Sharma, Chandradhara. *A Critical Survey of Indian Philosophy*. p. 122
15. Pande. p. 103
16. प्रमाणैरर्थपरीक्षणं न्यायः। Nyāyabhāṣya (introductory)
17. प्रत्यक्षागमैरीक्षितस्य अन्वीक्षणं अन्वीक्षा। तथा प्रवर्तते इति। Nyāyabhāṣya (introductory) interpreted by Chatterji S.C. in his article 'The Nyāya doctrine of Pramāṇa.' p. 2
18. Einstein, A. *The World As We See It.* p. 60
19. यत्र यदस्ति तत्र तस्य अनुभवः प्रमा। तद्वति तत्प्रकारकानुभवो वा।
    (Tr.) Datta D.M. : *The Six ways of Knowing.* p. 20
20. अक्षस्य अक्षस्य प्रतिविषयं वृत्तिः प्रत्यक्षम्। Nyāyabhāṣya
21. तद्धेदं तर्ह्यव्याकृतमासीत्तन्नामरूपाभ्यामेव व्याक्तियतासौ। Bṛ.Up. 1.4.7
22. षण्णामपि पदार्थानां अस्तित्त्वं अभिधेयत्वं ज्ञेयत्वम्। Praśastapādabhāṣya
23. सामान्यविशेषमिति बुद्ध्यपेक्षम्। Vai.Sū.1.2.3
24. द्रव्यादीनां त्रयाणां सत्तासम्बन्धः। सामान्यादीनां त्रयाणामपि स्वात्मसत्त्वम्। Praśastap:adabhāṣya
25. Gangopādhyāya, Mrinalakanti. *Indian Atomism.* p. 54
26. Radhakrishnan, S. Indian Philosophy, vol. 2. p. 276
27. Rodis Genevieve, Lewis *From Metaphysics to Physics.* p. 243
28. Wilson. John. *Ethics and Science.* p. 354

BIBLIOGRAPHY

Primary Sources

1. *Bṛhadāraṇyakopaniṣad.* 1974. Gorakhpur: Gīta Press.
2. *Kaṭhopaniṣad.* 1959. Gorakhpur: Gīta Press.
3. *Kiraṇārati.* 1991. R.T. Vyas (ed.). Vadodara: Oriental Institute.
4. *Muṇḍakapaniṣad.* 1959. Gorakhpur: Gīta Press.
5. *Nyāyabhāṣyam.* 1986. Swami Davarakidas Sastri. Varanasi: Sudha Prakashana.
6. *Nyāyavārtikatātparyaṭīkā.* 1989. Rajeshwara Sastri Dravid. Varanasi: Chowkhamba Sanskrit Samsthan.
7. *Praśnopaniṣad.* 1959. Gorakhpur: Gīta Press.
8. *Taittirīyopaniṣad.* 1959. Gorakhpur: Gīta Press.

Secondary Sources

1. Cohen, Robert S. 1987. "Ethics and Science". *Science and Quest for Reality.* Alfred I. Tauber. London: Macmillan.
2. Datta, D.M. 1922. *Six Way of Knowing.* London: George Allen & Unwin.
3. Drees, Willen B. *Problems in Debates about Physics and Religion.* pp. 188-223
4. Gangopadhyay, Mrinalakanti. 1980. *Indian Atomism.* Calcutta: K.P. Bagchi & Co.
5. Griffith, R.T.H. 1926. *The Hymns of the Ṛgveda.* Benaras: Lazerus & Co.
6. Pande, G.C. 1993. *Studies in Mahāyāna.* Saranath, Varanasi: Central Institute of Higher Tibetan Studies.
7. Pitte, P. Van De. "From Metaphysics to Physics". Trans. of Genevrive Rodis Lewis article. *Cartesian Science.* pp. 242-258
8. Radhakrishnan, S. 1948. *Indian Philosophy,* vols. 1 & 2. London: George Allen & Unwin.
9. Sharma, Chandradhara. 1979. *A Critical Survey of Indian Philosophy.* Delhi: Motilal Benarasidass.
10. Whiteman, Michael. 1966. *Philosophy of Space and Time.* London: George Allen & Unwin.

CHAPTER 30

Tāntric Theory of Consciousness: A Phenomenological and Critical Study

Kamalakar Mishra

A BRIEF SYNOPSIS

1. Introduction

The background of the Phenomenological approach in the West; the Upaniṣadic and the Tāntric traditions of consciousness-philosophy; Advaita-Vedānta and Kashmir Śaivism; a brief history of Tāntrism-Kashmir Śaivism with special reference to the theory of consciousness.

2. 'Spanda' (Spontaneity) as the Nature of Consciousness

Spanda as free and effortless activity of consciousness; difference of '*Kriyā*' (*Spanda* or *Vimarśa*—spontaneous activity) from '*Karma*' (voluntary and ethical action); difference from the Advaita-Vadāntic position; an analysis of the exampels of *Spanda* given in actual experience; the impurities that obstruct the full expression of pure *Spanda*; logical possibility of the state of consciousness with cent per cent pure *Spanda*.

3. 'Jñāna' (Knowledge) as 'Kriyā' (Activity)

The Advaita-Vedāntic theory: knowledge as a passive state of consciousness, the analogy of the reflection of the moon in the pond, inadequacy of the analogy; the Tāntric theory : knowledge as positive and active 'grasping' or 'catching' of the object; compatibility of *Jñāna* with *Kriyā* (Answer to the Advaita-Vedāntic objection); unity of '*Prakāśa*' (Illumination) with '*Vimarśa*' (spontaneous ideation); the meaning of the symbol of *Ardhanārīśvara* in this context; the epistemological meaning of the theory of '*Śiva-Śakti-Sāmarasya*' (the unity of *Śiva-Śakti*).

4. The Problem of Self-Consciousness (Ahaṁ-Vimarśa) in Pure Consciousness

Awareness of the not-self as the Advaita-Vedāntic logic of self-consciousness; '*Kriyā*' as the Tāntric logic of self-consciousness; logical possibility of '*Ahaṁ-vimarśa*' (self-consciousness) in the pure non-dual consciousness, answer to the Advaita-Vedāntic objection; self-consciousness as the natural *Spanda* of consciousness; the Tāntric criticism of the Advaitic position that consciousness is devoid of self-consciousness; consciousness as person; logical possibility of the 'cosmic person'.

5. *The Concept of Svayaṁprakāśa (Self-Illumination of Consciousness)*

Consciousness (self) is self-illuminated (*Svayaṁ-prakāśa*); knowledge too is self-illuminated; *Svayaṁ-prakāśa* (self-illumiantion) and *Ahaṁ-vimarśa* (self-consciousness); comparison and contrast with the Advaita-Vedāntic position; consciousness as the '*Ādi-siddha*' (self-proved as prior to every mental activity).

6. *The Question of the Intentionality of Consciousness*

Consciousness and '*Idaṁ-vimarśa*' (object-consciousness); object as *Pratibimba* (reflection) in consciousness; possibility of contentless consciousness (pure *Ahaṁ-vimará* without *idaṁ-vimarśa*); difference of the Indian position from the western Phenomenology in this regard; the phenomenon of the yogic experience of '*Nirvikalpa*' (contentless) consciousness, the analogy of the stage-light given by Swami Vidyāraṇya; '*Ahantā*' (consciousness-in-itself) and '*Idantā*' (consciousness-in-the object); the symbols of '*Śāmbhavi-mudrā*' (interiorised consciousness) and '*Naṭarāja-mudrā*' (exteriorised consciousness).

7. *The Pratibhā Theory (Knowledge and Talent as Spontaneous Spark or Flash of Consciousness)*

The '*Prātibha-jñāna*' (knowledge as spontaneous illumination from within consciousness); *Pratibhā* as talent or genius; talent (*Pratibhā*) as spontaneous spark or flash from within consciousness; examples of the spark of *Pratibhā* in the given experience of the practical life; cognitive *Pratibhā* and creative *Pratibhā*; *Pratibhā* or *Pratibhā-śakti*; the spiritual practices for the removal of the obstruction and attainment of the *Pratibhā-śakti.*

8. *The Aesthetic Element in Consciousness ('Rasa')*

Ānanda (joy) as the nature of consciousness; '*Rasa*' as the flow of *Ānanda*; the *Rasa*-theory of Bharata as explained by Abhinavagupta; *Śānta-Rasa* as the underlying unity of all the *Rasas;* the *Ānanda* derived from the object is the *Ānanda* of consciousness and the way of their removal.

9. The Moral and Spiritual Element in Consciousness

Factors of moral consciousness; factors of spiritual consciousness; moral goodness and spiritual goodness; spiritual state of consciousness as the state of natural and spontaneous morality. Examples of the lives of saints and sages; Goodness as the inherent nature of consciousness, and evil as the alien adoptation; animal consciousness and human consciousness; the phenomenology of the development of moral and spiritual consciousness among human beings (the concept of "*Saptapramātā*"—Seven hierarchical stages of the development of consciousness).

10. The Element of Desire (Kāma) in Consciousness

Kāma as the natural and spontaneous expression of the *Ānanda* of consciousness; different forms and levels of the manifestation of '*Kama*' *Kāma* as power (*Śakti*); the phenomenon of the transformation of *Kāma* from the gross to the refined level; ways of the sublimation and spiritualisation of *Kāma*; sublimation of *Kāma* into love, aesthetic experience and artistic creativity.

11. The Element of "Loka-Maṅgala" (Social Good) in Consciousness

The selfish and the altruistic elements in consciousness; selfishness as the surface nature and altruism as the deeper nature of consciousness; the feeling of unity with others (*Sarvātma-bhāva*); '*Loka-hita*' (social good) as the natural feeling of the evolved consciousness; self-enrichment and self-perfection by the feeling of '*Lok-hita*'; natural unity of the '*Preya*' (the pleasant) with the '*Śreya*' (the good) at the deeper level of consciousness.

12. Consciousness as Free-Will

'*Svātantrya*' (Freedom) as the nature of consciousness; the present predicament of the '*Apūrṇa-Aṇu*' (imperfect and limited self); comparison with the "Anguished freedom" of the Existentialist; factors which limit the freedom of consciousness; the possibility of the removal fo the factors and thereby attainment of the full freedom; the "freedom-from" and the "freedom-to"; Consciousness as will.

13. The Question of Accepting Consciousness as an Ontological Entity

The logical, epistemological and phenomenological status of consciousness; the self as formal consciousness; logical possibility of consciousness as an Ontological entity; the spiritual hypothesis; spiritualistic (psychical) researches; claims about the so-called phenomenon of rebirth; claims about the yogic "out-of-the body" experience of consciousness.

14. The Theory of Pratyabhijñā (Self-Recognition)

The question: 'who am I?'; Tantra and Upaniṣad as '*Ātma-śāstra*' (the discipline of the self); the self as consciousness, and consciousness as the self; the 'dual citizenship' of the self; the question of 'recognising' (*Pratyabhijñā*) of the real nature of the self; the question of *Ajñāna* (Ignorance) and *Ātma-jñāna* (Self-realisation); '*Bauddha-ajñāna*' (intellectual ignorance) and '*Pauruṣa-ajñāna*' ('existential' ignorance); individual consciousness as the mini-*Śiva*; *Śiva*-consciousness as the highest form of Self-consciousness; incorporation of the world-consciousness (*Jagad-vimarśa*) into Self-consciousness (*Ātma-vimarśa*); the concept of life as the sportive activity (*Līlā*) of consciousness; *Pratyabhijñā* as integral consciousness.

15. Consciousness as 'Vāk' (Speech or Language)

Linguistic approach to the understanding of consciousness; *Vimarśa* ('thinking') as the nature of consciousness, involvement of language in the process of thinking; discovery of consciousness in the process of understanding language; '*Parā-Vāk*'—Consciousness as the transcendental matrix of Language; '*Paśyantī Vāk*'—sprouting of Language from within consciousness; '*Madhyamā-Vāk*'—the full ideational formation of Language within the mind; '*Vaikharī-Vāk*'—external expression of language through spoken word; '*Nāda*'—language as primarily phonetical; the four stages of *Vāk* in the process of every creation; the anology of the mother producing the child.

16. Tantra as Deeper-Level Phenomenology

Limitations of empirical experience and possibility of extra-empirical knowledge; experience of the seers and the promise of verifiability of such experience; higher consciousness not as anti-rational but as clearer reason; continuity between the deeper and the surface levels of consciousness; the presence of enlightened persons in history.

17. Concluding Remarks

Significant points in the phenomenon of consciousness discovered by Tantra even at the ordinary (empirical) level of consciousness; Tāntric phenomenology as complementary to: (i) the western phenomenology both from the point of view of the ordinary consciousness and from that of the deeper consciousness, and (ii) the Advaita-Vedāntic conception of consciousness; significance of the Tāntric phenomenology in the realm of theoretical philosophy as also in the realm of practical life.

I

"THE TĀNTRIC THEORY OF CONSCIOUSNESS : A PHENOMENOLOGICAL AND CRITICAL STUDY"

Based on the use of the critical method of philosophy, the epistemological analysis (and the resultant discovery about the truth and extent of knowledge) made by Hume and Kant, brought a revolutionary and lasting change in the world of western philosophy. It became clear to the students of philosophy that generally and normally our knowing faculty is so constituted that knowledge (in the sense of cognition or experience) is limited to sense-experience, we can 'know' only what falls within the realm of senses. About what is beyond sense-experience, if any, we can only speculate or accept on faith; but that would be either a speculation of the mind or a matter of faith, and not knowledge proper. As a result of this startling discovery, it came to be accepted beyond any doubt that it is not possible for the human mind or intellect, limited as it is, to know 'Reality' or 'Essence' of life and the world.

Although the immediate successors of Kant (the Idealist philosophers of the Hegelian type) did not perhaps take note of this crucial Kantian discovery, it left a deep impact on the contemporary philosophy. It (the Kantian discovery) triggered two different trends or currents of the contemporary philosophy, namely, (i) Logical Positivism and its evolution in the form of Philosophical (Linguistic) Analysis, and (ii) the current of Existentialism-Phenomenology-Humanism. Both these trends, although moving in different directions, are based on the same Humanian-Kantian discovery that to go beyond the actual experience to land into the realm of speculation.

The object of philosophy, as accepted in the traditional thought, was to know Reality; but now as it became clear that the search for the knowledge of Reality is futile, the question arose: Should philosophy finally give up its endeavour of searching for the knowledge of Reality? Can we know nothing about the truth of life and the world? Phenomenology (including what is called 'Existential Phenomenology') came with an answer. The answer is that even if the reality or 'essence' of things may not be known, we can at least know the phenomenon of human existence, as it is within the reach of our experience. The object of philosophy is to know the phenomenon that means what is 'given in experience'.

Phenomenology developed primarily as a philosophical method—the method of taking cognizance of the phenomenon, that is, what is given in experience. The speculative formualtions and those just based on mere faith, are weeded out, and only the actual phenomenon is taken. This method can be applied for investigation into any field of knowledge.

The early phase of Phenomenology concentrates upon the study of consciousness. Consciousness is a phenomenon—a phenomenon of human existence, as is given in our experience. Phenomology has found out many important truths about the human consciousness. However, the phenomenologist, or anybody for that matter, bound by the limitation of the method, may not take the trouble of finding out if there are any deeper layers of consciousness beyond the reach of our normal experience or, if at all, there is any mode of experience other that what we normally have. S/he has to be confined to what is given in our normal experience. How can we know, s/he would ask, that there is a deeper or higher Consciousness (claimed by some philosophers and mystics), if it is not a phenomenon given in our experience?

When we come to the Indian side, we find a slightly different picture. In the Indian tradition, from the early times (say from the Vedic-Upaniṣadic period), it is held that our ordinary reason or understanding has no access to Reality, that our speculations about Reality are our own creation and therefore they do not touch Reality, and that our endeavour to conceptualize Reality is futile. Indian seers and philosophers were aware of this limitation, but they became also aware of the truth that there is at least one thing whose existence cannot be denied and that thing is 'oneself'—the knowing or thinking consciousness. Though *prima facie* the reality of this 'self' does not become known and only the formal nature of the knowing consciousness becomes evident, yet the seers had the suspicion that this self may be the surface consciousness and a vaster consciousness may be underlying it—the surface self may be just the tip of a larger reality. They sought to know the truth of it. Since the seers were more interested in discovering the laws of a healthy and happy life, they went on investigating into the real nature of the self in order to find out the way of ending suffering and attaining happiness. And they did succeed to a great extent. They made wide experiments, verification and research in their own way, and developed a 'technology' or 'Yoga' of purifying and transforming the states of consciousness and thereby achieving its deeper levels. Even at the phenomenal level of consciousness, they discovered many features which are yet unknown in the world of western phenomenology.

The discoveries and findings of the seers are recorded in the literature of the Veda-Upaniṣad (*Nigama*) on the one hand and in that of the Tantra (*Āgama*) on the other hand. However, with the use of literary device, the truth is presented by colouring it with allegories, symbols and myths in order to make the truth attractive and palatable. Later on, the record also got mixed up with many imaginary and untrue notions which can successfully be weeded out. In this respect, the Tāntric record can be considered more important, as it is fully based on experience, the *Śiva-Pārvatī* dialogue being a literary device. Abhinavagupta calls Tantra the 'tradition of experience' (*anubhava-sampradāya*). Kashmir Śaivism is the most prominent philosophical system of the Tāntric tradition, and Abhinavagupta is the principal philosopher of Kashmir Śaivism. In his writings, especially in his voluminous work *Tantraloka*, Abhinavagupta presents a comprehensive picture of consciousness at both the levels—phenomenal and noumenal. (In the context of Indian philosophy, it is not meaningless to talk about the noumenal level of consciousness, as the idea of the noumenal is not just speculation or mere faith but it is based on the actual experience of the seers and yogins).

The Tantra brings out the picture of a number of significant phenomena of consciousness, which are not normally taken cognizance of. '*Spanda*' ('*Vimarśa*' or '*Kriyā*'), '*Pratibhaā*', '*Vāk*', '*Svātantrya*', '*Kuṇḍalinī*', '*Rasā*' and '*Pratyabhijñā*' are some important phenomena to mention.. Even in ordinary consciousness we have glimpses of these phenomena, and Tantra points out the way or 'Yoga' to make them manifest more fully. Besides, the Tantra presents the all-encompassing nature of Self-realization (realization of the Higher Consciousness), vouchsafed by the experience of the yogins, saints and seers.

The dynamic nature of consciousness is also highlighted. Moreover, the possibility of an 'un-intentional' state of consciousness is accepted, as it is said to be actually realized partially or wholly in the logic experience of what is called '*Nirvikalpa-samādhi*'. But '*Sahaja-samādhi*' (the state of consciousness in which one is seated in the Self without doing anything, and yet benign and joyful activity flows through oneself in a natural and spontaneous way) or what is called '*Ātma-viśrānti*' (relaxing in the Self with the effortless flow of spontaneous activity), is the Tāntric paradigm of *Samādhi*.

Spanda or Kriyā

The key concept of the Tantric philosophy of Consciousness is *Kriyā* or *Spanda* which distinguishes it (the Tāntric philosophy) from other systems of thought, specially from the Advaita-Vedānta. All other points of uniqueness and distinction in the Tāntric philsophy can be logically derived from this single concept. We give here the concept of *Kriyā* in brief. In order that we understand the exact nature of *Kriyā* (*Spanda*), it must be distinguished, on the one hand, from what is called '*Karma*'—the ethical action which is voluntary and effortful, and, on the other hand, from the automatic activity which is mechanical and determined. While performing volitional or ethical action one has to exert one's will or make effort (*āyāsa*), and so it is not *Kriyā*, as *Kriyā* is effortless (*anāyāsa*) activity; it is spontaneous or natural (or automatic), so to say. But the same time it is not like the automata of the reflex action, nor like the mechanical activity of a robot, nor like the obsessional behaviour of a psycho-neurotic, as all these activities are determined and not free. In *Kriyā* there if freedom as one is not bound to perform the activity; one simply allows the activity to flow, as it were, as it (the activity) is perfectly in tune with oneself. One can, if one likes, check or dismiss the whole process. *Kriyā*, therefore, has both the merits—freedom and effortlessness (being automatic or natural). It is, therefore, called spontaneity (*spanda*). *Spanda* or *Kriyā* may be called a kind of natural activity, free and spontaneous.

We may find samples of actual experience in our ordinary life where can have some inkling of *Kriyā*. These samples, however, are not the perfect examples of pure *Kriyā*, but still they can help us understand the idea of *Kriyā*. Take the example of joy. When we are extremely joyful, certain jubilant activities like singing, etc., may automatically flow from us. Or, when per chance we happen to meet, after a long period of parting, someone who is very dear to us, we may spontaneously perform certain joyful activities in his or her welcome. When a child takes to playing, it is free and spontaneous on the part of the child. It does not result from some lack or want in the child; it ensues out of the joy and fullness of the child. The child's free play is a mini replica of the creation of the world out of the joy of the Absolute. A child's natural playing, free and spontaneous, is an example of *Kriyā* although not very perfect example. Such activities are not willfully done; they spring forth automatically; yet we feel free while doing them or rather allowing them to occur through us. There is no compulsion on our part, for the activity is not forced on us—neither from external factors nor from internal ones like urges and instincts. It is not the case that we do not like the activity and yet it happens against our will (as in the case of obsessional neurosis).

Such example of activity, howsoever incomplete they may be, suggest the possibility of a state of consciousness in which there is spontaneous or automatic activity plus perfect freedom. Hence, *Kriyā* concept is a legitimate hypothesis, to put it in scientific terms. The reason why we do not find hundred percent pure example of *Kriyā* in our ordinary life, is, the Tāntrist would say, that in ordinary experience the flow of pure *Kriyā* is obstructed as well as defiled by what is called *Mala,* one finds oneself exhibiting perfect currents of pure *Kriyā.* In actual life there is partial *Kriyā,* because there is partial freedom from impurtiy. Pure *Kriyā* is possible only in the state of perfection that can be found in the life of a *Jīvanmukta.* The imperfect examples of *Kriyā* in our actual life, anyway, give the inklings of pure *Kriyā.*

In the Advaita Vedānta and allied systems we do not find distinction between *Kriyā* and *Karma.* For the Advaitin all activity seems to be nothing but *Karma* which is volitional action and which arises out of some want or lack, and is therefore suggestive of imperfection. The Tāntric philosophers, however, are very careful in using the words *Kriyā* and *Karma.* They never equate *Kriyā* with *Karma.* In fact, they too like all other Indian philosophers hold that what is called *Karma* is bondage (*Kārma* or *Kārmaṇa mala*), and as such cannot go with *Jñāna.* But *Kriyā* is an independent category and is entirely different from *Karma.* This is the unique contribution of the Tāntric tradition. The Advaitin perhaps does not care to take into account such an important aspect of our actual experience.

Pratibhā

Another important phenomenon of consciousness is what is called '*Pratibhā*'. The natural spark or dawn (or flow) of the power of consciousness—in cognitive and/or creative way—is called *Pratibhā.* Any activity or awareness that is not learnt or acquired through labour but automatically springs forth from the inner consciousness, is *Pratibhā. Pratibhā* is a kind of automatic flash from within, which manifests in both cognitive and creative forms. Talent (or genius) is also not a learnt or acquired phenomenon but it comes as an automatic flash from within. So, talent is *Pratibhā,* and that is why *Pratibhā* literally means talent or genius.

Awareness or illumination that takes the form of knowledge and comes from within as an automatic internal flash of light, is called *Jñāna-Pratibhā* (cognitive flash). All knowledge, therefore, is *Prātibha*' (pertaining to *Pratibhā,* that is, coming as automatic dawn or flash). Creativity too is a matter of spontaneous flash; it is creative *Pratibhā* (*Kriyā-Pratibhā*).

In the consciousness of a scientist working in the laboratory, a sudden flash of understanding comes, which results in a new discovery. Simialrly in the musing mind of a philosopher, a sudden flash of thought or idea comes, which results in new revelation. All this is cognitive *Pratibhā.* Cognitive *Pratibhā* works in the field of science and philosophy. Creative *Pratibhā* works in all the practical fields of life—arts, sports, work, and so on.

Pratibhā is tne natural power of consciousness, but it is not equally manifest in everybody. The reason, Tantra points out, is that consciousness is covered by impurities (*Mala*), and the *malāvaraṇa* (covering of impurity) obstructs the manifestation of *Pratibhā.* The more the *mala* (impurity) is washed through the spiritual practice of self-purification, the more the *Pratibhā*-power is released. *Pratibhā* is the natural *śakti* (power) of consciousness; to automatically flow is also its nature, the only thing needed is the unobstructed passage.

Although *Pratibhā* is not created by effort, deliberate effort and exercise indirectly help in the manifestation of *Pratibhā*. Exercise and effort do not *cause* Pratibhā; they only facilitate the flow of *Pratibhā* by removing the obstruction from its path. This is like opening the window for the light to automatically come or like facilitating the flow of water by clearing the canal. Exercise is also significant because it cleanses the consciousness, and the cleansing of the consciousness results in the release of the captivated flow of the *Pratibhā-śakti.*

Vimarśa and Vāk

Tantra points out that consciousness is active or dynamic by its very nature. The activity of consciousness is in the form of thinking or ideation which is called '*Vimarśa*' (*Vimarśa* literally means 'thinking'.). Thinking (*Vimarśa*) is always in language (*Vāk*) or through words (*śabda*). Bhartṛhari says, "there can be no thinking or ideation without words or language" (*nāstyasau pratyayo loke yaḥ sabdānugamādṛte*). So, consciousness is linguistic (*sabdātmaka*). That is why consciousness is also understood as '*Vāk*' (speech or world or language). And language is primarily phonetic; therefore it is called '*nāda*' (sound). So, *Śakti, Kriyā, Vimarśa, Vāk* and *Nāda* denote one and the same phenomenon. Thus consciousness has two primal characteristics—(i) knowledge or illumination (*Prakāśa,* or *Jñāna* or *Bindu*), and (ii) power or dynamism or activity (*Śakti* or *Kriyā* or *Vimarśa* or *Vāk* or *Nāda*). Consciousness is energy, but it is sentient energy (*Citi-śakti*). It is sentience and energy—the two in one.

Language, which is the natural form of consciousness, is, according to Tantra, not conventional but *prātibha* (pertaining to *Pratibhā*), that is, 'innate' or coming out naturally from consciousness like the light coming out from the sun. If language orginates from convention, Tantra would argue, then in that case language is already needed to hold the convention; language must precede all convention. Actually, language stands *a priori* or already given in consciousness.

Svātantrya

Svātantrya (freedom), according to Tantra, is the key characteristic of Consciousness. Sentience and freedom go together. As against 'matter' (*jaḍa*) which is unconscious or insentient and therefore conditioned or bound by the laws of Nature, Consciousness is free, as it is sentience. However, at the phenomenal level of consciousness, freedom is limited, as it is partially marred by the obstructive elements of impurity (*Mala*). It is the 'anguished freedom' of the Existentailist. But, as Tantra points out and as is also vouchsafed by the experience of the seers, it is quite possible that freedom is attained in fuller degrees through the spiritual practice of self-purification. Again, the degree of freedom is proportionate to the removal of impurity; and it is possible to achieve the state of perfect freedom, which is attested by the seers and the *Jivanmuktas* (liberated souls). Liberated consciousness is also the state of perfection, as perfection and freedom is one and the same thing.

Freedom has two aspects that can be described in terms of 'freedom-from' and 'freedom-to'. 'Freedom-from' means that consciousness is not conditioned or bound or affected by anything whatsover—neither from within nor from without. 'Freedom-to' means the freedom to act or express or create. According to the Advaita-Vedāntic tradition, in *Brahman* (the ultimate consciousness or the Self), there is 'freedom-from' and not 'freedom-to', as *Brahman* is inactive (*Niṣkriya*). But according to Tantra, *Śiva* (or *Brahman*) is a state of both the 'freedom from' and 'freedom–to'. Creation is the freedom of *Śiva* or Consciouness—its free self-expression or self-manifestation. Even at the phenomenal level of the individual self, consciousness is mini-*Śiva*, so to say, which acts and creates within the sphere of its limited freedom.

The Advaita-Vedānta is not in a position to accept 'freedom-to' in the ultimate consciousness (*Brahman*), because for the Advaitin all activity is which is called *'Karma'* which arises out of lack or imperfection, and since *Brahman* has not imperfection, there can be no action (*Karma*) in *Brahman*. This logic leads the Advaitin to the position that Creation (of the universe) is not the work or activity of *Brahman*, rather it is super-imposition (*adhyāsa*) on *Brahman* due to Ignorance (*Avidyā*). The logic of *Karma* as imperfection, further leads the Advaitin to interpret the Upaniṣadic sentences (which declare the Creation to be the direct work of *Brahman*) as mythical story (*Ākhyāyikā*). Here Tantra would point out that the initial difficulty of the Advaitin is that he presupposes all activity to be '*Karma*', and this presupposition of the Advaitin makes him land into obviously absurd position. The Advaitin does not take cognizance of the phenomenon of what the Tantrist calls '*Spanda*' or *'Kriyā'* which is basically different from *'Karma'*. *Kriyā* or *Spanda* is the natural overflow of the fullness of *Ānanda*—from the state of perfection. As is in the general Indian tradition, the Tantra too accepts Karma as a sign of lack or imperfection; for the Tantrist too, the technical *Karma* is bondage, as it is a form of impurity (*Kārma* or *Kārmaṇa Mala*). But *Kriyā* is a quite different thing. Creation, according to Tantra, is not the *Karma* but *Kriyā* of Śiva or Brahman—the free and spontaneous overfloow of the *ānanda* of Consciousness (*Cidvijṛmbhā* or *Cid-vilāsa*).

Here it should be mentioned for clarification that the Tāntrist accepts the position of the Upaniṣad but differs from the Advaita-Vedāntin's inactivistic interpretation of the Upaniṣad. There is an implicit claim among the Tantri philosophers that if the Upaniṣad is construed in the Tantric way, the difficulties of the Advaitin would be solved. In this sense, the Tantric philosophy, specially or Kashmir Śaivism, is complementary to that of the Advaita-Vedānta.

II

THE TWO LEVELS OF CONSCIOUSNESS

The most significant contribution of the Indian thought, especially of the Upaniṣadic-Tāntric tradition, is the discovery that there is a deeper and cosmic level of consciousness or the self beneath its normal or 'surface' level. Man has duel citizenship, so to say; he/she is the citizen of the world terrestrial as well as that of the world celestial. The world celestial is hidden from the normal eyes because its sight is obstructed by the cloak of Ignorance (*Avidyā*) or by the predicament of self-forgetfulness (*Ātma-vismṛti*). But the fortunate thing is, and which is very significant, that the lost citizenship of the celestial world can be revived; the paradise is lost, but it can be regained as well. Tantra amply points out the most efficacious ways of regaining the lost paradise.

In this context one more thing is significant in the Tāntric theory. According to Tantra, the paradise or the deeper level of consciousness is not fully lost, it is partially working at the surface level, and it is a question of making the deeper level fully manifest by removing the obstruction. The Tāntric theory admits that the deeper level is not cut off from the surface, rather it is in continuaton. This position is differnt from the Advaitin's theory that the two levels of Consciousness are in rejection of each other.

We have already hinted that the acceptance of a deeper level of consciousness is not speculation or mere faith but is based on the actual experience of the seers, saints and yogins, and that it can be duly verified also.

Consciousness as Kuṇḍalinī

We have already pointed out that consciousness according to Tantra is energy (*Śakti*)—the sentient energy. As energy, it has the potential of creative activity. *Kuṇḍalinī* (literally meaning the 'coiled female serpent') is the symbolic name given to this energy in the language of the Tāntric Yoga. There is cosmic *Kuṇḍalinī* (the cosmic Consciousness) and there is individual *Kuṇḍalinī*—the individual point of consciousness or selves. All the individual *Kuṇḍalinīs* are connectd with the cosmic *Kuṇḍalinī* like the individual points of electricity at the consumption end, which are all connected with the one universal power-house from where the electric current flows to the individual points. Energy flows from the cosmic *Kuṇḍalinī* to the individual *Kuṇḍalinīs* partially or wholly, as the case may be.

There are actually three levels of the flow of *Kuṇḍalinī-śakti* in the individual: (i) at the gross biological-physical level, it is called '*Prāṇa-Kuṇḍalinī*' (the vital energy) which maintains the biological life; (ii) at the mental level, the *Kuṇḍalinī* flows or expresses itself in all the forms of thinking. This is called '*Nāda-Kuṇḍalinī*' (the 'sound' or 'word' or 'language' energy); (iii) at the spiritual level the *Kuṇḍalinī* expresses itself in the form of spiritual enlightenment—the state of Self-realization with universal love. This is called '*Bodha-Kuṇḍalinī*'. '*Bodha*' means enlightenment. The terms—*Prāṇa*', '*Nāda*' and '*Bodha*' *Kuṇḍalinī*—are attempts of understanding the flow of consciousness-energy at all the three levels—physical, mental and spiritual. Generally, *Kuṇḍalinī* is understood to be only the *Prāṇa-Kuṇḍalinī*; mostly people are unaware of the mental and the spiritual levels of *Kuṇḍalinī*.

Consciousness as 'Rasa' or 'Ānanda'

Consciousness is *Jñāna* ('knowledge' or illumination) and not only *Kriyā* or *Śakti* (Activity or Energy) but is also *Ānanda* (Bliss or Happiness). The nature of *Ānanda* is that it flows or overflows, and it is also experienced and enjoyed by the same consciousness in which it flows. The experience of the flow of *Ānanda* is called '*Rasa*'—the aesthetic experience of joy.

Tantra has given the *Rasa* theory of aesthetics. According to Tantra, *Ānanda* is present in the Self or Consciousness as its very nature like the light in the sun (and not like the light of the moon, which is acquired from the sun). All the *Ānanda* that we derive even from the external objects, really belongs to the self or consciousness. It is the *Ānanda* of the consciousness that is indirectly projected into the objects and apparently seems to be coming from the external world. To be clearer, the *Ānanda* which seems to be coming from the external object, really comes from within the consciousness.

Although *Ānanda* is inherently present in consciousness as its nature, it (the *Ānanda*) does not always become manifest. The external experience of art or the sight of a beloved person or anything of the kind, becomes an occasion for the manifestation of *Ānanda* from within the consciousness. For example, when we watch a drama or embrace a dear one, this temporarily removes the obstructive veil from the consciousness, and the '*Rasa*' (experience of *Ānanda*) is activated or released. The process of experiencing *Ānanda* is the process of unveiling or uncovering the consciousness. That is why it is said that 'consciousness unveiled itself is *Rasa*' (*bhinnāvaraṇā cideva rasaḥ*).

The Tantric Yoga of Conciousness

Tantra is primarily a 'praxis'. It has practical and pragmatic approach to philosophy. Tantra has given an applied form of its philosophy of consciouness. It has developed a 'technology' of consciouness in the form of what is called the Tāntric Yoga.

When we come to the side of *sādhanā* and forms of worship presented in the Tantric tradition, we find a very positive and constructive attitude towards the objects of Nature, towards every human relationship, and, in fact towards the whole world. Everything of the world is to be taken as divine and holy and be worshipped—the sun, the moon, the fire, the river, the mountain, the ocean, the tree, the animals and so on. Money and wealth are Goddess *Lakṣmī, Kāma* (libido) is Lord Cupid (*Kāmadeva*). Every human relationship is to be taken as divine. For example, for the wife the husband is *Śiva*, and for the husband the wife is *Śakti* or *Devī*. The parents, the teachers, the children—all are to be taken with what is called '*Īśvara buddhi*' or '*Deva-buddhi*' (the reverential attitude of taking it divine).

The sense of holiness of everything and the attitude of adoration towards everything is called *Śiva-bhāvanā* or *Īśvara-bhāvanā*, and this is Tāntric element in Hinduism. *Śiva-bhāvanā* is a deliberate spiritual device for melting or thinning the ego which is the main obstruction in the flow of our own divinity. It does not matter who or what is the object of worship, what matters is my attitude of worship, my humility and resignation of my ego.

I put off the coat of my ego, and the *Guru* or the other object of worship becomes an instrumental peg to hang the coat of my ego. Putting off or resigning my ego results in facilitating the flow of my own inner divinity. When I practice *Śiva-bhāvanā*, then for me the life and the world virtually change. This is because what realy matters is not the change of the world but change in my attitude towards the worlds.

Another significant element of the Tāntric Yoga is what is called *Kaula-mārga* or *Vāma-mārga*—the left-handed way of the spiritual *sādhanā* in which the five 'M's (*pañcamakāra*) are used as objects of worship. Apart from the natural and real difference between the good and the bad, we have artificially created many false distinctions of good and bad, or religious and profane. By using the so-caled impure objects in worship, *Kaula-sādhanā* aims at freeing the spiritual aspirant from false and vain distinctions.

Moreover, the *sādhanā* related to sex has the added significance of bringing about sex sublimation. The Tantric seers realized that sex is the most potent psychophysical energy and, if sublimated, can work wonders. The Tantric wisdom lies in winning over nature with the help of the laws of Nature itself. In accordance with the natural law of transformation or sublimation, the Tantric seers devised ways for transforming the base desires, especially sexual desire, into nobler and finer forms. Through the process of sublimation, sex energy can be made to flow through the highly beneficial channels of love, aesthetic creativity, devotion (*bhakti*), social service, and so on, on the one hand, and be used as the means of Self-realization on the other. The sexual attraction between man and woman may be transformed into true love between them, and then the conjugal love may be channeled into universal love, which is the sure means of Self-realization. This is the rationale of the *Kaula-sādhanā*. This much-misunderstood and much-abused *sādhanā* is of colossal significance if practiced in its true spirit.

Tantra has given a number of *sādhanās* or sets of *sādhanās* for the purpose of realizing the real nature of oneself and thereby becoming happy oneself and making others happy as well. The *Vijñānabhairava Tantra* itself gives more than a hundred forms of yogic practice or *sādhanā*. All the *sādhanās* presented in Tantra are integral and all-assimilative in nature. They tend to accept and transform in consciousness everything of life and the world, and not to derecognize and reject. Tantra gives the way of sublimation and not the way of rejection or repression. (However, everything of life and the world created by Nature or God is to be accepted and transformed, but there are many things which we ourselves have created out of ego, and these things may be evil. Such ego-creations of ours must be negated or rejected.)

Pratyabhijñā

The most significant part of the Tantric '*phenomenology*' is what is called '*Ātma-prāpti*' (Self-attainment) or '*Ātma-pratyaphijñā*' (Self-recognition). This concept is believed to have experiential basis, as it is said to have been realized by the yogins. It is further said that anyone can realize it, provided one fulfils the pre-requisites and follows the spiritual path of self-purification and universal love. As Tantra points out, actually everyone has partial Self-realization that varied in degree from person to person, proportionately depending on the degree of self-purification. By the yogic practice of self-purification, one can make the Self-illumination dawn in greater intensity in proportion to the amount of self-purification. The flow of *Pratibhā* (both cognitive and creative) or the flow of what is symbolically called *Kuṇḍalinī* (at all the three levels—biological, mental and spiritual) is the co-relate of the flow of Self-illumination. (Here it should be added for clarification that according to

Tantra, knowledge or illumination is flow or activity and not an inactive state of consciousness.).

Ātma-pratyaphijñā is not only conducive to the attainment of the spiritual goal but it helps in the acquisition of the worldly (material) values also. The reason is that is releases the captivated flow of *Pratibhā* from the inner Self, and the released *Pratibhā-śakti* becomes highly helpful in the mundane success too. Actually, in the Tāntric consciousness, the dichotomy between the spiritual and the physical (material) is abolished, and the so-called material becomes spiritualized; the '*Jagadānanda*' (worldly happiness) becomes the free manifestation of the '*Ātmānanda*' (the spiritual bliss of the Self).

(So far, we have tried to explain in brief some of the points of the Tantric theory of Consciousness. But there are many more; we have tried to cover all the points in the synopsis we have presented).

CHAPTER 31

Indian Atomism: Some Reflections

B. V. Subbarayappa

The theme of this paper is Atomism, but qualified by the word 'Indian'. Professor D.P. Chattopadhayaya, in his thoughtful background note, has posed a few questions. Some of them are: Is it misleading to speak of Indian science, European science? Must we maintain that Science is country-neutral and that is necessarily 'universal', i.e., has nothing to do with this or that culture or civilisation?

Atomism began to develop its universal character with the enunciation of the Dalton's atomic theory early in the nineteenth century. The concept of an atom was propounded by the pre-Socratic Greek thinkers, Leucippus and his pupil, Democritus (fifth century B.C.) elaborated upon by Lurectius (first century B.C.) and revived by Gassendi, Boyle and Newton (sixteenth –seventeenth century A.D.) after a gap of about 1,600 years. Though the atomism of Lucretius was a source of inspiration to Dalton, his own atomic theory was based upon some experimentation on air and inference. He had before him the chemical investigations of Joseph Black, Henry Cavendish, Priestly, Scheele and Lavoisier that had led to the discovery of oxygen and other new elements. In 1897, when the electron was discovered, the atomic or particle physics developed a sound scientific methodology and, through it, found universal applicability in that field.

But atomism conceived by the Greek thinkers was speculative and was not in the nature of any methodological approach. It was one of the philosophical adventures to explain the possible monistic world-stuff. If Thales thought of Water, Anaximenes of Air, and Heraclitus of Fire as the primordial stuff of the physical world, Democritus thought of atoms of only one class, spherical and indestructible as the basic world-stuff, outside the conceptual frame of the Greek theory of elements. In his speculation, atoms and void were both real. Even the soul was supposed to be made of atoms. Such views were not shared even by the later Greek philosophers like Plato and Aristotle, leave alone the universality of atomism at that time. Empedocles, a senior contemporary of Leuicippus, evolved a theory of four elements, earth, water, fire and air with their opposing qualities, hot and cold, dry and moist, which he called the 'roots of the world'; but Empedocles was disinclined towards atomism which had preceded his elemental theory. It is called Greek atomism because of the culture-area in which it originated as well as its particular characteristics, and confined to a group of Greek thinkers.

Atomism also originated in the Indian culture-area and its nature as well as structure was entirely different from that of the Greek, as will be seen later. Unlike the Greek atomism, Indian atomism arose after the appearance of doctrine of five elements (*Pañcamahābhūtas*). This doctrine gradually emerged from its upaniṣadic philosophical foundations, and later became a part of the systemic, or religio-philosophic matrix of the Vaiśeṣika, Nyāya as well as the syncretic Nyāya-Vaiśeṣika, Jaina and certain schools of Buddhism, and atomism was a part of this doctrine. It needs to be recognized that the content and the context go together. The contexts of atomism in Greece among some of the thinkers and that as developed in India were altogether different. Atomism in India should be viewed in its philosophic and epistemic roots, hence Indian atomism.

The innate strength of modern science lies in its method and the triumph of science is the triumph of its method. Scientific method does not make any distinction between one country and another, between a white man or a Negro, between male and female, as long as the scientific method is followed for which, as Eddington said, observation is the 'Court of Appeal', and in which the senses, the gateways of human knowledge, play a decisive role. Modern science, though powerful in its method, is sensorially determined, unlike the ancient intellectual or philosophical endeavours of which certain scientific ideas were an integral part, and such ideas were culture-specific. One can talk of Indian astronomy in the context of the performance of sacrifices and of Indian medicine or ayurveda, the foundational ideas of which were derived from the Sāṅkhya, Vaiśeṣika and Nyāya. One can also talk of Indian mathematics in the Vedic period, since it was a spin off of the *Śulba-sūtras* for the construction of sacrificial altars and of the Vedic metrical chanting of permutations and combinations leading to a pyramidal expansion of syllables. Such an exercise came up only in the sixteenth century in Europe, now known as Pascal's triangle as in the context of numbers.

I

ATOMISM: NYĀYA-VAIŚEṢIKA

The concept of whole (*avayavin*) and the constituent part(s) (*avayava*) as well as their belief in the eternal reality have shaped the Nyāya-Vaiśeṣika atomism. The Nyāya-Vaiśeṣika regards all compound substances (*avayavi dravya*) as non-eternal, since they undergo production and destruction. But the destruction would not be total or endless, but to a supra–sensible and partless or atomic stage. Of the five elements, the four (earth, water, fire and air) in their produced forms are non-eternal because they are subject to production and destruction. But in their atomic states, they are eternal. Such a conceptual linkage was necessary for the Nyāya-Vaiśeṣika as that alone would be in tune with their philosophic realism. It also thinks of mind being corporeal and atomic.

The basic tenets of their atomism are briefly as follows: Each element has its own class of atoms, spherical and indivisible, but with specific attributes, namely, earth atom-odour; water atom-taste; fire atom-colour; and air atom-touch. It is significant to note that these attributes are also of the elements themselves. Thus the atoms and the respective products have common specific qualities, no distinction being made in this respect between the gross substance and its atomic state.

As regards the production of gross matter from the atoms the Nyāya-Vaiśeṣika postulate is that atoms are in eternal motion. Hence, there always exists a possibility of the combination of some of them; but to begin with, only two atoms of the same element enter into combination, although during such a combination there would also be present the atoms of the other elements. Two like atoms are the material cause while those of the other elements could possibly play a supportive role. In any case, two unlike atoms, i.e., an atom of earth and that of air would not enter into combination, according to the Nyāya-Vaiśeṣika.

The term *dvaṇuka* (dyad) is used for the effect of the combination of two atoms. An argument advanced for this situation is that the magnitude of a dyad is derived by the number two only. An atom is so minute that it cannot be a causative agency for contributing any magnitude to the product (effect). Minuteness, in other words, cannot cause grossness, and further, atoms have no magnitude. This means that a dyad is not superior to the two atoms that give rise to it in magnitude. Hence it should be concluded that the magnitude of dyad must be derived from the number of atoms giving rise to it. Logically the minimum number of atoms that can be causative is two and therefore, only two atoms combine in the beginning and the first product is a dyad. Like the constituent atoms, the dyad is also invisible or supra-sensible. The minimum visible is designated as *tryaṇuka* or *trasareṇu* (triad) which, according to Nyāya-Vaiśeṣika is of the size of a mote in a sunbeam.

The postulate of the formation of a triad is intriguing and interesting alike. It has been stated that three dyads cause the coming into being of a triad and not six atoms directly. The reason adduced is that a thing of gross magnitude like a triad can only be formed by products like dyads. Atoms are eternal and if they were to produce directly a gross material, the process would go on and the resulting product, say earth or water, would also be eternal. But the experience is to the contrary as they are destructible. Hence it is only from the dyads that a triad could be formed.

Atoms and dyads are considered as having no extension in themselves, besides not possessing magnitude on a gross scale. These two concepts mean that the gross magnitude of a triad is not due to atoms nor even the inter–dyadic. Likewise a tetrad owes its emergence or formation to four triads and so on. The minimum standard of plurality of dyads is logically three. Hence at least three dyads are required for the formation of a triad. However, it is admitted that triads of different elements could also enter into combination to form a tetrad and the like. Since the atoms of the different elements have their own specific properties and there would be structural arrangement in the triads, tetrads and so on, Nyāya-Vaiśeṣika has explained the different qualities observed in substance(s) as being due to the structural arrangement (*vyūha*)–a refreshing concept even from the modern scientific print of view.

Speculative though, the Nyāya-Vaiśeṣika atomism is not devoid of any principle of causality. On the other hand, its postulate is that the effect, a new event, has always a cause. Atoms are the material cause of a dyad, and dyads are the material cause of a triad. The cause in each case brings about an effect, and is immediately absorbed or inheres in the effect which in turn performs the functions of a cause to continue the sequence. The Nyāya-Vaiśeṣika causality is known as *āramhhavāda* or *asatkāryavāda*.

There are also two question addressed by the Nyāya-Vaiśeṣika: (i) why do the primordial atoms enter into combination; and (ii) what causes the union of two atoms to begin with? The explanation of the Nyāya-Vaiśeṣika for the former is no doubt the motion of atoms, but in respect of the latter, it is explained in terms of an unforeseen force or power (*adṛṣta*) that would set off the process. In other words, the unseen force, is the efficient cause, while atoms are the material cause for the formation of dyads and so on.

II

JAINA ATOMISM

The Jaina metaphysics, regards matter (*pudgāla*) and spirit (*jīva*) as independent realities, under its two basic categorization of the Universe into *Jīva* (living) and *Ajīva* (non-living), the Universe being considered as without beginning and endless. *Ajīva* comprises five entities: *dharma, adharma, ākāśa, pudgla* and *kāla*. Each of them, excepting *kāla* or time, is known as *astikāya* i.e., that which exists, has pervasiveness and occupies space (*pradeṣa*), space being considered as an integral part of *ākāśa*, while the Nyāya-Vaiśeṣika regards *ākāśa* and space as two distinct entities, sound being the special quality of *ākāśa*. In Jaina metaphysics, matter is conceived as an eternal substance (*dravya*) which is undetermined by any processes of transformation of its quality or quantity.

The Jaina *Āgamas* have conceived of *paramāṇus* (ultimate atoms) as being infinite in number in respect of *dravya*. The characteristics of an atom are that it is the minutest particle from the point of view of locus or field (*kṣetra*), momentary in relation to time (*kāla*), and is capable of undergoing changes depending upon the condition (*bhāva*). In any case, in Jaina atomism, all atoms are alike without any classification or label is terms of those of earth, water, fire and air. The Jaina concept of atom is thus totally at variance with that of the Nyāya-Vaiśeṣika. Further, Jaina atomism regards atoms as being both cause and effect, the latter in the nature of transformations which the atoms are stated to undergo owing to both internal and external causes. The Nyāya-Vaiśeṣika, on the other hand, believes that atoms are the material causes of the world and the effect is a new event. Jaina atomism also makes another distinction between what is called *sūkṣma paramāṇu* (the minutest and the finest) and *vyavahāra paramāṇu* (*lit.* the practical ones) and regards that it is only the *sūkṣma paramāṇu* that is indivisible while the other type with its qualities (not specific to each atom) of colour, taste, smell and touch, could undergo infinite divisions—a view totally different from that of the Nyāya-Vaiśeṣika. Thus in Jaina atomism, both indivisibility and divisibility as well as eternality and non-eternality are equally real in the context of the eternality of substance and the practical mode respectively. Thus the Jaina atoms, infinite in number, of the *sūkṣma* type are indivisible, impassable (*abhedya*), indestructible, incombustible (*adāhya*) and non-receivable (*agrāhya*); but they have no qualitative differences at all. The atoms nevertheless could undergo transformation into gross materials like earth, water, fire and air depending upon the nature and extent of qualities like colour, taste, smell, touch and the like.

Jaina atomism differs from that of the Nyāya-Vaiśeṣika in some other ways too. It does not accept the latter's concept of the whole and the parts (*avayavin-avayava*). What is more, the Jaina atomism expounds that atoms are both the cause and the effect. It also regards time in the form of atomic state, *kālāṇu*, while Nyāya-Vaiśeṣika considers time as an eternal *dravya* and partless.

As for the motion of atoms, the Jaina view is that they are in motion and active but strangely holds that it may not be so always. The movement of an atom can be regular (*niyamita*) and irregular (*aniyamita*), depending upon the space and time conditions. It is pointed out that the motion of an atom can be natural and also due to its combination or an encounter with either other atoms or even a *skandha* (the aggregation of other atoms). Even the rate or speed of motion of an atom has been speculated upon by the Jaina thinkers. Although it is stated that the motion of an atom occurs in straight line in one unit of time called *samaya*, it could also be curvi-linear (*vigrahagati*), if during its motion, it is acted upon by others. Jaina atomism does not think of motion in an atom as its intrinsic quality like the Nyāya-Vaiśeṣika, but thinks of resistance experienced by an atom.

With regard to the process of atomic combination, the Jaina concept is that the combination of atoms takes place as a result of the qualities but of unequal degree, but not due to their inherent motion as the Nyāya-Vaiśeṣika has conceived. These qualities are in the nature of forces—cohesiveness or attractive force (*snigdhatva*); dryness or repulsive force (*rūkṣatva*); and (iii) even their combination, that are presumed to be present in atoms as well as in *skandhas* or aggregates—a scientific approach, though speculative.

III

BAUDDHA ATOMISM

Among the Buddhists, the Saravāstivādins have presented an atomic view of matter, but as part of their *kṣaṇabhaṅgavāda*. They consider that matter is a collocation of the fourfold substratum of colour, taste, odour and touch, and regard an atom as the minutest unit of *rūpa* or that which has the capacity to affect sense organ), thus relating it to an observational entity, indirectly though. According to them an atom is not only indivisible and invisible but also momentary in the sense they are continually in a flux or undergo phase-changes. Besides, the Sautrāntikas do not regard atoms in terms of particles of some matter. Instead they think of them in terms of dynamic force or energy in tune with their theory of momentariness or flux.

Two types of atoms, viz., simple (*dravya paramāṇu*) and compounded (*saṃghāta paramāṇu*) have been postulated. As for the compounded or the aggregation of atoms, some believe that it is a direct combination, while some others think that even so there always remains an intervening space between or among atoms, in contradistinction to the absence of such a postulate among the Nyāya-Vaiśeṣika. It is nevertheless pointed out that gross matter is a conglomeraton of a cluster of atoms having one atom at the center and the others around it, without any type of interaction or interpenetration.

The Sarvāstivādins have thought of eight types of atoms–four fundamental of earth (solid), water (fluid), fire (hot) and of air (moving) and four secondary (of colour, odour, taste, and touch), thus postulating that the specific qualities are also atomic. This is somewhat in consonance with the Jaina atomism. Even the organs of sense are regarded as modifications of atomic matter, in a way similar to the Nyāya-Vaiśeṣika. There is also an attempt at quantification: each secondary atom is believed to require four fundamental atoms for its support, the resulting aggregate consisting of 4x4 + 4 = 20 atoms if the body does not sound; if it is to sound, the aggregate consists of 5x4 + 5 = 25 atoms, taking into consideration the attribute, namely, sound.

A summary of the foregoing reveals that, the atomism of the Nyāya-Vaiśeṣika, Jaina and of the Bauddha developed in relation to their philosophical positions. The Jaina thinkers chose to retain the word *skandha* of Buddhists instead of *dvyaṇuka* (dyad), *tryaṇuka* (three dyads) and so on of the Nyāya-Vaiśeṣika. Though each of them conceived of an atomic or an indestructible or indivisible state, they differed from one another in the manner of the formation of gross bodies from atoms. Such differences too were governed by their philosophical or metaphysical persuasions. The Jainas thought of it, unlike the Nyāya-Vaiśeṣika, in terms of the qualitative transformations that would take place encompassing the atoms. In Jaina atomism there is also the distinction between that which is the minutest and indivisible (*sūkṣma paramāṇu*) and the practical one (*vyvahāra paramāṇu*). But this idea is noted for its absence either in that of Nyāya-Vaiśeṣika or that of the two Buddhist sects. Besides, while the Jaina atomism accepts that even one *paramāṇu* (*sūkṣma* type) could have the status of *skandha*, neither the Vaiśeṣika nor the Buddhist schools subscribe to such a view. Perhaps a common ground appears to be the characteristics of an atom, its indivisibility and indestructibility among the Nyāya-Vaiśeṣika, Jaina and the two Buddhists sects, despite their philosophical positions. It is significant to note that the structural details of atomism as delineated by the Nyāya-Vaiśeṣika as well as of the Jaina are far more than those of the two Buddhists sects. The reason for this may be the flexibility of the former's approach to the physical world and the *Kṣaṇikavāda* of the Buddhists in their interpretation of the basic stuff of world. However, the word, '*paramāṇu*', means differently among the three systems of thought.

In the West, the Miletian Leucippus (fl. c. 475 B.C.), speculated in an entirely different way and become the founder of the atomic doctrine of matter. His pupil, perhaps also of Miletus, was Democritus (c. 470-400 B.C.), a contemporary of Socrates, who developed an atomic theory that was not only different from the earlier Heracleitan conception that change alone was real but was also totally at variance with the Platonic doctrine of Ideas or the Aristotelian conception of matter. In a way Leucippus carried forward the new mood generated by Thales, Anximander, and Anaximenes, concerning the primordial stuff of the world. He expounded that all substances were made up of solid concrete atoms with the void or space between them. He emphasized that both void and atoms were a primary reality. Democritus also viewed the atoms as being different from one another only in size, i.e., quantitatively and not qualitatively in contradistinction to the Nyāya-Vaiśeṣika approach. He sought to explain the qualities of different substances as being due to the movement or rearrangement of atoms. Even the living beings were regarded as a temporary arrangement of atoms and, what is more, the soul was also believed to be composed of atoms. The atomic postulate of Decmocritus was propagated but with some elaboration or extension of his ideas by Epicurus of Samos (342-270 B.C.) and his followers known as Epicureans.

The greatest exponent among the Epicureans was the Roman Lucretius (c. 95-55 B.C.). He explained the origin of the entire world as being due to the interaction of atoms. And he emphasised that behind such an interatction there was no creator or creative intelligence, and pointed out that even mental phenomena were of atomic origin (similar to the Nyāya-Vaiśeṣika). He held that material objects were of two kinds—atomic and compounds of atoms.

As for the motion or movement of atoms, according to Lucretius, they do not move or travel generally as isolated or individual units, but massed together. Thus their pace is retarded by the one dragging back the other as well as by the opposing external objects. But when separate atoms travel through empty space, they encounter no obstruction from without and move as units on the course on which they have embarked. A somewhat similar idea can be seen in Jaina atomism with regard to its postulate of the maximum and minimum speed of atoms. Likewise the Jaina view that atoms move generally in straight course and also curvilinear sometimes, finds an echo in Lucretius. There could will have been a transmission of Indian atomistic ideas to the Greeco-Roman world in the closing centuries before the Christian era.

In the history of science, as we now know, it was Greek atomism and the exposition of Lucretius that has found a place. On the other hand, Indian atomism, a part of the Indian doctrine of five elements, perhaps because of its metaphysical or philosophical affiliations and other compulsions of purely logical nature, has not received due attention. Nevertheless, Indian atomism was a favourite proposition among its exponents and opponents alike till about the thirteenth century A.D. until the Navya-Nyāya came up with its own nuances. The Jaina and the Buddha atomism too did not make much headway from their original atomic ideas each somewhat bound by its metaphysical position. Among the opponents of atomism was the great Śaṁkarācārya whose Advaitic exposition was so penetrating and his antagonism against the Nyāya-Vaiśeṣika was so powerful that atomism, though it did not take a back seat, could no longer enjoy the status that it had earlier. Alongside, however, the commentators of the both Nyāya and Vaiśeṣika continued to be the torch-beares of atomism.

In Europe, on the other hand, Greek atomism lay dormant till about the seventeenth century A.D. Even at the time of Galileo, the Greek atomic views had come to the fore, but more in the nature of philosophical ideas. But they stimulated a curiosity specially among the biologists who posed for themselves the questions like: are atoms alive?. And are they tiny beings?. Among the early exponents of the atomic views were Pierre Gassendi (1592-1655) and Robert Boyle (1627-91). Christain Huygens, who was known for his wave theory of light also supported it. As noted already, in Greek Atomism both atoms void were real. Newton, in his computations concerning the motion of planets, found it necessary to assume interstellar space to be a vacuum. As he pointed out in his *magnum opus*, '*Principia*' *(The Mathematical Principles of Natural Philosophy)*, the conception of atom arose when he tried to extend the idea of vacuum to terrestrial matter. His corpuscular theory of light not withstanding, it is very difficult to know the exact nature of his 'corpuscles' or 'particles'. However, Lucretius had stated that the heat and the bright light which the sun emits would travel through empty space and therefore they would be forced to move more slowly, cleaving their way as it were though waves of air. He postulated that the atoms that compose this radiance would not travel as isolated individual units but linked and massed together' (p. 64). Perhaps these ideas of Lucretius might have influenced the thinking of Newton in formulating his corpuscular theory of light.

Newton's contemporary and opponent (as regards the priority concerning calculus), was the German, Leibniz (1646-1716) who was opposed to atomism. But in France Voltaire (1694-1778) was an able exponent of atomism which he tried to popularize in his own way. In any case, the physical investigators of the eighteenth century generally considered the constitution of matter as atomic. Early in the nineteenth century John Dalton (1766-1844) put forward his atomic theory (1808) both in quantitative and qualitative terms.

Greek atomism had one advantage. It did not make any distinction like the atoms of different elements, but considered them as being only different in size, and thus they could be conceived as the building blocks of any type of substance. The Jaina atomism also projected the idea that atoms were of only one class. Even so it thought of qualities like colour, smell, taste and touch as being atomic indirectly, in the context of the four elements earth, water fire and air. The Buddhists too thought of atomic nature of these qualities. This type of circumscribed thinking was perhaps not permissive of a broader vision of atoms as the possible building units of the universe. Moreover, the other dimension of Greek atomism, namely, void or vacuum became important in the physical investigations that came up later in Europe. In the Indian context, the idea of did not appear to have comedown from its philosophical position to the physical plane.

There is some evidence to indicate that the Nyāya-Vaiśeṣika atomism was known to Arabic savants in the nineth/tenth century A.D., as contained in the works of al-Ashari and al-Rāzi. While the Indian astronomical and medical texts, in their Arabic translations, were rendered into Latin in the twelfth/thirteenth centuries and thus were available to the European savants then, Indian atomism did not experience such a pathway because of the 'selectivity of translators from Arabic to Latin', as explained by Needham. Some of the Nyāya-Vaiśeṣika texts were known to the Chinese culture area through the Buddhist refutations. But any type of atomism did not appeal to either the Taoists or Confucians. In any case there is no denying that Indian atomism has a distinct place in the history of scientific ideas, although, by and large, it remained within the philosophical or metaphysical confines in India.

BIBLIOGRAPHY

Primary Sources

1. *Bhāṣāpariccheda of Viśvanātha* with commentaries of Dinakara and Ramarudra. 1933. Atmarama Sarma (ed.). Bombay: Nirnayasagar Press.
2. *Bhāṣāpariccheda with Siddhānta Muktiāvari.* 1954. S. Mukherjee (ed.). Calcutta: Advaita Ashram.
3. *Bhagavatīsūtra* with commentary of Abhayadeva Sūri. 1882. Nanak Chandaji (ed.). 4 vols. Benaras.
4. *Kaṇādarahasya of Śankara Miśra.* 1917. Damodar Shastri Goswami (ed.). Benaras: Chowkhamba Sanskrit.
5. *Kiraṇavalī of Udayana.* 1918. Vindhyeshwari Prasad Dvivedi. Benaras: Chowkhamba Sanskrit Series; 1991. Jitendra S. Jetley (ed.). Vadodara: Oriental Institute.
6. *Kiraṇāvatībhāskara of Padnanābha Miśra.* 1920. Benaras: Sarasvati Bhavan Text.
7. *Nyāyakandalī of Śridahra.* 1977. Pandit Durgadham Jha. Varanasi: Sampurnanand Sanskrit Series.
8. *Nyāyakandalī of Dharmottara.* 1951. Srinivas Sastri (ed. & trans.). Saranath: Sahitya Bhandar.
9. *Nyāyadarśanaṃ: Nyāyasūtrās of Gautama, Uddyotakaras' Vārtika and Vācaspatimiśras' Tātparayatīkā.* 1985. Amarendramohana Tarktatirtha (ed.). Delhi: Munshiram Manohar Lal.

10. *Nyāya Kusumāñjali* with commentaries. 1967. P. Upādhayāya and Dhundirāja Śāstri. Benaras: Chowkhamba Sanskrit Series; 1980. Utamur T. Viraraghavachar. Tirupati: Kendriya Sanskrit Vidhyapeetha.
11. *Nyāyatīilavatī of Vallabhacārya.* 1970. Dhundirāja Śāstri (ed.). Benaras: Chowkhamba Sanskrit Series.
12. *Nyāyaamañjarī of Jayanta Bhaṭṭa.* 1936. Pandit Sri Surya Narayana Shukla (ed.). Benaras: Chowkhamba Sanskrit Series.
13. *Nyāyasāra of Bhasarvajña.* 1922. V.S. Abhyankar and C.R. Devadhar (ed.). Poona. Oriental Book Supplying Agency.
14. *Nyāyasūtras of Gautama with Vātsyāyana Bhāṣya and Vishwanatha Pañcānanaś.* 1922. N.D. Joshi (ed.). Poona: Anandashram.
15. *Nyāya Vārttika of Udyotakara.* 1887, 1914. V.P. Dvivedi (ed.). Bibliotheca Indica; 1916. Benaras: Chowkhamba Sanskrit Series.
16. *Padārthadharmasangraha of Praśastapada with Nyāya Kendalī.* 1916. Ganganath Jhā. Benaras: Lazarus & Co.
17. *Pancstikāyasāra of Kundkundācārya:* Chakravartinayanar, Sacred Book of the Jainas. 1936.
18. *Puggalapaññatti.* 1924. Nalanda: Pali Text Society Translation Series.
19. *Samayasāra of Kuṇḍakundācārya.* Sacred Books of the Jainas. Sital Prasad.
20. *Saptapadārthi of Śivāditya.* 1932. D. Gurumurti. Adyar, Madras: Theosophical Publishing House.
21. *Tattvarthāsūtra of Umāsvāti.* 1944. A.S. Sastri (ed.). Mysore: Oriental Library Publications.
22. *The Vaiśeṣika Aphorisms of Kaṇda with Upaskāra and Vivṛti commentaries.* 1975. A.E. Gough (trans.). Delhi: Munshiram Manoharlal.
23. *Vaiśeṣika Darśana with commentary of Saṅkara Miśra.* 1961. Jayanaryana Pancanana. Calcutta: Bibliotheca Indica.
24. *Vaiśeṣika Aphorisms with commentary of Praśastapāda and glass of Udayana.* 1885. Vindhyeshwari Prasad Dube. Benaras: Benaras Sanskrit Series.

Secondary Sources

1. Baily, Cyril. 1936. *The Greek Atomists and Epicurus.* Oxford: Clarendon Press.
2. Barua, Benimadhava. 1937. *Early Buddhism, Cultural Heritage of India.* Calcutta. Belurmath.
3. Berridale, Keith A. 1921. *Indian Logic and Atomism.* Oxford: Clarendon Press.
4. Bhaduri, S. *Studies in Nyāya-Vaiśeṣika Metaphysics.* Poona: Bhandarkar Oriental Research Institute.
5. Bhattacharya, S. 1961. "The Nyāya-Vaiśeṣika Doctrine of Qualities." *Philosophy, East and West,* 11(3). pp. 143-152.
6. Bodas, Mahadev Rajasan. 1924. "A Historical Survey of Indian Logic". *Journal of Asiatic Society,* Bombay. pp. 306-347.
7. Chatterjee, S.C. 1935. *Nyāya Theory of Knowledge.* Calcutta: University of Calcutta.
8. ———. 1950. *Fundamentals of Hinduism, A Philosophical Study.* Calcutta: Dasgupta & Co.
9. ———. 1912. *The Hindu Realism.* Allahabad: The Indian Press.
10. ———. 1970. "Science of Motion in India, A Historical Retrospect". *Indo-Asian Cultures.* pp. 41-45.
11. Faddegon, B. 1918. *The Vaiśeṣika System Described with the Help of the Oldest Texts.* Amsterdam: Johannes Muller.
12. Gajendragadgker, Veena. *Atomism, Kaṇādai Doctrine of the Padārthas.* Delhi: Sri Satguru Publications. pp. 280-359.
13. Gopalan, S. "Jaina Epistemology: An Overview". *Outlines of Jainism.* New York: John Wiley & Sons. pp. 47-59.
14. Hiriyanna, M. 1932. *Outlines of Indian Philosophy* London: George Allen & Unwin Ltd.
15. ———. 1949. *Essentials of Indian Philosophy.* New York: Macmillan & Co.
16. Jwala Prasad. 1958. *Indian Epistemology,* 2nd edition. New Delhi: Motilal Banarasidass.
17. Matilal, B.K. 1977. "Ontological Aspects and Jainism". *Journal of Indian Philosophy,* Vol. V(1).
18. Mishra, Umesh. 1936. *Conception of Matter according to Nyāya Vaiśeṣika.* Allahabad: Allahabad Press.
19. ———. 1957. *Cosmological Speculations of Vaiśeṣika.* Allahabad: Allahabad Press.
20. Needham, Joseph. 1956. *Science and Civilization in China,* vol. 2. Cambridge: Cambridge University Press.
21. Rant, A. 1950. "Buddhism and Science". *Mahabodhi,* 58. pp. 128-134.

22. Stcherbhatsky, T.H. 1925. *Buddhist's Logic,* 2 vols. Leningrad.
23. Sikdar, J.C. 1970. "Jaina Atomic Theory". *Indian Journal fo History of Science,* 5(2). pp. 199-213.
24. ———. 1964. *Studies in Bhagavatīsūtra.* Mirzapur: Research Institute of Prakṛt and Jainology.
25. ———. *Jain Conuption of Substance (Dravya), Studies in Bhagwati Sūtra.* pp. 557-561.
26. Sinha, Jadunath. 1938. *Indian Realism.* London: Trench & Triiber & Co.
27. ———. 1952. *History of Indian Philosophy,* vol. 1 & 2. Calcutta: Central Book Agency.
28. ———. 1949. *Introduction to Indian Philosophy.* Agra: Lakshminarayana Agarwal Publishers.
29. Smart, Nimian. 1967. "Nyāya-Vaiśeṣika Atomism" under 'Indian Philosophy'. *Encyclopadia of Philosophy,* 4. pp. 157-158.
30. Story, Francis "The Buddhist Concept of Four Great Elements". *Mahabodhi,* 64. pp. 292-93.
31. Subbarayappa, B.V. "Physical World: Concepts and Views." *A Chapter in A Concise History of Sciences in India.* New Delhi: Indian National Science Academy.
32. ———. 1963. "On Indian Atomism". *Bulletin of National Institute of Science of India,* 21. pp. 118-129.
33. Tatia, Nathumal. 1951. *Studies in Jaina Philosophy.* Benaras: Jaina Cultural Research Society.
34. Ui. H. 1971. *The Vaiśeṣika Philosophy according to Dasapadārtha Śāstra.* Chinese Texts with Introduction (trans. with notes). London: F.W. Thomas.
35. Yamakai, Sogen. 1912. *Systems of Buddhist Thought.* Calcutta: University of Calcutta.

CHAPTER 32

On Historicism: Reconstructing the Relationship between Science and Philosophy

Amitabha Dasgupta

PROBLEMATICS DEFINED

The theme that defines the problematics of this paper is unquestionably metaphilosophical. Its metaphilosophical nature will be obvious if we consider the three basic questions that form the underlying framework of this inquiry. These questions are: First, what is the nature of philosophy? Second, what constitutes philosophical understanding? and, Third, what is the conceptual linkage between scientific knowledge and philosophical inquiry? As we can see, these questions though different, are nevertheless closely related. The present paper will take these questions together and will explore its implications and possible answers in order to arrive at a conception of philosophy. The basic thrust of this paper is to put forward the view that the notion of historicity has a fundamental importance in the context of knowledge, be it scientific or philosophical. Historicity will thus provide a general model explaining the background assumptions responsible for the growth of scientific knowledge and philosophical understanding. This thesis is supported by three interrelated arguments. First, philosophy is inseparably related to the sciences understood in the broad sense of the term. This close relationship is possible due to the conceptual linkages existing between these two forms of knowledge. The evidence to this is found if we look at the history of philosophy, which provides a living testimony exhibiting the deeply embedded structure of linkages existing between these two inquiries. This, in turn, shows that the history of philosophy is closely connected to the history of science. The second argument justifying historicity is that for the adequate understanding of the sciences, especially of the natural sciences, it is necessary to take into account of the historical dimension that these sciences assume. And, finally, on the consideration of the previous argument regarding the historicity of science the same claim may be made regarding the historicity of philosophy justifying the need to take into account of the historical dimension of philosophy.

The history of philosophy is thus meant to be important in the two primary senses. In the first sense, it is important because the study of it will make us aware of the genesis, context and development of philosophical doctrines. The second sense in which it is important is that since philosophy is intertwined with science, history of philosophy thus necessarily expresses the evolution of scientific consciousness. This constitutes the significance of the historicist model in the context of science and philosophy in general. The notion of historicity suggested here does not negate science. It, on the other hand, views science as historically defined phenomena. The notion of historicity in this sense has a foundational significance since it forms the theoretical background for the adequate understanding of both science and philosophy. But now a very pertinent question may arise: Why is historicity so important and so central? To answer this question, we need to talk about the internal structure of the problematics of the paper. This will reveal that the notion of historicity proposed in this paper has a wider meaning than what is thought of in philosophical traditions defending historicist conception of philosophy. The root to historicity, as this paper argues, lies in the relationship between science and philosophy.

To put it broadly, philosophy may be viewed in terms of two competing standpoints upholding two conceptions of philosophy. This results into two sharply demarcated views defining the nature of philosophy. Accordingly, there is a view that considers philosophy to be an autonomous inquiry representing an objective body of knowledge. This has been the most dominant and influential view prevailing since the time of classical tradition. It may be characterized as the autonomous view of philosophy. The basic argument of this standpoint is that philosophy has a nature similar to that of science. It is thus conceived as an objective body of knowledge about the nature of things. Philosophical knowledge, so conceived, can be thus formulated and expressed in terms of objectively true sentences. This preoccupation with objective nature of knowledge makes philosophy free from contingencies of reason. A pursuit like this will enable philosophy to achieve the ideal of objective truth—a truth that is eternal, and thus ahistorical. One of the methodological precepts of Kant, for example, was to reconstruct philosophy on the model of the natural sciences because his purpose was "to set metaphysics upon the secure path of science".[1] The quest for objectivity is not intrinsic to traditional philosophy. The same quest is found in the contemporary period, particularly, in analytic philosophers' pursuit of philosophy.

The alternative to a historical autonomous conception of philosophy is the historically oriented view of philosophy. Philosophy is thus viewed as an expression of man's historically developing self and world-understanding. Philosophy in this sense has a history. It is rooted in the historicity of man's understanding of himself and the world. Philosophy, so conceived, is not an objective enterprise to be modeled after the natural sciences. It is not a transcendental inquiry as that of Kant. It is, on the other hand, a historical enterprise. Historicism constitutes the general method of philosophy. Philosophy, in this sense, is not autonomous. As the argument goes, the fallacy of the autonomous view of philosophy is that it has failed to see the irreducible historicity involved in philosophical thinking. It has failed because of its sole reliance on natural science. It is due to this reason the advocates of the historicist view of philosophy suggest that philosophy must dissociates its connections from the natural sciences and instead it should tie itself to the tradition of *Geisteswissenchaften.*

We are now faced with a dilemma—a dilemma between autonomy vs historicity. To accept the former implies philosophy to be modeled after the natural sciences, whereas to accept the latter implies philosophy must cut off its connections with the natural sciences and to affiliate itself with the tradition of cultural and historical sciences. We are thus faced with the dilemma regarding what view to choose.

This paper argues that both the alternatives are unacceptable on the ground that there is a fundamental defect in the formulation of the problem itself. It is because of this that we are faced with the dilemma. But the dilemma posed here is not a genuine dilemma. It can be removed once the notion of historicity is situated in its broader context that will reveal its foundational significance. It will be a context that will transcend the conflict between the natural sciences and the tradition of *Geisteswissenchaften* because both will have a common core. In view of this, the controversy between autonomy vs historicity will be found to be spurious. Pursuing autonomy in philosophical inquiry can be shown to be unachievable. To this effect, arguments can be given to show that the questions (such as, 'What is knowledge?' 'What is human nature?') which constitute the autonomous nature of philosophy in its ultimate analysis depend on other disciplines. Similarly, the other alternative, namely, the historicist conception of philosophy cannot be formulated so narrowly that its entire focus ultimately rests on creating science-free space. But the idea of science-free space is an abstraction and is thus an unattainable state. It is because of its sole concentration on the extra-scientific experience of life the historicist conception of philosophy has ignored the problem of understanding the relationship between extra-scientific experience and scientific experience of life. This question can neither be ignored nor be bypassed, particularly, in view of the science-permeated character of our life. However, understanding of the relationship between these two domains of experience will be possible only when we take historicity of scientific knowledge into account. This justifies the need for having a broad based conception of historicity.

In view of the problematics stated above, this paper will have the following sections. The first section will present the autonomous view of philosophy in the light of Kant and the contemporary analytic philosophers. This will be followed by a critique addressing to the question: What is wrong with the autonomous view of philosophy? The second section will present the historicist standpoint and the justification it offers for the historicist conception of philosophy. In this respect, it will specially go into the discussion of the view which establishes the affinity between the historicist conception of philosophy and the *Geisteswissenchaften.* The view to be particularly highlighted is the hermeneutical philosophy of Gadamer. This discussion on the historicist conception of philosophy will be followed by a critique exposing the fallacy involved in the historicist mode of reasoning. The third section will go into the question explaining that in what sense the natural sciences can be said to be inherently historical. In the fourth or the final section, we will come back to our original question and will suggest that the relationship between philosophy and science can be reconstructed on the basis of the historicity of knowledge.

I

VINDICATING THE STANDPOINT OF AUTONOMY: KANT IN PERSPECTIVE

Speaking from the Kantian standpoint, philosophy assumes its own autonomy—representing its institutional and substantial distinctiveness from that of the sciences. Philosophy as a form of transcendental inquiry is thus engaged in the study of presuppositions of knowledge.

Kant addresses to the question: How is the knowledge of an objective order possible? The same concern for objectivity that Kant shows can be found in his approach to ethics where he seeks to develop a system of values to explain the objectivity of moral judgement. Thus, for Kant, examining the human reason under its two aspects—theoretical and practical—becomes the sole objective of philosophy. Accordingly, we find that the main thrust of Kant's philosophical project is to explain:

First: The possibility of the new scientific knowledge represented by the mathematical world-view of Newton
and
Second: The possibility of human freedom.

These two are brought under the two aspects of human reason with an explicit aim of relating the two in a unified conceptual framework of autonomous philosophy.

In his exploration into theoretical reason, Kant was highly influenced by the sciences of the seventeenth and eighteenth century Europe. The ideas that Kant finds most appealing are universality and objectivity that the new science represents. In contrast to this, speculative metaphysics failed to offer any such knowledge, which is worthy of consideration. In fact, the very possibility of metaphysics was questioned by Hume's radical scepticism. Kant, on the other hand, claims that all philosophy must address to the central question: How is metaphysics possible?[2] Through this question, Kant developed a systematic critique of human thought and reason. This results into his attempt to describe the nature and limits of knowledge. Accordingly, Kant designs his metaphysics with an explicit aim that it can serve as the foundation of discursive thought. His critical enterprise may be thus characterized by the following three-fold objectives. First, to show that there is a legitimate employment of understanding and the rules governing it can be made explicit. Second, the Humean scepticism is impossible on the ground that the rules of understanding alone can establish the existence of an objective world. The evidence to this can be seen from the fact that the world exhibits causal connections. Third, there are certain fundamental principles of science, such as, the principle of conservation of substance, the principle that every event has a cause and the principle that objects exist in space and time can be established *a priori*[3].

Kant's exploration of the nature and the structure of theoretical reason evidently indicates a distinct conception of philosophy that Kant upholds. Kant, though influenced by science, accepts that there is a fundamental difference between science and philosophy. The role of philosophy is not the same as that of science. Philosophy develops into a transcendental inquiry and thus makes explicit the presuppositions of objective knowledge embodied in science. The purpose of his Transcendental Deduction was to offer proof for the presupposition of scientific thinking represented in Newtonian physics and Euclidian geometry[4]. Philosophical knowledge in this sense assumes its own autonomy. It has its independent foundation and thus does not depend on any tradition. The conception of philosophy that Kant derives through his examination of theoretical reason unmistakably points out the autonomous and unhistorical nature of philosophy. The same conception of philosophy is found in Kant's treatment of practical reason. Reason under its two aspects—theoretical and practical—though different can be brought, as Kant's attempt shows, under the same conceptual framework. It is an unified approach both to theoretical and practical reason.

Kant finds that moral experience has a character, which is similar to that of natural experience. The similarity between the two can be asserted on the ground that moral experience is both universal and necessary and hence objective. Its objectivity follows from its law-governed nature. The chief concern of Kant's practical reason is thus to establish the objectivity of morals. In contrast to theoretical reason imparting understanding in terms of which we think or judge, practical reason involves formulating imperatives and the justification of imperatives. Kant argues that it is through such attempt that practical reason will be able to generate an objective system of morality based on the categorical notion of imperative. For to ensure objectivity, the nature of imperatives, as Kant argues, must be categorical and not hypothetical. Hypothetical imperatives cannot fulfil this requirement because their motivating force depends on the actual desires of the individual to whom they are addressed. The categorical imperative, on the other hand, for its validity does not depend on any empirical conditions. Unlike hypothetical imperatives, they do not contain any reference to the antecedent interest of the subject. As a result, the form through which they are expressed is: 'Do this!' or 'You ought to do this'.

The above exploration reveals that the concern for objectivity has been central to both Kant's preoccupation with science and ethics. In both these cases, his major concern is to establish the *a priori* validity of the universal laws, be it scientific or moral.[5] This allows him to show how these inquiries are possible on a legitimate ground. Kant's exploration of reason under its two aspects can be thus brought under the same framework. The reason is that their primary thrust is same no matter whether the subject of study is scientific knowledge or human conscience. This results into *a priori* conception of philosophy engaged in the study of presuppositions of these two areas of human concern. Through his attempt to vindicate the presuppositions of science and morality, Kant established the *a priori* certainity of these presuppositions. But this Kantian notion of *a priori* certainty can be achieved only when we accept that the presuppositions which Kant wants to study are not subjected to any conditions of historicity. They are trans-historical and due to this they are autonomous in nature. But can their validity be ascertained without caring for history? Can *a prioricity* defy historicity? These questions can be validly raised while considering Kant's presuppositional approach to both science and morality. A critical study of this approach will reveal that the *a priori* certainty that Kant claims for the presuppositions that explain the possibility of science and morality may not be tenable. Kant's fundamental plea that nature must conform to the pattern that he formulates and similarly morality must obey the dictates that he spells out may be found to have serious limitations on the ground of historical experience. This possesses a serious threat to the autonomy of the Kantian trans-historical presuppositions. We will now substantiate this claim by giving a brief account of what is wrong with the *a priori* nature of Kant's presuppositions both with respect to science and morality.

Does Nature Conform to Kant? An Argument from the History of Science

As stated earlier, for Kant, nothing will become an object of knowledge if it does not conform to certain *a priori* forms of our intuition and our understanding. If this attempt initiated by Kant is successful it will certainly have tremendous importance. On the basis of this principle, we will be able to deduce from it causality, premises of induction and many other important things. Similarly, by using the same token we will know the nature of space and time so thoroughly and so exhaustively that we will be succeeded in enunciating the principles of geometry without even assuming the possibility that they may be defeated by actual experience. Finally, it is through this Kantian project that we will be reassured that nature must obey causal laws and so on. Scientific knowledge is thus characterized by infallibilism and ahistoricism. But, can scientific knowledge be so characterized? Does nature conform to the design set by Kant? The lesson from the history of science shows contrary to what Kant claims.

Let us start with causality, which for Kant, is the *a priori* condition that understanding imposes on a given material. Accordingly, we cannot conceive of an event which do not conform to the principle of causality. It is, on the other hand, an inescapable form that rules out any violation of it. But this Kantian *a priori* determinism does no longer hold when we look at the development in post Newtonian physics, particularly, quantum mechanics. The discovery of quantum phenomena has forced physicists to rethink about such universal application of causality. They find that its application is inevitably restricted. Quantum mechanics thus offers an alternative picture of physics that allows departure from the principle of causality characterized by Kant as the *a priori* form of understanding. It is indeterminacy that matters when we try to take account of sub atomic particles. Thus, the theory makes it evident that the behaviour of a single electron cannot be predicted with absolute precision on the ground that causal laws do not govern it. The only possibility that the theory allows is to predict the average behaviour of particles. It is not causal determinism but probability that enters into this new scientific world-view. It may be good to caution here that though quantum mechanics does not subscribe to causal determinism it does not propagate chaos either. The theory has the two-layered structure. First, the particles whose motion is represented by certain waves known as the deBroglie waves obey rigorous causal laws. It is due to this reason that one can predict with absolute precision the propagation of the waves. The second layer constitutes the interpretation—the interpretation that we give to these waves. Waves are interpreted as 'probability clouds' where the density formed at each point indicates the probability of the occurrence of a particle. This implies that we cannot have definite statements but probability statements regarding the presence of a particle in a given place and time. We can never say for certain where exactly a particular electron will be found. Instead, we can say that with what probability we may expect to find the electron at a certain place. Quantum mechanics can only give average behaviour of particles. This signifies the breakdown of traditional determinism and the emergence of indeterminism in physics. What is indeterministic is the interpretation of deBroglie waves as formally representing certain probabilities. Particles, on the other hand, remain causally inaccessible. They themselves do not obey causal laws. This results into an ambivalent situation showing that even if the same experiment is repeated with all the conditions being kept intact the result will be different in each time. The principle 'like causes—like effects' thus no longer holds.

The result of quantum mechanics has a far-reaching significance on Kant's presuppositional approach to science. Kant argues that science will not be possible unless we accept causality. Causality is the basic presupposition of science. Quantum mechanics, on the other hand, shows the possibility of constructing a theory along the line that flatly contradicts Kant's claim for causality. It establishes the legitimacy of departing from the traditional notion of strict causality without resulting into the breakdown of science. If Kant is right we cannot even in principle entertain such views. To give up causality will mean to deny the very condition of gaining scientific knowledge. Kant's failure is that he did not think of possible forms of physical laws. Causality becomes the ultimate framework for him and thus it enjoys an *a priori* status. But, by doing this, Kant foreclosed the possibility of the alternative paradigm in science. He finds Newtonian paradigm to be the only paradigm expressing complete knowledge of the empirical world. But this proved to be wrong in view of the alternative picture offered by quantum mechanics. In other words, history of science shows that nature does not conform to Kant. His justification of science as embodying infallible and ahistorical knowledge becomes untenable. It is untenable because it does not take into account of the historical world of praxis. The historicity of science will show that science is not beyond falsification. Science being a creation of man is subjected to various sociological and historical conditions. The *a priori* certainity that Kant claims for science can be achieved only if we accept, to use D.P.Chattopadhyaya's phrase, that science is not "man-made but God-made".[6] In view of the historicity of science, philosophy can no longer be conceived as a transcendental inquiry explicating the a priori presuppositions of science. The autonomy ascribed to philosophy looses its ground due to the inherent historical nature of knowledge whether with respect to science or with morality.

Are Moral Laws Objective?

As we have seen, according to Kant since moral laws are universal and necessary they can be thus called objective. But are they really objective? This question can be significantly raised because the ground on which this claim is made can itself be questioned. Kant finds moral laws to be universal and necessary because moral laws, for him, are ahistorical, non-social and non-human. Moral laws, so conceived, turn out to be formal abstractions without having any relation to specific empirical situation. The notion of objectivity in morals is thus the outcome of a series of arguments constituting the Kantian perspective. Hence, to attack the objectivity of morals means attacking the entire perspective that Kant invoked. The line of attack conceived in this paper will have three major arguments. These three arguments together will form a systematic critique exposing the untenability of Kant's thesis on ethical objectivity.

First: The utopian concept of man. Kant's ethical theory is inseparably related to his theory of man where the latter may be characterized as a presupposition of the former because without it Kant's theory cannot stand on its own ground. This will be evident if we look into the main concern of his ethical theory. The main concern of Kant's ethical theory is to construct the ethical schema for the imaginary Rational Man removed totally from historically living human beings of the society. He is also the Universal Man not constrained either by space and time or by any other external influences. The reason is that he acts on his own. He acts according to the dictates of his own reasoning which, in other words, implies acting objectively. From this, Kant argues, that to act objectively means that on behalf of all rational beings, he can put forward the claim that the maxim or the principle of his action should become the universal law. This is the process through which the objectivity of moral law is attained. It becomes objective because it is the Rational Man who is the author formulating this universal law. Objectivity is thus directly connected with rationality ensuring universality. But, just as objectivity satisfies the condition of rationality, similarly, rationality, in turn, needs to satisfy certain conditions. Otherwise, it cannot be achieved. Hence, for Kant, for rationality to be achieved it is a requirement of the theory that the Rational Man must be unhistorical and unsocial. This is how Kant's system of ethics may be viewed as the vindication of the ethics of the Rational Man.

But ironically the truth is different. The ethics constructed on the basis of the Rational Man is really the ethics of the Utopian Man. Kant's formulation of the categorical imperative is a clear instance of this. For categorical imperatives to be possible, the moral subject must be autonomous in the sense that he must be free to create his own moral laws and the moral world. But is this not an utopian exercise? Imperatives are not unconditional. Imperatives, for human beings, are conditioned by various social customs and traditional practices. In a similar way, we are not free to create our own moral world. Our actions are conditioned by various situational factors. We thus act according to the logic of the situation. This points out inherent historicity of our existence. We are historically controlled beings and morality evolves through a dialectical relationship between man and history and man and society.

From the historical/social nature of man it follows that morality cannot be a static concept. Kant's universe is essentially a static universe where the possibility of new experience and the possibility of human failures are ruled out. It is a closed universe where everything is prejudged including human nature and moral experience. This indicates not the active but the passive role of the moral subject. If this is so then isn't it a retrogression from Kant's earlier Copernican revolution? Professor D.P.Chattopadhyaya[7], in one of his insightful papers, argued that the Copernican revolution through which Kant brought anthropo-centricity in philosophy of science surprisingly rejected it when he came to ethics. With this we now come to the second argument showing that the moral world cannot be separated from the social world.

Second: The Social World is the Moral World. In continuation to the earlier argument justifying the historicity of human existence, the present argument has been construed in the same manner justifying the inseparability of the moral world with the social world. The force of the objection is the same in both the arguments.

The inseparability of the two worlds can be established on the basis of a linguistic/ conceptual argument which will show that description and evaluation are not two logically distinct activities.[8] This implies that there is nothing called pure description nor is there pure evaluation. Such a possibility is conceptually ruled out on the ground that description involves evaluation and in the same way evaluation also involves description. This will be evident from the analysis of descriptive sentences and evaluative sentences. Take the case of description based evaluation. The sentence, 'The room is comfortable' is a descriptive sentence but it is also an evaluation. It is an expression of my attitude—the attitude of my approval of the room. If we notice, this statement is supported by a series of descriptions, such as, the room is well ventilated, cozy, airy and so on. This range of phenomena exhibit the qualities due to which the room is described as comfortable. This statement is thus both descriptive and evaluative. By saying that the room is comfortable, I am saying something about the room and at the same time by saying this I am expressing my attitude towards the room. This is the case of description-based evaluation.

The next is the evaluation-based description. Description is always context dependent. It is offered from a point of view. It is the particular point of view that influences me to look for relevant facts. Describing an event is also at the same time assessing the event. The reason is that providing the context implies that I am saying how the event is to be viewed. I can, for example, describe an event of someone committing a murder. The description provides the entire context of how the murder took place and the intentional nature of the action. This description may look like a pure description devoiding of any assessment. But this is not true because this description is also an assessment of the situation. The meaning of the word 'murder' implies that it is morally wrong. Hence, the description of murder cannot be value neutral. With this we now come to the third objection exposing the inherent limitation of Kant's notion of freedom.

Third: Freedom and its Opposites. Kant's notion of freedom has the following characteristics. First, moral laws will not be operative unless we accept the postulate of freedom and, second, freedom is constraint by reason. Kant's characterization of freedom makes it obvious that Kant subscribes to a notion, which may be described as the internalist perspective of freedom. Accordingly, freedom is taken to be internal to man. Now, to take freedom as internal means that it is contrasted with the external. Kant's internalist conception of freedom thus assumes a pair of opposites, such as, internal and external, subjective and objective, free will and determinism etc.[9] But this is where the problem lies. Freedom does not assumes any such contents or opposites. The root of the problem lies with the internalist notion of freedom, where freedom is understood in the sense of being pure, absolute and thus unconstrained by any external factors. It's main problem is that it fails to see that 'freedom' becomes a significant notion only in relation to a situation. In other words, freedom is essentially a situational concept within which all these opposites are reconciled. Freedom then is seen not in terms of its opposites but as a holistic notion, which is experienced in a situation. We may briefly point out here the reasons explaining why freedom due to its situational nature cannot be thought of in terms of its opposites.

It has been said that freedom is an internal notion undisturbed by the objective/ external standpoint. But can we have such a notion? Possibly not. Thomas Nagel[10] pointed out that the internalist conception of freedom leads to a predicament—an anamoly that follows from its logical structure. The basic force of the argument is that the external and the internal cannot be separated and attempt to do it will inevitably lead to a predicament. True, the internal and the external standpoints are different. But, as Nagel observes, they are not discontinuous because both belong to the same framework—"the framework of human life". That is the reason why the objective/external standpoint is never alien to our life which is reflected in our outlook i.e., our craving for being objective. In this situation we no longer confine ourselves to the internal perspective but place ourselves to the wider world and critically examine our attitudes and dispositions from this external/objective point of view. This is how we get more and more objective understanding about our own selves. This is also the requirement of freedom since without critical self-understanding we cannot act in the best possible way. But what do we gain out of this? We are now faced with a dilemma. Either, we have to give up the internal perspective on freedom and accept that freedom does not involve opposition between the internal and the external or we have to remain within the internalist perspective on freedom. But to accept the latter will imply facing a predicament. There is predicament because, on the one hand, we find that in order to achieve self-understanding which is necessary for attaining freedom we need to be objective and, on the other hand, this pursuit of self-understanding has no place within the internalist framework simply on the ground that self-understanding involves adopting more and more objective attitude. The internalist conception of freedom is thus logically trapped within its own theoretical framework. The only way to come out from this predicament will be to accept the view that freedom is a historically defined notion and thus the best way to understand it will be to see it as a situational concept. To view it as a situational concept means freedom will never be understood in terms of its opposites.

In the situational concept of freedom, freedom is always understood in terms of a set of restrictions or constraints. Unlike Kant, these constraints are not imposed by reason only. Further, these constraints are not obstacle to freedom. They will be viewed as obstacle only if we take freedom in the absolute sense. On the contrary, the presence of these restrictions will be necessarily felt whenever there is a situation involving freedom. As said earlier, there is freedom only in a situation and thus the first constraint of freedom is that it is restricted or limited to a situation. Along with this, freedom is limited to our capacities. There are things which we can do and there are things which we cannot do. Third, freedom is limited to knowledge. If we take freedom in relation to a situation then knowledge of the situation is important for the exercise of freedom.

The above discussion makes it apparent that moral laws are not objective in the sense in which Kant claims. Moral laws operate through the course of history. They evolve through social situations—through the dialectics operating between man and society. The *a priori* foundation on which Kant's system of ethics stands can be found to have serious flaws. These flaws in the foundation suggest that the Kantian attempt to construct ethics ahistorically ignoring, thereby, the social and human issues of life will inevitably fail.

Coming back to the autonomy question, the present study on Kant's theoretical and practical reason shows that Kant's *a priori* conception of philosophy has serious limitations. Its limitations become apparent when considered from the standpoint of historicity of knowledge and reason. Knowledge, be it scientific or ethical, must have a historical core. This undermines the *a priori* conception of philosophy. Philosophy can no longer be thus conceived as a transcendental project. With this downfall of *a priori* conception of philosophy, the autonomy question becomes an elusive ideal—an unattainable goal.

The search for this elusive ideal continues. It continues not in the same line as that of Kant. Its programme is not to discover presuppositions of science or to discover objective moral laws. Yet, there is an underlying similarity. The similarity lies in its conception of philosophy i.e., philosophy as autonomous. It is said that philosophy enjoys autonomy in the same way in which science enjoys autonomy. The contemporary analytic philosophy is a vivid expression of this metaphilosophical ideal.

Analytic Philosophy in its Search for Autonomy

Kant explicitly addressed the question of autonomy in philosophy. His objective is how to make philosophy autonomous and at par with science. This is how philosophy construed as a transcendental project by Kant came into existence. But analytic philosophers never explicitly addressed the autonomy question nor did they have the same Kantian dream in their pursuit of philosophy. Yet, the issue of autonomy looms large at the background of analytic philosophy. Analytic philosophers have been influenced by the scientific ideal of autonomy and, accordingly, in their methodology they tried to preserve the same conception of autonomy. This is evident from their programme itself. Analytic philosophy does not end with autonomy but begins with autonomy in the sense that the viability of its programme entirely depends on the condition that philosophy must be autonomous. Autonomy becomes a fundamental requirement of analytic philosophy. It is in this sense that autonomy is a methodological issue whereas, for Kant, it is a substantive issue.

How does then autonomy figure in analytic philosophy? This will be done at two levels. At the first level, we will give a brief description of the programme that analytic philosophy initiates highlighting orientation and the distinctive style that it assumes. At the second level, on the basis of this account we will show how the notion of autonomy figures in analytic philosophy.

Analytic philosophy starts with the assumption that philosophical problems are problems of language/meaning. The objective of philosophical inquiry is not to construct speculative theories of the world but to offer clarification of the meaning of concepts. Language thus becomes an indispensable tool for philosophical study. It is felt that problems in philosophy arise due to the misuse of language. An uncritical use of language can create hopeless confusion. Wittgenstein holds the view that philosophy starts with puzzlement. One such puzzlement is that a set of apparently true propositions may lead to an implausible conclusion contradicting that which is known to be the case. Metaphysics, for example, is an inquiry, which is largely an outcome of these philosophical puzzles. From the description of some of the classical philosophical problems like the mind-body dualism, the problem of perception, the nature of God, the knowledge of other minds, the nature truth, etc., one can see how philosophers are caught in a situation in which they go round and round and from which no escape seems possible. In such a state of affairs the only job which philosophy can perform is to cure conceptual illness. Thus, language must be properly investigated in order that we may avoid distorting it or be misled by it. This is what philosophers like J.L. Austin have called a “relook at the world without blinkers”.

That philosophy has an intimate relationship with language is further evidenced by the fact that in order to be conceived, thought and understood, a philosophical problem has to be formulated in a language. Language acts as a necessary condition for philosophical thought since it is impossible to think, to believe, to act or to be conscious without making vocal or sub-vocal use of language. Thus, the philosopher is interested in exploring and systematizing the logic of words. All this is evident from the recent development in analytic philosophy. We are no longer surprised when we are offered philosophical theories in the form of linguistic proposals. Gilbert Ryle goes to the extent of saying that "philosophical arguments have always, if not entirely, consisted in attempts to thrash out what it means to say so and so"[11]. From this brief account we can derive a few implications showing the internal structure of analytic philosophy. This, in turn, will reveal that in what sense analytic philosophy may be claimed to be autonomous in its approach and orientation[12].

First: Preoccupation with Problems. Analytic philosophy holds that the function of philosophy is to study concepts. Philosophical problems are thus characterized essentially as problems of language. Accordingly, philosophical inquiry may be viewed as a series constituting of problems expressed through concepts. But, what kind of series is this? Is it the same as historical series consisting of events, which are spatio-temporally continuous? Certainly, there is a view of history involved here. But this is different from the history of the usual kind where history is seen as a continuous process. But, when we talk of history of problems in analytic philosophy the sense of history involved there is a discontinuous history. It is discontinuous because of the spatio-temporal gaps existing between the problems. However, there is a internal connection maintained between them. The internal connection is formed due to interrelated arguments running through problems that constitute the history of philosophy. The evidence to this is found in philosophical practice where we see one philosopher criticizing another—criticizing essentially his arguments. This reveals an important truth. Since the internal connection is not temporal there is no sense of past or present involved here. Speaking metaphorically, past is dissolved into present. Hence, a present philosopher while criticizing a past philosopher considers him as if he is his contemporary. The central element involved in this perception is the logical structure that holds the internal connection expressed in the form of arguments that defy the externalities of history. All these trends unmistakably show the intellectual independence of the discipline that philosophy characterizes.

Second: Opposition between Problem and Theory. The second important implication that follows from our summary statement on analytic philosophy is that it is mostly preoccupied with problems and not with theories, doctrines or systems. Analytic philosophy thus ruled out theoretical continuity in favour of maintaining continuity at the level of problems in the history of philosophy. But why is this opposition to theory? It is a well-accepted fact that the continuity achieved through theories is much more stronger and substantial than the continuity achieved through problems. This is evident from the fact that theoretical continuity is normally taken as the basis for the existence of continuous discipline. In view of this, one is curious to know why analytic philosophy is an exception to this? The answer to this lies in analytic philosophers' hostility towards metaphysics.

Historically, metaphysics was involved in constructing speculative theories with a purpose to explain the ultimate nature of reality. But such speculative theories concerning the world lost their significance due to logical positivists' critique of metaphysics. It has been shown on a logico-linguistic ground that metaphysics does not form a significant discourse. This finding made a fresh ground for a new approach to philosophy. The purpose of philosophy is not construction of theories because that will lead to metaphysics. Philosophy, on the other hand, must be viewed as consisting of problems. This view follows from the linguistic characterization of philosophy. Accordingly, the study of problems becomes the main thrust of the history of philosophy. Keeping this view in mind, G.E.Moore named his book *Some Main Problems of Philosophy* and Russell published his book under the title *The Problems of Philosophy*. These titles are highly suggestive because they signify a view—a trend that saves the autonomy of philosophy. Opposition to theory in analytic philosophy is thus a prerequisite—a methodological device for achieving autonomy in philosophy.

Third: Conflict between Philosophical Systems and Scientific Knowledge. Apart from logico-linguistic reasons there are certain strong external reasons responsible for the untenability of philosophical theories/systems. It was increasingly realized that philosophical systems were losing their importance in view of the tremendous growth of scientific knowledge. Their explanations and world-views were not only found to be incompatible but spurious in relation to empirical findings of modern science. History of science shows how philosophical systems of the world have been gradually replaced by scientific systems of the world. This transition to science creates a vacuum in philosophy because the very survival of the discipline becomes a problem. In view of this crisis, the only alternative left for philosophers is to make a radical shift—a shift from construction of theories to problem solving. This allows space for autonomous research in philosophy and, thereby, ensures progress in philosophy. As Passmore pointed out, unlike other systems of history, problem history is "interested in periods of advance".[13]

Finally, there is an important feature involved in this approach, which brings analytic philosophy closer to Kant. Analytic philosophers, while asserting that there is an internal continuity between problems, implicitly assume that there is a permanent structure of human reason which is undefined and undisturbed by history. We find that Strawson, for example, while talking about his descriptive metaphysic states that language assumes a vast conceptual core which is totally unaffected by the contingencies of the history of reason. The standpoint of autonomy represented here is not thus essentially different from the standpoint of Kant though the respective approaches involved are different.

The above study shows how the notion of autonomy is figured in analytic philosophy. It states the conditions, the necessary requirements that make philosophy an autonomous inquiry being free from contingencies of history. But can philosophy be free from historicity of reason? Alternatively, can philosophy be autonomous if those above conditions are satisfied? The main source of the problem lies with those conditions. Analysis of these conditions will reveal that they are essentially intermingled with historicity. It will reveal that philosophy has a true historical nature. The autonomy view projected in analytic philosophy thus does not give a complete picture of philosophy. On the basis of this above line of argument we will now construct a critique exposing specifically the untenability of the problem view of philosophy offered in analytic philosophy.[14] To do so will be to refute the very ground on which the notion of autonomy lies in analytic philosophy.

First: Problem-Theory Nexus. Analytic philosophy holds the three following propositions. One: Problems are central to philosophical inquiry. Two: They can be studied independently of any theory. And, Three: the same problems persist throughout history of philosophy. But can problems be conceived and studied independently of theories? Again, in view of the assumption that history of philosophy implies recurrence of problems, how do we account for its progress? This is where we find a sharp contrast between philosophy and other disciplines. In other disciplines the objective of the inquiry is not the recurrence of problems but solutions of it and, most importantly, these solutions are offered in the light of theories. An example from the history of science may be immensely helpful here. Take the case of matter. The way the problems of matter are conceived in today's theoretical context is different from the way it is conceived in the work of Democritus. Note that these are not alternative views. They are not invariant through time. On the contrary, there is a long chain of succession of theories involved, which are responsible for replacing one particular problem situation into another. A problem is identified, theoretically structured, and explained through a theory. The change of theory by the rival theory thus naturally leads to the change of the problem. This is how science progresses from the Democritean theory of matter to the modern theory of matter conceptualized in terms of mechanics of waves. These theories though different from each other form a connection. This is what Karl Popper calls convergence of theories which is responsible for the growth of scientific knowledge. The growth of scientific knowledge is a cumulative process, which goes through a succession of theories leading to the gradual improvement of scientific knowledge. On the basis of this account we can reasonably conclude that there is a problem-theory nexus and the progress of an inquiry depends on a series of theories.

In view of this critique, the autonomy question in philosophy does not seem to stand on its own feet. Analytic philosophy finds a crucial dilemma. On the one hand, it finds that problem oriented approach cannot be practiced because problems have no independent existence apart from theories and, on the other hand, to accept theoretical continuity will mean accepting temporality which will mean giving up autonomy.

Second: From Where do Problems come from? This is the second level at which our critique of autonomy is construed. The issue of autonomy in philosophy cannot leave the question concerning the origin of philosophical problems unexplained. Since problems are one which philosophy studies, to find out its origin is thus an important task. This will reveal how far the study of concepts will enable philosophy to achieve autonomy. The study of the origin will reveal that philosophy receives its problems from society. The multifaceted nature of society expressed through science, religion, art, politics etc., becomes the constant source of new ideas and problems. In view of this, the sacrosanct nature of problems as upheld in analytic philosophy is no longer tenable. It reveals that problems are historically occasioned. If this is how problems are generated then in what sense will the study of it attain autonomy of philosophy? Philosophers, in general, and analytic philosophers, in particular, did not pay much attention to this aspect. Instead of accounting for it, they tried to bypass it by considering it as mere factual that did not have any effect on philosophical inquiry. This view is the result of the distinction made between the conceptual and the empirical. But to rule out the philosophical importance of this issue on the ground that it is empirical is naivety—a dogma that can hardly be justified. This is particularly true in the context of autonomy issue. Looking at the origin, we find that problems are historically rooted and, hence, they cannot be treated as ahistorical, non-temporal and autonomous.

Analytic philosophers, of course, have an escape route. Their line of argument is that even if we accept the importance of historical context, the fact remains that the context meant here is the context of problems and not of theories. As a result, problems are selected and discussed not in the light of theories. This, in a sense, will be asserting the independent nature of problems. If problems are delinked from theories then one can maintain the recurrence of problems. The problems of the past can be evaluated in terms of the philosophical needs of the present. This may be described as the contraction of the past into the present. This constitutes the non-temporal nature of philosophical problems through which the autonomy of philosophy is defended. But, is this a right argument? The central idea involved in this argument is the contraction of the past into the present so that the past/present distinction disappears. However, this is a lopsided and a false move. Is the past that is reduced to the present, really a present? Alternatively, what kind of present is this? The idea of present involved here does not have any existence. It is a false notion or what Kruger calls "spurious present". If this central argument collapses the idea of autonomy too collapses.

Third: Is there a Temporally Invariant Subject Matter of Philosophy? The autonomy of philosophy is directly related to the temporally invariant nature of the subject matter of philosophy. To have such a nature will imply that philosophy must be having a special domain of its inquiry. This will allow recurrence of problems without the necessary backing up of theories. In this respect, we may identify in the light of Rorty's critique the two "perennial and eternal problems" of philosophy. These two are problems of knowledge and human nature. They form the theoretical core of both traditional and modern philosophy. The existence of a theoretical core reveals that there is an unchanging internal structure of reason running all through the history of mankind. This, of course, keeps philosophy on a firm ground as an autonomous discipline.

But what is wrong with the idea of philosophy having a temporally invariant subject matter? The difficulty lies with the very idea itself. In this respect, we may point out two kinds of difficulty. One may be characterized as methodological and the other as empirical/practical. The methodological difficulty is essentially related to the issue of framework. The eternal problems of philosophy can be studied only through a framework suitable to it. Accordingly, it is realized that the framework constructed for this purpose must be permanent and neutral—natural to all cultures and traditions. This is where the problems lies. A neutral framework is constructed to engage in an impossible task. It is impossible because it attempts to provide what Rorty says "non-historical conditions of any possible historical development".[15] The so-called eternal problems like knowledge or human nature are essentially historically defined problems and accordingly their characterizations vary due to the historical needs or conditions. If this so then how could we construct non-historical conditions for those that are historical? Isn't it a contradiction inherent within philosophy itself? Next, the practical/empirical difficulties arise because the eternal nature of those perennial philosophical problems are increasingly found to be irrelevant in view of the rapid development of scientific knowledge. As a result, the *a priori* character of philosophy becomes a questionable assumption. The historical nature of philosophy shows that it does not have a temporally in variant subject matter. However, to say this is not to rule out that there are no common problems. But common problems are historically oriented. To explain, how do we learn these common problems? We learn them by fulfilling certain conditions, which are historical in nature. The outcome of all these arguments lead to the denial of the autonomy of philosophy.

Kant's transcendental project and the problem oriented approach of analytic philosophy suffered from a basic defect. Their defect was that they tried to model philosophy in the pattern of the natural sciences. The imposition of ahistorical character to philosophy thus became a necessity. Accordingly, Kant and analytic philosophers in their own ways tried to create a separate domain of philosophical inquiry. In this way the ahistorical model of natural science prevented them to see that philosophy had a historical character and hence it was a historical enterprise. The failure of the autonomy model raises two important issues. First, philosophy should cut off its relationship with the natural sciences and, second in fitness with its historical character it should tie itself to the historical and cultural sciences. This is how historicity as an alternative model of philosophical understanding came into existence. With this we now go to the next section elaborating the model of historicity as the mode of philosophical understanding.

II

HISTORICITY OF PHILOSOPHICAL UNDERSTANDING: A VIEW FROM HANS-GEORGE GADAMER

Just as Kant was the systematic exponent of the autonomy conception of philosophy so was Hegel the chief exponent of the historicist conception of philosophy.[16] The first thing that we notice in Hegel is his dissociation from natural science. For him, it is historical insights which are more important in philosophy than any thing else. This establishes a tradition linking philosophy to *Geisteswissenschaften*[17]. The methodological linkage gives rise to a systematic formulation of a historicist conception of philosophy represented by such diverse thinkers as Marx, Nietzsche, Dilthey, Heidegger, Gadamer etc. Among them, in Gadamer's work the historicist conception of philosophy finds its best expression. In the present study, we restrict ourselves only to Gadamer's thesis on the historicity of understanding. There are several reasons for it. But the main reason is that in view of the problematic of our paper we find that Gadamer's account will be more relevant for this purpose. Just as the autonomy standpoint seeks to relate philosophy to the methodological ideals of the natural sciences, the historicity standpoint of Gadamer on the other hand, explicitly situates philosophy, in the tradition of historical-cultural sciences or *Geisteswissenchaften.* In this respect, Gadamer's critical study on method is particularly invaluable. As a result, the historical nature of philosophy finds its clear and systematic expression in Gadamer's thesis on historicity.

We may begin our inquiry on Gadamer by distinguishing the two following questions. First is the general problem with which Gadamer is concerned which is expressed through his question: 'How is understanding possible?' He considers this transcendental question to be the starting point of his investigation into *Truth and Method.* Along with this general question, he has another question. This question he considers as 'the central question of the modern age' addressing to the problem: How do we relate our view of the world and our experience of the world to the 'unassailable and anonymous authority' that science personifies.[18] As we can see, these are two closely related questions and the second question is the question on method with which Gadamer starts his inquiry into the historicity of understanding. For the sake of brevity we identify the three key concepts that constitute Gadamer's view of historicity and accordingly present this discussion in terms of the three successive phases.

First: Understanding and Method. Gadamer subscribes to the view that there is a radical divide between explanation and understanding. Accordingly, he argues that the highest form of cognition to be achieved in the human sciences is not discovery or explanation of facts but understanding. This pronouncement is followed by his further arguments; namely, understanding is delinked from method because understanding is not an activity performed in accordance with certain methodological rules. Understanding, on the other hand, is essentially related to one's place in the continuing tradition.

The reason for Gadamer's rejection of the notion of method is primarily based on an epistemological consideration. Gadamer, when he rejects method, is rejecting the epistemological picture that is associated with the scientific research introduced particularly by Descartes. In order to understand the full implication of Gadamer's critique of method it is important to see how Gadamer defines the meaning and function of method. Gadamer remarks that the prevailing conception of knowledge that dominates western thinking is that knowledge is objective, universal and is thus free from bias, prejudice and tradition. Gadamer relates this conception of knowledge with method since, as he argues, this form of knowledge is achieved only through the construction of a universal method. This implies that there is an inseparable relation between knowledge and method where the former is determined by the latter. Considering its centrality, the method, in Gadamer's reading, consists "in pacing out a path of knowledge so consciously that it is always possible to retrace one's step".[19] Method in this sense as Gadamer defines, is meant to be "the path of repeated investigation". In view of this, to be methodical means the ability to once again go over the ground one has traversed. Repeatability is also the basic characteristics of the procedure of science. Gadamer point out that repeatability thus allows verification of scientific doctrines to be possible. These two establish certainty in knowledge and, as Gadamer observes, the ideal of knowledge is "the ideal of certainity" which, according to Descartes is the first rule of method.[20] This brief remark shows how the conception of knowledge as certain, objective and universal is attained through the application of method.

This, however, is not the universal picture of knowledge and truth. As Gadamer points out, we find a completely different picture when we come to human sciences. Truth in this domain cannot be known on the basis of method, i.e., verification and certainity. In his view, the universal claim of scientific method is no longer tenable where we experience truth "that transcends the domain of scientific method".[21] In this respect, Gadamer mentions the three different areas, namely, philosophy, art and history where the experience of truth is possible without being verified by the methodological rules of science.[22]

The idea of method, since its goal is to attain objectivity in knowledge and truth, becomes coextensive with objectivism. Method, so designed, thus assumes, as Gadamer points out, a fundamental epistemological dichotomy—a dichotomy between the subject and the object. This will be evidently found if we look into the process through which objective claims are made. Objectivism involves a double-movement process where the interpreter first goes back to the subjectivity of the author and then subsequently brings it back to the present, which is manifested, in the objectively graspable forms. Objectivism thus has its root in subjectivism while at the same time its entire effort is directed on how to over come subjectivism so that objective conception of knowledge, truth and meaning is possible. But, objectivism construed in this way ironically results into a paradoxical situation. The thesis that objectivism holds is that objectivity, whether in terms of knowledge or in terms of truth or in terms of meaning, is essentially a reconstruction of the subjective act or perspective of the author. The so-called objective reconstruction is supported by the subject-object dichotomy. In view of this, objectivism as a methodological thesis turns out to be conceptually anomalous. On the basis of this analysis, Gadamer concludes that any use of method contrary to its claims concerning objectivity falls under the concept of subjectivity.

Apart from its paradoxical nature, Gadamer's critique brings out another serious defect associated with method. His analysis shows that the use of method results into alienation of its object from the subject—the inquirer. According to Gadamer, alienation occurs due to the reason that for the application of method it is a necessary requirement that we must step out of our consciousness and view the text in itself. This is a methodological demand ensuring objectivity of understanding with respect to the text. That means we can understand the text once we abstract it from the entire relative/subjective conditions associated with it. As Gadamer points out, modern scholarship becomes scientific by virtue of the fact that "it objectifies tradition and eliminates the influence of the interpreter and his time on understanding".[23] Objectivism thus demands that in order to have understanding of the alien horizon one must leave out of his own horizon. This is where, as Gadamer points out, objectivism fails. It fails because it overlooks the fact that the interpreter's situation and his present interest entire into the process while making objective reconstruction of meaning. The subject-object dichotomy on which the idea of method stands leads to an unrealistic and untenable view of research.

Regarding the failure of objectivism, Gadamer's observation on Dilthey may be quite instructive. In Gadamer's reading, Dilthey became the unconscious victim of the Cartesian ideal of method and objective knowledge. True, Dilthey wanted to establish the autonomy of the human sciences as against the natural sciences but in the process he implicitly accepted the Cartesian method and thus introduced the dichotomy between the subject and the object. This leads to an utter ambivalence. The dichotomy of the subjective and the objective that Dilthey is accepting for the human sciences is the very same dichotomy that is used by positivists to question the cognitive legitimacy of these sciences. According to Gadamer, Dilthey is not bold enough in questioning whether the ideal of objectivity expressing through the Cartesian notion of knowledge is appropriate for understanding the *Geisteswissenschaften.* In Gadamer's finding, there is an "inconsistency at the heart of Dilthey's thought" which according to his diagnosis is the result of Dilthey's latent Cartesianism".[24] For Gadamer, *objective history* is thus ultimately impossible.

From Gadamer's critique of method and objectivism, the question that inevitably arises: Is Gadamer arguing for a relativistic world-view? His critique of objectivism, by no means, leads him to relativism. He is in the same way critical of relativism as he is of objectivism. For Gadamer, there is no absolute opposition between objectivism and relativism. In fact, relativism is an upshot of objectivism where the former is parasitic on the latter. Gadamer also describes the relationship between the two as dialectical where relativism figures as a dialectical antithesis to objectivism. This makes it evident that Gadamer cannot be sided with relativism. Hence, he looks for a way out, as Bernstein observes, to go beyond objectivism and relativism.[25] Keeping this perspective in view, Gadamer develops a system of ideas that offers "an entirely different notion of knowledge and truth". In this conception, knowledge or reason is not kept separated from prejudice, authority and tradition. There is no opposition between reason and these cultural notions. Reason, so conceived, cannot free itself from its historical context. It assumes its force within a tradition. This does not suggest, as Gadamer argues, the limitation of reason. It, on the other hand, expresses the essence of reason. This brings us to a very important aspect of Gadamer's notion of historicity, namely, understanding and prejudice.

Second: Understanding and Prejudice. Gadamer's idea of prejudice as constitutive of knowledge is the most controversial aspect of his theory of understanding. It is an attempt which challenges the thesis expressing the Cartesian and the Enlightenment conception of human knowledge. In this conception, a sharp dichotomy is maintained between knowledge and prejudice or reason and prejudice. Thus, it becomes a necessary requirement that in order to attain knowledge all prejudices must be bracketed. Gadamer, on the other hand, holds an opposite view which says that there is no knowledge without prejudices. Prejudices thus play a constructive role. It is through them that we get involved with the world. They become the preconditions of our experience of something. It is because of its constitutive nature, Gadamer maintains, "that all understanding inevitably involves same prejudice". This gives the hermeneutical problem its real thrust".[26] However, Gadamer is aware that prejudice is often understood in a negative sense suggesting something that is unfounded and false. Keeping this view in mind, Gadamer wants to rehabilitate the concept prejudice so that the centrality of its position and role can be evident to us. In Gadamer's reformulation:

> It is not so much our judgements as it is our prejudice that constitute our being. This is a provocative formulation, for I am using it to restore to its rightful place a positive concept of prejudice that was driven out of our linguistic usage by the French and the English Enlightenment. It can be shown that the concept of prejudice did not originally have the meaning we have attached to it. Prejudices are not necessarily unjustified as erroneous, so that they inevitably distort the

> truth. In fact, the historicity of our existence entails that prejudices, in the literal sense of the world, constitute the initial directedness of our whole ability to experience. Prejudices are biases of our openness to the world. They are simply conditions whereby we experience something—whereby what we encounter says something to us.[27]

Analysis of this passage reveals certain important implications pointing out the constructive role that prejudice plays in the context of both human existence and understanding. Prejudices are intrinsically related to our state of questioning which is an universal state for everyone. Prejudices thus form the passage through which we approach the world and experience the world. This encounter takes place in a state of questioning known as 'hermeneutical conditionedness' which is an universal state for anyone no matter whether he is a scientist or an artist. But in the sciences this state is never brought to the limelight and instead is pushed behind abstraction. However, as Gadamer points out emphatically, that in the sciences as well as in life "no assertion is possible that cannot be understood as an answer to a question, and assertion can be understood only in this way".[28] Given the fundamental nature of questions, Gadamer claims that it is not scientific methodology but asking of new questions that constitutes the key to new knowledge. This is how all experience including that of science necessarily incorporate a hermeneutical dimension. It is this hermeneutical dimension that constitutes the common element in all experience and reveals, as Gadamer points out, the fundamental level of the "linguistic constitution of the world".[29] We experience as well as understand the world through the medium of our pre-existing language and our linguistically based cultural tradition.

Gadamer's analysis of prejudice (which includes analysis of authority and tradition) shows that historicity is a distinctive feature of understanding which leads to the view that all understanding involves interpretation. His analysis shows that the act of understanding does not involve subject-object dichotomy. The aim of understanding is neither to discover objective truths nor its aim is to grasp the subjective intentions of the author of a work of art or of a text by an act of empathy. Objectivization of understanding is not possible because, as Gadamer's analysis of prejudice shows, we cannot abstract ourselves from our own historical contexts. Nor can there be any subjectivization of understanding possible because meaning and understanding are not psychological processes. They are, on the other hand, essentially linguistic.

The above analysis has a far-reaching consequence. The act of understanding instead of involving the subject-object dichotomy now becomes the ground for the subject-object synthesis. The subjective and the objective sides of understanding are thus fused together which results into a new form of understanding. The form that it assumes, as Gadamer claims, is that of the hermenutical circle. Understanding exhibits a circularly reinforcing relationship between a whole and its parts. To give a concrete example of this relationship, a historian who seeks to establish a relationship between a whole and its parts takes a socio-cultural totality to be a whole and the lives, actions, and products of individuals situated within its as its parts. We find a similar relational structure between the whole and its parts in the act of interpretation of a text and text analogue (e.g. an action or utterance). The starting point of the interpretation is the whole formed by the subjectivity of the author of the text. Only a person who shares a common cultural tradition with the author can understand this whole. It is by virtue of this mutual sharing that the interpreter could establish a connection between the text and its meaning. It also reflects the close relationship that exists between the interpreter and the object that he seeks to understand. Gadamer used the analogy of "play" to reveal this relationship. As he suggests, we must learn the art of how to be responsive to works of art, texts and traditions that we are trying to understand. To be responsive means to be able to participate in them. It will be lending us to their situations and will be thus participating in a common dialogue between them and us. This will be possible because of our inherent tendencies of human nature being guided by justified prejudices and prejudgement. In view of this, Gadamer claims that understanding and interpretation are same in the sense that they involve each other. With this, we now come to the last part of Gadamer's conception of the historicity of understanding.

Third: Understanding and the Fusion of Horizons. A theory of understanding cannot ignore exploring the possibility of how to understand alien phenomena, such as, a text or a tradition. In his inquiry, Gadamer explores this possibility and arrives at a firm conclusion that there exists an undeniable historical affinity between the agent and the alien object that he seeks to understand. The sense of affinity that prevails is realized through historical consciousness that ultimately culminates into the fusion of horizons.

The starting point of Gadamer's analysis is tradition. Human beings cannot be without tradition even though we may think that we are free of it. We are "thrown" into a tradition and being shaped by it. Further, what we are is mainly due to our tradition about which we may not be aware of it. This shows that tradition has an overimposing effect on us. But to say this is not to suggest that a tradition is the same as the nature or what Gadamer calls "nature like" implying that it stands in opposition to us. It is, on the other hand, as Gadamer suggests, "part of us" and thus there is no opposition between the two. Tradition and history are having inseparable relationship where the latter is the medium through which the former works.

The last point of the previous paragraph that tradition works through history brings an unique feature of historicality of thinking. This is characterized by Gadamer as effective historical consciousness. He explains it in relation to historical objectivism. The main defect of historical objectivism, as pointed out earlier, is that it treats the object as if it is ontologically independent of the subject. As a result, it fails to see the historical consciousness that is involved in this relationship, which overcomes the distance between the subject and the object. Understanding must be always in and through history. In this mode of understanding we will see in the object its counterpart also. This will be possible only when we achieve effective historical consciousness. As Gadamer points out:

> True historical thinking must take account of its own historicality. Only then will it not chase the phantom of an historical object which is the object of progressive research, but learn to see in the object the counterpart of itself and hence understand both. The true historical object is not an object at all, but the unity of the one and the other, a relationship in which exist both the reality of history and the reality of historical understanding. A proper hermeneutics would have to demonstrate the effectivity of history within understanding itself.[30]

Gadamer, while talking about effective historical consciousness, brings the notion of the "fusion of horizon". His claim is that the effective historical consciousness ultimately results into fusion of horizon. A horizon implies standpoint, which is limited and finite, and yet by its nature it is inherently open. Gadamer thus rules out the possibility of a closed horizon or a closed culture because they are simply false abstractions. In Gadamer's explanation, what is true of individual is also true of culture. We cannot see individual in isolation from others and so is the notion of culture which cannot be seen as something being enclosed in terms of its form. To put it in Gadamer's word:

> Just as the individual is never simply an individual, because he is always involved with others, so too the closed horizon that is supposed to enclose a culture is an abstraction. The historical movement of human life consists in the fact that it is never utterly bound to any one standpoint and hence can never have a truly closed horizon.[31]

This passage reveals that we are not prisoners of our own culture or horizons or paradigms. Openness to experience is a built-in feature of culture. Hence, the urge to understand what is alien is a natural tendency of understanding. Understanding too, as Gadamer points out, is limited but it is not closed. It is always open showing its readiness to transcend its limits so that it can bring under its manifold of that which is alien. This results into fusion of horizons through which our own horizon is enlarged and enriched. In this context, Gadamer points out the central role that language plays here. All human horizons are linguistically structured and thus we understand the other horizon only through language. Language in this sense is open to understanding alien horizons. It is through this process of fusion that we become critically aware of our prejudices—the prejudices that the justified and unjustified. Understanding of others thus involves understanding of us. To put it in Gadamer's characteristic phrase: "Only through others do we gain true knowledge of ourselves".[32] It is because of this dialectics operating between the self and the other dialogue or conversation becomes crucially important since they express the true essence of understanding.

With Gadamer's thesis on the historicity of understanding, philosophy takes a radical historical turn. He has laid down an argument structure that systematically leads to this conception of philosophy. Behind all his abstractions and complexities, the basic insight that Gadamer derived was from the nature of human existence. Historicity of understanding is thus not a theoretical abstraction but a view that expresses how human beings actually cognize. It is a parallel epistemological model relating philosophy to practical aspects of human existence. Hermenutical philosophy with is sole emphasis on historicity may be thus rightly characterized as practical philosophy.

There is, however, a problem here relating to the strategy that Gadamer adopted in order to give a historical turn to philosophy. Gadamer finds that to establish the historical nature of philosophy it must cut off its earlier relationship with the natural sciences and situate it within the tradition of *Geisteswissenschaffen.* This is how the entire direction of philosophy is changed from the standpoint of autonomy to the standpoint of historicity. Philosophy, instead of being oriented towards the natural sciences, is now oriented towards historical / cultural sciences. This, Gadamer argues, is a fundamental requirement without which the historical nature of philosophy will have no foothold. This is where Gadamer's position on historicity meets with problem. There are two distinct things to be noticed which cannot be confused. One is the historicity and the other is the orientation of philosophy towards *Geisteswissenschaften.* The two are different because the former can be attained without the help of the latter. Historicity is an independent notion. It is independent because it is an underlying and a primitive notion. Hence, it is not true that in order to attain historicity it must be related to *Geisteswissenschaften* tradition. The significance of the point raised here can be made evident if we look into Gadamer's programme of relating philosophy to *Geisteswissenschaften.* The question that necessarily comes here: Is Gadamer successful in his reorientation of philosophy towards *Geisteswissenschaften*? The attempt to answer this question will reveal shortcomings in Gadamer's programme itself. This failure suggests that historicity is not an exclusive property of *Geisteswissenschaften.* It is due to its primitive or underlying nature it can as well be related to the natural sciences. Historicity will be only then the right model that can successfully over throw the autonomy model in philosophy. Restricting philosophy exclusively to the *Geisteswissenschaften* tradition will result into a lopsided view of philosophy. It will be lopsided because there will be no place for the philosophical reflection of the natural sciences. The consequence of it will be to deny philosophy's relationship with the natural sciences. But such an attempt is not only historically incorrect but it is also conceptually wrong. For philosophy to cut off its relationship with the natural sciences will ultimately mean to be turning its back to the objective system of the world and, thereby, allowing itself to succumb into idealism. Gadamer's hermenutical engagement with philosophy is not an exception to this. True, through this process of reorientation he could establish the primacy of the historicist model over the autonomy model in philosophy but the price that he paid was much greater than what he gained. In fact, formulation of the historicist view of philosophy without acknowledging its conceptual linkages with the natural sciences is a gross distortion if not a falsification of truth. With this, we may now briefly go into the inadequacy of Gadamer's hermenutical enagement in philosophy pointing out how it distorts the basic truth of philosophy i.e., its relationship with science.

Idealism of Linguisticality

We know from our earlier exegetical remarks that the notion of understanding forms the conceptual core of Gadamer's philosophic hermenutics. But what is understanding? Understanding, for Gadamer, essentially implies understanding the meaning of a text or history or anything that is "handed down to us" through a tradition. Meaning is not something lying there to be discovered. Meaning and understanding, on the other hand, come together and merge in a single experience. Thus, the meaning of a text is realized only when it is understood. In view of this, Gadamer claims, "understanding belongs to the meaning of a text just as being heard belong to the meaning of music". This constitutes the linguistic turn of Gadamer's hermeneutics where language acts as medium of all understanding and tradition. This is very different from the view where language is seen as a tool or an instrument to be used. Language, on the other hand, is the very embodiment of human existence—a medium in which we live. Gadamer thus sets his task and, accordingly, wants to disclose "linguisticality" as the basic mode of human existence. But ironically, this involves hypostaizing language and tradition both. While disclosing linguisticality, Gadamer falls into, what Habermas calls, "idealism of linguisticality".[33]

It is because of his all-encompassing linguistic point of view that Gadamer ignored the objectively real framework of the world. This will be evident if we look at language in relation to society. Gadamer considers language as meta-institution (i.e., tradition) on which all other institutions are dependent. But can the linguistic infrastructure of a society be independent in the sense of being free from any constraints? The question raised here will not have affirmative answer. The reason is that language even if it is conceived as meta-institution is essentially a part of a totality—a system that itself is governed by the constraints of reality. The first constraint is, what Habermas calls "the constraint of outer nature". It is a constraint which regulates empirical-analytic sciences. The second is the "constraint of inner nature" which refers to social processes being dominated by power relation. Language is situated at the background of these constraints. As a result, both its functions and constitutive rules (i.e., grammatical rules) in terms of which we interpret the world are affected by these constraints. The point that Habermas is making is that we must "get behind" language and find out the conditions under which it historically develops. Language is thus not a self-sufficient independent system. We must see it in relation to a comprehensive framework that includes social labour, relations of power etc. In this respect, we must specially emphasize, as Habermas points out, on the role of social labour and political power in the understanding of culture and society. The notion of objective framework with which we have started is thus constituted jointly by language, labour and domination. Accordingly, understanding of social actions involves not just language but all these three together, which constitute the objective framework.

Coming back to Gadamer's philosophic hermeneutics, the account that it offers is highly one-sided because it underestimates and distorts the role of the natural sciences in the formation of social life. Further, the contrast made between the natural sciences and the *Geisteswissonschaften* in respect of historicity no longer holds. Natural science has historcity in the same way as *Geisteswissenschaften* has. As said earlier, historicity is the underlying framework unifying the both. In view of this, Gadamer's plea that philosophy should be reoriented towards *Geisteswissenschaften* in untenable because it commits the basic fallacy by denying the constitutive role that the natural sciences play in relation to philosophy. This takes us to the historicist view of science that we have already indicated while examining Gadamer's position. The task of the next section will be more focussed trying to bring out the inherent historicity of the natural science. Unless this is established the relationship between philosophy and science will be one sided, i.e., either philosophy will be viewed as autonomous or it will be exclusively the property of the cultural and historical sciences.

III

ON THE HISTORICITY OF THE NATURAL SCIENCES: THE TWO PERSPECTIVES—KUHN AND HUSSERL

There is a widespread belief that historicity has no place in the sciences. The two are incompatible notions where the former is essentially seen as curbing the autonomy of the latter. To accept historicity means to give up the autonomy of the sciences. The idea of the historicity of the natural sciences is thus an expression of a deviant thinking for those defending the autonomy of the sciences. They rule out the possibility that trans-historical character of natural science can ever be questioned. This is how transcendental philosophy came into existence and became the partner in the same pursuit i.e., a *priori* view of science and philosophy. But the scenario changed expressing the view that was once considered deviant. The change was initiated due to social reasons. There is a two way relationship observed between science and society. It is found that there is a growing impact of science upon social life, which, in turn, shows the conditions leading to the social production of science. This gives rise to the new historicist view of science eloquently presented in Kuhn's *The Structure of Scientific Revolution.*[34] Kuhn's presentation shows that scientific development is essentially historical pointing out its non-cumulative and non-convergent nature.

Non-cumulative and Non-convergent Model of Scientific Development: The Argument from Kuhn

The conventional view, represented by the Popper-Hempel model, depicts the progress of science as cumulative, meaning thereby, that it is a process where old theories are removed by the new theories because new facts are discovered that cannot be accounted for by the old theories. Similarly, small-scale laws are replaced by those which are more general in scope because they cover more and more of the facts. It is also important to note that there are several occasions when older theories are retained for a specific purpose. But they are never represented in their old formats. They are, on the other hand, taken as specialized forms of new emerging theories.

Kuhn argues that there is something fundamentally wrong with this conception of science as well as the activities that constitute science. In its formulation it was influenced by the traditional dogmas inherited from empiricism and rationalism. Kuhn thus makes an alternative attempt offering an image of science that according to him is the proper account of the way in which scientific inquiry in actually conducted.

On the basis of historical evidence, Kuhn argues that science does not progress by accumulation. Along with this, he also argues that methodological rules and guidelines that the earlier model of science formulates cannot provide unique answers to scientific questions.

Kuhn, while describing the stages of scientific development, made a crucial distinction between what he called normal science and revolutionary science. According to him, normal science is every day science—the science that is currently practiced. It represents a type of empirical investigation wherein the truth of current theories are presupposed and thus they are regarded as paradigms. Paradigms are "universally recognized scientific achievements that for a time provide model problems and solutions to a community of practitioners". Paradigms, so conceived, guide normal science in a particular direction. There are three major areas of activities with which normal science is concerned. First, it determines facts with more precision. Second, it investigates unexplained facts with a sole objective to explain them in the light of the current theory. And third, it seeks to resolve ambiguities as found in existing theories. These are the three vital functions that normal science performs which create the passage through which it proceeds. Kuhn's attempt here is to show how normal science explains nature by bringing it under its theoretical conceptual-complex. This constitutes the activity characteristic of normal science.

From normal science, Kuhn goes to extraordinary science. This is where scientific revolution occurs. It occurs occasionally. The reason for there being scientific revolution is that existing theories are found to be unsatisfactory for some reason or another. This results into a crisis situation characterized by the presence of rival theories existing at the same time. The theory that succeeds over other rival theories is the one that satisfies the two basic requirements. First, it must be able to solve problems which other rival theories cannot do. Second, it must be supported by a group of scientists who can successfully compete with the other group of scientists defending the rival theories. What makes the former group to succeed over their rival scientific group? In Kuhn's analysis, the success of the story does not lie on superior intellectual quality only. There are various sociological factors that are greatly responsible for a particular group to attain success over the rival group. Factors, such as, money, social prestige, political influence etc., are all important in this respect. The sociological dimension that Kuhn brought in the context of theory change radically transformed the Popper-Hempel picture of science. In fact, their idea of theory change appears to be a mere fiction in view of this present account.

Kuhn further argues that the suppression of historical fact and the picture of science described in science textbooks gave a highly distorted account of scientific inquiry. But unfortunately such an account is taken to be necessary because, as the argument goes, it enables the scientists to look at scientific theories in a particular way. It trains the scientists to withdraw completely from the theories that are not presently productive. That is why scientific textbooks, as Kuhn pointed out, describe previous theories as magic, superstition etc. But, according to Kuhn, this whole description is wrong. Previous theories are neither magic nor unscientific and they are in fact conflicting with newer theories. Similarly, with regard to current scientific theories, scientific text books consider them as final truth. But in science, there is no place for final truth because science is not static. There can be no science without anomalies leading to a conflict in the current theory. We thus find that there is a wide discrepancy between the actual practice of science and the account of science given in scientific textbooks. Scientists and philosophers of science both have been excessively influenced by the latter account. Philosophers of science have been engaged in explicating the logic of science. But what is the notion of science that they have while explicating its logic? In Kuhn's judgement, it is the textbook notion of science that forms the basis of their explication. The notion of science thus appears to be a monolithic whole exhibiting a fixed and ahistorical structure. But the historical practice of science, on the other hand, exhibits, as Kuhn points out, a "ramshackle structure".

This brief presentation of Kuhn's account shows how science is inextricably related to its historical practice. The two cannot be delinked. The attempt to do so will lead to a view of science which is more of a fiction than of a reality. Historicity of science is thus a reality. It is not a threat to science. It is, on the other hand, an essential component of science without which our view of science will be inevitably distorted and incomplete. Theoretical change does not consist in simple replacement of one theory by another. Science, on the other hand, is available as something historical. In this connection, we may also briefly state the view of Husserl offering justification for the historicity of science from the phenomenological standpoint.

Lebenswelt and the Galilean Science: The Argument from Husserl

In his *The Crisis of European Sciences and the Transcendental Phenomenology,*[35] Husserl seeks to redefine the meaning of science through a study of its historical foundation. His attempt is to show how the original meaning of science is lost through the period of its subsequent development. This deviation from original meaning results into a crisis in science. The crisis consists in the systematic rejection of the idea of 'reason', according to which, reason is both subjective and objective, theory and praxis and, therefore, serves as an instrument for changing the world in accordance with man's rational faculties and ends. But 'reason' as constituted in science is reduced to paradigmatic rules of deductive inference. Scientific rationality is divorced from the *rational humanities* and becomes a technological rationality without having any 'end' or 'telos' of its own. Galileo never asked for the validity of the foundation of mathematics and its extension to the natural sciences. For him this whole question is irrelevant since mathematics justifies its own foundation. Thus, science, as Herbert Marcuse observes, "contained an unscientific foundation".

Husserl characterizes modern science as the Galilean science whose chief activity consists of the physicist's programme of the "mathematization of nature". It exhibits a structure that is similar to the structure of a machine. In other words, the entire procedure of modern science can be better understood in the sense of a logical machine, which implies the algorithmic procedure used for the formalization of mathematics. These algorithmic procedures are purely mechanical in the sense that they can be applied in an absolutely routine manner. Methods of science, since they are rigorously formalized, assume the same character. This results in what is known as 'technization of science', which implies the mechanical application of scientific rules. Science can, thus, be compared with a machine, which can be handled by any one who knows the rules of the operation of the machine. This gives an instrumental character to the very structure of science. By the *logos* of pure science one now understands only technology whose purpose is to serve some external ends.

Here, at this stage, a basic philosophical question concerning the machine itself arises. For a philosopher the actual functioning of the machine is not of great interest. He goes beyond this and inquires about how and why this machine functions. That is to say, from the functional aspect he goes to certain foundational aspects of a machine. They are: the mechanism which makes functioning of a machine possible; the principle by which the machine is constructed; and, finally, the condition in which the entire construction is conceived. These philosophical activities clearly show the distinction between the machine and the presuppositions of a machine. On the same grounds a distinction can be maintained between Galilean science and presuppositions of it. These presuppositions are like the underlying structures from which science derives its sense. They indicate the manner in which modern science becomes possible. This, in other words, is to define the meaning of modern science in its entirety. But one who adopts the view of a technician of science understands science without its presuppositions and foundation. In such a view, philosophy of science is confined to the study of the mere logic of science. The study of the logic of science has its merit within the theoretico-logical superstructure of science. But it does not constitute the whole of science. Being a superstructure the universe of science requires a foundation upon which it rests and upon which it is constructed. The foundation is the common social experience or what Husserl calls *Lebenswelt.* A comprehensive study in philosophy of science will be possible only when it is able to take these two (i.e., theory and its foundation) together. We will now give a brief description of the mutual interaction of these two, and shall argue how an objectively valid scientific theory evolves essentially through a common atheoretical knowledge constituted in *Lebenswelt.*

The *Lebenswelt* is a pre-given world which exists independently of and prior to all scientific activity. But it pervades all our activities in the sense that it enters as a premise or presupposition of all our activities. This pre-given world includes nature which is not the idealized nature of physics. It is nature as given in direct and immediate experience. It is this pre-given world into which we are born and every moment we are aware of the fact that we are within it. We also find that we are surrounded not only by natural things, e.g., colour, shape, size, weight, etc., but also instruments, books, objects of art, and so on. These objects have human significance in the sense that they serve human purpose, desires and need. Besides objects, we encounter within *Lebenswelt* our fellow men, and we find that we stand in diverse relation to them. We take it for granted that our fellow men exist in the same way in which we exist, and that they confront the same thing and the same object as we do. The only difference is that depending on our standpoints the objects appear with their varying aspects. This realization that the world is one and the same for all constitutes the core of our social knowledge or atheoretical knowledge.

Following Husserl, certain predominant features of *Lebenswelt* can be spelt out. First of all, the world of common experience is extended in space and time. This provides a frame of reference in which items of experience can be related and described in spatial and temporal terms with one another. Furthermore, things exhibit some kind of spatial forms, and they are also grasped accordingly. Trees, for example, present a cylindrical shape. This, of course, should not be understood in a strictly geometrical sense. The phrase 'cylindrical shape' actually refers to a physiognomic aspect of spatial forms. It refers to a spatial configuration within which variation takes place.

Secondly, we find that there are various kinds of regularities exhibited at *Lebenswelt.* We experience various changes, and try to establish a regularity among these changes. The alternation of day and night, changes of season, for example, indicate a simple type of regularity. Again, people know without knowing science that water boils when heated and after a point it evaporates; or a stone falls down when dropped from the hand. This means that we know that events do not take place in isolation. Events are coordinated in a certain manner. Therefore, occurrences of one type are regularly followed by occurrences of another type. This is the idea of universal causality, which is embedded in the practical life of our day-to-day existence. The idea of universal causality is the basis of our everyday conceptualization by which we anticipate the future, and regulate our future course of action for the desired result. Anthropologists like Levi-Strauss have emphasized this aspect of social knowledge when they talk about rational behaviour of primitive man. On the basis of everyday causal connection, primitive man within his own framework provides a rational explanation for various phenomena.

The third feature of common social knowledge is that it is perspectival in character. By perspectival it is meant that things in the *Lebenswelt* appear as relative with respect to the human subjects. The same object may be perceived by us from our respective points of observation. Intersubjective argreement is sought about in order to make adjustments in these different perspectives. As a result, we find that we live in the same world of common experiences having the same intersubjective knowledge. However, a degree of relativity exists; but it exists not with regard to individual but with regard to social groups.

These three features constitute the core of our social or atheoretical knowledge. They are the basic coordinates of man's thinking. Atheoretical knowledge is the rudimentary form of conceptualization through which we comprehend and explain the world. Since it is atheoretical, the nature of this knowledge is vague, inexact, and indeterminate; but nevertheless it is the basis of man's mental operation in the everyday world. Theoretical pursuit evolves through this atheoretical knowledge with the purpose of making knowledge clear, exact, and determinate. In a similar way, theoretical pursuits in science should be seen and understood with reference to the theory-atheory matrix.

Husserl's account of science with respect to *Lebenswelt* shows that science is a collective experience. The *a priori* view of science, on the other hand sees science as an individual enterprise expressing creative endeavour of an individual. In this view, science is thus posed as unrelated phenomena, which is a product of the present only. Contrary to this, the Kuhn-Husserl argument makes a convincing case showing that science is a product of a long chain of history. It thus exposes the view that science is *a priori* an illusion. In the light of our discussion on the historicity of philosophy and the historicity of science, let us come back to the issue with which we have started our paper, namely, the relationship between philosophy and science. This will be the final section where we will reconstruct the entire relationship between philosophy and science at the background of historicity.

IV

RECONSTRUCTING THE RELATIONSHIP BETWEEN SCIENCE AND PHILOSOPHY

The contemporary historical turn of philosophy and of science makes a new ground allowing the possibility of a new form of relationship—a new order of conceptual linkages existing between science and philosophy. This changes the entire scenario—the entire thinking on the earlier relationship between philosophy and science where both were taken to be autonomous on their own right. It is the idea of autonomy that becomes the driving force behind this relationship. Philosophy is autonomous in the same way in which science is. If the concern of science is to discover the timeless and eternal order of things then philosophy too, it is argued, has the same concern aiming to discover the time-transcendent structure of human reason and human nature. It is not only in their respective goal that they are ahistorical but also in their practice the same ahistorical thrust is conspicuously present. In the past, problems in the natural sciences were investigated in isolation from their context and historical development. We have seen that the same approach was adopted while conducting philosophical inquiry. This strategy worked well and was proved to be a success.

However, the situation changes radically with the historical turn in the natural sciences. The newly founded relationship of the sciences to history becomes a model that changes the ahistorical approach of philosophical-inquiry. This led to the historical turn in philosophy. It is felt that philosophy is related to history in the same way in which science is related to history. History thus becomes the underlying framework for both these disciplines.

The historical turn thus initiates a new approach to philosophy. The shortcomings of the earlier ahistorical approach became too apparent. It is found that some of the basic philosophical problems get distorted when they are conceived in an ahistorical perspective. The questions like, as Kruger pointed out, 'what is knowledge?' and 'what are the foundations of morals?' will have proper answers only when we take scientific knowledge and cultural practice into consideration. A discussion on knowledge will be incomplete if we do not take scientific knowledge with its historical dynamics into account. There is hardly any dispute over the fact that scientific knowledge after all qualifies to be the paradigm of knowledge. Similarly, in today's context, there cannot be any ethics that does not recognize the seminal importance of cultural plurality.

The above description shows that the historical turn in philosophy and the historical turn in science are not two isolated unconnected events. They are, on the other hand, conceptually connected. With the historical turn the character of science undergoes a change. Science is now perceived as a historical force. This, in turn, as we have argued caused the historical turn in philosophy. Thus, to account for the historicity of philosophy the historicity of science must be accounted for as a part of philosophical requirement. The historicity of science is the topic that itself becomes a philosophical agenda. We have seen that Gadamer failed to recognize that the historical turn in philosophy originated from the historical turn in the natural sciences. As a result, he was exclusively concerned with *Geisteswissenchaflen* and, thereby, carefully avoided any trade with the natural sciences. The same tendency one will find in Heidegger and in Husserl too. All of them are indifferent to the issue how historical turn in philosophy is conceptually connected to the historical turn in science. It is due to this indifference that they always look for a science free space. Husserl's *Lebenswelt* was introduced explicitly to serve this purpose which became the ultimate basis of all our scientific theorizing. But, as Kruger asks the question, can there be a science free space? His answer is that science free space is an abstraction—"an artifact" which is not actually available in our everyday life. It is more of a fiction than of a fact. The reason is that science has become the indistinguishable part of our form of life and thus to attempt to create a science free space is an abstraction that lacks any real basis. *Lebenswelt* and the world as viewed by science cannot be distinguished. *Lebenswelt* in this sense cannot be the basis of the critique of science.

The historicist model of thinking commits a basic error due to which it developed such indifference or aversion towards the physical sciences. It identifies the physical sciences with the nature in the sense that it becomes the object of study for the sciences. There is an implicit assumption involved here. The nature is assumed as something invariant, alien and a reality out there. This is essentially a nonhuman conception of nature that science studies. The truth that reveals is that there is a fundamental opposition between man and nature and the origin of science presupposes this dichotomy as a necessary requirement for its progress. This is the reason why the historicist model of thinking seeks to eliminate the physical sciences from its paradigm. But this is a wrong assessment of the physical sciences. It over looks the relationship of the sciences to history. The historical turn gives an alternative picture of science where the opposition between man and nature is overcome. The two get closer through human activity. In other words, labour and science are the embodiments of this activity. Science bridges the gulf between man and nature.

The question that confronts us is the relationship between man and nature. This is a context where we can most effectively use the Marxian insight that offers a holistic picture binding man and nature within the framework of history.[36] As Marx argues, man exists primarily by producing things. It is through the activity of production that he transforms nature that becomes a necessary means for his own subsistence. To produce a wooden table is to transform the natural object called wood into a "human subject". To produce means to humanize nature. The activity of production makes nature no longer alien to man. The distance between the two gets dissolved in this activity. This brings a drastic change in our conception of reality. Reality is not something independent of man but it is a product of his activity, a property of praxis. Labour thus assumes a far-reaching significance. Its meaning becomes identical with the humanization of nature. Science being the expression of social labour is connected with the same humanization process and, thereby, removes the distance between man and nature.

The above discussion shows that since man and nature are in the state of interdependence, the study of these two cannot take two radically different courses. The Marxian term that explains the interrelationship is the notion of historical practice which connects these two separate elements. History thus comes as the underlying framework that unifies the history of man and the history of nature. These two are the two sides of the same history; the two aspects of the single science. As Marx says:

> We know only a single science, the science of history. One can look at history from two sides and divide it into the history of nature and the history of men. The two sides are, however, inseparable; the history of nature and the history of men are dependent on each other so long as men exist.[37]

The idea of unity that is expressed here is not a methodological unity achieved through the imposition of the natural sciences on the human sciences nor does it bypass the natural sciences and takes recourse in the *Geisteswissenchaflen.* It is, on the other hand, a substantive unity based on the reciprocal relationship between man and nature. History, according to Marx, is the science which is the concrete expression of this unity.

Coming to the final outcome, the study conducted in the present paper subscribes to the historicist conception of philosophy, which comprises of the three basic elements. First, it defends the historicist standpoint as opposed to the autonomy standpoint in philosophy. Second, the historicist standpoint does not negate the constructive role of the natural sciences in establishing its close relationship with philosophy. Third, the best way to do it is to make a reconstruction of this entire relationship so that history of philosophy and history of science will have an inseparable conceptual linkage. To conclude, history will be thus the underlying framework for both philosophy and science.

NOTES

1. Kant, I. *The Critique of Pure Reason.* N.K. Smith (trans.). London: Macmillan. Preface.
2. A similar Kantian attempt engaged in the formulation of an autonomous philosophy is found in Kalidas Bhattacharyya's work on *Presuppositions of Science and Philosophy and Other Essays.* He takes philosophy to be the study of metaphysics. Philosophy is a "systematic study of the basic structure of the universe". The idea of basic structure is crucial to this understanding since it distinguishes philosophy from the sciences. The structure of the world with which science is concerned is empirical. It may not be always empirical in the strong sense. But, in principle, it must be imaginable as more or less concrete. There is a third sense in which it is also empirical. The structure that science reveals is always hypothetical in nature and thus it is subjected to empirical verification. Philosophy, on the contrary, studies the structure that is non empirical or *a priori.* There are three senses in which it is non empirical. First, there is no logical requirement on the part of the structure that it should be known only in context of empirical phenomena. The philosophical structure is unaffected by any empirical consideration. The structure that philosophy discovers is an autonomous structure. Second, the philosophical structure and its constituents can in no way be conceived as abstractions from empirical phenomena. Scientific entities are admitted as the result of useful hypotheses. Whereas, philosophical entities are not of the nature of hypotheses. Philosophical entities are discovered through analysis. Space, time, self, for example, are studied as autonomous metaphysical entities. Third, the *a priori* nature of the philosophical structure of the world is never be in the form of a hypothesis. Constituents of the basic structure are since revealed a priori are thus revealed as autonomous.
   See Bhattacharyya, Kalidas. 1974. *Presuppositions of Science and Philosophy and Other Essays.* Santiniketan: Centre of Advanced Study in Philosophy, Visva Bharati.
3. To explain the implication of these three objectives: First, Objects of our knowledge are constructed by the understanding i.e., by the rules given by the understanding. Whatever we know must be thus necessarily conditioned by the forms of our understanding. From this it follows that since objects of our knowledge are conditioned by the things which are unconditioned, namely, things itself can never be known by us. In the light of this basic argument, Kant draws his conclusion that rational theology is not just unbelievable, but unthinkable.
   Second, skepticism in philosophy is logically untenable. 'Every change has its cause' in an instance of a priori knowledge. The reason is that we cannot learn from experience that every change has its cause. It is assumed in everyday life and it forms the basic presupposition of the natural sciences. Hume is wrong in supposing that the causal principle is derived from experience. He is wrong on the ground that causal the causal connection is universal and necessary and thus cannot be derived from experience. Hence, this knowledge is a *priori.*
   Third, human mind, according to Kant, possesses two fundamentally distinct capacities—the capacities of sensibility and understanding. Human sensibility has the forms of space and time in which all objects

of our experience are ordered. Human understanding is the faculty by which we think or judge. It has also certain forms, which are called categories. The categories are not derived from experience. The two such typical categories are substantiality and causality. Kant's idea of space and time as forms of sensibility assumes for reaching significance, particularly, in the context of Newtonian science. The metaphysical possibility as well as the epistemology of Newtonian absolute space remained a mystery till Kant came on the scene. Kant's doctrine was able to solve the mystery by showing that the certainty of the spatio-temporal framework of Newtonian physics could be established only by recognizing it to be the form of our own experience.

See Brittan G. 1978. *Kant's Theory of Science.* Princeton: Princeton University Press.

4. Brittan, G. (ed.). 1986. *Kant's Philosophy of Physical Science.* Dordrecht: D. Reidel.
5. "Two things fill the mind with ever new and increasing admiration and awe, the starry heavens above one and moral law within me. I see them before me and connect them immediately with the consciousness of my existence." Kant, I. *Critique of Practical Reason.* Lewis White Beck, (trans.). Macmillan. Sec. 5, pp. 161-162.

   In this connection, Paul Geuyer's observation is quite significant. As he says, "Kant ultimately came to see that the validity of both these laws of starry skies above as well as the moral law within had to be sought in the legislative power of human intellect itself."

   Geuyer, Paul (ed.) 1992. *The Cambridge Companion to Kant.* Cambridge: Cambridge University Press. Introduction.
6. Chattopadhyaya, D.P. 1992. *Anthropology and Historiography of Science.* Delhi: Motilal Banarsidass Publishers, Private Limited.

   In the contemporary Indian philosophy, D.P.Chattopadhyaya's work on history of science is remarkably insightful. He shows a new way of doing history of science. His approach involves philosophical reconstruction of history of science. He rejects analytic philosophy of science because of its ahistorical approach to science. Similarly, he is highly critical of the narrative approach to the history of science. A narrative approach is characterized by its lack of philosophical concern and insight. He thus suggests philosophical reconstruction of the history of science which, in concrete term, involves showing how facts and theories are interwoven in any approach to science be it philosophical or historical. In this respect, he points out the need for taking a transcendental point of view in the history of science. His argument is that first a philosophical study of science must view science as a part of definite historical culture and, second, it must be studied from a transcultural or transcendental point of view. The transcendental point of view does not oppose empiricism or realism in science. For the proper understanding of facts such a point of view is methodologically indispensable. Another extremely important feature of his study is to go into the works of anthropology of science, such as, the works of Levi-Strauss along with the history of science. He shows on the basis of an elaborate study that the anthropology of science and the history of science are not conflicting but complementary to each other. Their complementary nature has been established in the light of a new concept that he introduced called human universals. The final argument that emerges from his work is that philosophy of science in order to be a significant study of science must embrace both history of science and anthropology of science in its conceptual and methodological fabric.
7. Chattopadhyaya, D.P. 1976. "Copernicus Betrayed". *Individual and World: Essays in Anthropological Rationalism.* Delhi: Oxford University Press.
8. Das Gupta, A. 1999. "Fact/Value Holism and the Ethics of Human Freedom". *Persons, Mind and Value,* S.K. Mohanty (ed). Delhi: Decent Books.
9. Strawson, P.E. 1974. "Freedom and Resentment". *Freedom and Resentment and Other Essays.* London: Methuen & Co.
10. Nagel, T. 1987. *The View From Nowhere.* New York: Oxford University Press.
11. Ryle, G. 1967 "Systematically Misleading Expressions". *The Linguistic Turn,* R.Rorty (ed). Chicago: University of Chicago Press.
12. Das Gupta, A. 1996. *The Second Linguistic Turn: Chomsky and the Philosophy of Language.* Frankfurt am Main: Perter Lang.
13. Passmore, J. *Encyclopedia of Philosophy,* P.Edwards (ed.) vol. 6, pp. 226-30.
14. Kruger, L. 1984. "Why do we Study the History of Philosophy?" *Philosophy in History,* R.Rorty et al (ed). Cambridge: Cambridge University Press.

15. Rorty, R. 1972. *Philosophy and the Mirror of Nature.* N.J.: Princeton University Press. p. 9.
16. Beiser, F.C. 1990. "Hegel's Historicism". *The Cambridge Companion to Hegel,* F.C. Beiser (ed.). Cambridge University Press.
With Hegel, historicism enters into philosophy as a self conscious and self critical method of philosophy. Hegel argues that philosophy needs historical explanation in the same way in which politics and religion need it. Philosophers view their doctrines as the product of eternal reason. The notion of eternal cannot be seen in isolation from human activity. It is the product of human activity performed in a cultural context. In this sense, the notion of eternal reason does not have any material basis. It is an illusion that can be exposed only through the process of historicizing philosophy. The basis of Hegel's historicism lies in his central argument that society is an organic whole having parts which are inseparable from one another. Art, religion, constitution, tradition and language are all parts being harmoniously blended and thus form a systematic unity. Philosophy does not have any existence apart from this whole and being a part of this social whole it implies that philosophy cannot be uprooted from its social context. It is due to its inherent contextuality that a philosopher cannot go beyond his own age. Similarly, it cannot be separated from its past because it is the product of past achievement. Philosophy is thus not an outcome of a priori reasoning. Hegel developed the basic premise of his historicist conception of philosophy in his *Lectures on the History of Philosophy.* His argument for the historical nature of philosophy is that philosophy has a subject matter whose nature is different from the subject matter of other disciplines. According to Hegel, the subject matter of philosophy consists of thoughts, ideas and concepts. They form the basic mechanism in terms of which we think about the world. But what is distinctive about thought, as Hegel argues, is that by its very nature it is historical. Thought is not a fixed state of being. It is, rather, a continuous flow of activity involving a process of development leading from one state to another. In this historically oriented conception of thought, the object of thought cannot be separated from thinking about it. The nature of the former is changed through the involvement of the latter. Hence, Hegel's plea is that if thought is historical can philosophy be anything other than historical?
17. Hegel, C.W. 1990. *Lectures on the History of Philosophy.* Berkeley: University of California. pp. 23-24.
18. Gadamer, H.G. 1980 "The Universality of the Hermeneutical Problem" *Contemporary Hermeneutics.* London: Routledge and Kegan Paul. p. 128.
19. Gadamer, H.G. 1994. "What is Truth". *Hermeneutics and Truth,* B.R. Wachterhauser (ed.). Evanston: North Western University Press. p. 37.
20. Ibid.
21. Gadamer, H.G. 1975. *Truth and Method.* New York: Seabury Press. pp. 1-2.
22. Ibid.
23. Ibid. p. 333.
24. Gadamer, H.G. 1979. "Problem of Historical Consciousness". *Interpretive Social Science: A Reader,* P. Rabinow and W.M. Sullivan (ed.). Berkeley: University of California Press. p. 124.
25. Bernstein, R.J. 1983. *Beyond Objectivism and Relativism: Science, Hermeneutics and Praxis.* Oxford: Basil Blackwell.
26. Gadamer. *Truth and Method.* p. 239.
27. Gadamer, H.G. "The Universality of the Hermeneutical Problem". *Contemporary Hermeneutics.* J.Bleicher (ed.).
28. Ibid. p. 135.
29. Ibid. p. 136.
30. Gadamer. *Truth and Method,* p. 267.
31. Ibid. p. 271
32. Gadamer, H.G. "Problems of Historical Consciousness". p. 107.
33. Habermas, J. 1970. "A Review of Gadamer's Truth and Method". Reprinted in *Understanding and Social Inquiry,* F.A. Dailmayr and A.Mc Carthy (ed.). 1977. University of Notre Dame Press.
34. Kuhn, T.S. 1962. *The Structure of Scientific Revolution.* Chicago: University of Chicago Press.
35. Husserl, E. 1970. *The Crisis of European Science and the Transcendental Phenomenology.* Evanston: North Western University Press.
36. Das Gupta, A. 1993. "Unity in Marx", *Economic and Political Weekly,* February.
37. Marx, K. *The German Ideology.* Moscow: The Foreign Publishing House. p. 28.

ACKNOWLEDGEMENT

This paper will be incomplete if I fail to acknowledge the three authors whose works constitute the thematic core of the paper. The works of Late Professor Kalidas Bhattacharyya, Professor D.P.Chattopadhyaya and Professor Lorenz Kruger have laid down the three basic conceptual strands within which this study has been conceived. The influence of their thought has been thus evidently found in all through the present work. Finally, I am specially grateful to Professor D.P.Chattopadhyaya for his patience and generous help without which the work could never be completed.

CHAPTER 33

Philosophy, Civilization and Conceptual Categories in Sociology

Yogendra Singh

Philosophy constitutes the foundation of all social sciences. Indeed, it is at the root of all forms of knowledge. Sociology is, therefore, no exception. From its very beginning, sociology has been deeply influenced by philosophical discourses and its theoretical constructs. The Indian sociology has historically been deeply impacted by the western sociological traditions despite its being self-conscious about it from its inception. Rooted as the western sociology was in its own philosophical heritage and its major paradigms, we witness that the debate on this issue in the early stages of the growth of sociology in India reflected itself in two directions: first, it was felt by some sociologists that the various constructs of the western philosophy contained elements which could be meaningfully integrated with the Indian philosophical traditions selectively, and secondly, there was also an attempt made to offer an alternate paradigm of the Indian sociology anchored entirely in the Indian philosophical tradition. Nevertheless, the entire Indian debate on the relationship between sociology, its categories and discourses with philosophy cannot be disassociated from the historicity of its relationship with the western sociological paradigms and their own grounding into the various western philosophical theories.

I

PHILOSOPHY AND SOCIOLOGY IN THE WEST

The social sciences, with their grounding in the empirical realities, do suffer from the limitations of what Karl Popper calls the 'poverty of historicism'. Philosophical paradigms that have shaped their epistemology have, therefore, provided them a level of enduring significance. A very apt, though controversial, example of this may be found in the contemporary retreat of the theories of economic and political Marxism; the philosophical Marxism, however, survives and integrates well with other theoretical paradigms in the social sciences. Nevertheless, it cannot be denied that theoretic tensions have continued both in the paradigms of philosophy and sociology. For instance, the controversy, particularly in the French philosophy between those who deem philosophy to be essentially professional, analytic and formal in essence and those who would seek its essentiality in praxis has raged vigorously. If we come across a passionate support to the tradition of the 'analytic philosophy' in the writings of Jacques Bouveresse or Claud Lefort, we also witness equally strong defense of the humanistic and praxis oriented philosophy of Maurice Merleau-Ponty, Jean Paul Sartre, Marcuse, Foucault and Jean Toussaint Desanti, etc. Bouveresse is particularly critical of Desanti's criticism of the analytic philosophy that "philosophy would write its own death warrant if it did not seek to connect up with the needs of everyday man, if it were to shut itself up in the new clergyship".[1] In his own defense Bouveresse writes:

> Rather than incriminating, as does Desanti, a certain propensity of contemporary philosophers to overlook their fundamental obligations to the unspecialized public in order to confine themselves to purely technical tasks, it would no doubt be preferable to recognize that their apparent capitulation on this point corresponds also to an objective situation, a situation constituted by the fact that the professionals are today in many respects the last to be a able to provide what society generally demands of them under the name of 'philosophy'. Those who propose any sort of reply at all obviously have a better chance, in any case, to make themselves heard than those who feel themselves constrained, not, as is ordinarily supposed, by pusillanimity but by a sense of professional honesty, to confess their own ignorance.[2]

In sociology, a similar tension in its professional worldview emanates from the two sources: first, from the discontent with the formalization of the basic sociological categories or attempts to elevate sociology to the levels of a positive science by experiments in the formulation of the nomological theories. C. Wright Mills' criticism of Talcott Parsons', or A. Strauss' focus on the 'grounded theory' can be quoted as appropriate instances.[3] Secondly, the popularity of the 'post-modern' worldview of epistemology leading to the total rejection of the notion of a rational actor or the operability of a social system has created for some sociologists the poignant dilemma to profess a sociology or post-sociology without social system.[4] Pierre Bourdieu writes: "The vanity of attributing immense and immediate effects to philosophy, and to the utterances of intellectuals, seems to me to be example par excellence of what Schopenhauer called 'pedantic comedy', by which he meant the ridicule one incurs when performing an action that is not included in one's concept, like a stage horse that defecates on stage. Now, if there is one thing that our 'modern' or 'post-modern' philosophers have in common, beyond the conflicts that divide them, it is this excessive confidence in the powers of language. It is the typical illusion of the *lector* , who can regard an academic commentary as a political act or critique of text as a feat of resistance, and experience revolutions in the order of words as radical revolution in the order of things."[5]

This similarity in the worldview both of philosophy and sociology regarding commitment to social purpose and normative critique of social order exists side by side their orientation towards the abstract or axiomatic theorizing.While in the field of sociology it is self-evident, in philosophy too it is widely existent both in the Anglo-Saxon and the French traditions of philosophy. In his correspondence, Ludwig Wittgenstein writes: "What is the use of studying philosophy if all that it does for you is to enable you to talk with some plausibility about some abstruse questions of logic etc., and it does not improve your thinking about the important questions of everyday life, if it does not make you more conscientious than any...journalist in the use of the *dangerous* phrases such people use for their own end."[6]

This convergence of the vocation both of sociology and philosophy and the common nature of the theoretic tensions in their paradigms and definition of their 'calling' constitutes a meaningful context in which the relationship of categories and discourses between the two could be evaluated. This may be witnessed both at the levels of formulation of epistemology, ontology and ethics of social realities, conditions and processes as also towards the commitment to social praxis.

The philosophical presuppositions permeate through and through in the western sociology. Auguste Comte, who made the first systematic and formal contribution to sociology called it 'positive philosophy'. He had, of course, a linear view of, what he called the 'hierarchy of sciences' which evolved, according to him, from the 'theological' to the 'metaphysical' and then finally to the 'positivistic philosophical' stage of evolution. Positivism provides a link to philosophy in the early sociological formulations in the west. This linkage is between the two contending philosophical paradigms, that of the German idealistic philosophy and the French and the British philosophies of the radical and utilitarian positivism. Both the contending philosophical paradigms have their own construction of the concept of rationality which has deeply influenced the European sociological theories during 1889-1930, and its dialectic has not come to an end even now. The strategic sociological categories through which the implicit philosophical presuppositions are reflected prior to this period are, for instance, the nature of social order and change. Comte characterizes sociology as 'social physics' and makes ample uses of the notions of 'static' and 'dynamic' equilibriums to explain order and change in society. In Britain, Herbert Spencer introduces the notion of contract grounded in the philosophy of rational utilitarianism to explain the nature of the industrial social order in the process of evolution and change.

Between 1889-1930, however, the philosophical debate in the western sociology focuses primarily on the role of 'reason', 'un-reason' and 'normative principles' in the constitution of social order and its change. The impact of the German idealistic philosophies of Immanuel Kant and Hegel seem to be pre-eminent in the sociological contributions of Karl Marx, Max Weber and Emile Durkheim. A theoretic, critical and creative tension seems to be palpable in their writings as between the uses of the notions of rationality-irrationality, representation- presentation, materialism-idealism and order-change in the processes of a society. We notice, in the contributions of Karl Marx a dialectical response to the Hegelian philosophy; this is evident in all his works but it seems to be particularly manifest in his, *The Economic and Philosophical Manuscript of 1884* and his, *Hegel's Philosophy of Right.* Even though Marx may claim to have reversed the Hegel's idealistic paradigm, replacing it with 'historical-materialism' and 'dialectical materialism', the essential notions of Hegel's philosophy, such as 'alienation', 'systematic replacement (superceding) in structural forms and the 'dialectic of contradictions' etc., permeate through his sociology. One may also witness in his writings the uses of structural-linguistic technique of the binary opposites, for instance, he reformulates Feurbach's statement 'God created Man' by 'Man created God' or on feudalism, 'lord owns the estate' is inversed by him as 'estate owns the lord' etc.

True to his generation, Marx implicitly and explicitly demonstrates in his writings the theoretic tension about the notions of rationality-irrationality. He locates its dialectics in history. The significance that 'history' assumes in his sociological analysis bears intimate resemblance to Hegel's heritage. But on the issue of reason and unreason in history Marx makes probably a distinction between 'micro-history' and 'macro-history'. The debate as to whether Marx has a concept of 'social structure' which implies a degree of stability and integration or his sociology recognizes social realities only as appearances of a 'historical moment' ever in the process of dialectical-historical transformation can be resolved to my mind if we view his notion of 'social structure' at two moments of time. First, the social structure as a part of the life-world of 'here and now' which one could call the 'micro-history' of society. Then, one could view social structure in the perspective of 'historical materialism' through its stages of evolution and change which belongs to the domain of 'macro-history'. This distinction in the notion of history is essential to grasp the role that Marx attributes to rationality-irrationality in the social processes of a society. From this point of view, we could maintain that Marx treats 'capitalism' as being a rational institution in the perspective of 'micro-history' but at the same time, capitalism contains the seeds of its self-destruction in the long term 'macro-historical' unfolding of the revolutionary social transformation.

The philosophical disposition of Max Weber reflects multiple orientations. His writings mirror influences of German historicists like W. Rickert, W. Dilthey and W. Windelband; his critical evaluation of the nature of social order and social institutions such as, capitalism, democracy, religion and ethics and historical contexts of civilization etc., lead him towards critical uses of the contributions of Marx, Neitzsche, Kant and the neo-Kantians. Weber's sociology, despite exposure to these multiple and often contradictory orientations has its own unity of discourse, and offers a systematic philosophy of civilization. The unit-actor in Weber's notion of social order is individual and not the 'species man' and the 'emergent properties' of social cooperation. Weber attributes to civilization and its moral order a quality of historicity; it is driven by forces of tradition, legal (regulatory) norms and 'charisma' of individual leaders. The march of civilization is governed by the manner in which these three forces are integrated, become creatively functional and over a period of time have the tendency to get routinized. The totality of this process of cultural and ideational changes constitutes, according to Weber the process of rationalization. It constitutes the ideological basis of a social order which undergoes continual changes. The process of change takes place due to the pressure building up in a social order which is overly routinized or where the existing principles of rationalization have lost their meaning necessitating a new normative principle and social order; it provide the scope for a 'charismatic' rupture in the established normative principles of the society. The various forms of prophecies, the 'innovations' in the normative principles of social order, trigger a new cycle of change-order-change in the established social system.

Weber criticizes Marx for his mono-causal explanation of social change. Like Marx he also considers capitalism to be driven by rationality. But the basis of this rationality in the European industrial capitalism lies, to begin with, in the ethical revolution (the role of prophecy) brought about by the 'protestant ethic'; through further rationalization this ethical rationality gives way, according to Weber, to a utilitarian-materialist rationality; capitalism thus loses its ethical sheen and is converted into an iron-cage. Weber also implicitly rejects Marx's premise which claims socialist order to be entirely egalitarian and free from the stratagems of power and hierarchy. Despite differences of ideology, according to him, both socialism and capitalism share the need for the rational-bureaucratic institutions in common. As C. Wright Mills aptly concludes, Weber's sociology shows complimentary features similar to those found in the contributions of Hegel, Marx, Nietzsche, and Adam Smith and yet goes beyond them. He writes: "In using the structural principle of explanation, Weber comes quite close to the analytical procedure of Marxist thought, which, in a 'de-spirituaized' way, makes use of the originally Hegelian and conservative way of thinking. In his methodological emphasis upon understanding the individual as the ultimate unit of explanation, Weber is polemical against this organicist thought of conservatism as well as the Marxist use of objective meanings of social action irrespective of the awareness of the actor. Like Hegel and Adam Smith, Marx ascribed meaning to the process of social interaction. Adam Smith's 'unseen hand' and Hegel's 'ruse of the idea' appear in Marx's system as an objective logic of dynamic institutions that work themselves out behind the backs of the actors".[7] He adds further, "Weber attempts to incorporate the point of view both of Marx and of Nietzsche in his discussion: With Marx, he shares the sociological approach to ideas: they are powerless in history unless they are fused with material interests: And with Nietzsche, he is deeply concerned with the importance of ideas for psychic reactions."[8]

As in Marx and Weber, Emile Durkheim's sociology too is deeply grounded in philosophy. In his, *The Division of Labour in Society*, he directly postulates a theory of division of labour which links it to the changes in the nature of social solidarity, which in turn condition the moral order of the society. He uses the evolution in the legal systems, from the 'penal' to the 'restitutve' laws as indicators of changes in the social solidarity and the moral order in the society. The division of labour emerges as a result of the need in the social system to reintegrate itself through the differentiation in occupations and its normative order. It does not result from the rationality and utlitarianism of the individual as Adam Smith and Herbert Spencer opined, nor is it related to the realization of 'happiness' in society implicit in Bentham's hedonistic calculus. In his, *Elementary Forms of Religious Life*, Durkheim attempts a sociological theory of knowledge and is critical of the Kantian epistemology. Offering illustrations from the religious rituals of the Australian tribe, he proposes that the basic categories of knowledge, such as the notions of 'space', 'time', 'number' etc., which according to Kant exist in *a priori* state, are in fact products of 'representation' of social solidarity through the manifestation of collective behaviour, for instance, the religious rituals.

The 1890-1930 generation of sociologist of which we have discussed the three most important representatives, share in common the philosophical debate on the nature of rationality, its sources and its role in constituting the nature of society and its processes. We also notice in their sociological paradigms a theoretic tension between the positivistic and interpretive (symbolic) approaches to sociological explanation. This tension progressively increased in sociology from 1930s onwards with the increasing influence of Freud not only in theorizing but also in ethnographic observations and analysis. The ensuing Second World War added a new edge to this process. It is reflected in the emergence of the 'Critical School' of sociology. The rise of Fascism and Nazism and the systematic racial violence that Nazism perpetrated in Germany, shifted the centrality in sociological researches to the study of the phenomena of 'collective irrationality' and the ideology of 'authoritarianism', the 'roots of prejudice' and other forms of 'totalitarian' ideologies. The rise of the 'Critical School' of sociology in Germany is a historical development of this phase. The writings of Adorno, Horkheimer, Habermas and Eric Fromme etc., amply reflect this new theoretic tension. They address through their writings and research project some of the basic philosophical issues, such as, the notion of history and its relationship with the ideological forces of rationality and irrationality, the relationship between 'freedom' and 'power', the roots of collective irrationality in the ideologies of culture and civilization and its 'negative dialectics' etc. Some of the most prominent sociologists of the 'Critical School' migrated from Germany to America and Great Britain where they made innovative contributions. Eric Fromme blended the conceptual categories and the premises of the Freudian approach in his treatment of the nature of social order; Karl Mannheim made his celebrated contribution to the exploration of the nature of 'ideology and utopia' and offered a philosophical critique of the theory of knowledge from a sociological perspective. Paul Lazersfeld made innovative contributions to the techniques of conceptual operationalization, observation and measurement of attitudes, opinions and ideologies. We find a centrality of the philosophical issues in the contributions of these sociologists. Also there is a manifest effort in these writings to blend several paradigms drawn from Marxism, phenomenology, functionalism and Freudian or neo-Freudian theories to evolve a systematic and integrated approach in sociological theory.

During the Second World War and the following three decades, not Europe but America held the position of pre-eminence in the contributions to sociology. The American sociology from the very beginning had been anchored in the pragmatic philosophical tradition. It had a problem-solving orientation, and most early studies had a focus upon the issues of acculturation, migration, urbanization and urban settlements, crime and delinquency and industrial productivity and workforce etc. During the 1940s and 1950s decades, the American sociology and social anthropology got deeply involved in researches in the areas of 'national character', 'morale of soldiers and their aspiration levels', 'value-orientations' of communities and groups and comparative studies of social structure and cultural values of ethnic communities. The philosophical presuppositions implicit in the categories used in these researches were multidimensional but their overpowering orientation was towards a behavioural and structural-functional explanation of social realities. It signified a revival of a new mode of positivistic sociology with many innovative additions to its techniques and conceptual categories resulting from cross-cultural and comparative studies.

A marked change in this orientation takes place by the end of 1960s, and one may witness in sociological theory a growing disenchantment from the functional and behavioural models of studies. It also inaugurated a period of wider cultural and social unrest among the youth and their questioning of the philosophical and normative premises of the mainstream American sociological contributions. Particularly, the uses of the sociological and social anthropological knowledge and techniques for promoting the political- strategic objectives of the state in general and in the USA in particular, was now highly resented, and sociology in a major shift of paradigms began to return to the philosophical foundations of the European sociology. Alvin Gouldner, C. Wright Mills, E.Horowitz, A. Strauss and several other American sociologists challenged the relevance of the functional theory, its positivistic grounding and teleological presuppositions. Instead of the 'power of generalization', the preference in the sociological practice now shifted to the quality of 'reflexivity' and the depth of 'interpretive understanding.' The philosophical pre-eminence that was initiated by the 'Critical School' sociologists once again became the central concern in sociology. Neo-Marxism, neo-Freudianism, structuralism, semiology, phenomenology and ethnomethodology etc.now came into vogue in most theoretical and methodological discourses in sociology.

In this process, sociologists now began to re-evaluate and re-search most of the themes of the previous sociology. For instance, the notions of 'modernity', 'political ideology and the nature of state', 'the theories of development', 'culture and identity' and 'ideology and social structure' etc. which were studied earlier were now given new analytical and theoretical interpretations. In addition, some new themes were also introduced in the sociological discourse: the study of 'democracy and citizenship' the issues of 'legitimation, communication and power structure', the 'ideological foundations of nationalism and nation-state' and the 'processes of restructuration in the modern industrial societies' etc. were now increasingly engaging the sociologists. This development made it possible for sociologists to introduce a range of philosophical discourses in their analytical designs. It is well reflected in the writings of Anthony Giddens, Earnst Gellner, Jurgen Habermas, Allain Touraine, Schultz, Berger and Luckmann and a host of other sociologists. Pierre Bourdieu, probably continuing the tradition of Emile Durkheim in the French sociology, offers us an excellent example of the emerging new interface between sociology and philosophy.

In in his *Pascalian Meditations*, Bourdieu examines the relationship between sociology and philosophy in greater depth and with an unprecedented centrality. A major hurdle in this relationship, according to Bourdieu, has been the detachment of philosophy from its original concerns with the practical matters of the every day life and in its being ensnared by, what he calls, "epistemic doxa" or *skhol'e*. He writes: "Nothing, paradoxically, is more dogmatic than a *doxa*, a set of fundamental beliefs which does not even need to be asserted in the form of an explicit, self-conscious dogma. The 'free' and 'pure' disposition favoured by *skhol'e* implies (active or passive) ignorance not only of what happens in the world of practice (brought to light by the anecdote of Thales and the Thracian servant girl), and, more precisely, in the order of the *polis* and politics, but also what it is to exist, quite simply, in the world".[9] He finds a mirroring of this limitation in the philosophies of Kant, Heidegger, Rickert, Dilthey, Husserl and the post-modern philosophers. About the philosophers of post-modernity, he writes:

> Only a critique aiming to make explicit the social conditions of possibility of what is defined, at each moment, as 'philosophical' would be able to make visible the sources of the philosophical effects that are implied in those conditions (i.e. professional position of philosopher). This alone will fulfil the intention of liberating philosophical thought from presuppositions inscribed in

> the position and disposition of those who are able to indulge in the intellectual activity designated by the term 'philosophy'...To those who ask why, and above all by what right, one can call for such a 'liberation' of philosophy, I will reply first that one has to liberate philosophy in order to liberate the social sciences from the reactive—not to say reactionary—critique that philosophy never ceases to make of them, being content, most of the time, to orchestrate unwittingly the commonest vision of these sciences. Thus, turning against social sciences the 'philosophy of suspicion' that they so readily attribute to it, the so-called 'postmodern' philosophers almost all concur in denouncing the scientific ambition that social sciences affirm by definition. Inclined to see an assertion as just a disguised injunction or order, to see logic as a 'thought police', to see claim to scientificity as a mere 'truth-effect' designed to secure obedience or as a disguised aspiration to hegemony inspired by the will to power—when, that is, they do not go so far as to transform sociology, a somewhat undisciplined discipline, into a disciplinarian discipline, authoritarian, even totalitarian and thought-policing, they can, some-times in contradiction with their conscious and declared political options, restore a philosophically and politically acceptable form to the most obscurantist accusations and anathemas that spiritualistic (and conservative) criticism has always made of the sciences, and especially the social sciences, in the name of the sacred values of the person and the imprescriptible rights of the 'subject'.
>
> But I also have the conviction that there is no more philosophical activity, even if it is bound to scandalize any normally constituted 'philosophical mind', than analysis of the specific logic of the philosophical field and of the dispositions and beliefs socially recognized at a given moment as 'philosophical' which are generated and flourish there, thanks to philosophers' blindness to their own scholastic blindness. The immediate harmony between the logic of a field and the dispositions it induces and presupposes means that all its arbitrary content tends to be disguised as timeless, universal self-evidence. The philosophical field is no exception to this rule. Sociological critique is therefore not a mere preliminary, preparing the ground for a more radical and more specific philosophical critique, it leads to the principle of the 'philosophy' of philosophy, which is tacitly engaged in the social practice, in a given place and time, is defined as philosophical.[10]

From this perspective, Bourdieu unravels the basic convergence in the discourse of philosophy with that of sociology. The appearance of the schism between the two, according to him, is due to the 'scholastic enclosure' of philosophy resulting from its self-limiting epistemology and its institutional location both in Europe and America which aim at promoting academic elitism.

II

PHILOSOPHY AND SOCIOLOGY IN INDIA

We have discussed the philosophical moorings of the western sociology at some length in order to illustrate the contrasting situation that we encounter as we begin to deal with the historicity of the Indian sociology. The political and cultural (civilizational) encounter with the West, the colonial domination and its institutionalization in India which, on the one hand, triggered the processes of its economic exploitation and, on the other, led to the institution-building and social movements towards its modernization, has left a historical imprint on the nature of the growth of the Indian sociology. Long before 1920, when sociology began to establish itself as a discipline in the universities in India , the Christian missionaries and the British administrators contributed to writings, journals and reports on various aspects of the Indian society and its culture. In totality, its objective was to construct a 'pre-sociology' of India, which, in other words, implied the interpretation of the Indian social and cultural reality from their own religious and philosophical frame of reference. The missionaries whose objective it was to christianize India, confronted major hurdles in their objective due to the resistance from the Indian institutions like caste, village councils and the network of the indigenous religious institutions, folk values and beliefs. Their construction of the reality of the Indian society was, therefore, selective, fragmented and culturally biased to say the least. Even the worldview of Christianity that is reflected in their writings is highly self-limiting, and often it is sectarian.

In addition to the missionaries, the two other sources from where the philosophical discourses in sociology were drawn have been the contributions of the 'orientalist' philosophers and the 'English utilitarian' administrators. The orientalist's focus was mainly on the textual-philosophical foundations of the Indian civilization and most of them present Indian tradition in positive or even laudatory terms. Scholars like Max Mullar and M. Jones specialized in Indology, translated many Vedic and other philosophical-religious texts into the European languages , and in a way their attempt was to interpret the Indian civilization for the West. Yet, we may also notice another kind of orientalism in the construction of the Indian society and its civilization among the philosophers and social scientist in Europe which is reflected, apart from a short reference to India in Hegel's *Philosophy of History*, in the writings of Marx and later on Max Weber's interpretation of caste and Hinduism. These writings too have an orientalist ideological nuance. Marx neglects the linkages, in the so called, segmentary social structure of India. Max Weber locates the Indian social structure and culture almost entirely in the Brahamanical traditions, such as the role of the 'priest'and the 'other-worldly asceticism' in Hinduism. Both of them have, in a manner, relied heavily upon the ethnographic and sociological data generated by the British administration during the late nineteenth and the early twentieth centuries, and the ideological perspective of their interpretation of India also seems to be in consonance with the 'colonial, utilitarian' approach.

In what sense have these contributions influenced the philosophical context of the 'pre-sociology of India'? The answer is that it did so in many ways; for instance, the 'historical materialistic' philosophical foundation evident in Marx's writings on India, triggered a methodological and analytical trend in the Indian sociology of the coming decades which continues, despite many fluctuations, even to this day. Max Weber's writings too have influenced the Indian sociology, once again, in terms of its methodological orientation e.g. its focus upon interpretive and historical analysis, the generation of concepts through construction of 'ideal types' based upon historical specificity of institutions and processes. His hypotheses about the limitation that Hinduism may create in the path of India's capitalist development and its modernization, have, however, proved to be fallacious.

The philosophical framework in the evaluation of the Indian social reality as reflected in the writings of the British administrators remained embedded in the British tradition of rational-utilitarianism. One can also witness in their analysis elements of the 'progress ideology' reigning supreme in Europe during that time. These administrators not only designed institutions of social and economic cartography of India through Census operation, land settlement reports, survey of the material resources of India, and the preparation of the District Gazetteers etc., but they also initiated the ethnographic and linguistic surveys of India. This was in addition to the codification and institutionalization of modern legal system, educational institutions and other organs of the state. Through these reports and writings one comes across the value-presuppositions of these 'utilitarian' administrators which was derived mainly from the cultural foundations and historical experiences of the western civilization. We find a focus on the question of 'origin' and 'evolution' in the analysis of many social institutions they studied in India, for instance, the caste system, tribal structures, languages and the village communities. Comparisons were primarily made with the stages of growth of similar institutions in the west.

Sociology as it began to establish itself as an academic discipline in the universities in India inherited these 'pre-sociological' antecedents and led to debates among not only the Indian sociologists or social anthropologists but also among the historians, philosophers, social scientists and intellectuals. This debate was organic to the Indian renaissance movement, which had its main centers in Calcutta and Bombay.[11] These scholars offered logical and substantive evidence to expose the implicit fallacies in the propositions about the Indian social and cultural reality formulated by the British and the European sociologists and social scientists. They also tended to offer philosophical counterpoints from the Indian tradition to refute the value-premises implicit in their writings about India.

Radhakamal Mukherjee and G.S. Ghurye can be named as the two most outstanding founders of the academic sociology in India. Both of them have addressed philosophical issues in their writings. Radhakamal Mukherjee, enunciates it in a more systematic form in his *The Philosophy of Social Sciences* (1960), where he challenges the validity of the philosophical presuppositions of the western sociology and social sciences. He defines man as 'homo symbolicus' with the capacity for value creation and self-transcendence. He rejects Marxist or other positivistic philosophies of the West which deny autonomy to human actor or even offer a deterministic view of the existential condition of man. He proposes a general theory of society based on the philosophies of Hegel, Vedānta, Buddhism and Taoism constituting an integrated paradigm. He writes: "The philosophy of dialectical materialism today promotes the universal notion of an inevitable pattern of social development through struggles and conflicts of global revolution and war and subsumes all human progress within the dialectic of the economic movement. Modern evolutionary naturalism, Spencerian, Marxian, or Bergsonian, reduces man's mind and values as passive entities manipulated mechanically by a vast process that he cannot intelligently direct or control."[12]

Mukherjee retains the notion of dialectics in his sociology even though he is critical of dialectical materialism. He writes: "...man thinks and lives dialectically. All social relations and behaviours and the values that lie deep seated in them embody polar principles and tendencies...through the dialectic of the vedantic *neti neti* , Buddhist *satya* and Taoist namelessness, the self identifies itself with the reality and the supreme value".[13] Moreover, dialectic means, to Mukherjee, the capacity of man to transcend through interplay of opposite forces to higher and higher planes of ethical and cognitive awareness, endowing ultimately in him the capacity for self-transcendence. In terms sociological practice, he offers a 'middle way' between liberal democratic and the planned model of social development.

His colleague, D.P. Mukherji attempts yet another effort to arrive at a 'middle path' between the dialectical logic of Marxism (he calls it 'marxology') and the dialectic of the Indian class, community and other structural forms that are deeply embedded in the tradition. He, like Radhakamal Mukherjee, rejects the positivistic atomism implicit in most sociological propositions about social categories in the western sociology. He favours the formulation of the categories in the Indian sociology by abstracting them from the indigenous institutions and the Indian tradition. He accords primacy to the tradition in the understanding of the Indian social reality and for evolving methods and concepts for its study in the processes of continuity and change. Philosophically, his paradigm offers a synthesis between the 'meat-theories' of Dilthey and Marx, but he also sees the need for its operationalization into sociological categories by grounding it into the Indian tradition. The unit of social action in India, he argues is not the individual but the *sangh* or the community. He prefers a historical-dialectical approach in the Indian sociology rather than its being overwhelmed by empirical positivism of the western sociology. His collection of essays *Diversities* (1958) contains his basic ideas regarding the relationship between philosophy and sociology and between sociology and the Indian tradition. He accepts the need for objectivity in sociology, and also the desirability of planned development. But planning for development must not be detached from human development and the grounding of its objectives into the values and traditions of the society. This emphasis on historicity and tradition in the determination of the goals of planned development of society shows dual philosophical tension in his sociology: on the one hand, between the universalism of the Marxist paradigm and historicism of Dilthey, and on the other hand, a tension between his formulation of sociology as an objective science and his reiteration to ground its paradigm in the Indian tradition. His student and colleague, A. K. Saran aptly comments on this philosophical tension; Saran writes: "The historic roots of the idea of a planned social order go back to the breakup of the worldview founded, among others, on the idea of the Great Chain of Being. The immediate positive reaction to the traditional worldview was to substitute the transcendental intuition of order by an immanentist conception of the social system. This was the logico-philosophical basis of the competitive, individualistic society which supplanted the traditionai order in the West...The implicit auto-apotheosis (of Man) which characterizes modern thought on planned socio-economic systems is the result of this effort. With the addition of the idea of a collective secular Providence to the competitive worldview, there arises an inner tension between the notion of self-adjustment and the notion of planning".[14] According to Saran, the logic of D.P. Mukherji's search for a middle path leads him "towards traditional sociology not far removed from that of Coomarswamy and Schuon."[15]

It is curious how the continual focus on the category of 'tradition', in the conceptualization of 'social structure' and 'change' has persisted in the Indian sociology. This is further evident from the writings of G.S. Ghurye, yet another 'pioneer' of the Indian sociology. He concurred with the view that the Indian social reality could not be grasped fully through the western sociological categories and their implicit philosophical assumptions. He criticized the postulate of dissociation between the ethnicity of tribe and caste and the treatment of the Indian tribal social reality through the category 'aborigines' by Verrier Elwin, and attempted to demonstrate the cultural and social linkages between the tribal and other forms of social structures and values in India through out its history and tradition. He also enunciated the sociological significance of the 'epistemological theories' in the Indian philosophical traditions, even though he did not make use of such categories in his own ethnographic and historical analyses.[16] This may also be true in case of the empirical and ethnographic researches of most other Indian sociologists. The discourse of philosophy in the operationalization of sociological categores in the Indian sociology has, therefore, remained confined largely to the domains of interpretation and analysis. It offers us a very relevant problem for critical analysis on the relationship between philosophy and sociology in India.

III

A SOCIOLOGY FOR INDIA

The identity of sociology as a discipline was enlarged following Independence. Its institutionalization through teaching in the universities and colleges increased multifold. Several research institutes for specialized sociological researches were founded and the state came forward to aid teaching and research in sociology by providing funds through institutionalized means. Indian sociology, by this time had started broadening its Euro-centric worldview and was exposed systematically to the theories, methods and substantive studies conducted by the American sociologists and social anthropologists. This, enlarged and also refocused the sensitivity in sociology about its relationship with philosophy. Its discourse, however, remained circumscribed as earlier, in terms of the philosophical significance of the Indian tradition to the paradigm of the Indian sociology. Louis Dumont and David Pocock initiated the debate in their journal the *Contributions to Indian Sociology* (1957-1966) and offered a view of their appraoch to 'a sociology for India'. Louis Dumont's *Homo Hierarchicus* (1970) further contains his treatise in an analytical and systematic manner, where he tries to establish the linkages between the Indian social structure and its civilization. In his subsequent writings, Dumont contrasts the European notion of the *Homo*

Equalis, with its Indian counterpart the *Homo-Hierarchicus* , as the basis of the civilizational differences between the Indian and the European traditions.

Dumont and Pocock's writings on the sociology for India enkindled a wider debate for many reasons: first due to their effort to place the Indian sociological paradigm in a cross-civilizational and comparative perspective; secondly, because it is grounded essentially in the theory of structuralism and finally, because it is linked with the tradition of continuing debate upon this theme right from the days of the 'pioneers' of the Indian sociology. Dumont's writings raise many questions which have relevance to the inter-face of philosophy with sociology. This is particularly evident in his distinction between the' universal' and the 'particular' categories in sociology on the one hand, and on the other, his distinction between the 'insider' and 'outsider' perspectives in the study of any society.[17] Dumont and Pocock make a distinction between the 'representation' of social reality and its 'facticity' in actual behaviour.[18] They hold that the aim of sociology is to unravel the central codes of a people's culture and civilization and to analyse it in a comparative perspective by movement from a particularistic to a universalistic domain of analysis. Comparison, thus involves the transposition of meanings from one level to another in order to facilitate the social construction of reality in terms of a global ideology. Dumont, further elucidates this methodology in his, *Homo Hierarchicus: The Study of Caste and Its Implications,* by treating 'caste', its structure and representations as the core of the Indian social reality and its ideology. Sociology, in his view, entails essentially the study of ideology. He writes: "The word 'ideology' commonly designates a more or less unified set of ideas and values. Thus one can speak of the ideology of a society, and also the ideologies of more restricted groups such as a social class or of a movement, or again of partial ideologies bearing on a single aspect of the social system such as kinship. It is obvious that there is a basic ideology, and a kind of germinal ideology tied to common language and hence to the linguistic group or the global society. There are certainly variations–sometimes contradictions–according to social milieu, for example social class, but they are expressed in the same language...The sociologist needs a term to designate the global ideology, and he cannot accept the special usage whereby ideology is limited to social class and given a purely negative sense, thus discrediting ideas or 'representations' in general for the sake of partisan aims."[19]

The thesis of Dumont and Pocock on the sociology for India has come under severe criticism by the Indian sociologists and social anthropologists for its various limitations. First, their commitment to a structuralist theory delimits their perspective to a narrow domain through which their notion of ideology is elaborated; even though they accept the distinction between the specific and global ideologies, the methodology of structuralism based on the notions of dialectic, transformational relationship and comparison in their analysis of ideology does not take into account the enormous plurality, not of the 'partial ideologies' but in the 'core ideologies' coexistent in the Indian tradition. The debate on the 'sociology for India' following Dumont-Pocock's formulation illustrates it; the exclusiveness of the Indian civilization or ideology being defined as entirely Hindu is challenged by counterposing it to the Islamic culture and values in India,[20] and within the Hindu civilization itself the role of the Hindu and non-Hindu or non-Brahamanical elements of Hinduism have been found to be of great significance[21] in sociological analysis. Secondly, the emphasis upon the study of 'representations' rather than 'actual behaviour' or institutions excludes from sociological studies a vast domain of the Indian social realities, for instance, its economy, industries, technologies and political values etc. from the scope of sociology which is unacceptable to its profession. Finally, Dumont's approach to 'ethno-sociology' is also problematic. He, while recognizing the significance of the 'particular', ultimately rejects it as a frame of reference for sociological analysis, which according to him, is basically global in its explanatory pursuit.

The criticism of Dumont has also come from A.K.Saran, who champions a staunchly traditionalist view on sociology and social sciences.In an essay on "The World Renunciation in Indian Religion"[22] in the *Contributions to Indian Sociology,* Dumont equates the notions of *dharma, artha* and *kāma* in the *varṇa* scheme of Hinduism to the Talcott Parsonian categories of 'moral universalism', 'calculating egoism' and 'rational action' as in economic theory respectively. He writes: "In the language of Parsons, *kāma* is expressive action, *artha* instrumental action, *dharma* moral action. The triology gives an exhaustive classification of the types of action and is based upon a system of opposition."[23] Saran's objection arises from Dumont's indifference in this comparison to the basic antinomy between the Parsonian worldview of culture and values and the 'traditional worldview' of Hinduism on which the *varṇa* scheme of values is based. As to Dumont's defense of his position as being 'an outsider's point of view', Saran says, "social reality qua reality has no 'outside'...the only outside is its interpretation in terms of an alien culture", and "taking in the name of science, modernity or objectivity, a firmly provincial standpoint for the study of traditional or tradition-haunted societies."[24] Saran's objection to Dumont's interpretation of the traditional Indian categories arises also from his rejection of all 'modern' sciences including sociology because he treats the discourse of modernity as a deviance from the 'traditional worldview' based on the sanctity of the eternal 'revelation'.

Indeed, from a traditional standpoint and its logic Saran's position is irrefutable as, for instance, "the Mimamsākas, who believed the Vedas to be unquestionable, inerrant and eternal...defended the inerrancy and irreducible authority of scripture by contending that scriptures have a unique subject matter and that inference or logic and epistemology, unlike scriptures, are fallible."[25] Louis Dumont errs not only in his conception of tradition but also his notion of caste as a sociological category by locating its normative boundary entirely within the notion of "purity and pollution". From a philosophical standpoint, the generation of social categories or conceptual classifications (from a Vaiśeṣika theory of universals) of the organization of the Hindu society in the context of the South Indian anthropology by Daniel offers an alternative perspective. Daniel writes: "Several principles have been identified as underlying or generating the caste system, the most popular being that of purity versus pollution. Unfortunately these present but half the truth....The inability to go beyond or beneath caste arose from the failure to see that *jāti* meaning 'genus' (the source concept of the ill translated 'caste') is not applied to human beings only, but to animals, plants and even inorganic material, such as metal and minerals as well....There is no better term than *substance* to describe the general nature of these variously ranked cultural units. In other words, differentially valued and ranked substances underlie the system known as the caste system, which is but one of many surface manifestations of this system of ranked substances."[26]

There are at least two other systematic attempts towards a sociology for India initiated first, by the ethno-sociological approach and the second, in the recent contributions to, what is called, *dalit* sociology. The ethno-sociological approach is deeply influenced by the American social anthropological contributions to the theories of cultural analysis based on the distinction between the 'core' and 'peripheral' values of a specific society. Its observations are based on the analysis of the texts, standardized forms of myths, legends, and other forms of social and cultural representations of the social reality. Recently, attempt towards an ethno-sociology of India based on the observation of cultural and philosophical presuppositions central to the social structure and values of specific communities or even at a general level of society, have been made by several sociologists and social anthropologists.[27] The contribution of McKimm Marriott and R. Inden stand out as distinct examples.[28] There is no attempt, however, in these writings to correlate the constructed categories with the empirical social and cultural situation in India. But a kind of philosophical sensitivity or even centrality is noticeable in the analysis of social and cultural forms. Instead of the universal categories, the ethno-sociological analysis has its focus upon the specificity and intrinsic historicity of the conceptual structures.

Since long, there has been a persisting criticism from many sociologists in India and abroad about the treatment of caste and other social structures in India from a Brahamanical (scriptural-normative) perspective. Edmund Leach, C. Parvattamma and a few other sociologists have criticized M.N.Srinivas' concepts of 'sanskritization-westernization' for its location in the Brahamanical ideology and its sponsored structures of power.[29] This debate, however, has remained feeble until in the decades of the 1980, following which, the momentum for the dalit sociological approach towards 'a sociology for India' has gained a new pace. Philosophically, its paradigm draws extensively from the Hindu counter-mythologies and legends, from the Buddhist philosophical traditions which challenge the irreducibility of the Vedas and other scriptures and from Marxism and neo-Marxism in a selective manner. B.R. Ambedkar's historiography of India which offers a counterpoint to the Brahamanical viewpoint often constitutes its basic frame of reference. Its scope extends from the study of the *dalit* ideology and its historical evolution during the nineteenth century,to the study of continual subaltern movements from among the tribals, scheduled caste and other marginalized communities and the rise of their cultural self-consciousness. There is also extensive discursion on the concept of '*dalit*' and its ethnological and social boundary. Nevertheless, the recent processes of the social and economic mobility among the scheduled castes, tribes and other deprived communities which have resulted into the emergence of the *dalit* elites and intellectuals has also contributed to the rise in *dalit* consciousness. Even though its roots go far back in history its contemporary resurgence is a historical product of recent social, political and economic changes in India. Gail Omvedt who has made rich contributions to the study of the backward class ideology and movement has recently made a penetrating study of the *dalit* consciousness. Many sociologists, social anthropologists and other social scientists have contributed further on the ideology, structure, mobility and conflict arising out of the dialectic of the *dalit* movement and the relative impact that processes of social change have had on the *dalit* community. Apart from Omvedt, Joan Mencher, Kathleen Gough,

Owen Lynch, J.M. Mahar, Nandu Ram, Gopal Guru and several others have made substantial contributions to a sociological corpus of knowledge which could in totality add a new dimension to the debate on the "sociology for India".[30] The centrality of the Buddhist philosophy in the meta-theoretical issues implicit in these studies have, however, not been fully articulated. It finds reflection, if at all, in the rejection of the Brahamanical model of *jāti* and *varṇa* systems and its legitimation in the social order of the Hindu society.

The Marxist philosophy of dialectical-materialism or historical materialism has influenced sociological studies in India since very early days. Among philosophers, affinity of dialectical materialism with the Lokāyat philosophical tradition has been often highlighted. In sociology, the Marxist paradigm has been operationalized through the historical manifestations of successive modes of production which constitute the basis of social relationship (class structure) and its inner dialectic in society. If we locate Marxist philosophy mainly in the conceptualization of the 'modes of production' and its historical evolution (historical materialism) manifested in the dialectics of social change in a society, then both sociologists and economists in India may seem to have integrated the core elements of this philosophy in their studies to a much larger extent and in a more conscious manner. The same may not be true in case of the uses of philosophy in other types of sociological researches and analyses in India where philosophical linkages are manifest only by implication. For instance, Kathleen Gough in her study of the political economy of the Thanjavur district in Tamil Nadu analyses the historical processes of change through the use of the 'three modes of production—Asiatic, feudal and capitalist' as being most suited to undertake a comparative sociological analysis.[31] Marxist sociology in early phases made use of mainly the historical and textual materials for analysis. For instance, A.R.Desai's *Social Background of Indian Nationalism* makes use of historical texts and documents as the basis for a Marxist interpretation of the rise of nationalism in India.

The Marxist studies have, however, slowly moved towards the empirical observation of social institutions and processes; this has exposed it to the challenging task of the operationalization of the concepts of the modes of production into specific and observable indicators which could determine whether an observed social system qualified for being 'pre-capitalist', 'feudal' or 'capitalist' in character. Much of the contemporary debate in Marxist political economy and sociology hovers around this issue. This also constitutes the basis for debate on the relevance of Marxism for sociological study of the Indian society.

The application of Marxist theory in sociological studies in the European context can be found, during the cold war years, in two forms; first, as instruments of rationalization of the empirical social observations through the Marxist discourse disregarding a strict logical fit between fact and theory. This type of the use of Marxism was widely patronized by the socialist states, particularly the former USSR. The second attempt was to develop it maintaining its philosophical centrality. In the European continent, particularly in France and Italy the philosophical debates on Marxism was kept alive and innovated upon in a creative manner. The disintegration of the USSR saw a triumph of philosophical Marxism over political Marxism all over Europe, even in the USA, which gave impetus to a much wider discourse on Marxism and its innovative uses. The Marxist theoretical applications in the Indian sociology, have been confined to a much limited discourse in epistemological sense, even though in scope their application has been widened beyond the study of modes of production and class structure to the study of a diverse set of social formations. The reference could be made to a series of studies in 'gender relationship', political economy of urbanization and the new social movements, in the fields of ecolog,, human rights and the dialectics of civil society.

From 1980s onwards, most sociological studies have shifted their focus from the study of structures to the processes in society. The study of socials movements has gained momentum. In these studies, we find increasing uses of multiple theoretical paradigms. In some studies, particularly in the context of the 'new' social movements, the uses of even the 'post modern philosophical' discourse is quite discernable.[32] The European discourse on 'post-sociology' and 'post-society' emerging out of the new forces of information revolution and 'hyper-industrial' society there, have also found expression, at least at the comparative if not analytical level, in some sociological studies of contemporary structural forms and movements in India. The discourse of the 'post-modern philosophy' and its impact on sociology constitutes now a widely debated theme.[33] A reflection of these can be seen in *Social Movements, Old and New: A Post-modernist Critique,* by Rajendra Singh (2001). In his appraisal of the notions of 'society', 'modernity', 'post-modernity' and his uses of the concepts of 'post-sociology' and 'post-society' one could easily see the influence of several contemporary critics of positivism and reductionism in the theoretical constructs of the mainstream sociology. The writings of Jacque Lacan, Jacques Derrida, Michel Foucault, Ernesto Laclau, Alain Touraine, Peter Berger etc. have been used to evolve a theoretical approach to the study of social movements. A totalistic and reductionist view of society in which the 'subject' has no centrality is questioned in favour of a notion of post modernism having features, such as 'non-deterministic polymorphous pattern of change', 'decentring of faith in reason, rationality and western materialism', 'consumerism', 'post-industrialism' and finally, 'return to the past and return to the nature'.[34] In operational terms, however, unlike most post-modernist formulations, the notion of society, as a frame of reference is not rejected in this study: Singh writes: "Post-modernity symbolizes both, a critique of modernity as well as a new apperception of the current nature of *a new conception of society and social movement* (italics added).[35] There is a conscious recognition in this study of the relevance of multiple theoretic paradigms (instead of singular reductionism, e.g. Marxism), reflexivity and 'homophilic' orientation in the sociological studies.

In philosophical terms, sociology at present does not seem to have altered the nature of its pre-established categories, but it has indeed, moved many steps forward to undertake a critical appraisal of the interpretive or analytical uses of the structural-functional and 'abstracted' empirical or statistical-mathematical models in sociological studies rooted in the philosophy of positivism. While the sociological categories may be the same, the philosophical premises from which they are now being operationalized shows new awareness to the utility of the ethno-methodological, phenomenological and cultural-analytic paradigms in the formulation of categories. This orientation in the contemporary Indian sociology also mirrors the global epistemological tension that sociology in general is confronted with today.

IV

PHILOSOPHY AND THE DILEMMA OF THE INDIAN SOCIOLOGY

In contrast to the western sociology, the philosophical moorings of the Indian sociology and its categories have right from the beginning been hanging on the horns of a dilemma, that is: how to integrate the categories of the Indian sociology with the Indian philosophical traditions. In a way, it is a dilemma which is not confined to sociology alone, but extends to all social sciences where a discourse on culture and ideology has relevance to the observation of reality. At another level, it also symbolizes the dilemma or cultural crisis of the Indian discourse on modernity or post-modernity itself.

The structural foundation of the sociological theories and its categories in the West have evolved through a processes of continuity and change in the western philosophy and its discourses. It is reflected in the textual formulation of the principles of sociology in the West, which at various stages of evolution and change have systematically grounded sociology into varied philosophical traditions, ranging from analytical philosophy, positivism, dialectical materialism, phenomenology or existential phenomenology etc., respectively. Many major sociological categories such as 'community', 'capitalism', 'rational action', 'alienation of individual' and 'imperative norms' etc., as Max Weber, Charles Nisbet and Werner Stark etc. have demonstrated, have their origin in the western Christian thought and its inner dialectics, and later were grounded in philosophy. The categories of sociology and its theoretical discourses in the West are, therefore, fully integrated with its own theological and philosophical traditions, and reflect the processes of its change and continuity.

In contrast, sociology in India has right from its beginning faced the problem of its categories and theoretical paradigms, derived as they were from the West, being alien to the Indian philosophical traditions. The realization of this lacunae has resulted in three major directions: first, attempt to formulate an alternate sociological paradigm, as we find in the writings of Radhakamal Mukherjee; the second response, as we see in the contributions of A.K.Saran, is to reject sociology itself which is deemed to be a product of a deviant worldview alienated from Tradition, which Saran describes as the Great Chain of Being. This type of response is, according to him not only valid for India, but also for the West, because alienation from Tradition is a common malaise of all humans living in contemporary 'modern' society. Saran's is a voice of minority in the Indian sociology, but his views have been widely acclaimed by a vast circle of intellectuals professing theology and philosophy. The third response to the dilemma faced by the Indian sociologists is to locate its categories and discourses within the ethno-cultural tradition specific to a community or society. Known as 'ethno-sociology', this type of response has led to several studies in India, each grounding their categories in the specificity of the local traditions, or as we see in McKim Marrott, in a specific Great Tradition of the Indian philosophy. A variation on the ethno-sociological approach, which is gaining momentum is to use a multiplicity of theoretical orientations and categories in sociological observation that are operationally feasible and are drawn from a variety of philosophical traditions whether from the West, East or India. This pragmatic approach to resolve the basic dilemma is in harmony with the contemporary debate on the emerging shape of a global society facing the challenges of post-modernity. But the basic dilemma in the Indian sociology, that is, to resolve the problem of integration of its categories and theoretical paradigms with the Indian philosophy remains a question mark which is waiting for a solution.

This dilemma is compounded by the fact that most Indian sociologists, who have realized the need of grounding sociological categories within the Indian philosophical systems, have not attempted to operationalize such categries for application in their own empirical or observational studies of the Indian social realities. Instead, most of their empirical or observational studies make use of the categories and concepts drawn from the western social sciences, even while they, like Radhakamal Mukherjee, profess the need for an alternate model of the Indian sociology grounded in the Indian philosophy of the philosophies of the East. The influence of the writings of the western philosophers and theologians is manifest even in A.K.Saran's critique of sociology. So is the case of the ethno-sociological theory which bears deep imprint of the American social anthropological influence. How to resolve this dilemma? Can it be accomplished by taking an ethnocentric view of philosophy and sociology? How have other non-western sociologists all over the world responded to similar dilemmas? These questions can be answered only by viewing the problem in a comparative cultural perspective. In the meantime, there is a need for a new beginning and to re-orientate the discourse of the Indian sociology so as to make it operationally viable at a meta-theoretical level which ensures grounding of the sociological categories in the discourse of Indian philosophy.

NOTES

1. Bouveresse, Jacques. 1983. "Why I am so very un-French". *Philosophy in France Today.* Montifiore Alan. London: Cambridge University Press. p. 27.
2. Ibid. pp. 29-30.
3. See, Mills, C.W. See also, Strauss, A.
4. See, Singh, Y. 2003. "The Worldview of Sociology and the Challenge of Post-Modernity." Mimegraphed.
5. Bourdieu, Pierre. 2000. *Pacalian Meditations.* Cambridge: Polity Press. p. 2.
6. Wittgenstein, Ludwig. Quoted in Bourdieu. p. 42.
7. Gerth, H.H. and Mills, C. Wright. 1952. *From Max Weber: Essays in Sociology.* London: Routledge & Kegan Paul Ltd. p. 58.
8. Ibid. p. 60.
9. Bourdieu. p. 15.
10. Ibid. pp. 29-30.
11. Singh, Y. 1986. *Indian Sociology: Social Conditioning and Emerging Concerns.* New Delhi: Vistar.
12. Mukherjee, R. 1960. *The Philosophy of Social Science.* London: George Allen & Unwin. p. 118.
13. Ibid. p. 4.
14. Saran, A.K. 1965. "The Faith of a Modern Intellectual." *Towards a Sociology of Culture in India.* T.K. Unnithan et al (ed.). Delhi: Prentice Hall of India. pp. 129-30.
15. Saran, A.K. 1951.
16. Singh, Y. *Indian Sociology.*
17. Singh, Y. 1984. See also, Singh, Y. *Indian Sociology.*
18. Dumont, L. and Pocock, David. 1957. *Contributions to Indian Sociology,* Paris. p. 11.
19. Dumont, L. 1970. *Homo Hierarchicus.* London: Weidenfeld & Nicolson. p. 263.

20. Ahmed, Imtiaz. 1972. "For a Sociology of India." *Contributions to Indian Sociology* (New Series), Delhi.
21. Burghart, R. 1983. "For a Sociology of India: An Intracultural Approach to the Study of Hindu Society". *Contributions to Indian Sociology* (New Series), 17(2).
22. Dumont, L. 1960. "For a Sociology of India: A Rejoinder to Dr. Bailey". *Contributions to Indian Sociology*, pp. 33-62.
23. Ibid. p. 41.
24. Saran, A.K. 1962. "For a Sociology of India". *Eastern Authropologist*, 1(15). p. 68.
25. Tiwari, H. 1994. "One and Many: The Early Naiyaikas and the Problem of Universals". *Journal of Indian Philosophy*, vol. 23. p. 144.
26. Daniel, E.V. 1984. *Fluid Signs, Being a Person the Tamil Way*. Berkeley. pp. 1-2. See also, Matilal, B.K. 1985. *Logic, Language and Reality: An Introduction to Indian Philosophical Studies*. Delhi.
27. Singh, Y. *Indian Sociology*.
28. Marriot, M. and Inden, R. 1977. "Towards an Ethno-Sociology of South Asian Caste System". *The New Wind: Changing Identities in South Asia*. Kenneth Davis (ed.). The Hague: Monton.
29. Singh, Y. 1973.
30. Singh, Y. *Indian Sociology*.
31. Gough, Kathleen. 1979. "Dravidian Kinship and Modes of Production". *Contributions to Indian Sociology* (New Series), Delhi. p. 286.
32. Singh, Rajendra. 2001. *Social Movements, Old and New: A Post-Modernist Critique*. New Delhi: Sage Publications.
33. Singh, Y. *The Worldview of Sociology*.
34. Singh, Rajendra. pp. 28-65.
35. Ibid. p. 62.

BIBLIOGRAPHY

1. Bourdieu, Pierre. 2000. *Pacalian Meditations*. Cambridge: Polity Press.
2. Bouveresse, Jacques. 1983. "Why I am so very un-French". *Philosophy in France Today*. Montefiore Alan. London: Cambridge Unviersity Press.
3. Burghart, R. 1983. "For a Sociology of India: An Intracultural Approach to the Study of Hindu Society". *Contributions to Indian Sociology*, New Series, 17(2).
4. Gerth, H.H. and Wright Mills, C. 1952. *From Max Weber: Essays in Sociology*. London: Routledge & Kegan Paul.
5. Daniel, E.V. 1984. *Fluid Signs, Being a Person the Tamil Way*. Berkeley.
6. Dumont, Louis. 1957. "For a Sociology of India". *Contributions to Indian Sociology*. Paris.
7. ———. 1960. "For a Sociology of India: A Rejoinder to Dr. Bailey". *Contributions to Indian Sociology*.
8. ———. 1970. *Homo Hierarchicus*. London: Weidenfeld & Nicolson.
9. Gough, Kathleen. 1979. "Dravidian Kinship and Modes of Production". *Contributions to Indian Sociology* (New Series). Delhi.
10. Matilal, B.K. 1985. *Logic, Language and Reality: An Introduction to Indian Philosophical Studies*. Delhi.
11. Marriott, M. and Inden, R. 1977. "Towards an Elthno-Sociology of South Asian Caste System". *The New Wind: Changing Identities in South Asia*. Kenneth David (ed.). The Hague: Mouton.
12. Imtiaz Ahmed. 1972. "For a Sociology of India". *Contributions to Indian Sociology* (New Series), Delhi.
13. Mukherjee, Radhakamal. 1960. *The Philosophy of Social Science.*. London: George Allen & Unwin.
14. Mukherji, D.P. 1958. *Diversities*. Delhi: Peoples Publishing House.
15. Saran, A.K. 1962. "For a Sociology of India". *Eastern Anthropologist*, 1(15).
16. ———. 1965. "The Faith of a Modern Intellectual" *Towards a Sociology of Culture in India*. T.K. Unnithan et al (ed.). Delhi: Prentice Hall of India.
17. Singh, Rajendra. 2001. *Social Movements, Old and New: A Post-Modernist Critique*. New Delhi: Sage Publications.
18. Singh, Yogendra. 1986. *Indian Sociology: Social Conditioning and Emerging Concerns*. New Delhi: Vistar.
19. ———. 2003. *The Worldview of Sociology and the Challenge of Post-Modernity*. Mimegraphed.
20. Tiwari, Heeraman. 1994. "One and Many: The Early Naiyāikas and the Problem of Unviersals". *Journal of Indian Philosophy*, vol. 23.

CHAPTER 34

Cultural and Ethical Response to Science: Indian Methodology

S. Panneerselvam

The relation between science and human life has been always emphasized both by philosophers and scientists. The following questions are inevitable when we talk about the above relations. The paper basically aims at answering the following issues: (1) Can we accept the view that science is absolutely objective? (2) What are the limitations upon the objectivity of science? (3) Can we say that technology is applied science? (4) Can it possess autonomy? (5) If science and technology are value-laden, then what are their internal and external values? (6) Will the challenge of science and technology to traditional Indian culture produce a creative response? (7) Or will science and technology become a universal solvent dissolving traditional values? (8) Should science be religious? (9) What does the cultural model of science mean? (10) Can there be an interaction between the two?

Science plays an important role in the modern society. Science is often seen as possessing an absolute objective character that God held in medieval theology. It is often claimed that technology is nothing but applied science. According to A.N. Whitehead, there is a "fallacy of the detached observer" by which, modern science had wrongly separated the experimenter from the experiment. The traditional view of science that it is absolutely objective is nothing but a myth and we need a more humanistic view of science. The view that science as absolutely objective and completely removed from the cultural context of the scientist has been questioned by the philosophers of science. Kuhn formulated the view that social and institutional factors directly influence the nature of scientific theories. Similarly, the Socialists who have studied the scientific knowledge claim that science arise from the "social construction of facts". For them, different social conditions will produce different facts. This to some extent implies that because of the cultural differences, Indian science is different from Western science because of different facts. This rejects the fundamental assumptions of the universality and objectivity of science. Similarly, Latour and Woolgar, by adopting the role of anthropologists looked upon the laboratory as the site of an unknown native tribe called "scientists".

Science and technology are humanistic disciplines but of course one can make a distinction between science and technology. In science, we investigate the reality that is given to us, the empirical reality, and the world around us. In technology we create a reality according to our designs. It is a man-made reality. In other words, science deals with what is whereas technology deals with what-is-to-be. In science we have reality first and then its description whereas in technology we have description or design first and only afterwards reality—the object that is produced according to our design. Though we consider the fact that science and technology are humanistic disciplines scholars like, C.P. Snow have made the distinction between the worlds of science and the humanities into "two cultures". It must be understood that the same human cognitive process underlies both disciplines and that this process is necessarily value-laden. Science not only expresses internal values but also produces external values through its impact upon society and the world. The claim that science is value-neutral cannot be correct. Science depends upon and expresses human values. Science is to be not only shaped by human motives and attitudes, but this knowledge process depends heavily and properly infused with human values. These values are not external values imposed upon science from outside, but honesty, beauty and knowledge as intrinsic values stand at the very heart of the scientific enterprise. Those thinkers who claim value neutrality for science dehumanize science and distract us from the realization that the very choice of what constitutes a scientific explanation depends upon the value-laden choice. Science without internal human values could not be science.

Philosophers have tried to explain the distinction between science and non-science. Popper for example has explained the progress of science in terms of bold conjectures which scientists attempt to falsify rather than confirm. What makes a conjecture a scientific one is that it is open to be tested and perhaps refuted. Theories, which are in principle immune to the refutation, are not scientific. Similarly, Kuhn described a psychological experiment, which explains the nature of scientific discovery. The history of science is characterized by periods of normal since within which scientist work. Scientists working within the received paradigm will not give it up easily, even in the face of anomalous results. Feyerabend attacks science and scientific education. He claims that science is simply a form of ideology like any other ideology.

India seems to be living in two or more conceptual worlds at the same time: (1) the world of the great tradition in which the mythological past lies in the present, time exists in a mosaic of different periods, matter and mind appear on the same continuum, and the dominant conceptions are of groups, clusters, and patterns and (2) the modern world of science and technology in which mathematics plays a major role in describing the world, matter and mind though related are discrete entities, and conceptions are deductive, linear and of individual events. But which one is the need of the hour?

We need to develop alternative world-views, alternative metaphysics, as the basis for reflection on technology vis-à-vis society and civilization. The way towards understanding the metaphysical roots of technology, must lead through the creation of an alternative world-view which will enable us to grasp sharply and clearly ramifications and consequences of present technology for a future human society. It is here people from non-western cultures have much to contribute. But how to start? The starting point is that we must re-examine our intellectual heritage and tradition in the light of our present situation. Tradition is always hermeneutical and accommodates new interpretation and understanding. This reconstruction means the reconstructing the present categories of knowledge. Man's mode of being-in-the world helps a person to evaluate the tradition. It is not possible for a person simply to follow the tradition, but he has the right to evaluate the tradition. The world of historicity will have an impact on the tradition and it accepts evaluation and reinterpretation. This does not mean that we are revolting against the tradition, but interpreting them in the context of present historicity. The cultural world, which one belongs to, allows a radical interpretation of the tradition. This sort of interpretation teaches a way of looking at the tradition afresh from a new perspective, which will suit for our present situation. Husserl, for example, who used phenomenology to investigate the *a priori* of the life-world, develops a concept, "the surrounding world" to explain this. It is a concept that has its place exclusively in the mental-spiritual sphere. He argues that we live in our particular surrounding world, which is the locus of all our cares and endeavours. Our surrounding world, according to Husserl, has a spiritual structure in us and in our historical life. It is absurd to look upon the nature of the surrounding world as something alien to the spirit. This explains how a particular person is placed in the surrounding world or tradition though his physical world is supported by scientific and technological society. Every man is placed in a tradition or culture, which cannot be avoided.

In science as well as in the post-metaphysical thinking the role of reason is unique. But the role and definition of reason differs among them. Some like Rorty considers it as a social phenomenon. "We have to resist the urge to see social practices of justification as more than just such practices".[1] Foucault attempts to disempower the ideas of reason by totally objectivating them. "What is this reason that we use? What are its historical effects? What are its limits, and what are its dangers?" asks Foucault.[2] Derrida attempts for a totalized critique of reason. He believes that the ideas of reason are built into thought, and give rise to illusions and therefore he wants to renounce the ideas of reason by interrogating, disrupting and displacing them. Similarly, Habermas reconstructs the Kantian notion of reason so as to explain the importance of comprehensive reason. As a critic of scientific-technological rationality, he constructs social rationality. He, for example, has rejected both Adorno and Horkheimer who considered that the development of western rationality as the totalisation of reification, domination and repression. Against this background, Habermas defended the positive aspects of enlightenment and also of modernity and Western rationality. He wanted to emphasis the role of rationality in the economy, culture and morality. This means that for him social rationality has implications in social life, which cannot be neglected. In his comprehensive concept of rationality, different dimensions of social life, *i.e.* values, norms, interests, are studied and preserved.

Marcuse defines reason as "the fundamental concept of philosophical thought, the only one by means of which it has bound itself to human destiny... it is not only a category of bourgeois philosophy, but a concern of mankind".[3] Horkheimer and Adorno in their *Dialectic of Enlightenment* attempted a critique of instrumental reason. Instrumental reason is now not identified with a particular period of history, society or class. Rationalization has thus moved from a historically specific to global context, thus expanded its scope to the whole of human society. Both Horkheimer and Adorno argue that unfortunately, the Enlightenment project, which had the agenda of liberating humanity, has turned into a new and powerful force of domination. In *Dialectic of Enlightenment*, both Horkheimer and Adorno explain how reason turned into its opposite and resulted in new rationalized forms of social domination. Social rationality turned into irrationality and enlightenment into deception. Not only this,

Enlightenment reason has resulted in domination and regression. Thus for them, instrumental reason and science have become myths which resulted in worship and praise for superior powers and social domination. Habermas wanted to revise the project of Enlightenment rationality. His idea was to offer an alternate to the subject-centered tradition of rationalism. Along with Horkheimer and Adorno, Marcuse also criticized the scientific-technological rationality and instrumental reason. He argued that the very form of technical reason is ideological and believed that not only the application of technology, but technology itself is domination. He says: "Specific purposes and interests of domination enter the very construction of the technical apparatus. Technology is always a historical-social project; in it is projected what a society and its ruling interests intend to do with men and things. Such a purpose of domination belongs to the very structure of technical reason."[4]

We need alternative view of knowledge. For example, philosophers, futurists, and others who are interested in the future of technology and thus with the future of culture would be benefited by a dialogue with the alternative world views of Indian culture in which alternative basis for knowledge and of life is admitted. The western or the technological society is based to a great extent, on the qualitative-instrumental values. It is true on the basis of these values, the social and political assessments are made. As long as the quantitative instrumental basis remains unchanged and channels its imperative via descriptive science, through industrial profit-efficiency-oriented technology, the order of things will remain the same. It must be noted that even the prevalent approaches to values cultivated by the majority of contemporary philosophers are reductions, and indirectly serve the cause of the quantitative world-view. Some of the reductionist approaches are (1) the Linguistic approach (for example, J.L. Austin) (2) the Formalist approach (for example, George Henrick Wright) (3) the Simple-minded approach (for example, E. Mesthene) and (4) the Simplistic Mathematical Approach (for example, A. Rosenstein). What is interesting is that in all these approaches, values are reduced to something other than they are, linguistic utterances, logical structures, technological commodities and mathematical functions. Thus to change the predominantly quantitative temper, our civilization will require a through-going change in our modes of understanding.

The West is now in search of quality of life. It has understood the emptiness of the quantitative approach. The modes of life governed by quantity are simply not sufficient. Quality of life is hard to define, although its absence is readily apparent. We know what is within the structure of our experience of it. Quality of life adds to our stature as human beings. Quality of life cannot be understood without a purpose in life. The purpose in life cannot be secured unless we ascribe some meaning to the world or at least some meaning to the human life—beyond the immediate gratification of our sensual desires. This means that the quality of life requires a transcendental dimension of life. Traditional cultures and religions, by providing these transcendental dimensions can contribute to our experience of the quality of life.

The issues connected with the quality of life can be known through the issues connected with needs. Needs, here include both genuine and artificial. Under genuine needs one can include basic needs, cultural needs and subjective needs. The biological needs are the needs, which are necessary for survival, and the subjective needs are the needs, which make the individual unique. But what is important is the cultural needs which are the specific needs, and which contributes to the well-being of human beings as socio-cultural entities. They are specific to a given society at a given time. They may vary from society to society and from epoch to epoch in the same society. Although acquired, they are not subjective but rather trans-subjective, for once a culture develops a certain set of needs, an individual raised in this culture regards these as necessary. The artificial needs appear to contribute to our well-being, but in reality it is not. It maybe seen as an outgrowth or continuation of cultural and individual needs. But they are parasitic. Their satisfaction not infrequently leads to the suppression of other significant needs. Man spends more time with computers and internet than with nature or with other human beings.

We talk about the "universality of science" and the "diversity of cultures". Often we think that science is reliable whereas culture is ephemeral. But the fact is other way round. It is culture that is enduring and universal whereas it is science that is transient and ephemeral. The only viable framework for development is culture and not economics fused with technology as at present. Development must mean the fulfillment within a culture that nourishes and sustains. It is argued that the scientific method is infallible. This reliability condition is used by the scientists to claim the superiority of science over culture. Can this be a proper criterion? Often it is shown that the scientific method is a myth. It is not possible to define the scientific method adequately and also it is difficult to show exactly what makes the scientific method scientific. For Popper and others, scientific method does not exist. Also there is no one single method in science. There is multiplicity of methods. For example, the astrophysics has its own method of exploring phenomena like quasars, blackholes, the origins of the universe etc. Physics and Chemistry differ in their methods. The methods used for understanding the Newtonian Universe is different from that of the universe of sub-atomic particles. Similarly, the scientific method as applied to social sciences cannot be a mere transposition of the methodology of physics. Here also one can ask a further question. Which physics? Is it quantum physics or classical physics?

Here one may give a counter argument. Even if there is no single method for science, science proceeds within well-ordered structures called paradigms which are conceptual structures that outline the territory and provide strategies for scientific endeavors. But even this argument cannot be right for the main reason that each scientific revolution is different from the other and each seems to have been guided by the logic specific to it. In our over enthusiastic mood to make science universal and to make the scientific method hold for realms of human inquiry, we have simply distorted the nature of phenomenon. But in reality science is as diverse as other modes of knowledge. But in the scientific frame of reference, culture has been claimed to be relativistic, pluralistic, diverse and transient. This maybe so at the superficial level of appearance, but there is also the essence and purpose of culture. It has a purpose of uplifting human beings. There is an underlying unity among seemingly diverse cultures and that this is the unity of purpose to assure a quality of life to the individuals within a culture. Culture in the final analysis maybe considered to be one of many instruments man has inherited, but it is an instrument of quality. The fundamental difference between science and culture is that while science is concerned with the quantity of life and the quantitative aspects of the universe, culture is concerned with the quality of life and the qualitative aspects of the universe. The model of development used in the present-day society fails for the main reason that it is only concerned with quantity. "Development while preserving the cultural values" should be our motto.

In the scientific model, there is only kind of value, which will be measured in monetary terms. In such a model, culture is a disvalue. It is outside of the model. It is one of the externalities. The cultural model on the other hand, recognizes a plurality of values and science is one of the positive values. It is of secondary importance whether we regard religion as part of culture or as a phenomenon more important than culture and in fact determining the nature of culture. We must adopt the cultural model as the basis for future development. As long as our model of development remains scientific and economic, culture will inevitably be a casualty, and indirectly we shall be its victims, as repositories of culture. The cultural model recognizes a plurality of values and science is one of the positive values. We must adopt the cultural models as the basis for future development. Science will become a stimulus to cultural growth rather than universal solvents reducing culture to a meaningless homogeneous world of uniform practices. India alone can give a direction and serve as a model for the West and other developing countries of how science and culture can interact for the good of mankind.

The increasing awareness that western culture maybe breaking down has made us search for causes and examine facets of modern society which we have hitherto ignored, neglected and overlooked. In technology, there is a focal point, in which conceptual and ideological paths meet. To understand these converging paths is to understand the main configurations of the network within which our civilization operates. For example, notions like progress, nature, invention, rationality, efficiency etc. have a link with culture. To put in simple terms, the philosophy of culture is the philosophy of society, a philosophy of man in a civilization which has found itself at an impasse, which is threatened by excessive specialization, fragmentation and atomization and which is becoming aware that it has chosen a mistaken idiom for its interaction with nature. All these problems to some extent are due to our wrong approach to science and technology. Philosophy teaches how to live with our environment with peace and free from conflict. Sufficient care has not been taken to understand the traditional methods of preserving nature. This has led to innumerable environmental problems. The degradation of the environment is leading to vast areas of the world and as a consequence of this, the world, which we live in, is becoming more and more unsuitable for human habitation. A clean and hygienic environment is a basic necessity for healthy living. Industrialization, unplanned development and mechanization have spoiled the environment considerably. The solution to the problem is possible only through the understanding of indigenous culture, which would result global understanding. If sustainable development is to succeed as a new way of life, its moral content should be well justified. The need of the society is to transform the behaviour of the societies towards the biosphere. A new ethic of embracing plants and animals is required so as to live in harmony with nature. Eminent environmental thinkers like R.C. Clark, R. Ellot and P. Singer have emphasized the need to protect the living beings on earth. It is the duty of man to take care of non- human beings also and hence has more moral responsibilities towards earth.

We live in a civilization that is threatened by the uncontrolled growth of technology, deriving from the empirical sciences, which have nothing to say about human values. Modern civilization is radically rotten, and only a complete transformation in theory and practice could cure it. The environmental crisis facing industrial society is so grave that man has to do something to save the human society, as well as nature and other living beings. In the present society, there is a public demand for particular ethics for single profession of vocation, a demand which is as unwarranted as if one were to demand specific civic rights and laws for different groups, communities within the same political entity called state. The different professions and communal groups of people may have different mores, but there should only be one underlying set of ethical maxims, principles as obligatory for all human beings, irrespective of this race, religion, nationality or other secondary qualities. In our present scientific technological civilization, there is a need for protecting man as well as environment. Every individual and every creature has intrinsic dignity and inalienable rights, and each one of them has an inescapable responsibility for what he does.

Our ancient Indian thinkers have spoken elaborately on these issues. But the issue is more significant in this millennium because of the fact that the problem we face today is to be tackled immediately if humanity wants to survive in the future. It is not only concerned about the living of human beings. Man has to protect the plant and animal kingdom. He should not think that the nature exists for his use alone. He has to take care of every aspect of nature. The rights and wrongs of our treatment of animals are discussed at length in ethics. The ethics of population growth and the use of natural resources have an important part to play in the discussion of social or distributive justice between nations. Now philosophers understand their responsibility to consider questions of moral responsibility and political organization in a global contact, otherwise known as "global ethics". The sense of a need to think afresh about questions of ethics in international relations gains importance from the belief that ecology has altered us to potential crisis of, earth-shaking proportions. This means till now we have been talking about issues connected with national boundaries like, self-determination of peoples, implications of war, nuclear deterrence etc. But now, environmental disaster is a common threat to the whole humanity and hence must be tackled immediately if it wants to survive in the future. This means there is a demand for a radical re-thinking of moral parameters.

The role of philosopher is very important in this context. The Norwegian philosopher, Arne Naess, for example, talked about what is known as deep ecology. He made a distinction between "shallow ecology" and "deep ecology". Shallow ecology attributes value and importance to the processes of nature only in so far as they are important for human welfare and interests. Such a view believes that global warming for example represents danger because it threatens agricultural production and human habitation. Deep ecology on the other hand is concerned with changes in the biosphere in themselves and not just to the extent that they work to the benefit or detriment of human beings. To think in this way is to hold the view that there are things of value and importance whose value do not lie in their connection with human interest, that there are strictly environmental values. From this standpoint, shallow ecology is objectionable because it makes human beings the sole focus of value and thus expresses a kind of self-centredness. The fact that environmental crisis are multiplied and take different forms shows that we are still in search of a truly environmental value which can be supplied only by philosophers.

Ethics as the study of right and good is always studied in relation to man. This has been the approach of many of the western ethical thinkers. But this type of ethics is always man-centered. It starts with the assumption that all the values exist for the sake of humanity. This has led to lot of problems because man has failed to understand the importance of other living beings. In the contemporary period, the need for such ethics has been felt very much. Albert Schweitzer defines ethics as man's unlimited responsibility towards every living being. Philosophers like Immanuel Kant, Max Weber, Hans Jonas, Jurgen Habermas, Richard Hare, John Rawls, and others have stressed this. Kant developed the moral philosophy or philosophy of practical reason during 1785 and 1797 and published three important books, namely, *Foundation of the Metaphysic of Morals, Critique of Practical Reason* and *Metaphysics of Morals.* The philosophy of practical reason or ethics is concerned with that only which ought to be done, i.e., what should be enacted by man's action grounded in a free will, whereas the philosophy of theoretical reason or nature is concerned merely with everything that is. Max Weber's ethics is known as "responsibility ethics". He was guided in his historical-sociological research by an idea which was decisive in his construction of concepts and his formation of theories; the idea of the rationalization of all social fields. Max Weber who rejected the dogmatic interpretation of history and society, whether idealistic or materialistic has pointed out that in every investigation of historical and social events one must observe strictly one main question, namely, that is, such an inquiry is strictly, beyond doubt, factual. His study on *Protestant Ethics and the Spirit of Capitalism* (1901) is a typical example of his approach to the socio-hisorical phenomena. Similarly, Hans Jonas' *The Imperative of Responsibility in Search of an Ethics for the Technological Age* is an investigation with a reconsideration of the ethical key-concept freedom and like Kant he takes man's free will as the metaphysical condition of morality. According to him, in so far as technical science has extended man's educative power up to the point where it becomes sensitively dangerous to world as such, it also extends man's responsibility for future life on earth. Thus man's responsibility becomes for the first time cosmic. It needed the obvious endangering of the whole system, the factual beginnings of its destruction, to make us discover or rediscover our solidarity with the whole world. Habermas' Discourse Ethics or theory of Communication is meant to serve the purpose of critically discussing various possibilities of morally responsible acting, aiming at guidelines for a morality justifiable life in our scientific-technical world. He considers as the objective of Discourse Ethics to re-formulate and re-assess Kant's formalistic moral theory, in particular the justification of ethical norms and principles, by employing the means of communication by saying that moral questions can be answered by rational reflection and discourse.

The Promethean science and the Faustian science though were in quest of knowledge, but because of their differing views of man's nature and life's goal for, have entirely different purposes. For the Promethean science, knowledge was an instrument of liberation and self-perfection leading to the divine, whereas for Faustian science, knowledge was an instrument of power, untrammeled and absolute, over everyone and everything leading to self-destruction and eternal perdition. Ultimately, the Promethean science lost out to

Faustian science, first in the West and later all over the world. Technology is not a thing-in-itself. It is and always has been part of the social structure, belonging to a larger cultural framework in which man functions as a human being. There is and always has been a continuos dialogue concerning society, its needs and aspirations, and the technical means potentially contained in technology for satisfying those needs and fulfilling those aspirations. The nature of science cannot be understood without understanding the nature of this dialogue. To consider science as entirely autonomous is wrong though it has secured for itself a great deal of autonomy. It is a mistake to think that the technological system is self-justifying in its own terms. There should be a dialogue between science and culture.

Two such models explaining the interaction between science and culture/philosophy are available in the Indian context. The one offered by Professor R. Sundara Rajan and the other by Professor D.P. Chattopadhyaya. Professor Sundara Rajan's book, *Beyond the Crisis of European Sciences: Towards New Beginnings* criticizes the eurocentric bias of science and explores the possibility for a new path. He talks about the "European themata" i.e., the general features of style and motivation, which seem to characterize the modern sciences, and to explain the need to develop a conceptual framework for understanding of science and also to support the relationship between science and philosophy. Professor Sundara Rajan wants to develop a four-fold framework of science—science as a possibility, science as a fact, science as a problem and science as a hope,[5] which he thinks, can solve the crisis of the natural science. In the first context, i.e., science as a possibility, philosophy is facilitative. The critical approach of philosophy is helpful to science. In the second, science as a fact, there is a radical change in the relation between philosophy and science.[6] Philosophy has to help science by analyzing social reality. Analysis and clarificatory procedures of philosophy are immensely helpful in the understanding of the basic principles and methods of sciences. In the third context, i.e., science as a problem adopts the critical function of philosophy. Here philosophy takes the possibility of a critique of sciences in terms of a normative understanding of life. The crisis of the sciences is approached by philosophy to solve it. For example, the role of science in the politics of domination and colonization has been questioned and here philosophy comes to its rescue. In the fourth and final context i.e., science as hope, we allow new possibilities, taking into consideration its failures and limitations. This means one needs new self-understanding. This is possible through the "thematic dimensional approach" which for example, Holton prescribes.

There is a relationship between philosophy and human sciences. This relationship is quite often not approached seriously. But one needs the other and one is not a threat to other. Each discipline must enter a dialogue with the other thus giving the scope for new thinking both in philosophy and science. Taking two paradigms of Popper and Khun, Professor Sundara Rajan argues that for Popper, science and philosophy are very close in spirit and motivation.[7] But for Kuhn the relation is a variable one and sometimes they are indistinguishable also. The difference between the two thinkers is that while Popper insisted on the role of philosophers in science, Kuhn is of the view that philosopher misses the rhythm of science.

Another important thinker who has been emphasizing the need for the interaction between science, technology, philosophy and culture is Professor D.P. Chattopadhyaya.

This interaction according to him can be approached in many ways.[8] First, it can be shown from the commonsensical or pre-theoretical point of view that every man combines in his world-view the basic aspects of his life, scientific, technological, geographical, historical and economic. Second, one may try to redo the same thing in a more systematic and refined way at the theoretical plane. Third, we may focus on the distinction as well as relation between civilization and culture, between the material and the spiritual aspects of human life. Fourth, one may explain the importance of relationship between man and the environment and in the process show that even the higher forms of culture cannot be free from the environmental conditions. Fifth, one may argue that even the disciplines like mathematics are influenced by practical and social considerations. Sixth, comments may be offered to show that there is close relation between the environment, human nature, medicine, ethics language technology, and philosophy. Lastly, one may try to say that philosophy, science, technology and culture are in fact, an interwoven fabric of human civilization and their specialization, differentiation etc., are mainly due to theoretical needs for specialization. According to Professor Chattopadhyaya, man has a past behind him and a tradition to support and regulate him. His very being is embedded, or, one might even say, he is born in a culture, marked among other things by its tradition and modernity, language and culture. Since man is sustained by tradition and culture, he questions them both. His sense of values can never be completely dominated and determined by his tradition and culture. He cannot transcend the challenge of modernization. Because of this, he questions his own tradition and cultural past. Professor Chattopadhyaya very rightly says: "Continuous growth of knowledge, particularly of its scientific form, and advancement of technology often make us question our own traditional heritage and cultural past."[9]

In his interesting paper, "Rationality, Culture, and Values,"[10] he deals with the correct relation between rationality and culture. He rejects the claim that there is a unique and universal relation between culture and rationality. He believes that culture-bound rationality is a sort of relativism. He examines the three different concepts of rationality developed in the three branches of human knowledge, namely, the economics, evolutionary biology and psychological behaviourism. By examining all the three concepts Professor Chattopadhyaya comes to the conclusion that all these concepts of rationality are limited and they underestimate the diversity of human nature born out of freedom and cultural circumstances. They are outer and inner aspects of human nature. Since all the theories of rationality are derived from human experience, their validity and correctness must be tested only through human experience.

Professor Chattopadhyaya is of the view that some philosophers have been very much attracted by the model of physical science, because of its testability and precision criteria. Some others accept the model of analogy of God, His comprehensiveness and power. But Professor Chattopadhyaya feels that in all philosophical positions, there is an inarticulate anthropological presupposition. Since philosophy is a reflective enquiry, every philosopher consciously or unconsciously touches the principle of anthropological root. "Criticised, corrected and corroborated by the objective details of experience, the philosopher broadens and deepens his theoretical visions."[11]

We always find different conceptions of culture. The culture of people takes into account the language, ideas, customs, taboos and other related components. One must always consider the following aspects with regard to culture: (1) culture unifies men into one cultural group and (2) the development of many cultures is due to various external causes like, physical habitats and resources, and inner causes like range of possibilities inherent in various areas of activity. If conflict among cultures follows from the very concept of culture, then there emerges a theory where there is a relation between culture and rationality. The difference between cultures and rationality is that a culture unifies all those who belong to that culture, whereas all men unite in rationality by sharing this essential feature. Culture endows people with their identity.

The relation between science and culture is similar to that of system and life-world which are defined as two aspects of human existence. In the writings of Schutz and Goffman, we can see these two-fold aspects of human existence playing important role. There is always a tension between these two aspects of life, namely, the system and life-world. This is explained in Kantian writings also. Kantian deduction is the basis for the above distinction. Kant identified the life-world with the Newtonian world. He assimilated the life-world with the world of natural science, says Husserl. Kant failed to make a distinction between *a priori* of science and *a priori* of the life world. Space, time and causality of the life-world are not to be identified with the space, time and causality of mathematical natural science. But Kant believed that the space of our immediate experience is the same as that of Newtonian space. Kant failed to note that the life-world is more basic and primordial than that of the objects of science. Life-world is first and foremost intersubjective. Kant wrongly identified the world of mathematical science with the life-world. A system is always defined in terms of structures and life-world by hermeneutics of culture. Truly speaking, these two aspects are not opposite to each other. It is the one world, which is pictured, in two different perspectives. In the system or structural perspective, otherwise known as the "perspective of nature", the categories like space, time, causality etc., are discussed. In the life-world, the end and means, norms and values and their meaning are important. Goffman also explains the above distinction in terms of natural and social. A close observation of this would reveal that both are intimately connected and both represent different dimensions of human existence. Whether it is dichotomy between the objective and subjective, or the causal and meaningful, or the nature and life-world, it must be admitted that both are invariably important.

Technology is always has been part of the social structure, belonging to a larger cultural framework in which man functions as human being. There is and always has been a continuous dialogue concerning society, its needs and aspirations and the technical means potentially contained in technology for satisfying those needs and fulfilling those aspirations. The nature of technology cannot be understood without understanding the nature of this dialogue. The place of technology in the scope of human knowledge is determined by the nature of the dialogue concerning the aspirations of society and the potentials of technology. It is in this sense that we can talk about the dialectical approach to technology. The crucial questions are: How do the forms of technological knowledge arise? What are they? How are they developed? In what sense do they represent knowledge? All these questions must be answered in relation to the peculiarities of this dialogue.

NOTES

1. Richard Rorty. 1979. *Philosophy and the Mirror of Nature.* Princeton: Princeton University Press. p. 390.
2. Foucault, Michel. 1984. "Space, Knowledge, and Power". *The Foucault Reader,* Paul Rainbow (ed.). New York: Pantheon Books. p. 249.
3. Marcuse, H. 1968, "Philosophy and Critical Theory". *Negations.* Boston. pp. 135, 147.
4. Ibid.
5. Sundara Rajan, R. *Beyond the Crisis of European Sciences.* Shimla: Indian Institute of Advanced Study. p. 203
6. Ibid., p. 21.
7. Ibid., p.17
8. Chattopadhyaya, D.P. "On the Nature of Interconnection between Science, Technology, Philosophy and Culture". *Science, Philosophy and Culture,* part-1, D.P. Chattopadhyaya and Ravinder Kumar (ed.). New Delhi: PHISPC in association with ICPR. p. 35.
9. Chattopadhyaya, D.P. 1973, *Societies and Cultures.* Bombay. p. x.
10. Chattopadhyaya, D.P. 1991. "Rationality, Culture and Values", *Journal of Indian Council of Philosophical Research,* vol. 8.
11. Chattopadhyaya, D.P. 1967. *Individuals and Worlds.* Delhi: Oxford University Press. p. 83.

CHAPTER 35

Consciousness in Science and Scientific Omnijectivity

Minakshi Roy Choudhuri

PREFATORY

The term consciousness used in contexts with which most people are familiar is not seen as an ambiguous term. Common people are not puzzled by the references of the expressions "loss of consciousness" or "return of consciousness". But many who hope to express the meaning of consciousness in the form of a definition find that to answer "What is . . ." question about consciousness is not an easy matter. In English language there are a large number of synonyms of the term consciousness. "Sensation", "perception", "apperception" all are its synonyms. But each of these terms expresses the nature of consciousness from a specific context and offers only its partial meaning. Even the terms "understanding" and "intelligence" are onesided expressions of the nature of consciousness.[1] There being a pool of synonyms it is indeed difficult to state precisely what is meant by consciousness. But a semantical analysis of the concepts brings to focus the feature which is implicit in the uses of all the synonyms whatever might be the differences in their nuances. Almost all the synonyms of consciousness have reference to awareness. Consciousness as awareness is present in our sentient experiences, volitional freedom and also in states of contemplation and meditation. It is present in our cognates when we think, doubt, remember or perceive and also in our experiences of sensing, feeling or willing.

Ancient Indian philosophers contributed substantially to the study of Pure Consciousness from the standpoints of knowledge and reality. In *Munduka Upaniṣad* it is said that there are two kinds of knowledge, *pārā-vidya* and *aparā-vidyā*. *Pārā-vidyā* is the higher knowledge about the knower, i.e. Pure Consciousness. Systematic study of matter is *apārā-vidyā*. The field of enquiry which received primary importance in *parā-vidyā* is not the world of mundane, material objects but internal modifications of the sensory world, culminating in *citsvarūp* — Pure Consciousness which is also *jñānāsvarupa* i.e. knowledge. Referring to this distinction between Pure Consciousness and relational consciousness J Needham comments that ". . . what we feel to be the best of ourselves as human beings is only part of a total structure containing layers of mind . . . These layers . . . need to be peeled back . . . one by one, along the path of inner growth . . ."[2]

Perhaps Needham had in his mind the idea of *pancakoṣa* as, the sheaths or succession of cases which make up the various frames of the body enveloping the objectless Pure Consciousness. Essentially man is *citsvarūpa* and not merely a physical body. In *Taittiriya*

Upaniṣad it is said that true nature of man is *sat-citānanda* — existence-knowledge-bliss. Since the true nature of man is covered with gross physical and complex of physical and mental sheaths, in *Taittiriya Upaniṣad,* the study of Self or *Ātman* begins with matter, (*ānandamayakoṣa*), then proceeds to energy (*prāṇamayakoṣa*), and this is followed by uncovering of the nature of mind (*manomayakoṣa*), intellect or soul (*vijñānamayakoṣa*) and finally the spirit, (*ānandamayakoṣa*)[3]

The approach is different in the West. There is resistance among philosophers of mind to treat consciousness as a transcendental, objectless, pure being. This resistance is due to the influence of the Descartes-Newton paradigm of cognitive enterprise. Descartes in the seventeenth century divided the world into two kinds of substances — mental and physical and excluded *res cogitans* from the subject matter of science. Science is concerned only with the physical body, *res extensa.* Though a spiritual man Newton held that mechanical laws of motion are comprehensive enough to account for actions and reactions of physical bodies. According to Einstein, awareness of man's intellectual love of reality has only emotive value in scientific enquiry. His unified field theory relegates consciousness as a transcendental principle to a tertiary or secondary level of importance.

With certain new principles emerging out of twentieth century scientific discoveries some of the founders of quantum mechanics, Erwin Schrödinger and Eugene Wigner among others, considered consciousness as an essential principle in the universe. For a proper understanding of the universe and formulation of laws of quantum mechanics, principle of consciousness is as much necessary as any physical principle. Given this new perspective some of the philosophers of mind, Searle among others, is trying to locate consciousness in nature without demolishing its distinct character.

This paper has a few major sections. In the first section I propose to sketch the nature of consciousness from Indian perspective. In the second section I propose to concentrate on the recent philosophical views of the nature of consciousness as propounded by philosophers of the West. This will be followed by attempts to show how in recent years professional scientists are trying to explore the relation between consciousness and physical science. In the third section I propose to present how I understand the relation between consciousness and scientific knowledge. This section will be on the epistemological role of consciousness and primacy of consciousness in scientific knowledge. I propose to conclude the paper with a brief analysis of the meeting point of western science and Indian mysticism.

I

Ages ago philosophers in India tried to study and investigate the nature of consciousness through mental means. In the Indian tradition it is called *adhyātmāvidyā* — the science of self or mind. The approach of *adhyātmāvidyā* is reflective and critical. Through reflection and criticism (*vimarśa and pramāṇa parīkśa*) *adhyātmāvidyā* moves towards the unfoldment of truth that self is the Pure Subject, i.e. in-itself self is the Transcendental Consciousness. The philosophers in India discussed the nature of Consciousness which is technically called *cit* or *caitanya* in accordance with their metaphysical commitment.

The streams of classical Indian thought which extensively studied the phenomenon of consciousness are Sāṁkhya, Yoga and Advaita Vedānta. It is a widely held belief that the elements of Sāṁkhya philosophy are rooted in or derived from *Chhāndogya Upaniṣad, Kathaponiṣad, Manusmṛti, Buddhacarita, Carakasṁhita* and different *Purāṇas.* The original development of Sāṁkhya philosophy is attributed to Kapilā, Iśvarakṛsna, Patañjali of *Yoga Sutra,* Vācaspati Miśra and Vijñānabhikiṣu. K.C. Bhattacharya highlighted the principle of spirituality in Sāṁkhya philosophy. Regarding consciousness Saṁkhya held that consciousness-in-itself is the eternal being (*sat*). It is immutable and transcendental and obviously beyond spatio-temporal determinations. In its pure, isolated form consciousness which is named *puruṣa,* is contentless and devoid of any activity, initiative and enterprise within it. Because of its transcendental presence *puruṣa* or pure consciousness makes co-ordination of experiences possible. It is the foundation (*adhisthāna*) of empirical knowledge. According to Sāṁkhya, *puruṣa* or pure consciousness is a metaphysical reality which exists side by side with *prakṛti,* the primordial material reality[4]. *Puruṣa* and *prakṛti* both are eternal and have independent existence possessing mutually opposite nature.[5] *Puruṣa* is neither mind (*manas*), nor ego (*ahaṅkāra*) nor intellect (*buddhi*). It is pure transcendental consciousness. It is beyond change and activity. *Prakṛti,* on the other hand, is essentially dynamic but unintelligent and unconscious (*jaḍa*). Vedāntins attacked the notion of cooperation between *puruṣa* and *prakṛti* which Sāṁkhya holds in the context of explaining the world of sense and science. Vedāntins rejected Sāṁkhya dualism and together with it the doctrine of real transformation (*parināmavāda*) according to which the world is the actual transformation of *prakṛti* and that cooperation of *puruṣa* and *prakṛti* is the pre-condition of evolution. From Vedāntist standpoint it is necessary to admit God as the bridging principle between the opposed elements of *puruṣa* and *prakṛti.* Necessity for admitting God in the context of explaining empirical world was realized by later Sāṁkhya writers like Vijñānabhikṣu among others. The decline of Sāṁkhya dualism was substantially explained by the gradual emergence of God in the Yoga system of Patañjali. This situation has a striking resemblance with Descartes' effort to counter the attacks against dualism between mind and body by invoking the idea of non-deceiving God in his system.

Yoga represents the practical side of Sāṁkhya. It is intimately related to Sāṁkhya. Gita regards Sāṁkhya and Yoga as one. Yoga accepts epistemology and metaphysics of Sāṁkhya and emphasises the path of meditation which would lead to the cessation of *antaḥkaraṇa* or ego-consciousness. Patañjali, the *yogi* philosopher of ancient India explained that purity of consciousness is due to the cessation of the modification of *citta. Citta* is the first evolute of *prakṛti* and has the predominance of *sattvā. Citta*-in-itself is unconscious. But due to the primacy of *sattvā* element it is in the state of serenity and calmness in which the restlessness of mind ceases. It therefore appears as if it is conscious. *Citta* assumes the form of that object with which it gets related. The form which *citta* assumes is called *vṛtti* or modifications. The light of consciousness which comes from the *puruṣa* and illuminates the modification of *citta* is called *jñāna. Citta* is the 'physical medium' of the manifestation of *puruṣa. Puruṣa* is the unchanging pure consciousness. On account of the reflection of *puruṣa* on *citta, puruṣa appears* to be changing and active and *citta* appears to be conscious. But neither *puruṣa* is active nor *citta* is conscious. When *puruṣa* realizes that it is a passive spectator it ceases to identity itself with its own reflection in *citta*. Modification of *citta* thereby ceases. This cessation is the result of meditation and *Pātañjali Yoga* also called *Rāja yoga* is defined as the effort to attain perfection through cessation of the modifications of *citta* (*yogāscittavrittinirodh*). The point to be noted here is that the phenomenon of consciousness is something more than mind or *citta*. The range of consciousness transcends the range of ordinary mind. It is the supra-conscious level of mind the higher state of existence which is beyond the discursive realm of reason. At this supra-conscious state all mental modifications are checked and *puruṣa* returns to its original perfection, i.e. passivity.

The contention of Sāṁkhya thinkers that *puruṣa* is formless, contentless, irreducible principle, is pushed to its logical consequences in Advaita Vedānta of Sāṁkara where consciousness is referred to as Self or *Ātman*. Self or *Ātman* is identical with *Brahman*. Being identical with *Brahman* consciousness is one, homogeneous, indivisible and eternal being. It is formless, Pure Consciousness. It is transcendental and revealing principle which reveals everything other than consciousness but is not revealed by anything else. It is subject but not in the sense of 'knower' or 'cognizer' (*jñāta* or *pramātā*) but subject which never becomes an object. Pure Consciousness as subject is non-dual. Though reality is non-dual Śaṁkara does not completely negate empirical world (*Saṁsāra*) and our knowledge of the empirical world. Due to the association of consciousness with mind îhe internal organ or *antaḥkaraṇa* we conceive the physical or material world as the object of knowledge and mind as the knowing subject, i.e. a duality between subject and object. Mind is endowed with the capacity "of being affected through the mediation of the senses by the energy emanated from the physical/material object." There is awareness of the object because of the unifying function of the mind under the witnessing of consciousness. In other words consciousness is the spiritual force which enables the mind to objectify its affections. The matter can be explained in a different way. The functions of sense organs are regulated by the mind while mind, in its turn, can perform its unifying and objectifying function and can regulate the functioning of the senses by virtue of the Self or Consciousness. But Consciousness as such is not in any way affected by the activities of the senses and that of mind. It is therefore said to be the Witness (*sākṣīn*) of the cognitive function of the mind. It is due to our ignorance we wrongly regard mind as the knowing subject. Continuous association of Consciousness with mind makes our knowledge of object possible but left to itself Consciousness transcends all possible descriptions. In other words Sāṁkara makes a distinction between empirical and trans-empirical consciousness. Empirical consciousness is real from practical (*vyabahārika*) standpoint but the state of trans-empirical consciousness is the state of *turīya* where Self or *Ātman* or Consciousness is entirely identical with Brahman. Realization of this identity is the Supreme Knowledge, *Brahmātmaiktva-Vijñāna*. This non-dual truth is a matter of direct experience (*anubhava*). To be more precise, it is pure experience freed from nescience and all delusions of empirical delimitations. Knowledge in its trans-empirical sense is the realization of 'knowing-being identity'.[6]

Summarily stated, to the Advaita Vedāntins Consciousness as identical with *Brahman* reveals the nature of things and beings of the world—but revelation of its nature does not depend on anything other than itself. Consciousness is self-revealing and what is revealed is the identity between Being and Consciousness. In-Itself Consciousness is Infinite. Infinite Consciousness appears as individuated and differentiated due to the difference in adjuncts or conditions (*upādhi*). Associated with *antaḥkaraṇa* consciousness appears as individual self. Conscious human subject of the mundane world looks at consciousness from the point of view of empirical being. His vision is impaired due to the veil of ignorance enveloping real self. Hence he obtains only a distorted picture of Ultimate Reality and finds Consciousness inseparably associated with embodied self. When the veil of ignorance covering the true nature of Consciousness—the undifferentiated Reality, is removed he realizes that Consciousness transcends spatio-temporal determinations and exists as Pure, Indeterminate Being.

The nature of consciousness is understood in a different way by the ancient Indian philosophers of materialist persuasion. In the classical Indian philosophy materialist school was referred to as the Lokāyatā. According to *Bhārspatisutra* there are four gross material elements viz. fire (*tejas*), water (*apah*), air (*vāyu*) and earth (*pṛthvi*). The followers of Lokāyata, Cārvākas among others, conceived the world with all its variety as the outcome of the various combination of the material elements. The properties of the material bodies are due to the nature of the gross material elements, i.e. the ultimate constituents of bodies. Consciousness also emerges naturally from the conglomeration of material elements. When material elements are transformed into the particular form of a body a new phenomenon, consciousness emerges. The later Lokāyatā, such as *Kambalāivata*', further assumed that vital breaths and the senses provide causal support to the senses for the production of consciousness. In other words, consciousness comes into existence when primordial material elements combine to create physical body and disintegrates with the disintegration of the body. Consciousness, from materialist standpoint, is not therefore eternal in nature.[7]

Today Indian philosophy stands at a critical point. It aspires to preserve the ideas of tradition through which it flourished yet it cannot ignore the significance and value of the present day scientific attitude and scientific explanation of the empirical world. Contemporary Indian philosophers try to get away of this dilemma by pronouncing that traditional ideas and present day scientific temper are not opposed to each other. The outcome of this modified attitude of Indian thinkers is a sort of east-west synthesis which in Sri Aurobindo's synthetic and comprehensive work has been described as Cosmic Consciousness. Cosmic Consciousness is the Supreme Reality. According to Sri Aurobindo Consciousness as Supreme Reality is not synonymous with consciousness as subject which is associated with individual's will, intention, desire, belief etc. It is not the reflective consciousness of human beings. Cosmic Consciousness is marked by supra-human transcendence. It is the Omnipresent Reality called *Brahman* which from the spatio-temporally constrained dualistic standpoint is unknowable. According to Sri Aurobindo a Creative Force is inherent in Cosmic consciousness. Supreme Reality is not only Pure Existence but Consciousness-Force. As he puts it "*Siva* and *Kāli*, *Brahman* and *Śakti* are one and not two who are separable. Force inherent in Existence may be at rest or it may be at motion, but when it is at rest, it exists nonetheless and is not abolished, diminished or in anyway essentially altered."[8] Consciousness or Pure Existence by its nature is a Force. It is the One all-embracing principle underlying the material, the vital, the mental and the supramental. Sri Aurobindo calls this principle *cit*, the Divine Power behind the world process. The universe is created and sustained by *cit.* It is with reference to the empirical world of objects and individual beings that the question of creation is normally raised. This creation has been described as the *plunge of the Spirit into Ignorance.* The world is created by the Consciousness-Force through Ignorance. Sri Aurobindo says, Ignorance is not the negation of Divinity but the Power of Divine Consciousness Itself. It is a Power inseparable from Consciousness-Force. It is the Power to descend and build the world in which we live, move and have our being. For Its Power of Ignorance Divine Consciousness can withold Itself partially. Finite appearance is shaped out of the Infinite Reality by this Divine Power of Ignorance.[9] This conception of Consciousness-Force as the power of partially witholding Itself distinguished Sri Aurobindo's notion of Consciousness as Supreme Reality from Advaita Vedāntist's conception of the same. To the latter Pure Consciousness is identical with knowledge (*jñana*). In other words, as said before, in Advaita Vedānta epistemology and ontology are identical under the aspect of eternity. Appearance of object with its attribute as something distinct from subject in consciousness are superimposition (*adhyāsa*).

The superimposed world is illusion. The object is unconscious but the subject is Pure Consciousness. Due to our ignorance (*avidyā*) we mingle subject and object and regard the phenomenal world of subject and object as real world[10] Through his sustained efforts in the form of spiritual discipline man is able to remove the veil of ignorance and is able to 'see' or experience directly Consciousness in its trans-empirical form which is the true form of consciousness. Sri Aurobindo's conception of creation of the phenomenal world through Ignorance does not make the world essentially illusory. Unlike Saṁkara he gives a status and a reality to the empirical or the phenomenal world.

Classical Indian philosophers have separated spiritual consciousness and material nature. In Sāṁkhya philosophy the being of contentless pure consciousness (*puruṣa*) is utterly distinct from all-pervading eternal but unintelligent and unconscious material principle of the universe (*prakṛti*). The extreme form of opposition between consciousness and matter is found in Advaita Vedānta where Consciousness, empty of all contents, is the pure homogeneous Reality devoid of all kinds of differentiations. As I go through Sāṁkara's Advaita view of Consciousness, I often recall Kant who also said that although phenomenal world is constituted of consciousness, the latter in its transcendentality is the pure function of thinking and sensory contents are 'presented to it for categorical formation'. Close scrutiny of the writings of Sri Aurobindo reveals that he is affiliated to the Vedic tradition of transcendence and Oneness of Being, viz. "all is consciousness", or *sarvaṁidaṁ caitanyaṁ* but also recognizes a two way relation of ascent and decent-evolution and involution between the levels of existence, matter life and mind.

Sri Aurobindo intends to overcome the devaluation of cosmic existence and individual human life to which extreme form of monism, spiritual or material leads. From the standpoint of spiritual monism the phenomenal world ultimately turns out to be illusory while all mental or spiritual experiences are mere epiphenomena from the standpoint of material monism Sri Aurobindo aims at reconciliation of these opposite positions of spiritual monism and material monism. It was his vision that reality is both spiritual and material and spiritualist and materialist need not compromise or contradict each other. Unlike Śaṁkara, Sri Aurobindo argues that Omnipresent Reality, i.e. *Brahman* is both transcendent and immanent. Transcendence and immanence are not irreconcilable opposites but are attributes of *Brahman.* As Transcendent Being *Brahman* is beyond all cosmic and individual existence. As Immanent Being *Brahman* is in the cosmic and individual existence. The nature of *Brahman* is such that It manifests Itself as a Universal-Cosmic-Force and creating world of multiplicities. Physical bodies (matter), individual human beings (body-mind complex) both are manifestations of *Brahman* but *Brahman* as Transcendent Being is the Primary Existence. The existence of the world consisting of the physical bodies and human beings depends on the Transcendent Being. The empirical world is due to the descent of the spirit in Matter, Life and Mind. This is the involutionary aspect of creation. It is on account of the presence of the Spirit that Matter, Life and Mind ascend to the higher regions of Spirit. The Spirit is the original involutionary element and the final evolutionary emergence. The process of evolution reminds us of upward causation from physics and chemistry via psychology and epistemology to abstract entities like theory, number and musical notation. Similarly involution is the downward causal movement from the world of abstract entities via psychological consciousness to the world of physics. An excellent exposition of this two way causal movement is given in the book *The Self and Its Brain* jointly authored by Popper, the philosopher-physicist, and Eccles, the neurologist-philosopher.

II

From the survey of the works of philosophy of mind in the West since the era of positivism it appears that large majority of philosophers purport to develop materialist theories of mind and materialist interpretation of consciousness. First, there is the radical materialist or behaviourist view of consciousness. It denies the existence of mind and anything called mental including consciousness. Whatever is real is amenable to objective behaviour. Behaviour of entities other than physical cannot be so observed. Mind is not an entity in any ordinary sense and consciousness does not exist as inherent quality of mind. According to Wittgenstein the substantive notion of mind is the result of *language game.*[11] In a similar vein Ryle says that the category of existence is applicable only to certain behaviour and dispositions. To postulate the existence of mind as a substantive entity over and above the behaviour and dispositions of objects is a mistaken application of the category of existence.[12] In their early works Smart and Place assert the identity of the mental with the physical. They wanted to deny the existence of any mental state in addition to behaviour. Consciousness as an irreducible phenomenological property does not exist.[13] Interestingly enough, Churchland, Jackendoff and Lycan have used the word "consciousness" in the titles of their books but have not found it worth putting any effort 'to give an account or a theory of consciousness'.[14]

The epiphenomenalists also reject the substantive notion of mind but unlike the behaviourists they accept the existence of conscious mental states. These states are causally ineffective by-products of physiological processes. Both behaviourism and epiphenomenalism seem to eliminate consciousness by denying its importance and relevance in a cognitive discourse. As an uncompromising materialist Stanovich has argued that introduction of the phenomenon of consciousness muddles the issues in psychology. Theoretical progress in psychology has been attained 'independent of the concept of consciousness'.[15]

Some of the materialists instead of eliminating conscious mind try to locate it in the brain and what we call conscious, mental states which, on their view, are nothing but brain-states. Such states are caused by the central nervous system. So this particular materialist version of mind and consciousness is called the central state-materialism. In support of this version Armstrong argues radically that every mental state not only corresponds to a brain state but is really identical with it. All the properties of brain states are physical. Accordingly consciousness as intrinsic property of the so-called mental phenomena does not exist at all.[16] This identity thesis was further influenced by the antimetaphysical theories of functionalism. The functionalists engaged in studying artificial intelligence discredits the non-physical notion of consciousness and define it in terms of the input-output system of human organism. Input-output model which the functionalists use in explaining consciousness is comparable to the pattern of the working of the computer. Comparing consciousness with software program it is said that consciousness runs on the hardware brain and conscious mental states are identical with artificial thinking of computers.[17]

Let us try to understand why do a large number of philosophers follow a reductionist strategy in one form or other in explaining the nature of consciousness? It is the strong influence of the dominant mechanical paradigm of Newtonian science with its machine like universe that led philosophers to think that the consequence of the admission of a non-material entity over and above matter would mean entertaining dualistic universe of matter and consciousness. Dualism is inconsistent with the mechanistic world view of Newton. From the thesis of mechanistic determinism emerged the doctrine of scientific materialism the crux of the doctrine being that matter is the ultimate reality and is the object of scientific enquiry. This situation led the philosophers to think that reductionist explanation of conscious mental states conforms with the materialist view that matter is the ultimate reality and also with its basic principles such as strong objectivity, causal determinism and epiphenomenalism.[18]

There are philosophers, Searle and Popper among others, who deviate from the mainstream view of either eliminating or reducing consciousness to a material base. According to Searle[19] consciousness has a special feature of subjectivity which is not present in any physical state. The weakness of eliminative and identity theses is that it purport to explain consciousness in terms of a material/physical framework which from the very beginning excludes the item of subjectivity. The notion of subjectivity might be used as a mode of justification of a subjective judgment which would be the epistemological way of understanding subjectivity. But in the context of comprehension of the nature of consciousness it is the ontology of subjectivity which is primary. Subjectivity of consciousness stands for the mode of existence of consciousness. Conscious mental states are always states of a person and these states can be most adequately studied within the first person parameter. As suggested by Searle, brain and consciousness are the contents of two separate domains of existence the domain of objective existence and the domain of subjective existence. Brain is real and it has its specific properties. Consciousness is also real and ineliminable subjectivity is its special character. Subjectivity cannot be replaced by sheer physical states. The notable feature of the two modes of being of brain and consciousness is that they are not completely dissociated but causally linked. Mental states are produced by particular operations in brain. This puzzling problem of causal linkage between and co-existence of incompatible systems within the same body-mind complex is solved once we submit to biological naturalism and try to grasp the truth that brain and consciousness both are parts of human biology.

A comparable approach towards understanding consciousness is found in Popper's hypothesis that evolution 'produces mind, and human language'.[20] Searle suggests that consciousness has place in nature and explains its reality in terms of particular cause-effect link between brain states and conscious states. Popper's conjecture is that 'matter can transcend itself, by producing mind, purpose and a world of the products of the human mind'. There is also interaction between mental and physical states. The reality of mental states can be explained in terms of this interaction. Popper tries to make his point considerably clear by introducing a tripartite division between the world of physical entities (W_1), the world of mental states (W_2) and the world of he products of human mind (W_3). There is interaction between $World_2$ and $World_3$ and also between $World_2$ and $World_1$. In the interaction between three worlds the world of conscious mental states W_2 is at the interface between W_1 and W_3. In different ways Searle and Popper are trying to explain the interaction between physical states and consciousness without disturbing the autonomy of consciousness. Higher forms of life, having purposes, aims and conscious pursuits of goals have place in nature and for that matter laws of physics are not affected.

Interestingly enough with the advent of quantum mechanics physicists are approaching towards placing consciousness in the order of nature. The materialist thesis that matter is the ultimate reality started disintegrating with the explanation of matter and its properties like occupying space, having mass and unchanging substantive character in terms of new discoveries of eminent physicists, Thomson, Faraday, Rutherford among others. The Searle-Popper evolutionary thesis of emergence of consciousness figures well in this new perspective of science. Electron as the tiny splinter of matter was discovered by Thomson while particles of electricity which atoms contain discovered by Faraday. By probing more deeply into the nature of atom Rutherford discovered that inside the atom there is nucleus round which electrons rotate. Cartesian-Newtonian science failed in the world of subatomic stratum of reality particularly with the celebrated uncertainty principle of Heisenberg. It substantiated inherent indeterminacy of position and momentum of subatomic entities like electrons. Scientific materialism seemed to crumble down further with Schrödinger's wave equation proving that electrons are 'standing waves' which can also be quantized.

Nobel Prize winning physicist Josephson says that events of subatomic world are naturally found to be too subtle and elusive. Their actions and reactions cannot be recorded by experimental observation. Physical theories of the micro world cannot therefore be based upon conventional scientific observation however subtle instruments might be designed.[21] Further, Josephson, referring to Chaos theory of Gleick points out that it is in principle impossible to capture the subtle elements of the micro world and give a precise description of that realm. Because of the limitations of experimentation quantum physicists assert the necessity of subjective experience in theorizing about the quantum world. Prior to the discoveries of the entities of subatomic world the principles of subjectivity and consciousness were excluded from the methodological principles of scientific investigation. Today's physicists seem to have shifted their attitude from pure objectivity to the fusion of subjective and objective and develop an *omnijective* world view.[22] Unlike the observer of classical physics, the observer of quantum physics looks through the microscope as an active participator in building up the omnijective world view. Now the quantum physicists are heading towards the view that hindrances of observing the elusive entities of nature may be overcome by direct experience. Josephson[23] and Schrödinger[24] suggest that first person perspective of observation should be added to the convention of the third person perspective of observation in physical science. Both these outstanding physicists believe that for the success of science, for a 'complete' understanding of nature, mystical perception might have an useful application. The notable point is that Schrödinger's defence of the relevance of subjective experience in physics moves towards the idea of subject as spirit which cannot be examined or experimented upon but has to be experienced. In a similar vein Wigner says that as physical theory encompasses micro-world phenomena ". . . through the creation of quantum mechanics the concept of consciousness came to the fore . . ." [25] The case of consciousness should not be ignored. Until science comes to find a place for consciousness its claim for completeness would remain a pretension.[26]

The truth which modern science seems to establish is that the scientist at the observational level no longer plays the role of passive observer but gets involved into what is observed. Involvement of the observer is the distinctive feature of quantum mechanics. Wheeler's suggestion is that the word "observer" should be replaced by the word "participater".[27] This suggestion brings science closer to the mystical tradition of ancient India when philosophers indifferent ways had repeatedly asserted that truth can only be obtained by participation and not by observation.

III

There is a basic epistemological function of consciousness in science. A scientific theory is a set of connected statements about the items of experience. For this purpose the items of experience need to be brought together. It is consciousness which glues the discrete sensory items and this gluing activity of consciousness is there even at the lower level of awareness, viz, perceptual awareness. A careful analysis would show that perceptual awareness is in fact conceptual in character. For example, if one says, 'this table is wooden' he is actually conceptualizing a piece of matter. Uninterpreted given matter is not epistemologically available. The predicative expression 'is wooden' is not peculiar to 'this table'. It is also applicable to 'that chair', to 'that bookshelf'. Besides one's image of a table at different times or one's image of a table compared to others' image of the same for geometrical reasons, perceptual considerations and also because of variation in attention are different. The idea of a table though more abstract than the image of a table is rooted in this perception or that perception. We can well think of a society where all tables (what *we* call table) are round in shape. Their idea of table will never be oblongish or squarish as their concept or idea of table *is* determined by their perception and image of the table. But for all items of experience–perceptual, imaginational or conceptual one question can always be raised and pertinently. This is a question about the subject who perceives, imagines and conceives. Here by the subject we mean the enquiring subject, the knowing subject. When we view consciousness relative to the enquirer of the scientific world we are concerned with consciousness vis-a-vis empirical and verificational level.

The consciousness of the person who owns the items of experience has an unificatory role and for this unificatory role of consciousness the person has to be credited with a relation called identity relation. The person growing over the years, decades maintains an identity–biological identity and also psychological identity. Therefore all the experiences which happen to him and which are generated by him get related between themselves by virtue of the fact that they are being owned by that particular person. There is a difference between what happens to a person and what is generated by him. The very reasonable way of doing it is what we call in terms of external stimulus (e-stimulus) and internal stimulus (i-stimulus). Light falls on one's eyes and he sees the wall—i.e. the object in the external world affects his sense organ and he is having sensory awareness. This sort of awareness happens to a person due to e-stimulus. Sometimes we do something on our own. For example, one wants to read Karl Popper's *Conjectures and Refutations* and he starts reading it. His action is internally generated. Strictly speaking, it is intentionally rooted. The significant point to be noted here is that what we intend over time have unity between them. This is one way of explaining the unificatory function of consciousness. Now this unificatory function of consciousness can also be understood in relation to our knowledge of scientific objects. In most cases experience and observation in science are purpose-oriented and are rooted in scientist's intention to know the nature of objects of a particular domain. So i–stimulation is at work in scientific inquiry.

To account for the unity of the items of experience, sensory or intentional, we have to posit a self. Without some such essential gluing concept underlying person's empirical life, items of experience are dissociated from one another. In the context of science the notion of consciousness stands for self-consciousness–reflectivity of self vis-a-vis what happened to him and what were generated by him at t_1, t_2, t_3. Mental act of remembering what the subject had known before at t_1 and gluing it with what he later experiences at t_2 would be impossible if the mental states of the subject are entirely separated across t_1, t_2, t_3 . . . It would create difficulties analogous to those which the followers of the doctrine of momentariness (*Kṣṇabhangurvāda*) of Buddhism had to face.[29] The Naiyāikas however did not believe in the cognitive character of memory but our general understanding is that scientific theories are set of connected statements of which some are observational and others theoretical. At the observational level and also at the theoretical level connecting the statements would be impossible by the knowing subject without the identity of the subject himself across t_1 t_2 t_3... The identity of the subject presupposes identity of self who acts as witness of experiences and also of acts of thinking of the subject across time but itself is not affected by the imprints of time. Reflectivity of self presupposes identity of self over time. The knowing subject must maintain some sort of the identity of itself. Otherwise he cannot continue to be the knowing subject at t_1, t_2 t_3 and so on. In other words, if there is disruption in the identity of the knowing subject and mental states occurring at different times fall entirely apart then the subject himself who existed at t_1 cannot claim to exist at t_2, t_3 and so on. The subjects across t_1, t_2, t_3 . . . turn out to be entirely different subjects and re-identification of the subjects would be impossible.[28] In brief, it is in the being of the self the objective world is somehow held together. The representations of the objects of the world are given as ordered in space and time which are further organized by knower in terms of the categories like quality, quantity and causality. For this the self must maintain its identity across what it receives from the external world and in organizing the same in terms of categories.

The object known at t_1 will not be cognitively available to the knowing subject at t_2 if the identity of the subject is not maintained. It is for the identity of the knowing subject that science can claim to provide a well connected world-view. Cognitive availability of object at other time means that mental act of remembrance is not sheer remembrance but remembrance of an object or experience. Since knowledge of object involves remembrance the later also has a cognitive component in it. Similarly, in it cognitive mode consciousness has the character of object-directedness (*ākankṣādharmita*) and not pure consciousness.[29] To put it differently a sort of knower-known duality is there in scientific knowledge but not to that extreme which would make subject and object fall entirely apart. It is the self existing behind the subjectivity and objectivity which settles the problem of unity and identity of the subject and its experienced items.

Primacy of the epistemological role of consciousness in theorising about the world is suggestive of the principle that objects of knowledge or items of experience are apperceived by the self behind the knowing mind. Even the perishable micro-world entities are subject to this principle. Otherwise the categories of probability and quantity would be inapplicable to the quantum world.[30] To discover the unitarian character of reality, the discoverer, i.e. the subject as scientist must be conscious about his own identity across what he discovers gradually. Primacy of consciousness does not mean refusal to recognise the objective realistic claim of the world of science. Self-consciousness accompanying the different levels of the cognitive activities of the scientist cannot unify 'all items of experience of nature' unless nature itself has a pre-epistemic and ontological unity of its own. Identity of self-consciousness is as important as the unity of the world discovered gradually by science.[31] Further, nature does not always oblige the scientist by conforming to the epistemically unified world. There are surprises in nature. There is every possibility of the epistemically unified world-view being disconfirmed by the unified and diversified structures of the micro-levels of nature. Actually nature may be supportive of the hypothesis which the scientist frames in conformity to his comprehension of the unity of the world and one can say nature verifies or justifies the hypothesis. Interestingly enough at times facts of nature falsify the hypothesis and it also happens that the scientist is obliged to reject his hypothesis as false in view of the recalcitrant facts. But it is also true that the relation between the epistemologically drawn hypothesis and facts of nature is such that neither verification nor falsification is decisive and we can conclude like Duhem that no crucial experiment is really crucial.

It is a misconception of the inductivist to believe that science has an observational base. Newton explicitly admitted priority of hypotheses over experience in construction of scientific theories. For example, the basic concept of classical mechanics—the concept of pure mass-point—a material point free from all external influences clearly cannot be obtained empirically. Michael Polanyi, the professionally trained chemist considered theoretical knowledge as more subjective than objective.[32] He maintained that knowledge in general is bound to be personal and scientific knowledge is not an exception to this generic feature of knowledge. Every stage of scientific knowledge is largely determined by scientist's power of intellectual insight and thought. It is with ideas that the scientific enquiry starts but there are no rules of production of such ideas. Ideas which motivate scientist's pursuit of truth are due to creative insight or constructive imagination of the scientist. In other words, scientific enquiry is inextricably linked with human perspective and its claim of autonomy, pure objectivity and impersonality right from its beginning to its current stage falls through. The more we probe deep into the human roots of science it becomes clear to us that scientific descriptions, explanations and predictions are not detached from the influence of the scientist himself who purports to describe, explain or predict facts of nature.

What Popper says about the nature of scientific enquiry is very close to Polanyi's view. He agrees with Polanyi that scientific theories down from empirical generalizations to higher order abstract theories are rooted in the scientist's self-conscious, creative insight of what the world order is really like. By a sort of mysterious mental exploration and conceptual mapping of the given, mind is capable of grasping the world at large. Laws and theories are explanations of the world as captured by the knowing mind. Evolution of man as a mentalized being with reflective awareness has been traced by Darwin and this lends support to the primacy of reflective activity in building scientific theories. In the subhuman creatures there is body, there is organized body but not what we call the power of reflective activity. It is this reflective activity of man which accounts for the emergence of knowledge in general and scientific knowledge in particular.

Lending support to the Darwinian evolution Popper argues for the evolutionary approach in epistemology. He argues that unlike downward copying movement of Plato's world of ideas towards the world of science and art, three worlds of theories, (W_1), mental states (W_2) and physical states (W_3) are related in a circular-causal manner. When we look into the contents of $World_3$ i.e., the work of the scientists we become convinced of what we call upward causation—the movement from the world of physical and chemical states to the $World_2$ of mental states, psychology and epistemology, and therefrom the movement is towards $World_3$—the world of theories and problems. But then what happens? By reflecting critically on the results of others' thought, i.e. theories, the knowing minds belonging to $World_2$ bring out some solutions of the problems of some theories of $World_3$ and this shows the members of $World_2$ can act on the members of $World_3$. Then again the mind and body, the content of the $World_2$, die and return to the level of $World_1$. Thus between the three worlds of Popper there is upward causal movement from $World_1$ to $World_2$ and from $World_2$ to $World_3$. Then there is down .ward causation from $World_3$ to $World_2$ and from $World_2$ to $World_1$.

Both Popper and Eccles agree that the concept of self is more fundamental than the concept of brain. That self exists and it has a brain is explicit in the very title of their book *The Self and Its Brain.* But while Popper stops at $World_3$ and scrupulously avoids the question of existence of soul, Eccles is not ready to stop there. He says, the circular causation—the upward and downward movement is not repeatedly cyclical but *creatively* so. Talking in the vein of Bergson, Eccles says that rightly speaking, the cycle is virtuous and beyond $World_3$ there may be world yet to be explored. The unexplored realm is what is called the realm of spirituality—Eccles is willing to recognize the transcendental promise of biological evolution and even asserts that 'non-physical mind' enters our physical brain during embryological development. Survival of non-physical *beyond* death cannot be ruled out in principle.

It is to be borne in mind that in the context of scientific knowledge attempts at theorising cannot begin unless there are sufficient facts known to be awaiting, so to say, a theory. Scientific knowledge is preconditioned by the scientist's understanding of the problem, insightful thinking and experience of the relevant data. What is most important is the connecting activity underlying scientific theorisation. This activity is possible because of consciousness which transcends the temporal order and witnesses the experience and cognitive activities of the theoriser. Object of knowledge, in a sense, is present in consciousness and it is in consciousness that the knower builds up a unified world view. The behaviour of objects is explained in terms of the experience of the unified structure of the real world. There are surprises in nature and the unified structure built in consciousness is not necessarily confirmed by the experience of complex actions and reactions of the objects in the real world. Science grows through criticism and test of theoretically formulated laws and this is also intertwined with the reflective activity of consciousness.

IV

Modern physics with its new discoveries has profoundly influenced our general philosophical framework of understanding reality. The concepts of matter, object, space, time, cause, effect are undergoing revisions with the emerging patterns of atomic and subatomic reality. As the limitations of the classical physics are being revealed by quantum theory, new world-view is now coming up which turns out to be closely related to the mystical tradition of the ancient India.[33]

The close relation between the world-view of quantum physicists and Indian philosophical thinking is quite evident in the idea of Cosmic Web or cosmic entanglement.[34] In contrast to the solid material objects, modern physicists have discovered that at the atomic level there are wave-like patterns of probabilities. These patterns are not representations of probabilities of behaviour of objects but of patterns of interconnections. The new picture of interconnectedness is not the picture of "things". There are no such entities which in classical sense were called "thing",—i.e. entities locatable in space and time and connectable in terms of cause-effect relations. Subatomic entities are viewed as "interconnections" between interconnections. Quantum physical interpretation of the subatomic world ends up with interconnections.

Underlying the Cosmic Web world-view there is the idea of "basic oneness" of the universe.[35] That universe is holistic has been proved by David Bohm and others who experimented successfully on Bell's thesis and came to the conclusion that there could be instantaneous communication between distant objects. This phenomenon of "non-local instantaneous communication" has been explained by Bohm in terms of the theory of *implicate order.*[36] It is the theory that all things and events are entangled in a 'total or unbroken wholeness' or unity. It implies a strict denial of absolute individuality both to objects and systems of objects. This interconnectedness or *implicate order* is the order of the physical world and the life world.

The crucial feature of this holistic world-view is that human observers are not external to the entangled, unified world but are necessarily connected as a participater in bringing about the properties of Cosmic Web. In other words the new truth is that we cannot speak about nature without at the same time speaking about ourselves. Instead of split there is interaction between nature and conscious knower. Thus the dualistic paradigm of Descartes, Newton and Laplace has been replaced by the 'Holistic Paradigm'. The holistic universe consists of entities which seem to have opposite nature. It consists of objects and subjects, matter and consciousness. Objects or matter are open to experimentation while subjects or consciousness are revealed in experience. Reality consisting of opposite elements cannot be grasped by ordinary perception. Hence today's physicists come closer to mystical tradition in Indian philosophy which makes a distinction between transcendental consciousness and consciousness as awareness of phenomenal objects. Transcendental consciousness is the consciousness of the basic Oneness of the universe. The cosmos is seen as One inseparable reality which is spiritual, organic and material at the same time. From the empirical standpoint (*vyavahārika*) the categorizing mentality of men divides nature into individual things and beings. But it is an illusory picture of reality drawn for the purpose of coping with the environment. In reality all things are interconnected and transcendentally unified. Upaniṣadic enquiry into the consciousness of the transcendentally unified world starts from sensory level, moves towards super-sensory level and ends up with holistic view of reality. Hence Sāṁkara asserts 'Absolute Consciousness is an act of direct mystical experience or (*Aparokṣanubhuti*)'. The scientific advancement confirms the Vedāntic truth—'I am the whole world (*Ahaṁ Brahmāsmi*)'. Schopenhauer's prediction that beneficial and elevating Vedāntic mysticism of Upaniṣads one day will have 'epoch making impact on thoughts of the ages' is an emerging truth since last century.

NOTES AND REFERENCES

1. Pribram, K.H. refers to Webster's Dictionary and says that there are twelve different meanings of "consciousness". See, Pribram, K.H. 1971. "Self-Consciousness and Intentionality: A Model Based on an Experimental Analysis of the Brain Mechanisms Involved in the Jamesian Theory of Motivation and Evolution" *Consciousness and Self-Regulation,* G.E. Schwartz and D.Shapiro (ed.). New York: Plenum Press.

2. Quoted in, Swami Smarānanda. 2003. "Philosophy and Science". *Philosophy and Science: An Exploratory Approach to Consciousness.* Kolkata: The Ramakrishna Mission Institute of Culture.
3. *Taittiriya Upaniṣad,* 'Ananda Valli'.
4. *Sāṁkhyakārikā.* Isvarakṛsna, (ed.) and S.S. Suryanarayana Shastri (trans.). Madras.
5. Ibid.
6. Pande, G.C. 1994. *Life and Thought of Śaṁkaracārya.* New Delhi: Motilal Banarasidass. See also, Chattopadhyaya, D.P. 2003. "Consciousness and Scientific Knowledge". *Philosophy of Science Phenomenology and Other Essays.* New Delhi: Indian Council of Philosophical Research.
7. Chattopadhyaya, D.P. in collaboration with Gangophdhyaya, M.K. (ed.). 1990. *Cārvāka Lokayāta.* New Delhi: Indian Council of Philosophical Research.
8. Sri Aurobindo. 1955. *The Life Divine,* vol. 1. Pondichery. p. 104.
9. Ibid. p. 108.
10. *Vedātasāra.* 1929. Isadananda (ed.) and M. Hiranmoy (tr.) Poona. Section on *adhyās.*
11. Wittgenstein, L. 1953. *Philosophical Investigations.* Oxford: Basil Blackwell.
12. Ryle, G. 1949. *The Concept of Mind.* New York: Barnes and Noble.
13. Smart, J.J.C. 1959. "Sensations and Brain Process?", *Philosophical Review,* 68. pp. 141-156; Place, U.T. 1956. "Is Consiousness a Brain Process?", *British Journal of Psychology,* 47. pp. 44-50.
14. Churchland, P.M. 1984. *Matter and Consciousness: A Contemporary Introduction to the Philosophy of Mind.* Cambridge: MIT Press; Jackendoff, R. 1987. *Consciousness and the Computational Mind.* Cambridge: MIT Press; Lycan, W.G. 1987. *Consciousness.* Cambridge: Harvard University Press. See also, Searle, J.R. 1992. *The Rediscovery of Mind.* Cambridge: MIT Press.
15. Stanovich, K.E. 2002. "Damn! There Goes That Ghost Again!", *Behavioral and Brain Sciences,* 7. pp. 696-698. See also, Rao, R.K. *Consciousness Studies: Cross Cultural Perspectives.* London: Mc Farland and Company, Inc.
16. Armstrong, D.M. 1968. *A Materialist Theory of Mind.* London: Routledge.
17. Turing, A. "Computing Machinery and Intelligence", *Mind,* 59. pp. 433-460. See also, Rao, R.K.
18. Goswami, A. 1995. *The Self-Aware Universe.* New York: Penguine Putnam. p. 17.
19. Searle, J.R.
20. Popper K.R. and Eccles, J.C. 1977. *The Self and Its Brain.* Springler International.
21. Josephson, B.D. 1922. "The Elusivity of Nature and the Mind-Matter Problem". *The Interrelationship between Mind and Matter,* B. Rubik (ed.). Philadelphia: P.A. Centre for Frontier Sciences, Temple University. pp. 219-222.
22. Talbot, M. 1981. *Mysticism and The New Physics.* New York: Bantam Books.
23. Josephson, B.D.
24. Schrödinger, E. *My View of the World.* Cambridge: Cambridge University Press.
25. Wigner, E.P. 1972. "The Place of Consciousness in Modern Physics" *Consciousness and Reality: The Human Pivot Point.* New York: Avon Books. p. 133.
26. Penrose. 1994. *Shadows of the Mind: A Search for the Missing Science of Consciousness.* Oxford: Oxford University Press. p. 8.
27. Capra, F. 1984. *Science and Consciousness: Two Views of the Universe,* Cozenave (ed.), A. Hale and Callander (trans.). Oxford: Peragment Press.
28. Shoemaker, S. 1971. *Self Knowledge and Self-Identity.* New Delhi: Allied Publishers.
29. Chattopadhyaya, D.P. "Consciousness and Scientific Knowledge".
30. Ibid.
31. Ibid.
32. Polanyi, M. 1964. *Personal Knowledge: Towards a Post-Critical Philosophy.* New York: Harper and Row.
33. Swami Jitatmananda. 2002. *Modern Physics and Vedanta.* Mumbai: Bharatiya Vidya Bhavan.
34. Capra, F.
35. Swami Jitatmananda; Capra, F.
36. Bohm, D. 1952. "A Suggested Interpretation of the Quantum Theory in Terms of Hidden Variables, I and II", *Physical Review* 85.

Index of Names

Index of Subjects

*	Part 5	Development of Modern Indian Thought and the Social Sciences	S. Bhattacharya	(ed.)
*	Part 6	Aspects of India's International Relations 1700 to 2000: South Asia and the World	Jayanta Kumar Ray	(ed.)
*	Part 7	Political Ideas in Modern India: Thematic Explorations	V.R. Mehta & Thomas Pantham	(eds.)

Volume XI Consciousness, Science, Society, Value and Yoga (CONSSVAY)

*	Part 1	Philosophical Consciousness and Scientific Knowledge: Conceptual Linkages and Civilizational Background	D.P. Chattopadhyaya	(ed.)
*	Part 2	Self, Society and Science; Theoretical and Historical Perspectives	D.P. Chattopadhyaya	(ed.)
*	Part 3	Consciousness, Indian Psychology and Yoga	Kireet Joshi & Matthijs Cornelissen	(eds.)
*	Part 4	The Enworlded Subjectivity: Its Three Worlds and Beyond	R. Balasubramanian	(ed.)

Volume XII Levels of Reality (CONSSVAY)

*	Part 1	A Conceptual-Analytic Study of Indian Philosophy of Morals	Rajendra Prasad	
*	Part 2	A Historical-Developmental Study of Classical Indian Philosophy of Morals	Rajendra Prasad	(ed.)
*	Part 3	Vedic Vision of Consciousness and Reality	S.P. Singh	
>	Part 4	Modern Atomism in Europe and India	J. Pasupathy	(ed.)
>	Part 5	Materialism and Immaterialism in India and Europe	Partha Ghose	(ed.)
*	Part 6	Life and Organicism	N.S. Rangaswamy	(ed.)

Volume XIII Theories of Natural and Life Sciences (CONSSVAY)

*	Part 1	India in the World of Physics: Then and Now	A.N. Mitra	(ed.)
>	Part 2	From Physiology and Chemistry to Biochemistry	D.P. Burma & Maharani Chakraborty	(eds.)
>	Part 3	Psychology and Psychoanalysis	Girishwar Mishra	(ed.)
>	Part 4	Cognitive Sciences: Brain, Psychology and Computer	Shobini L. Rao	(ed.)
>	Part 5	Foundations of Sciences	B.V. Sreekantan	(ed.)
>	Part 6	History of Science and Philosophy of Science	Pradip Kumar Sengupta	(ed.)
>	Part 7	History of Science and Philosophy of Science	Pradip Kumar Sengupta	(ed.)
>	Part 8	Science in India	J.V. Narlikar	(ed.)

Volume XIV Natural and Cultural Sciences (CONSSVAY)

>	Part 1	Nature and Culture	Roddam Narasimha	(ed.)
>	Part 2	Social Sciences: Communication, Anthropology and Sociology	Yogendra Singh	(ed.)
>	Part 3	Economics and Ethics	Ashok Sanjay Guha	(ed.)
*	Part 4	Different Types of History	Bharati Ray	(ed.)
>	Part 5	History of India's Polity, Governance and Constitutional Culture	Subhash C. Kashyap	(ed.)

Volume XV Science, Technology and Philosophy (CONSSVAY)

*	Part 1	Science, Technology, Imperialism and War	J. B. Das Gupta	(ed.)
>	Part 2	Science and the Public	Ashok Jain	(ed.)
>	Part 3	Science, Literature and Aesthetics	Amiya Dev	(ed.)
>	Part 4	Science, and Modern India: An Institutional History c.1784-1947	Uma Das Gupta	(ed.)
*	Part 5	Old Wisdom and New Horizon	Manoj Kumar Pal	

Volume XVI Yoga (CONSSVAY)

>	Part 1	Cognitive Anomalies, Consciousness and Yoga	K. Ramakrishna Rao	(ed.)
>	Part 2	History of Yoga in India	S.P. Singh	(ed.)
>	Part 3	Varieties of Yogic Experience	Manoj Das	(ed.)
>	Part 4	Synthesis of Yoga	Kireet Joshi	(ed.)
<	Part 5	Yoga, Evolution and Mutation of Human Species	(Under Plan)	

Monographs

*	1.	Science, Philosophy and Culture in Historical Perspective	D.P. Chattopadhyaya & Ravinder Kumar	(eds.)
*	2.	Some Aspects of India's Philosophical & Scientific Heritage	D.P. Chattopadhyaya & Ravinder Kumar	(eds.)
*	3.	Mathematics, Astronomy and Biology in Indian Tradition: Some Conceptual Preliminaries	D.P. Chattopadhyaya & Ravinder Kumar	(eds.)
*	4.	Language, Logic and Science in India: Some Conceptual and Historical Perspectives	D.P. Chattopadhyaya & Ravinder Kumar	(eds.)
*	5.	Primal Spirituality of the Vedas: Its Renewal and Renaissance	R. Balasubramanian	
*	6.	Interdisciplinary Studies in Science, Technology, Philosophy and Culture	D.P. Chattopadhyaya	
*	7.	Ancient Yoga and Modern Science	T.R. Anantharaman	
*	8.	Prolegomena to Any Future Historiography of Cultures & Civilizations	Daya Krishna	
*	9.	Science and Spirituality: A Quantum Integration	Amit Goswami and Maggie Goswami	
*	10.	On Rational Historiography	V. Shekhawat	
*	11.	*Kauṭilīya Arthaśāstra* Revisited	Surindra Nath Mital	
*	12.	The Ways of Understanding the Human Past	D.P. Chattopadhyaya	
*	13.	The Architecture of Knowledge	Subhash Kak	
*	14.	Karnataka Music as Aesthetic Form	R. Sathyanarayana	
*	15.	Indian Philosophy and Philosophy of Science	Sundar Sarukkai	

* Already Published
> In the Process of Publication
< Under Plan